Hitchhiker's
Guide to
Visual
Basic® &
SQL Server™

FIFTH EDITION

D0746412

William R. Vaughn

Microsoft Press

PUBLISHED BY

Microsoft Press
A Division of Microsoft Corporation
One Microsoft Way
Redmond, Washington 98052-6399

Library of Congress Cataloging-in-Publication Data
Vaughn, William R.
    Hitchhiker's Guide to Visual Basic and SQL Server / William R.
  Vaughn. -- 5th ed.
       p. cm.
     Includes index.
     ISBN 1-57231-567-9
     1. Microsoft Visual BASIC. 2. SQL (Computer program language)
   3. Client/server computing.   I. Title.
   QA76.73.B3V39   1997
   005.26'8--dc21   97-10659
                                                             CIP

Printed and bound in the United States of America.

  4 5 6 7 8 9   MLML   2 1 0 9 8

Distributed to the book trade in Canada by Macmillan of Canada, a division of Canada
Publishing Corporation.

A CIP catalogue record for this book is available from the British Library.

Microsoft Press books are available through booksellers and distributors worldwide. For
further information about international editions, contact your local Microsoft Corporation office. Or contact Microsoft Press International directly at fax (206) 936-7329.

Acquisitions Editor: Eric Stroo

Project Editor: Kathleen Atkins

Technical Editor: Dail Magee, Jr.

I dedicate this guide to my wife and daughters, who did without my personal attention while it was being written.

CONTENTS AT A GLANCE

PART VI # THE ODBC API

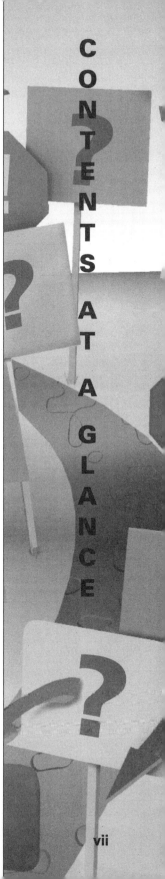

C
O
N
T
E
N
T
S
A
T
A
G
L
A
N
C
E

?

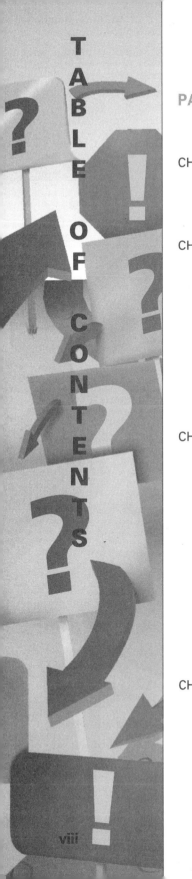

T
A
B
L
E

O
F

C
O
N
T
E
N
T
S

ACKNOWLEDGMENTS

As I saved the last file for the 5th edition of *Hitchhiker's Guide to Visual Basic and SQL Server,* I began to tally the cost of this and all of the previous versions of this work. I vaguely remember all of the evenings and weekends and the entire month of December when I was sequestered in my cave. While I would have preferred completing this last revision while my daughters were away at school, this wasn't possible due to delays in Visual Basic's version 5.0 release. I would, therefore, like to take this opportunity to thank my daughters for their indulgence and support and to apologize for missing their company over the holidays. I would also like to thank my wife and best friend Marilyn, who tolerates far more than she should have to, and who kept me fed, healthy, and loved through all of this.

Like any other technical book, this guide is a compendium of information drawn from a variety of sources. Many of those sources were people, and the information was drawn from their comments in the halls, from their reviews of early drafts, and from the code, articles, and books they have written. I thank Rick Nasci, Ken Nilsen, Emily Kruglick, Peter Tucker, and especially Dave Stearns for their technical guidance. I would also like to thank my "fans" from all over the world, who send me corrections, encouragement, war stories, success stories, and busts of Homer. I am very gratified to hear how much help this book has been to those in the field trying to solve real problems.

There are probably a few people I've forgotten to mention. And as with earlier editions, a few others are best forgotten, lest I burn any more bridges.

Bill Vaughn
Redmond, Washington
January 1997

PART I

Client/Server Computing:
An Introduction

1 Chapter

The Road Ahead

Where We Are Now

And Where We're Headed

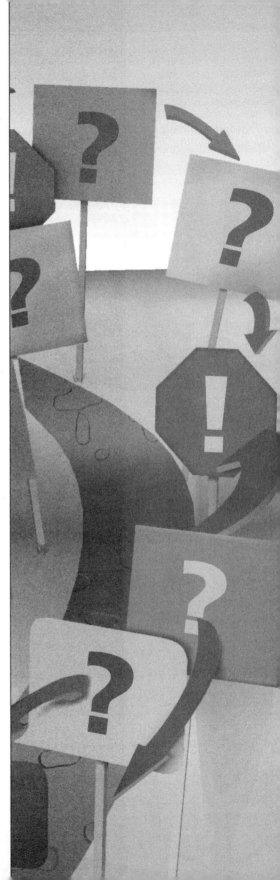

Change happened again, and frankly, it caught a lot of us flat-footed. Over the last year, client/server computing has just gone through *another* revolution. What used to be fairly simple to explain has grown in complexity and sophistication, well beyond what many of us were prepared for. I guess change is inevitable, and much of it is for the good. Most of these changes—but not all—were brought about by the tsunami of the Internet and Microsoft's headlong plunge into it. Last year, little in Visual Basic really addressed this hitherto unexplored technology. And most of you didn't care. The Internet seemed like a leap in the wrong direction—back toward the dark days of centralized databases and 3270 workstations. Many of you (like me) said: "Been there. Done that. No thanks," and discounted the trend as a fad that would ebb away like the Tandy 2000, IBM's "chicklet" keyboard, and the "Bass-O-Matic."

But it hasn't gone away. Anyone roaming the halls at Microsoft can tell you the word "Internet" is on everyone's lips and in every staff study of proposed applications and technologies. But if you poll the developers and their managers at VBits (which I do several times a year) and ask them "Let's see a show of hands—as of today, who is developing for the Internet?" not many hands go up. Lots of people are *thinking* about the Internet and have long-term plans for the Internet, but not many traditional client/server developers are launching new Internet-based applications. Why not? Well, as a number of recent news stories have told us, the Internet has been an expensive experiment for many companies, who have yet to see their first dime of profit after having poured millions into development of web-based applications. In addition, not many companies are convinced that a public web is better than (or as good as) their existing private networks. Many are afraid of security leaks, unpredictable network availability, and that their employees will spend too much time looking for weather forecasts and smut. Corporate America is not completely convinced that it's ready to give up its private LAN limousines in favor of public transportation for its data.

What all this means for this book is that I don't intend to add much to this volume on Internet implementation. I'll leave that for the sixth edition (if there is one). Here we will stay focused on *intra*net implementations. Yes, many of the techniques we look at can be used for Internet (public) networks—many, but not all. However, the philosophy behind each of these approaches is very different. In the traditional client/server case, you build a state-based interface. The server knows who you are, and you remain connected until you get the data you need—even if it takes hours. In the Internet case, you build stateless connections to host resources. The host sees you as simply a place to send a web page full of fetched information. Sure, this oversimplifies the differences, but the point is that most of us are still developing for the state-based interfaces, and that's what this guide addresses. Welcome to the ever-changing world of personal computing. Blink and you're behind, take a week off and you're out of touch, take a month off and you're lost. I just hope the time I am taking "off" to finish the fifth edition won't put me so far behind I won't recognize my desk when I get back.

Meanwhile, Visual Basic went through another phase of its evolution. While many think that Visual Basic version 4.0 was a Jurassic throwback, it was really a big step forward—but perhaps too far. Visual Basic was not reborn this time—as we moved from version 4.0 to 5.0—but you would think so. When Microsoft shipped Visual Basic version 4.0, they knew that it was not as fast as Visual Basic version 3.0 in a number of ways (not in *all* ways because the tests showed it to be somewhat faster here and there). This made it easy(ier) for Delphi and PowerBuilder to get a toehold in the Rapid Application Development (RAD) tools market. And then came the infamous *InfoWorld* review, where Visual Basic 4.0 was impaled on the underside of a 48-pin DIP. While some of the points made in the article were on target, many were not (IMHO) and showed just how difficult it is to accurately review these complex platforms. But Visual Basic version 5.0 should put a lump in the throats of the Delphi and PowerBuilder crowd. Independent tests show that the new compiled code is much, *much* faster than Visual Basic version 4.0. So fast that the C++ developers have taken note. All tests show that Visual Basic–compiled programs are within a couple of percentage points of their C++ equivalents (some were actually faster). Suddenly, one of the biggest excuses for *not* using Visual Basic has been quashed. Forms load faster, p-code programs are smaller and run faster, and there are so many new features that we had a dickens of a time getting the top 50 of them on the data sheet. And the other principal reason for *not* using Visual Basic has also fallen. Yes, you can create your own controls with Visual Basic. It looks like Visual Basic has come of age, and it's a big, mean, hungry tiger.

Visual Basic's C-like execution speed and ease of use for development continue to make it far more cost-effective than other compile-link-test languages. And because more than 80 percent of Microsoft Windows-based applications access databases, an increasing number of Visual Basic applications are serving as front ends to database management systems of all sizes and every degree of complexity. Many applications are still not concerned with the complexity of data sharing, but the trend is toward more sophisticated multiuser/multitasking systems that place significant demands on the application, the workstation, the network, the server, and the developer. For example, MIS shops have discovered that Visual Basic is a viable platform for developing applications that access databases, which allows them to leverage their development talent and produce customized solutions more quickly.

As Visual Basic applications have expanded and as their roles have matured, the mechanisms for connecting Visual Basic to databases have also multiplied and matured. Visual Basic 5.0 is no exception, as it adds support for several new methodologies to the list of supported techniques and a litany of new approaches to existing paradigms. While some of these new methods, such as the Client Batch cursor library for Remote Data Objects (RDO), are relatively subtle refinements of RDO, others, such as the use of Microsoft Transaction Server (Viper) to manage remote business objects, really require quite a bit of conversion and some fundamental architectural changes. Pressure exerted on Microsoft by developers has yielded much of this better performance, especially when it comes to accessing data. Those companies that used Visual Basic 4.0's performance as a springboard for launching competitive database interfaces or simply for performance-tuning applications will soon discover that this differentiating factor is gone.

If high-performance and an optimizing compiler is the good news about Visual Basic version 5.0, the really good news is that Microsoft SQL Server "Developer" Edition now ships with Visual Basic version 5.0 Enterprise Edition. This underscores how serious Microsoft is about making sure that developers have the best tools to do the job. I think you will be pleased with the combination of tools Microsoft has bundled together for this edition—designed with you, the client/server developer, in mind.

But the rest of the story is sobering for many developers. Visual Basic version 5.0, with all of its speed and features, is 32-bit only. Yes, that's right— 32-bit only. It won't run or create a control or compile an executable that runs on any 16-bit platform. But you've figured that out by now. If this is a surprise, you had better check on your stock of candles. For those of you stuck with 16-bit clients, you'll have to stick with Visual Basic version 3.0 or 4.0. Microsoft has been saying for years that there is no 16-bit development going on. They didn't lie. It might be time to bite the bullet and catch up.

Where We Are Now

In some ways, Visual Basic version 5.0 fundamentally redefines the way we approach programming because it adds a number of important new paradigms and lets you implement many of the technologies we have only alluded to in the past. Included in this litany of new features is yet another way to access remote databases like SQL Server—namely ODBCDirect—and, more important, an entirely new programming paradigm: event-driven and (virtually) fully asynchronous operations. In addition, for the first time since the introduction of VBSQL, where you had event-driven error and message handling, you now have the ability to start an asynchronous operation and simply wait for the event to fire that indicates its completion. Remote Data Objects (RDO) 2.0 also adds the concept of optimistic batch updates, dissociated result sets, and an entirely new cursor library to support all of this. It's now easier and actually practical to create Visual Basic–based ActiveX (OLE) Automation servers as executables that live on the server and implement common business objects.

Another fundamental change is the ability to create your own controls—using Visual Basic, just Visual Basic. Microsoft has chosen to call this technology the *ActiveX Platform*. It really isn't just OLE; it is far more flexible and means so much more. This technology means you can write your own bound controls or take existing controls (yours or Microsoft's or anyone else's) and make new controls from them—and make composites from these new controls. By itself, this is enough to radically change the way that we approach forms design, team development, and using (or not using) the Data or RemoteData controls. But there's more. This same technology lets you create stand-alone DLLs. These can be linked into an application or run out of process either on the workstation or on the remote server. Suddenly, the three-tiered techniques we have been harping on for years are easier to implement—and all in Visual Basic.

And even that's not the whole story. Remember what I said about Microsoft being totally committed to client/server technology? Well, they put their money where their mouth is. Visual Basic version 5.0 Enterprise Edition now includes (along with SQL Server) Microsoft Database Tools to help model databases and build queries (which you had to use Microsoft Access to do before), Transact SQL Debugger to track every single stored procedure being executed on your connection, and Microsoft Transaction Server to help implement three-tiered client/server applications. Microsoft's Visual Basic team now seems to understand what we need.

Unhappy with the Data control and the RemoteData control? Find them too limited? Too few bound controls, and those too limited and inflexible to use? Wait until you see the DataBindings collection. With Visual Basic version 5.0, you can now bind more than one property of a control to the columns of a result set—even with the controls you build yourself. You can also intercept the update operation and substitute your own code when it comes time to change a row. At this point, you can execute a stored procedure to do the update. Gee, it looks like the Data control and the RemoteData control have a few more weeks of life left in them after all.

While all of this seems really cool (and it is), you can still encounter a couple of dangers out there. Working with client/server development tools is something like leading your development team on a walking tour of a Florida swamp. While there are plenty of safe paths through the razor grass and slimy cypress logs, some of those mossy bumps sticking out of the muck aren't stones—they are the backs of alligators—and that attractive low-hanging vine is really a water moccasin basking in the sun. I hope to be able to point these out as we go.

Case in point: Microsoft has formally introduced another programming paradigm for client/server developers and unannounced another. Yes, the Microsoft Visual Basic team wants to talk about ODBCDirect but not about ADO. One is supported but might not make sense; the other makes sense but doesn't really exist yet for Visual Basic. Get the idea? If you hear Twilight Zone music in the background, that's perfectly normal—I hear it all the time.

Here's another problem: Microsoft, anxious to corral the wild herds of xBase flat-file developers, is now promoting at least eight development platforms: C++ (and Visual C++), Excel, SQL Server, FoxPro, Access, J++, and Visual Basic. (And I probably left a couple out.) Visual Basic also has been ported to a dizzying array (several hundred at last count) of third-party applications as well as to Microsoft Office 97. And that doesn't count Visual Basic Script and Active Server Pages. Developers, architects, and managers are all confused: Which platform will yield the best performance at the lowest cost? To add to the confusion, if you stick just with Visual Basic, you can now choose from at least six distinct ways to access client/server data (and these are just the Microsoft ways):

- *The Microsoft Jet database engine,* available in several versions. All versions are referenced through Data Access Objects (DAO) with or without the Data control.

  - Jet 1.1, supplied with Visual Basic 3.0 and accessed whenever you use the Data control or the Jet Data Access Objects (DAO), is now obsolete even for 16-bit platforms.

  - Jet 2.0 and Jet 2.5, available for use with Visual Basic 3.0 through "compatibility layers" and service packs for Microsoft Access. (This approach yields better efficiency from the engine, although many of Jet's features and objects aren't implemented in DAO 1.1.) This method is also obsolete. (It was obsolete when it was introduced.)

  - Jet 2.5 and Jet 3.0 and the new DAO, as available for use with Visual Basic 4.0, all enable new DAO features and are fully supported by Visual Basic 4.0 DAO. This method is almost obsolete, but useful for 16-bit platforms.

  - Jet 3.5, as available with Visual Basic version 5.0, enables even more DAO features—but only in a 32-bit version.

- *The RemoteData control (RDC)* and *the Remote Data Objects (RDO) version 2.0* merge the flexibility of RDO and ODBC with the ease of use of bound controls. This lightweight middleware 32-bit technology was introduced with Visual Basic version 4.0 and has emerged as the interface of choice for most SQL Server front ends.

- *ODBCDirect,* the newest official member of the data access team, lets you use DAO to connect directly through RDO instead of through Jet. Mostly useful from Microsoft Office where your choices are fairly limited without a Visual Basic version 5.0 Enterprise Edition license.

- *The Visual Basic Library for SQL Server,* now provided in both VBX and OCX forms (this was the *first* native interface to SQL Server), is obsolete (or at least terribly outdated) and already has been replaced by the ODBC API but eventually will be replaced by ADO.

- *The ODBC API*—that is, the application programming interface to open database connectivity—is available through the use of API DECLARE statements, as provided in the ODBC Programmer's Toolkit. (This is the *new* native interface to SQL Server and is quickly becoming the Esperanto of the database industry.)

- *ActiveX Data Objects (ADO)* is the newest programming interface to emerge from the badger works at Microsoft. Sure, you can use it in Visual Basic version 5.0, but you won't find a word of documentation on it with Visual Basic. Because it's simply an ActiveX object library like RDO, you can use it anywhere that hosts ActiveX components. As initially implemented, ADO exposes a small subset of RDO 2.0's functionality. When it emerges from its chrysalis stage, it will encompass all the functionality of RDO, DAO, and VBSQL and become the new "all-in-one" programming interface. Right now it's a little too limited to be used in place of any of these. I don't talk much about this pupa-stage technology in this book—again, more fodder for the next edition.

Figure 1-1 on the next page shows these six major players and the component layers needed to implement them.

This guide is designed to help you write Visual Basic applications that interact with SQL Server, using any of these six models. I devote a section of the guide to each of them—well, I combine the ODBCDirect information into the Jet/DAO and RDO sections. But this is still not the whole story. Now that Visual Basic 5.0 can create high-speed compiled executables and DLLs, the practicality of creating server-side or even out-of-process COM (or DCOM) business objects becomes a reality. This was not a real option with Visual Basic version 4.0 due to its limitations, so I suggested in the fourth edition that this relatively unbeaten path should be trod carefully. In Visual Basic version 5.0, this new approach can be safely added to the cornucopia of viable options available to you as a front-end developer.

Since there are so many choices, choosing the *right* interface will not be a simple undertaking. In the chapters that follow, I'll attempt to tie many of these development methodologies together and make some sense of the choices. The methods are presented in ascending order of complexity, from DAO/Jet to the ODBC API, and are loosely connected by how they are implemented (except for ADO, which is stuck out on the right of the chart because it is not really ready for any traditional client/server role). For example, the DAO/Jet, RDC/RDO, and ADO methods use programmatic object models; VBSQL and ODBC use API-driven programming models. My intention in these pages is to provide a single, definitive source of focused information on using Visual Basic to access SQL Server.

Some developers inflict their DAO/Jet performance problems on themselves. Many of the same developers who are attracted to Visual Basic and Jet also belong to the Flat Earth Society, where dBASE and flat-file ISAM databases put bread on the table. When the flat-earthers incorrectly port age-old techniques and designs over to relational schemas, they often doom their systems to pitifully low performance from the start.

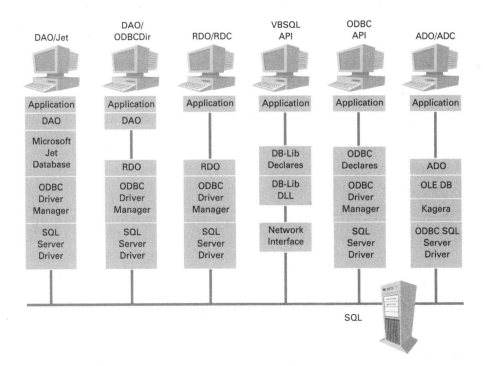

Figure 1-1 *Six ways to access SQL Server from Visual Basic*

One thing that we all have to learn while using Visual Basic version 5.0 is that we can't simply assume we're using the Jet database engine when we refer to DAO. From now on, we'll see a clear line drawn between DAO and any particular database engine. As a result of this trend, I expect to see eventually a new, combined object model to emerge from the DAO/RDO/ODBCDirect hodgepodge—ADO. But that's a story for a later time. Are you worried that your existing code won't work with the new design? Don't be. Microsoft is doing everything that makes sense to help you leverage all of your existing code. We won't be moving to ADO for some time yet.

One more thing: as we've already seen, the ODBC API has become the new *native* interface to SQL Server because over the past few years Microsoft has adopted this interface as the primary way to access its family of database products. However, that does *not* make it the interface of choice when developing front ends for SQL Server. While the ODBC API *is* the new native interface, it leaves a lot to be desired when it comes time to build successful client/server applications. Certainly, existing DB-Library–based applications will continue for some time to work on Microsoft-supported versions of SQL Server, but the future of the DBLIB API is clouded.

Unfortunately, Sybase and Microsoft have chosen to split their support of SQL Server. Because of this split, it's not at all clear how and if Sybase will support DBLIB applications, and therefore VBSQL, in the future. For now, Sybase really has no choice but to support DBLIB applications to some limited extent, and I think Sybase will also continue to support them for some time to come. But this does mean that many of the techniques discussed in this guide might not work as expected on Sybase systems.

VBSQL and C-language (DBLIB) applications can both be developed with an object-oriented architecture, and they are based on APIs that are virtually identical. Because of this similarity, many of the development techniques discussed here apply equally to C and to Visual Basic, especially the techniques for error and message handling, row buffering, using cursors, and handling stored procedures. If you are a C-oriented developer, the techniques discussed in this guide can help you gain valuable insights into writing SQL front-end applications, but you might have to spend some time learning Visual Basic.

And Where We're Headed

Before we really hit the road, let's get our bearings. Specific sections of this guide discuss the rest of this chapter's topics in detail, but here's where we'll take a first look at some recent and upcoming changes and improvements.

DAO/Jet

Visual Basic 5.0 uses Jet 3.5, the newest version of the Microsoft Jet database engine, first implemented in Microsoft Access 97 (Microsoft Office 97). Jet 3.5 can be used only in 32-bit operating systems like Microsoft Windows 95 and Microsoft Windows NT. We were really lucky to get 16-bit support in Visual Basic version 4.0—it was nearly dropped in that development cycle. Each of the Jet engine interfaces is implemented with a type library, which provides a means of making components available in the engine interface so that a developer can choose the most suitable object model. The various Jet object models support different sets or subsets of the Visual Basic DAO model.

Because Jet 3.5 as supplied with Visual Basic version 5.0 no longer runs in 16-bit environments, your type library choices are fairly limited. However, you can still choose a type library that continues to recognize your older (and generally obsolete) 16-bit code. Before you start to code a new application, or once you have imported an existing Visual Basic application, you need to choose one of the three matching type libraries:

- *The Microsoft DAO 3.5 Object Library* is for 32-bit systems only. This type library supports all the new Recordset objects but not the outdated Dynaset, Snapshot, or Table objects, properties, and methods used with Visual Basic 3.0. This library is used to help filter out the outdated objects and should be used for all new Visual Basic development.

- *The Microsoft DAO 2.5 Object Library* is for 16-bit systems only and isn't provided in Visual Basic version 5.0. It supports all the new Recordset objects *and* most of the outdated DAO objects, including the Dynaset, Snapshot, and Table objects. Some objects and methods introduced with Visual Basic 2.0 aren't supported (such as the ListFields and ListIndexes methods). This is the *only* library supported in 16-bit systems.

- *The Microsoft DAO 2.5/3.5 Compatibility Library* supports the new Recordset objects and the same set of objects supported by the Microsoft DAO 2.5 Object Library. This library is used to provide the widest compatibility for Visual Basic application conversions.

The dialog box for choosing a library is found in the Visual Basic References dialog box (available via the Project menu), as shown in *Figure 1-2* on the next page.

In an attempt to improve Jet's performance against ODBC back-end servers, a number of changes were made in the Jet database engine to help it deal with external databases and their special needs. Most of the changes were made in Jet 3.0, but one important new change is the addition of the ODBCDirect interface, which appears officially for the first time in DAO 3.5.

Many of you are trying to decide whether to use the Data Access Objects (DAO) partly implemented in Visual Basic 2.0, fully implemented in Visual Basic 3.0, further enhanced in Visual Basic 4.0, expanded to support RDO in Visual Basic 5.0, and replicated for ODBC back-end databases with the RDC/RDO model. A number of considerations make this a tough decision, but after you've read the chapters that follow, you'll have a pretty good idea of what to do. Or maybe you'll decide to go into decorative landscaping instead—it's a lot more soothing.

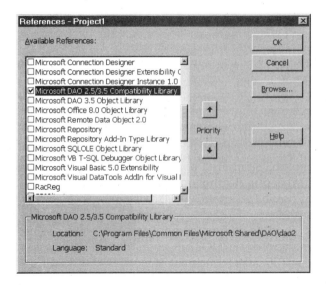

Figure 1-2 *Dialog box for choosing a type library*

The Jet 3.0 and 3.5 enhancements did make Jet faster—to an extent. In some respects, these versions are *much* faster than Jet 1.1. For one thing, the new versions delegate more query processing to the back end instead of trying to pull the data over the net to process queries locally. For another, their caching and buffering have improved. They populate Data control Resultset objects in a background task, and they support multiple result sets from stored procedures, though they do it in a somewhat strange way. The new versions of DAO/Jet trap errors and build a collection of all those encountered while running a query. They support the transaction model better by basing transaction scope on the new Workspace object. They also support SQL pass-through better, even with attached tables, and they provide better and more intelligent connection management schemes, permitting you to override connection sharing.

Unfortunately, however, even the newest versions of DAO/Jet don't utilize all the new SQL Server features and some of the more sophisticated aspects of Transact SQL (TSQL) and stored-procedure programming. The principal reason for these omissions is the desire to have DAO/Jet act as a generic interface. Therefore, no substantive functionality can be added to support SQL Server–specific features that aren't supported elsewhere. For example, DAO/Jet doesn't support server-side cursors, and stored-procedure output parameters and return codes are still unavailable. Using DAO/Jet, there is still no way to limit the number of rows returned by a query (other than through the WHERE clause) and queries are still canceled by embedded TSQL RAISERROR statements. Queries that are executed through DAO are still run synchronously, with no way to cancel a query that has run amok, and messages and PRINT statements returned from the server are still ignored.

The ODBCDirect Model

Just before the senior product manager for the DAO/Jet team left for Australia (literally), he sent out a memo announcing the introduction of another new DAO programming model: ODBCDirect. This new interface decouples Data Access Objects from the Microsoft Jet database engine and reconnects DAO to ODBC databases (only) through RDO. The intent was to create a database-independent interface that used the familiar ISAM-oriented DAO programming model but broke its ties to the Jet engine, which is not particularly well suited to remote data access. Frankly, that was the intent in the first place—to create a programming interface that didn't lean toward one database architecture or another. Unfortunately, that's not what was originally implemented. DAO/Jet proved to be very ISAM-oriented and couldn't deal adequately with the realities of client/server design without the help of some pretty careful coding. Sure, you could write front-end applications to SQL Server using Jet/DAO, but you had to remember to watch where you stepped.

When it came time to make DAO do what remote developers needed in Visual Basic version 4.0, its ties to Jet made easy changes virtually impossible—and this is when RDO was created. ODBCDirect leverages the work done by the RDO team by cross-wiring DAO objects to the RDO ODBC interface instead of to Jet. No, ODBCDirect doesn't mean that you can run Visual Basic version 4.0 (which supported the ODBCDirect beta) applications in 16-bit mode. Remember that ODBCDirect uses RDO, and RDO is strictly 32-bit. The new Office 97 applications also use ODBCDirect—but not RDO unless you have a Visual Basic version 5.0 Enterprise Edition license (or one of the other RDO development platforms). ODBCDirect also doesn't implement all of the RDO interface—but nearly all. For example, it doesn't expose the event-driven operations, but I expect this to arrive sooner or later (just not as soon as Visual Basic version 5.0). Should you use RDO over ODBCDirect? Let's leave that question for the sections on RDO and ODBCDirect.

The RDC/RDO Model

One of the most powerful features of Visual Basic 5.0 is the new RemoteData control (RDC). This custom control addresses the specific needs of remote ODBC database engines, especially SQL Server. All the features unsupported by the Jet/DAO interface are supported by the RDC/RDO model. The Remote-Data control has been generally overhauled for Visual Basic version 5.0, as the 1.0 version was pretty "challenged," and it sports a couple of enhancements to accommodate the client batch cursor library.

The Remote Data Objects are also broadly enhanced in Visual Basic version 5.0, as the following features were introduced:

- *Event-driven asynchronous operations*, which means you no longer have to poll for completion of asynchronous operations. All by itself, this feature is a pretty powerful enhancement that can revolutionize the way we approach asynchronous operations.

- *Virtually complete coverage of asynchronous operations*, which means fewer times when your application is blocked, which means smoother-running applications.

- *Optimistic batch concurrency*. This feature is implemented by a new cursor library developed using technology provided by the FoxPro team. It also permits you to create a stand-alone rdoResultset object, update it, and reconnect it later to post batch updates.

- *Stand-alone rdoConnection objects*, which means easier programming and the ability to attach connections to queries so that they can be easily executed against a set of selected connections.

- *A new stand-alone rdoQuery object*, which makes programming easier by replacing the cumbersome rdoPreparedStatement object. Basically, all of the rdoPreparedStatement methods and properties are supported in the rdoQuery, so don't worry about backward compatibility.

The RDC is used as a replacement for the standard Data control, and it totally eliminates the need for the Jet database engine. With the RDC, you can create applications that use bound controls, just as you can with the standard Data control, but the Remote Data Objects (RDO) implemented by the RDC are somewhat different from the DAOs implemented by the Jet database engine. I think you will find, however, that the RDO model has all the functionality you need; in fact, many of the Jet methods and properties that the RDO model lacks were in the DAO model only to support Jet's ISAM heritage.

The RDC/RDO model also exposes the ODBC handles you need for using direct ODBC calls against a variety of data sources. This way, if the interface doesn't support some required feature, you can attempt to use the ODBC API to implement it. The RDO model is designed around the ODBC API: it supports an object hierarchy identical to that used by the API. This approach gives you more control over the user interface and the back-end interface, as well as a lot more flexibility—however, this technique can be very dangerous.

VBSQL

Let's take a short detour here and look at some changes to Visual Basic that have had implications for the Visual Basic Library for SQL Server (VBSQL). Between 1993 and 1995, Microsoft completely rewrote Visual Basic, and it's no longer the mostly assembly-language monolithic application that Visual Basic 3.0 was. In most ways, as I began this chapter telling you, Visual Basic 4.0 was an entirely new product. As such, it is now heavily dependent on object linking and embedding (what Microsoft now calls "ActiveX" technology), Visual Basic for Applications (VBA), and other loadable "components," including Jet and RDO. As a result of this redesign, Visual Basic 4.0 was able to create OLE DLLs and applications that act as OLE servers and clients. It can also support development add-ins like SourceSafe. Visual Basic version 5.0 is no different except that it can also create fully compiled ActiveX executables and DLLs. It starts from the Visual Basic version 4.0 platform and builds on additional functionality—still using component architecture.

While Visual Basic 4.0 was provided in both 16-bit and 32-bit versions, for use on 16-bit Windows and 32-bit Windows 95 and Windows NT systems, Visual Basic version 5.0 (as I have said) is 32-bit only. Upon close inspection, these two versions are very different in many respects. For example, the 32-bit versions of Visual Basic are designed to work with 16-bit Unicode strings. (Unicode, for your information, is a 16-bit-per-character storage format used to support languages that need additional bits to represent their alphabets.) This single aspect of the 32-bit versions can have a significant impact on the conversion of 16-bit Visual Basic 3.0 applications that pass strings to DLLs; VBSQL applications are among these. In addition, since the Microsoft Windows operating system itself has changed drastically, calls made from Visual Basic applications to Windows APIs must be recoded and, in some cases, completely redesigned. Because of these differences, application conversion to the Windows 95 or the Windows NT platform can be a challenge, especially with a larger application. You can make it easier by studying the documentation and Knowledge Base articles on conversion that are included with Visual Basic. In most cases, you should be able to port existing Visual Basic 3.0 applications to 16-bit Visual Basic 4.0 without trouble—assuming you don't use any nasty tricks based on inside knowledge of the Visual Basic or Windows architecture. Moving from 16-bit Visual Basic version 3.0 applications to 32-bit Visual Basic will be increasingly difficult as we move toward future versions of Visual Basic that are less accommodating to 16-bit nuances.

NOTE Can you say "rewrite"? VBX custom controls are supported in the 16-bit version of Visual Basic 4.0, but you have to use OCX equivalents of all custom controls for 32-bit programs. And guess what—not all control vendors are ready with 32-bit versions. (The slowest to convert will probably be those who have gone out of business.) Most of the applications written for Visual Basic 3.0 can be imported into Visual Basic 4.0 or 5.0 and recompiled, but some will require significant recoding, rethinking, and other adjustments before they will work as before.

Though Visual Basic itself has changed radically, the methods and techniques used for developing VBSQL applications are generally unchanged. Even though Visual Basic version 5.0 permits implementation of user-written event handlers, you still need a custom control to implement the DB-Library error and message callback routines for both the 16-bit and the 32-bit operating systems. The Microsoft SQL Server group has developed a new VBSQL.OCX to support 32-bit operating systems. It's designed to be a virtual clone of the 16-bit version. The latest version of this control is on the CD that is included with this book.

The ODBC API

The ODBC API continues to be an enigma. Thanks to some unclear messages being sent out by Microsoft (myself included), many of you are confused as to its role. While ODBC is of vital importance for Microsoft's connectivity strategy, it is *not* an ideal programming interface for Visual Basic client/server developers. If you think of the ODBC API as a low-level interface and not as a primary development path, you will be a lot happier. The API becomes interesting only when the other interfaces (like RDO) fail to meet immediate needs—then, and only then, should you consider programming to this API.

The ODBC API has some competitors: DB-Library and VBSQL, DAO/Jet, ODBCDirect, the RDC/RDO model, ADO, and third-party interfaces. Widespread acceptance of the ODBC API will be affected by how widely its competitors are accepted (or rejected). The ODBC API is every bit as fast as DB-Library and VBSQL; those who say otherwise are misinformed. Only time will tell which of these programming models will become the most widely accepted one, but my money is ultimately on RDO 2.0, the new kid on the block.

Many developers coded to the ODBC API on 16-bit platforms when they didn't have (or couldn't use) RDO or VBSQL. I can tell you that those folks are in for a fairly tough job when it comes time for them to convert to 32-bit. They'll discover that many of the rules have changed, as is bound to happen with an API approach. Many of the routines they coded so carefully before no longer work in the 32-bit Unicode world. Because of these and other problems, I don't currently recommend this interface for Visual Basic developers.

2 Chapter

Data Access: A Jump Start

Creating a Sample Application

Using DAO/Jet

Using the RemoteData Control and Remote Data Objects

Using ODBCDirect

Using VBSQL and the ODBC API

Comparing the Samples

This chapter walks you through eight rudimentary applications—two accessing DAO/Jet, two using the RDC/RDO model, two using ODBCDirect, and one each for VBSQL and the ODBC API—that contrast the programming models described in Chapter 1. Each sample application performs the following three tasks:

- Opens a connection to SQL Server

- Executes a query based on a user-supplied value

- Returns values from the result set into a grid control or to a set of text boxes on the Visual Basic form

Because the sample applications are not expected to edit the results, I haven't provided the additional code that you would need for managing updates. The applications use the *Pubs* database, so you can test them with any version of SQL Server. (Note, however, that the ODBC drivers that ship with Visual Basic 5.0 don't work with Sybase SQL Server; Visigenic and other ODBC driver vendors have suitable Sybase drivers—or so I am told.) Source code for all the sample applications is on this guide's companion CD. For the most part, the sample applications use Visual Basic 5.0 coding conventions; significant differences are noted.

Each of the programming models used for the sample applications requires one or more supplementary data access components in order to function. Generally, these components provide a programmatic or bound-control interface between Visual Basic and SQL Server. Most, but not all, of the components are included in Visual Basic 5.0. In the case of VBSQL, however, you must do some shopping before trying the code: only the Enterprise Edition of Visual Basic includes any of the VBSQL components. To make your evaluation of VBSQL easier, I have included the latest version of the VBSQL controls on the CD that comes with the book. But you still need to get a copy of Microsoft SQL Server "Developer" or "Workstation" Edition to get a license for this control. *Figure 2-1* shows where each programming model's components can be acquired.

Figure 2-1
Sources of Supplementary Components for Programming Models

Programming Model	Components	Source
Jet DAO, Data control	DAO 3.5 libraries, Jet engine, ODBC driver manager, ODBC SQL Server driver	Visual Basic 5.0, as installed with setup, Professional, Enterprise Editions
RDO, RemoteData control	RemoteData control, RDO object library DLLs, ODBC driver manager, ODBC SQL Server driver	Visual Basic 5.0, Enterprise Edition, installed with setup (32-bit only)
ODBCDirect	DAO 3.5 libraries, ODBC driver manager, ODBC SQL Server driver	Visual Basic 5.0, Enterprise Edition, installed with setup (32-bit only)
VBSQL	VBSQL.OCX (32-bit), DBNMPNTW.DLL (32-bit), VBSQL.VBX (16-bit), DBNMP3.DLL (16-bit), W3DBLIB.DLL (16-bit), MSDBLIB3.DLL (16-bit), VBSQL.BI (16-bit), VBSQL.BAS (32-bit)	Now included with Visual Basic 5.0, Enterprise Edition, via SQL Server 6.5 Programmer's Toolkit (only in SQL Server Developer or Workstation Edition) or on Microsoft Developer Network (MSDN) CD
ODBC API	ODBC driver manager, ODBC SQL Server driver	As included with Visual Basic 5.0 Professional, Enterprise Editions, and SQL Server 6.5

It's a little early to be thumbing for rides on that new RDO UserConnection Designer freeway over on the left or the ActiveX skyway over on the right. We will get to those new architectures after a while. Let's just get the basics down first. I would feel pretty bad if you were hit by a passing beer truck before you knew the ropes.

Creating a Sample Application

As part of the development process, before you can get the samples using the Data control, the RemoteData control, and VBSQL to work, you will have to add an appropriate custom control for your project to the Visual Basic form by using the Controls tab of the Visual Basic Components dialog box (available by choosing Components on the Project menu) to activate the specific type of data access library you need. When you use the Data control, for example, you automatically activate the DAO/Jet mode, the Jet database engine, and its associated dynamic-link libraries (DLLs). Once activated, the libraries become part of your application—not physically attached to your executable, but logically linked to it and brought into memory when they are first accessed at run time.

If you wanted to cross the desert, you probably wouldn't visit a used-camel lot in downtown Cleveland to shop for a suitable beast of burden. After all, you can't tell how your camel will ride or deal with the heat until you get it out on the sand, and if you're not careful, you just might end up with a beast that bites. But choosing complex development tools can feel like that kind of shopping.

To get started, position the controls on a Visual Basic form. You'll need one TextBox control to accept the name of the title that will be used as a search argument. You'll also need either the DBGrid control or a set of text boxes for displaying the results. It's possible to use the DBGrid control without having bound it first, but it might be easier to use the standard Grid control or text boxes for those applications that don't use the Data control. In some cases, you'll need to add the Data control, the RemoteData control, or the VBSQL custom control to the sample form.

If you're using Visual Basic Jet Data Access Objects (DAO) and aren't using the Data control, you'll need to register the Jet database engine by choosing one of the Microsoft DAO *x.x* Object Library options from the References dialog box. If you don't, your application will compile, but when you encounter the first Data Access Object or method—usually OpenDatabase—at run time,

Visual Basic will complain about an undefined user-specified object. Which DAO version should you choose? For now, choose the Jet 3.5 version if you're using 32-bit Visual Basic. Choose the Jet 2.5 version if you're using the 16-bit version of Visual Basic. (And if you're still running the 8-bit version, heaven help you.)

Figure 2-2 displays the controls and interfaces used for the eight sample applications. In the case of the DAO model and the ODBC API, no additional controls are needed; everything necessary is already included with Visual Basic. To use the RemoteData control, you'll need the Visual Basic Enterprise Edition—the RDC won't work in the other editions. (And, no, you won't be able to buy a single Enterprise Edition and then develop on a Professional Edition workstation because of registry license key issues.)

Figure 2-2
Controls and Interfaces for the Sample Applications

Interface	Engine Interface	User Interface	Automatically Access Bound Controls
Data control	Jet/DAO/ODBC 	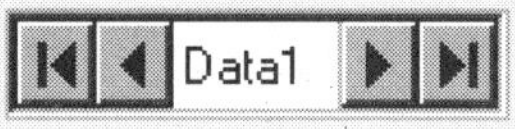	Yes
Data Access Object (DAO/Jet)	Jet/DAO/ODBC 	None	No
RemoteData control	RDO/ODBC 	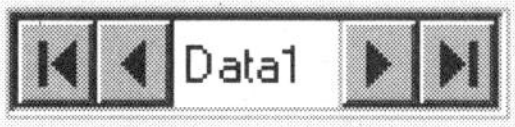	Yes
Remote Data Object (RDO)	RDO/ODBC	None	No
Data control with ODBCDirect	DAO/RDO/ODBC	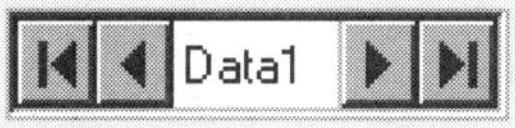	Yes
ODBCDirect (DAO) Data Access Object	DAO/RDO/ODBC	None	No
ODBC API	API only	None	No
VBSQL	VBSQL.VBX/ OCX DB-Library 	None	No

Using DAO/Jet

As already noted, the sample applications using the Data control and DAO access the Microsoft Jet database engine by default. We'll consider these two sample applications together here, but you'll also see that much of what we have to say about procedures that use the Data control will also be true of those that use the RemoteData control. Remember that while you do use DAO to access the ODBCDirect interface, Jet isn't involved, so we'll postpone that side trip until later.

An Application Using the Data Control

The Data control is a bound-control interface that by default connects the Jet database engine with SQL Server through the ODBC driver manager and the SQL Server driver, as you see in the following illustration:

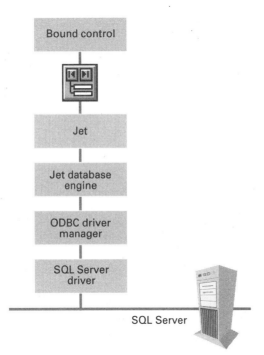

I'll show you how to bypass Jet completely a little later when we use ODBCDirect with the Data control. This technique hasn't been used extensively in larger SQL Server shops up to now, but it's easy to set up and program. The Data control's real advantage is its ability to access the heterogeneous-join capability of the Jet engine and map complex page-based data (like Text and Image columns) to picture box controls. To implement the sample application that uses the Data control, you need very little additional code. Simply set the form-control properties at design time. To set design-time properties, you will need to add the Data control, set the Connect property, and set the DatabaseName property.

Adding the Data control

Add the Data control to the form, as shown here:

The Data control icon appears on the toolbar and looks like this:

Visual Basic 3.0 doesn't require you to register object libraries. In Visual Basic 5.0, once you add the Data control to your form, DAO is automatically registered; with no additional hassle, you can now use both the Data control and the DAO that it creates.

Setting the Connect property

NOTE The Connect property is simply a string that tells the ODBC driver manager which driver to use and who is using it. It has about a dozen parameters—most of which are optional. Since most of the techniques we look at here use ODBC, they end up using the connect string one way or another. These examples code the ODBC connect string with the minimum number of parameters, to keep your life simple.

Using the Properties window in Design mode (set focus to the Data control and press F4), set the Data control's Connect property as follows:

```
ODBC;UID=<your user ID>;PWD=<your password>;DATABASE=Pubs
```

Use your own SQL Server user ID (UID) and password (PWD) in this string. (If you don't know your user ID and password, check with your SQL server administrator.) If you're using integrated security, one of the new features available with SQL Server 4.2 and later versions, you won't need a user ID or password, since the Microsoft Windows NT environment can manage user security, in which case your Windows network domain logon name and password will be used to validate your access to the SQL server. If you want to use domain-managed (integrated) security, use the *UID=;PWD=;* syntax in the connect string. This is interpreted by the ODBC layer as a signal to attempt to use integrated security. Note that this connect string sets the default database to *Pubs*.

What if your user ID is *Fred* and your password is *MidField* and your default database name is *PUBS?* The connect string will look like this:

```
ODBC;UID=Fred;PWD=MidField;DATABASE=PUBS
```

Don't try to pretty this up by adding extra spaces—these are seen as part of the values, so leave 'em out.

Setting the DatabaseName property

32bit ODBC

Set the Data control's DatabaseName property to the ODBC data source name (DSN) that you have already established. If you don't have a data source set up yet, start the Control Panel in Windows and click on the ODBC setup icon. Visual Basic offers two of these, one for 16-bit ODBC drivers and the other for 32-bit drivers. Use the version that matches the version of Visual Basic you are using. (The illustration to the left shows the version for 32-bit Visual Basic.)

Visual Basic version 5.0 includes the new ODBC driver manager and support code that has an entirely new set of interactive ODBC DSN dialog boxes. While these might not be familiar to old ODBC hands, they are pretty intuitive and offer far more flexibility.

At this point, you'll be prompted to add, change, or delete one of the existing ODBC DSNs. Add one if you don't already have a DSN, or choose one of the existing names to modify. If you choose to add a new DSN, select *SQL Server* as the driver name. If you don't see *SQL Server* in the list of available drivers, you didn't check it in the Visual Basic Setup dialog boxes or it has been misplaced. Go back and reinstall it now—without those drivers, you won't get anywhere. In the next dialog box, be sure to enter the following information. (All the other entries for this dialog box are optional.)

- *The name of your data source.* This doesn't have to be any particular name, but it should be something that identifies where the SQL Server data is coming from. I usually name my data sources after the database, *not* the server. (For the purposes of this sample application, use *Pubs* as the new DSN.)

- *A description of the data source.* Again, you have free rein; enter anything that helps to identify this data source. This information shows up in the ODBC dialog boxes.

- *The network name of the server that is running SQL Server.* Nope, don't add \\ to the name. For Windows NT or OS/2 servers, simply give the server name. It's more complicated if the server is somewhere out on the WWW, but we'll talk about that later.

- *The name of the SQL Server database.* These sample applications use *Pubs*, so if your SQL Server database is case-sensitive, be sure to use a capital *P*. If you don't provide a default database here or in the connect string, the default database is automatically changed to the default database that was chosen by the server administrator (SA) when your SQL Server logon account was created.

When the time comes to establish a connection, any details you don't provide at design time to the Data control's ODBC connection properties are gathered via ODBC-created dialog boxes at run time. Values from the DSN provide the default values. Notice that the DSN does *not* include either the user ID or the password, although the values that were last used might be stored in the DSN as a default UID and PWD. To avoid these dialog boxes, be sure to provide all the required parameters to the Data control's Connect property or DSN entry. But if the values you or your user supply are wrong, these dialog boxes will always appear. We'll come back to this again later.

All the programming models except VBSQL require you to use a connect string and a DSN. (All models, including the ODBC API, support DSN-less and file-based DSN connections.) Once you have created a DSN and a working connect string, you can use this information each time it's called for in the sample applications. In Visual Basic 3.0, DSN entries are maintained in an ASCII file (ODBC.INI). In later versions of Visual Basic, this information is kept both in the ODBC.INI file *and* in the Windows system registry.

Setting the DBGrid properties

The sample applications for the Data control and the RemoteData control both use the DBGrid control to expose the result set returned from the query. To get a feel for how easy this is, you can set up the DBGrid control in Design mode, or you can simply use the sample from the companion disc. Once the DBGrid control is installed on your form, set the DataSource property of the DBGrid control to the Name property of the Data control: Data1. This *cannot* be done in code at run time. Because we're going to execute a parameter query that is built on the fly, you also can't use the Retrieve Fields feature of the DBGrid control. Sure, you can set up a dummy query that returns the same columns that the working query returns, but let's use the manual method for now.

Click the right mouse button on the DBGrid control, and choose Edit. Once in the DBGrid Edit mode, you can select one of the columns and, again clicking the right mouse button, insert a new column. Since the DBGrid control is initialized with two columns, you have to do this only once. While still in Edit mode, right-click on the control and choose Properties. Set the column properties as shown in *Figure 2-3*. The SQL parameter query we are going to use returns the Title, Price, and Author fields, so you need to set the data field and column headings accordingly. If you want to see formatting for the Price column in the grid, set the NumberFormat property in the column Properties

CAUTION

In setting up a data source, be sure to leave the default language alone unless you are well aware of what it does. If you use English-language applications, you should leave the default set to English—even if your application keeps track of French fries.

It's a bad idea to change the entries in the ODBC.INI files or the registry without using the ODBC administration tools. In fact, mucking with the Windows system registry is a lot like doing brain surgery on yourself in the bathroom mirror: just about the time you think you've got it right, your daughter, demanding instant access to her makeup, barges in and bumps your elbow. "Sorry, daddy" might be the last words you understand.

window. The remaining properties don't play a significant role in our sample application, so just leave them alone for now. All the work that remains for setting up this sample application is done in code. These procedures are fairly short in general, especially when you use the Data control.

Figure 2-3
Column Properties Settings

DBGrid Property	Setting	Notes
DataSource	Data1	Points to Data control, which creates Recordset object
AllowUpdate	False	No changes planned
Caption	"Example 1"	To identify the grid
DBGrid.Columns		Set each column's properties
(0).Caption	"Title"	Set with Edit mode
(1).Caption	"Price"	To label the columns
(2).Caption	"Author"	
(0).DataField	Title	To identify the columns
(1).DataField	Price	
(2).DataField	Author	
(1).NumberFormat	"Currency"	To format the dollar amounts

Coding the SearchButton_Click event procedure

For the SearchButton_Click event procedure, simply set the Data control's RecordSource property to the SQL query, as shown in the sample code that follows. (OK, this *is* a little complicated, but it's not unusual for a real-world application. After all, in most serious client/server applications, you don't just point to a single table and pull back all the rows; when your database tables have 100,000,000 rows, that would be a fatal mistake, not just an inconvenience. But *you* know that!) Note that the SQL parameter query filters rows by using the value from the TitleDesired text box, concatenating the contents of the TextBox control with the SQL query and surrounding it with single quotes. When the result set is created with the Refresh method, I make sure the whole result set gets populated so that we can run another query later. I also use the new With statement that makes object coding simpler. To make sure you get this right, use a Debug statement to view the syntax before it is executed; leaving out the Debug statement is arrogant and angers the Saints:

```
Private Sub SearchButton_Click()
SQL$ = "Select Title, Price, Au_Fname + ' ' + Au_Lname Author" _
    & " From Titles T, TitleAuthor TA, Authors" _
    & " Where T.Title_ID = TA.Title_ID" _
    & " And TA.Au_ID = Authors.AU_ID" _
    & " And Title like '%" & (TitleDesired) & "%'"
```

```
Debug.Print SQL$

End Sub
```

Setting the Data control options property

If the syntax of the preceding SQL statement seems a little unusual, note that it does *not* use Jet database engine SQL syntax. It was written in the Transact-SQL (TSQL) dialect, used exclusively by the SQL server. Therefore, you must tell the Jet database engine not to parse the query or check its syntax but simply to pass it through to the SQL server for processing. To do this, set the Data control's Option property to 64 (*dbSQLPassThrough*). You can do this at design time by using the Data control's Property window, or you can do it in code. Because the query is using SQL PassThrough, the resulting Jet Recordset object allows only read-only access. You can set the Data control's ReadOnly property to True if desired, but this really isn't necessary; it gets set automatically at run time:

```
Data1.Options = dbSQLPassThrough
Data1.ReadOnly = True
```

Executing the query

After the RecordSource property and Options properties are set, use the Data control's Refresh method to establish a connection and execute the query automatically. This procedure is coded as follows:

```
Data1.Refresh
```

The Jet database engine processes the request and returns when (and only when) the first qualifying row is ready. The Data control then populates any bound controls and manages the current-row pointer.

Coding the CloseButton_Click event procedure

Since the Data control automatically manages the Data Access Object that it creates, you don't need any special code here to close databases or result sets. To end the application gracefully, however, add the following code to the CloseButton_Click event procedure:

```
Unload Form1
```

Note that we did not just use an END statement here. That statement should be avoided like a cheap lawnmower, since it doesn't permit Visual Basic procedures to finish their applications correctly.

Evaluating the results

Once control returns to your application, Visual Basic and the Data control automatically display the rows of the Recordset object according to the latest results of the SQL parameter query. In accordance with the size of the DBGrid control, the first and *n*th rows of the Recordset object are displayed. If more

SQL Server 6.0 made a fairly radical change in its SQL parser. Basically, it adopted a SQL syntax virtually (but not exactly) identical to that used by the Jet database engine. This means that the join syntax you use when working with Microsoft Access should work almost without change in TSQL queries. I have left these examples in the old format because they still work against SQL Server 6.0 and older versions of SQL Server as well. It's tough to teach this old dog new tricks. I'll talk about the differences again later.

than one title matches the query criteria, you can use the Data control buttons to move either forward or backward to another row in the Recordset object. Note that as you manipulate the Data control, one row after another in the DBGrid control becomes the current row. To end the application, click the Close button. This action unceremoniously unloads the first form.

TIP When you install Visual Basic 5.0, the VB.INI file is reinstalled. The Visual Basic 5.0 version of the file doesn't include a line to activate the Data control, however, so if you expect to continue using the Data control from Visual Basic 3.0, add a line to the VB.INI file:

```
DataAccess=1
```

An Application Using Data Access Objects with Jet

By default, the Data Access Object (DAO) programmatic interface connects to the Jet database engine, which interacts with the SQL server through the ODBC driver manager and the SQL Server driver, as you see in the following illustration:

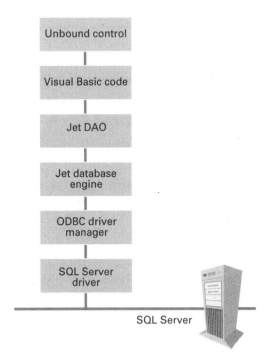

A little later, we'll take a look at using DAO with the ODBCDirect (RDO) interface. In the past, when Visual Basic developers have needed to access SQL Server with a data object model, the DAO interface was their first (and sometimes only) choice. DAO objects, methods, and properties can be used in conjunction with the Data control or by themselves. That is, once you open a connection using the Data control, the Data Access Objects it exposes through its properties can be used as if you had created them in code.

This sample application illustrates the basic use of the DAO model for accessing SQL Server without benefit of the Data control. In this case, we implement the data binding and create the data objects in code. We also include code to clean up the DAO interface when we are done. (All these ancillary operations were managed automatically by the Data control in the previous sample application.)

Start with the form used in the sample application for the Data control. To display the current row of the result set, create a form that has three text boxes instead of the DBGrid control. Sure, you could use the common Grid control or even the DBGrid control in unbound mode, but that would be overkill for this sample application; besides, use of the TextBox controls illustrates a more basic type of front end—a model that many serious front-end applications still use. Set up your form to look like this one:

Registering the Jet Data Access Objects

Using the References dialog box in Visual Basic (available via the Project menu), make sure that the Data Access Objects (DAO) are registered. As we saw in Chapter 1 (Figure 1-2), you can choose from two to a half-dozen different Jet DAO libraries; for now, choose the Microsoft DAO 3.5 Object Library if you are working with 32-bit Visual Basic and the Microsoft DAO 2.5 Object Library if you are working with 16-bit Visual Basic (Visual Basic version 4.0). If you don't register DAO, your application will fail to compile as you make your first reference to a DAO method or object. (In the previous sample application, DAO registration was automatic when the Data control was added to the form.)

NOTE   If you didn't follow the advice in the Visual Basic 5.0 README file and you installed Visual Basic 5.0 without first uninstalling Visual Basic 4.0, you'll see all of the old 16-bit libraries, too.

Adding data navigation buttons

Add a pair of buttons to navigate up and down the result set. When you click those buttons, your event procedure will move the current record pointer to the adjacent record. This sample application, as mentioned, uses the DAO interface without also using the Data control. If we were using it along with the Data control, however, we would note that the Data control also has buttons that reposition the current record pointer to the first and last records of the result set, and we could add those buttons if we wanted to; they would make the code for this sample application only a couple of lines longer.

The rest of the work for this sample application is done in code. Since you won't be using bound controls, you need to code procedures that move data from the current record to the TextBox controls. You also have to code procedures to open the database, create the result set, and close the Data Access Objects when you are done with them. (I added code to disable the Previous Record and Next Record buttons when clicking them would have caused problems.) For the most part, you don't need to worry about data type binding. This is done for you automatically.

Coding the global variables

To start with, declare global variables that are used to contain the Database and Recordset objects created in other procedures:

```
Dim SQL As String
Dim Db As Database
Dim Rs As Recordset
Dim i As Integer
```

Coding the Form_Load event procedure

Now we'll write code to open the database connection and instantiate the Database object. In this case, instead of just setting design-time properties, code the Form_Load event procedure, as shown here. Note that the code refers to the *Pubs* data source name (DSN). (If you need to review the details of creating a DSN, see the previous sample application.)

Set the connect string to

```
ODBC;DSN=Pubs;UID=<your user ID>;PWD=<your password>
```

Enter your SQL Server user ID and password in this string, just as you did in the previous sample application. (And if you *still* don't know your user ID and password, consider getting into a new line of work.)

NOTE Notice that the connect string starts with *ODBC;*. This is required by DAO to differentiate how it handles parameters destined for other ISAM interfaces. You won't include it with RDO or elsewhere.

The following example assumes that the workstation running the sample application has already been logged on with a valid user ID and password to a Windows NT domain and that the SQL server has been set up with domain-managed (integrated) security:

```
Private Sub Form_Load()

' The TestPubs DSN simply points to my local server's
' Pubs database.

Set Db = OpenDatabase("TestPubs", False, False, _
            "odbc;uid=;pwd=;database=Pubs;")
End Sub

FLErrors:
    Debug.print "Error:"; Err, Error$
    Resume Next
End Sub
```

If your error handler gets a 429 error ("ActiveX component can't create object or return reference to this object"), you didn't register the DAO objects properly or you misspelled one of the objects. Press F1 to get more details on this error. If you get a successful open, the Database object in the *Db* variable is valid and can be used to create your record set.

Coding the SearchButton_Click event procedure

In this procedure, the query is executed and data from the first row is moved into the TextBox controls (in your code). Use the same SQL statement that was used in the sample application for the Data control.

As you did in the previous sample application, filter the query with the value passed in from the TitleDesired text box. Notice that we use the MoveLast method to fully populate the result set (and free up the connection for another operation). This SQL syntax is still not compatible with the Jet engine, however, so we use the SQL pass-through option again. In this case, it is specified in the OpenRecordset method with the value *dbSQLPassThrough*:

```
Private Sub SearchButton_Click()
SQL$ = "Select Title, Price, Au_Fname + ' ' + Au_Lname Author" _
    & " From Titles T, TitleAuthor TA, Authors" _
```

In the object-oriented world, you have classes or types of objects. You also have $12 words like *instantiate*, which means "to create an instance or copy of one class of object." Thus a rabbit is a *class* of object, a specific lop-eared bunny is an *instance* of the rabbit object, and what two consenting lop-eared bunnies do in the privacy of their own hutch is a form of *instantiation*.

(continued)

```
        & " Where T.Title_ID = TA.Title_ID" _
        & " And TA.Au_ID = Authors.AU_ID" _
        & " And Title like '%" & (TitleDesired) & "%'"

Debug.Print SQL$

Set Rs = Db.OpenRecordset(SQL, dbOpenSnapshot, dbSQLPassThrough)
Rs.MoveLast: Rs.MoveFirst        ' To fully populate the Recordset
If Rs.RecordCount > 0 Then
    ShowRecord
End If
End Sub
```

Coding the ShowRecord procedure

Once the data has been fetched into the Recordset object, the next step is to move the data into the TextBox controls, where the user can see it. This procedure assumes that the Recordset object has been created. If there is no current record—as when the current record pointer is positioned beyond either end of the Recordset object, or when there are no records at all—the appropriate buttons are disabled and no attempt is made to reference the current record:

```
Sub ShowRecord()
'
' Fill the form fields from the Recordset.
'
If Rs.BOF = False And Rs.EOF = False Then
'
'   Note the three different ways to address the Recordset fields.
'
    DataFound(0) = Rs!Title
    DataFound(1) = Format$(Rs("Price"), "$###.##")
    DataFound(2) = Rs(2)
End If

PreviousRecordButton.Enabled = Not Rs.BOF
NextRecordButton.Enabled = Not Rs.EOF

End Sub
```

Coding the Recordset navigation buttons

The navigation buttons can allow the user to see any additional rows of the result set. These buttons use the MoveNext and MovePrevious methods to position the pointer for the current record within the record set. Note that this code does not prevent movement past either end of the Recordset object; the ShowRecord procedure automatically deals with this contingency:

```
Private Sub NextRecordButton_Click()
Rs.MoveNext
ShowRecord
End Sub
```

```
Private Sub PreviousRecordButton_Click()
Rs.MovePrevious
ShowRecord
End Sub
```

Coding the CloseButton_Click event procedure

To make sure your application leaves no operations pending and closes the connection to the SQL server cleanly, close both the Recordset object and the Database object before quitting the application. In addition, to end the application gracefully, unload the form in the CloseButton_Click event procedure:

```
Private Sub CloseButton_Click()
Rs.Close
Db.Close
Unload Form1
End Sub
```

Evaluating the results

When your code executes the OpenRecordset method and when control returns to your application, your code displays the first row of the Recordset object in the TextBox controls. If more than one title matches the query criteria, you can use the navigation buttons to move to another record (either forward or backward) in the result set and display the data from the new current record. Once you position the current record pointer off either end of the result set, the controls are disabled.

Using the RemoteData Control and Remote Data Objects

The following two applications demonstrate features available with use of the RemoteData control (RDC) and the Remote Data Object (RDO) interface. While RDO can be used via ODBCDirect, this example shows how to access RDO directly.

An Application Using the RemoteData Control

The RemoteData control is the Visual Basic Enterprise Edition bound-control interface that connects the SQL server directly through the ODBC driver manager and the SQL Server driver, as you see in the following illustration. Only the Visual Basic Enterprise Edition includes the RemoteData control—and then only with 32-bit versions of Visual Basic. The RDC needs no intermediate layer like Jet to function.

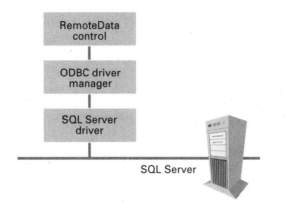

Like the Data control, the RDC is easy to set up and program. Its primary advantage is that it is a direct interface to the ODBC driver manager and is designed specifically for use with ODBC data sources, especially SQL Server. The RemoteData control and the Data control use the same form layout, so this sample application leverages the sample application for the Data control; a few minor changes will accommodate the differences.

Remove the Data control from the form file used for that sample application, and replace it with the RemoteData control. To do this, select the Data control on the form and press the Delete key. Next, select the RemoteData control on the Controls tab of the Components dialog box. In the References dialog box, choose Microsoft RemoteData Control 2.0 and Microsoft Remote Data Object 2.0. The RemoteData control, once it is checked in the Components dialog box, appears in the Toolbox. Double-click the RemoteData control, or drag it to your form in place of the Data control you just deleted. Change the DataSource property of the DBGrid control to the name of the RemoteData control (MSRDC1); the other DBGrid settings don't have to change.

Setting the RemoteData control properties

As already mentioned, the RemoteData control shares many properties with the Data control, but these properties must be reset. Set the RemoteData control's Connect property as follows:

```
UID=<your user ID>;PWD=<your password>;DATABASE=Pubs;
```

Note that there is no need to precede the connect string with *ODBC;* as you *must* do when you code the Connect property for Jet. Enter your SQL Server user ID and password in this string, just as you did in the sample application using the Data control, and be sure to add the default database to the end of the string, as shown. (Yes, you can set the user ID and password with the RemoteData control's UserName and Password properties, but this isn't necessary if they are already included in the Connect property.) Now set the DataSourceName property (DSN) to the name of the ODBC data source that you have already established, using the DSN from the sample application for the Data control—yes, they can use the same ODBC data source.

Coding the procedures

The RecordSource property isn't implemented in the RemoteData control, so instead of setting this property, as we did in the sample application using the Data control, we'll set the SQL property to the same SQL query. Because it isn't necessary to bypass the Jet database engine, it's also unnecessary to set the Option property. To execute the query, use the Refresh method, as before. In this case, however, it applies to the RemoteData control (MSRDC1). As in the sample application using the Data control, here too the Refresh method automatically establishes a connection (if one isn't already open) and executes the query. The RemoteData control then populates any bound controls and manages the current-row pointer, as was also the case in the sample application using the Data control. Here is the entire code listing for the RemoteData control:

```
Private Sub CloseButton_Click()
Unload Form1
End Sub

Private Sub SearchButton_Click()
SQL$ = "Select Title, Price, Au_Fname + ' ' + Au_Lname Author" _
    & " From Titles T, TitleAuthor TA, Authors" _
    & " Where T.Title_ID = TA.Title_ID" _
    & " And TA.Au_ID = Authors.AU_ID" _
    & " And Title like '%" & (TitleDesired) & "%'"

Debug.Print SQL$

MSRDC1.SQL = SQL$
MSRDC1.Refresh
```

Evaluating the results

Once control returns to your application, Visual Basic and the RemoteData control automatically display the rows of the record set in the DBGrid control. And, as we also saw in the sample applications using the Data control and the DAO interface, if more than one title matches the query criteria, you can use the RemoteData control buttons to move to another row in the result set. Note that as you manipulate the DBGrid control, one row and then another becomes current.

You can see an important difference between this sample application and the one for the Data control if you use the SP_WHO stored procedure to determine the number of connections this sample application has opened.

This example seems to be about the slowest so far. By checking the SQLTrace log, you can see that the MSRDC1 is doing an individual SQL row fetch for each row in the result set—that makes about two dozen ODBC operations for each two dozen rows. Not good. But the team is still working on this control.

Note that even after the data has been extracted from the SQL server, the connection remains open, but it can be closed instantly, on demand. If you are running in Design mode, you might find it interesting to execute the SP_WHO stored procedure once again after the application has ended but while Visual Basic is still running in Design mode. Note that there are *no* orphaned connections.

As we did in the sample application using the Data control, we'll click the Close button to unload the first form and end the application.

ODBCDirect does *not* route calls directly through to the ODBC API; it takes the long way around by going through a DAO to the RDO mapping layer before it goes "directly" to the ODBC API.

An Application Using Remote Data Objects

The Remote Data Object (RDO) programmatic interface connects the SQL server *directly* through the ODBC driver manager and SQL Server driver, as you see in the following illustration. As already mentioned, RDO objects, methods, and properties can all be used in conjunction with the RemoteData control, and they can also be used by themselves. The RDO interface is destined to have a significant impact on how Visual Basic developers access SQL Server. It was designed from the ground up to interface with intelligent database engines like SQL Server, so it can't help being an ideal solution for front-end developers. Like the RemoteData control, the RDO interface doesn't need an intermediate layer such as the Jet database engine; it relies on the intelligence of the remote SQL server engine.

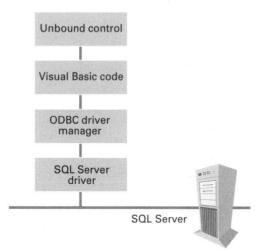

To illustrate, this sample application uses Remote Data Objects (RDO) to perform the same functions that we saw performed in our previous samples. The techniques used here are very similar to those used with the DAO interface. In both cases, your code has to work with each column's data on a row-by-row basis, and you must add code to clean up the RDO interface when you are done. This sample application uses the same form, as you see in the following illustration, used in the sample application for the DAO interface.

```
┌─────────────────────────────────────────────┐
│ ⌐┐ Quickstart Example              _ □ X      │
│ ┌─────────────────────────────────────────┐  │
│ │     Visual Basic Data Access Sample       │  │
│ │              Application                   │  │
│ └─────────────────────────────────────────┘  │
│                                               │
│  Enter Title  ┌──────────────────────────┐   │
│     Wanted    └──────────────────────────┘   │
│                                               │
│        Title  ┌──────────────────────────┐   │
│               └──────────────────────────┘   │
│                                               │
│        Price  ┌──────────────────────────┐   │
│               └──────────────────────────┘   │
│                                               │
│       Author  ┌──────────────────────────┐   │
│               └──────────────────────────┘   │
│                                               │
│            ┌─────────┐          ┌─────────┐   │
│            │Previous │          │  Next   │   │
│            │ Record  │          │ Record  │   │
│            └─────────┘          └─────────┘   │
│  ═══════════════════════════════════════════  │
│  ┌────────┐                     ┌────────┐    │
│  │ Search │                     │ Close  │    │
│  └────────┘                     └────────┘    │
└─────────────────────────────────────────────┘
```

Registering Remote Data Objects

Using the References dialog box in the 32-bit version of Visual Basic, register the Remote Data Objects. If you don't, your application will fail to compile as you make your first reference to an RDO method or object. RDO registration is *not* automatic when you add the RemoteData control to your form.

Adding data navigation buttons

We can use the same form here that we used in the sample application for the DAO interface, so we can also use the same pair of buttons to navigate up and down the result set. When you click these buttons, your event procedure moves the current record pointer to the adjacent record. The RemoteData control, like the Data control, has buttons of its own that move the current record pointer to the first, last, and adjacent records. If you want to use the RDO interface in conjunction with the RemoteData control, you can choose those buttons and add only a couple of lines to the code for this sample application.

As in the sample application for the DAO interface, the rest of the work involved in this sample is done in code. We won't be using bound controls, so you'll need to code procedures that move data from the current row to the TextBox controls. Again, as in the DAO sample application, you must code procedures to open the connection, create the result set, and close the Remote Data Objects.

Coding the global variables

To start with, declare global variables that you'll use to contain the rdo-Environment, rdoConnection, and rdoResultset objects:

```
Dim SQL As String
Dim Db As New rdoConnection
Dim Rs As rdoResultset
Dim Ps As rdoQuery
Dim i As Integer
```

In Visual Basic 3.0, and even in the 16-bit versions of Visual Basic 4.0, it is *not* possible to register Remote Data Objects. Technically, it is possible to produce 16-bit versions of the RDO interface and the RemoteData control, but it's not going to see the light of day. Microsoft stopped working on 16-bit software years ago. I suppose some third party will find the resources to build them if the market demands them loudly enough.

Coding the Form_Load event procedure

Now we'll write code to open a connection and instantiate the rdoConnection object. In this case, instead of just setting design-time properties, code the Form_Load event procedure as shown in the sample code that follows. Note that the code refers to the same DSN and connect string as those used in the sample application for the RemoteData control.

In this example, the value of the Prompt property forces the RDO interface to return a trappable error if the user ID and password are incorrect. I use this technique when I depend on integrated security to provide the logon name and password.

As in the previous examples, the WHERE clause of the query is filtered by the value passed in from the TitleDesired text box. In this case, however, we take advantage of the RDO interface's ability to execute parameter queries by creating an rdoQuery and setting its parameter to the value passed in from the TitleDesired text box. The rdoQuery is created during the Form_Load event procedure; the parameter is set in the next step:

```
Private Sub Form_Load()
With Db
    Db.Connect = "DSN=TestPubs;uid=;pwd=;"
    Db.EstablishConnection rdDriverNoPrompt, True
    SQL$ = "Select Title, Price, Au_Fname + ' ' +" _
        & " Au_Lname Author" _
        & " From Titles T, TitleAuthor TA, Authors" _
        & " Where T.Title_ID = TA.Title_ID" _
        & " And TA.Au_ID = Authors.AU_ID" _
        & " And Title like ? "
    Set Ps = .CreateQuery("Sample", SQL$)
End With
End Sub
```

NOTE Did you notice that the rdoPreparedStatement was *not* used in this example? That's because it has been replaced with the rdoQuery object. This new RDO object has lots of new features we will be talking about later.

If your error handler gets a 429 error ("ActionX component can't create object..."), you didn't register the Remote Data Objects properly, you are running in 16-bit mode, or you misspelled one of the objects. Press F1 to get more details on this error. If you get a successful open, the rdoConnection object referred to by the DB variable is valid and can be used to create your rdoResultset object.

Coding the SearchButton_Click event procedure

In this procedure, the query is executed and data from the first row is moved into the TextBox controls (in code):

```
Private Sub SearchButton_Click()

Ps.rdoParameters(0) = "%" & (TitleWanted) & "%"
Set Rs = Ps.OpenResultset(rdOpenStatic)
Rs.MoveLast: Rs.MoveFirst          ' To fully populate the Recordset

If Rs.RowCount > 0 Then
    ShowRecord
End If
End Sub
```

Another approach would be to use the Refresh method to rerun the rdoQuery query.

Coding the ShowRecord procedure

Once the data has been fetched into the rdoResultset object, the next step is to move the data into the TextBox controls, where the user can see it. This procedure assumes that the rdoResultset object has been created. If there is no current record—as when the current record pointer is positioned beyond either end of the rdoResultset object or when there are no records at all—the appropriate buttons are disabled and no attempt is made to reference the current record. Note that this code is identical to the code for the DAO ShowRecord procedure:

```
Sub ShowRecord()
'
' Fill the form fields from the Recordset.
'
If Rs.BOF = False And Rs.EOF = False Then
'
'   Note the three different ways to address the Recordset fields.
'
    DataFound(0) = Rs!Title
    DataFound(1) = Format$(Rs("Price"), "$###.##")
    DataFound(2) = Rs(2)
End If

PreviousRecordButton.Enabled = Not Rs.BOF
NextRecordButton.Enabled = Not Rs.EOF

End Sub
```

Coding the Recordset navigation buttons

A user who wants to see additional rows of the result set can use the navigation buttons to view those records. The navigation buttons use the MoveNext and MovePrevious methods to position the current record pointer within the rdoResultset object. Note that this code doesn't prevent movement past either end of the rdoResultset object; the ShowRecord procedure automatically deals

CAUTION

In Visual Basic version 4.0, when a new rdoResultset object is created, any existing rdoResultset objects are maintained. They are accessible through the rdoResultsets collection. To ensure that unneeded rdoResultset objects are *not* kept, use the Close method against the rdoResultset collection before you create any new rdoResultset objects. In Visual Basic version 5.0, RDO automatically drops existing rdoResultset objects when you assign a value to a variable that is set to an rdoResultset.

with this contingency. Again, this code is identical to the code for the same procedure in the DAO sample application, which means that in many cases the transition from DAO code to RDO code can be fairly painless:

```
Private Sub NextRecordButton_Click()
    Rs.MoveNext
    ShowRecord
End Sub

Private Sub PreviousRecordButton_Click()
    Rs.MovePrevious
    ShowRecord
End Sub
```

Code the CloseButton_Click event procedure

To clean up any pending operations and cleanly close the connection to the SQL server, you need to close both the Recordset object and the Database object before quitting the application. To end the application gracefully, you should also unload the form in the CloseButton_Click event procedure:

```
Private Sub CloseButton_Click()
Rs.Close
Db.Close
Unload Form1
End Sub
```

Evaluating the results

When your code executes the OpenResultset method and when control returns to your application, your code displays the first row of the rdoResultset object in the TextBox controls. If more than one title matches the query criteria, you can use the navigation buttons to move to another row (either forward or backward) in the result set. Once you position the current record pointer off either end of the Resultset object, the controls are disabled.

Using ODBCDirect

Starting with Visual Basic version 5.0, the Data control can be used without Jet. That is, you can create an ODBCDirect Workspace object and use the Data control as a bound-control interface that connects with SQL Server through the ODBC driver manager and the SQL Server driver. However, using this technique disables any benefit DAO derived from Jet.

The following two sections show how to use ODBCDirect with and without the Data control. In the final analysis, the Data control's new RDO interface might be especially interesting for client/server developers—a lot more interesting than using DAO to access RDO.

An Application Using the Data Control with ODBCDirect

To implement the sample application that uses the Data control in ODBCDirect mode, you need very little additional code—simply set the form-control properties at design time. To do this, add the Data control, set the Connect, the DefaultType, and the DatabaseName properties as described below.

Adding the Data control

Add the Data control to the form just as you did in the earlier Data control example. Once you add the Data control to your form, DAO 3.5 is automatically registered. Even though ODBCDirect uses RDO, you don't have to register the RDO 2.0 library—unless you plan to use it elsewhere. Once these reference changes are made, you can use both the Data control and the DAO that it creates. No, you can't use the RDO objects that the Data control references—these are hidden by DAO.

> **NOTE** In case you missed something, ODBCDirect still requires a 32-bit system to function. That means you must have Microsoft Windows 95 or Windows NT to run an application that uses ODBCDirect or RDO.

ODBCDirect is probably not as interesting to SQL Server front-end developers as it is to Microsoft Office and other VBA hosts that need to access SQL Server. Since these platforms don't include a Visual Basic version 5.0 Enterprise Edition or other RDO license (which is required to access RDO directly), use of the ODBCDirect interface to RDO is a viable, albeit circuitous, approach.

Setting the Connect property

Using the Properties window in Design mode (set focus to the Data control and press F4), set the Data control's Connect property as follows:

```
ODBC;UID=<your user ID>;PWD=<your password>;DATABASE=Pubs
```

Enter your SQL Server user ID (UID) and password (PWD) into this string. Yes, you RDO types, you still need to prefix the connect string with *ODBC;*—this is still DAO. You still don't need to include your user ID and password if you are using integrated security.

> **NOTE** If you don't prefix your connect string with *ODBC;*, you get nada, nothing, no error, zippo—including no data.

Setting the DatabaseName property

Set the Data control's DatabaseName property to the 32-bit ODBC data source name (DSN) that you have already established. You can use the new drop-down menu on the Data control's property sheet for this.

Setting the DBGrid properties

The DBGrid control is set up the same way it was in the earlier Data control sample.

Coding the SearchButton_Click event procedure

Again, this routine is identical to the code we used for the Data control. That's the advantage to using this technique—your existing DAO applications and code can often be used without change.

```
Private Sub SearchButton_Click()
If Len(TitleDesired.Text) > 0 Then
    With Data1
        .RecordSource = "Select Title, Price, " _
        & " Au_Fname + ' ' + Au_Lname Author" _
        & " From Titles T, TitleAuthor TA, Authors" _
        & " Where T.Title_ID = TA.Title_ID" _
        & " And TA.Au_ID = Authors.AU_ID" _
        & " And Title like '%" & (TitleDesired) & "%'"

    Debug.Print .RecordSource
        .Refresh
        If .Recordset.RecordCount > 0 Then
            .Recordset.MoveLast: .Recordset.MoveFirst
        End If
    End With
End If
End Sub
```

(Not) Setting the Data control options property

Because we aren't using the Jet query processor in this example, we don't really care if the syntax of the preceding SQL statement seems a little unusual—ODBCDirect expects you to use the SQL dialect required by the remote server. Because of this, you don't need to set the Options property—as a matter of fact, you shouldn't.

Executing the query

After the RecordSource and Options properties are set, use the Data control's Refresh method to establish a connection and execute the query automatically—just as you did in the earlier Data control example. This procedure is coded as follows:

```
Data1.Refresh
```

When you execute this method, DAO processes the request via RDO and returns when (and only when) the first qualifying row is ready. The Data control then populates any bound controls and manages the current-row pointer.

Coding the CloseButton_Click event procedure

Since the Data control automatically manages the Data Access Object that it creates, you don't need any special code here to close databases or result sets. To end the application gracefully, however, add the following code to the CloseButton_Click event procedure:

```
Unload Form1
```

Note that we did not just use an END statement here. That statement should be avoided like undercooked hamburgers, since it does not permit Visual Basic procedures to finish their applications correctly.

Evaluating the results

You won't notice much difference between this example and the other Data control example—except perhaps for the difference in speed. Just as in the earlier example, once control returns to your application, Visual Basic and the Data control automatically display the rows of the Recordset object according to the latest results of the SQL parameter query. In accordance with the size of the DBGrid control, the first and nth rows of the Recordset object are displayed. If more than one title matches the query criteria, you can use the Data control buttons to move either forward or backward to another row in the Recordset object. Note that as you manipulate the Data control, one row after another in the DBGrid control becomes the current row. To end the application, click the Close button. This action unceremoniously unloads the first form.

An Application Using Data Access Objects with ODBCDirect

Earlier we saw how the Data Access Object (DAO) programmatic interface connects by default to the Jet database engine, which interacts with the SQL server through the ODBC driver manager and the SQL Server driver. This example shows how to bypass the Jet database engine completely and create a DAO interface to SQL Server via the ODBCDirect interface added to Visual Basic version 5.0. DAO objects, methods, and properties created using ODBCDirect can still be used in conjunction with the Data control or by themselves. That is, once you open a connection using the Data control, the Data Access Objects it exposes through its properties can be used as if you had created them in code. Even though ODBCDirect uses the 32-bit RDO libraries under cover, you can't use the objects yourself. But there's no reason why you can't create your own RDO objects—even with an application that also uses ODBCDirect. You'll need the Enterprise license, however.

NOTE When you choose to use DAO objects with the ODBCDirect option, be aware that many of the neat features on which you depended when you used Jet are no longer available.

This sample application illustrates the basic use of the DAO/ODBCDirect model for accessing SQL Server without benefit of the Data control. The code differs from the earlier DAO example because of a couple of limitations of ODBCDirect, which I discovered while creating this example. For example, the ODBCDirect Database object doesn't support the use of parameterized

QueryDef objects. If you open an ODBCDirect connection instead, you can create QueryDef objects that require parameters. Just as we did before, start with the form used in the sample application for the Data control. To display the current row of the result set, create a form that has three text boxes instead of the DBGrid control. Sure, you could use the common Grid control or even the DBGrid control in unbound mode, but that would be overkill for this sample application; besides, use of the TextBox controls illustrates a more basic type of front end—a model that many serious front-end applications use. Set up your form to look like this one:

Registering the Jet Data Access Objects

Using the References dialog box in Visual Basic (available via the Project menu), make sure that the 32-bit Data Access Objects (DAO) are registered. No, this feature is not supported in 16-bit versions of Visual Basic. Choose the Microsoft DAO 3.5 Object Library. If you don't register DAO, your application will fail to compile as you make your first reference to a DAO method or object. (In the previous sample application, 32-bit DAO registration was automatic when the Data control was added to the form.)

Adding data navigation buttons

The button procedures used to move around in the Recordset are identical to those you coded for the DAO/Jet example—again, another advantage to using this model.

Coding the global variables

Declare global variables that are used to contain the Database and Recordset objects created in other procedures this way:

```
Dim SQL As String
Dim Db As Connection
Dim Ws As Workspace
Dim Rs As Recordset
Dim Qd As QueryDef
Dim i As Integer
```

Coding the Form_Load event procedure

Here is where the differences arise. First we need to tell DAO that we *don't* want to invoke Jet. To do this, we need to create a new Workspace object using the new Type property set to *dbUseODBC*. Without this step, Jet is loaded the first time you reference a DAO object. Next, we'll write code to open the database connection and instantiate the Database object using the new DAO OpenConnection method that closely matches the equivalent RDO method. Finally, we create a QueryDef to hold our parameter query.

The example assumes that the client workstation running the sample application has already been logged on with a valid user ID and password to a Windows NT domain and that the SQL server has been set up with domain-managed (integrated) security:

```
Private Sub Form_Load()
Dim Connect As String
On Error GoTo FLErrors
Connect$ = "ODBC;DSN=TestPubs;UID=;PWD=;"
Set Ws = DBEngine.CreateWorkspace("ODBCWS", _
    "", "", dbUseODBC)
' Note that we open a "Connection" object here… not a
' Database object.
Set Db = Ws.OpenConnection("Pubs", False, _
    False, Connect$)

SQL$ = "Select Title, Price, Au_Fname + ' ' +" _
    & " Au_Lname Author" _
    & " From Titles T, TitleAuthor TA, Authors" _
    & " Where T.Title_ID = TA.Title_ID" _
    & " And TA.Au_ID = Authors.Au_ID" _
    & " And Title Like ?"

Set Qd = Db.CreateQueryDef("", SQL)

Exit Sub

FLErrors:
    For Each er In Errors
        MsgBox "Error:" & Error$
    Next er
    Resume
End Sub
```

Coding the SearchButton_Click event procedure

In this procedure, the query is executed and data from the first row is moved into the TextBox controls (in your code). This code is very similar to that used in the previous DAO example except we are using RDO's (and ODBCDirect's) ability to run parameter queries. Note that there is no need to specify the dbSQLPassThrough option.

```
Private Sub SearchButton_Click()
    Qd(0) = "%" & TitleWanted & "%"
    Set Rs = Qd.OpenRecordset(dbOpenSnapshot)
    If Rs.RecordCount > 0 Then
' To fully populate the Recordset
        Rs.MoveLast: Rs.MoveFirst
        ShowRecord
    Else
        MsgBox "No rows returned"
    End If
End Sub
```

Coding the procedures

The operational procedure code is identical to that used in the earlier DAO example. That's the whole idea behind ODBCDirect. While not all DAO code works against ODBCDirect, most of the basic (so to speak) operations do.

Evaluating the results

After your code executes the OpenRecordset method and control returns to your application, your code displays the first row of the Recordset object in the TextBox controls. If more than one title matches the query criteria, you can use the navigation buttons to move to another record (either forward or backward) in the result set and display the data from the new current record. Once you position the current record pointer off either end of the result set, the controls are disabled.

I think you will find that this technique is only slightly more complicated than using DAO/Jet, but it can yield much better performance. Unfortunately, many of the techniques you used to deal with data using DAO won't work with ODBCDirect. But I'll talk about that later.

Using VBSQL and the ODBC API

The Microsoft Visual Basic Library for SQL Server (VBSQL) is the function call interface to DB-Library (also known as DBLIB). DB-Library has been the "native" application programming interface (API) to both Microsoft SQL Server and Sybase SQL Server since their inception. Now, however, Microsoft and Sybase are in the process of replacing DB-Library with more elegant interfaces; in fact, Sybase's newest versions don't even support DB-Library. Nevertheless, VBSQL provides access to virtually all the SQL Server features—even to some that can't be accessed by the ODBC API, though that interface is now being hailed as the "new" native interface to SQL Server.

An Application Using VBSQL

The following example application shows how to use VBSQL to build a simple client/server application as you see in the following illustration. Yes, this technique is obsolete—but an awfully large number of people are still baking bread the old-fashioned VBSQL way.

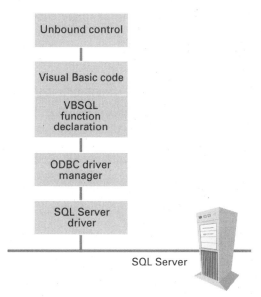

To implement this sample application, you will have to implement the data binding and create the result set in code, just as you did when you implemented the DAO sample application. You will also need to add code for navigating through the result set and cleaning up the VBSQL linkage when you are done.

NOTE For the 5th edition, I have dropped the extra code needed to cross-compile the VBSQL code for 16-bit Visual Basic version 3.0 and Visual Basic version 4.0 systems. This code is still available in the 3rd and 4th editions of the book.

Installing the VBSQL custom control

Using the Components dialog box in Visual Basic 5.0, add "Vbsql OLE Custom Control module" to your project. I guess the SQL Server folks didn't hear about the switch to "ActiveX." Once it's installed and available in the Toolbox, you still need to add the VBSQL custom control to the form.

Yes, the VBSQL custom control is kinda funny looking. It appears as a rectangle with a white circle in it. I guess the VBSQL folks didn't have time to get the icon working—and since they have not touched it since it was released, it still looks that way. Just set the Visible property to False, because there are no interface elements on the control.

Importing the VBSQL DECLARE statements

To execute the VBSQL interface directly, create a Visual Basic module from the VBSQL.BAS file that is included with the VBSQL control. Once you add this file to your project, the Visual Basic version 5.0 Quick Info tips are activated. Now *this* is a neat feature.

Adding data navigation buttons

As in the sample application using the RDO interface, you must add a pair of buttons to navigate up and down the result set. When these buttons are clicked, your event procedure will move the current record pointer to the adjacent record. The sample application for the Data control used buttons that permitted you to move to the first, last, and adjacent records, and you can add those buttons here, too, if you choose; they'll add only a couple of lines of code.

NOTE VBSQL uses more calls than the ODBC API does, but the calls are designed specifically for SQL Server. That's what makes VBSQL's coding interface simpler than the ODBC API's.

In this sample application, the code creates a simple cursor to fetch the data—a somewhat unwieldy procedure for such a simple task, but I use it here *not* because cursors are the primary means that many developers use for accessing SQL Server data, but because I want you to compare apples with apples. That is, each of the other object-level interfaces use cursors and I didn't want you to get the wrong impression about VBSQL. (Personally, though, I rarely use cursors. I find them too cumbersome, and they're usually unnecessary for most of my applications.)

The rest of the work involved in this sample application is done in code. Since the application won't be using bound controls, you will again need to code procedures that move data from the current record to the TextBox controls. You will also have to code procedures to open the connection, create the result set, and close the VBSQL connection.

Coding the global variables

Declare global variables that will be used to manage the connection and cursor:

```
Dim SqlConn As Long          'To hold the connection handle
Dim CursorID As Long         'To hold the cursor ID
Dim R As Long                'To hold result codes
Dim RCols As Long            'To hold number of cursor columns
Dim RRows As Long            'To hold number of cursor result rows
Dim CurRow As Long           'To hold the current-row pointer
Dim RowPointers(100) As Long ' We expect fewer than 100 hits
```

NOTE The biggest difference between the 16-bit and 32-bit versions of VBSQL is in the declaration of variables used and arguments passed to the interface: 16-bit uses Integer constants, and 32-bit uses Longs.

Coding the Form_Load event procedure

Now write code to open the database connection. Once the connection is open, the VBSQL interface returns a handle that is used in all subsequent references to this connection. In 16-bit Visual Basic, this is an Integer; in 32-bit Visual Basic, it's a Long.

The SQLOpenConnection function expects you to provide a valid user ID and password, as in all the other sample applications. Once the connection is open, you must change the default database to *Pubs* to ensure that your queries reference the right tables. Code the Form_Load event procedure as shown next. (This code works for both 16-bit and 32-bit implementations.)

```
Private Sub Form_Load()
Dim A As String
Show
A$ = SqlInit$()
SqlConn = SqlOpenConnection("BetaV1", "", "", "Test Station", _
    "Test VBSQL")
If SqlConn = 0 Then
    MsgBox "Could not open connection"
    Exit Sub
End If
R = SqlUse(SqlConn, "Pubs")
End Sub
```

Coding the SearchButton_Click event procedure

This procedure executes the query and uses the same SQL statement used in the previous examples. As before, the query is filtered with the value read from the TitleDesired text box:

```
Private Sub SearchButton_Click()
Dim SQL As String
Dim MaxRows As Long
MaxRows = 100
If TitleDesired.Text = "" Then Exit Sub
SQL$ = "Select Title, Price, Au_Fname + ' ' + Au_Lname Author"
SQL$ = SQL$ & " From Titles T, TitleAuthor TA, Authors"
SQL$ = SQL$ & " Where T.Title_ID = TA.Title_ID"
SQL$ = SQL$ & " And TA.Au_ID = Authors.Au_ID"
SQL$ = SQL$ & " And Title Like '%" & TitleDesired.Text & "%'"
Debug.Print SQL$

CursorID = SqlCursorOpen(SqlConn, SQL$, CURKEYSET, _
    CURREADONLY, MaxRows)
' Position to last row to populate cursor.
R = SqlCursorFetch(CursorID, FETCHLAST, 0)
' Position back to first data row.
R = SqlCursorFetch(CursorID, FETCHFIRST, 0)
CurRow = 1
' Determine number of rows returned.
R = SqlCursorInfo(CursorID, RCols, RRows)
'
' Set state of navigation buttons based on number of hits.
'
MoveUpButton.Enabled = False
' We are positioned at the first record.
MoveDownButton.Enabled = False
If RRows > 0 Then FillTextBoxes
If RRows > 1 Then MoveDownButton.Enabled = True

End Sub
```

Coding the FillTextBoxes procedure

Once the data has been fetched into the cursor, the next step is to move the data into the TextBox controls, where the user can see it. This procedure assumes that the cursor has been created and that there is a current record:

```
Private Sub FillTextBoxes()
TitleFound.Text = SqlCursorData(CursorID, CurRow, 1)
PriceFound.Text = Format$(SqlCursorData(CursorID, CurRow, 2), _
    "$.##")
AuthorFound.Text = SqlCursorData(CursorID, CurRow, 3)
End Sub
```

Coding the Recordset navigation buttons

A user who wants to see additional rows of the result set can use the navigation buttons to view those records. The navigation buttons use the MoveNext and MovePrevious methods to position the current-row pointer within the cursor. Note that this code must also prevent movement past either end of the cursor:

```
Sub MoveUpButton_Click()
If RRows = 1 Then Exit Sub
If CurRow = 0 Then Exit Sub
CurRow = CurRow - 1
If CurRow = 0 Then MoveUpButton.Enabled = False
If RRows > 1 Then MoveDownButton.Enabled = True
FillTextBoxes            ' Display the current record
End Sub

Sub MoveDownButton_Click()
If RRows = 1 Then Exit Sub
If CurRow = RRows Then Exit Sub
CurRow = CurRow + 1
If CurRow = RRows Then MoveDownButton.Enabled = False
If RRows > 1 Then MoveUpButton.Enabled = True
FillTextBoxes            ' Display the current record
End Sub
```

Coding the CloseButton_Click event procedure

To make sure your application cleans up any pending operations and cleanly closes the connection to the SQL server, you need to close the cursor and the connection before quitting the application. To end the application gracefully, you should also unload the form in the CloseButton_Click event procedure:

```
Private Sub CloseButton_Click()
SqlClose (SqlConn)
SqlWinExit
Unload Form1
End Sub
```

Coding the error and message handlers

All VBSQL applications must provide code to handle the Error and Message events. These events provide a mechanism for SQL Server to communicate with your application. As the processing of your requests proceeds, SQL Server uses these events to notify your application when the current database changes, when the SQL query creates a message, or when an error occurs. These event handlers are discussed in detail in later chapters; for now, the code shown here simply filters out unimportant messages and errors, and it prints the rest in a message box:

```
Private Sub VBSQL1_Error(ByVal SqlConn As Long, ByVal Severity _
    As Long, ByVal ErrorNum As Long, ByVal ErrorStr As String, _
```

(continued)

```
    ByVal OSErrorNum As Long, ByVal OSErrStr As String, _
    RetCode As Long)
    MsgBox "VBSQL Error:" & "Sev:" & Severity & " Number:" & _
        ErrorNum & " - " & ErrorStr
End Sub

Private Sub VBSQL1_Message(ByVal SqlConn As Long, ByVal Message _
    As Long, ByVal State As Long, ByVal Severity As Long, ByVal _
    MsgStr As String, ByVal ServerNameStr As String, ByVal _
    ProcNameStr As String, ByVal Line As Long)
Select Case Message
    Case 5701
    Case Else
        MsgBox "VBSQL Message:" & Message & " State:" & State _
            & " Sev:" & Severity & " - " & ServerNameStr & _
            " - " & ProcNameStr & " - " & Line & " - " & MsgStr
End Select

End Sub
```

Evaluating the results

The code for this sample application seems far more complex than the code
for any of the others, partly because using a cursor for this type of work is
really unnecessary and needlessly complicates the implementation. VBSQL
has a number of other, simpler (and faster) buffering schemas that would be
more appropriate in this case. Nevertheless, despite the more complex interface, this application should still perform at least as fast as (and usually faster)
and use fewer resources than any of the others we have tried so far.

An Application Using the ODBC API

One point cannot be over-
stressed: there is no such
thing as a crashproof API.
Whenever you bind incorrectly,
you get a GPF. Whenever you
forget to initialize variables
properly, you get a GPF. And
often when you simply enter
incorrect SQL syntax, you get
a GPF. This last kind of GPF
has to do with an ODBC API
bug that is probably fixed by
now. All the others occur for
one reason: when you're
working with a C-oriented
dynamic-link library like the
ODBC API, you're expected
to know what you're doing.

Our final sample application, which you see diagrammed on the facing page,
uses the ODBC API without benefit of an object model or a Visual Basic–
friendly interface. The approach here is not unlike what we used for the VBSQL
cursor implementation, but it uses even more code.

The ODBC API, as we've seen, is being touted as the new "native" interface to SQL Server, but it's not quite there yet. In its current state, however, it
does have a certain appeal: no matter which back-end server you code to, the
approach is roughly the same. Since the ODBC API's performance can be as
fast as or faster than VBSQL's, it's a viable alternative for client/server front-
end developers who are not afraid of wading hip-deep into the code. What the
ODBC API lacks is speed of development and stability. The sample application
that follows took almost an entire day to code and debug. The length of time
was due to a number of factors, including my attempts to keep the example
simple, but it was due mostly to about a dozen general protection faults (GPFs)
along the way.

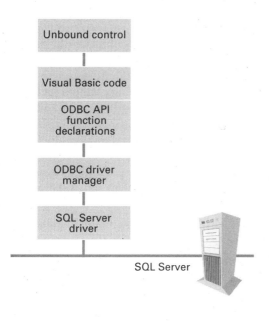

Unbound control

Visual Basic code

ODBC API
function
declarations

ODBC driver
manager

SQL Server
driver

SQL Server

NOTE   VBSQL is an API, but with VBSQL you don't have to bind or pre-allocate space for incoming variables. All of that is handled automatically by the VBX/OCX or by the interface library itself.

Loading the include file

You don't have to register anything to use the ODBC API, but you do have to locate the ODBC API include file and add it to your project. The include file contains the function declarations and constants you'll need for exposing the ODBC API, and they're carefully hidden. As I write this section, it's not clear where the ODBC API include file will be (if it will be) included on the Visual Basic version 5.0 CD. You need to use ODBC32.TXT for 32-bit Visual Basic applications and ODBC16.TXT for 16-bit applications. Use the Add File command on the Project menu to add the appropriate file to your project.

CAUTION
When a DLL or code that loads a DLL dies, the operating system might not unload the library. It remains in memory, usable as far as Windows is concerned, but otherwise dead. In a 16-bit operating system, the only way to clear it out is to use WPS or restart. If you're working in Windows for Workgroups, plan to reboot the system often to clean up zombied dynamic-link libraries. (Now you know why we moved to Windows 95 and Windows NT.)

NOTE   To make things easier for you, the include file for the ODBC API is on this guide's companion CD. A couple of constant declarations were left out of the file supplied by Visual Basic; the version on this book's companion CD includes these statements. (You'll never miss them until you try to use the GetFocus function.) The Visual Basic include files that come with the SQL 6.5 ODBC Programmer's Toolkit are *not* suitable for use with Visual Basic, and we'll find out why a little later. Just remember not to use them for now.

One more point about this sample application: in order to simplify the design, I chose *not* to implement a prepared statement that would permit execution of a parameter query, even though generally you would use a SQL prepared statement for this type of application. We did this in the RDO sample application; in terms of extra lines of code and more chances for GPFs, however, a prepared statement is far more expensive to implement with the ODBC API.

TIP   When you're working without a Visual Basic–friendly interface, and especially when you're working with the ODBC API, any mistake you make can result in a GPF that kills Visual Basic. In most (but not all) cases, Windows 95 and Windows NT won't be damaged, so you can simply restart Visual Basic, reload your application, and party on. To be safe, though, save often.

Adding data navigation buttons

Here, we're using the same form that we used for the VBSQL sample application, so the pair of buttons used to navigate up and down the result set is already in place. When these buttons are clicked, your event procedure moves the current record pointer to the adjacent record.

The rest of the work involved in this example is done in code. Since we won't be using bound controls, you'll need to code procedures that move data from the current row to the TextBox controls. Just as in the VBSQL sample application, you must code procedures to open the connection, create the cursor, and close the cursor and connection when you are done. You also need to create environment, connection, and statement handles in code and free them when the application no longer needs them.

Coding the global variables

Declare global variables that will be used to contain the environment, connection, and statement handles created in other procedures:

```
Option Explicit
Dim rc As Integer
Dim hEnv As Long
Dim hDbc As Long
Dim hStmt As Long
Dim SQL As String
Dim MaxRows As Integer
Dim RowStatus(100) As Integer
Dim RowsFetched As Long
Dim RRows As Long
Dim CurRow As Integer
```

Coding the support procedures

To deal with errors and other contingencies more easily, you must code a couple of support routines for handling function errors and general error-description routines. Several procedures use the Attempt function to simplify error handling: you have to check the error status after each call, so the Attempt function does this with less code. ODBC error handling, compared to VBSQL event-driven error handling or the integrated error handling provided by all the other programming approaches, is far more burdensome. The code for the Attempt function is as follows:

```
Private Sub Attempt(ResultCode As Integer, ErrorMessage As String)
  ' If ResultCode <> SQL_SUCCESS, then exit.

  If (ResultCode <> SQL_SUCCESS) Then
    Screen.MousePointer = vbDefault
    MsgBox ErrorMessage, vbCritical, _
      "Unexpected ODBC Driver Function failure"
    Stop
  End If

End Sub
```

The DescribeError procedure is used to illuminate errors. It uses the SQLError API function to return error strings and native error numbers, which should give you a hint about what went wrong:

```
Sub DescribeError(ByVal hDbc As Long, ByVal hStmt As Long)
  ' Print an error message for the given connection handle
  ' and statement handle.
  Dim rgbValue1 As String * 16
  Dim rgbValue3 As String * 1024
  Dim Outlen As Integer
  Dim Native As Long
  Const SbufferLen = 1024

  rgbValue1 = String$(16, 0)
  rgbValue3 = String$(SbufferLen, 0)

  Do
    rc = SQLError(hEnv, hDbc, hStmt, rgbValue1, Native, _
      rgbValue3, SbufferLen, Outlen)
    Screen.MousePointer = vbDefault
    If rc = SQL_SUCCESS Or rc = SQL_SUCCESS_WITH_INFO Then
      If Outlen = 0 Then
        MsgBox "Error -- No error information available", _
          vbOKOnly, App.EXEName
      Else
        If rc = SQL_ERROR Then
          MsgBox Left$(rgbValue3, Outlen), vbCritical, _
            App.EXEName
```

(continued)

```
            Else
                MsgBox Left$(rgbValue3, Outlen), vbOKOnly, _
                    App.EXEName
            End If
        End If
    End If
Loop Until rc <> SQL_SUCCESS

End Sub
```

Coding the Form_Load event procedure

The Form_Load event procedure allocates the environment, connection, and statement handles by using the allocation functions, which trap errors with the Attempt function. The Form_Load event procedure also establishes a connection by using the same connect string we have used for the other ODBC examples. This application uses the same connection strategy as in the RDO sample application. It depends on integrated security to connect. Once this procedure is complete, the application has a valid connection. You don't have to worry about registration errors or unknown objects here. (There are plenty of other things to worry about.)

```
Private Sub Form_Load()
Dim A As String
Dim Connect As String
Dim Server As String * 128  ' Holds the completed connect string
Dim cbOut As Integer
    Attempt SQLAllocEnv(hEnv), _
      "Cannot allocate environment handle"
    Attempt SQLAllocConnect(hEnv, hDbc), _
      "Cannot allocate connection handle"

  ' Make the connection.

  Connect$ = "DSN=TestPubs;UID=;pwd=;"
  rc% = SQLDriverConnect(hDbc, GetParent(GetFocus()), _
    Connect$, Len(Connect$), Server, Len(Server), cbOut%, _
    SQL_DRIVER_NOPROMPT)
  If (rc% = SQL_ERROR) Or (rc% = SQL_INVALID_HANDLE) Then
    DescribeError hDbc, hStmt
    Exit Sub
  ElseIf rc% = SQL_NO_DATA_FOUND Then
    Exit Sub
  End If

End Sub
```

Coding the SearchButton_Click event procedure

In this procedure, the query is executed and data from row *n* is moved into the TextBox controls (in code). The SQL statement is roughly the same, but in this case we make sure to concatenate the % values to the parameter.

As in the previous sample applications, you filter the query with the value passed in from the TitleDesired text box. This application is different in that it deals with statement-handle allocation each time the query is to be executed, which essentially flushes any previous queries and frees the connection for another operation:

```
Private Sub SearchButton_Click()

' Free previous handle.
If hStmt <> 0 Then SQLFreeStmt hStmt, SQL_CLOSE
' Allocate a statement handle.
Attempt SQLAllocStmt(hDbc, hStmt), _
  "Cannot allocate statement handle"
Attempt SQLSetStmtOption(hStmt, SQL_CURSOR_TYPE, _
  SQL_CURSOR_KEYSET_DRIVEN), "Cannot set statement option"

If TitleDesired.Text = "" Then Exit Sub
SQL$ = "Select Title, Price, Au_Fname + ' ' + Au_Lname Author"
SQL$ = SQL$ & " From Titles T, TitleAuthor TA, Authors"
SQL$ = SQL$ & " Where T.Title_ID = TA.Title_ID"
SQL$ = SQL$ & " And TA.Au_ID = Authors.Au_ID"
SQL$ = SQL$ & " And Title Like '%" & TitleDesired.Text & "%'"
Debug.Print SQL$

rc = SQLExecDirect(hStmt, SQL$, Len(SQL$))
If rc = SQL_SUCCESS Or rc = SQL_SUCCESS_WITH_INFO Then

Attempt SQLExtendedFetch(hStmt, SQL_FETCH_LAST, 0, _
  RowsFetched, RowStatus(0)), "Could not fetch last"
Attempt SQLGetStmtOption(hStmt, SQL_ROW_NUMBER, RRows), _
  "Could not get statement option"
Attempt SQLExtendedFetch(hStmt, SQL_FETCH_FIRST, 0, _
  RowsFetched, RowStatus(0)), "Could not fetch First"

'
' Set state of navigation buttons based on number of hits.
'
MoveUpButton.Enabled = False
' We are positioned at the first record.
MoveDownButton.Enabled = False
If RRows > 0 Then CurRow = 1: FillTextBoxes
If RRows > 1 Then MoveDownButton.Enabled = True
Else
    DescribeError hDbc, hStmt
End If
End Sub
```

Coding the FillTextBoxes procedure

This procedure is used to move data from the current row into the three unbound text boxes on the form. It forced me to use Text formatting for all three columns, since the ODBC API gave me fits when I tried to convert the Price column into a numeric value. (The Price column is defined as Money in the database, and since the values came back correctly, it doesn't matter that much.) Note the use of fixed-length string value holders. These must be preinitialized and cleared between uses to prevent trash from creeping in:

```
Private Sub FillTextBoxes()
Dim InText As String * 129, InVal As Double
Dim TextLen As Long, ValLen As Long
rc = SQLExtendedFetch(hStmt, SQL_FETCH_ABSOLUTE, CurRow, _
    RowsFetched, RowStatus(0))
If rc = SQL_SUCCESS Then
    rc = SQLGetData(hStmt, 1, SQL_C_CHAR, InText, 128, TextLen)
    TitleFound.Text = Left(InText, TextLen)
    InText = String(128, " ")
    rc = SQLGetData(hStmt, 2, SQL_C_CHAR, InText, 16, TextLen)
    PriceFound.Text = Format$(Val(InText), "$.##")
    rc = SQLGetData(hStmt, 3, SQL_C_CHAR, InText, 128, TextLen)
    AuthorFound.Text = Left(InText, TextLen)
    InText = String(128, " ")
Else
    Beep
End If
End Sub
```

Coding the Recordset navigation buttons

The user who wants to see additional rows of the result set can use the navigation buttons to view those records. The navigation buttons simply increment our own internal *CurRec* counter. Note that this code does not prevent movement past either end of the cursor; the ShowRecord procedure automatically deals with this contingency:

```
Sub MoveUpButton_Click()
If RRows = 1 Then Exit Sub
If CurRow = 0 Then Exit Sub
CurRow = CurRow - 1
If CurRow = 0 Then MoveUpButton.Enabled = False
If RRows > 1 Then MoveDownButton.Enabled = True
FillTextBoxes              ' Display the current record
End Sub

Sub MoveDownButton_Click()
If RRows = 1 Then Exit Sub
If CurRow = RRows Then Exit Sub
CurRow = CurRow + 1
If CurRow = RRows Then MoveDownButton.Enabled = False
If RRows > 1 Then MoveUpButton.Enabled = True
FillTextBoxes              ' Display the current record

End Sub
```

Coding the CloseButton_Click event procedure

To make sure your application cleans up any pending operations and cleanly closes the connection to the SQL server, you need to close both the Recordset object and the Database object before quitting the application. You should also unload the form in the CloseButton_Click event procedure, if you want to close the application gracefully:

```
Private Sub CloseButton_Click()
    rc = SQLFreeStmt(hStmt, SQL_CLOSE)
    rc = SQLDisconnect(hDbc)          ' Disconnect
    rc = SQLFreeConnect(hDbc)         ' Free the connection handle
    rc = SQLFreeEnv(hEnv)             ' Free the environment handle
    Unload Form1
End Sub
```

Evaluating the results

When your code opens the connection and creates the cursor with the SQLExecDirect function, and when control returns to your application, your code displays the first row of the cursor in the TextBox controls. If more than one title matches the query criteria, you can use the navigation buttons to move to another row (either forward or backward) in the result set. Once you position the current record pointer off either end of the result set, the controls are disabled.

As in the other ODBC examples, use the SP_WHO stored procedure to determine the number of connections this application has opened. And, again as in the other ODBC examples, the connection remains open even after the data has been extracted from the SQL server; it remains open until you deallocate the statement handle or close the connection handle. If you are running in Design mode, you might find it interesting to reexecute the SP_WHO stored procedure after the application has ended but while Visual Basic is still running in Design mode. Look familiar? Are we establishing a pattern?

To see how many connections are being used, open another window on your workstation or server and start ISQLW or Enterprise Manager. Log on to the SQL server and, using the SP_WHO stored procedure, determine the number of connections your application has opened. Note that one or more connections might remain open even after the data has been extracted from the SQL server, or extra connections might stay open for a time, until their result sets are fully populated.

CAUTION
It is not at all wise to click the square Stop button on the Visual Basic toolbar; apparently, this kills the application *and* its data interface before it has a chance to shut down its connections. What this means to you is that a number of zombied connections can be created and held as long as Visual Basic is still running. If you have a limited number of connections (as most servers do), you can cripple the server—or, worse, your workstation can run out of handles and be unable to save your application. Not good.

NOTE An important way to compare the Visual Basic programming models described in this chapter is against Visual Basic 3.0 and other programming environments, such as PowerBuilder or Delphi. One thing I've noticed is that the Jet-based environments have stopped holding connections open after they're closed at design time. When it comes to orphaned connections, you have to be especially careful if you're working with any of the other models, including VBSQL.

Comparing the Samples

I hope you learned something from this overview. *Figure 2-4* summarizes key points of comparison. Can you gauge speed or overall suitability from the sample applications described in this chapter? I don't really think so. What you should be able to tell is how easy or difficult each model is to code, at least in a general sense. Real-world applications are composed of the same kinds of data access logic as those found in these sample applications: logic for opening a connection, gathering query criteria, submitting a query, and displaying the results. But so many other factors gate application speed and suitability that this sort of evaluation is by its very nature extremely complex.

Looking Closer at the Results

SQL Server 6.*x* brought a number of important innovations to developers writing front-end applications. One of the most useful features is SQLTrace. This application is brutally simple to use and yields a plethora of information about what is sent to the SQL server from whatever programming model you choose. Basically, you run SQLTrace on the server or on a workstation connected to the server. It establishes a connection and, using the new SQL tracing hooks added to SQL 6.0, displays exactly what was sent by each connection. You can set up filters to see specific users, applications, or only certain aspects of the operation. In any case, you should take a look at the logs when choosing a programming model and, once you do, when choosing one data-retrieval strategy over another. For example, a typical RDO query operation might return a log that looks like this:

```
-- 8/17/96 10:18:21.853 New connection (ID=29, SPID=13,
User=sa(REDMOND\BILLVA), App='', Host='BETAV1'(fffe2e85) )
-- 8/17/96 10:18:22.393 SQL (ID=29, SPID=13,
User=sa(REDMOND\BILLVA), App='', Host='BETAV1'(fffe2e85) )
set quoted_identifier on use "WorkDB"
go
-- 8/17/96 10:18:23.426 SQL (ID=29, SPID=13,
User=sa(REDMOND\BILLVA), App='', Host='BETAV1'(fffe2e85) )
select usertype,type,name from systypes where usertype>=100
select 502,'',USER_NAME() exec sp_server_info 500 select 501,'',1
where 'a'='A' set textsize 2147483647 set ansi_defaults on set
cursor_close_on_commit off set implicit_transactions off
go
-- 8/17/96 10:18:24.526 RPC (ID=29, SPID=13,
User=sa(REDMOND\BILLVA), App='', Host='BETAV1'(fffe2e85) )
sp_datatype_info 0, 0
go
-- 8/17/96 10:19:14.550 SQL (ID=29, SPID=13,
User=sa(REDMOND\BILLVA), App='', Host='BETAV1'(fffe2e85) )
SET FMTONLY ON select  email from workdb..phones SET FMTONLY OFF
go
```

(continued)

Figure 2-4

Comparison of Sample Applications

	Data Control Jet	Data Control ODBC-Direct	DAO/Jet	DAO/ODBC-Direct	Remote Data Control	RDO	VBSQL API	ODBC API
Data access	DAO/Jet/ODBC	DAO/ODBC-Direct	DAO/Jet/ODBC	DAO/ODBC-Direct	RDO/ODBC	RDO/ODBC	DB-Library	ODBC interface
Ease of coding[1]	1	2	4	4	1	3	6	10
Lines of code	14	14	45	45	16	50	67	127
Sample implementation	DBGrid	DBGrid	Text-Boxes	Text-Boxes	DBGrid	Text-Boxes	Text-Boxes	Text-Boxes
Query type	Concatenated	Prepared statement	Concatenated	Prepared statement	Prepared statement	Prepared statement	Concatenated	Concatenated
SQL Server features	Some	Most	Some	Most	Most	Most	All	Most
GPFs[2] likely	None	Few to none	None	Few to none	Few to none	Few to none	Few to none	Many
Visual Basic–friendly interface?	Yes	Yes	Yes	Yes	Yes	Yes	Yes	No

1. Scale is 1 = easy; 10 = hard
2. General protection faults (that is, crashes)

```
-- 8/17/96 10:19:17.113 SQL (ID=29, SPID=13,
User=sa(REDMOND\BILLVA), App='', Host='BETAV1'(fffe2e85) )
create proc #odbc#billva953253 @P1 varchar(10) as select * from
workdb..phones where email = @P1
go
-- 8/17/96 10:19:18.136 RPC (ID=29, SPID=13,
User=sa(REDMOND\BILLVA), App='', Host='BETAV1'(fffe2e85) )
sp_cursoropen NULL, " EXEC #odbc#billva953253 'lbates'
", 8, 1, NULL
go
-- 8/17/96 10:19:19.176 RPC (ID=29, SPID=13,
User=sa(REDMOND\BILLVA), App='', Host='BETAV1'(fffe2e85) )
sp_cursorfetch 14310192, 1, 0, 1
go
-- 8/17/96 10:19:21.260 RPC (ID=29, SPID=13,
User=sa(REDMOND\BILLVA), App='', Host='BETAV1'(fffe2e85) )
sp_cursorclose 14310192
go
```

Notice that each notation in the trace log indicates the time when the command arrived and which connection sent it. This kind of detail can be a telling indicator of object-level interface efficiency. That is, you are seeing what the SQL server was told to do based on the high-level command you executed in your application. Be careful though—this type of logging can also adversely affect server performance.

3
Chapter

Choosing an Architecture

Asking the Right Questions

Understanding Client/Server
Architecture

A Hypothetical
Client/Server System

A Hypothetical Distributed-
Engine Configuration

Client/Server or Distributed-
Engine Architecture?

Accessing a Centralized
Database Engine with a
Distributed Database Engine

Implementing a
Client/Server Front End

can't tell you how many times I've worked on a team that didn't make the tough decisions early enough to avoid having to rework almost an entire database system after it was discovered that the system had been built on a weak foundation. Without the discussion that follows, you might choose a database management system (DBMS) design that seems to meet or exceed your immediate needs, or a design that your team is comfortable with, but then discover a year from now that your choice was the wrong one—maybe even so wrong that you have to redesign or reimplement existing applications before you can find a workable long-term solution.

This chapter compares two different approaches to database systems architecture: a client/server configuration and a distributed-engine configuration. Both approaches are in widespread use throughout the world, because both are applicable to a variety of business situations. One of these configurations—or, according to your business needs, some combination of the two—might be the most suitable approach for you.

Asking the Right Questions

When you're developing an application to connect to SQL Server, one of the first questions you need to ask yourself is this one: "What is the *best* database engine architecture for *our* system?" Fortunately, you have many choices—and even more now that you can consider web-based deployment strategies. Unfortunately, just because there are so many choices, this question becomes a hard one to answer. The decision-making process is even more complicated in systems where SQL Server is only one of several databases or database engines that are accessed. As you look for the best choice for your application, you'll need to put a few questions to those members of your team who have the most complete understanding of the overall system design and development strategy:

PART I CLIENT/SERVER COMPUTING: AN INTRODUCTION

- Which type of database management system best matches the *performance* needs of our system?

    - Why use a systems architecture that we or our company will soon outgrow or one that is too complex for our needs?

    - With the number of active users we expect to support, will our proposed system be able to handle the load?

- Which strategy best matches our development skills?

    - Why lead our developers into the outback of unfamiliar territory?

    - Why use a strategy that only the most skilled developers on our team can implement?

    - Why develop another application that takes months or years to write and even longer to modify when it needs fixing?

    - Why use unproven technology?

    - Why use the same approach we have always used if it isn't meeting any of our needs except our need to be comfortable?

    - Are we really talking about design strategy, or are we talking about personnel, company politics, our company's skill set, and our staff's desire or ability to learn and grow technically?

- Does the application prototype *really* scale to the size we will need in production?

    - Will the *n*-user model that we created and tested work the way we've predicted it will when we go on line with 10 or 100 or 1000 × *n* users?

    - Will the system—the entire system—bear up under production network traffic loads?

    - Are we going to design a little-red-wagon–size application for hauling loads of gravel?

    - Will the system deal with the way end users *really* work?

    - Are the end users skilled enough and well enough trained not to have problems, or will their lack of skill and experience lead to more problems than our design can tolerate?

    - How will this strategy apply to our needs in the near future? the midterm future? the extended future?

    - If the system we've chosen will get us from here into late next year, when it will go into full production with 100 times the volume, why not build a strategy *now* that will work for today and tomorrow and for several quarters of tomorrows?

- Does our strategy work with our existing workstation or server application mix?

- Why plan a strategy that means we have to buy and install lots of expensive equipment and retrain most of the workstation users?

- Why plan a strategy that doesn't leverage the movement of our organization into the graphical user interface (GUI) world of applications development?

- Are our workstations capable of running the applications we've designed, along with all the other applications currently running on the workstations?

- Will our new application so overload or block the system that no other work can be done while our application is running?

- How much will it cost for hardware, software, licenses, and development?

    - Are we measuring all the real costs: money, time lost in production, development costs, and training costs?

    - Are we digging ditches with spoons?

    - Has anyone successfully implemented a similar system, or are we asking our company and our developers to perch astride a cutting-edge razor?

- Is the systems architecture stable enough to support our design?

    - Does it suddenly die or lock up, with no rational explanation?

    - Does the system vendor provide independent references who will testify to the system's features and foibles in full production mode?

    - Will only a leading-edge implementation do the job, or will existing implementations work almost as well?

NOTE There is no single "best" solution. If you have a C-language–based development shop, for example, you'll be unlikely to accept a DBMS design decision using Visual Basic or Pascal. And solutions at IBM are unlikely to include a Compaq ProLinea running the Microsoft Windows NT operating system, regardless of how well such a configuration would match IBM's needs.

In many, many cases, your design decisions will be made on the basis of what your *people*—your developers, managers, and support staff—know best. All in all, many design decisions boil down to personnel or political problems, not to technical problems. In any system, you need to factor in the ability of your developers to implement and support the design against the complexity of the application. If your staff is not skilled or confident enough to develop API-based client/server applications, you might feel that you have only one alternative: to use one of the integrated development environments, or the Data control and its snap-together data access solutions, and then live with possible performance problems and design constraints. But if you want to use

SQL Server as a back-end server, you're faced with at least the number of development platform options shown in **Figure 3-1** on the next page.

The development options shown in the figure are organized on the basis of development language. This is a consideration for sites with developers who are trained in only one programming discipline, a situation that limits the available choices. A C-based development strategy doesn't make sense if your organization has only Visual Basic developers. But if your shop is FORTRAN-based, you might gain some insights into the development costs associated with one language or another, not to mention the challenging task of creating applications for Windows in FORTRAN. If you haven't decided between Visual Basic and C or C++, consider the development, training, and support costs involved with your choice of development strategy. You'll find that Visual Basic makes development of the interactive connection to SQL Server far easier, which means not only faster, less trouble-prone applications but also applications that come together faster and with fewer support headaches later on. The Microsoft Foundation Class (MFC) C++ object libraries for Windows can trim development costs for C-based Windows applications, but, like any other C-based development strategy, this approach doesn't provide Visual Basic's or even QuickBasic's "stop and ask" mode, an invaluable aid when you're working with SQL Server's interactive connection.

If you have chosen to program in C, I would make sure that whoever made that decision didn't come to this dubiously correct conclusion based on Visual Basic version 4.0. Now that Visual Basic version 5.0 has a full-blown native code–optimizing compiler, your tests should show that Visual Basic runs within a couple of percentage points as fast as C++ in virtually all cases—but is far easier to use to develop client/server applications.

If you're concerned with speed of execution, I think you'll find that Visual Basic applications wait at the same speed as C programs. That is, both programming models wait at the same speed for users, RAM access, network latency, disk drives, and video retrace—the factors that can make all applications slow to a crawl. One of your primary concerns, however, should be *perceived* performance of the front-end application: how fast or slow the application *appears* to the user to be running. The performance of different applications can be radically different; it depends on the front-end architecture and other factors, and these factors have little to do with the language used to compile the application. In many cases, application speed has more to do with the use and number of controls in the application than with the database or how it was accessed. With Visual Basic, it's much easier to create lots of forms using lots of complex control arrangements, so a developer sitting at a 64 MB, P6/200 MHz-based machine might not realize or appreciate the frustration of a user on a more conservative system.

NIHS—Not-Invented-Here Syndrome—results from a virus that is fairly common among the more experienced and entrenched developers, here and abroad. Engineers and managers too often decide that a solution from outside cannot possibly meet their special and specific needs, and they settle for a 70 percent implementation of their own before attempting to implement an 80 percent solution from someone outside. "If we didn't create it," the logic goes, "how good can it be? No one knows *our* business like our own people."

If you aren't sure, ask someone who has developed in both languages which one he or she prefers. If you choose to program in C, you can still use most of the strategies discussed here (but you will need a note from your mom).

One more thing—don't let ignorance be an excuse for failure. Don't let anyone on your staff decide to use an architecture, language, or technique just because he or she doesn't understand the alternatives. Too often, I have seen corporate Not-Invented-Here Syndrome (NIHS) kill or hobble a project. I also find it frustrating to hear that a development language has been dropped, along with SQL Server, because a prototype developer couldn't get the test case to work. Throwing out both Visual Basic and SQL Server because a developer has misunderstood the implementation of a high-performance front end is like junking a Maserati because cheap tires can't hold traction when the power is applied.

Figure 3-1
Development Platform Choices for SQL Server

Language (OS)	Interface	Comments
Visual Basic (Windows)	Visual Basic SQL Server Library (VBSQL); VBSQL.VBX/OCX 16-bit and 32-bit support.	Similar to DBLIB. High-speed, low-level API. Accesses virtually all SQL Server features. Very small footprint and broad acceptance as a production-level interface. Used only with Microsoft SQL Server. Uses custom DECLARE files to access C functions especially adapted for Visual Basic.
	ODBC API 16-bit and 32-bit support.	High-speed, low-level, database-independent interface. Accesses virtually all SQL Server features, although fewer than VBSQL does. Uses custom DECLARE files to access C-based functions. Little specific Visual Basic support. Binding and 32-bit string issues make interface complex.
	Data Access Objects (DAO) via Microsoft Jet database engine. 16-bit (Visual Basic version 3.0, 4.0) and 32-bit support (Visual Basic version 4.0, 5.0).	Upper middleware for ODBC. Faster development, slower performance. Limited support of SQL Server features—especially stored procedures and multiple result sets. Can bind to specific Visual Basic controls.
	RemoteData control (RDC) and Remote Data Objects (RDO). 32-bit support only.	Thin interface for ODBC API. Same support for SQL Server as ODBC API but far easier and safer to program. Advanced batch-mode cursor library. Extensive asynchronous and event-driven support. Application can use bound controls or RDO programmatic interface. Faster than Jet, somewhat slower than API-based models.
	ODBCDirect—DAO interface to RDO. 32-bit support only.	Object interface that remaps DAO objects to equivalent RDO objects. Same support for SQL Server as RDO. Asynchronous operations, but no events. Faster than Jet, slightly slower than API-based models.
	Third-party property-driven controls.	Some use ODBC, some use DBLIB, some are proprietary. Limited support and compatibility.
Microsoft Access (Windows)	DBMS user interface.	Packaged-product DBMS. It implements distributed-engine technology. Accesses SQL Server via Jet and ODBC drivers.
	DAO via Microsoft Jet database engine. 16-bit (Access 2.0) and 32-bit support.	As implemented in Visual Basic, but better buffering and background processing than in Visual Basic. Upper middleware for ODBC. Faster development, slower performance. Rich reporting, query design.

Language (OS)	Interface	Comments
	ODBCDirect—DAO interface to RDO. 32-bit support only.	Object interface that remaps DAO objects to equivalent RDO objects. Same support for SQL Server as RDO. Asynchronous operations, but no events. Faster than Jet, somewhat slower than API-based models.
Visual Basic (MS-DOS)	VBSQL for MS-DOS. 16-bit support only.	Similar to DBLIB. High-speed, low-level API. Functional subset, given RAM constraints. (Obsolete.)
C or C++ (Any)	DBLIB API. 16-bit and 32-bit support.	High-speed, low-level API. Hard-coded binding of data fields. No interactive authoring or de-bug. Full support for two-phase commit and all SQL Server features.
	ODBC API. 16-bit and 32-bit support.	Database-independent interface. High-speed, low-level API. Accesses most SQL Server features.
	Jet API. 16-bit and 32-bit support.	Jet Programmer's Toolkit now exposes same API as used by other Jet clients, such as Microsoft Visual Basic and Microsoft Access.

Since you're thinking about using SQL Server—after all, you *are* reading a book on the subject—you're probably trying to decide on a design in which more than a few records will be accessed by more than a few people. If your system is expected to implement a single-user application that accesses a 5000-row table, I doubt that SQL Server will be cost-effective (although now that Microsoft has reduced the price of its Workstation version of SQL Server, per-haps a valid choice for small offices would include Microsoft SQL Server). But if your implementation will need enough power for 2 to 2200 or so transactions per second (TPS) sometime in the future, or even a year from now, SQL Server will be an appropriate choice.

The discussion in this chapter is also intended to bring those who have been using PC-class database systems like dBASE up to speed on client/server architecture. I'll attempt to make your decision about using a centralized or a distributed-engine approach somewhat easier—or at least better informed. I make a few basic assumptions that you can either accept or reject, but they do serve to illustrate the religious differences between two general models, both of which are gaining wider and wider acceptance. Before we examine those models, however, let's take a side trip through the major components of cli-ent/server architecture.

One other point before we get started. Many of you are considering use of a Jet database to prototype a SQL Server production database. The decision to do this is often based on the premise that Jet is a relational database engine and so is SQL Server. Well, that's true, and it's also true that both systems have tables, stored queries, referential integrity constraints, security systems, and support very similar dialects of ANSI SQL. But these features and subsystems

are implemented very differently. Frankly, it would be most unwise to make design decisions based on the performance, security, referential integrity management, or even the way queries are executed in a Jet database. In other words, just because a query seems to work in a Jet database doesn't mean that it will scale or even work in a SQL Server system. SQL Server database systems are more than just a set of tables and referential integrity constraints. Most production systems are simply not designed like 2- to 20-user Jet databases. These systems don't expose base tables to the developer—they expose SQL views or stored procedures or ActiveX business objects. These systems don't depend on broad cursors to expose thousands, or even hundreds, of rows to the user—especially not the systems that support more than a few dozen users. The fundamental design philosophy of a production SQL Server database is very unlike the type of database system that you can create with the Jet engine.

Understanding Client/Server Architecture

On the client side of this configuration, we find a fairly simple front-end application running on a fairly simple personal computer. (See *Figure 3-2*.) The application might be asked to do data validation or present lists of valid options, but most of the data integrity and business rules are enforced with the server's validation rules, defaults, triggers, and stored procedures. The server is designed to accept SQL queries from the front-end application—usually in the form of calls to stored procedures that return clearly defined and limited-scope result sets. On the server side, we find an intelligent database server engine. We've seen the term *engine* before—with the Microsoft Jet database engine, for example—but we haven't defined it as such. Briefly, an engine is a body of code that is used for performing a specific set of functions. An engine can be a mathematical processor, a business rule processor, or some other set of code that can be intelligently controlled.

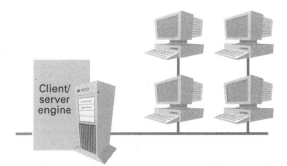

Figure 3-2   *Client/server configuration*

The Client's Responsibilities

Generally, the client application is responsible, at the least, for *connection management, data capture, data retrieval, data presentation,* and *error management.* Front-end applications often have responsibilities far in excess of these, but virtually all front ends must perform these fundamental tasks. Note that the term "client" in this context refers to the client application and its supporting database files, connection interfaces, and other components of the client system.

Connection management

The client application connects to the SQL server by way of a user-supplied or application-generated user ID and password. (This task might also mean that the first line of defense for the database security system is built into the application.) The client often disconnects from the server when the connection is no longer needed and reconnects, as required, when activity returns. The client must also deal with connection problems due to trouble on the server, network, in the application itself, or simply due to an inept user. Yes, some of the new architectures use the Distributed Component Object Model (DCOM) to assign the connection tasks to a remote server. That is, the client application uses a DCOM link to attach to a class module or an ActiveX component running on the server. This remote object still needs to make a connection to the server. Because the object can't (or shouldn't) pass on the user ID and password (and remain reentrant), it often must use its own connection ID and password and assume security is performed through other means.

This is where Microsoft Transaction Server comes in handy.

Data capture

This means that the client presents forms for the user to fill in with data, or it simply gathers information from the ether. The client facilitates this process by presenting lists of valid options based on database- or application-derived data. For example, on the basis of validation tables in the database, a client application presents lists of valid states or part numbers. The client also validates data values before they are sent to the database. This prevalidation often involves cross-checking form fields against other fields, either on the form or in the database. Validation can take place as fields are filled in or completed, or as the form is committed. Another responsibility of the client is submission of prevalidated rows as updates to the database and management of exceptions when database rules, triggers, or other checks fail. This task involves getting the user to decide what to do if an update fails because of a multiuser collision or a simple validation error.

Data retrieval

The client application creates data queries that are based on user or situational input. This task might mean that the application creates a SQL query on the fly, passes parameters to a local or system stored procedure, or invokes methods on business objects. The client also submits queries to the database engine for processing and retrieves the result sets, as required. This task includes processing result sets and making logical decisions based on the data returned. Another responsibility of the client is to manage data returned to the application, which might mean storing data in local arrays or passing it to subsystems that display it for the user. This might also mean maintaining the currency of one or more controls. Depending on the way that the data is fetched, it's often the client's responsibility to consume what it has asked for. That is, if the query or other operation asks for 50 rows, the client application must retrieve that data as quickly as possible. This responsibility should *never* fall on the user—users have a tendency to walk away (physically or mentally), leaving work undone.

Data presentation

The client application is responsible for displaying results from queries, as needed. This task might involve filling a Grid or ListBox control or filling out a complex form containing fields that require complex conversion, as when you're working with graphics or Rich Text Format (RTF) data. Since many applications use a master-detail methodology, it might be necessary to place the rows from several result sets into two or more display areas. Finally, the client keeps data presented to the user current and valid, which usually means executing background queries on exposed data to maintain currency or executing queries to keep hidden validation rules current.

Error management

The client is also responsible for trapping and dealing with the errors that can, and do, occur in the course of handling user demands and server and network vagaries. In no case should the user be presented with dialog boxes that indicate a fatal error unless all other methods of managing the error have been exhausted. Effective and comprehensive error management is the sign of a successful client application. In many cases, the client application will be forced to make a number of decisions on its own to determine the cause and scope of the error and attempt recovery. Only when it's unavoidable should the client application solicit additional information from the user, who is often the person least able to assist in the resolution of the problem. While error management is fairly easy for the developer, the user is rarely as informed about or concerned with the intricacies of the application or the overall database system. Would you be happy with a car that demanded that *you* supply precise fuel-air ratios on an especially cold morning when the car's computer couldn't figure out how to get your gas-guzzler started?

The Server's Responsibilities

In any client/server implementation, the server is not just a data repository. The server is also responsible for intelligent *security management, data management, query management, database system management,* and *error management.* The emphasis in this chapter is more on the client side of this architecture, but you really *must* understand the role played by the server before you can create an efficient, trouble-free client application. In many cases, your DBMS design will include quite a bit of development on the server. That is, you will be required to not only lay out tables but also develop the constraints, rules, triggers, views, stored procedures, and security constraints on all of the above— not to mention the replication, backup, log-file management, and the administrative procedures you need to devise to make all of this work.

You must also define the boundaries of the middle layers, the client, and the server. More and more middleware in the form of intelligent server-side (or even client-side) objects is performing logical and physical disk input/ output (I/O) to the database. I expect that developers of most applications, using object-oriented techniques, will spend considerable resources developing and managing these objects.

Security management

The server prevents unauthorized access to itself and your database while permitting guarded access to those with valid permission. This task involves safeguarding not only the data itself but also views, procedures, and administration of the database. The server enforces the checking of data types as well as enforcing rules, triggers, and index structures. This means that incoming data must conform to a complex set of criteria that are based on permissions granted to the user or to the group to which the user belongs. Data might be accepted, or it might be rejected because of database inconsistencies, violations of rules or triggers, checks of index duplicates, or other kinds of problems. To complicate matters, SQL Server runs on Windows NT, which has its own idea about who can get access to the server. Unless your code can find its way through the Windows NT minefields, it won't be able to knock on SQL Server's door to beg for a connection.

Data management

The server is also responsible for the validity and integrity of the data sent to the database system from your application and every other application that has permission to access your database. This task involves writing data to database tables once it has passed the security screen and recording these changes in the transaction logs. At the lowest levels, it means allocating and initializing database pages and blocks of pages as well as managing the physical disk I/O and any indexes or temporary database objects. The server is responsible for data validation using any rules assigned to data columns and for executing any triggers assigned to those data tables that are being changed. Another task of the server is to maintain the transaction log so that the system maintains a recoverable state at all times and operations can be rolled back or committed, as necessary. The server also maintains database statistics, the error log, and other supportive structures for tracking changes in the data and the schema.

Query management

The server processes SQL queries from the clients, a task that involves syntax and object checks and compilation of the query into a valid and efficient processing plan—even if the query is a stored procedure. The server also fetches data rows according to the plan and returns the rows to the client (often via a remote server-side object), as requested. This means opening a dialog with the user to support client management of individual result sets. The server might also keep cursor keysets locally if the query builds a server-side cursor. Management of these and all other temporary objects can consume considerable resources on the server, so it is the client application's responsibility to ensure that these resources are managed intelligently.

Database system management

In managing the database system itself, the server manages all connections to the database, using network and database security criteria to coordinate use of and access to the connections. The server also maintains tables, indexes, procedures, rules, triggers, data types, lists of valid users, and other database objects. Other tasks of database management performed by the server include allocation, initialization, and deallocation of space for all database structures; management of the procedure and data queues, the database memory, and database threads of execution; and efficient sharing of CPU time among users and internal tasks.

Error management

The server must also be capable of handling a variety of errors that, in most cases, client applications never see, nor should they. When problems or conflicts arise that the server can't resolve, it can often be programmed to inform the administrator (even by e-mail or a voice page) or simply to report back to the client. Again, sending error reports back to the user is counterproductive if the user can't do anything about it. For example, if the amount of space available on a device is nearly exhausted, sending a message to the user does little to solve the problem. The user can't adjust the free space or do anything but worry about it, ignore the error, or call the System Administrator (SA) to fix the problem. Having the system e-mail the SA when things start going wrong makes much more sense. Having a warning light go on in the client application might also be helpful—something like an "Oil" light on your car's dashboard. Any message shown to the user must provide enough information for the user to make an informed decision regarding what action to take.

The Interface

A principal difference between the client/server and distributed-engine architectures involves the interface—the way, in a client/server model, these two components are interconnected. In a SQL Server client/server model, the interface is designed to pass queries to the server and return result sets to the client, as you see in **Figure 3-3**, over a network link—a LAN or WAN. The client/

server interface in a SQL Server model is actually somewhat complex—it uses an unpublished form of Metadata called the Tabular Data Stream (TDS)—but it does not pass disk sectors or anything resembling raw disk I/O data to or from the server. This means that the interface can be simple and, since there is such a low volume of data, relatively slow without severely affecting the performance of the overall system or even the performance of the client system. It can also mean that if the link is fast enough, a far greater number of users can share the server than is possible when raw data I/O is sent over the wires.

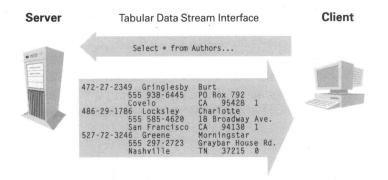

Figure 3-3 *SQL Server model*

NOTE   Even though DCOM, Remote Automation, and ActiveX technology are here, remember that the SQL server still speaks, reads, and writes in TDS. The objects that talk to the server must speak TDS to be understood—this condition hasn't changed. How the client speaks to the objects is new.

A Hypothetical Client/Server System

In the hypothetical client/server configuration that will be described here, the centralized server is dedicated to the task of running the database engine. Too often, the database engine is forced to do at least double duty, as both a file server and a print server and even as a user workstation. Using the database engine as a file server is not so bad, since there is very little counterproductive overhead involved. But when the database engine has to share RAM space and resources with a print spooler, the performance of the engine can really suffer as it contends with large, complex print images being crammed bit by bit into the slowest pile of iron connected to your computer: the printer.

In our hypothetical client/server model, front-end applications are designed to be used on fairly low-powered client PC workstations running anything from straight MS-DOS (using DB-Library from C, or the Microsoft Visual

CAUTION
Don't plan to use the Windows NT Server system as a workstation *and* as a host for SQL Server. That's like asking someone to be a monk and an underworld attorney at the same time.

A Quick Point About File Servers

In the general sense, I don't think you should share CPU and I/O resources by sharing files on the same server as the SQL server. However, one of the database designs that I am finding more and more appealing is that of an image file server. In my humble opinion (IMHO), images and large text chunks have no business being stored in the database. Sure, it's possible to store gargantuan images or files as database pages, but SQL Server is not particularly efficient about the way these are stored, retrieved, or backed up. Image and Text data pages are stored with all of the other ordinary row-data pages and must be backed up as such. These data types gobble space on the server's devices, and since they can't be accessed separately, they can't be compressed (unless you do it in your own code) or backed up separately—even though the data might never change.

There are better ways to store this type of data. In many cases, I have recommended storing page-based data in separate files on a separate file server, leaving only a pathname and offset in the database. This increases access performance dramatically and speeds up backup, recovery, and transaction-log handling (when the image operations are logged—which is rarely done). This also means that you can use a variety of compression and file media to store data. For example, you can use read-only CDs or even tape (no, not paper tape) to store the data, managing it through your own set of retrieval routines. This approach also means that you don't always have to transmit the page-based data over the LAN or WAN because it can be stored on a CD right on the client's system. That is, you can distribute the page-based data (especially when it doesn't change very often) on a CD that includes the front-end application. Sure, the application might need updating, but in many, many cases, the page-based data doesn't.

Here's an additional tip: A company I worked with distributes an application that retrieves medical imagery. The company's original plan called for the database to hold complex (and rather disgusting) images of people's insides, but the final implementation simply included the data on a companion CD—the application pulls up the pictures by retrieving the path and image coordinates from the database, which are also on the CD. Likewise, if your design uses the database to retrieve large read-only data blocks, it might be a good idea to use the database to store the file's pathname instead of its contents.

Basic Library for SQL Server [VBSQL] from Visual Basic for MS-DOS) to the Microsoft Windows, Windows NT, and Windows 95 operating systems; you'll have little need for extra CPU horsepower, local disk space, or more RAM— that is, assuming you use one of the less RAM-hungry programming models.

The Local Area Network (LAN) Contribution

Local area network (LAN) performance plays a significant role in some architectures. Ask yourself (or your system architect) if the LAN interface on SQL Server is expected to carry any of the following:

- SQL queries and result sets related to database access.

- Print spooler traffic.

- Direct shared-disk I/O as a file server, with files simply copied or moved to and from the server.

- Traffic generated by applications using the net as the motherboard of the computer. (In this case, files shared over the net are opened by multiple users and are searched and manipulated as if they were local files on a single-user system.)

- Traffic generated by Internet or e-mail servers.

- Packet protocols that clog the net with broadcast messages (such as NetBIOS).

- Any of the new network connectivity applications—such as the ones that broadcast video or live audio over the net.

- Traffic generated by Internet access—as when using a proxy server on the net.

If more than a few of these are possible, the net could become a performance bottleneck in your design. Another factor to consider is network load as affected by external factors, time of day, increased latency, efficiency, and bandwidth. If the network is already running at capacity, it might be wise to consider faster LAN hardware or a secondary dedicated network. If the LAN is really a WAN and your application is expected to work across continents or oceans, bounced from satellite to satellite, you'd better be prepared for some dramatic restrictions in the type of topology and programming model you can choose.

In any case, if your LAN is expected to carry a significant load, be sure to test a sample configuration under *live* load conditions. This is also a good idea if you want to try to connect external workstations via remote access service (RAS) or some other low-speed link. Another question to ask is whether the LAN can take the additional load. If your LAN is already heavily burdened, it might not be such a hot idea to add another LAN-intensive application to the load. Don't expect your test with 5 users to reflect what will happen with 25 or 2500 users.

CAUTION
In a 16-bit Windows 3.*x* environment, switching to another window is extremely problematic when other programs fail to yield to the Windows message loop. The multitasking afforded by the Windows NT family is a real advantage for developers. In virtually no case are the keyboard and mouse locked up while applications contend for system resources. Windows 95 is almost as generous with CPU time—but it does block on occasion.

In our hypothetical client/server installation, you can use a fairly low-performance LAN or even a serial remote access service link. The principal reason why you *can* use a relatively low-performance LAN has to do with what the LAN carries. In this hypothetical design, it carries relatively minuscule queries (of usually fewer than several dozen bytes) in one direction and retrieves only those data rows that are needed. Unless you use cursors extensively—that is, incorrectly—your LAN won't be required to carry anywhere near its capacity, multiplied by a dozen or a dozen dozen users. However, some of the object-based designs can dramatically affect the amount of LAN traffic if you aren't careful.

This design assumes that the LAN is dedicated to your application and isn't required to support significant amounts of high-volume transaction processing. For example, if the application is going to upload complex bit-mapped graphics, a faster net would only make operations faster. But if your application makes complex queries that yield only a limited number of result rows (say, a few hundred to a few thousand), a faster net might prove unnecessary.

I got up in a SQL Server user's group meeting some time ago to address a question about performance. Others had offered advice on changes to the schema, using faster or more processors, or a different front-end programming model. I simply suggested more RAM. "Sixty-four megs or more of RAM," I said, "can solve a litany of schema problems and make many poor design decisions irrelevant."

Typical Client/Server Configurations

Figure 3-4 shows three client/server configurations that will provide adequate user response. CPU type and speed are shown for the low end of the number of users. If you don't have enough data cache RAM, you will generally find that SQL Server systems are disk-bound. But once most active data pages are in memory, you'll generally find that SQL Server systems are CPU-bound. Increasing CPU speed or moving to a Windows NT–based multiprocessor hardware platform can also improve server performance.

Figure 3-4
Typical Client/Server Configurations

System Component	Typical 1–10 User Configuration	Typical 10–50 User Configuration	Typical 40–100 User Configuration
Server system	50-MHz (or faster) 486, Windows NT, 16 MB (or more) RAM, 1-GB hard disk, VGA video, 8-bit network adapter	60-MHz (or faster) 586, Windows NT, 24 MB (or more) RAM, 1.5-GB hard disk, VGA video, 16-bit network adapter	Multiple 120-MHz (or faster) Pentium-class processors, Windows NT, 64 MB (or more) RAM, 2-GB hard disk, VGA video, 32-bit network adapter
Workstation	PC XT[1], AT, or better (depends on OS)	PC XT, AT, or better (depends on OS)	PC XT, AT, or better (depends on OS)

1. This can be any XT-class system if you run MS-DOS, even an Osborne. For the client system's Windows operating system, a 486/50 is barely enough nowadays, especially if you are running Microsoft Office 97.

Note that the suggested server system doesn't have a particularly fast video adapter. It shouldn't need one. The server should have just enough video hardware—no more—to tell what's going on in character mode (or in low-resolution VGA mode). The hard disk is big enough to store the operating system (about 70 MB) and a small database (about 50 MB). SQL Server and its new GUI-based utilities take up a lot more room than the old IBM OS/2 versions. The Windows NT operating system is also much greedier than the older versions of OS/2 when it comes to hard disk space. I originally started working with a 350-MB drive on my lab server; once the Windows NT operating system and SQL Server were loaded, I had almost no room left for the rest of the ancillary utilities or for a test database of reasonable size.

There has to be sufficient allocation for swap and temporary database space, which is directly related to the number of users your system will have and to how you intend to build your cursors. And, no, the server should not be configured so that it has to swap out the server software in favor of some other program or subsystem; adding more hard disk space for a larger database or more RAM and processors for better performance is something you can expect to do as your system grows.

With most systems, both server and workstation will probably require at least a single-speed CD-ROM drive to load software (at least initially). Visual Basic and SQL Server are now distributed exclusively on CD. Since the whole CD is not full, maybe the SQL Server group should have included some hit tunes by Elton John. (And maybe they did...)

TIP   I am often asked, "Is it better to buy one 2-GB disk or two 1-GB disks?" While it would probably be cheaper to buy a single large disk and possibly easier to set up, back up, and maintain, remember that SQL Server uses one thread for each logical device. By having each device on a separate drive, you end up with multiple threads, but more important, multiple heads, actuator mechanisms, and logically independent disk I/O channels. Two are better than one in this case.

As the number of users increases, the increased need for performance eventually will require you to add more RAM so that more pages are in the memory queues. With this configuration, once you approach the level of 20 to 50 users, you might want to add another processor or upgrade to a more powerful CPU (or both). The Windows NT operating system needs more RAM and more disk space, so you might be tempted to use OS/2. This is an option if you stick with OS/2 1.3; more recent versions have a distinct disadvantage for SQL Server, and the most recent versions won't run SQL Server at all. At some point, you will find that the system is net-bound and that the server needs to be upgraded to 16-bit or 32-bit power on the net card.

The workstation system shouldn't be any more powerful than it needs to be to run the operating system, whether MS-DOS, Windows, or Windows NT. I don't recommend an XT to run the Windows operating system—unless you work for the government or are into waiting. An XT won't run Windows 95 or even Windows 3.x for that matter. If you are running an MS-DOS–based front end, an XT is fine, especially if you can add an expanded RAM card. In most cases, the operating system will take up far more resources than the SQL front-end application. CP/M will be problematic.

Cost per User

Startup costs for the three hypothetical configurations shown in *Figure 3-4* must include the server hardware and the license for the server engine. Add to that the cost of a single copy of the language (assuming that you choose a language, like Microsoft Visual Basic, that doesn't require multiple-use licenses) and the API interface. The disk space listed in the figure is not for data in the database but for OS overhead and user-related temporary space. The operating system, base database, temporary tables, swap file, applications, and a copy each of *Doom* and *Solitaire* will easily take about 150 MB for a serious server system. Add your database disk requirements to this total—more if you plan to run *Hearts* or *Doom* over the net.

Figure 3-5 plots the cost of our hypothetical client/server installation, with costs shared by all users. The chart assumes a single server and one additional workstation for each additional user. Incremental costs include the workstations and their LAN hardware. This is a fairly asymptotic plot, up to the point where a larger server (or maybe just more RAM) is needed to support the additional users. I put this point where the number of users exceeds 50. As you see, the initial cost of the server is quickly amortized. The model depicted here forms the foundation of many client/server cost-effectiveness studies.

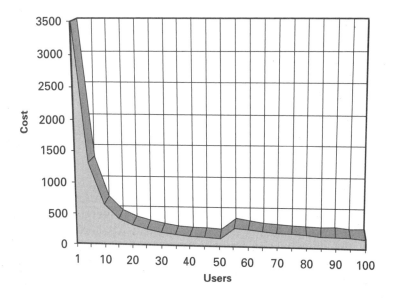

Figure 3-5 *Cost of client/server installation*

Client/Server Performance

Without going into a long-winded treatise on client/server performance, I'll invite you to consider this fact: some server-based client/server systems, including SQL Server, actually have *higher* per-user throughput as new users are added.

In other words, adding more users makes processing *faster* for each user. The reason for this is commonality. Performance doesn't improve when the extra users aren't sharing the same database and shared procedures. When they are, however, the server doesn't have to take the time to load them into memory; they're already there. When multiple users share the same stored procedure, as in SQL Server, the engine doesn't have to stop, load, and compile the procedure before executing it. Additional users might be able to use the procedure that is already sitting in RAM. This means that the server can handle significantly more users and process information faster than systems that cannot share work already processed for other users.

Actually, SQL Server doesn't really *share* stored procedures—they aren't reentrant. SQL Server *does* cache unused procedures so that they don't have to be reloaded once a user is done with them. That is, when a stored procedure ends, it is marked as unused but otherwise left in memory until SQL Server needs the RAM to load another procedure. If another user comes along who needs the procedure, SQL Server simply reactivates any dormant copy that happens to be in memory. The chances of a specific procedure being in RAM is a function of the following conditions:

- How much procedure cache RAM you allocate

- How many instances of the procedure fit into the cache

- How many procedures are used

- How many users access the procedures

NOTE Imagine a home where each of 10 children and 2 parents had to eat something different at each meal. Instead of one big pot of soup on the stove at suppertime, there would be 12 tiny ones, each with a different kind of soup. In the same way, it's entirely possible to create single-server client/server systems that manage large numbers of databases, but these implementations couldn't share anything but the CPU's attention and the server's code.

Figure 3-6 on the next page shows that as more users are added to this hypothetical dedicated system, performance actually improves. And as each user is added, the chances get better that a needed page is already in memory or that a necessary stored procedure has already been loaded. (Of course, this performance model assumes that an effective locking strategy is used.) This particular system's performance per user drops off at around 500 users; the point at which performance drops off depends on the following factors:

- *Amount of data in the database.* Smaller databases might be more prone to throughput problems as the number of users increases, with more users fighting over fewer core pages.

- *Number of page collisions.* Page collisions can occur when multiple users are accessing the same page. The number of page collisions is inversely proportional to the size of the database core—that is, the set of data most likely to be accessed or updated. Page collisions are not really a problem unless multiple simultaneous updates are being attempted.

- *Number of simultaneous users.* A 500-user system that has only 50 active users needs a very different hardware mix than one with 500 active users.

- *Ratio of updates and inserts to queries.* How many changes are being made at any one time and by how many users? This question is tied to the issue of page locks. Are updated pages evenly distributed, or do most updates occur on the same shared pages?

- *Broadness or specificity of update transactions.* Are update transactions broad in scope, or are they focused on specific rows? For example, do update operations change a broad range of rows in a single operation, and must these operations be completed before other, similar transactions can proceed?

- *Efficiency of updates.* When an application, while holding a locked page, takes an inordinate amount of time to complete an update, the overall performance of the database can be dramatically reduced.

- *Data distribution.* How is the data spread out over the database? Are there update or query hot spots that increase locking problems or decrease data I/O?

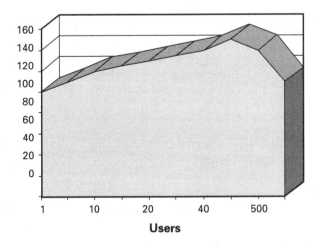

Figure 3-6   *Client/server engine performance*

- *Commonality of data and procedures.* Can the engine share cached data pages and procedures, or are the queries so broad in scope or so specific that they eliminate any efficiencies gained by commonality? Or when database operations access common pages, does update and access locking reduce performance? This also implies that the database server is dedicated to the task at hand and doesn't have to deal with several databases at once or with ancillary processes such as acting as a print or file server or even as a workstation.

- *Number of queries per second.* Is the system an online transaction processing (OLTP) system, or is it used for decision support?

- *Amount of data processed per query.* Are some front-end applications uploading or downloading large numbers of rows—using the SQL server as an ISAM data source?

- *Production schedule.* Can bulk updates or database synchronization routines be done at nonpeak hours, or does the currency of the system data demand immediate across-the-board updates?

- *Number and complexity of triggers and rules.* Are complex, time-consuming triggers needed to maintain complex database relationship constraints?

- *Number and usability of indexes.* More indexes mean faster access for retrieval but slower updates.

- *Speed and efficiency of hardware.* Hardware would include the LAN. In most cases, disk caching does not help here. To maintain the database's viability, the database engine needs to manage the caches.

- *Amount of work done on the front end.* Does the front-end application prequalify the updates so that all (or most) will pass centralized rule and integrity checks?

- *Replication.* Is the server having to take time out to replicate or mirror some or all of the data store?

A Hypothetical Distributed-Engine Configuration

What I am calling the distributed-engine configuration places a dedicated database engine or query processor at each workstation. (See *Figure 3-7* on the next page.) In this design, either a central file server or one of the workstation clients acts as the central data repository. The distributed-engine configuration requires significantly more intelligence in the workstation front-end application than the client/server configuration, and it needs more and faster hardware to support it. Each workstation contains a stand-alone database engine closely coupled to a front-end application, and each workstation acts independently—ignorant, for the most part, of database activity on other workstations. Sure, the file server operating system is aware that there are a number of competing users for a single file, but it has no idea what's happening at the level of the database—especially at the logical level, where the data is more than just clusters and sectors of a disk file. For a single-user database, this approach makes considerable sense. It also throws more CPU horsepower at the problem—which is both good and bad, as I'll explain.

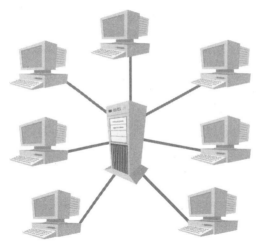

Figure 3-7 *Distributed-engine configuration*

The Local Area Network (LAN) Contribution

In the distributed-engine configuration, the LAN hardware plays a critical (and often limiting) role. (See *Figure 3-8*.) Each workstation uses the net as a local disk channel. What this means is that when an application accesses a *local* hard disk, it accesses the operating system file I/O primitives after having passed through a number of complex logical data object layers. Once the system file I/O takes over, local hard disks are accessed via the motherboard bus, the local hard disk controller card, and the on-drive controller. Data I/O throughput is limited by the bandwidth of the motherboard bus (which generally is very fast), the power of the disk controller card, and the performance of the drive and its own controller. (The hard disk controller can include caching logic and perhaps even pre-fetch or lazy-write hardware-assisted logic that can really improve performance for this type of system. Caching controllers can help most disk operations, but in some cases they can interfere with database integrity. To deal with this contingency, the lazy-write feature is often disabled.)

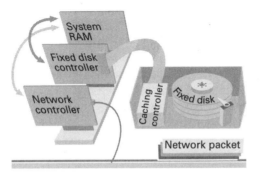

Figure 3-8 *LAN hardware in the distributed-engine configuration*

What this means for you is that when you execute a query, the database query processor has to read and update the indexes and any tables *over the net*. And this can mean, in a worst-case scenario, that many, many index and table blocks are passed over the net, sometimes several times in a single query.

When you access a hard disk drive over the net, you add two net controller cards, a lot of cable, and perhaps a half-dozen or more multiplexers, concentrators, and maybe even modems to the circuit. You also have to make a packet of every disk I/O request. This means that for each block of data, which can range from a few hundred to several thousand bytes, a network driver has to add addressing, protocol, and checksum data to create an addressable *packet* of data. In some cases, the packets must be enclosed in packets that are themselves enclosed in packets as you traverse through TCP/IP, SNA, and named pipe protocol mazes. Each packet is placed on the net as space becomes available. If the LAN is busy, the driver and the net card block until they can cram another packet in edgewise. Having the LAN loaded up with mail, HTTP, other low-level file I/O, and network overhead packets doesn't make this system work any better.

At the server end, the data packet is picked off the net by the server's network controller card—when it isn't busy reading other users' packets. The packets are opened by the network driver, and the data is quickly routed to the file server's operating system as an I/O request. The file server takes the request and performs the disk I/O operation by reading or writing the requested data. The file server software then sends the requested sectors or write confirmations back—through the same gauntlet.

Each workstation can cache parts of the database locally, in volatile RAM or temporary disk space, so if the workstation shuts down without posting "dirty" cache pages and closing the database file, the central database file can become corrupted. Because users often turn their computers on and off as if they were television sets, this form of database damage can become a way of life unless you have some heart-to-heart discussions with your users. Fortunately, most of the more recent versions of the databases designed to use this architecture limit their exposure to this kind of damage by using carefully orchestrated write operations. If one of these physical writes is interrupted, the database is marked suspect. This approach is also subject to failure modes triggered by LAN storms or disruptions—but you never have those. (Yeah, right.) For this design to work, the LAN must be a screamer: a device so fast that if you held it up to your ear, you could hear the bits running into each other and crying out in pain.

Since the type of net traffic is very different in this configuration, you might discover that as you add more users (though I can't tell you exactly how many more) the system gets bogged down performing even the simplest query. You will also find that different net protocols can significantly affect scalability and throughput. For example, an Ethernet network tends to be fairly fast, and it scales nicely—up to the point where it breaks down completely. Arcnet is somewhat slower but more linear in performance. It tends to be stable even as more users are added, but its lack of overall speed keeps that number relatively low. Often a significant amount of data must be sent up and down a network so that contact can be maintained with all the network nodes and resources. This overhead is a function of the network protocol in use and can account for a significant amount of the total network traffic.

NOTE   Microsoft uses one of the largest networks in the world. The network is basically all Ethernet and was recently converted to all Transmission Control Protocol/Internet Protocol (TCP/IP) for better performance and less overhead.

When you attempt to determine whether your network can carry the load of a distributed-workstation design, be sure to consider the network load as it is currently implemented. In other words, how many users are *already* tied to the net, and what load are they putting on the existing servers and network routers? Running your tests against a dedicated LAN is a great idea for crash tests, but not for evaluating production performance.

Typical Distributed-Engine Configurations

Figure 3-9 shows three typical distributed-engine hardware configurations that will provide adequate user response. CPU type and speed are shown for the low end of the range of users. Generally, you'll find that the system becomes netbound or begins to be tied up because the server is waiting for disk access. Increasing the CPU speed or upgrading the server to the Windows NT operating system can improve performance. Using DoubleSpace or DriveSpace disk compression or Windows NT compressed data files has just the opposite effect: the compression/decompression activity adds to the overall load on the server.

This type of system has an entirely different set of configuration constraints from those in our hypothetical client/server configuration. Here, the shared file server is not expected to do double duty as a workstation, but it still must have the horsepower to deal with any number of data-hungry workstations. This won't be a problem in some situations, as when a system has 40 users connected to the database but only half or fewer of them are working at any one time. Unfortunately, however, there is nothing to stop the other half from going back to work just as the first half starts a complex set of queries. As more users are added, the strain on the disk controller, the system bus, and the CPU—not to mention the load on the net card—grows more intense. In many cases, the focus of this intense activity might be data pages that all or most applications must access in common. With smaller databases, it is far more likely that a page is already being accessed (and perhaps locked) by another user.

The workstation in this configuration is expected to run not only the database engine but also a complex Windows-based front end. Using MS-DOS as a low-cost alternative is not an option, since our hypothetical distributed database engine runs only on the Windows or Windows NT operating systems. Each workstation will need more RAM and hard disk space—at least 4 to 6 megabytes—just to support the operating system. The front-end application is

Figure 3-9
Typical Distributed-Engine Configurations

System Component	Typical 1–4 User Configuration	Typical 5–20 User Configuration	Typical 18–50 User Configuration
"Server"[1]	33-MHz (or faster) 486, Windows for Workgroups, 8 MB (or more) RAM, 150-MB hard disk, VGA video, 8-bit network adapter	Dedicated 66-MHz (or faster) 486, Windows for Workgroups or Windows NT, 16 MB (or more) RAM, 400-MB hard disk, VGA video, 16-bit network adapter	Dedicated 133-MHz (or faster) Pentium-class processor, Windows for Workgroups or Windows NT, 24 MB (or more) RAM, 500-MB hard disk, VGA video, 32-bit network adapter
Workstation	33-MHz (or faster) 386, Windows for Workgroups, 6 MB (or more) RAM, 150-MB hard disk, SVGA video, 8-bit network adapter	33-MHz (or faster) 486, Windows for Workgroups, 6 MB (or more) RAM, 150-MB hard disk, SVGA video, 16-bit network adapter	66-MHz (or faster) 486, Windows for Workgroups, 8 MB (or more) RAM, 150-MB hard disk, SVGA video, 32-bit network adapter

1. In this case, the server can be one of the workstations, but this arrangement might not make sense if there are very many users. Remember to add more CPU and RAM capacity for a system that plays the role of both server and workstation.

also more demanding of system resources and will require more RAM and more hard disk space. Note that this configuration stores working result sets (keysets) on local disk space; once that has been used up, the engine gives up trying to build result sets. To deal with this problem, the workstation must dedicate another 10 to 50 or more megabytes of local disk space to temporary and swap space, or it must create queries that don't require as much space. The first of these options requires more hardware; the second, more programming discipline.

Cost per User

The startup cost for this hypothetical configuration must include the server hardware and the operating system. In this case, the workstation software must also include a license for the Windows operating system. The workstation hardware is also far more expensive, and the cost goes up as the number of users increases.

Figure 3-10 on the next page plots the cost of our hypothetical distributed-engine configuration, with costs shared by each user (and remember that all the data in this and other figures is generated on the basis of particular assumptions). Incremental costs include the additional workstations and their LAN hardware. This model shows a significant difference from the slope of our hypothetical client/server system because the workstations in this case are more expensive and tend to cost even more as they try to compete in a more heavily populated environment. Until you have about four or five users, you don't really need an additional dedicated server.

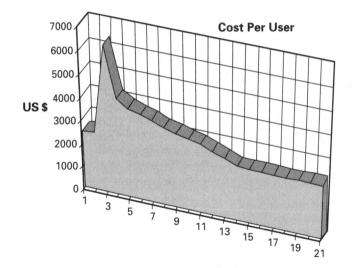

Figure 3-10 *Cost of distributed-engine installation*

Distributed-Engine Performance

Consider this fact: the distributed-engine configuration can share data pages, but only if they are cached on the file server. Unfortunately, the file server can't tell the difference between a database page, a page of code, or a page from this guide. The file server knows only about clusters of sectors. Heavily caching the server improves performance, since it places frequently accessed data pages in its local RAM, but you had better have the server protected with an uninterruptible power supply to prevent n megabytes of cache from getting cashiered into the bit bucket when the power fails. Caching systems can use lazy-write techniques to defer writing to the hard disk until a more opportune time; however, this feature must often be disabled to protect database integrity.

If the server is running on the OS/2 High Performance File System (HPFS), the Windows NT File System (NTFS), or the Windows operating system with SMARTDrive installed, intelligent data caching tries to keep the most frequently used data pages in RAM. But, again, because the file server can't understand the structure of the database, it can't make caching anywhere close to as efficient as it could be. This problem is exacerbated by the remote workstation database engines, each with a mind of its own when it comes to how its own query should be dealt with. No workstation database engine knows what any other engine is doing; it might know that there are other users competing for its data, but that's all. Sure, there is a shared-lock page file that all of the workstation database engines can see and jointly maintain, but this file simply maps the pages of the database file and helps other workstation database engines know which data pages of the shared file are locked. If one engine locks a page, all the engines know it, but they don't know *why* it's locked, and they don't know if they might be holding pages needed by other engines: the deadly embrace.

In this model, users who simply have a shared database file open will have little overall impact on the performance of the system. But as more active users are added to this hypothetical dedicated system, the chances increase that a needed page will be locked, and the chances of a network collision also increase. (See *Figure 3-11*.)

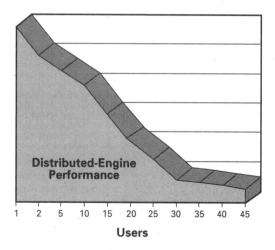

Figure 3-11 *Performance in the distributed-engine configuration*

Client/Server or Distributed-Engine Architecture?

Figure 3-12 summarizes costs and performance of the two hypothetical models. Let me emphasize again that these hypothetical models may or may not reflect your actual situation; I mean now to expose many of the questions you should be asking as you think about choosing the most suitable back-end/front-end architecture for your specific situation.

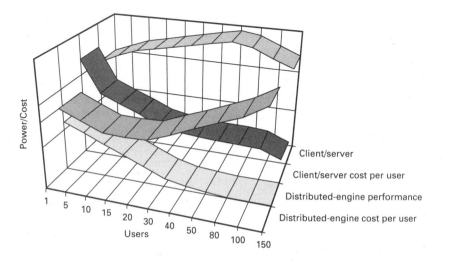

Figure 3-12 *Summary of costs and performance*

As you can see, the efficiency of our hypothetical distributed-engine architecture pretty much peaks out at around 25 users. Beyond that number, the amount of workstation, server, and net hardware you will need to maintain performance for the active users starts to get prohibitively expensive. The following factors also can affect the system's performance and predisposition for success.

Database Size

None of the figures included in this chapter puts much emphasis on the size of the database. I think we could probably come up with a factor called *user rows* that multiplies the total number of users by the number of the rows that need to be processed.

The two architectures we've been considering deal very differently with user rows. Both have to read data pages containing rows from a hard disk while searching or simply fetching the rows, but the distributed-engine system has to perform this disk I/O over the net—while all the other users are doing the same thing. As the number of user rows fetched or searched increases, network activity increases, collisions increase, and the network hardware moves toward saturation. The client/server architecture also has to use the net to get the data to the users, but that's it; except when the data is being backed up or bulk-loaded from external disk drives, the net is used to deliver the *results* of the query, not to perform the search. And since queries in a client/server model often fit into a single network packet, this side of the operation is extremely fast.

Input/Output Ratio

When you're measuring the performance of a database and the front-end application, be sure to design tests that accurately reflect not only the raw query speed (the time it takes to run a typical decision-support query) but also the update speed. In many configurations, the ratio of writes to reads can be very low, so a database that has unspectacular update speed might perform with total adequacy in read-only situations. When you update a database, the engine has to perform the following tasks:

- Lock one or more pages
- Allocate space for the new row
- Delete the old row
- Write the new row
- Rebuild the index (which also involves page locking)
- Unlock the pages

When you simply execute a query, however, the engine only has to find one or more records in the database. The number of suitable indexes plays a big role here, as does the number of triggers and rules that the engine has to run on every update. More indexes will mean more work whenever the data changes, but fewer indexes will mean more scans in which all the rows in a table are read one at a time.

Data Page Management

In some databases, the data is stored in a physically sequential order on disk. You may be able to request this arrangement by asking for a "clustered" index. Clustering complicates updates, since multiple rows often have to be moved around on the pages, though it can mean faster retrieval—but only in cases where the data is accessed in sorted order. When a row is deleted from some databases, the space freed is not released until the database is brought down and restarted in maintenance mode and empty rows are purged. This arrangement saves time during an update, but it isn't as fast as updating in place, which changes the row in situ, nor is it as efficient as dynamic page allocation and deallocation. More important, after a large update you might discover that your database has doubled in size through the action of a single user. Be sure you know how page management methodologies will affect your design.

Index Management

Make sure you also know what kinds of indexes are available to your developers. In some cases, a simple ISAM-style index with a few keys will suffice. Remember, though, that for every index you add, you gain query speed but lose update speed. Go back and rethink your write-to-read ratio. If you are doing more writes than reads in real time, then perhaps you need fewer indexes, not more. It might make sense to minimize the number of indexes you use during the bulk of the update activity and then rebuild them later in the cycle, before the bulk of the queries is made.

Lock Management

Is the system that you are designing limited by the total number of page locks available on the file server? Watch out for an upper limit of locks. Both data and index pages require locks. In the distributed-engine model, you will be capped by the number of locks supported at the MS-DOS level (SHARE.EXE), not by some number you set on the server.

Some LAN implementations (like Novell's) require additional tuning parameters to prevent the system from running out of network locks. If you exceed the maximum number of locks set per connection for the Novell server, you will get the following error message on the server: *Record Lock threshold exceeded*. This error can also cause the Novell server to crash. To solve this problem, follow these steps:

1. Obtain the TTSFIX.NLM dynamic patch, either directly from Novell or from CompuServe. On CompuServe, look for 311PTD.EXE in the NOVFILES forum.

2. Set the Record Lock threshold to some high value greater than the default of 500, preferably between 6,000 and 10,000. Even though the server should no longer crash, Jet might still encounter problems when the server exceeds the lock count. There are no reports of any problems with the Record Lock threshold set to a high value. Even with this maximum set, if the threshold is reached, Jet will stop; with the fix, the Novell network won't crash.

3. Load the TTSFIX.NLM dynamic patch on the server to ensure that it won't crash if a lock count is exceeded.

The 311LPTD.ZIP file also contains PATCHMAN.NLM and TTSFIX.NLM; these files should be loaded in the server's AUTOEXEC.NCF file. This action requires the command LOAD PATCHMAN.NLM, followed by LOAD TTSFIX.NLM in the AUTOEXEC.NCF.

The following table details possible lock settings:

Value to Set	Range	Default
#1 SET Maximum record locks per connection	10–10,000	500
#2 SET Maximum file locks per connection	10–1,000	250
#3 SET Maximum record locks	100–200,000	20,000
#4 SET Maximum file locks	100–100,000	10,000

Remember, the error I've just been talking about is related to the record locks setting on the Novell server. This problem isn't related to the MS-DOS SHARE.EXE locks setting.

Recovery

If you are going to bet your company on a database, is that database capable of repairing itself when the system reboots, or do you have to bring the system back up manually, restore or repair it manually, and then restart it? Watch out for systems that don't support full transaction logging. When transactions aren't logged, an unexpected interruption while the engine is writing a cached transaction to disk might result in a partial transaction and a corrupted database. And the first time you get called in over the weekend to repair a corrupted database, don't forget I told you so.

Periodic Maintenance

All databases need to be serviced, and SQL Server needs to have its transaction logs backed up and cleared at least daily on most production systems. But if your workstations are spread out all over the map, how do you get the users in the next city or county to get off your database so you can back it up? Fortunately, SQL Server lets you do this with a full load and without bringing down the database. It's something like changing the tires on a race car without having the car leave the track. Make sure you can back up your database without having to get all the users off—or have a plan for getting them off.

Accessing a Centralized Database Engine with a Distributed Database Engine

The preceding discussion focused on the choice of either a centralized or a distributed database engine. But what about using a distributed database engine to access data on a centralized database engine? This is a programming mode that reflects the trend toward highly decentralized database management.

Let's say that relatively small divisions are spread out all over a company. Each subgroup has its own idea about how to prepare, manage, and store its data, and the composite data is transmitted to a central site for weekly reports. (Sound familiar?) But this company finds that weekly summaries are insufficient for timely decision making. Because many other companies have reached the same conclusion, fairly complex mechanisms have evolved for keeping departmental data synchronized with central corporate data.

A distributed-engine system can manage local data effectively as long as volume and number of users are not too great. Centralized data can also be integrated through attachment to corporate database tables (and views) that are constantly kept up to date. And the departments, by posting changes from distributed sites to corporate tables, can also keep the central site current. At least that's how its supposed to work in theory. This strategy can be hobbled easily by slow WAN performance or sloppy application design.

Visual Basic permits implementation of any of the programming models examined so far. With the Microsoft Jet database engine, you can easily set up a department-size database and make it available to everyone. By attaching to SQL Server tables (the new Microsoft Access documentation calls this *linking*), you can tie corporate data to departmental data so that both the central site (and therefore other departments) and your local department can share in a common data pool. This is a viable way to manage data in large and small companies alike.

There are pitfalls, however. The distributed engine often expects to access data by using its own intelligence—that is, its own query engine. Because the centralized server expects to do the same thing, conflicts arise. When a workstation query processor has to perform an operation that can't be completed by remote execution of a query on the central server, the workstation's query processor must do the search itself, the hard way—by downloading data from central database tables. When it has to resort to this strategy, Jet's latest version does it in a fairly intelligent way. Instead of trying to read and join entire tables—something that, obviously, must be avoided—Jet attempts to draw a subset of the table rows to join with local data. In other cases, however, Jet simply creates a temporary stored procedure to fetch the rows and makes iterative calls to this procedure. Let's see, a 50,000-row table accessed by a stored procedure would still take 100,000 trips to the server (and back) over the LAN (or worse yet, the WAN). Ah, no, not a particularly viable solution.

Because the Jet engine can't create its native table-type Resultset object against external database tables, Visual Basic front ends are forced to build either dynaset-type or snapshot-type Recordset objects. I won't go into great detail here; I will say only that these objects consume local resources (RAM and temporary disk space) for either keysets or data rows, which means that it's impractical to attach to tables of any size and perform simple queries without setting specific row limits in the WHERE clause of the SQL query. When the Jet engine accesses the central server, it does so via what we call a *connection*. The number of available connections is limited by license, by physical limitations of RAM, and by server resources. And even though Visual Basic developers have more control than ever over these connections, the number of connections can easily get out of hand through injudicious use of the Data control or incorrectly managed Recordset objects. Another consideration is the accessibility of SQL Server–specific features. For example, the Jet engine doesn't utilize SQL Server 6.*x* server-side cursors or parameters passed from stored procedures, and it doesn't know how to access certain SQL Server data types.

What does all this mean? In general, it means that you can create completely adequate front-end programs without resorting to API-based programming models. If your applications are designed carefully and with the limitations of the architecture in mind, you'll be able to create applications that are easy to assemble and support.

Implementing a Client/Server Front End

From here on, this chapter (and the rest of the book) assumes that your primary goal is to develop a high-performance front-end application that interacts with SQL Server. If your data needs are so limited that SQL Server is not really an option and won't be one in the near future, you need to consider Jet Data Access Objects (DAO) or some other development strategy. If that's your situation, take this guide back to the store and try to get your money back—or, better yet, put it on the shelf and take it back down a year from now if you discover that your design isn't giving you the performance you expected. Otherwise, let's go ahead and consider two front-end applications that interact with SQL Server: the Microsoft Visual Basic Library for SQL Server (VBSQL) and the Microsoft Open Database Connectivity (ODBC) application programming interface (API).

VBSQL

If you don't own a copy of VBSQL, you can purchase one by ordering the SQL Server Workstation Edition, which includes the Microsoft SQL Server Programmer's Toolkit. It also includes the SQL Server Transact-SQL Reference. VBSQL is also included with Visual Basic 5.0 Enterprise Edition, on the Microsoft Developer Network (MSDN) subscription service CD, and on the CD included with this book—yes, the latest 16-bit and 32-bit versions. If you use the control on this book's companion CD, you still need to get a license for it by buying MSDN, SQL Server Developer Edition, or Visual Basic 5.0 Enterprise Edition.

Conversing with SQL Server

If a fairly complex application under development can't hear what the server says until run time, the task of creating the application is significantly complicated. In fact, many problems associated with the creation of front-end applications to SQL Server are due to the inability of the development language to *interact* adequately with SQL Server during the development cycle. SQL Server expects to be told what to do in specific terms, and it will respond in a fairly predictable way. In fact, conversing with SQL Server is like having a conversation with a blindly obedient, highly specialized, highly skilled (but somewhat anal) assistant. Transact-SQL truly is an interactive, two-way language, and Visual Basic's interactive mode is an efficient and relatively trouble-free way to develop these applications.

Visual Basic, unlike C or other edit-compile-link-debug languages, permits developers to step through the phrases of the conversation, examine the server's response, adapt the code as needed, and continue the conversation. In a radical departure from traditional C-language debugging techniques, Visual Basic developers not only can change the source code interactively, they can also alter program logic and flow. For example, developers can jump over code or instruct Visual Basic to repeat code that has already been executed. This way, unanticipated responses from the server can be dealt with as they occur, and alternative code can be created or branched to while the tested logic condition still exists. Visual Basic's interactive debugging window also permits you to execute code, including all written procedures, on the fly—right in the middle of an application.

As any experienced developer will confirm, one of the toughest tasks is to set up various logic states once a problem has been found. With Visual Basic's interactive watchpoint, setting a breakpoint at a particular state is now easier than ever. Once at the problem point, a developer can easily step through the code or make source changes as they are needed. More important, it is possible to send SQL Server additional commands or even ask additional questions regarding its current state. Having developed applications using C, Visual Basic, and other languages, I find Visual Basic's interactive approach by far the most flexible, and what used to take weeks now takes hours: Visual Basic dramatically reduces the time needed for developing interactive TSQL code. And since Visual Basic version 5.0 has added an optimizing compiler, performance is no longer an issue.

What about DBLIB?

DB-Library (DBLIB) is the set of C-language API functions that do for C developers what the VBSQL functions do for Visual Basic developers. Not all DBLIB functions are supported by the VBSQL libraries—but, fortunately, not all of them are needed. For example, C developers spend a significant amount of time dealing with fairly involved binding of SQL arguments to C data types. This is completely unnecessary in Visual Basic, since virtually all arguments are returned in the form of variants that can be converted, as necessary, with built-in Visual Basic functions.

NOTE VBSQL is really a "VB-ized" interface to a C library, making it very different from a purely C interface as implemented by the ODBC API.

In actuality, most VBSQL functions are merely linkages to C-based DBLIB functions. You will see, however, that a number of Visual Basic functions have no C equivalents. For example, the SQLOpenConnection function is not supported in C; this VBSQL "utility" function is provided to perform a series of C calls that are normally sent as a set.

Two-phase commit

Another set of C functions not supported in VBSQL is the two-phase commit protocol, which is used to keep two or more SQL Server databases in synchronization. This is a fairly complex protocol, as DBLIB logic goes. It involves setting up a special dialog with each of the servers concerned. To ensure completion of the transaction if something goes wrong before all the servers can complete the operation, the protocol logs the transaction with a mother server. Since the VBSQL interface does not support this protocol, I recommend that a separate C-language program (or dynamic-link library) be written to perform this operation with DBLIB if the two-phase commit is needed. Even C developers think long and hard before implementing two-phase commit, and once you take a close look at automatic Distributed Transaction Coordinator (DTC) features in SQL Server 6.*x*, you might decide you won't miss two-phase commit at all. Better yet, consider using Microsoft Transaction Server to do the job.

ODBC

Open Database Connectivity (ODBC) is one of the most misunderstood interfaces that Microsoft supports. The term *ODBC* has been used to mean everything from a database-independent application programming interface to the data access interface used in Microsoft Visual Basic 2.0.

ODBC is really a database-neutral API based on the SQL Access development group's specification. To be more specific, an application can write to the ODBC API and access different data sources simply by attaching different ODBC drivers. Theoretically, an ODBC application could connect to SQL Server via the SQL server driver, and to Oracle via the Oracle driver, with no need for a change in the application's executable. (And, theoretically, an application could also connect in the same way to a Microsoft Jet database via the Jet ODBC driver. Yes, Microsoft did develop an ODBC driver, a limited one, that can read and write to Jet databases by using the ODBC API. It ships with Microsoft Office 97 and now with Visual Basic version 5.0.) At this point, there are dozens of ODBC drivers that permit ODBC application front ends to reach virtually every kind of database; I also hear rumors about an 80-column-card driver being supported by IBM.

NOTE   As a developer of ODBC drivers, you have a choice: Do you want your driver to expose some or all functionality of the database management system, or should your driver make the database management system look like a lowest-common-denominator generic database? The Microsoft SQL Server ODBC driver can exploit much of the SQL server's functionality, and it allows an application to make the ODBC equivalents of most of the calls it normally would have made via DBLIB. Execution of stored procedures and triggers that generally aren't supported in other server-based database engines is fully supported here. If your code takes advantage of specific database engine features that aren't universally supported, you may end up where you started—with a database-specific application. This time, however, you will have written this database-specific application with a generic interface that might not be able to use all the database features you need.

The difficulty you might experience in programming to the generic ODBC interface is similar to what you'll experience when you use any other API-based interface. There are about 55 ODBC APIs; VBSQL has over 120. ODBC is as fast an interface as DBLIB or VBSQL, but ODBC is less aware of SQL Server–specific features. The ODBC functions are more complex than their VBSQL equivalents, however. Each ODBC call is designed to accept many, many more arguments— and each argument has many, many options. As a point of comparison, the *Microsoft ODBC Programmer's Reference and SDK Guide* contains over 800 pages of options, but the VBSQL programmer's reference for Visual Basic is not even half that long.

What about Visual Basic and ODBC?

The Microsoft Jet database engine, which ships with Microsoft Visual Basic, Visual C++, and Microsoft Office applications, connects to external non-ISAM databases via the ODBC API as do Remote Data Objects (RDO) and ODBCDirect. When you use DAO/Jet to access ODBC databases, you use Visual Basic Data Access Objects (DAO) or the Data control to write your code, not the ODBC API. Jet builds and submits queries to the external server via the ODBC API and driver manager. Without stealing the thunder from later chapters, let me just say here that the DAO implementation first introduced in Visual Basic 4.0 is a significant improvement over the DAO implementation in earlier versions. Part III of this guide details how all the Jet/DAO pieces fit together in Visual Basic. Part IV of this guide mentions how the new ODBCDirect interface adds another dimension to the matrix, letting you write code using DAO, but which ultimately calls RDO, which calls the ODBC API.

What about the Enterprise Edition?

To better address the special needs of client/server developers, Microsoft bundled together a number of applications, special documentation, and custom controls to create the Visual Basic 4.0 Enterprise Edition. It includes the RemoteData control (RDC) and supports the RDO programming interface. The RDC and the RDO interface are specifically designed for connecting to remote database engines via the best available ODBC drivers. In short, the RDC/RDO model provides a thin, tightly coded object interface to the ODBC API. Visual Basic version 5.0 Enterprise Edition extends the RDO interface and also includes the ODBCDirect interface and a litany of new applications, designers, and add-ins to support client/server development. These include the Visual Database Tools, the Microsoft Transaction Server, and SQL Server itself. In addition, the Visual Basic version 5.0 Enterprise Edition also includes a sophisticated TSQL debugger and UserConnection designer to help work with stored procedures. (Part IV of this guide is devoted to the RDC, the RDO interface, and these tools.)

What about VBSQL for MS-DOS?

In the fall of 1993, Microsoft released its new SQL Server Programmer's Toolkit for Visual Basic, which included a newly engineered VBSQL for MS-DOS. The API used with MS-DOS is a subset of the one used with Visual Basic for the Microsoft Windows operating system and C. The new version is a big improvement over the first one, but it still requires a great deal of conventional RAM.

Are there really any developers out there who want one application that connects to a multitude of different databases without really taking advantage of the features of any of them? There are times when you'll want an application to manipulate data from a corporate SQL server and then connect easily to a local laptop version of the data. We're getting closer to that with the server-replication features provided with SQL Server 6.*x* and the Briefcase feature of Jet and Windows 95. One day they might all work together.

Nevertheless, this implementation is important to those who are still programming for MS-DOS, even if the rest of the world is moving on to the Windows operating system. At this writing, no further updates are planned for this implementation, which also means that Visual Basic for MS-DOS will never support the Jet database engine technology or be ported to the Windows NT or Windows 95 environments.

What about other interfaces?

Jet, DBLIB, and ODBC are not the only choices for Visual Basic programmers. Any number of third-party database engines and SQL Server interfaces are also available, but most of the attention has been drawn away from property-driven interfaces or stand-alone front-end development systems, in favor of the new data-aware bound-control interfaces that connect via the Data control.

We used to recommend use of Microsoft Access as a way to help develop queries and database schemas—but no more. Since Microsoft Visual Database Tools have arrived in the Enterprise Edition, this need is gone. By itself, Access can be an excellent choice when it comes to a reporting or ad hoc query engine. Access and Visual Basic also share the Jet database engine dynamic-link libraries (DLLs)—well, sort of. (See *Figure 3-13*.) Do yourself a favor, though: be sure not to venture too far into Access land without a guide.

Figure 3-13
Access and Visual Basic with Jet

Application	Jet Engine Version	Notes
Microsoft Access 1.0	1.0	Not compatible/integrated with Visual Basic 2.0.
Microsoft Access 1.1	1.1	To sync with Visual Basic 3.0.
Microsoft Visual Basic 3.0	1.1	Reads/writes 1, 1.1.
Microsoft Access 2.0	2.0	Requires compatibility layer for Visual Basic 3.0; can import data from 1.0 and 1.1 but can't change structure without conversion.
Microsoft Visual Basic 4.0	2.5	Same database format as 2.0; same restrictions.
Microsoft Visual Basic 4.0	3.0	Same database format as 2.0, with additional support for database replication, but additions not supported in Visual Basic 4.0. Uses IISAM drivers to read older versions of Jet databases.
Microsoft Access (Office 95)	3.0+	Same database format as 3.0, but different DLLs. Visual Basic version 4.0a synced with this version.
Microsoft Access (Office 97)	3.5	Same database format as 3.0, but different DLLs. Visual Basic version 5.0 synced with this version.
Microsoft Visual Basic 5.0	3.5+	Same database format as 3.0, but different DLLs. Supports ODBCDirect.

4 Chapter

The Development Workstation

Hardware

The Server

Software

consider myself a power user. I'm not content unless I have the fastest, largest, most reliable system on the market. Nothing is more frustrating for a developer—or a developer's manager, for that matter—than the time wasted on waiting for a compile, a search, or a screen repaint. I can justify buying the sharpest ax in the store by showing how many more trees I can cut down with the best tools.

This chapter walks you through the less intuitive concepts involving hardware, server connections, and systems software for a Visual Basic front-end development workstation. While we cover these points, keep in mind the programming model you intend to use. For example, if you choose the Jet model with its Data Access Objects (DAO), you'll need considerably more local RAM, hard disk space, and CPU power for your front end, especially if you depend heavily on Recordset cursors.

Hardware

Before you can choose a suitable hardware platform, you need to be aware of its specific needs. I assume that most readers of this guide probably will be using Visual Basic 5.0 rather than earlier versions of Visual Basic. And if you need to create 32-bit applications for the Microsoft Windows 95 or Microsoft Windows NT operating systems, you must use at *least* version 4.0. Recall that the standard edition of Visual Basic 4.0 is a 32-bit version; the 16-bit version of Visual Basic 4.0 is available only with the Professional or Enterprise editions that support both 16-bit and 32-bit compilers. Visual Basic version 5.0, in case you hadn't noticed, is a 32-bit–only product.

Developing with Visual Basic

The Enterprise edition of Visual Basic includes the RemoteData control; Remote Data Objects; an unbound mode for the DBGrid control; the ability to create dynamic-link libraries (DLLs), in-process servers, and ActiveX components and controls; and a number of add-on applications that make team development easier. Client/server developers can benefit from virtually all these enhancements.

PART I CLIENT/SERVER COMPUTING: AN INTRODUCTION

Since Visual Basic 4.0 came on the scene, you might have quickly discovered that a 100-MHz Pentium processor and 16 MB of RAM seemed like a must. Visual Basic version 5.0 helps that situation because it loads and runs quite a bit faster than Visual Basic version 4.0. Most of the new Visual Basic features are now interconnected with the new ActiveX (what they used to call OLE) "glue" and are treated like objects. Visual Basic version 5.0 changes the user interface (again) and introduces the new multiple-document interface (MDI) development mode. The single-document (SDI) user interface is similar to what it was in the earlier versions, and Visual Basic still looks like a Windows-based application. Visual Basic version 4.0 converted all of the Visual Basic version 3.0 assembly language code to C++, and the Jet database engine was ripped out and reattached with an OLE interface. Visual Basic version 5.0 kept this new ActiveX foundation, so for some operations you might find Visual Basic 5.0 somewhat faster than Visual Basic 3.0.

When you compare Visual Basic version 3.0 and Visual Basic version 5.0 directly, especially for VBSQL applications, the root executable size doesn't seem to be significantly larger but the number and size of the DLLs that get loaded and the number of files you have to ship with the EXE (according to the Setup Wizard) has grown considerably. Unless you distribute on 100-MB Zip media or on CD, this increased volume in itself may be problematic if your 1.4-MB installation disk is already full. The increased number of libraries and controls will certainly mean longer load times for workstations that don't already have the DLLs and controls loaded.

Generally, the performance of Visual Basic version 4.0 16-bit leaves a lot to be desired. But considering what the developers had to go through to get a basically 32-bit application to run on a 16-bit OS, I think they did pretty well. Thankfully, Visual Basic version 5.0 is significantly faster—especially if you create a *native* code executable. If you consider that Visual Basic version 5.0 and C++ applications run at roughly the same speed, you begin to get the point—Visual Basic version 5.0 is a very different beast from version 4.0.

TIP If you write an application that does nothing but load the appropriate DLLs and run that application at start time, you can make application loading much faster.

That said, you need to ask how much power is *sufficient*. How much is enough to get the job done in a reasonable amount of time? For front-end development using Visual Basic 3.0, I recommend at least a 25-MHz 386DX with 6 MB of RAM. For Visual Basic 4.0 or 5.0, make that a 66-MHz 486 with 12 MB of RAM, at the *minimum*. In any case, I recommend a fast, high-resolution VGA (noninterlaced), running with at least 800 × 600 resolution. You will need enough disk space for the Windows operating system, including its tools, applications, and documentation. Visual Basic 5.0 has grown to over 25 MB of disk space for a low-impact development installation and to over 200 MB (not counting the extra material on the CD) for a complete installation. Yes, 200 MB—especially if you load the Visual Database Tools and TSQL debugger and don't install SQL Server on your workstation (you shouldn't). If you are running a dual Visual Basic/C++ development station, double your disk space requirement because these two environments share very few components beyond the ActiveX libraries. The last Visual Basic 3.0 development system I used—for courseware, applications, graphics, and documentation development, as well as for some multimedia testing—was a 33-MHz 486 with 16 MB of RAM, 1024 × 768 VGA, and two 200-MB hard disks that ended up being about

85 percent full. That system worked just fine. My new Visual Basic version 5.0 development system is a Gateway P5/133. This puppy has a 1280 × 1024 video adapter and two 1.6-GB hard disks with an 8-speed, 5-disc CD-ROM drive. Without the 17-inch monitor, I would need new glasses—but it makes for a great workstation when I want all the windows open at once. Why so many CDs? Well since the help files and documentation are now all on line, you'll want to dedicate a CD spindle to the Visual Basic installation disc.

Visual Basic 5.0 development mode is considerably faster than Visual Basic version 4.0 because Microsoft worked quite a bit on form and control load times, memory footprint, and a refined P-code interpreter. As far as the video requirements are concerned, even if you plan to use only the Windows operating system, having the space to open the Properties window and a 640 × 400 form, with room left over for a code window (or six), means you will need lots of pixels—and the horsepower to get them to the video controller before you die of boredom. All that RAM means room for all the ActiveX components, the VBA engine, the object libraries, type libraries, and so forth.

One of the more frustrating aspects of developing Visual Basic applications is the lack of space on the standard VGA desktop: 640 × 480 pixels is simply not enough real estate to work on when you add a Toolbox window, a Properties window, and a debugging window to the application under development. For this reason, I recommend a high-resolution VGA or Super VGA video card and monitor. You may also want to consider a local bus video system; it will speed up the work that the Windows operating system has to do.

With a 1024 × 800 or higher-resolution system—and a good pair of glasses—you can build applications for the target 640 × 480 systems far faster and with fewer problems. Be careful, though—you might be tempted to use more screen space than is available on the target system. Limit the size of your forms to 640 × 400 or 640 × 480 pixels if that is the maximum resolution on the target system. This is a lot easier with Visual Basic version 5.0 because it supports a Form Layout window that lets you preview the form as it will appear and be positioned on the screen.

Your manager should be looking for faster systems for you and your team. On any given day, you always need to ask yourself how much of your time is going to waste while you wait for your system to do what you asked it to do. When you have an answer, multiply it by your fully burdened hourly rate and out will pop a dollar figure that your manager should not be able to argue away when you justify the purchase of a new system.

TIP   To increase the performance of any system, simply change to a video mode that supports fewer colors—16 is ideal. When you display 256 colors or more, the Windows video drivers and the video hardware must deal with 8 to 24 (or more) bit layers for each pixel you change. Significant system and user time are wasted while you wait for the video card to catch up. Choosing a Windows-aware video board also boosts overall performance.

The Operating System

The new 32-bit operating systems like Windows 95 and Windows NT are easier to use and have considerably more resources to share, but they don't seem to be dramatically faster, especially on a low-budget workstation, which is why you need so much horsepower. The Windows NT operating system brings a true multitasking engine to the desktop—it's a joy. No matter how nasty the background application or how much I/O it needs, you are rarely more than a couple of seconds away from a task/context switch to another window. The problem with Windows NT is that it is tough to install because it's not nearly as smart about hardware changes as Windows 95 is. You can also run remote access service (RAS) applications from modems without having to worry about crashing the connection while you're doing work in the foreground. The Windows 95 operating system features task switching, too, and it's far better than what the Windows for Workgroups system provides. The last time I looked, though, Windows 95 task switching was still not as crisp as what you get with the Windows NT system. With the new Windows 95 user interface incorporated into Windows NT 4.0, most of us will be switching—for good.

The Server

One of the thorniest problems you will face with SQL Server is getting connected to it for the first time. With all the security layers you have to go through, it's like trying to crash one of Bill Clinton's private parties with a 16mm movie camera tucked in your shirt. You have to be logged on to the workstation, the net, the domain, and SQL Server itself, and then you need permission to access the desired table, view, or procedure. If you're using the right network protocol, Windows NT lets you set up integrated security that automatically keeps user names and passwords synced up from server to domain. Unfortunately, though, the error messages you get back are still not very clear.

Can you say "16 MB"? All the developers here in Building 2 at Microsoft have Pentium-class machines, and so should you. But, yes, you can do with less. A 66-MHz 486 will still be enough —but you will want more before too long.

You shouldn't plan to use your server as a workstation. I tried that on my 32-MB P5-60 and soon discovered (via Task Manager) that it quickly ran out of physical RAM and began to swap (the kiss of death). It's OK to run a "lesser" system as your testbed server.

The RAS Alternative

If you have a suitable server but no LAN cards, you can still set up a workstation to a SQL server by using the Microsoft Windows Network RAS–based protocol. This feature of the Windows for Workgroups, Windows NT, and Windows 95 systems permits workstations and servers to be interconnected via modems or direct RS-232 cabling. Since the Tabular Data Stream (TDS) used by the workstation to communicate with the SQL server is a highly efficient communications channel, using lower-throughput transmission means is often practical. If you give the server intelligently thought-out questions (queries), you can significantly reduce the amount of data sent to the server and back (and clogging up the net), and thus you can increase the overall speed of your application. But consider that many, many of the application's transmissions are simple queries to check on status or ask for only a few rows. With RAS's somewhat slower performance, what might have been a transmission time of half a second changes to one, two, three, or even four seconds. Try it. Perhaps your application is written in such a way that the RAS alternative can't possibly be useful. Be sure to test RAS on applications that already perform fairly well.

I have tested hardware setups using 2400-bps modems to connect my VBSQL workstation to a remote server. Yes, it's slower, but not unacceptably so. Because the overall applications strategy is designed to maximize work on the server instead of on the workstation, I can often achieve acceptable performance—usually in the range of two to eight times slower than conventional Ethernet LANs; it depends on modem speed. Because 28.8-Kbps and faster modems are commonplace today, much higher throughput can be ensured.

Can you use RAS with an ODBC connection from DAO/Jet? Sure. But if you're not really careful, you'll drag down the whole works. The extra overhead imposed by the behavior of the ODBC and DAO/Jet default cursors really loads up the net (and therefore the communications link) with a lot of traffic. I think you'll find that using RAS with an ODBC connection from Jet doesn't work very well at all unless you can somehow get the Jet query processor to refrain from bringing back rows to process locally, and unless you can reduce the data definition language (DDL) queries that run each time a record set is opened. Even then, it's pretty slow. Can you use RAS with RDO? Again, sure, but again, you need to be careful. RDO isn't nearly as verbose as Jet, so it can work out just fine.

Growing Your Own

Some time ago, I saw an editorial in *PC Week* that advocated the abandonment of all 8088 and 80286 systems. But I have found a good use for my old 8088 XT clone (besides keeping my lab warm). I use it to stress-test my MS-DOS SQL applications (and now my Visual Basic for MS-DOS applications). It also runs SQL Server Administration Facility (SAF) and Microsoft ISQL, so I can submit administrative commands and put additional load on the server without having to disturb other workstations. This old XT clunker runs the standard monochrome CGA Windows 3.0 operating system, with a 2.5-MB expanded RAM card. (Nope, the Windows 3.1 system won't run on an 8088, which means it won't run Visual Basic for Windows applications at all.) The system has uncovered a number of problems related to the user interface, memory constraints, and time—problems that would have been harder to find on a faster, less memory-challenged system.

My 10-MHz 80286 AT clone, with 10 MB of RAM and EGA video, functioned for many years as my only OS/2 file and SQL server. I was informed that OS/2 1.3 would not work correctly on an 80286, especially when I was using the High Performance File System (HPFS). Since I don't use HPFS—you shouldn't with SQL Server—this didn't pose a problem, and that AT server was fast enough. It performed as if there were already several users competing for its resources, so for my lab it was perfect. I have since pushed it into a support role (holding up the edge of a desk), and into its place I've moved an old NCR 386/25 running OS/2 1.3. This system is a little faster, but with midresolution video (VGA) and 10 MB of RAM. With the XT and another couple of 386-based workstations, I have the ability to test many of the interactive problems that are hard to duplicate outside a production environment. All these systems are interconnected via LAN Manager 2 and Windows NT networking on thin Ethernet. I have to run the NetBIOS API, as well as the TCP/IP and IPX protocols.

Over the past few months, I have upgraded my lab again and moved the old 386/33 16-MB workstation over to the role of Windows NT domain controller and SQL server. This gives me the chance to test interserver applications and the role of a domain controller on the net. Again, I was told that the new Windows NT/AS 3.51 system wouldn't run on a 386, so I used one of those plug-in upgrades, and it's now a 486SX with 16 MB. In many cases, simply more RAM can make up for a slower processor. Granted, the processor does have to work very hard in the new operating systems, but if the time wasted on swapping to disk is eliminated, a fair percentage of this overhead can also be eliminated.

I recommend that you find your own dedicated server to work on, too. Many companies have surplus 486-based systems lying around gathering dust and waiting for another purpose in life. Resurrect one of these, add as much RAM as you can (at least 16 MB), and free up 100 MB or more of disk space to work on. But you can't do front-end development on an OS/2 1.3 workstation. You might be able to get OS/2 2.0 to work, but I wouldn't wish that on you or anyone else; apparently, OS/2 2.0 is actually slower running SQL Server than OS/2 1.3 is. (I don't have a clue about Warf or Woof or Warp—you know, that other IBM OS thing—but I do know it doesn't run SQL Server.)

The real advantage of using your own servers and workstations, if you can afford to, is that no matter what you do to *your* server, you can't disturb anyone else's work. And if you have your own dedicated server, it is far easier to administer it directly, which is often necessary in the front-end development cycle.

TIP If you want to use your old 486 system as a server and it has a proprietary memory card that is difficult or expensive to populate, get one of the third-party add-on memory expansion cards that can accept standard SIMMs. That way, you can move the low-density (1–4 MB) SIMMs out of your development workstation and into the server.

One more point: do *not* try to use your Windows NT server, running SQL Server, as your development workstation—not unless you're running a fast Pentium-class (or better) processor with at least 48 MB of RAM. You are destined to a life of delay and frustration if you don't have enough RAM to keep SQL Server, the Windows NT user interface, the Visual Basic 5.0 development environment, and your application in memory without swapping.

Software

What development software is needed for creating client/server front-end applications for Microsoft SQL Server? I have never tried to use Visual Basic or any of the other tools in a Novell/Digital Research operating system, but I have used the new Visual Basic and VBSQL controls under the Windows NT and Windows 95 operating systems. Yes, the Windows 3.*x* operating system will work, too. (And remember that you must use the Windows 3.*x* system if your workstation is an 8088.) The Windows 3.1 and 3.11 environments have much better memory management and font handling than previous versions do, and Windows 95 goes beyond that. The Windows NT 3.5 or 3.51 operating systems would also be serious alternatives—but be sure to install SP3. (Older versions of the Windows NT system might not give you any problems—but they can't be used with Visual Basic version 5.0 and getting support on the older versions is harder.) Windows 95 will prove to be a required investment if you're developing true 32-bit applications.

Both the Professional and Enterprise Editions of Visual Basic include a number of very useful custom controls and extra tools that you will greatly appreciate. (And recall that the Enterprise Edition comes with the RemoteData control and Remote Data Objects.) You can use the Standard Edition of Visual Basic to do VBSQL development and do without the custom controls; all the controls you'll need are in the SQL Server Programmer's Toolkit (PTK) or on the Microsoft Developer Network (MSDN) CD. The latest SQL Server PTK is also on the web along with a trial (time bomb) version of SQL Server 6.5. See the download area starting at http://www.microsoft.com. I put all of this free stuff on the book's CD (which is a whole lot easier to load).

Visual Basic 5.0 includes a number of new features— thanks to Sybase, Borland, and IBM. There's nothing like competition to make product managers push the envelope. The resulting death march for the Visual Basic 5.0 team and Microsoft Consulting Services yielded the new Enterprise Edition.

When the Windows NT version of SQL Server shipped, Microsoft rebundled the programmers' toolkit into the Microsoft SQL Server Workstation and later into the Developer Editions. This package contains the libraries and include files packaged with the previous kit. Now that SQL Server 6.5 has shipped, the new SQL 6.5 Programmer's Toolkit contains the VBSQL libraries and controls. (These are also on this book's CD.) The graphical user interface tools that come with SQL 6.5 are useful when it comes to creating the databases and managing them once they're set up.

> **TIP** When I set up a development system, I create a VBTest directory that is separate from the Visual Basic or SQL directories so that I can find the needed components more easily. You can install a number of other SQL applications as well. These include the SQL tools and libraries needed to create C-based applications.

SQL Support Applications

You'll need one or more of the following support applications in order to set up the SQL server and check the progress of your own application. You may already be familiar with some of them—they are all included with Microsoft SQL Server 6.*x*. Be sure to install them on your Windows 95 or Windows NT workstation. That way, they can run without disturbing the SQL server.

Microsoft SQL Enterprise Manager

This powerful tool runs on the Windows NT or Windows 95 operating system, and it's invaluable when it comes time to add additional users or manually drop a pipe that has been abandoned by Visual Basic. It really combines the features of several of the older applications. I highly recommend installing this one on your development workstation. It permits total control of one or more servers from a single interactive application.

ISQL

This MS-DOS–based, console-style application is perfect for sending scripts to the SQL server when you're developing on an MS-DOS workstation, or when, for whatever reason, you can't get the Windows operating system to work or are just using an MS-DOS session under Windows. In my classroom, the term *script* has been used to mean a set of SQL "batches," which are defined as series of logically connected TSQL statements. If you're not familiar with the concept of batches, you had better go back and read about them in the Transact-SQL manual; you'll be using batches extensively as you write VBSQL applications.

Microsoft ISQLW

This is a Windows version of the character-based Microsoft ISQL program. Unlike ISQL, however, it still tries to buffer all query output. That can be a pain, but ISQL does let you see the execution plan in glorious detail—sometimes in goriest detail—as well as statistics about the query that is being run. This application doesn't require the use of the INSTCAT or other scripts in order to run.

SQLTrace

This SQL Server 6.0 Windows-based application permits you to monitor the query activity on a selected server. This is an invaluable tool when you're working with any of the programming models. Frankly, I don't know how we have managed to do without it for this long.

Microsoft Windows NT Administrator's Tools

These are used to check on the status of network connections. (As we'll see later, many of the problems that your users—and therefore your application—have to deal with are due to the state of the network connection.) The Windows NT Administrator's Tools are also critical when you need to set up or test permissions for a VBSQL application. More important, this application is used for dropping orphaned pipes left behind when a VBSQL application is improperly terminated.

TIP Microsoft SQL Enterprise Manager can create scripts to define a database and all its components (tables, rules, defaults, triggers, and stored procedures)—but not its data. SQL Transfer Manager, which is now built into SQL Enterprise Manager, creates scripts that also include data. Once you provide a destination database, these scripts replace the database completely. You can run them with ISQL, ISQLW, or the query window in Enterprise Manager to document the structure of your new database or to distribute the database to other developers.

PART II

Designing Client/Server Applications

5

Chapter

Planning
Your Design

The State Machine

A Panoramic View
of Cursors and Buffers

Basic Design Decisions

Avoiding the Top 10
Design Mistakes

Creating a Virtual Application

O ver the past few years, many industry periodicals have caught client/server fever. Week after week, we hear about one implementation after another—some successful, some not. From case after case, a few critical design guidelines have emerged, and I've mentioned a number of them in Part I.

The chapters in Part II of this guide focus more closely on the steps involved in using Microsoft Visual Basic to create successful Microsoft SQL Server front-end applications that avoid common pitfalls and leverage what has been learned from successful implementations. This chapter compares the SQL Server development environment to a "state machine," offers a brief overview and review of cursors and buffers, poses some fundamental design questions, and describes how to create and use what I call a *virtual application*. I have also included a section detailing the top 10 reasons that client/server applications fail.

The State Machine

A state machine, when it's not a political organization, is a body of logic that expects known responses to a known number of input requests. Most of my front-end applications are designed around the model of the state machine because each state is fairly easy to code, debug as an independent unit, and reuse from program to program. Now that the concept of multithreaded business objects has matured, knowing how and why to create objects that do or don't maintain a specific state is even more important than it used to be—but we will consider this later. For now, let's focus on how the client application must build a state machine in order to communicate with SQL Server.

The early PC game *Adventure* was an example of a state machine. To move from room to room in that game, you had to examine the properties of the room you were in by asking questions. Invalid questions were rejected, and valid ones returned deterministic responses. Using valid questions and action words, you could gather treasure and investigate properties or alternate paths. Once you found an exit (there could be several), you made the transition to another room—another state. The new room had different properties, exits, and pitfalls.

In a SQL Server "adventure," any particular path you take might not provide an immediate pathway back to the previous "room," but you can continue stepping from state to state—asking questions at each level, making requests of the system, and gathering treasure in the form of returned data or Metadata. Generally speaking, each of the programming models we'll be examining expects you to perform the following operations:

- *Initialize the data interface,* as required, which includes setting default properties, timeout values, and user names.

- *Establish a connection* to the SQL server.

- *Create a query from scratch,* or use one stored in a local repository, such as a Microsoft Jet MDB database or an ODBC prepared statement.

- *Execute the query.*

- *Process the result sets* (there could be several), which includes dealing with sets of rows returned in the result sets.

- *Close the connection,* deinitialize the interface, and terminate it, as necessary.

NOTE Even when you create a remote business object, you have to consider state. You must often create the object so that it remains "stateless"—that is, it can be run without having to remember details from any previous invocations.

Basically, each of these operations is a state, and your options for proceeding from state to state are fairly limited: you can't open a connection before initializing the interface, and you can't send a query before you open a connection. Each state has its own set of messages and errors, too, which you have to deal with before you can move on. (Interstate flight to avoid handling errors is a felony, you know.)

A Panoramic View of Cursors and Buffers

In general, and for lots of good reasons, I'm against the extensive use of cursors for retrieving data. If you haven't worked with the client/server paradigm before, you might not be entirely familiar with what cursors are or with what they do in this context. Let's stop and take a look at them here so that you'll know what I'm talking about in later chapters, where I tell you why I don't care much for cursors, and so you'll be able to follow along in the next section of this chapter, where we'll consider some basic design decisions. While we're at it, let's take a look at buffers, too.

A cursor is simply a set of pointers to the rows returned by a query. It's like a result set except that most of the data usually remains on the server—only a pointer to the base rows is maintained in the cursor. When a query is written, it describes a subset of the rows in one or more tables, and the cursor points to those rows in a result set.

A buffer is a client-side RAM repository where result set data is held temporarily until it can be moved to another place for storage. Buffers are usually managed by the interface layer, such as DB-Library. A buffer is very different from a cursor in that the buffer is simply a copy of the data extracted from the SQL server based on the result set; once the data is fetched into the buffer, subsequent changes made to the data aren't reflected. In contrast, because a cursor is a pointer, if the addressed row changes in the database, the data referenced by the cursor also reflects this change.

Figure 5-1 on page 121 displays the types of cursors and buffers and shows where they are (or aren't) supported in the SQL Server programming models we're looking at. Since you can access only one row at a time with a cursor, you must have some mechanism for positioning a current-row pointer to a selected row. Each programming model provides a rich set of mechanisms to make it easy to point to a specific row, the next row, the previous row, the last row, the first row, or any row in between. For example, each of the programming models supports the ability to use methods like MoveFirst, MoveLast, MoveNext, MovePrevious, AbsolutePosition, PercentPosition, or Move to select the next current row.

Writing a front-end application to a client/server relational database engine is a new experience for many developers, especially those who have worked with ISAM or other flat-file systems. In many cases, the development skills and techniques that were required in the past are inappropriate to the new context, but they are applied anyway—and SQL Server ends up being used as a file server. Then, when it fails to perform as expected, it is discarded for a "faster" system. Months or years later, the application design itself is discovered to have failed, not SQL Server.

The difference between the various kinds of cursors comes down to how they handle *membership,* how and when they move data to the workstation, how they scroll (or don't), and where the keyset is built. The data columns from one or more rows are said to be *members* of the cursor if the query's WHERE clause includes them. These columns, combined into logical rows, become member rows of the result set.

For example, consider the following query:

```
SELECT Name, Type from Animals
WHERE Age > 10
```

When the query is executed, SQL Server immediately begins selecting members for the result set. In this case, the members of the result set will include all rows of the *Animals* table in which the number in the *Age* column is greater than 10.

If sorting isn't required, SQL Server passes the first rows of this result set back to the workstation as soon as they are fetched and then it stops processing; further processing is delayed until the workstation retrieves the fetched rows. Generally, however, the SQL server stays 1 to 2 KB ahead of the workstation, so if there are many users updating the database, the chances are good that another row qualifying for this result set will be added before the workstation retrieves the fetched rows. When the workstation does retrieve them, the added row will be included as a member of the result set as long as the SQL server hasn't already passed the point where that row would have been inserted. (This point is determined by the internal sorting order for the data.) But if the row is added after the workstation has begun processing the result set, that row is *not* included as a member. (A row accepted as a member may be deleted later by another user, but its "corpse" is still considered a member of the result set.)

The cursor's membership roll isn't complete until the last row of the result set has been determined by the SQL server. This process of completing the cursor's membership is called *cursor population*. Once the last row has been fetched by the workstation, the cursor is considered to be fully populated.

When working with SQL Server versions 6.0 and later, your application can choose to build server-side cursors. In this case, the keyset is built on the server itself—in the TempDB database. This means that before control returns to your application, the entire keyset is created—which results in considerably different behavior than when you're using client-side cursors. You also must ensure that TempDB has sufficient space to accommodate the keyset multiplied by the number of users using your application. Consider that the task of managing these cursors consumes CPU horsepower on the SQL server but doesn't consume any LAN or client-side resources. In my experience, you can choose from a couple of ways to really get server-side cursors to sing. First, if you have a lot of RAM on the server, consider setting some of it aside to put TempDB in RAM. If you can keep the server-side cursors small (as you should anyway), you can gain considerable performance. Check out "When to Use Tempdb in RAM" in the SQL Server Books Online. In any case, using TempDB in RAM could be beneficial if all of the following conditions are true:

- *You have a significant amount of available system RAM.* This means at least 64 MB, with 128 MB or more being typical.

- *Your applications have a locality of reference* such that the SQL Server cache hit ratio is poor, even with a lot of available buffer cache. You can see your hit ratio by using SQL Performance Monitor to monitor the Cache Hit Ratio counter in the SQLServer object. For information about using SQL Performance Monitor, see the section in Chapter 19 titled "Monitoring Server Activity and Performance" in the SQL Server Books Online.

- *Your applications do a lot of TempDB operations.* Rather than guess whether this is the case, you can use sp_lock to observe the lock activity in TempDB while queries are running. Or you can monitor TempDB space consumption by issuing this (or a similar) query interactively or from a looping batch file:

```
SELECT SUM(DPAGES) FROM TEMPDB..SYSINDEXES
```

- *The TempDB operations are sized* so that they will fit on the TempDB made possible by your RAM configuration.

If you decide to use TempDB in RAM, you should verify the performance benefit obtained from this. To do this, follow these steps:

1. Select a query or small set of queries that typify your most frequently performed TempDB-intensive operations.

2. Run these several times, noting the execution time.

3. Reconfigure for TempDB in RAM, run the identical queries, and note the difference in execution time.

If the amount of improvement isn't significant, it's probably best to give the RAM back to the SQL cache. Using TempDB in RAM is safe and won't harm database integrity or recoverability. This is because TempDB is used only for intermediate operations and is created from scratch upon each server restart.

Types of Cursors

With each of our programming models, at least four major types of cursors can be used for fetching result sets from SQL Server: *keyset* cursors, *snapshot* or *static* cursors, *dynamic* cursors, and *mixed* cursors. Each programming model supports cursors differently, but all of them support at least two of these basic cursor types. Some programming models, like RDO, support enhanced cursor management, which not only extends the concept of cursor handling but changes the way you handle offline use of the data returned by a cursor. The process of choosing a cursor is further complicated by differences in terminology and, more significantly, by differences in implementation between ODBC drivers and the other programming models. I suggest you try out the various cursors before expecting one behavior or another.

When it comes time to decide which cursor to use, choose the cheapest. That is, don't choose a scrolling cursor or an updatable cursor if you don't need those features. Very few situations justify opening a cursor on a whole table. Most cursors should be a couple of hundred rows at most. If you find a need to build a larger result set than this, as when you're importing or exporting data, don't use a scrollable cursor.

As we examine cursors, consider that they are built from sets of rows from one or more tables. Cursors can also be built from the result set generated by a SQL View or a stored procedure. Not all cursors are updatable—this capacity is a function of the programming interface and its ability to identify the rows to be updated. Some models, such as DAO/Jet, support complex (expensive) schemes to update the accessed rows—no matter which table contains the data. In any case, if you have update permission for the data, you can always use your own stored procedure or update query to change the underlying data tables, as long as you can identify the set of rows to change or to delete.

Cursorless result sets

All of the programming interfaces except DAO/Jet support at least one other way of returning data—the *cursorless* result set. In this case, the interface doesn't create a cursor at all but simply passes the data rows to your front end for processing. In all cases, this is the fastest way to get data from the server into the workstation RAM, but it provides few of the benefits of a cursor. While this type of result set *can* be updatable, it often isn't—you usually have to roll the update queries yourself. Because these high-speed "fire-hose" result sets are not scrollable (only one row is exposed and you can move the current-row pointer forward only), they are often called *forward-only* result sets.

Scrolling cursors

One of the most expensive aspects of cursor management involves supporting the ability to scroll. This means that once you have executed a query, a scrollable cursor permits you to position to virtually any specific row in the result set. Remember that only one row can be the "current" row, so this functionality can be very important if you need to browse through the data randomly. These repositioning methods are expensive in that they consume system resources much the way those little fishes in the Amazon River go for an explorer's toes. To increase performance, choose a cursor that has limited or no scrolling—such as the forward-only result sets described above. Gee, it looks like we are back to cursorless result sets again.

Keyset cursors

A keyset cursor stores a set of keys—basically a set of pointers—and allows a selected row to be refetched according to row-specific information stored in those keys. The keyset cursor requires separate storage for the data in each of the keys that it comprises. The remaining row data columns stay on the server where other users can access them. This means that other users can make changes, deletions, or additions to the rows you include in your cursor. A keyset cursor's membership is fixed once the result set is fully populated. When you or other users who share the database make changes to the data, these changes are returned to your workstation when you position to a changed row. When your code adds data to the underlying database using an updatable keyset cursor, some implementations add the row to the cursor—but not all do. When other people add one or more rows to the database that would qualify for your cursor, the data is never added to a keyset cursor. If other people delete rows in the database your keyset points to, those rows still exist in your cursor. If, and only if, you position to one of these deleted rows, the underlying cursor logic detects that the row is no longer fetchable and trips an error. None of the keyset cursor implementations automatically inform you when a row has been deleted—not until you ask for the deleted row.

Snapshot/static cursors

A snapshot or static cursor also provides keyset addressability, but it moves all selected data rows to the local workstation, from which any subsequent fetches will now retrieve the data. Generally, this cursor's membership is fixed once the result set is fully populated. But not all static cursors are read-only—some can be updated and some support additions to their membership. The snapshot or static cursor requires workstation storage for the keyset and for the data in each row of the result set. As a rule, when others add, change, or delete rows in the database, the changes are *not* reflected in a snapshot cursor that has been fully populated.

Dynamic cursors

Like a keyset or snapshot cursor, a dynamic cursor stores a block of keys. But with this type of cursor, the query that was used to generate the result set is constantly reexecuted. Because of this background activity, dynamic cursors are expensive to implement and comparatively slow, but they never limit or close out their membership: any rows that qualify for membership in a dynamic cursor are fetched whenever the cursor is positioned within a fixed range of rows that are near the subject row. You'll find, however, that most implementations don't support bookmark repositioning as commonly supported by other types of cursors.

Mixed cursors

A mixed cursor is a special type of dynamic cursor. It can be tuned to set the size of its keyset buffers. In most other respects, it functions the way a dynamic cursor does. Most models don't implement this hybrid.

Types of Buffers

In this section, we'll be looking at two kinds of buffers: single-row buffers and *n*-row buffers.

Single-row buffers

A single-row buffer isn't really a cursor at all because the same membership rules that apply to a forward-only keyset cursor apply here. With a single-row buffer, you can view data from only one row of the result set. Previous rows are not accessible, and the current row is not accessible once you move to the next row in the result set. (*Figure 5-1* shows that single-row buffers are *not* supported by the Jet/DAO programming model. Jet does provide a dbForwardOnly option for creating cursors, although the resource impact for single-row buffers with Jet is very different from that of single-row buffers used with the other models.)

n-row buffers

An *n*-row buffer expands the scope and scrollability of the single-row buffer. In this case, a fixed number of the rows in the result set can be exposed to the workstation and the application is permitted to move freely within those rows. While the GetRows method supported in DAO/Jet, ODBCDirect, and RDO is similar to this low-level buffering, it is not really the same because the GetRows result set isn't scrollable until you move it to your own array.

Implementing Cursors

Visual Basic version 5.0 has brought another nuance to cursor management. RDO 2.0 has implemented another ODBC cursor library and made a number of other changes that affect how cursors are implemented by the programming models. To understand these changes, you need to understand that the ODBC-based programming models all use the same ODBC driver manager and share

Figure 5-1
Cursors and Buffers and Their Support in Programming Models

Cursor and Buffer Types	Jet/DAO	ODBCDirect	RDO/RDC	VBSQL	ODBC API
Keyset cursor	Dynaset-type Recordset object	Keyset-type Recordset object (RDO keyset)	Keyset-type Resultset object	DB-Library or server-side keyset cursor	Keyset cursor option
Forward-only cursor	Forward-only Recordset object	Forward-only Recordset object (RDO forward-only)	Forward-only Resultset object	DB-Library default single-row buffer	Forward-only cursor option
Static cursor	Snapshot-type Recordset object	Snapshot-type Recordset object (RDO static)	Static-type Resultset object	DB-Library or server-side static cursor	Static cursor option
Dynamic cursor	Not supported	Dynamic-type Recordset object (RDO dynamic)	Dynamic-type Resultset object	DB-Library or server-side dynamic cursor	Dynamic cursor option
Mixed cursor	Not supported	Not supported	Not supported	DB-Library or server-side mixed cursor	Limited support (based on driver support)
Single-row buffer	Not supported	Forward-only option	Forward-only option	Forward-only option	Default result set
n-row buffer	Not supported	Not supported	Not supported	RowBuffer option	Not supported

the same cursor libraries as described below. Remember that each driver vendor is responsible to implement this functionality, so your results will vary from driver to driver:

- *ODBC (standard) cursor library:* This is the oldest of the cursor libraries and has been characterized as a "kludge." It creates client-side cursors and little else. It's notorious for its lack of performance and its simplistic approach. Unfortunately, it's probably the most widely used library. Because of a RAM leakage problem with this cursor library, I recommend that this library be avoided for asynchronous or event-driven work, at least until it's fixed. Check the Web for a repaired ODBC driver.

- *Server-side cursor library:* This was introduced with RDO 1.0 and is the first implementation of a server-side library against any back-end server—but only the SQL Server driver was provided by Visual Basic version 4.0. While some people opt to use this driver, it must be disabled if you want to use this library with multiple result set queries.

- *Client Batch cursor library:* This is the newest member of the RDO cursor family. It was developed by the FoxPro team at Microsoft and is far more efficient, sophisticated, and flexible than the ODBC client-side cursor. It supports "dissociate" result sets and optimistic batch updates. Basically, it's designed to do everything the standard ODBC client-side cursor library can do—only faster and better.

Note that if you are working with databases other than SQL Server (even Sybase or Oracle), you will have to dig up your own ODBC drivers. *InfoWorld* recently roasted Sybase for its lack of support for RDO ODBC drivers. The problem faced by Sybase and other vendors and driver builders is that the RDO drivers in Visual Basic version 4.0 required ODBC Level II compliance—at least to some extent. Basically, RDO 1.0 requires SQLExtendedFetch and SQLSetPos. These APIs are usually implemented by the ODBC cursor library, so it's not hard to do. You need other ODBC Level II APIs only for specific functionality. (See *Figure 5-2*.) If the driver doesn't support the API, RDO loses the associated feature.

Figure 5-2
ODBC Level II Compliance Requirements for RDO 1.0

To Support	Requires Implementation of the Following APIs
Parameters ("?" in SQL statements)	SQLDescribeParam, SQLNumParams
Stored procedures (Call syntax)	SQLProcedureColumns
Multiple results (MoreResults method)	SQLMoreResults
Reporting of supported features	SQLGetInfo

RDO 2.0 has relaxed these requirements because it now polls the SQLGetInfo API to determine which features are supported by the driver. Wherever possible, RDO 2.0 attempts to circumvent the lack of support by using its own code. This helps those drivers that lack support for full ODBC Level II conformance get by, especially when you use the new Client Batch cursor library.

Basic Design Decisions

Now that we've admired the view of cursors and buffers, let's step back next to the main highway. Regardless of the programming model you choose, you will have to make a number of design decisions before and throughout the implementation phase of development. You'll have to decide how your application will access data at the lowest level, no matter whether you want to add a new record to the employee table or count the number of rooms available on the fifth floor. For most problems, it won't be appropriate to use a single approach and you'll have to choose among several implementations in a number of areas:

- How many users are expected to run your front-end client application at any one time? Are there enough connections to manage the load? What about space on the server—including TempDB? What other applications, databases, or users are accessing the server?

- Can your application tolerate more than one instance running on the same machine? Do the instances affect each other?

- How should server connections be made? Should a connection be established when the user first logs on, and should it be kept in place indefinitely?

- Will a more sophisticated connection management or sharing technique be required?

- How should security be managed? Should the application use Windows NT domain security or a custom brand? How should the application differentiate among users with different degrees of authority?

- Will the users be connecting through a LAN or WAN or over the Internet?

- How should queries be created? Should they be created, compiled, and executed on the fly? Should you leverage stored procedures? Should you depend on parameterized queries stored in QueryDef objects or stored procedures? Should you simply build parameter queries in code?

- How should rows be fetched? Should you use a cursor, a row buffer, or a cursorless result set? Should the cursor be created on the server or on the workstation?

- Should rows be sorted, searched, and processed on the server, or should these operations be performed after the rows have been brought to the workstation?

- What about bound controls? Should you depend on data-aware controls tied to the Data control or the RemoteData control? Can you use a data-aware control without binding it to the Data control, using the control's "unbound" mode instead to add data to the control?

- How should data be updated? Should you create updatable cursors, use special stored procedures, or use action queries? Does your user have permission to update base tables or only to make changes through stored procedures?

- What type of concurrency should you use? Can you afford to lock a page the whole time it is being edited, or must you add code to deal with pessimistic locking?

CAUTION

When you're creating a new client/server system, plan to spend at least as much time on research and design as you do on coding. If your front-end design is flawed, the best database implementation on the planet will look like leftover pizza.

- Will it take so much time to execute queries that asynchronous operation will be justified? Should you include code that keeps data constantly updated when it's exposed to the user? Should you inform the user of changes only when data on the screen is touched?

- Have you worked out query strategies that account for the use of server-side resources? When you sort result sets or create server-side cursors or temporary tables, are there enough resources on the server to maintain these structures? Can they be maintained for all active users?

- What fallback plan has been established to deal with contingencies like the main server's illness or demise? Is there a mechanism for supporting users even when access to a remote server is unavailable? Can the front end be designed for tolerance of intermittent remote server access?

- What provisions have you made for many people to work on a project at the same time? Is the code broken down into pieces so as to lend itself to this type of development? Or is your front end a monolithic beast? Does it consist of one program or several?

Am I prejudiced toward one of the client/server programming models? You might think so since I was a co-founder of RDO and a real fan of VBSQL for a number of years, but I think there are suitable applications for each one. Each model supports a range of development experience. Some support developers with API-level experience, and some don't. And each model addresses the client/server paradigm differently. Some use an object model, and some don't. All but one of the models depends on the ODBC interface, and three of the remaining expose the internal ODBC handles that permit low-level API operations. Three of the models support bound controls, but all of them support data-aware controls that have unbound modes. Confused yet? I never promised you a rose garden.

Avoiding the Top 10 Design Mistakes

When a project is finally wrapped up and delivered, the managers gather to decide what went right, what went wrong, whom to promote, and whom to blame. All too often, it can seem that the tools and developers are assigned a significant part of the blame and the architects and systems analysts are given most of the medals. But many designs are flawed long before the first line of code is written—though the developers working in the trenches often contribute to the fallibility of the design. With apologies to David Letterman, I suggest you take note of the following top 10 reasons for systems (especially client/server systems) not meeting expectations:

- **The design didn't deliver what the customers wanted.** In many cases, this is because the customers didn't know what they wanted until you didn't give it to them. Generally, a design that fails this way is the result of an implementation without a clear (as in written) specification. When one creates a specification, one has to study what needs to be done, come to an understanding about the end result, and *write it down*. This way the designer and the customer can come to a common understanding about what the design does.

- **The architect or analyst who designed the system knew how to lay bricks but not how to use a hammer—so you end up with a lot of brick outhouses.** Invariably, people build what they know how to build, using the tools they are comfortable with. If they are experts at ISAM designs, they think about ISAM solutions to the problems at hand, even if they don't always work very well. The customer has no way of knowing what the best implementation would be, and perhaps management doesn't know either. Sometimes a better understanding of the alternatives is in order before charging off to implement old or inadequate concepts. Too many times, we have seen complaints that Visual Basic or Microsoft Access or whatever was seemingly incapable of building a cursor against a giant table, when the real problem was lack of a complete understanding of how a multiuser client/server system is designed in the first place. For the most part, client/server applications that support dozens to dozens of dozens of users don't build SELECT * cursors on base tables—they use stored procedures, views, or server-side intelligent objects to return information—not just rows.

- **The design assumed that since the application worked for 5 users it would work for 50 or 500 or 5000.** Too often, we see designs that account for neither the volume of traffic generated by their application nor all of the applications that use the same design taken as a whole. In today's world of 500-KB e-mail messages broadcast throughout the net to announce the birth of the new group administrator's son, network bandwidth is already pretty much taxed to the limit. Scalability of any application depends on the quantity of resources consumed by each individual application. This includes workstation resources but also must include network packets sent and received, round-trips to the server, and resources on the server. If a single application creates a 40-MB TempDB sorted result set, how is the system going to support 50 or 500 instances of the same application—each consuming server resources like teenagers eating M&Ms?

- **The developer forgot the oldest maxim of all: "Stuff happens."** In a robust client/server application, much of your code should be dealing with the errors (and messages) returned from the server or the OS running the application. Not only should the application deal with all of these errors, it should be designed to do so from the beginning, when the developer best understands where the problems can best be trapped and addressed. All too often, one assumes that the network or the available resources will be just as readily available as they are when the application is written.

- **The design called for mustard on the buns, so mustard was added to the bread recipe.** We have seen a migration away from fairly simplistic two-tier client/server applications that baked many of the business rules and field edits into the application instead of putting them on the breakfast table, where all of the developers could reach them as needed. While this does not seem to have much of an impact when you write the first application, and perhaps not when you write the second, by the time you get to the fourth or fourteenth, you can really see the problem arise. Each time business rule code is included in an application, you risk having to go back and change each and every application when the rules change. For those shops where the business rules never change, you can disregard this problem.

- **The design didn't account for everyone wanting to use the same clerk.** Imagine a fast-food restaurant designed to deal with dozens of people at once but with only one cash register that all of the teenagers behind the counter have to share. This same problem is often duplicated in client/server designs when insert/update activity is focused on the pages containing the most current rows. This is the "hot spot" problem many of us have seen. Unless you deal with this problem by adding a few more cash registers, your system is destined to bog down as individual applications vie for the most often used pages. Generally, for a database design (for example), the easiest way to deal with this situation is to change the data indexing scheme to make sure new rows are added to different pages in the database. That way, when the page is locked by someone down the counter ordering a full-meal-deal, another operation can complete without having to wait.

- **The design didn't account for that cookie-hungry kid in the back room who used a pair of binoculars to watch the cook open the combination lock on the pantry.** Security is a prime concern where I work, and it should be a concern for your designer as well. Since Visual Basic and all the rest have made client/server data access so simple, even a well-meaning bungler can easily get access to the corporate cookies and stomp all over the data—especially when the user ID and password you assign is granted permission to access the base database tables. By building stored procedures (or server-side ActiveX objects) to gate access to the data, you prevent the kids from wandering through the pantry fingering the goodies. This design also gives you a way to implement business rules on the server and simplify application design and dissemination. Since the stored procedures can change without the applications having to be recompiled, you can make some pretty significant changes without having to change a single installed application.

- **The design called for colorful ad copy to be delivered to the customer, and instead of including it in the Sunday paper, you baked it into each loaf of bread.** Not everyone is a fan of putting binary large objects (BLOBs) in the database. While it is possible to do so, there are not many cases where this yields the best performance. Yes, there are cases where the alternative was tried and was ultimately rejected, but in many, many cases, abysmal performance can be turned around overnight by simply leaving the photos, documents, and other BLOBs in the original source files and putting a pointer (preferably an HTTP pointer) to the file in the database.

- **The design failed to account for tornadoes.** A data backup and restore regimen must be part of any workable client/server design. When it isn't, it is just a matter of time before you're faced with a mob of people angry because they can't get at their data. Few problems are more job threatening than not having a backup and restore strategy. Be sure it works, too. In many cases, you might not be able to restore a single table or even restore at all if you don't have the proper utilities and procedures in place.

- **The design called for the bread to be rewarmed in a toaster oven (because that's what we know how to do)—even when the customer uses a microwave oven.** The NIH (not invented here) problem has hamstrung companies large and small since the dawn of time. How could someone else's solution be as good as one we make right here in River City? More often than not, decisions are made based on tradition and comfort level as opposed to what works best for the situation. While this is a valid concern, it must be tempered with the realities of future viability and support. In many cases, the decision to buy or make has had more to do with people skills than technical merits. That is, if you have a shop full of APL programmers and you need to implement a PC solution, you can either retrain the staff and start from scratch or buy an outside solution and have your staff sit on their 80-column cards—neither is particularly easy to do. Companies that don't make these tough decisions die or are absorbed sooner or later.

Creating a Virtual Application

Any database front-end application has to screen data accepted from the user. For example, when the dialog box in *Figure 5-3* is presented to the user, nothing beyond the user's training and your code can guarantee the quality of what is entered and accepted into the field. If the user is totally untrained—say, a customer at a bank's ATM—the available choices must be very narrow indeed; an open field that invites any number of answers invites ambiguous responses and failed applications, too. And many fields cannot be tested for validity unless values in a table are looked up or examined in relation to other values. For example, an application that captures telephone area codes might compare the user-provided value with a list of known area codes in the particular state and a list of zip code zones, and until all the validating data is complete—the statewide area codes and the zip codes—full validation can't be had. Since most front-end applications use dozens of input fields or more, a question arises: Where and when should field validation take place?

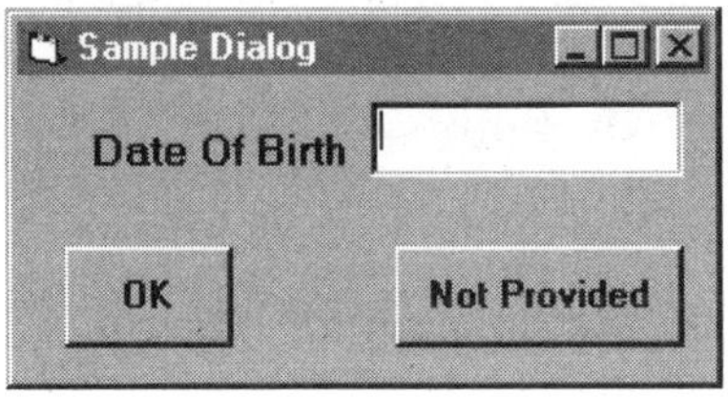

Figure 5-3 *Dialog box representing an open field*

There is no true consensus on this question. Most approaches taken by front-end development applications like Microsoft Access or PowerSoft PowerBuilder don't leverage the extensive power that can be made available through the establishment of rules and defaults on the SQL server. These rules and defaults are the most powerful tools a database administrator has for combating violations of column integrity. When specific criteria are established for each column, the database is protected from all applications that attempt to make changes in the data.

But applications that rely completely on server-side validation are difficult to code, besides making life more difficult for data entry operators. And rules are blind: they don't know who is making a change or why, and without a lot of ugly code, there's no way to bend the rules for certain users and the inevitable special case. Regardless of the front end or utility accessing the table, all changes must pass muster before being accepted.

The problem with this approach is timing. Rules and defaults are applied when data is added or changed; the mechanism for invoking the rules is an INSERT or UPDATE SQL statement or a method applied to a remote object. This usually means that by the time the rules and defaults are applied, the form fields have all been completed and the user has already moved on mentally to the next form. If there are problems with the data, the user is generally forced to completely reconstruct the incorrect field, so your code has to be more complex because it has to parse the field in question from the error message before anything else can happen. And that can be difficult, since some base columns are derived from a number of form fields.

By contrast, many database front-end development applications, such as Microsoft Access, permit you to create forms with built-in field validation. These edits are done independently of the remote database, so they don't reflect changes made to rules or defaults in the root tables. This type of field validation is fast, and it's fairly easy to code, but it's also application-centric: its benefits can't be shared between applications or even between forms in the same application. And when remote database defaults or rules change, the applications in question must be recoded, recompiled, and redistributed.

One way around this dilemma is to create to a single executable, which all users can access over the net. This is a limited solution, however—it doesn't take account of changes made while an application is running or of cases in which an application is too large to download over a slow network link. This solution also requires each application to be changed when base-table field validation criteria change, which can be quite expensive if a variety of applications use the database. Some Internet applications take this approach, while others make use of ISAPI or DCOM interfaces in an attempt to alleviate this problem.

Another fairly common approach is to turn off all column rules so that responsibility for field validation resides in the front-end application. This solution is workable when only one or two applications perform data entry; any more than that, and the problem of how to validate fields gets highly complex.

Another newly emerging approach to validation issues is to encapsulate data entry rules into one or more ActiveX controls. Since you can now write these in Visual Basic, this alternative makes a lot of sense. These custom controls can be as simple as a smart TextBox control with extra code behind its Click event or as sophisticated as a whole set of controls aggregated into a single ActiveX control. Either way, a control can be passed around the development team and used by everyone. If the underlying rules change, you have to rebuild the control and recompile, but that's far better and faster than ferreting out all of the rules when they are hard-coded in a dozen different applications. Another approach would be to move this functionality out of process and onto the remote server, letting Microsoft Transaction Manager manage the logic for you.

What I call the *virtual application* leverages server-side rules and still provides field-level validation. The virtual application automatically adapts field and form validation criteria to changes in database rules, defaults, and sometimes triggers. The following section discusses the implementation of the virtual front end and how to make the best use of its features.

Local and Database-Driven Validation

Data entry operators often work "head down" and don't like to cursor back to correct mistakes in fields already entered. One school of thought says that field validation should be performed as the data is entered or as soon as possible thereafter. This approach is hospitable to field-level validation and can be supplemented with form-level checks as a form is committed. These tests carry out cross-checks that might include several fields. One approach to field-level validation, an approach used by Microsoft Access, builds edit masks and tests into the local application form and its validation code. But what this means, unless you are clever, is that your field- and form-level validation must be designed to match the eccentricities of the database's schema and validation changes: when the database changes, your application must change as well.

NOTE In the context of a form, the term *field* means a control or other element in the form for capturing or displaying data. A field is derived from one or more columns in a database row, and one or more fields can be used to determine one or more columns in the database.

Another school of thought insists that field validation be done with the rules, triggers, and stored procedures maintained in the database. In this scenario, as the operator changes focus from one of the form's input fields to another, or at least from section to section of the form, a database query is executed that validates the data entered up to that point. One technique updates a "dataless" table that contains only a subset of the columns that are about to be updated but which are bound to the same rules as the base table. If the pseudo update or insert fails because of a rule violation, it is abundantly clear which column or columns caused the failure. This type of query is very quick and can be done in the background as the operator begins work on the next input field. When the operator commits the form, a "true" update can be executed, one that is sure to succeed—unless there are duplicate or missing records. The hitch with this approach is that it doesn't lend itself to the use of control-level validation, which can significantly reduce your code. For example, many of the checks performed by Visual Basic's masked edit control can simplify data entry and validation as data is entered—but the control is not normally cognizant of database rule changes that might affect the control's default, range, and mask property settings.

Data-Driven Validation

In a virtual application, regardless of the programming model you choose, you can create a data entry validation test by using the rules maintained in the database. While the application or form is loading, you query the SQL Server *SysComments* table, a repository of all the database's procedures, rules, defaults, and triggers, for the rules and default values that apply to specific fields in the form (if you know which rules are assigned to those fields). Each row in *SysComments* is an index with its ID object. (A listing of all SQL Server objects is kept in the *SysObjects* table.) By using a simple join or subquery between the *SysObjects* and *SysComments* tables and basing it on the *name* column of *SysObjects*, you can get the rule or default you want. The following sample query illustrates the subquery technique that extracts *pub_idrule* from the database:

```
Select text from syscomments where id =
    (select id from sysobjects where name = 'pub_idrule')
```

> **NOTE** On some SQL servers, all objects are case-sensitive. If the SQL server in our example were set to case-sensitive mode, and if the rule were entered as *Pub_IDRule*, the sample query would not work.

Here are the results of our sample query: the text of the rule as returned from the *Pubs* database's *SysComments* table. This rule's job is to validate changes made to the pub_id field in the *Publishers* table or wherever else the pub_id column is used:

```
create rule Pub_IDRule as @pub_id in ("1389", "0736", "0877",
"1622", "1756") or @pub_id like "99[0-9][0-9]"
```

Making Virtual Rules

With a virtual application, validation is performed in the field's LostFocus event. To use *pub_idrule* in your form field's LostFocus event, you have to create a procedure that reads the rule from the database (as already shown), parses the arguments, and creates an array that contains valid values. The rule arguments are the operator (such as =, <, >, !=, BETWEEN, IN, or LIKE) and the value or expression being tested for.

Unless your procedure is particularly smart and you are very good at parsing non-Polish expressions, your database administrators and the developers who set the rule text will have to be aware that your application expects a fairly fixed and carefully written rule—at least one that has been written within known guidelines. For example, *pub_idrule* uses an IN clause to provide a list of valid field values. If a rule developer changed this to a set of specific tests instead, your rule parser might fail.

TIP   When your application depends on the syntax of a rule, it might be a good idea to tell those who are likely to change the rule. That way, your application has half a chance of working when changes are made.

Using LIKE tests in rules

The second part of *pub_idrule* uses a different approach to validate the pub_id field. In this case, the TSQL LIKE operator is used to accept certain characters in specified positions. Since Visual Basic now supports its own *Like* keyword, you can parse out the criteria string, convert it to Visual Basic syntax, and use it to filter the field in question, as in the following form and code:

```
Private Sub Form_Load()

Dim SQL$
Dim i%, Qry$
Set db = OpenDatabase _
    ("pubs", False, False, "uid=;pwd=;database=pubs;")
SQL$ = "select text from syscomments where id =" _
    & "(select id from sysobjects where name = 'pub_idrule')"
Set rs = db.OpenRecordset(SQL, dbOpenSnapshot, dbSQLPassThrough)
Qry$ = rs(0)
i% = InStr(Qry$, "like")          ' Search for "Like" value test
If i% > 0 Then
    LikeTest$ = Mid$(Qry$, i% + 6)  ' Strip off test criteria
    i = InStr(LikeTest$, Chr$(34))  ' Search for trailing quote
    LikeTest$ = Left$(LikeTest, i - 1) ' Trim trailing quote
Debug.Print " LikeTest ="; LikeTest$
Else
MsgBox "Could not parse rule"
End If

End Sub
```

In the Validate event—or, in this case, in the TestButton_Click event—
you can now create a test that changes when the rule changes in the database:

```
Private Sub TestButton_Click()

PassFail = ""
Dim r$
If PubID Like LikeTest Then
r$ = "passed"
Else
r$ = "Failed"
Beep
End If
PassFail = r$
End Sub
```

Converting LIKE expressions

Wouldn't it be nice if both TSQL and ANSI SQL LIKE expressions used the
same syntax? I guess that's too much to ask—but it's not that hard to convert. *Figure 5-4* shows the differences. (Notice, however, that the previous
example doesn't need to be converted: the bracket operator "[n]" syntax is
roughly the same for both syntaxes.)

Any rule expression can also contain TSQL expressions or functions, such
as GETDATE() to return the current date. For example, the following rule checks
whether the value being tested is within three of days of the current day:

```
@value between Getdate() and dateadd (day,3,getdate())
```

Figure 5-4
Differences Between TSQL and ANSI SQL LIKE Expressions

TSQL	Visual Basic	Notes
%	*	Any string of zero or more characters, as in *LIKE "do*"* returns "dog", "doggy" and "do".
_	?	Any single character, as in *"_og"* returns "dog" or "bog" but not "og" or "oggle".
_	#	Any single digit (0–9). TSQL does not dif- ferentiate between the characters 0–9 and the letters, so you can specify a single digit using the bracket [ ] syntax.
[]	[]	Any single character within the specified range (for example, [a–f]) or set (for example, [abcdef]).
[^]	[!]	Any single character not within the speci- fied range (for example, [!a–f]) or set (for example, [!abcdef]).

If you come across a rule containing an expression, you can try substituting the Visual Basic equivalent of the statement, but this gets a little tricky since you cannot create Visual Basic code on the fly and expect Visual Basic to execute it. What you can do is use a CASE statement to branch to an equivalent Visual Basic code handler and pass the parsed parameters to the statement. (You can also work out a compromise with the developer to rephrase the rule. Try a bribe—say, a case of Mountain Dew.)

Setting edit masks

What if a particular type of test would be handled better by a masked edit control? You might consider parsing the test value from the rule and creating a masked edit mask—but that seems like a lot of trouble. It might be more useful to include a mask right in the rule. Rules can have comments, so I suggest creating a mask and placing the text for the mask in a comment. For example, locating the mask would be easy if our *pub_idrule* contained the following text:

```
create rule Pub_idRule as @pub_id in ("1389", "0736", "0877",
"1622", "1756")

or @pub_id like "99[0-9][0-9]"
/* MASK={####} */
```

In this example, the mask simply permits the entry of four numbers. In more complex statements, it would be easy to specify the appropriate mask in the rule.

Virtualizing Defaults and Parsing Default Strings

Defaults, like rules, are kept in the SQL Server *SysComments* system table. Parsing default strings poses a few problems, but most of them are less complex than those you faced working with rules.

A default can contain only a constant (value) or constant expression, but this constant can be a global variable, such as *@@Connections*, or it can be a fairly complex expression; it just can't reference database tables or other columns. Many of the expressions and functions can be generated on the workstation end. For example, GETDATE() is simply the current date. You can execute DATE$ or TIME$ to get current values, unless the server is in a different time zone.

CAUTION
When rules are created or used, SQL Server doesn't check masks for correct syntax, since a mask is only a comment. Syntax is checked only when an application is executed and a rule is invoked, so your code has to do the error checking to ensure that your mask is right. Make sure you have a backup mask in case the SQL administrator sets an incorrect mask value. I keep a Richard M. Nixon mask handy for just those occasions.

TIP If your default is simply a value, you have no worries. All you have to do is parse the value and test for it in a simple comparison statement. But if the default uses an expression that contains a global variable, you are up one nasty creek—unless your initialization routine requeries the remote server for the current value.

The following query fetches a default value for a named column in a named table. This is probably the syntax you will need to use, since it doesn't assume that you know the name of the default; it assumes only that there is a default on a particular table's column. In the process of developing this test code, I noticed that the default names in the *Pubs* database were hardly user-friendly: most of the time, a default name ended with a fairly long number, which was probably generated by the automated routine that created the table and its components in the first place. Therefore, this technique is probably a better choice when you know the table and column names:

```
select text from syscomments where id =
    (select cdefault from syscolumns
    where name = "city" and id = (select id from sysobjects
    where name = "Authors" and type = "U")
)
```

The return string from this query contains the syntax you need to create the default:

```
create default CityDefault as "Redmond"
```

In this case, simply parse the value between the quotes, and use it for the test value in your form field GetFocus or LostFocus validation routine. (Note that if the default is a money value, it may be preceded with *$*.)

CAUTION

System clocks might be manually synchronized every now and then, but they are notoriously inaccurate and tend to drift. If the SQL server is in another state or country, it will also be set to a different time from your workstation. Be wary of any strategy that depends on date and time values to be completely accurate.

> **NOTE** When I used the new Enterprise Manager to examine and attempt to change the defaults in the *Pubs* database, I noticed a number of areas where the program returned incorrect information or otherwise failed to work correctly. For example, I tried to bind a default to the *Titles* table, but it would not accept the name of the default as entered. I fell back to the BINDEFAULT stored procedure, which correctly bound the new default. I used a query to verify that the default was correctly bound, but it didn't appear in the table when I examined it with Enterprise Manager. It appears that the table data is extracted from the database but not requeried when the table changes.

Administration of Virtual Applications

The kind of virtual application I have been describing can ensure that minor changes (and some that are not so minor) made to field criteria in the database won't force you to recompile your front end. Here are a few more points to consider:

- *Changes made to the database are not propagated to the front end* until it requeries the *SysComments* table. Since your code is replicating the rule tests, no update rule violations should occur. If they do, it means that the rule has changed or that your code is bogus. Requery *SysComments*, rebuild your rule test, and retest the field.

- *If the SQL administrator changes the rule so that your code fails to parse the new syntax, your code should quietly report the error* back to the system administrator and use a fallback rule or default. Notification can take place by e-mail or with a call placed to the SQL administrator through a workstation modem playing a WAV file that contains an appropriate message.

- *Your application should load default values when the form loads*, and again if notified to do so. The notification mechanism is up to you. It can take the form of an e-mail message sent from the server or a time value set in a special table designed for this purpose. One thing you can do is limit the times when this type of change is permitted: choose a time when all applications are off line.

6 Chapter

Making Connections to SQL Server

Security

Connection Management

Handling Connection Errors

A connection is a fairly complex set of interface, network, and Microsoft SQL Server structures, agents, and protocols that temporarily link your application to a SQL server. No matter which programming model you use, its database interface must be connected to the SQL server before any other operations can take place. Each interface manages connections differently, which can be a deciding factor in your choice of programming model.

The checklist in *Figure 6-1* shows which of the programming model interfaces perform which connection-related operations.

Figure 6-1
Connection Operation Checklist

Operation	Jet	ODBC-Direct	RDO/RDC	VBSQL	ODBC
Open connection via Data control or RemoteData control	✓	✓	✓	—	—
Support missing-argument logon dialogs	—	✓	✓	✓	✓
Open additional connections automatically to update rows	✓	—	—	—	—
Defer releasing of connections after they have been closed	✓	—	—	—	✓ (3.0)
Clean up connections in Design mode	✓	—	—	—	✓
Return handle to connection	—	✓	✓	✓	✓

PART II   DESIGNING CLIENT/SERVER APPLICATIONS

Security

If the data you are accessing has any value, you must take steps to secure it. Without security systems, your data is subject to theft, damage, and accidental access. Setting up and maintaining database security is the responsibility of the SQL server administrator, who establishes a schema of database users and data objects. Each user is given or denied permission to access portions of the database; the portions vary from a single column in a single table to the entire database itself.

In Microsoft Visual Basic version 5.0, all ODBC interfaces, including RDO, now support ODBC connection management. That is, unless you (or the underlying interface) disable it, the ODBC Driver Manager will attempt to share your connections with other parts of your program using the same transaction scope. RDO and DAO intentionally disable this feature. If you decide to enable it, be especially careful because it can significantly impact how many users are permitted to gain access to your server.

> **NOTE** Generally, your client application must be granted access to the database tables and columns you need, but no more. In any case, data retrieval and update are often performed against views or stored procedures, not on database tables themselves, a practice that filters and protects delicate referential or data integrity constraints.

Either the user establishing a connection to the SQL server provides a valid user ID and matching password or the interface uses the user ID and password supplied by the Microsoft Windows NT domain. When you build business objects that need connectivity, this stateless object must pass its own "user" ID to gain access to the SQL server. The user ID and password are the keys to the security system and should be guarded as carefully as physical access to the server is guarded.

For each user, the SQL server administrator must create a logon ID that corresponds to the user-provided ID (or to the Windows NT user ID). In some cases, the logon ID is used to identify a function rather than a person. For example, an application that everyone in a department uses to order lunch could have a departmental ID as a logon ID. This kind of logon ID is usually built into the application or the component: anyone granted access can manipulate the data.

Getting the User ID and Password

If you choose to let the user enter the user ID and password, you can create a dialog box that doesn't echo the password as it is being typed. Fortunately, Visual Basic provides this feature as the Password property of its TextBox control; simply set it to an asterisk (*). You can also store the user ID and password in an INI file or in the registry so that users need not enter it each time.

Getting a Valid Server Name or Data Source Name

I rarely ask the user for the name of the SQL server or the data source name (DSN). If you *must* ask the user to enter the resource name, however, you should present a list of valid SQL servers or DSNs instead of having the user type a name into a Text control. To present such a list, you must poll the network for all *visible* SQL servers or use the ODBC DSN APIs and then show just those servers or DSNs the user has rights to. (This guide's companion disc includes an example of using the ODBC APIs to get DSNs.)

NOTE I still experience problems with the visibility of SQL servers, so don't be alarmed if your SQL server isn't on the list of valid servers presented by the SQL Server graphical user interface (GUI) tools. Sometimes this aberration can be caused when the LAN server is marked as not being visible. In a Microsoft Windows 95 environment, the LAN APIs used to poll for SQL servers don't work as they do in Windows 3.*x* or Windows NT. Basically, this means that you won't be able to troll for servers in Windows 95—not until Microsoft decides to fix it.

I used to recommend the Visual Basic LAN Manager custom controls for presenting the user with a list of SQL servers, but then the Microsoft SQL Server development team added a new call, SqlServerEnum, to VBSQL 4.2 (created to support the Windows NT environment). This call returns a list of servers that have identified themselves as SQL servers. If you are using the Windows NT operating system (but not Windows 95), you can use this call to search the local system or the net domain and all the systems that have SQL Server installed appear on the list, even if the servers aren't running at the moment. (This call is understandably slow; in my tests, it took SqlServerEnum almost 25 seconds to return any results.)

Avoiding the ODBC Login Dialog Boxes

In no case should you permit your users to be confronted with the ODBC login dialog boxes. This is a fairly common and unavoidable occurrence if you use DAO/Jet or don't set the proper options when using RDO or ODBCDirect. Whenever the ODBC driver manager receives a failed logon attempt notification from the driver, it checks its option flags and if not reset (I'll show you how in a minute), it throws up the dialog box shown in *Figure 6-2*. Notice that this is radically different from the dialog boxes you might have been used to seeing in the past. I triggered this dialog box because my code didn't pass a DSN, login ID, or password. This dialog box prompts a user to choose from the list of visible DSNs or make one up on her own. Not good. Do you want *your* users making up their own DSNs? I wouldn't. If you provide a valid DSN, the dialog box shown in *Figure 6-3* appears, which (fortunately) does *not* let the user choose an alternative DSN.

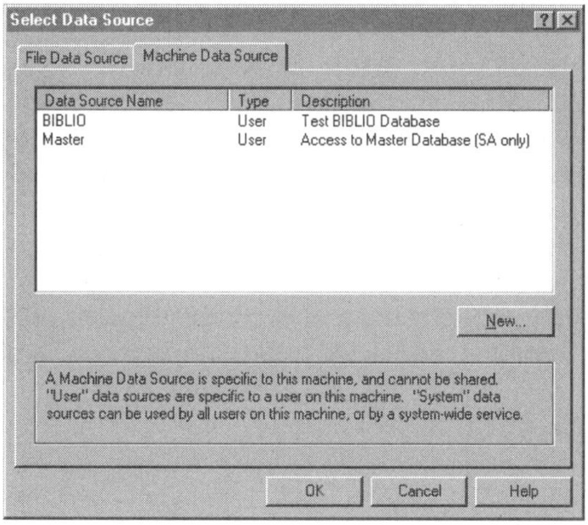

Figure 6-2 *ODBC prompts the user for the missing DSN*

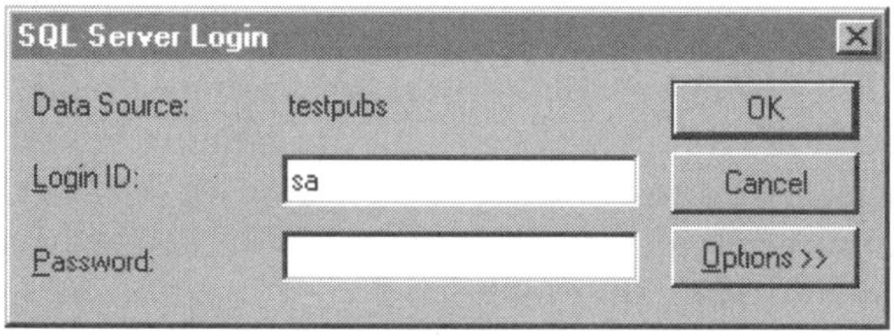

Figure 6-3 *The SQL Server Login dialog box*

Unfortunately, the login dialog box does let the user choose the Options button, which exposes all kinds of tempting options, as you see in **Figure 6-4**, including the database name. Swell. This lapse in security is completely preventable in all of the non-DAO/Jet programming models; simply specify that the ODBC option must return all ODBC connection errors to the application. While this means that you actually have to code an error handler, this shouldn't be a big problem.

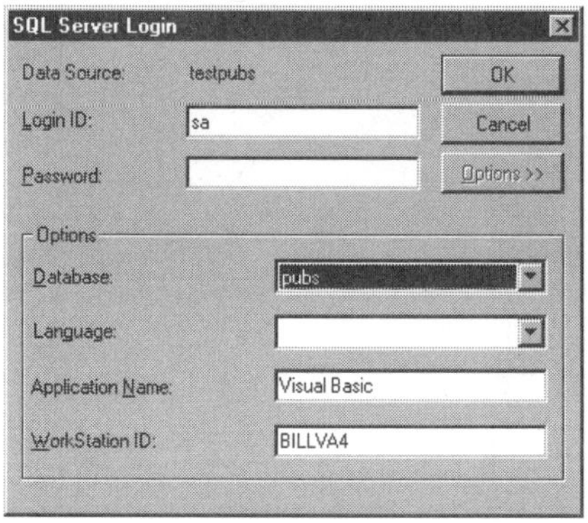

Figure 6-4 *The expanded version of the SQL Server Login dialog box*

The other ODBC connection options

You no longer need a registered data source name (DSN) to connect to an ODBC data source. The new ODBC drivers included with SQL Server 6.5 now support two additional connection options. Actually, one of these options (DSN-less connections) has been around for some time. Now you can, in addition, specify a file-based data source. These are stored on your system in *\Program Files\Common Files\Odbc\Data Sources* under the name you specify. The advantage here is that you can simply add this file DSN to your setup script and install it on the client's system without having to go through the pain of registering a new DSN on the client's system. I just created one of these, and it looks like this:

```
[ODBC]
DRIVER=SQL Server
UID=sa
DATABASE=pubs
WSID=BILLVA4
APP=Visual Basic
SERVER=Betav1
```

Notice that it has most (but not all) of the information captured by the DSN dialog boxes. This means that if your DSN doesn't use the default network library (named pipes) and network address or needs to use ODBC-to-ANSI conversion or any of the other nondefault options, you can't use a file-based DSN—instead, you must create one using the dialog boxes or the appropriate RegisterDSN function in code.

If you *do* need finer control over your DSN, you can use the interactive ODBC applet launched from the Windows Control Panel, as shown in *Figure 6-5*. This dialog box can be used to build any kind of DSN you can imagine (and some you probably couldn't). You can also use this dialog box to set the Tracing option, a System DSN, and other, more obscure options like network library and address.

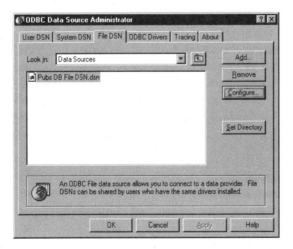

Figure 6-5 *The ODBC Data Source Administrator Control Panel*

Let's look at some of these options and see what impact they have on your application. While some are fairly intuitive, others aren't so easy to understand or don't work as you would expect. The ODBC SQL Server Setup dialog box offers the following options:

- *Data Source Name:* The name of the data source—for example, "Personnel Data." Yes, DSNs can have embedded spaces.

- *Description:* A description of the data in the data source—for example, "Hire date, salary history, and current review of all employees"— strictly optional.

- *Server:* The name of a SQL server on your network. Don't add the \\. While the ODBC help file says, "You can select a server from the list," you can't—at least not in Windows 95. You must enter the server name. You can also use *(local)* as the server on a Microsoft Windows NT computer if the client is running on a Windows NT system running SQL Server. The user can then use the local SQL Server engine (that listens on named pipes), even when running a non-networked version of SQL Server. Note that when the 16-bit SQL Server driver is using *(local)* without a network, the MS Loopback Adapter must be installed. For more information about server names for different types of networks, see "SQL Server Setup" in SQL Server Books Online.

- *Network Address:* The address of the SQL Server database management system (DBMS) from which the driver retrieves data. For Microsoft SQL Server, you can usually leave this value set to *(Default)*. You use this option when you're setting up TCP/IP connections.

- *Network Library:* The name of the SQL Server network library DLL that the SQL Server driver uses to communicate with the network software. If the value of this option is *(Default)*, the SQL Server driver uses the client computer's default network library, which is specified in the Default Network box on the Net-Library tab of the SQL Server Client Configuration Utility. If you create a data source using a network library other than the default and optionally a network address, ODBC SQL Server Setup will create a server name entry that you can see in the Advanced tab in the SQL Server Client Configuration Utility. These server name entries can also be used by DB-Library applications.

- *Options:* A button you can click to reveal the following options.

  - Database Name: The name of the SQL Server database, for example, *Pubs*. This option is case sensitive, but only on a case-sensitive SQL server.

  - Language Name: The national language used by SQL Server. Leave this alone unless you want SQL Server to converse with you in French.

- Generate Stored Procedures For Prepared Statements: Stored procedures are created for prepared statements when this option is selected (the default). The SQL Server driver prepares a statement by placing it in a procedure and compiling that procedure. When this option check box is clear, the creation of stored procedures for prepared statements is disabled. In this case, a prepared statement is stored and executed at run time.

- Translation: The description of the current translator. To select a different translator, click the Select button and select from the list in the Select Translator dialog box.

- Convert OEM To ANSI Characters: If the SQL Server client computer and SQL Server are using the same non-ANSI character set, select this option. For example, if SQL Server uses code page 850 and the client computer uses code page 850 for the OEM code page, selecting this option will ensure that extended characters stored in the database are properly converted to ANSI for use by Windows-based applications. When this option check box is clear and the SQL Server client machine and SQL Server are using different character sets, you must specify a character set translator.

DSN-less connections

When we get to Part IV, we'll see how to set up a DSN-less connection. This option needs no DSN in any form and has most of the same restrictions and benefits as a file-based DSN. DSN-less connections open faster (there is no registry search) and can help speed up applications that depend on connection conservation techniques.

Connection Management

Your application, when it's working with SQL Server data, is expected to communicate with the SQL server in a fairly structured way. Now that there are a number of alternative interfaces to SQL Server, some of the details might be taken care of for you, but you must always be aware of what is happening in the background on your behalf.

As SQL Server and its interface drivers improve, fundamental aspects of front-end design must change to accommodate or take advantage of the improvements. For example, SQL Server 6.0 supports a way to use a single connection for performing more than one operation at a time. If you're writing an application that is expected to communicate with both SQL Server 4.0 and SQL Server 6.0, you might consider the cost benefits of this feature.

Permitting More Active Connections

To get the most out of a server, you might want to keep connections open only if they are going to be used immediately. Several techniques can permit more active connections to the server by eliminating or at least reducing idle connections—those left open between requests to the server. The first technique is *opening just in time*. With the exception of the first connection, most SQL connections take only a second or less to complete when you use the VBSQL model. The other programming interfaces can take considerably longer, especially if you open a database object directly by using DAO/Jet or if you reference a registered data source name. The "just in time" technique slows the workstation down somewhat—how much depends on the number of operations—but it can be an effective way to increase the number of users who can access the SQL server at any one time.

A second technique—*watchdog timer disconnect*—drops connections that aren't being actively used (and that don't have active queries pending). It's very much like a screen saver. This technique uses conventional logic, but it sets up a timer that watches for any activity that would reset its wait time. Once that time has expired, the timer closes the connection. The next attempt at database access is expected to fail because of a null connection or missing object, and when it does, the error handler reopens the connection and passes control back to the requesting call.

A third method—new for Visual Basic version 5.0—is the ability of the ODBC 3.0 Driver Manager to "pool" connections. When connection pooling is enabled, the ODBC Driver Manager, in conjunction with the Resource Dispenser Manager (new for ODBC 3.0), maintains a pool of connections from which a connection is drawn when your application asks to establish a new connection—as with the OpenConnection or EstablishConnection methods in RDO. Connections are returned to the pool (but not necessarily disconnected) when you use the Close method. Because not all connections are interchangeable, connections are pooled based on their type and transaction scope. The pool itself is sized dynamically, based on demand and idle connections. By default, if a connection is idle for more than 10 minutes (far too long in my opinion), it is "destroyed." There are rumors that the intelligence of this aspect is expected to increase as the use of this feature broadens. By default, RDO and ODBCDirect *disable* this feature, but you can enable it through API calls.

Personally, I find this kind of connection management a little *too* helpful. For the most part, my applications do just fine managing their connections without having the driver maintain a pool. However, some of the ITG applications written for internal use here at Microsoft do need connection management. The problem for these applications will be how to keep the ODBC Driver Manager's pool manager from kicking sand in their faces.

NOTE If you're designing connections to the Windows NT version of SQL Server, you *should* consider leaving them open. Since the number of connections supported by the Windows NT version can be virtually unlimited, and since these servers can support gigabytes of RAM, a few dozen extra connections are not much of a burden. The amount of overhead involved in opening a connection, closing it, and reopening it later can impose a greater burden than the extra resources the additional connections take.

Microsoft's ITG group implements connection managers for several internal applications, and the concept seems to work quite well. I'm sure if you call, they will be happy to send you the source code. (In your dreams.)

A New Connection's Impact on the Server

SQL Enterprise manager shows the host (workstation) name when you view server activity. You and the system administrator will both find the host name and the application name useful in identifying your connection. That way, you can kill your connection if you need to, or you can identify what resources or locks it is using. In the ODBC *Connect* argument, and in the VBSQL functions that are used for opening connections, you can expose the parameters via the sp_who stored procedure or an sp_who query. But most of the time, I use SQL Enterprise Manager's Current Activity window to see what's going on. *Figure 6-6* shows what will be returned.

Figure 6-6 *Viewing connections in Microsoft SQL Enterprise Manager*

Notice that the application-provided workstation ID (WSID) and application name (APP) values are given along with the current database and which user is connected. What would you use these parameters for? With SysProcedures queries, you could develop an application that kept a current record of who had logged on when and of what the users were doing in general at any given time. For an application like that, it would be especially helpful to have the name of the program spelled out. You might also want to set the Workstation Name string to reflect the current time of logon or additional user-specific information.

Setting the Timeout Value

The default logon timeout value for establishing a connection can vary from 15 seconds to over 60 seconds; the exact value depends on the programming interface you choose and the way you set timeout arguments. This means that if you pass an incorrect or misspelled server name, or if the server is down or otherwise unavailable, you might have to wait for a full minute or longer before control is returned to your application (and the Windows operating system might be blocked for that whole time).

Most SQL servers on a LAN, as opposed to a WAN or RAS, connect in a few seconds. (ODBC connections can take longer to complete, but the initial wait for the server to respond is usually still within 1 to 5 seconds. The *first* time a workstation opens a connection to a server, however, the time for completing the process tends to be longer by 50 percent, even if the application ends and another begins. I can only account for this extra time as LAN overhead that's not needed after the initial connection has been made and after the workstation engine components (including DLLs) have been loaded and initialized. The Windows operating system holds DLLs and EXE files in memory until the space is needed, even when their instance count is reduced to 0, so this may explain the shorter waiting times for subsequent connections.

NOTE   I usually set the login timeout value to about 15 seconds to accommodate fully loaded networks. If you set the login timeout value any higher, users have a tendency to give your application the three-finger salute: Ctrl-Alt-Delete. Perhaps you should use an option flag for those sites that are on remote services and need more time.

Handling Connection Errors

The client/server interface is very much like a conversation between master and servant, with occasional moans or complaints from the servant. These protestations are called *error messages*. Each error message is accompanied by a number and a details string that describes the situation. If you develop your applications at one sitting, without errors, you may put this book down and take your place in the Museum of Living Legends. But every good front-end developer I know spends a great deal of time anticipating errors and the other contingencies of working with a remote server.

Because the various programming interfaces handle errors differently, it's not always clear what the problem is when something goes wrong with a connection. When I'm debugging these problems, I ask my users the following set of questions before attempting to guess what went wrong.

- *Has the application ever connected? If so, what has changed since then?* This tells me whether we're searching for a user-security problem or for a link problem that has affected the network. If the user has been able to get connected in the past, then the likelihood of a setup, security, or net protocol problem is reduced—unless some new application or a new version of the operating system has just been installed. Upgrading drivers can impact connectability.

- *What messages are displayed? What do the modem or net interface lights do?* The messages can lead me in the right direction, or they might only be symptoms of a problem that is masked by other configuration problems. If the modem or net lights are not showing typical traffic, then a problem with the physical link is likely.

- *What were you doing when the application didn't connect?* Was the user using the program in a new way or in some unexpected manner? Is the program current and appropriate for the intended use? Was the program being pushed beyond its limits or beyond the limits of the net? Is the user connected to other net resources? Perhaps too many other applications or net resources are already being used.

- *Did the application handle the error, or did it just crash?* This helps me identify problems that need to be addressed by better error handling on the part of the application.

- *Are the system, modem, and network plugged in*? This seems silly, but I can't tell you how many times the simplest things have made a system malfunction.

Application-Related Problems

Once you discover that something is wrong, you can start looking at your application, if it has just been installed, or at the LAN, if everything was working up to the point when the connection failed. The workstation depends on your application and the operating system, including its LAN software component, to manage client-side resources like RAM and device handles. If these are already stressed or exhausted before you attempt the connection, there is no way to predict how the operating system and your application will resolve the dogfight for the last of the resource scraps.

Problems Caused by Support Libraries

Many problems are caused because dynamic-link libraries and controls are in the wrong places or were not installed on the user's machine in the first place. If the libraries are mismatched or incorrectly installed, there is no way to tell how your application will be affected. I have seen several instances lately of problems that were caused by installing a "newer" version of the ODBC drivers on top of "older" drivers. Remember that the ODBC setup dialog boxes support overriding the version checking—if you really feel brave.

The libraries are in the form of DLL, OCX, VBX, and other files that must be placed where the Windows loader can find them at run time. Most libraries are placed in the WINDOWS\SYSTEM directory by your setup program. In some cases, the components must also be registered in the Windows system registry; your setup program is responsible for this as well. (See the Visual Basic documentation, or search online help for more information.)

On all Windows platforms, the Windows loader behaves the same way when it starts to look for a library. If you understand the loading sequence, you can more easily understand what's going wrong when your application fails to connect or function according to design. When your application is launched by Program Manager, Windows Explorer, File Manager, the File Run command, or any other means, the Windows loader searches for the executable and all its components in the following places and in the following order:

I installed the VBSQL.OCX last year using the early version of PTK setup. Guess what? It didn't copy the required NTWDBLIB.DLL into the WINDOWS\SYSTEM directory. The result? The VBSQL.OCX wouldn't register. Just copy this file over manually—being sure to check the version number as you move it. Remember that these must be a matched set, so get the copy of the OCX and the DLL from the same source.

- *In memory.* If an existing copy of the executable or library is in memory, all Windows has to do is create a new instance of the data segment and provide a pointer to the existing code. The library doesn't have to belong to a running application. It can be sitting in memory from a program that ended hours ago but was not purged because Windows didn't need the RAM. The DLL might be there because it is dead or roadkill—left over from a failed program sometime in the past. You might have to reboot or at least scrape off the corpse with Pview. (See the Visual Basic version 5.0 TOOLS directory.)

- *In the current directory.* If the user is browsing a removable media drive, some networked drive, or a local hard disk, the loader searches whichever drive and directory the user is browsing. If the connection or removable media drive isn't there next time, the loader might not find the library or might load it from some other place further down the search tree. When your application profile resets (or fails to reset) the default directory, the libraries that get loaded or don't can change sporadically.

- *In the WINDOWS and WINDOWS\SYSTEM directories (in that order).* Most DLLs are expected to be located in the WINDOWS\SYSTEM directory, but, as you can see, this is not the first or even second place that the Windows loader searches.

- *In the directories specified by the PATH environment variable, in the order specified.* This is the usual place for applications to install their code if they haven't built proper setup programs. In some cases, they actually munge the PATH environment variable to put their directory high in the list, hoping that it will be searched before other locations. Unfortunately, by the time Windows gets to the PATH, it has already searched many other locations.

Windows reports that the program or library can't be found only when *all* these locations have been searched. Note that if a DLL matching the 8.3 name of the DLL being searched for happens to be in memory or in the current directory, that matching DLL is used *instead* of the version in the WINDOWS\SYSTEM directory, which might be more (or less) current.

When I'm debugging a VBSQL application, the first thing I want to know is whether a matched set of VBSQL libraries is being used. There might be four different versions of a library installed on the user's system, and any one of them might get loaded; it depends on the current directory and the search path of the Windows loader. It seems that several of Microsoft's applications (and those of other vendors) ship a copy of DBNMP3.DLL without the companion W3DBLIB.DLL or VBSQL.VBX. The ODBC libraries use the DBNMP3.DLL to connect their TDS interface to named pipes; since the W3DBLIB.DLL is used only for DB-Library applications, ODBC has no need of it. Unfortunately, however, if these two libraries are installed without the matching support library, the resulting behavior will be unpredictable. Since SQL Server 6.0, the names of these libraries have been changed to eliminate conflict with Sybase SQL Server, but the same rules apply to the replacements. *Figure 6-7* shows the new names. Most SQL Server front ends running on Microsoft networks use named pipes to communicate with the server. To support named pipes, all interfaces use either a 16-bit (DBNMP3.DLL) or 32-bit (DBNMPNTW.DLL) library. Again, your setup application must install this library in the WINDOWS\SYSTEM directory or somewhere else where the Windows loader can find it.

One of the easiest ways to wreck a user's system is to improperly install an application. Since we have long since (OK, not that long) moved away from programs that can be installed with a single floppy by simply copying over a few files, the Setup program and regimen have grown in importance. To make it simple, just follow this advice: never, never *copy* libraries of any kind—or even applications—to the user's system. No, not *anywhere* on the user's system. Always use a program (like Setup) that tests to see whether the libraries being overlaid are already registered or are a more recent version of the code. This is essential.

Figure 6-7
New Names for Libraries

Visual Basic 3.0 and 5.0 VBSQL Library	Visual Basic 4.0 and 5.0 (16-bit)	Visual Basic 4.0 and 5.0 (32-bit)
W3DBLIB.DLL	MSDBLIB3.DLL	NTWDBLIB.DLL
DBNMP3.DLL	DBNMP3.DLL	DBNMPNTW.DLL

LAN-Related Connection Problems

A litany of network-related problems can make connecting difficult, if not impossible. To exacerbate this difficulty, network failures are often masked as other problems, since they are not always reported by specific error messages. Too often, the error reported to and by the user is a generic "could not connect" message. When we add the complication of Internet and WAN variations to these problems, it's no wonder, to me, anyway, that I lost so much hair trying to connect to the network. To debug these situations, I start with the following questions:

- *Has the user logged on to the LAN?* This problem is especially prevalent with security systems that don't require users to log on to the network before using the workstation. If the user bypassed the network logon dialog box when first booting, the only options for getting on the LAN are to log on (in Windows for Workgroups) or shut down all applications and log on as a new user in Windows 95 or Windows NT.

- *Are there enough available file or LAN connections (handles)?* If the user has created too many persistent connections on the workstation (the user might not be using them but hasn't closed them, either), the operating system might not be able to create any more. On some systems, the total number of LAN connections is limited. In general, with the default settings, if a user has more than four or five remote drives connected, the user could have problems connecting to SQL Server. In some cases, you might not be able to connect without mapping to a shared drive on the SQL server.

- *Can the host server support additional users?* It's entirely possible to exceed the limit for LAN users long before the maximum number of SQL connections has been reached. Both Windows NT and SQL Server are sold and licensed in configurations that put a cap on the total number of connections. Once this limit is reached, no additional users are permitted to log on. (This restriction should not apply to a share-level security system, as far as SQL connections are concerned.)

- *Is the LAN down?* Let's say I get a call from a user whose e-mail is down. I explain that the net is down. A few minutes later, the same user calls to report a SQL Server application that is also down for some reason or one that is really slow. At that point, I'll check to see if the bridge to the SQL Server host server is down, and I'll test other shares on the net or on the host server to see if I can still access these.

- *Has an improper share been established for IPC$ (named pipes) on an OS/2 server?* The STARTUP.CMD file on an OS/2 host server must contain a NET SHARE IPC$ statement if LAN Manager is running share-level security. With user-level security, permissions to access the IPC$ share are set on a user-by-user basis by the LAN administrator. A user who does not have permission to share IPC$ is out of luck.

- *Have improper permissions been assigned in user-level security, or is there an invalid LAN configuration?* Perhaps the user does not have permission to access the SQL server.

- *Have you run the new Client Configuration Utility to set the default device drivers and network address of the server?* This is a new requirement introduced when SQL Server began supporting TCP/IP. This utility collects the parameters and addresses needed to connect the user's workstation to the specified server. This is required when you use a TCP/IP-addressed server because it isn't referenced by name.

Just last week a user reported that he couldn't get connected via TCP/IP, and the documentation lacked a degree of clarity on the subject. While I was unable to help much, he did indicate that he had discovered that the problem had to do with missing entries in the WIN.INI file. After some investigation, I discovered that SQL Server 6.0 uses the WIN.INI file to hold the needed parameters for the new TCP/IP drivers. Apparently, these WIN.INI entries are created when you use the SQL Client Configuration Utility on a 16-bit system. See SQL Server Books Online "Setting the Default Net-Library" for details.

SQL Server–Related Connection Problems

If the LAN is functioning properly, the fault might lie with the SQL server itself. To debug these situations, I start by working through the following possible problems and solutions.

- *Did the user enter an improper SQL logon ID or password?* If the logon ID and password are valid, maybe the user doesn't have permission to access this SQL server.

- *Is the server running?* Did the host server include a command to launch SQL Server when the server starts? Check the services list from Control Panel or the STARTUP.CMD batch file. Use SQL Server Manager to see for sure.

- *Did corrupt data prevent the SQL server from starting?* If a running query that is making changes is terminated, there is a chance that the SQL server might be unable to roll back the change and so the database will be marked as suspect. Check the SQL Server error logs.

- *Has the database been improperly restored?* On occasion, when an attempt is made to move or restore a database (or just a table), the permissions, logon IDs, and passwords are not properly restored, or they end up being assigned to the wrong databases.

- *Is there too little disk or RAM space on the host server?* If it depends on local swap or temporary space, and if this space is exhausted, the SQL server might be unable to start.

- *Is the SQL server in single-user mode*? Or maybe the SQL administrator is doing maintenance work.

- *Are your user ID and password on the list for valid users?* Are you in the group of valid users as far as Windows NT is concerned?

- *Has the server been hit by an 80mm mortar round?* You never know.

Errors Related to Connections and Licenses

A SQL server can connect from one to more than a thousand users; the number depends on how many connections have been installed by the SQL administrator—and how many are licensed. Each connection consumes between 37 KB and 42 KB of system RAM, which can be allocated to additional procedures or data cache space. Therefore, the number of connections on any SQL server might be changed by an administrator who is trying to free additional RAM, and a not uncommon error is generated when the SQL server runs out of available connections. Because this is a common problem with limited-access SQL servers, you should always test your application to see how it behaves in these circumstances.

On SQL Server 6.0 systems, the administrator can also set the number of *licenses* that the server supports. Licenses are a new feature and are managed separately from connections. You can easily exhaust all the available licenses before you exhaust the number of logical connections. For example, when you set the maximum number of "connections" to 5, SQL Server 4.2 allows 15 connections before failing to permit another, which is consistent with the understanding that a single application can use several connections (and 3 connections per application should be enough, unless you use a lot of Data controls or cursors). SQL Server 6.0 is somewhat stricter with its connections. If you set a *license* limit to 5, then you get 5 connections, period—regardless of the number of connections that has been set. The error returns a very informative message:

```
Msg:18458 State:1 Sev:14 Login failed- The maximum simultaneous
user count of 5 licenses for this server has been exceeded.
Additional licenses should be obtained and registered via the
Licensing application in the NT Control Panel.
```

An error also occurs if you try to open a connection after the server has allocated its last one. How the error is manifested will be determined by your programming model and the version of SQL Server that is running:

- In SQL Server 1.0 and 1.1, a message indicating that the server has unexpectedly lost the named pipe interface is returned when there are no more connections. This message is technically correct but hardly indicative of the root cause. Apparently, the workstation opens a named pipe to the SQL server. When no more connections are available, SQL Server responds by closing the named pipe at the SQL Server end—thus the "unexpected EOF" error from the server.

- In SQL Server 4.2 (and in the Windows NT version), when the SQL server connection limit has been set to 5 but another front-end application is started, DBLIB reports a SQLEWRIT error message: "Write to SQL Server failed. This error number is unused." With VBSQL applications, DBLIB returns this SQLEWRIT error message but also sends a SQLECONN message (which would indicate some sort of LAN failure).

Because of this ambiguity, you should expect any one of a number of possible error messages when a connection to SQL Server fails.

Logon-Related Problems

In too many cases when an error occurs during an attempted connection to SQL Server, the front-end application merely passes through the error strings returned by the SQL server or the data interface. The user is then confronted with an enlightening message like this one:

"And just what, exactly, *is* an error number 10004?" your user asks you over the phone as you're trying to watch *America's Funniest Home Videos*.

This little gem is generated by a SQL administrative program when a valid server name has not been provided. To decode this message, would it help your user to have *SQL Server Programmer's Reference for Visual Basic,* Appendix B? Not really: the only reference there is to the error SQLECONN, but if the user looked up SQLECONN in the VBSQL.BI that comes from the VBSQL developers and searched for 10004, he or she would be referred right back to SQLECONN. At least the application came right out and said, "Couldn't connect with server." It could have sent back the text supplied by DBLIB: "Unable to connect. SQL Server is unavailable or does not exist." (Actually, this message is much better than the one that goes on to ask whether the user wants to *start* this non-existent server.)

CAUTION

SQLESQLPS, an error code mentioned in the SQL Server Progammer's Toolkit documentation, is supposed to indicate that the maximum number of connections has already been allocated. But this constant isn't defined in VBSQL.BI, nor is it in the DB-Library C documentation. But, hey—what difference does it make? Running out of connections doesn't return this value anyway.

The point is that passing raw error codes and error messages directly to the user generally doesn't suffice. Users already know that something has gone wrong; now they want to know what they can *do* about it. Perhaps they simply need to be patient and wait a little longer. Maybe they should send e-mail to the person in charge of the server—and maybe your application could do that automatically. In fact, the more information I give the *application* about what to do automatically when things go wrong, the fewer calls I get during my favorite TV programs. And the more information I give the *user* about corrective options or things to check for, the better. That way, the user can check his or her own system with some degree of intelligence, and the tech-support people dragged away from *their* television sets will have more of a clue about how to correct the problem. In any case, the user should not be presented with a cryptic error message or an hourglass cursor that won't go away.

So, what can you do for the user when an attempted connection to SQL Server fails? You can make sure your application has a fallback plan for each of several contingencies. One of the more successful fallback plans I have used involves the use of INI files. If the OS/2 host name is recorded in WIN.INI, a replacement server can be specified more easily (say, when the original server is being repaired, or at other times, as necessary).

When I create a general-purpose query utility that an entire group has access to, the application often does not require a user ID or password. With this method, it is more important to limit access to the SQL server, physically and logically, by limiting access to the LAN and to the room where the server is maintained. I do this through the LAN user-level or domain permissions scheme. In this case, the application uses a logon name that is known only to the developer (me), the application (where it is hard-coded), and the SQL administrator. The user must gain access to the application EXE and the SQL Server IPC$ by entering a valid domain user name and password. Since the application cannot be used to gain access to any but the hard-coded tables and queries specified by the application, the chances of losing data integrity are no greater than if the user had logged on with a specific SQL user ID. Nevertheless, this method does make the fact that SQL operations are taking place totally obvious to the user.

7 Chapter

Designing and Building Queries

Types of Queries

Designing Queries for Performance

Building Queries

Query-Related Error Messages

Once your application is connected to SQL Server, your next task is to send a query. Like a dutiful but often over-zealous servant, SQL Server does its best to give you whatever you ask for. If your query demands 100,000 rows, the server does what is necessary to deliver every last one of them to you. It might take hours, consume every bit of hard disk space on your client system, and bring the server and the net to their knees, but SQL Server assumes you know what you're doing. This chapter is about making sure that you do.

Types of Queries

Queries are of two types: *select* queries, which might return data rows, and *action* queries, which contain one or more Transact-SQL (TSQL) commands that update data, insert and delete data, execute data definition language (DDL) operations, or simply run maintenance operations. A select query always contains at least one SQL SELECT statement. An action query can contain any TSQL statement, including code to invoke a SQL utility like DBCC (Database Consistency Checker). I lied. Some queries can also be composites of select and action operations, but these are really *batches* and must be treated differently.

In general, select and action queries are handled differently because the programming interface (such as RDO or DAO) is expected to manage the data rows resulting from a select query. Some programming interfaces let you send either type of query almost without restriction. Others generate trappable errors if you use the wrong method or the wrong function to execute a row-returning query.

More often than not, a single query is used repeatedly throughout a program. A query might be created and stored in workstation RAM or in an MDB database. You can also define and keep queries on the SQL server as stored procedures, and it's possible to create your own repository of queries on disk, calling them up as required for execution. Stored queries can be either select or action queries. With Visual Basic version 5.0, you can now create a UserConnection object, which can define queries that you write or can act as an intermediary to stored procedures. But since the UserConnection Designer works only with RDO, I'll defer talk about it until later.

A query can contain as many SQL statements as needed, and it can combine statements that return rows with those that perform an action. Sometimes a query generates multiple sets of results—that is, a single query might return rows from several select queries, followed by the result set from one or more action queries, followed by the return rows from one or more select statements, in any combination. The TSQL documentation refers to this type of query as a *batch* (and recall, as I mentioned in Chapter 4, that a set of batches is called a *script)*. Batches can be difficult to manage, but they can also improve performance, and they provide a mechanism for logically binding related operations. Handling a query that generates multiple result sets is a little tricky, so each programming interface takes a different approach, and we'll cover those in the relevant sections of this guide.

Designing Queries for Performance

Your application's overall performance is judged by how quickly it fetches data, and the way you phrase queries can have a significant impact on the work that the interface and the server are required to do. The harder you make the system work, the longer it takes to retrieve your data. As you design your queries, keep the following points in mind:

- *Make sure your query returns only the rows needed in the immediate situation.* In a user-interactive front end, there is usually no need to return more than a few hundred rows at a time.

- *Return only the columns that are needed.* Never use the * operator to return all columns from the tables involved in a query unless you really need *all* the columns. If you accidentally select a Text or Image column, performance can be adversely affected. By the same token, update only those columns that have changed. Each column might have a separate rule, and update trigger processing is always complicated when you update columns unnecessarily. Each column you reference in the query means more overhead on the server, more data to transmit over the net, and more overhead on the workstation—whether or not you ever touch the data. Normalization can help this.

- *Given the power of SQL Server and TSQL logic, you now have fewer good reasons for bringing rows to the workstation for updating.* With ISAM database systems, bringing each row to the workstation was considered a basic part of application design. In client/server systems, however, it's no longer necessary to bring each row to the workstation, update it, and send it back to the server. Bulk operation TSQL UPDATE statements or stored procedures can do this for you—and far faster.

- *Whenever possible, use stored parameter queries.* RDO will automatically create a stored procedure for most queries (unless you tell it not to), but this doesn't help performance if the make procedure operation is repeated every time. You can help make this faster by creating rdoQuery or QueryDef objects or by using the UserConnection Designer to create UserConnection objects to which you pass parameters as needed.

- *Use stored procedures whenever possible.* Most MIS shops insist on gating access to base tables through SQL views or stored procedures that restrict access to specific operations and users. Stored procedures can also help improve performance, since they don't have to be compiled each time they are used and they often can be executed directly from the procedure cache. Any query that can be written in the form of a stored procedure should be written that way, even if it takes a number of parameters.

- *If at all possible, avoid using cursors.* But if you think that you must use cursors, try read-only, forward-only, single-row *cursorless* result sets first. In any case, use the cheapest cursor possible and the smallest number of rows.

- *Don't ask for an updatable connection or result set if you don't plan to update the data.* Don't send a ship when a rowboat will do.

- *Don't create a scrollable cursor.* If you don't intend to move to random rows in the result set, you don't need a scrollable cursor.

- *Limit the scope of your queries, especially update queries, when there are other interactive users on line.* In my mainframe days, we never performed global database management operations during the day, when the data entry crew was using the system. All bulk processing was deferred to the swing and graveyard shifts, when the system could be dedicated to backup, bulk insert, and delete operations, as well as to nightly maintenance. That way, the interactive users were not affected by our heavy use of the system, and the constant changes being made by the users did not upset our reports and audits.

- *Multiply the effect of each operation by the number of other users performing the same operation at the same time.* Each query consumes workstation and server-side RAM and disk space, including database pages, procedure and data queue pages, and CPU time on both ends of the wire. Although each query carries a measurable startup overhead, it's easier for the server to manage queries that can be executed quickly than it is for the server to manage larger, more data-intensive queries.

- *Making a subset of the data to query against can often improve performance dramatically.* For example, when I need to look up valid help context IDs, I must execute a complex query that joins three tables and produces a single-row result set. Normally, this query would take about 2 seconds to execute, which wouldn't be a problem if only one query were being executed. But this query is executed by an unattended Microsoft Word for Windows macro, which performs the query for each hidden word in the document, so 2 seconds per word is a long time. To make this query faster, I create a temporary table the first time the macro is called. This table is a result set product that contains just the rows for the section I am working on. Next, I create an index on the temporary table, using the desired help context ID column as the key. After that, each query is a simple key-based lookup, and query response time drops to .02 second or less.

- *Avoid using multiple UPDATE statements in a batch.* By combining update operations, you can improve performance but you also complicate error recovery and database integrity—that is, unless you use the optimistic batch update feature of RDO 2.0. This new interface manages the errors and collisions for you, making this type of operation less painful.

- *Consider the use of remote business objects.* Now that Visual Basic can create compiled ActiveX executables and Microsoft Transaction Server can be used to manage these remote server-side objects, the practicality of implementing a DCOM interface to your data is more realistic than ever.

- *Remember that data retrieved from the server begins to get stale the instant it arrives at the workstation.* This is especially true in systems where multiple users are constantly changing the data. When you execute a query, you're essentially taking a snapshot of the data at a particular point in time. Using a cursor gives you a window on the underlying data, but what the user sees and what is buffered in memory doesn't refresh itself. Unless you are using a dynamic cursor, membership of the cursor might be fixed until the cursor is rebuilt. And no, I'm not recommending dynamic cursors; they're just too expensive.

- *Never, never create a situation in which the user can open a row for editing and then walk away from the system or otherwise hold the row for an extended period.* It's really very easy to create a situation like this when you use the pessimistic schemes that lock the data (pages) the instant the Edit method is invoked and keep it locked until the data is committed with the Update method. Either use the optimistic locking option or prohibit intervention of the code between the Edit and Update methods.

CAUTION

Because of the interactive nature of SQL Server, you can't be completely sure about whether a hard-coded query submitted to the server is syntactically correct or exactly how many result sets will be generated by the query. I find it easiest to develop queries one piece at a time, letting the code loop through the statement until the syntax is correct for each case, especially when queries are generated on the fly. Step into the code line by line in Visual Basic by using the F8 key.

Building Queries

You can find any number of ways to come up with the right SQL query to perform the task at hand. More and more GUI interfaces do chores that not only make it easier for you to build SQL statements but also encourage standards and optimal techniques. This means that when you drag a couple of related tables to one of these tools' query windows, a correctly phrased JOIN statement is generated—regardless of the back end you are accessing. This means you make fewer mistakes and build better performing queries the first time. Frankly, I prefer these applications to write my joins for me. They are, at least, a good starting point. I like to take what they create and add my own subtleties to the query to get the right combination of criteria and functionality.

The following sections walk through the SQL generators provided in Visual Basic 5.0 (in the Enterprise Edition) as well as several techniques that you will need when you try to roll these queries yourself or tinker with the ones generated by the GUI tools.

Using Microsoft Query and Visual Database Tools

I used to tell everyone that I didn't like to figure out the nuances of Jet SQL syntax, so I would use Microsoft Access to build the query for me. The problem wasn't cured by SQL Server switching to an ANSI-like syntax for TSQL because the JOIN syntax is every bit as complicated as Jet's (albeit similar). But now Visual Basic version 5.0 has two new ways to help develop queries interactively: Microsoft Visual Database Tools (VDT) and Microsoft Query. The rub? They come only in the Visual Basic version 5.0 Enterprise Edition or Microsoft Developer Studio boxes. If you haven't done it already, now would be a great time to install these.

Microsoft Query

When you fire up the UserConnection Designer (by choosing Add ActiveX Designer from the Project menu), it helps you build a new UserConnection object (UCO). A UCO is a prestuffed class that contains all the code needed to open a connection against a back-end RDO data source and expose all or a selected set of the data source's stored procedures. You can also create your own queries using Microsoft Query by clicking the Build button in the Query Properties dialog box. I won't go into the nuances of creating a query this way because I found that the VDT tools were far more sophisticated (but not as closely integrated).

Visual Database Tools

Microsoft Visual Database Tools is far more than a set of interactive graphical query design tools. It also includes a way to manage your database schema and structure. While it is beyond the scope of this guide to get into these features, they are useful, and they are well documented elsewhere. Be sure to check out VDT's ability to change a table's definition—yes, it can even automatically change the data type or data length of a column of an existing SQL Server table (with or without data).

VDT comes in really handy when you need to develop a query against an ODBC back end. It is designed to work against a variety of back ends—including SQL Server (natch). VDT uses a GUI interface to let you "draw" queries very much the way Microsoft Access does. The real (neat) difference is that you can see all four phases of the operation at once, as shown in a typical query development window:

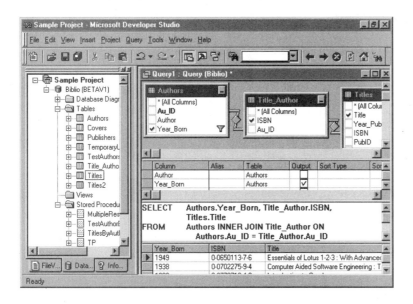

TIP Generally, you have to launch VDT from within a Visual Basic design session. It doesn't show up on the external menus—at least it didn't for me. You might also hunt around for the Developer Studio executable MSDEV.EXE, which should launch the stand-alone version of VDT.

Basically, it works like this:

1. Launch VDT from Visual Basic. Notice that it comes up saying it's "Visual Studio 97."

2. Choose New Project from the File menu. I named mine *Test Pubs*.

3. Select or create a DSN to point to the *Pubs* (or your) server and database.

4. Enter the login name and password to gain access to the server. I usually blank out the user ID because I use integrated security. Click the Options button if you aren't sure the right database is selected.

5. If VDT logs you on, you can go on. Otherwise, you need to work out the connection problems first. If it works, you will see, once you choose the Data View tab at the bottom of the dialog box, the screen shown at the top of the following page.

6. I clicked "pubs (BETAV1)" and then Tables so that all of the underlying *Pubs* tables were exposed.

7. Double-click one of the tables. I chose the *Titles* table, as you see here:

At this point, the Query toolbar is exposed along with a grid containing the first 500 rows of the chosen table. This 500-row limit is set by using the Options dialog box. I clicked all of the Window option buttons on the Query toolbar to show all four query design windows.

8. Next, I dragged the *TitleAuthor* and *Authors* table icons over from the left pane into the top window of the query designer. VDT figured out the relationships and painted appropriate connective tissue.

9. When I clicked the ! on the Query toolbar, the query I developed was executed and the resulting rows appeared in the bottom results window. Neat, huh?

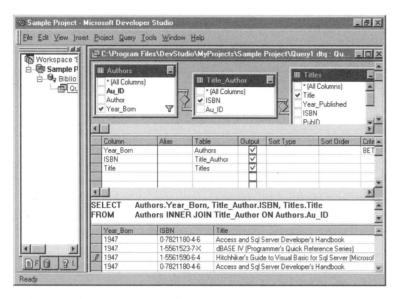

10. When you are ready to save the query, you can easily use VDT to build and save your query as a stored procedure.

Remember that most sites require you to work exclusively with stored procedures, so your SA might not have exposed the root tables for you.

Doing It by Hand

If you need to tune the queries built by Microsoft Access or Visual Database Tools or simply write your own queries, here are a few hints and techniques to make this a more positive experience.

It is somewhat unusual to ask your server the same question over and over, but it's not unusual to ask *almost* the same question repeatedly, with subtle variations. Here's what I mean:

```
Select * From Authors Where City = 'Detroit'
```

and

```
Select * From Authors Where City = 'Redmond'
```

In general, either queries are created on the fly, when SQL statements are concatenated with arguments generated by the user, or they're specially written parameter queries that depend on the interface to fill in the missing arguments.

In concatenation, which I use quite a bit, the program logic takes a fixed SQL statement and substitutes values in the WHERE clause to return a known set of columns. For example, if I want to query a database on farm animals to return information about all pig-type animals over the age of four, the code for performing the query will look like this:

```
SQL$ = "SELECT Name From Animals" _     ' This does not change
& " WHERE AnimalType = '" _     ' Nor does this
& TypeWanted & "'" _          ' Substitute variables
& " AND AGE > " & AgeWanted
```

I think that the VDT is far cleaner and much more closely integrated with Visual Basic than Microsoft Access is.

The *TypeWanted* and *AgeWanted* variables will be supplied by the user or the program logic—in the case of my query, *TypeWanted* = "PIG" and *AgeWanted* = 4. All of this code is executed each time the query is used. This also means that the query must be syntax-checked and compiled by the SQL server, by the Jet query processor, or by the ODBC layers each time the query is executed.

TIP When building concatenated queries, be sure to separate arguments and parameters with white space. TSQL syntax ignores all white space but doesn't tolerate a query that incorrectly jams two arguments together. You must also surround dates and quoted strings with quotes—usually single quotes.

Quote Management

One of the most challenging parts of creating a concatenated query is managing quotes. Fortunately, the ODBC interfaces know how to handle quoted parameters, so this should not be a problem—at least the chore of adding framing quotes should not be a problem. But you still have to make sure that the strings you pass as parameters don't contain single quotes.

SQL Server 4.*x* and earlier versions expect TSQL string arguments to be surrounded with quotes, either single ('MyString') or double ("MyString"), as long as they are used in matching pairs. Not all TSQL variables require quotes, however. In TSQL queries, only dates and strings must be quote-delineated. All other kinds of numbers are simply surrounded by white space or commas.

SQL Server 6.0 added support for quoted identifiers. According to ANSI syntax, you need to use double quotation marks (") to delimit keywords (quoted identifiers) and single quotation marks (') to delimit string constants. This requirement resolves the conflict with quoted identifiers and string constants during expression evaluation at the parser level and is included to provide ANSI compatibility for delimited identifiers. Additionally, although the practice is not recommended, keywords specified within double quotation marks can now be used as object names. If you want your object names to use keywords, reserved words, database technology terms, or names that could cause conflict with future keywords, first attempt to resolve possible conflicts by choosing another word for the object name. When this isn't possible, use quoted identifiers—in other words, surround the keywords in double quotes. These quoted identifiers can contain as many as 30 characters. The delimited string can contain any combination of characters represented by the current code page, except double quotation marks.

To enforce or remove quoted identifier and string constant resolution at the session level (for each connection), use the SET statement. This causes the current session to differentiate between single and double quotation marks when evaluating an expression. When QUOTED_IDENTIFIER is turned on, strings in double quotation marks (") won't be evaluated or checked against keywords. When you use keywords for object names or portions of object names, the QUOTED_IDENTIFIER option *must* be set when creating that object, as well as when accessing that object.

> **NOTE** If an object name or part of an object name (for example, a column) is created using a keyword when the QUOTED_IDENTIFIER option is turned on, then all subsequent references to that object must be made with the QUOTED_IDENTIFIER option on. In general, it's best to avoid using keywords as object names.

When you're qualifying a column name and a table name in the same statement, be sure to use the same qualifying expressions for each; they are evaluated as strings and must match or an error is returned.

Basically, SQL Server 6.0 (and good programming practice) expects you to use *only* single quotes to delineate strings and dates. This isn't so hard to do until you come across a string with an embedded single quote. For example, the last name *O'Hara* poses a problem if you attempt to delineate this string in single quotes. How is the SQL parser to know where the string ends and the SQL syntax starts? It's tempting to use single quotes to delineate TSQL strings because Visual Basic prefers double quotes to delineate string expressions, and it uses single quotes to start comments.

> **NOTE** Jet SQL statements require that dates be quoted and surrounded with the pound (#) symbol: "#12/31/95#". TSQL simply requires single quotes.

I usually write string-concatenating routines that contain a quote on either side of TSQL string and date variables, as shown in the farm-animal example. When you concatenate a string already containing an embedded quote that matches your delineator, Visual Basic dutifully passes it on to SQL Server, but when the string arrives at the server, the query fails the syntax check because of unbalanced quotes. A number of solutions have been proposed, most of them somewhat messy—but that's why developers get the big bucks:

- *Replace all embedded single quotes with two single quotes.* For example, *O'Hara* becomes *O''Hara*. This is the method I prefer and use most often.

- *Quietly replace the single quote with another character before it is sent to the server, and then resubstitute the single quote when the data is presented to the user.* The problem with this approach is that it upsets the collating sequence and makes searching more complex. More important, every program that references the data must decrypt the quote substitutes.

- *Switch to double-quote instead of single-quote delimiters.* This solution makes the Visual Basic concatenation of strings a little tougher but not impossible. It can lead to problems with strings containing double quotes, but names generally don't contain double quotes. This approach requires you to set the SQL Server Quote Identifier option to double quote (").

- *Work with Text data types instead of VarChar or Char data types.* In this case, data is passed to the SQL server without the use of concatenated strings. The downside is that Text data types for small strings are expensive to store.

As a last resort, you can work through the courts to get all the O'Haras in your database to change their names, and eliminate embedded quotes that way.

NOTE When you're working with double quotes, don't forget about using CHR$(34) (or some variable set to this value) as a substitute for a double quote or CHR$(39) (or some variable set to this value) as a substitute for a single quote. If you need to embed double quotes, simply double up the quotes: "< >"< >"< >"

Parameter Queries

All the programming interfaces support at least one type of operation in which you predefine a query and then use special syntax or object properties to bind the parameters to the query at run time. Although VBSQL doesn't directly support this kind of query, there is nothing to stop you from either implementing it in code (which would take about 10 lines) or using stored procedures that can provide the same functionality. The advantage of a parameter query is that the query is precompiled (in the form of a stored procedure or a DAO/Jet QueryDef) and an execution plan is stored on the server for repeated use. For complex queries, or for those that are executed frequently, a parameter query can save a significant amount of time.

An advantage of using parameter queries with any of the ODBC interfaces (including RDO and ODBCDirect) is that string delineation is handled automatically. With ODBC, strings are managed by the ODBC driver and driver manager, so there is no need to add additional quotes around the strings. And to create my farm-animal query with the RDO interface, I simply substitute ? in the SQL statement for each parameter to be supplied at run time and create an rdoQuery object, as follows. (Note that I don't need to surround the ? parameter placeholder with delineators.)

```
Dim Qy As rdoQuery
SQL$ = "SELECT * From Animals" _          ' This does not change
  & " WHERE AnimalType = ? and AGE > ?"
```

```
Set Qy = cn.Query("PickAnimal", SQL$)
Qy(0) = TypeWanted
Qy(1) = AgeWanted
⋮
```

In this case, the application can set the SQL statement once, create the rdoQuery object, and execute the query. If I need to run the query again, I simply set the rdoParameter values to the new values and use the Requery method to automatically substitute the current parameters into the query and reexecute the code.

NOTE The *Qy(0)* notation references the rdoParameters collection of the rdoQuery object.

Does it make sense for your application to use this type of parameter query? Sure, in some cases. In most shops, however, it's far more sensible to create stored procedures on the SQL server that define all the normally executed procedures. This approach simplifies your application and improves overall system performance. When you're using the RDO or ODBC interfaces, passing parameters to and from stored procedures is simplified through use of the UserConnection Designer.

Overlapping Queries

One of the limitations of SQL Server 4.2 is its inability to manage more than one operation on a connection. When you open a connection and submit a query for processing, you *must* process all the rows resulting from the query before you can submit another. To get around this problem, you can open an additional connection and create a separate query context that is independent of the first.

SQL Server 6.0 introduced server-side cursors, which enables you to create a cursor and immediately (well, almost) turn around and perform other operations on the same connection—once the keyset is built. This is possible because the keyset has already been populated and is being managed by SQL Server on the server, not on your workstation. What is really going on is a little shell game with concurrency. Basically, when you create a synchronous server-side cursor, control doesn't return to your application until the cursor is created and fully populated. If you choose asynchronous mode, you must wait until StillExecuting has changed to False or the QueryComplete event fires before proceeding. While this might seem like a subtle difference, it can make it far easier to use a single connection to perform multiple operations.

When you're using Jet/DAO, Jet's connection manager attempts to share the first connection as you open the second, which prevents operations on either connection until the first result set is fully populated. In this case, you *must* execute a MoveLast method or find another way to position the current-row pointer past the end of the result set. Jet 2.5 performs the MoveLast operation for you, but this means that your workstation is locked until the last row is processed, whether you want it or not.

While SQL Server 6.0 does permit multiple operations if you use server-side cursors, Jet/DAO doesn't attempt to use server-side cursors, and it can't share the connection with another result set. When you're using any of the other interfaces, you have to use SQL Server 6.x server-side cursors before attempting to share a connection, or you simply have to open another connection.

Allowing a text box to be exposed so that its contents can be accepted as a valid query is especially dangerous—it's what I call an *employment longevity–limiting* error. For this reason, I have not written a single production application that permits totally ad hoc queries.

Ad Hoc Queries

An ad hoc query is a user-defined SQL statement, and you might feel the need to permit such queries in your application. Microsoft ISQLW and the query manager window in SQL Server 6.x Enterprise Manager applications permit the user to create and execute ad hoc queries. Microsoft Visual Database Tools, Microsoft Access, and Microsoft Query also permit this type of query, and they provide a slick user interface for generating desired SQL statements. Many of my applications permit the user to choose from a wide selection of options that generate virtually infinite combinations of SQL statements—but the resulting SQL statements are carefully designed, and they have been screened to prevent the user from entering random UPDATE, DELETE, DROP, and other destructive SQL statements; the only available TSQL options are chosen from a menu. Yes, the user can create queries that bring the server to its knees—but this adverse effect is limited by carefully designed timeout and row-count governors.

Multiple Result Set Queries

Some situations call for the creation and execution of related sets of SQL statements that perform a number of steps before completion. For example, you might submit a query containing several SELECT statements and a few UPDATE and INSERT statements, which are followed by a couple of additional SELECT statements. This approach is very typical of the kind of code executed by stored procedures. Your code might be interested in only the final result set, but the data interface must be designed to deal with all result sets generated by a query, batch, or script. *Each* statement in a batch returns a result set, regardless of the type of statement. Only SELECT statements return rows, but each TSQL statement returns a result set that the data interface and your application *must* acknowledge. How each of the programming models handles multiple result sets is discussed in the sections of this guide devoted to the respective models. Keep in mind that some cursor libraries don't know how to build scrollable cursors on this type of query.

NOTE While it's necessary to deal with all of the result sets generated by a query, you can disable quite a bit of background "noise" generated when you're calling stored procedures, including when trigger code is running. For a more detailed explanation of what's going on and an explanation of a problem with this, see Knowledge Base article Q113674, *"INF: -T3640 Flag May Block Updates to an ODBC Application."* Basically, each time a statement in a stored procedure is completed, the server sends a DONE_IN_PROC token to the client. (These are buffered until the network packet is full.) If you have a loop in your procedure, you can guess how this can add up. The 3640 trace flag (or NOCOUNT option) turns off the generation of the token and can decrease LAN (or WAN) traffic considerably. The 3640 trace flag sets the behavior for the whole server as a default. If you think you might run into this situation, instead of using the 3640 trace flag, use the SET NOCOUNT ON statement at the start of your stored procedure and you will get the same effect.

Asynchronous Queries

Queries can take milliseconds to complete, or they can take hours—especially action queries or complex select queries that involve large numbers of rows. If you don't use an asynchronous option, Visual Basic will block until the query returns its first row or the result set is fully populated. *Figure 7-1* shows how the various programming models support asynchronous operations. Visual Basic version 5.0 supports asynchronous operations better than ever. In addition, you don't have to poll for completion as required in Visual Basic version 4.0—just catch the event that fires when the operation is complete.

Figure 7-1
Support for Asynchronous Queries

Programming Model	Support for Asynchronous Queries	Event Notification
Jet/DAO[1]	None; all DAO access blocked until query is completed	None
ODBCDirect	dbRunAsync option on Execute, OpenRecordset, MoveLast methods	None
RDO	rdAsyncEnable option on Establish-Connection, OpenConnection, Requery, MoveLast, Execute, and OpenResultset methods	All synchronous operations
ODBC	SQL_ASYNC_ENABLE as SQLSetStmtOption	None
VBSQL	SQLSend, SQLReady, SQLOk functions	Only on errors and messages

1. The Jet database engine used with the Data control supports limited background population as well as control-break termination.

You should be concerned with a basic problem here—how to prevent Visual Basic from blocking while these operations occur:

- The connection is being opened.

- The result set is being created or re-created with the Requery method.

- You move to the last row to repopulate your result set with the MoveLast method.

- You subsequently move the current record pointer.

Let's take a closer look at these events.

As *Figure 7-1* shows, all the models except DAO/Jet support some kind of mechanism for preventing lockups while the result set is being created. With Visual Basic version 4.0, either your application's data interface is notified when the first row is ready or the application polls constantly to see whether the first row is ready. And therein lies one of the problems: if your application polls too frequently, the server takes longer to complete processing of the query, like a cook checking the oven every 10 seconds to see if the TV dinner is done. (It isn't, because the oven temperature never gets above 110 degrees.) When you use an asynchronous option, control is returned to your application immediately after you request the operation—dinner isn't ready yet, but it's in the microwave and the clock is running. It's your responsibility to check for completion of the operation before using the results. Wouldn't it be nice if you got an event when the operation completed—something like the "ding" from your microwave? Well, there's good news. For the first time ever, Visual Basic supports a robust and easily programmable event model. However, only RDO supports these events. ODBCDirect does *not* support them. This means that you don't need to (actually you really shouldn't) poll the StillExecuting or StillConnecting properties to see if the asynchronous operation is complete.

NOTE In a 16-bit Windows environment, there is no support for preemptive multitasking, so the entire environment is locked while a blocked component (like Jet) waits for something to complete. In 32-bit Windows environments, only the current application is blocked and then only if you use the synchronous option.

What *are* you allowed to do while the query engine is running? Well, even though you can't use the connection for other data access operations, you can open additional connections and run other queries on all the interfaces except DAO/Jet. You can also complete population on other result sets from other connections—or you can launch *Myst* while you wait and try to figure out how to open the sea chest at the bottom of the pump-tower pit.

Counting Your Rows

I don't know how many times I have been asked, "How can I tell how many rows are going to result from the query?" Developers often ask this question because they want to build an array or initialize a grid to hold the rows or simply display a status bar to indicate the progress being made to fetch the rows. The problem is that SQL Server *does not know* how many rows will result from your query—it doesn't know until the result set is fully populated, *after* the query has been completed. It's like asking a farmer how many eggs he will be collecting in the morning. He has no way of knowing until he leaves the barn.

"Well," you say, "Access seems to know because it shows a progress bar that shows how far it has proceeded for any specific query." While it's true that Access shows a status bar, it's not true that it knows how many rows are going to result from a complex query—especially against an ODBC database. What that Access progress bar is really showing is *progress*. That's it—just that Access is still working on the query. Yes, you see a number down there, but it is an educated guess at the percentage of work done—just a guess. Ever notice what it does when it starts approaching 60 percent? It slows down. Until you get control back from testing the RowCount or RecordCount properties after having done a MoveLast in RDO or DAO, there's no way of knowing how many rows have been found.

Setting Query Timeout

When you execute a query, it might take milliseconds or hours for the first row to be returned. Even if you are using one of the asynchronous modes, you need to set a reasonable upper limit on the time the query should be permitted to run. Using past history as a benchmark, set the query timeout to a value roughly two to three times longer than the query should take—but not much longer than that. For example, with a query that normally takes 30 seconds to run, I set the timeout at 90 seconds. I've found that some updates take considerably longer to execute than others. I speculate that if the SQL server must create another allocation unit to complete the operation, the query can take considerably longer.

Only VBSQL and RDO permit you to tell the SQL server to continue working on a query that has timed out. With the other interfaces, the query has been canceled by the time you get the timeout error. If you are using VBSQL or RDO (in Visual Basic version 5.0), you can set the timeout value to a fairly low number—expecting a timeout error. Once it fires, you can give the user an opportunity to either cancel the operation or keep the server working on the solution.

Query-Related Error Messages

What should the user see when a query returns an error message? That's up to you and your application. In some rare cases, it makes sense to display the message string with a MsgBox function. In other cases, messages can be ignored. Keep in mind that a single query can return a whole laundry list of errors and messages. All of the interfaces provide a way to see all of these errors in the order in which they appear. For example, in RDO you need to check all of the rdoError objects in the rdoErrors collection. The first message you see can be a generic something-went-wrong message that is not particularly descriptive. The real reason is kept in the error-message collection.

Some errors, generally caused by the user, are simply the results of incorrect query syntax. Others might signal the death of the query, the net, the connection, or of the server itself. Your code needs to be cognizant of what was being attempted when the error occurred—it needs to know. An error usually means that the query is dead and cannot be resurrected. But sometimes it means that the LAN or the WAN is too busy to get the job done.

When you're working in Visual Basic's Design mode and a query's syntax fails to pass muster, you can change the query string and then reexecute the query by changing the current Visual Basic statement (what I still call the *instruction pointer*) to rerun a section of code. You can also use this feature to examine the properties of the returned data. For example, you can ask the data interface if any rows were returned (unfortunately, it won't tell you how many are in the result set), and for each of those rows, the data interface can be queried for the content and description of the columns. Select the appropriate line of code, and press Ctrl-F9 to reset the next statement to execute.

Virtually all the data access methods, properties, and API functions can be executed interactively in the Debug window. For example, you can open additional connections, submit queries, perform administrative work (like dropping tables or changing permissions), or clear result sets simply by executing the code from the Debug window. I encourage you to use this feature to work yourself out of problems at design time.

I have made an interesting discovery about users' willingness to wait for a computer to complete an operation: they are generally willing to wait *as long as there is activity*. If they see the gears moving in the background, they assume that the system is doing the best it can and eventually will finish. But as the waiting period approaches 62.7 seconds, the number of users who will reboot the system approaches 98.7 percent—and not all users are this patient.

TIP One of the oldest available aids to Visual Basic developers is the Windows help file. Visual Basic 5.0 integrates the help file as no other version has done before and makes it easier than ever to use. Because virtually all controls now support help linkages, I encourage you to develop your own application help file so that users can simply press F1 when they get into trouble.

8
Chapter

Retrieving Data and Working with Result Sets

Using Single-Row Result Sets

Using Cursors

Updating and Inserting Data

Much of the early part of in this chapter refers to *populating* result sets. To be sure this term is clearly understood, let's take a close look now at this phenomenon.

When you execute a query that creates a cursor, the cursor keys (or the actual rows selected) are recorded so that the system and your application can refer to them later. The process of populating keyset cursors involves creating a pointer or bookmark for each row that qualifies for inclusion in the result set. These pointers are transmitted back to the client over the net unless you use a server-side cursor, in which case they are stored on the server in TempDB. As population proceeds, more rows are added to the result set until all qualifying rows have been located and added. Once this process is completed, the cursor is considered to be "fully populated."

Let's say your query is finally ready to return the first row of data. Now what? At this point, at least one row of the result set is ready to process. In some cases, the result set will be fully populated, so your application won't have to wait again while the result set data or keys are moved to the workstation. But if your result set isn't populated beyond the first row (or buffer), your application might block each time you move the row pointer to another row in the result set.

Generally, it doesn't take long to fetch a single additional row, as when you use the MoveNext method. But if you end up having to move to the last row in the result set, or beyond the scope of the buffer, your application will block again while the data interface finishes populating the result set. This can take quite a while for a large result set. Fortunately, RDO and ODBCDirect support asynchronous operations on the MoveLast method, so your application no longer has to wait. Well, you still have to wait, but your application is no longer blocked while the result set is being fully populated. This is another argument for smaller result sets.

Using Single-Row Result Sets

A cursor can be overkill for many query operations, so cursors shouldn't be used unless they are necessary. Personally, I prefer the simplicity and speed of a single-row, forward-only result set, since it's the fastest way to get rows back. In many cases, I don't intend to change the rows that have been fetched, and most applications for decision support and reporting are designed to extract data, not update it, so the extra overhead that the interface adds for supporting updates just goes to waste. The single-row, cursorless result set is ideal for these applications. Single-row result sets are also useful for fetching the final results from a complex query—one that might return only a single value. I expect this is the type of result set used to fetch the answer for the famous ultimate question about life, the universe, and everything—since the answer was "42."

NOTE Most of the interfaces support at least one type of cursorless result set that minimizes the impact on workstation RAM and disk space. Jet supports a forward-only, read-write option but still creates a keyset or snapshot-type Recordset cursor to implement it. The default result set in VBSQL is a forward-only, single-row result set. This is similar to the default ODBC API result set, where only one row is available at any one time—both RDO and ODBCDirect expose this type of result set. VBSQL provides no mechanism for directly updating its cursorless result set rows, whereas the ODBC and RDO interfaces support forward-only, read-write result sets, though at a slightly higher cost. But VBSQL does support Browse-mode queries that permit updates via a separate connection.

When a user working with a Windows application wants to see more than just a single row at a time, the application can fill a Grid control with the set of rows that meets the user's requirements. For example, an order-entry system might support a form containing information about a specific customer, with a detailed form underneath the first form, that contains order-item rows, as shown in the illustration on the following page.

In this case, using a single-row query to fetch a small buffered result set might make sense. Even if the chosen data is to be updated, a separate query using the Customer key and (possibly) a second connection can take care of the necessary changes. The details of the order information on this specific customer can be fetched with a limited-scope updatable cursor.

Remember that even though you specify a simple, cursorless result set, you can always update the underlying data—assuming you have permission to do so—by issuing an update action query. Invariably, this requires a separate connection unless you cancel the current row-fetch operation on the first connection.

Using Cursors

Any cursor, regardless of its type, exposes only one row of the result set at a time. Each of the programming models permits movement of the current-row pointer to other rows in the cursor, but when you're using one of the forward-only cursors, you will probably be limited to the MoveNext method. You won't be able to use the MoveLast method on forward-only cursors. Why would you want to? Since you can see only the current row at any one time, moving to the last row would serve only to throw away all rows from the current row to the last—with no chance at seeing the rows in between. If this is your intent, simply use the Close method.

After a cursor has been created, you can use a variety of techniques for moving the current-row pointer to one of the other rows in the result set. All of our programming models use somewhat different techniques, and these are discussed in the remaining parts of this guide. With the current-row pointer positioned to a row, you can change the data in the base table—if and *only* if the cursor is updatable; not all cursors are. According to how the cursor was created, its data source, and which programming model you are using, one or more columns of the result set, or even the entire result set, might be read-only.

Remember, even if the cursor is not updatable (and I often create read-only cursors to save time and space), you can update the data using an update action query. In many cases, you can't update tables directly anyway because they can be updated only via stored procedures; using update queries that call stored procedures is standard operating procedure. (SOP as we said in the army.)

> **NOTE** One of the new RDO 2.0 features lets you trap the WillUpdate-Rows event to change how RDO handles a pending alteration of a cursor. This way you can create a cursor that ordinarily would not be updatable and execute appropriate code (possibly a stored procedure) when the data is to be updated. Using this event (and others), you can now use the RemoteData control against read-only data sources and still permit changes to the database.

It is entirely possible to create a cursor with no member rows or to position the current-row pointer off either end of the cursor or on an invalid row. Therefore, it's not a good idea to attempt to blindly change data. For example, if the current row of a cursor is suddenly deleted, the current row is invalid, and you must reposition to another, valid row before you can perform an update operation. This is an all-too-typical error in a heavily used system. It's not unusual for other users to delete or change the data you are working on, forcing you to deal with the contingencies that arise.

Limiting the Rows in a Cursor

It's important to limit your cursor to fewer than a few hundred rows so that you can minimize the system resources required to build it. The upper limit will depend on the interactive nature of the application and the density of the display mechanism. Limiting the rows in a result set is easy with SQL Server. Just execute the following code, where *nnn* is the maximum number of rows:

Don't depend on this behavior in future versions of SQL Server when ROWCOUNT will limit result set rows but not Insert, Update, or Delete operation rows.

```
SET ROWCOUNT nnn
```

Is it really *that* easy? Of course not. When you execute *SET ROWCOUNT*, you also cap the number of *updatable* rows!

Consider this example:

```
SET ROWCOUNT 100
Update Animals
Set Age = Age + 1 WHERE Birthday >= GetDate()
```

In this case, only the first 100 rows of the *Animals* table meeting the WHERE clause are updated. Does any programming model support limiting rows? Yes, both the RDO and ODBCDirect models support the MaxRows property on the rdoQuery and QueryDef objects. The MaxRows property caps the number of rows returned by the query but also can affect the number of rows modified by an associated update. What about using *SET ROWCOUNT* with Jet? The code looks like this:

```
' Set maximum number of rows to be returned to 20
db.Execute "SET ROWCOUNT 20", dbSQLPassThrough
```

In this example, I use a globally declared database object, *db*, that is affected by the *SET ROWCOUNT* operation—that is, all subsequent operations on this query, regardless of type, are affected by this row limit. Of course, I'm assuming that the Execute statement doesn't have to open another connection to execute its query. For this reason, I recommend that you turn off this cap when you are done with the query:

```
' Set no maximum number of rows to be returned
db.Execute "SET ROWCOUNT 0", dbSQLPassThrough
```

TIP   Some SQL Server ODBC drivers might be confused about the impact of the SQL_MAX_ROWS option. Some versions of the driver do not account for the fact that the ROWCOUNT setting affects UPDATE statements, too.

Limiting Rows with the WHERE Clause

When you can't use *SET ROWCOUNT* or don't want to, you should cap the number of rows returned by using the SQL statement's WHERE clause. Frankly, this technique is far more reliable and more in keeping with relational database theory and practice. This technique works with all programming models and doesn't affect updates unless you apply the same WHERE clause to the UPDATE statement. For example, here's how to make sure the query contains enough qualifying information to limit its scope to a few hundred rows:

```
SELECT Name, Type, Age, Sex
FROM Animals
WHERE ID_NO BETWEEN 1 AND 200
```

Updating and Inserting Data

Let's say the user has decided to change a data field on the form. How will the change be posted to the database? All the programming models have their own update methodologies, but you might feel that you have to use a cursor to update the row or rows involved. (You can also use bound controls to expose and update data more or less automatically.) You don't need to use a cursor. As a matter of fact, I don't even encourage use of updatable cursors. I suggest a fundamental database design that doesn't support the concept of updatable cursors because all updates are performed instead through action queries that execute stored procedures.

If an update affects more than one table in the database, you should bind the operations into a transaction. That way, the entire transaction can be rolled back if one update or insert fails. Transaction management and error detection are mostly up to you and your code. Some operations are rolled back by trigger code, but your code is expected to execute the rollback when an error indicates that the transaction cannot be completed. Again, using a stored procedure for this type of operation makes abundant sense.

As I have said before, many MIS shops don't permit direct access to underlying tables in a database. Instead, access is gated through protected stored procedures and views. In this case, updating is very easy—you simply pass parameters to the data update or insert procedure. This method used to preclude the use of bound controls, since they expected access to updatable cursors created against basic tables or views. With Visual Basic version 5.0 and RDO, you can now intercept the actual update operation by catching the WillUpdateRows event, substituting an appropriate stored procedure call, and then simply canceling RDO's update operation.

Unless you can gain access to an updatable view or use the WillUpdate-Rows event, you won't be able to update protected underlying tables using the Data control or the RemoteData control. Even a stored procedure might also limit changes to certain users and certain times of day, or it might impose other restrictions that help protect database integrity (and the system administrator's job). Your application might have to connect via a special logon ID and password to gain access to the update or insert procedures.

An example of this methodology is Microsoft's RAID front end, which is used to track applications and documentation bugs throughout the company. RAID permits anyone to access the database by using a common user ID and no password. Updates are handled strictly by the application. It uses stored procedures that verify the user's ID, the type of change, and the validity of the data. The database itself is locked for most other access, so you can't open it with Microsoft Access and fix a few bugs by hitting the tables directly.

Using Optimistic Batch Updates

When we get to the RDO chapters in this book, we will fully examine the new Client Batch cursor library. But let's take a brief look at this new feature now. Basically, the Client Batch cursor library and its ability to perform optimistic batch updates is designed to let you fetch a set of rows and perform a set of operations—such as Insert, Update, and Delete—on the result set. When you open one of these result sets in *batch* mode, the changes are queued and *not* posted to the database as they're made. When you're ready to commit the changes, you use the BatchUpdate method, which sends the entire group of operations to the server as a set. Since this type of operation is expected to be executed against an easily updated set of rows, you shouldn't get any errors. But if you do, RDO builds an array containing the bookmarks of the rows that failed to be changed. This important new technique can improve performance and make handling form-based multirow updates far easier to manage.

PART III

Using DAO
with the Microsoft
Jet Database Engine

9
Chapter

The Microsoft Jet Database Engine and the DAO Model

**DAO/Jet and
SQL Server: Some History**

**How Jet Accesses
Remote Databases**

Understanding the DAO Model

et me be the first to admit it: I still don't call myself an expert on the Microsoft Jet database engine. What I know of Jet is drawn from my having worked with Jet to access SQL Server, not dBASE or even Microsoft Access databases. I'm well aware that Jet is far, far more than an easy-to-use programmatic interface to SQL Server. My opinions about how Jet is suitable for one SQL Server application or another are based on my having created applications that worked (or didn't) after I used documentation that I might have written in the first place. So I guess I have no one to blame but myself when it comes to misunderstandings about Jet.

Nevertheless, I can report that a very significant change has been made to the Jet database engine—it's now designed to break away from DAO on demand. That is, you can now program DAO to load and use RDO instead of Jet as its data access interface. This is the ODBCDirect mode of DAO. From now on, we need to think about DAO and Jet separately. When I say *Jet* from here on in, I mean to describe how the Jet database engine operates on its own. When I say *DAO/Jet,* I mean to describe how DAO behaves when it is using Jet to implement the programming model. When I want to refer to DAO's behavior when it's connected to RDO, I use the term *ODBCDirect*.

DAO/Jet and SQL Server: Some History

SQL Server developers faced a number of different hurdles when it came to developing with DAO/Jet. Since DAO/Jet originally had been designed to make SQL Server look like another of the ISAM back ends, many of the techniques described in the Jet documentation encouraged ISAM-style development methodologies for implementing relational front-end requirements.

These techniques worked, but they often degraded system and front-end performance, and sometimes Jet simply got in the way. For example,

DAO/Jet 1.1 supports a Database object that can be used interchangeably by ISAM and SQL Server database developers. With virtually the same code as that used for ISAM databases, a developer could either open a database file or connect to SQL Server (and to any ODBC back end, for that matter). This apparently easy way to get at SQL Server led many developers to use the attachment without link (AWOL) technique to open SQL Server tables just as they opened ISAM tables.

Other ISAM optimizations tended to make Jet 1.1 merely *appear* slower than competitive front ends in connecting to SQL Server, especially when result sets contained more than a few hundred rows. For example, to remain backward-compatible with Visual Basic 2.0, DAO/Jet preloaded the result sets returned from ODBC data sources to make second-row access as fast as possible. The first row's fetch time cost a relative fortune, but all the subsequent rows were basically free. Since many SQL Server customers were working with fairly large tables or could use only stored procedures to access or update data, the basic ISAM approach led to disappointing performance and some frustration. There *were* ways to make Jet 1.1 work faster and deal with many SQL Server front-end development issues, but these techniques weren't widely known or understood—not even by yours truly.

With pressure to make the version of Jet destined to be used with Visual Basic 4.0 a more responsive, more flexible, and better performing front end to SQL Server, the Jet team redesigned the connection handler and tuned the ODBC interface and query optimizer to be more cognizant of remote database intelligence. A sophisticated buffer manager and new result set population strategy were added. The team also redesigned the query optimizer to perform many queries as interactive stored procedures on the remote server. The Jet ODBC interface was reengineered as well, to stop prepopulating ODBC result sets. Connection and query times dropped, and perceived performance significantly increased. Unfortunately, Visual Basic version 4.0's new architecture ate up most of these speed improvements—we had not gained much ground.

More important, the Jet group became acutely aware of the issues that you and I face daily when we work with databases that contain millions or billions of rows and are accessed by hundreds of concurrent users. The Jet documentation team continued to work with the Visual Basic 4.0 team to create development guidelines and documentation for making any Jet-based front end as efficient as it was designed to be, emphasizing the special tuning and optimization techniques needed to make a production-quality front end.

I use it, but I don't like the term *ODBCDirect*. As far as I am concerned, it's confusing and misleading. When in ODBCDirect mode, DAO doesn't speak "directly" to ODBC—it speaks to RDO, which speaks directly to ODBC.

How Jet Accesses Remote Databases

Jet is designed to access at least three different database formats. According to how you open the Database object or attach external databases, Jet chooses the interface and drivers for accessing data in the following kinds of databases.

- *MDB (Microsoft Access–format) databases.* These are a cross between true relational databases and ISAM databases. Jet databases are maintained in a single file that integrates data, indexes, reports, forms, macros, and all other support data. This is Jet's native format. It's a very common practice to attach a SQL Server table to a Jet database. This model uses a separate SYSTEM.MDW file to manage user security. (You can't create a user-security file without a utility provided by Microsoft Access; the Visual Basic group chose not to include this applet.)

- *True ISAM databases like dBASE, FoxPro, Paradox, and Btrieve.* These databases are accessed via installable ISAM drivers. This type of database characteristically has many files, and Jet treats each one as a table. (Jet 3.5 now uses an IISAM driver to access Jet 2.0 files as well.)

- *External databases accessible through an ODBC driver.* Jet can access virtually any database that has an ODBC level 1–compliant driver. SQL Server is connected through this type of interface, even when you attach one or more SQL Server tables to a Jet database.

Jet manages each of these databases differently while trying to make the interface with them as seamless as possible. The objects, properties, and methods used to manipulate data are generally the same, regardless of data format. Accessing SQL Server through Jet's ODBC drivers is also generally the same except that the Jet table-type Recordset object and its associated index-based methods aren't available.

Jet and SQL Server: Coding Queries and Creating Cursors

Let's look more closely at how Jet deals with SQL Server databases and creates cursors against SQL Server data. Jet can create a forward-only snapshot-type DAO Recordset object, which you can count as a separate type of cursor if you want to. (It's still possible to create the outdated Dynaset and Snapshot objects with Visual Basic 5.0, but I'm going to ignore these.) Jet can also create a dynaset-type or snapshot-type Recordset object. Altogether, then, you have three different cursors from which to choose when you use Jet to access SQL Server databases. The dynaset-type Recordset object is an updatable cursor containing bookmarks for each member row. The snapshot-type Recordset object contains a static copy of the data rows. Cursors store either bookmarks or data values in workstation resources. This means that a 1000-row dynaset cursor brings 1000 times the number of bytes per bookmark into local RAM, with the data for retrieved rows overflowing to local disk space if it can't fit in RAM. (The Windows swap file is *not* involved in this type of RAM allocation.) Any of these cursors can be created with code using the DAO interface or with the Data control, which now has much broader functionality than it did in Visual Basic 3.0.

NOTE Since the ODBC API and SQL Server don't expose ISAM-level calls such as OpenTable and Seek, DAO/Jet can't create a Table object or table-type Recordset object against ODBC data sources. This type of access is reserved for native and ISAM databases that use separately accessible indexes to walk the data rows.

When you code a query against an ODBC data source and ask DAO/Jet to execute it, you start by executing a method that uses a SQL query as one of its arguments or you execute a DAO/Jet QueryDef that contains a SQL query. Even if you simply specify the name of a SQL Server table, Jet executes a SELECT * query to fetch its data. For example, using the OpenResultset method against an attached SQL Server table in a Jet database starts a new query.

The SQL query is then studied by Jet's query processor. Let's assume you're using Jet's SQL syntax. (If you choose Transact-SQL instead, the Jet query processor must be bypassed.) At this point, the query processor checks the statement for correct syntax, permissions, and object references. If the query fails muster, processing goes no farther and you get a trappable error.

Next, a decision is made about how to deal with the request. Jet will always send the entire SQL request to the server—unless the server can't perform the request, for one of several reasons. First, the data might come from two different sources. For example, one table could be a Jet table and the other a SQL Server table, or you could be attempting to join data from two SQL Server sources. Second, your query might have user-defined, Jet-specific, or Visual Basic–specific functions. If so, Jet evaluates and processes the functions locally. (Statistical or financial functions, for instance, force local execution.) If a user-defined function (UDF) doesn't reference any data from the server, however, then the UDF is evaluated first and the result is included in the SQL statement sent to the server for processing. Third, the query might be Jet-specific. Queries must be executed locally when they contain SQL commands unique to Jet (such as the TOP operator) or when the data can't otherwise be derived from data on the server.

Regardless of how Jet decides to process the query, it executes the ODBC API SQLPrepare function, which causes the SQL Server ODBC driver to create one or more temporary stored procedures to perform the actual operation. Jet also attempts to create a parameter query that can be run interactively if it finds that at least some of the data must be drawn from the workstation. Each query is associated with a DAO Database object, which in turn is associated with a specific connection. As the query is executed against SQL Server, the connection is blocked for all other activity because SQL Server can't support multiple operations on a single connection unless it uses server-side cursors, which DAO/Jet can't use.

As Jet completes the query, it prepares a DAO Recordset object containing either the data rows stored locally on the workstation, in the case of a snapshot cursor, or pointers to the data rows back on the server, in the case of a dynaset cursor. If the query calls for the data to be sorted, as when the query contains an ORDER BY clause, SQL Server orders the rows of the result set before returning control to your application. If there's no need to perform further ordering, SQL Server returns control when the first block of rows is ready. In some cases, Jet continues working on your query in the background after the first block of data is returned to your application.

Once Jet returns control to your application and completes processing of the query, the connection is released for another operation—but not before. Again, this is because of the single-threaded nature of SQL Server connections. Unlike Visual Basic 3.0, in which any query to SQL Server locks the system until the query is complete, Jet attempts to return control to your application sooner. This isn't always possible, however, as when you ask for a sorted result set. When you are working on a 32-bit operating system such as Windows 95 or Windows NT, this isn't as serious a problem as it is when you're working on a nonpreemptive multitasking system that doesn't let other applications run while you wait for the results of a long query.

The Jet Query Processor

Let's take a critical look at the Jet query processor. In virtually all cases that you're working with queries whose data is derived solely from the SQL server, you *don't* want Jet to perform the join locally. If it does, you're treating SQL Server like a file server. Who cares, if only a few rows are involved? But when you're dealing with more than a few dozen rows, local joins can slow your application to a crawl.

So that Jet can work to its full potential in a sophisticated client/server environment, you have to set a number of tuning options. Unfortunately, some of these options are difficult to reach from code, since they are embedded deep in the system registry. Visual Basic offers little support for querying or updating the registry, so you must resort to Windows calls or to actually changing the registry entries manually, which is scary.

So that Jet can process the logic involved in your query, Jet's query processor must understand how your database schema is laid out. This information must include table and column names, index names, and what features your database server supports. Jet gleans this information by executing a series of ODBC API functions against the SQL Server system tables and the special tables installed when the ODBC drivers are set up. This process can take some time, so if you don't use an attached table, the information isn't cached and the process must be repeated many, many times—unless you are careful. I'll point out the techniques that trigger this DLL dump later on, in Chapter 12.

A concept that confused me until one of the Jet program managers set me straight—they love to do that—is the difference between asynchronous operations in Microsoft Access and Visual Basic Data control background Recordset population. By default, Jet runs all of its queries in asynchronous mode. This means that Jet periodically polls SQL Server for completion of the current query. While it's waiting to poll again, Jet yields to the operating system (Windows 95 or Windows NT), which can permit other Windows-based tasks to complete. Because of limitations in Visual Basic, the DAO/Jet interface is *not* capable of providing an asynchronous development environment, as supported in Microsoft Access and RDO. The Visual Basic application that has made a request (such as to open a record set) must wait until at least the first rows have returned to the workstation. Therefore, DAO/Jet programs must populate their record sets by using their own code, and they begin that work *after* the first records have been returned. The Data control *does* support asynchronous operations, however. By default, it attempts to populate a result set in the background. Just don't move to another row while this is going on—moving turns off the fetch.

Another basic problem with the Jet query processor architecture is Jet's attitude toward your request. Jet assumes that you know what you're doing. (This assumption might be somewhat optimistic.) But working from this idea, the DAO/Jet interface creates the most expensive, powerful, and flexible cursor it can, unless you tell it to do otherwise. Visual Basic 3.0 gives developers few choices about the type of cursor to create, but Visual Basic 5.0 gives you lots of choices. It still creates a read-write, full-access dynaset cursor by default, however. I suggest that you investigate forward-only scrolling snapshot-type Resultset objects, accessed via the GetRows method. This is the cheapest, fastest way to access data from SQL Server with Jet. If you don't intend to update data through this connection, set the Database object's ReadOnly property to True for even better performance.

When you're using Jet to access SQL Server, limit the scope of every operation. This means making sure that you ask for only the specific rows you need. Don't ask for columns you don't need, and that goes double for Text and Image data types. And don't fill lists with more than a few hundred rows. Users can't or won't read them, and keeping the data current will be a problem. You should also perform sorting and filtering operations via SQL queries that run on the SQL server; don't plan to filter or sort once the data is returned to the workstation.

Comparing DAO/Jet with ODBCDirect is something like teaching someone how to fly an airplane using the rudder pedals, the yoke, and the throttle and then expecting the student to immediately transition from a Piper Tomahawk trainer to an F-111—the controls are the same, aren't they?

CAUTION

No matter which interface you use, every cursor feature that you enable slows the process down, since more code must be executed to support it. Because 90 percent of this code is executed on your workstation, you have to pay the price in slower response and more lost time. Everyone sharing the server and network also has to pay in increased server and net load. If you regularly use expensive cursor strategies, be sure to leave your home phone number where everyone can find it when things go wrong.

Understanding the DAO Model

Now that you have an idea about the inner workings of the Jet engine, let's take a look at the Data Access Objects programming model and how it behaves when connected to Jet. While the same DAO programming objects are used with ODBCDirect, they might behave differently when connected to RDO.

Before Visual Basic 4.0, every object, method, property, and event (except those provided by the VBX controls) was hard-coded into the language. Unless you added a custom control, there was no way to extend the list of known Visual Basic 3.0 objects or their attributes. For components hard-wired into Visual Basic 3.0, however, such as data access, it was impossible to extend the object model. This limitation became painfully evident when Jet 2.x was released with Microsoft Access 2.0. Visual Basic could access the new engine indirectly through the compatibility layer, but it couldn't reach the new Recordset object or its properties and methods. Moreover, all the new security and replication features were also unavailable.

Visual Basic 4.0 departed radically from this hard-wired design when Microsoft implemented a new OLE-based architecture. Each object, property, method, or event that Visual Basic recognizes in code is now defined through a type library. Basically, a type library is a dynamic description of each object, coupled with its properties and methods. This list is loaded either when the Visual Basic run-time component is created or at design time when the developer chooses a new custom control or object library from the References dialog box. That way, new object models can be loaded as they evolve. These object models can be developed in any language, by anyone—even by other Visual Basic programs.

To deal with the various scenarios Visual Basic developers are expected to use, Visual Basic version 4.0 provides three Jet object models: the Jet DAO 2.5 Object Library, the Jet DAO 3.0 Object Library, and the Jet DAO 2.5/3.0 Compatibility Library. Since Visual Basic version 5.0 is 32-bit only, it supports only the Jet DAO 3.5 Object Library and the Jet DAO 2.5/3.5 Compatibility Library. Each of these object models has a specific function. The Jet DAO 2.5 models are designed to provide compatibility for existing Visual Basic 3.0 DAO applications so that at least they can compile in Visual Basic 4.0, even when they use outdated Data Access Objects. The Jet DAO 3.*x* object models are designed strictly for 32-bit Visual Basic, since this version provides no support for the obsolete objects. This model also helps you identify all instances of outdated objects. For 16-bit applications, your only choice is the Jet DAO 2.5 Object Library. For 32-bit applications, you can choose the Jet DAO 2.5/3.0 Compatibility Library, which provides backward compatibility with older versions of the DAO interface, allowing you to recompile existing Visual Basic 3.0 or Visual Basic version 4.0 code (Jet 1.1 or 2.0) for 32-bit applications. In future versions of Visual Basic, however, some of these older properties, methods, and objects won't be supported. To ease your move to the new Jet 3.*x* model and ensure that your existing code will continue to run properly, you should use the Jet DAO 3.5 Object Library for new projects. This library contains only the new DAO functionality.

If you open the Visual Basic help file, you can find the Jet 2.5/3.0 object model laid out in a neat graphic, but not all the objects in the Jet object model can be accessed when you're working with remote SQL Server databases. **Figure 9-1** on the next page shows which objects can be used in accessing SQL Server data. The obsolete Resultset objects in the figure are leftover objects from Visual Basic 2.0 and Visual Basic 3.0. Depending on the type of library that is loaded, you might be able to reference these, but you should still migrate your code away from them—you can't be certain that these objects will be supported in any future releases. **Figure 9-2** shows how to translate them to their more current equivalent objects. **Figure 9-2** also lists a number of statements that have been replaced and gives a tip or two about converting your code. Several of the changes made to the Jet engine were done under the cowling, so your code won't appear to change. For example, when you use the BeginTrans statement in Visual Basic 3.0 code and convert to Visual Basic 4.0, this statement becomes a method of the default Workspace object. Your code doesn't change, nor does the impact of the statement.

TIP Using the Jet DAO 3.5 Object Library ensures that your new projects will continue to function correctly in versions of Visual Basic later than Visual Basic 5.0. Therefore, your *new* projects should use the Jet DAO 3.5 Object Library, and any existing projects should be migrated to it. Before you get started, however, be sure to read about using Remote Data Objects in Part IV of this guide.

When Microsoft shipped Access 7.0, the Access sub-version of Jet replaced the Visual Basic 4.0 version. At that point, some Jet bugs were fixed, some parts began to work better, and some new bugs were uncovered. That's the nature of component architecture. It's like having a car made of parts from all over the country. Ford has been trying to get this kind of thing right for almost 70 years; this is Microsoft's first year or two with ActiveX-based component architecture. Since Microsoft Office 97 shipped ahead of Visual Basic version 5.0, we shouldn't have a reoccurrence of this problem.

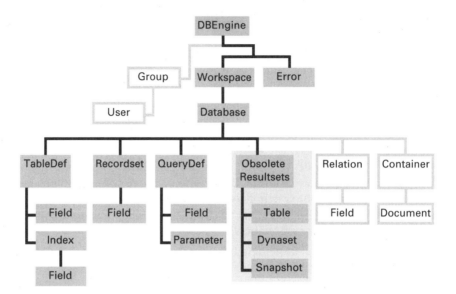

Figure 9-1 *Jet 2.5/3.x object model for SQL Server databases*

Figure 9-2
Conversion of Outdated Jet 1.1
Objects and Methods to Jet 2.5/3.*x*

Outdated Objects, Methods, or Statements	How to Convert to Jet DAO 2.5/3.*x* Code
Dynaset	Use dynaset-type Recordset object
CreateDynaset	Use OpenRecordset(<sql>, dbOpenDynaset)
Snapshot	Use snapshot-type Recordset object
CreateSnapshot	Use OpenRecordset(<sql>, dbOpenSnapshot)
Table	Use table-type Recordset object (not available via ODBC)
OpenTable	Use OpenRecordset(<sql>, dbOpenTable) (not available via ODBC)
OpenQueryDef	Access existing QueryDef objects in the QueryDefs collection
ListIndexes	Use TableDefs Indexes collection
ListFields	Use TableDefs Fields collections
ListParameters	Use QueryDefs Parameters collection
FreeLocks function	Use DBEngine.Idle method
SetDefaultWorkspace	Use DBEngine DefaultUser and DefaultPassword properties
SetDataAccessOption	Use DBEngine INIPath property
RA = ExecuteSQL	Use Execute method, RecordsAffected property
DeleteQueryDef	Use the QueryDefs collection Delete method

Properties and Methods

Each of the Data Access Object classes permits your code to manipulate properties that activate options, set operational parameters, or execute methods that carry out actions (such as opening a result set or closing a database on SQL Server). Visual Basic objects are instances of class procedures that have instance variables: their *methods*. Each of the DAO classes also supports a set of variables that affect or reflect their behavior and operation: these are called *properties*. When you want one of the objects to perform some operation or when you want to perform an operation on an object, you use one of its methods.

TIP Since Visual Basic now supports a dynamic object model, your objects have to be registered before they and their associated properties and methods can be available. A common mistake we all make when first working with Visual Basic 4.0 (or 5.0) is forgetting to register Data Access Objects or other object models of choice. Since Visual Basic no longer compiles the whole program when you press the Run key, you won't encounter a problem until you attempt to reference a procedure that references one of the unregistered objects. To avoid this problem, choose the Start With Full Compile option on the Run menu (or press Ctrl-F5).

These objects, like many in Visual Basic 5.0, are loaded dynamically when you choose them from the References dialog box available via the Tools menu. When you first drag the preloaded Data control to your form, the Jet Data Access Objects are registered and loaded for you automatically so that the Visual Basic version 5.0 integrated development environment (IDE) will work the way the Visual Basic 3.0 IDE does.

Several of these objects aren't available to you when you're writing applications to access SQL Server via the Jet Data Access Objects. Those objects are shown in *Figure 9-3*. *Figure 9-4* on the next page shows the objects that can be used and describes how they relate to SQL Server front-end development.

Figure 9-3
Objects Not Available to SQL Server Front-End Applications

Object	Description
Group	Maintains group- and user-level security for Jet databases
User	Maintains group- and user-level security for Jet databases
Relation	Manages Jet database referential integrity; can't map to attached tables or reflect SQL Server referential integrity constraints
Container	Holds information that describes a group of objects
Document	Includes information about one instance of a type of object (database, saved table, query, or relationship)

Figure 9-4
Dynamically Loaded Data Access Objects

Data Access Object	What It Does
DBEngine	Holds all other objects. Addresses overall engine options.
Workspace	Maintains a unique transaction scope. All transactions are Workspace-global. Holds the Databases collection. Can be set to connect to either Jet or RDO (ODBCDirect mode).
Database	Permits user to address a specific SQL Server database and holds the TableDefs collection. Database objects are used to establish a connection to SQL Server, so opening a Database object opens at least one ODBC connection.
Connection	ODBCDirect only. Used to map to the RDO Connection object and its unique behavior.
TableDef	Describes database tables. One TableDef is created for each table in the SQL Server database. Each TableDef contains a Fields collection and an Indexes collection.
Field	Describes the columns of a database table and their attributes. There is one Field object for each defined column. The Field object is also used to hold QueryDef and Index field definitions.
Index	Describes a table index. There is one Index object for each table index in the database. Each Index object contains a Fields collection that contains one Field object for each table field included in the index.
Recordset	A cursor. Permits sequential or random access to data rows in a result set. Contains either data rows, as in a snapshot-type Recordset object, or pointers to data rows, as in a dynaset-type Recordset object.
QueryDef	A stored query maintained in a Jet database. Roughly equivalent to a simple stored procedure containing only a single SELECT statement or action query. QueryDef objects have a Parameters collection, which is used to hold query parameters.
Parameter	Maintains the parameters passed to a specific QueryDef object when it is executed.

Collections

Collections aren't new to Visual Basic, but they now play a very important role in the development of DAO-based applications (or, for that matter, in the development of any object-based Visual Basic application). Collections are described in the Visual Basic documentation, but the focus there isn't particularly data-oriented.

A collection holds a set of related objects. It functions basically as a linked list, with behavior somewhat different from what you may be used to working with, unless you are familiar with the ListBox or ComboBox controls. Each element of a collection is called a *member*. Collection members are always added to the end of a collection, but they can be removed randomly. When a member is deleted, all the other members move up in the list—not physically, just logically. Therefore, when you use an index to reference the individual members of a collection, the index number is valid only until you delete a member. For this reason, you can delete member 0 a number of times—each time, the remaining members logically slide up to take the freed space.

Since collections are rebuilt through the Refresh method, you can't count on the order number of any one element. A TableDef object that was the fourth member a second ago might be the third, fifth, or fifty-fifth after you refresh the collection. And you do have to refresh collections on occasion, especially when you make changes that bypass Jet.

Collection members are added and removed either automatically or via such methods as Append or Delete. As new Database or Recordset objects are created, references to the new objects are automatically placed in their associated collections.

Visual Basic 3.0 supports only a few object collections, such as the TableDefs collection of TableDef objects. Visual Basic 4.0 and 5.0 support many more, as well as the creation of user-defined collections. All the objects shown in *Figure 9-4* except the DBEngine object itself are maintained in associated collections. For example, all Database objects are maintained in the Databases collection, and all Field objects are kept in the Fields collection.

NOTE The TableDef, Recordset, Index, and QueryDef objects each have a Fields collection to manage the columns associated with each object.

To refer to collection members in code, you can use one of a half-dozen (or more) syntax forms. Let's assume that the first table in the TableDefs collection is named *Titles*. Any of the following DAO syntax variations will be supported for referring to the first table:

```
TableDefs(0)              ' By ordinal number
                          ' All collections are zero-based
TableDefs(n%)             ' Indirectly by ordinal where n% = 0
TableDefs("Titles")       ' Directly by name
MyTable$ = "Titles"
TableDefs(MyTable$)       ' Indirectly by name
TableDefs!Titles          ' Directly by name
```

Using the "bang" operator (!) is the fastest way to reference objects. If the name has embedded spaces, enclose the name in brackets or pass it in a string:

```
TableDefs![My TableName]
MyLongTableName$ = "My TableName"
TableDefs(MyLongTableName$)
```

Populating the Object Model

When your application makes a code reference to a Data Access Object, the DBEngine object is started automatically. A new Workspace object isn't created until you reference one of the underlying objects. If you need to use ODBCDirect, be sure to create a separate Workspace object for it—otherwise, you get a Jet Workspaces(0) object by default. When you subsequently open a Jet Workspace connection to SQL Server, as when you use the OpenDatabase method against the default Workspaces(0), Jet simply establishes a connection to the SQL server and fetches a few initialization values from a tuning configuration table. The SQL Server connection interface assigns your connection a default database, or your connect string specifies a specific SQL Server database to use. No further DAO/Jet object population takes place.

Consider the number of behind-the-scenes queries that have to take place to fetch all this information. That's what makes the DAO/Jet interface so slow to connect and to prepopulate the DAO/Jet DDL objects.

Since we're focusing on the DAO/Jet interface, let's assume that we haven't created an ODBCDirect Workspace. When you make your first reference to the TableDefs collection, DAO/Jet calls the ODBC API, which selectively populates the object model so that all relevant DAO objects reflect the current schema of your SQL Server database. Simply creating a Resultset object doesn't populate the DAO data definition language (DDL) structures. All DAO DDL information is stored in structures addressed by reference to the Database object. For example, once the DAO object model is fully populated, the TableDefs collection contains a TableDef member for each table in the SQL Server database, and each Fields collection of each TableDef object contains a description of all columns in each table—whether or not you ever reference them in code.

In most cases, you do *not* want Jet fully populating the rest of the object model to reflect the schema of your SQL Server database—trust me. One of the most expensive and time-consuming operations Jet performs is populating the Databases, TableDefs, Fields, and Indexes collections. For better performance, DAO/Jet should populate only what it needs. DAO/Jet doesn't walk the entire SQL Server database schema when you open a DAO/Jet TableDef object; it simply uses the SQLTables ODBC function to pull back selected tables' DDL information. When, and only when, you touch a Field object in code, DAO/Jet drills down using the ODBC SQLColumns function. To make matters worse, this information is cached in the Database object. However, declaring this information globally doesn't pose a serious problem, since it can be used by all procedures in the form. But if it's defined in a procedure, the entire operation is repeated each time the SQL Server database is opened—not good. This warning should make it abundantly clear that Jet was designed to access ODBC data sources through *attached* tables. Jet shows its best performance (at OpenDatabase time) if the work required to map a table's schema is done once, when the ODBC data source table is attached.

TIP When changes are made in the database schema—as when tables, fields, or indexes are added or deleted—the process of fetching the DDL information *must* be repeated if you're depending on accurate mapping of the database schema. To repopulate the collections, use the Refresh method against the TableDefs, Indexes, or Databases collections. If you don't repopulate, the local copy of the DDL schema kept in the DAO interface doesn't change. That's the good news. The bad news is that when you execute a query based on a stale schema, it might fail because of an unknown object reference. Generally, a SQL Server front-end application doesn't need to query the database schema at run time—this information is useful at design time as you set up your forms and bound controls. But if your application creates new SQL Server tables via non-DAO means, as when you use SQL pass-through queries, you must refresh the TableDefs or Indexes collections.

Chapter

Data Access Objects Up Close

Component Architecture

The DBEngine Object

Workspace Objects

Database Objects

TableDef Objects

Field Objects

Index Objects

Tables and Indexes

Creating or Adding
Tables and Indexes

Now that you have a sense of DAO/Jet's evolution and basic developmental approach, let's take a tour of how it is exposed to programmers. This chapter describes the Data Access Objects in detail, emphasizing how they interact with Microsoft SQL Server when connected through the Jet database engine. We'll see how DAO connects to SQL Server using the ODBCDirect mode later.

The DBEngine object provides top-level addressability for all local DAO objects, and for DAO/Jet it represents the Microsoft Jet database engine—DBEngine properties are applied to the Jet engine itself. Depending on the type of Visual Basic loaded, the following Jet engine is loaded:

Figure 10-1
Jet Engines Used According to Visual Basic Type

Visual Basic Version	Microsoft Jet Engine
3.0—16-bit	Jet 1.0, 1.1, or 2.0
4.0—16-bit	Jet 2.5
4.0—32-bit	Jet 3.0
5.0 (32-bit only)	Jet 3.5

But before we pull completely off the road, let's take a look at one of Visual Basic's most important architectural buttresses.

Component Architecture

A principal difference between Visual Basic 3.0 and Visual Basic 4.0 and 5.0 is the concept of Component Object Model (COM) architecture. What it means for you is that as newer versions of any of Visual Basic's components are developed, you can take full advantage of their bug fixes, new objects and methods, or improved performance simply by installing the new dynamic-link

PART III USING DAO WITH THE MICROSOFT JET DATABASE ENGINE libraries (DLLs) and registering them with the Windows operating system. Jet is also provided in many other Microsoft products, including Microsoft Access, Microsoft Visual C++, Microsoft Excel, and Microsoft Office applications, so when one of these applications is installed on your system, it can bring a newer version of Jet or other Visual Basic 4.0 components (such as VBA) with it. The bottom line? Well, it might very well mean that the functionality of your application could change as these components evolve within versions. You won't need the compatibility layer or anything else to access these changes, even if they are quite significant, because of the way components like Jet are plugged into Visual Basic through OLE and COM architectures. You should be aware, though, that these components might be installed whenever you add any application that updates one of Visual Basic's components. Be especially wary of any third-party application that has its own setup routine, which might overlay an older DLL on the current version of a component.

The DBEngine Object

In Visual Basic version 5.0, starting a DAO application no longer automatically initializes the Jet database engine because it might never be invoked if the application chooses to use ODBCDirect. When the first reference to a DAO/Jet Workspace is made, the Jet engine is loaded, initialized, and started. At this point, Jet takes a look at the Windows registry for initialization option settings. You must restart the DBEngine in order for any changes to its options to take effect. How does this affect other applications that share the engine? Each time an application that uses the Jet engine is launched, it gets its own instance data segment, which permits independent configuration and operation.

> **NOTE** All applications using the same version share the same *code* segments, but each is allocated its own *data* segment. The Jet engine is *not* shared if you run a Visual Basic 3.0 DAO application or some other Jet 1.*x* application on the same system as a Visual Basic 4.0 or 5.0 application. They do compete for the same resources, however.

All 32-bit DBEngine (Jet 3.*x*) settings are made by way of the Windows system registry. The 16-bit version of the engine (Jet 2.*x*) uses INI files to maintain the initialization settings. For virtually all production applications, you should set up an application-centric INI file or Windows registry location and point to this location by using the DBEngine.INIPath property. The INIPath property doesn't contain a value unless you set it because there is no default path—the underlying code uses the current file directory or the Windows registry entries.

To restart the Jet engine, you must first stop it. Try setting the DBEngine object to Nothing:

```
Set DBEngine = Nothing
```

Using this technique does have a drawback: all the DBEngine objects' open Database and Resultset objects are closed, somewhat rudely. It might be a good idea to close these ancillary objects before using this technique. To restart Jet, simply reference one of its objects, which brings it back on line.

Workspace Objects

One of the new objects added to Visual Basic 4.0 is the Workspace object. In Visual Basic version 5.0, this object is used to choose how DAO is implemented—whether through the Jet engine or RDO. If you choose to use ODBCDirect to connect your DAO objects to their equivalent RDO objects, you have to set up a new Workspace—the default Workspace automatically connects DAO to the Jet database engine. Yes, you can do both—that is, you can have both a DAO/Jet Workspace *and* a DAO/RDO (ODBCDirect) Workspace at the same time.

To activate an ODBCDirect Workspace, simply create your own Workspace like this:

```
Dim Ws as Workspace
Set Ws = DBEngine.CreateWorkspace ("MyODBCDWs", "", "", dbUseODBC)
```

CAUTION

Don't expect the DAO/Jet objects you create to work the same way when you switch over to ODBCDirect. You'll find lots of subtle and not so subtle differences between these two interfaces—and no, the documentation does *not* detail what ODBCDirect does *not* do in relation to DAO/Jet. ODBCDirect objects don't even do what straight RDO objects do.

In a general sense, the Workspace object provides a transaction scope and manages security for Jet databases that have security enabled. But I'm not going to drive into that quicksand for you; if you feel the need to implement a secured Jet database, I highly recommend taking along someone with a strong back and a long rope. Note, however, that when you set up a new DAO/Jet Workspace object, you must provide a user ID and password to gate access to secure Jet databases. Once you set the Workspace object user ID and password, Jet also uses these values when attempting to open connections to remote ODBC databases such as SQL Server. But if these values don't match those intended for the SQL server, you trip a trappable error. To turn off this automatic authentication, simply change the registry entry JetTryAuth to 0, or include a user ID and password in the connect string.

When you're writing DAO/Jet-based front-end applications, the Workspace object gives you a significant level of control over transaction scope that simply isn't available in Visual Basic 3.0. Now you can create a separate Workspace object for databases that need to participate in a transaction, and you can exclude those that shouldn't.

When you start the Jet database engine without indicating that the Workspace should use RDO, Jet automatically creates the default workspace, DBEngine.Workspaces(0), which is used if you don't specifically reference a Workspace object in using the OpenDatabase method. When you use transactions, all databases in the specified DAO/Jet Workspace are affected, even if multiple Database objects are opened in the Workspace. For example, if you use a BeginTrans method, update several records in a database, and then delete records in another database, both the update and delete operations are rolled back when you use the Rollback method. Now you understand why it is important to be able to create additional Workspace objects to manage transactions independently across Database objects. Generally, all transaction operations are passed on to SQL Server for processing—Jet doesn't buffer or manage ODBC transaction operations.

New Workspace objects are created with the CreateWorkspace method of the DBEngine object. If newly created Workspace objects must be referred to after creation, you must manually append them to the Workspaces collection. You can, however, use newly created Workspace objects without appending them to the Workspaces collection. You can refer to any other Workspace object that you create and append to the collection by its Name property setting or by its ordinal number.

Using the IsolateODBCTrans Property

In some situations, when you need to have multiple simultaneous transactions pending on the same ODBC database, you open a separate Workspace object for each transaction. Although each Workspace object can have its own ODBC connection to the database, this slows the system's performance. Because transaction isolation normally isn't required, ODBC connections from multiple Workspace objects opened by the same user are shared, by default. The IsolateODBCTrans property returns or sets a Boolean value that indicates whether multiple transactions that involve the same ODBC database are to be isolated. The default value is False—don't isolate transactions involving the same ODBC database.

SQL Server doesn't allow simultaneous transactions on a single connection, so if you need to have more than one transaction at a time pending against such a database, set the IsolateODBCTrans property to True on each Workspace object as soon as you open it. This forces a separate ODBC connection for each Workspace object.

Workspace Methods

The Workspace object also has a number of methods that are detailed in the Visual Basic help file. Note that you can execute the transaction methods against either a specific Database object (but *only* in Jet 2.5) or a chosen Workspace object. I would recommend, however, that you *not* use the Database method. Instead, use the Workspace method, for forward compatibility. If you reference neither a Database object nor a Workspace object when you're using the transaction methods, the default Workspaces(0) object is used. The Workspace object also enables the OpenDatabase method, which is used to establish a SQL Server connection.

Database Objects

The Database object provides addressability to the connection established by the OpenDatabase method. The Visual Basic 5.0 Database object, unlike Visual Basic 2.0's, doesn't provide a transaction scope. Sure, when you execute a transaction method against one of the tables in the database, all pending transactions on this database (connection) are affected, but so are all pending transactions on all other Database objects in its Workspace—which is usually not what you have in mind. Remember, the Workspace object is what provides top-level transaction scope; the Database object maintains information about the connection and a TableDefs collection.

> **NOTE** A DAO/Jet Database Object is *not* the same as an ODBCDirect Connection object, although it serves basically the same function—it establishes a connection to the remote server. But the ODBCDirect Connection object can create temporary QueryDef objects while the DAO/Jet Database object cannot—not while it is connected to Jet.

You manipulate an open database and the connection associated with it by using a Database object and its methods and properties. You can examine the collections in a Database object to map the tables, views, and stored procedures of the underlying SQL Server database and the QueryDef objects in a local Jet database. None of the forms, reports, or macros associated with a Jet database are accessible from Visual Basic. You can also use the Database object collections to modify or create SQL Server tables and indexes and Jet database queries and relationships. The Database object is also the basis for creating cursors against SQL Server data. For example, you can perform the following operations:

- Use the OpenRecordset method to create a new Recordset object directly from the Database object

- Use the Execute method to run a query against SQL Server that doesn't return rows

- Use the OpenRecordset method to execute a SQL pass-through query, with or without use of a QueryDef object, so that you can bypass the Jet query processor

- Use the Close method to close an open database and return the connection to the connection pool

The Workspace object's CreateDatabase method can't be used to create a new SQL Server database. But once you create a new SQL Server device and database, using the tools provided with SQL Server, you can create new tables and indexes with Visual Basic DAO methods. Why you would want to do this when there are tools like SQL Enterprise Manager is beyond me, but you can use the CreateTableDef and CreateIndex methods if you really want to. Frankly, I prefer Visual Database Tools or SQL Enterprise Manager, Transact-SQL statements, or, better yet, SQL OLE for creating my tables—even from inside Visual Basic applications. You can't use any of the Jet relationship methods to create or manipulate SQL Server intertable constraint relationships. None of the Jet Relation object properties or methods maps to SQL Server relations (not even to a distant cousin); they are strictly for Jet databases. To open an existing SQL Server database, use the Workspace object's OpenDatabase method,

CAUTION

There is no such thing as a "default" database in the Visual Basic DAO interface. Despite what the Visual Basic documentation says, the CurrentDB method has no meaning and doesn't compile. It does have a use in Microsoft Access Basic applications, however, since it refers to the Jet database currently opened by the user. When you see references to this object, simply substitute Workspaces(0).Databases(0) if you have already opened a database. If not, the reference to Database(0) is bogus.

which automatically appends it to the Databases collection.

When you use one of the three transaction methods (BeginTrans, CommitTrans, or Rollback) on the Database object, the transaction applies to all databases opened on the Workspace object from which the Database object was opened. If you want to use an independent transaction, you must open an additional Workspace object and then use it to open another Database object. Here is how to create two independent Database objects:

```
Dim Db1 As Database, Db2 As Database, Ws As Workspace, _
    Ws2 As Workspace
Dim MyUserName As String
Set Ws = Workspaces(0)                    ' Use the default Workspace
Set Db1 = Ws.OpenDatabase("DSN1",0,0, _
    "ODBC;UID=;PWD=;Database=Pubs")       ' Create new Workspace
Set Ws2 = DBEngine.CreateWorkspace _
    ("Special", MyUserName, "SpecialPW")
Ws2.ODBCIsolateTrans = True
Set Db2 =
Ws.OpenDatabase("DSN1",0,0,"ODBC;UID=;PWD=;Database=Pubs")
```

It isn't necessary to specify the DBEngine object when you use the OpenDatabase method. You need to do that only when you open a Database object in a transaction context in which a specific Workspace object needs to be referenced.

You can also open a Jet database that contains *attached* tables—links to SQL Server tables—instead of opening a remote SQL Server database directly. Opening a Jet database that has attached tables doesn't automatically establish links to the specified external ODBC databases until the table's TableDef or Field objects are referenced in code or until a Recordset object is opened against the Database object. If links to these tables can't be established, a trappable error occurs. You might also need permission to access the database, or the database might already be open for someone else's exclusive use. In these cases, a trappable error also occurs.

After you open an external database, you can examine the Connect property of the Database object to determine the parameters used to access the database. When an external ODBC database is opened directly, you can't use a table-type Recordset object, nor can one be used to access any ODBC-accessed table. Each time you open an external ODBC database directly, you establish a connection to the external database server. Since the Jet engine executes additional queries on the database to determine the structure of accessed tables, don't open external databases directly. (The ability to do so is provided only for the sake of backward compatibility.)

Attached Tables vs. Direct Links

As already mentioned, there are two fundamental ways to gain access to SQL Server data via DAO/Jet. You can open a Database object against a SQL Server data source or against a Jet MDB database containing attached SQL Server tables.

Each of these techniques has advantages and disadvantages. If you choose to open the SQL Server database directly, you can execute either Jet queries or Transact-SQL queries to create Recordset objects or execute action queries that change data or perform administrative functions. The downside to this approach is the expense incurred when the Database object is first opened—the data definition language (DDL) queries can take considerable time to perform. And this isn't a one-time penalty, either: additional DDL queries are required when the Recordset object is created against nonattached tables. The Database penalty *is* a one-time cost, however, if you open a Database object and its associated connection and leave it open for the duration of your operation. But this strategy assumes that the connection, which is tied up for the duration of the operation, isn't a system resource that needs to be conserved.

One technique that can reduce the time needed to open a connection involves preconnecting to the SQL server during form load. You pay a price as the program loads, but all subsequent OpenDatabase operations are *very* fast. If you leave this connection open, Jet can use it as required, and since the DDL operations have already been done, it also keeps Jet aware of the available tables on your SQL Server database. This technique ties up a connection for an indefinite period of time, however.

When you need to access SQL Server data with attached tables (or *linked* tables, as the Microsoft Access documentation now says), you simply open a Jet database that contains linkage information about chosen SQL Server tables. The data in the tables remains in the tables. It isn't downloaded into the Jet database and is really manipulated only when you create a cursor or execute an action query that references it. When you query these attached tables or use them in a join, Jet opens a connection (or shares one that is already open) and performs whatever input/output is necessary to access the data.

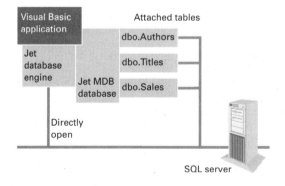

Just before Visual Basic 4.0 shipped, the Jet team added a new feature that permits you to create TSQL query–based Resultset objects on MDB databases. To perform a SQL pass-through query on a table attached to your MDB file, you can first set the Connect property of the attached table's Database object to a valid ODBC connect string. This new Jet feature removes one of the serious impediments to using attached tables, but it still means that you must create a Jet database and attach SQL Server tables to it, or attach your SQL Server tables to an existing Jet database. Yes, this database can be shared, and other people can use the attached tables. You can create it on the fly, too, in code.

Use the Close method to remove a Database object from the Databases collection and release the connection back to the pool. (The Databases collection should really be called the OpenDatabases collection—it doesn't actually hold databases, but rather Database structures that describe open database connections.) Any open Recordset objects in the database are closed automatically when the Database object is closed.

CAUTION
You can write code in a Visual Basic application to attach tables on the fly. But if you repeat this process every time the application runs, you negate most of the advantages you gained when you avoided opening the Database object directly.

TIP   To ensure that *all* of the resources allocated to an open Database object are released, set the Database object to Nothing.

When a procedure that declares a Database object is finished, the local Database objects are closed along with any open Recordset objects unless their Recordset variables are declared globally. Any pending updates are lost, and any pending transactions are rolled back without warning or error messages. Both Jet and Visual Basic manage the status and instance count of the Recordset and Database objects, so if you have Recordset objects open in other contexts, these remain open. The instance count is decremented, however, and the Database is closed and cleaned up once the instance count reaches 0.

CAUTION
You should explicitly complete any pending transactions or edits and close Recordset objects and Database objects, before you exit procedures that declare these object variables locally.

The first database that is opened is assigned to Databases(0). The Name property setting of a database is a string that specifies the ODBC data source name or the pathname if you open a Jet database. The Connect property specifies the database type and other parameters used to connect to SQL Server external databases. For example, if you don't provide enough parameters in the *Connect* argument of the OpenDatabase method or if some of the parameters are incorrect, the user is prompted for correct information. Whatever is provided by the user and passed back from the ODBC driver is reapplied to the Connect property.

Examining the Connect property after the Database is open can be quite informative, and you can also do this in subsequent OpenDatabase operations. When you are opening SQL Server databases directly, the *Exclusive* argument is basically ignored. You can't gain exclusive access to a SQL server without logging on as server administrator and setting administrative options. The *ReadOnly* argument is observed, however, and can be used to indicate your intention not to update any cursor that has been created. But this option doesn't prevent you from executing action queries that update rows independently of the read-only cursors that Jet creates.

The RecordsAffected property was introduced in Visual Basic 4.0. It contains the number of rows deleted, updated, or inserted in the running of an action query. When you use the Execute method to run a QueryDef, the RecordsAffected property setting is the number of records affected. The RecordsAffected property setting is the same as the value returned by the (obsolete) ExecuteSQL method.

Database Properties

Figure 10-2 shows a list of database properties and what they do.

Figure 10-2
Database Properties

Property	What It Does
Updatable	Indicates whether the database is read-only or read-write. Reflects the *ReadOnly* argument of the Open-Database method.
QueryTimeout	Determines the number of seconds that the underlying interface (in this case, ODBC) will wait for the current query to complete.
Connect	This connect string is built up on the basis of the parameters passed in the OpenDatabase method.
Transactions	This Boolean value indicates True if a database supports the transaction model (always True for SQL Server).
RecordsAffected	Shows how many rows were affected by the latest action query.

Database Methods

The Database object has a number of methods that are used to control the functionality of the queries to its tables. The CreateDynaset, CreateSnapshot, and ExecuteSQL methods are all outdated, which means that they aren't likely to be supported for much longer. (They are visible only if you use the "Compatibility" libraries.) Their functionality has been replaced with the OpenRecordset and Execute methods.

The CreateTableDef method can be used to create either Jet or SQL Server tables and is instrumental in creating attached SQL Server tables. *Figure 10-3* summarizes the current methods that apply to SQL Server. *Figure 10-4* lists obsolete methods that were supported in earlier versions of Jet, including Jet 2.5, but that are no longer supported in Jet 3.*x* and should be avoided.

Figure 10-3
Current DAO/Jet Methods Applicable to SQL Server

Method	What It Does
Close	Closes the database. Releases the connection to the pool.
CreateQueryDef	Creates a Jet QueryDef object in a Jet database. Can refer to SQL Server data by using TSQL queries.
CreateTableDef	Creates a new table definition, in either a Jet or a SQL Server database.
Execute	Runs a SQL action query.
OpenRecordset	Creates a cursor against Jet or SQL Server data.

Figure 10-4
Obsolete DAO/Jet Database Methods

Method	What It Does
BeginTrans	Begins a new transaction. Basically equivalent to the TSQL command of the same name. Works only if the Transactions property is True. Convert to Workspace method.
CommitTrans	Equivalent to the TSQL Commit Transaction command. Convert to Workspace method.
Rollback	Equivalent to the TSQL Rollback command. Convert to Workspace method.
CreateDynaset	Creates a Dynaset object from a specified table or SQL query. Convert to OpenRecordset method.
CreateSnapshot	Creates a Snapshot object from a specified table or SQL query. Convert to OpenRecordset method.
ExecuteSQL	Executes a SQL query that doesn't return rows. Use Execute method.

NOTE   In Jet 2.5, you can't close a database if transactions begun with BeginTrans are still pending. Use the CommitTrans or Rollback methods before trying to use the Close method. In Jet 3.x, however, using the Close method *forces* a close and a transaction rollback.

TableDef Objects

TableDef objects hold descriptions of tables and their associated indexes. When you open a Database object directly, the TableDef object is populated as soon as it is referenced. When you open an attached table, the TableDef object is already populated. This is done when the SQL Server table is first attached.

Each Database object has only one TableDefs collection, which contains a TableDef object for each base table and view in the database. It can also include system tables. In turn, each TableDef object contains two collections: Fields and Indexes. You don't need to define the database before you open it; these structures will be filled in for you.

You can access (point to) individual TableDef objects either by using the name of the table or by using the TableDefs collection ordinal number. It makes no difference how you open the database; the access syntax is the same:

```
Set MyDB = OpenDataBase("Work", False, False, Connect)
TableName$ = MyDb.TableDefs("Pigs").Name
TableName$ = MyDb.TableDefs(1).Name
TableName$ = MyDb.TableDefs!Pigs.Name
TableName$ = MyDb.TableDefs(1)
```

All of these address the same TableDef property (*Name*). The number of tables—TableDef objects defined for a particular database—can be returned through use of the Count property. As in all Visual Basic collections, the ordinal numbers range from 0 through Count −1.

TableDef Attributes

The TableDef object's Attribute property specifies characteristics of the table represented by the TableDef object and can be a sum of the Long constants shown in *Figure 10-5*. Generally, you just examine these bits to see if a particular option is enabled, since we rarely create SQL Server tables using this set of attributes. When you are creating attached tables, however, you can set the *dbAttachSavePWD* option to tell Jet that the password and user ID are to be saved in the linkage information.

Figure 10-5
DAO/Jet TableDef Object Attribute Properties Applicable to ODBC Data Sources

Constant	Description
dbAttachExclusive	For databases that use the Microsoft Jet database engine, indicates that the table is an attached table opened for exclusive use
dbAttachSavePWD	For databases that use the Jet database engine, indicates that the user ID and password for the attached table are to be saved with the connection information
dbSystemObject	Indicates that the table is a system table provided by the Jet engine (read-only)
dbHiddenObject	Indicates that the table is a hidden table provided by the Jet engine (for temporary use; read-only)
dbAttachedTable	Indicates that the table is an attached table from a non-ODBC database, such as a Jet or Paradox database
dbAttachedODBC	Indicates that the table is an attached table from an ODBC database, such as Microsoft SQL Server

TableDef Data Types

When Jet populates the TableDefs collection, it maps the SQL Server data types to equivalent DAO/Jet types—or tries to. Not all these assignments make sense, but remember that Jet isn't communicating with SQL Server directly; it gets everything through the ODBC driver, which has its own ideas about data type mapping. I'm not going to describe how to create a new table by using the DAO interface, where you must perform this mapping in reverse; you're better off using Visual Database Tools or SQL Enterprise Manager for this chore, and the Visual Basic documentation includes a short treatise on the subject.

When you describe a new table or access an existing table with the DAO/Jet TableDef object, you'll need to define (or at least understand) the data type and size for each type of data to be accessed. A big change from earlier versions of Visual Basic is the lack of CONSTANT.TXT files. Since Visual Basic now uses type libraries to manage all constants, you no longer need to manually import constant files. That's the good news. The bad news is that now you must conform to the defined constants when you create your code.

Figure 10-6 shows how the Visual Basic Field object Type property maps to SQL Server data types. I thought it would also be interesting and useful to have a map showing how SQL Server data types would be represented in a Visual Basic TableDef and which SQL Server data types would be used for each of the defined FT_data types. To find out how existing SQL Server tables are mapped, I wrote a small application that dumped the mapping for each of the defined SQL Server 4.2 and 6.*x* data types. (Most of the applications I used to create this guide are on the companion disc, and most of them are very simple, but they do show how I arrived at my conclusions.) There were no great differences between the two in most cases, but there were some subtle ones that you should be aware of. *Figure 10-7* on the next page shows those subtle differences. Note that reported size doesn't always reflect the amount of space used to store the data. Since all columns were defined with their default lengths, the size does reflect how much space is reserved for the data type—or, in some cases, the maximum space that can be allocated.

Figure 10-6
Field Object Type Property Settings

Value	Setting	Description	SQL Server Data Type
1	dbBoolean	True/False	Bit
2	dbByte	Byte	TinyInt
3	dbInteger	Integer	SmallInt
4	dbLong	Long	Int
5	dbCurrency	Currency	SmallMoney, Decimal,[1] Numeric
6	dbSingle	Single	Real[2]
7	dbDouble	Double	Real
8[3]	dbDate	Date/Time	DateTime
10	dbText	0–255 string bytes	Char
11	dbLongBinary	Long binary (OLE object) 0–2 GB binary	Image
12	dbMemo	0–2 GB strings	Text, VarBinary, TimeStamp[4]

1. The dbCurrency type can map to any of these currency-type SQL Server data types.
2. The dbSingle type did not get mapped by any SQL Server data type but would be recognized as a Real SQL Server data type.
3. Value 9 is currently undefined by Visual Basic.
4. The dbMemo type is used when any of these three types is referenced.

Figure 10-7
SQL Server Data Types Mapped to DAO/Jet Data Types

SQL Server 6.0 Data Type	Value	Reported Size	Visual Basic Data Type
Binary	12	255	Memo
Bit	1	1	Yes/No
Char	10	255	Text (string)
DateTime	8	16	Date/Time
Float	7	8	Double
Image	11	2147483647	Long binary (OLE object)
Int	4	4	Long
Money	5	21	Currency
Real	7/6[1]	8/4	Double/Single
SmallDateTime	8	16	Date/Time
SmallInt	3	2	Integer
SmallMoney	5	21/12[2]	Currency
SysName	10	30	Text (string)
Text	12	2147483647	Memo
TimeStamp	12	8	Memo
TinyInt	2	1	Byte
Varbinary	12	255	Memo
VarChar	10	255	Text (string)
Decimal[3]	5	20	Currency
Numeric	5	18	Currency
Identity	4	4	Long

1. The Real SQL Server data type is reported as type "7" (double) when a SQL Server 6.0 database is read but as type "6" (single) when a SQL Server 4.2 database is read.
2. The size reported by Visual Basic is 21 for SQL Server 6.0 but only 12 when a SQL Server 4.2 database is being mapped.
3. The Decimal, Numeric, and Identity columns are all new for SQL Server 6.0. The Identity column isn't a specific data type, but I thought it would be interesting to show how it is mapped.

Figure 10-8 shows data type mapping with the Visual Basic DAO interface to create a new SQL Server table on SQL Server 4.2 and 6.0. The figure contains each of the Visual Basic 4.0 data types. Note that the only difference between the two versions involves the dbCurrency and dbSingle data types. This mapping should be the same when Microsoft Access is used to create a SQL Server table.

Figure 10-8
Visual Basic DAO/Jet Data Types Mapped to SQL Server

Visual Basic Data Type	Creates SQL Server 6.0 Data Type	Creates SQL Server 4.2 Data Type
dbDate	DateTime	DateTime
dbText	VarChar (255)	VarChar (255)
dbMemo	Text	Text
dbBoolean	Bit	Bit
dbInteger	SmallInt	SmallInt
dbLong	Int	Int
dbCurrency	Decimal (18, 0)	Money
dbSingle	Real	Float
dbDouble	Float	Float
dbByte	TinyInt	TinyInt
dbLongBinary	Image	Image

The results have not changed much from those for Visual Basic 3.0. Since SQL Server 4.2 supports 17 data types and SQL Server 6.0 supports 20 data types, not all of them can be created by Visual Basic, which supports only 11. I did note that all three integer types were supported now that the dbByte data type is fully supported. Both types of floating-point numbers are supported as well. Binary, VarBinary, SmallMoney, SmallDateTime, and TimeStamp columns could *not* be created, however. Most of these are of relatively minor importance in the bigger picture, since they are represented by similar data types that can easily be substituted. But the inability to create TimeStamp columns is a real problem if you use Jet to create your SQL Server tables.

Field Objects

Field objects are used in a variety of ways to define or declare the columns defined in tables, indexes, and Jet queries and relations. Row data can be reached (if the Field object is part of a Recordset object) through the Value property. Each Field object is maintained in a Fields collection associated with the TableDef, Index, QueryDef, or Relation object. The properties of a Field object that are available in accessing SQL Server data are shown in *Figure 10-9* on the next page.

TIP One Field object attribute that (still) didn't make it to online help is dbRandomIncrField, which indicates a counter-type field that is generated randomly. By setting this attribute bit (64), you can create new tables, including Identity columns using the DAO interface.

Figure 10-9
DAO/Jet Field Object Properties

Property	What It Does
Name	Indicates name of the SQL Server table column.
Size	Indicates size of the field. This is a Long value. Size is determined by the Type property. It bears no relationship to the size of the data held in this field.
Type	Indicates data type of the field.
Value	Holds the data for this element, if this Field object belongs to a Recordset object.
AllowZeroLength	Indicates whether a zero-length string (" ") is a valid setting for the Value property of a Field object with a Text or Memo data type.
Attributes	Indicates one or more characteristics of a Field object.
DataUpdatable	Indicates whether the data in the field represented by a Field object is updatable.
Required	Indicates whether a Field or Index object requires a non-Null value. This maps to the NULL or NOT NULL declaration.
SourceField	Indicates the name of the field that is the original source of the data for a Field object. Used for attached tables.
SourceTable	Indicates the name of the table that is the original source of the data for a Field object. Used for attached tables.

There are a number of ways—I count at least eight—of referring to the data Value property of the current row's Field object. The Value property of the current Fields collection can be addressed by ordinal number, directly:

```
Ms$ = Rs.Fields(1)
```

Or it can be addressed by ordinal number, indirectly:

```
N% = 1
Ms$ = Rs.Fields(n%)
```

It can also be addressed by column name, directly:

```
Ms$ = Rs.Fields("FootSize")
```

And it can be addressed by column name, indirectly:

```
N$ = "FootSize"
Ms$ = Rs.Fields(N$)
```

You can use the Recordset object's default collection and property (Fields.Value), so you don't really need to reference the Field object directly at all:

```
Ms$ = Rs(1)
Ms$ = Rs(N%)
Ms$ = Rs(N$)
```

Using the "bang" (!) syntax is the fastest way:

```
Ms$ = Rs!FootSize
```

Clear? Many of the examples in the documentation use the Visual Basic feature of not having to include the default property that's being referenced. For example, it's no longer necessary to code *Text1.Text = "SomeString"* because *Text1 = "SomeString"* does the same thing.

TIP What's the fastest way to address Field objects? Well, consider that all "late"-bound methods must perform additional lookup work at run time—each time the field is referenced. A late-bound Field object is one where you use a variable to reference a column. I expect that you'll find using the ordinal number is the fastest.

NOTE The OrdinalPosition property for fields in a Recordset object will differ according to whether the dbSQLPassThrough option is used. This is because Jet can't control the order in which columns are maintained in ODBC tables.

Index Objects

The DAO/Jet Index object defines an index for a table. These objects are kept in the Indexes collection. An Index object contains a Fields collection, which in turn contains one or more Field objects designating the columns that define the index keys. A table can have several indexes, but at least one must be defined as unique in order to satisfy Jet. When you are creating new indexes in code, you can examine or change Index object properties up to the point where they are appended to the Indexes collection. After that, they are read-only. The properties of the Index object that are of interest to SQL Server front-end developers are shown in *Figure 10-10* on the next page. (Other index properties do not apply to SQL Server front-end applications.)

Tables and Indexes

One of the most common questions that Visual Basic developers ask when they are using the Data Access Objects is, "Why can't I change the data in the tables?" The principal reason is the lack of unique indexes, or the lack of a designated set of fields uniquely identifying each row. If SQL Server data is to be modified by Data Access Objects, the table or tables used to create the Recordset object must have unique indexes. Since SQL Server doesn't require indexes of any kind, it's entirely possible to have tables containing duplicate rows; but you don't need SQL Server indexes to update tables with Jet—only a field or combination of fields that uniquely identifies the rows.

Figure 10-10
DAO/Jet Index Object Properties

Property	What It Does
Name	Names the index.
Fields	Contains a string holding one or more field names that refer to the keys for a table. Multiple fields are separated by a semicolon (;).
Clustered	Doesn't apply to ODBC indexes, just to Paradox.
IgnoreNulls	Doesn't apply to ODBC indexes.
Primary	Indicates whether an Index object represents a primary index for a table. At least one Index object must have Primary = True to support updatability.
Required	Indicates whether an Index object requires a non-Null value. Since indexes in SQL Server require non-Null values, this should always be True.
Unique	Indicates whether this index is to be unique. (At least one of the indexes must be unique.)

TIP It seems that rebuilding databases doesn't always restore the primary key index—at least not to ODBC's satisfaction. Before you send embarrassing mail, be sure that a primary key is established for the table that you are trying to update via ODBC.

A powerful aspect of DAO/Jet's index implementation is how it deals with external indexes. For example, you can designate a field in an attached table or view as the "unique" identifier. Jet then assumes, on the basis of this designated field, that the SQL server will maintain the unique characteristics of the row, or of a combination of several fields, *and* allow you to update the data.

Despite this flexibility on the part of SQL Server, in order to use Visual Basic's Data Access Objects to do any data modifications you'll have to establish unique indexes on the SQL Server tables that are to be accessed. This might mean a general redesign of one or more tables and their ability to accept duplicate rows—or at least rows with duplicate primary keys.

Creating or Adding Tables and Indexes

If you want to use Visual Basic Data Access Objects to create new tables and indexes, there is a set of objects and methods for doing so. But unless you are really bored and need something to occupy your time, there are better and easier ways to perform DDL housekeeping—such as using Visual Database

Tools or SQL Enterprise Manager. There are also a number of limitations as far as the table is concerned. For example, you'll be able to create only 11 of the 20 supported SQL Server data types. You won't be able to create TimeStamp columns or use any of the new SQL Server 6.*x* constraint types. You won't be able to set up any SQL Server 6.*x* relationships, replication, or any of the other new features not directly exposed by Jet. All the indexes created are established as nonclustered, so setting up a specific data ordering sequence isn't an option. Of course, there's nothing to stop you from sending TSQL queries or SQL statements via the Execute method to create the tables.

The following SQL query could define DAO code for creating a table. Note that we are able to establish a TimeStamp column and to make sure that the Text data type and Age columns are defined as permitting nulls:

```
CREATE TABLE Implements
(Name char(30) NOT NULL,
 Type char(5) NOT NULL,
 Age SmallInt NULL,
 Location char(30) NOT NULL,
 Condition Text NULL,
 Working bit NOT NULL,
 TIMESTAMP timestamp NULL)
```

Now for the DAO code. Note that there is no way to set the null characteristics of the fields. The Required property has no effect, and we can't create the TimeStamp column. The syntax is tighter than in the DAO 1.1 interface, but it still falls short of being able to create SQL Server tables:

```
Private Sub MakeNewTable_click()
Dim db As Database
Set db = OpenDatabase _
    ("workdb", 0, 0, "odbc;uid=;pwd=;database=workdb")
Dim tb As TableDef
Dim fd As Field
Dim ix As Index
db.TableDefs.Refresh
Set tb = db.CreateTableDef(Name:="DAOExample")
Tb.Fields.Append tb.CreateField _
    (Name:="Name", Type:=dbText, Size:=30)
Tb.Fields.Append tb.CreateField _
    (Name:="Type", Type:=dbText, Size:=5)
Tb.Fields.Append tb.CreateField(Name:="Age", Type:=dbInteger)
Tb.Fields.Append tb.CreateField _
    (Name:="Location", Type:=dbText, Size:=30)
Tb.Fields.Append tb.CreateField(Name:="Condition", Type:=dbMemo)
Tb.Fields.Append tb.CreateField(Name:="Working", Type:=dbBoolean)
db.TableDefs.Append tb
db.Close
End Sub
```

Chapter

Configuring and Tuning the Jet Engine

The Windows Registry Database

Understanding Jet Engine Options

Before we plunge directly into the whole topic of configuring and tuning the Microsoft Jet database engine, let's go over some basics about how the Microsoft Windows registry works. That way, it will be easier for you to tell what's what when it comes time to make a few changes in the registry.

The Windows Registry Database

One of the highlights of the Windows 95 adventure is the Windows registry database. This is used to keep the thousands of settings for every imaginable option in the operating system and for every 32-bit application that runs under its control. Your 16-bit or 32-bit applications can still use INI file settings for whatever purposes you choose, but the Data Access Objects (DAO) and the ODBC drivers now depend heavily on the registry in all 32-bit systems.

TIP   For Jet 2.5 in 16-bit applications, initialization settings are saved in the VB.INI (or <APPNAME>.INI) file. Before these option settings can take effect, you must ensure that your application creates an application-specific INI file containing them and that it uses the DBEngine.INIPath property to point to the file. Going to the trouble of creating an INI file or a set of complicated registry entries won't do much good if you don't tell Jet where to find them.

Registry Scope

Let's assume you're going to work with a 32-bit application that needs to initialize some Jet engine options. If so, your settings can be applied on either of two levels. First, they can be applied *systemwide*. Changes will affect all instances of your application, as well as each instance of the Jet engine used by every application running on the machine. In this case, you need to modify the HKEY_LOCAL_MACHINE tree, especially if only one Jet-based application is running on the workstation or someplace else where all applications can

PART III   USING DAO WITH THE MICROSOFT JET DATABASE ENGINE

tolerate using the same initialization values. This isn't the best way to proceed, however, since these settings will be used as the defaults unless an application specifically overrides them with its own settings. Be careful what you change here, unless you enjoy getting calls in the middle of the night from irate users. Second, your settings can be applied so that they affect only the *currently logged-on user*. In this case, you need to reference the HKEY_CURRENT_USER folder, especially if you expect to be running more than one Jet-based application on your workstation. Generally, each Visual Basic application should use settings in a tree that it provides for itself. If you already have such a tree for your application, you should add a Jet section to it—something like this:

HKEY_CURRENT_USER\Software\Visual Basic\5.0*appname*\Jet\3.5\\...

You can also have settings that apply just to *one application* but that are *unique for every user*. For this option, use your own application-specific path, but use HKEY_LOCAL_MACHINE in place of HKEY_CURRENT_USER. That way, every logged-on user gets his or her own set of keys for this application.

Remember that the Jet engine is shared by other applications—not just Visual Basic but also by the entire Microsoft Office suite of tools, Visual C++, and third-party applications. Eventually, most, if not all, applications will have access to Data Access Objects and the Jet engine. Therefore, any changes you make to global engine settings might very easily disturb other applications, just as their settings might disturb yours.

Once your application starts, you have an instance of the DAO/Jet DBEngine object assigned to your application. Basically, separate code segments are created for you, and all your specific parameters are maintained there. As a result, what other applications do has no immediate effect on your running application once it begins. If you change the initialization settings used by some other application, however, or if some other application changes your settings, the results can be unpredictable. How do you solve this problem? As a general rule, you never change the global Jet engine initialization settings; you create separate settings for your application. And if you have several related applications that run on the same machine, you can share initialization settings.

Creating and Using New Registry Keys

To establish a place in the registry database where your settings can be saved, you must open the Windows registry by using the REGEDIT application and then add the required folders and individual key entries. Although Visual Basic supplies a few intrinsic functions for altering the registry, you can't use them to change numeric values; you can change only string settings. This means that you must work through the Windows APIs to make the changes, make the changes manually, or find a third-party source for a control or dynamic-link library (DLL) that makes these changes.

When you are working in Visual Basic Design mode, the Jet engine searches the registry for ODBC initialization settings in the following location:

HKEY_LOCAL_MACHINE\SOFTWARE\Microsoft\Jet\3.5\Engines\ODBC

The Microsoft Jet database engine, not unlike the SQL Server engine, has a small myriad of options that permit you to configure it for different application requirements. Ignoring these settings is like building a race car from components bought at Kmart: the car will work, but it won't be particularly competitive outside the parking lot.

The contents of that location are shown here:

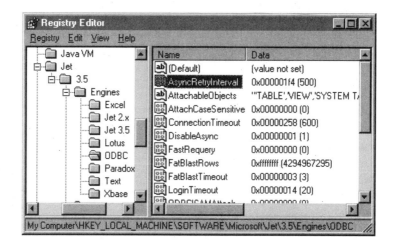

Since Jet uses HKEY_LOCAL_MACHINE as a default, you must change the registry path by using the DBEngine object's INIPath property to point to your application's private registry or INI file. Once you get your application working, you need to create an application key that can be installed in the Windows registry on any system where the application is expected to run—that is, on the *target system*. For example, you can create a key for an application named SQLFrontEnd in the following registry location:

HKEY_CURRENT_USER\SOFTWARE\SQLFrontEnd\Jet\3.5\Engines\ODBC

When you are working with Jet-based ODBC applications, you need to make your ODBC settings in a newly created ODBC section of the Jet\3.5\Engines registry folder. As we already know, making changes to the registry is dangerous, especially changes to the HKEY_LOCAL_MACHINE registry: other applications are going to be depending on these settings, and if you mess up the registry, your system is toast. But since it's a good idea to create the default-override registry entries in a separate registry key, you must discipline yourself to set the INIPath property each time you start a Jet application. Locate your new key under the HKEY_CURRENT_USER registry, and set the DBEngine.INIPath property to this location. It would also be good programming practice to establish this key on your development machine. Then, each time you start a new DAO application, you can make sure you reference an application-specific registry location as the first line of code in the Form_Load event procedure.

Once you establish another key location, be sure to keep the last three keys the same. For example, if your application is called SQLApp, you can create a new entry as follows:

HKEY_LOCAL_MACHINE\SOFTWARE\MyApps\SQLApp\Jet\3.5\

If you use a generally accepted technique when you create registry keys, what you create might not clash with another application that your user happens to be running on your system. But anytime you blindly create a registry entry, you might inadvertently overlay settings established by another application—perhaps even one of your own.

To use this new key, set your INIPath property before any other DAO references in your application. Note that you can't set up the Data control to start automatically, because it starts the Jet engine before your first chance to set the INIPath in the Form_Load event procedure. To set the INIPath property to the new location in code, use the following syntax:

```
DBEngine.INIPath = _
    "HKEY_LOCAL_MACHINE\SOFTWARE\MyApps\SQLApp\Jet\3.5"
```

To create an ODBC key and establish a few values, take the following steps. (If you plan to make changes or additions to the non-ODBC key settings, simply add the setting key values to the Engines key; this is where Jet looks for non-ISAM and non-ODBC settings.)

1. Run the Windows application REGEDIT. Once the application starts, and before you do anything else, you should back up the current registry by choosing Export Registry File from the Registry menu. This backup file might be helpful when it comes to repairing any inadvertent damage. But if *you* never make mistakes, move on to the next step. Just don't call me at four in the morning to complain that your system is dripping solder.

2. When you have backed up the registry, examine the initial REGEDIT window, which displays the top-level registry keys, as shown here:

3. Click on the plus sign (+) to the left of the HKEY_LOCAL_MACHINE icon. This action exposes the next level of keys.

4. Click on the plus signs for SOFTWARE, for Microsoft, for Jet, for 3.5, and finally for Engines. This exposes the list of Jet engine options that you chose when Visual Basic was installed. See if the ODBC key is already installed. If so, you need to decide how you want to proceed. Do you want to change the existing settings or create new ones of your own? If you decide to change them, skip down to Step 6. If you want to create your own key, go up to the HKEY_CURRENT_USER key

and create the following set of keys by choosing New Key from the Edit menu. Be sure to substitute the name of your application EXE for *AppName:*

> SOFTWARE\MyApps*AppName*\Jet\3.5\Engines

5. Now create a new key under the Engines key. Enter *ODBC* for the name. You now have an ODBC key.

6. Select the ODBC key under Engines, and choose New DWORD Value from the Edit menu. Name the new value *QueryTimeout.* You now have an ODBC key value entry.

Double-click on the new ODBC QueryTimeout entry. The Edit DWORD Value dialog box appears. Use this dialog box to set the new QueryTimeout value to 60 (hex 3C).

Perform Steps 5 and 6 for each default override setting you need to create. When your work on the registry is complete, it's a good idea to back up again. You can choose to back up either the whole registry or just the part you changed. For now, export just the part you changed—the ODBC key.

The easy way out

Now that you have waded through the preceding steps, grab a towel and take a look at the exported file you just created. The one I created in preparing this guide looks like this:

```
REGEDIT4
[HKEY_LOCAL_MACHINE\SOFTWARE\Microsoft\Jet\3.5\Engines\ODBC]
"QueryTimeout"=dword:0000003c
"LoginTimeout"=dword:00000020
"ConnectionTimeout"=dword:00000258
"AttachableObjects"=
    "'TABLE','VIEW','SYSTEM TABLE','ALIAS','SYNONYM'"
```

Since you can also edit this file, you could create your own REGEDIT import file and use it to set up the registry when you install an application on the target machine. (This assumes, of course, that the keys don't already exist.) If you install these keys over existing keys, your new version replaces the existing set. Note that it would still be a good idea to use the HKEY_CURRENT_USER key instead.

Be sure to follow the format shown here, including the use of hexadecimal values. Need to convert them? Use the Windows Calculator. It has a built-in hex option. (Unless you own an old Pentium, it ought to get most of the math right.)

Testing a new key

To make sure your new registry key works, try a few lines of code. The following Visual Basic procedure sets the location for a new registry entry in HKEY_CURRENT_USER and tests for a correct QueryTimeout value:

```
Private Sub Command1_Click()
DBEngine.IniPath = "HKEY_CURRENT_USER\SOFTWARE\MyApps\SQLApp\Jet\3.5"
Dim db As Database
Set db = OpenDatabase _
    ("workdb", 0, 0,"odbc;uid=;pwd=;database=workdb")
Debug.Print db.QueryTimeout  ' Should match default override value
End Sub
```

I checked this out, and the INI file settings, which were taken from the registry, were preempted for the new value set in the registry, despite what the help topic says for the QueryTimeout property of the Database object. I did note that neither the INI file settings nor the registry settings had any effect on the default QueryTimeout value when a 16-bit Visual Basic application was running.

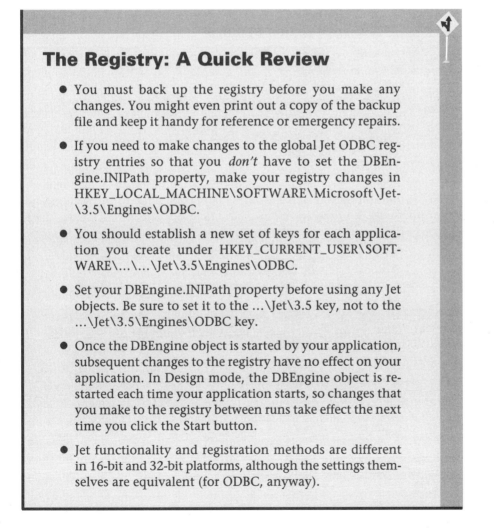

The Registry: A Quick Review

- You must back up the registry before you make any changes. You might even print out a copy of the backup file and keep it handy for reference or emergency repairs.

- If you need to make changes to the global Jet ODBC registry entries so that you *don't* have to set the DBEngine.INIPath property, make your registry changes in HKEY_LOCAL_MACHINE\SOFTWARE\Microsoft\Jet\3.5\Engines\ODBC.

- You should establish a new set of keys for each application you create under HKEY_CURRENT_USER\SOFTWARE\...\...\Jet\3.5\Engines\ODBC.

- Set your DBEngine.INIPath property before using any Jet objects. Be sure to set it to the ...\Jet\3.5 key, not to the ...\Jet\3.5\Engines\ODBC key.

- Once the DBEngine object is started by your application, subsequent changes to the registry have no effect on your application. In Design mode, the DBEngine object is restarted each time your application starts, so changes that you make to the registry between runs take effect the next time you click the Start button.

- Jet functionality and registration methods are different in 16-bit and 32-bit platforms, although the settings themselves are equivalent (for ODBC, anyway).

Understanding Jet Engine Options

The following sections describe initialization and ISAM format settings for both 16-bit (Jet 2.5) and 32-bit (Jet 3.5) Microsoft ODBC drivers.

Microsoft ODBC Driver Initialization Settings

When the Jet database engine is first initialized, it reads the ODBC initialization settings shown in *Figure 11-1*. Changing the settings has no effect on the engine once it is started. These settings are the same for both Jet 2.5 and Jet 3.*x*, but the Jet 2.5 settings are located in an appropriate INI file, and the Jet 3.*x* settings are located in an appropriate registry key. When stored in the registry, all these settings are described as DWORD values, with the exception of the AttachableObjects and Win32 settings, which are strings.

Figure 11-1
ODBC Initialization Settings

Setting	Description
AsyncRetryInterval	The number of milliseconds between polls to determine whether the server is done processing a query. This entry is used for asynchronous processing only. The default is 500.
AttachableObjects	A list of server object types to which attaching will be allowed. The default is 'TABLE', 'VIEW', 'SYSTEM TABLE', 'ALIAS', 'SYNONYM'.
AttachCaseSensitive	An indicator of whether to match table names exactly when attaching. Values are 0 (attach the first table matching the specified name, regardless of case) and 1 (attach a table only if the name matches exactly). The default is 0.
ConnectionTimeout	The number of seconds a cached connection can remain idle before timing out. The default is 600 (10 minutes).
DisableAsync	An indicator of whether to force synchronous query execution. Values are 0 (use asynchronous query execution if possible) and 1 (force synchronous query execution). The default is 0.
FatBlastRows	(New to Jet 3.5.) Number of rows to "FatBlast." 0 = don't FatBlast, < 0 = (default) handle automatically, > 0 = number of rows. Determines how Jet caches "fat" cursors.
FatBlastTimeout	(New to Jet 3.5.) If main query takes longer than this setting (in seconds), don't use FatBlast. Determines how Jet caches "fat" cursors.
FastRequery	An indicator of whether to use a prepared SELECT statement for parameterized queries. Values are 0 (no) and 1 (yes). The default is 0.

Setting	Description
LoginTimeout	The number of seconds a logon attempt can continue before timing out. The default is 20.
ODBCISAMAttach	(New to Jet 3.5.) Used to gate access to "Simba" and "Pecos" drivers. (These were predecessors to the Jet ODBC "Brazos" drivers.) If set to 0, these drivers aren't supported except from Microsoft Excel and Text IISAMs.
PreparedInsert	An indicator of whether to use a prepared INSERT statement that inserts data in all columns. Values are 0 (use a custom INSERT statement that inserts only non-Null values) and 1 (use a prepared INSERT statement). The default is 0. Using prepared INSERT statements can cause Null values to overwrite server defaults and can cause triggers to execute on columns that weren't explicitly inserted.
PreparedUpdate	An indicator of whether to use a prepared UPDATE statement that updates data in all columns. Values are 0 (use a custom UPDATE statement that sets only columns that have changed) and 1 (use a prepared UPDATE statement). The default is 0. Using prepared UPDATE statements can cause triggers to execute on unchanged columns.
QueryTimeout	The number of seconds Jet (ODBC) waits for a query to return the first row of the result set. The default is 60.
SnapshotOnly	An indicator of whether Recordset objects are forced to be of snapshot type. Values are 0 (allow dynasets) and 1 (force snapshots only). The default is 0.
TraceODBCAPI	An indicator of whether to trace ODBC API calls in ODBCAPI.TXT. Values are 0 (no) and 1 (yes). The default is 1.
TraceSQLMode	An indicator of whether the Jet database engine will trace SQL statements sent to an ODBC data source in SQLOUT.TXT. Values are 0 (no) and 1 (yes). The default is 0. This entry is interchangeable with SQLTraceMode.
TryJetAuth/JetTryAuth	An indicator of whether to try using the Microsoft Access user name and password to log on to the SQL server before prompting. Values are 0 (no) and 1 (yes). At one time, this was "JetTryAuth" (and it is still so in the Jet Database Engine Programmer's Guide). The default is 1.
Win32	The location of ODBC32.DLL. The full path name is determined at the time of installation.

There seems to be some confusion about when timeouts occur with the ODBC API. On the basis of the ODBC API documentation and my own experience, I can tell you that the timeout duration starts when you submit the query and ends when the first row is returned to the workstation. The Visual Basic 4.0 documentation, which says that the timeout duration is the number of seconds a query can run before timing out, is inaccurate. Once the QueryTimeout period expires, the query is abandoned—even if it took nine hours to reach the point of failure. With the ODBC API, you can't restart a query once it times out. Your only option is to resubmit the query.

The Details

The following paragraphs shed some additional light on several of the more important Jet engine options, with special attention to their use with ODBC connections and queries.

AsyncRetryInterval, DisableAsync

The Visual Basic 4.0 DAO interface doesn't support asynchronous operations, so these options are of no consequence except when you are using the Data control—which supports some asynchronous operations, right? Nope. Jet *does* support asynchronous operations behind the scenes, when it sends queries to the ODBC driver manager. It polls for completion on the basis of the AsyncRetryInterval setting. Too-frequent polling slows the workstation down, but not polling frequently enough can also slow the response to completed queries.

AttachableObjects

This option shouldn't be touched unless you need to limit the types of SQL Server objects available to your application.

AttachCaseSensitive

When working with case-sensitive SQL servers, you might consider setting this option to prevent any case shifting during name mungeing.

ConnectionTimeout

This is a must-set option: the default of 10 minutes is far too long. Jet is now better about closing unneeded connections than it was in Visual Basic 3.0. Until the timeout period expires, however, Jet doesn't drop idle SQL Server connections—even after you close your Database object. Not only that, but the engine must remain idle long enough for the connection handler to get a chance to time out. That's why you need to set the timeout value to 1 and then use the DBEngine.Idle method to give Jet a chance to catch up and drop idle connections. I like to set the ConnectionTimeout option as high as 1 to

2 minutes and as low as 1 to 10 seconds; the setting depends on how many users are fighting for connections and on how often I open and close my Database objects. Setting the ConnectionTimeout option to 0 disables the timeout, so connections never close—been there, seen that; no, thanks.

FastRequery

Apparently, whenever the ODBC driver submits a query, this option tells the driver to build one or more temporary stored procedures. The use of temporary stored procedures does make subsequent execution of a parameter query faster—assuming that the query lends itself to this form of automation. But the problem with this option is that your application might need to submit some parameter queries that lend themselves to the creation of ODBC prepared statements, as well as some queries that do not. Since this is a DBEngine option, not an option on the OpenRecordset or CreateQueryDef methods, you have to decide before your application starts whether all parameter queries are to be converted to SQL Server temporary stored procedures. The ODBC 2.5 drivers and SQL Server 6.x support temporary stored procedures as part of the overall server design. Stored procedures, instead of being placed in the working database, are all placed in TempDB space. That's the good news. The bad news is that your TempDB space, which also stores server-side cursors, hasn't grown since you started using the new drivers, and it now needs to be larger—a whole lot larger.

PreparedInsert, PreparedUpdate

These options are very important to SQL Server front-end applications that don't use dbSQLPassThrough to send INSERT or UPDATE statements to SQL Server. I rarely allow Jet to update tables directly, and most of my database changes are done via SQL Server–based stored procedures, so this option doesn't make me lose any sleep.

QueryTimeout

This option can be set through the Database object's QueryTimeout property. In 32-bit Visual Basic, the default value can be set in the registry. In 16-bit Visual Basic, the registry and INI file settings have no effect on the 60-second timeout; you can change the value only by specifically setting the property after each Database object is opened. The ODBCTimeout property is used for executing QueryDef objects. Like the QueryTimeout property, it determines how long Jet waits for an ODBC query to return its first row. It defaults to 60 seconds or to the value assigned to the QueryTimeout property.

SnapshotOnly

Since you get to choose what kind of Recordset object is created through the dbOpen*xxx* options in the OpenRecordset method, the need for this option is unclear. If anyone finds a good reason for it, let me know.

TraceODBCAPI

This option lets you review the lowest-level interface to the ODBC driver. The data file created is named SQLOUT.TXT, and its location is hard-coded to be saved in the current directory. In Design mode, this is generally where the VB.EXE is loaded. This option can be very handy when it comes to investigating how Jet has parsed out a chosen query. Basically, it lets you eavesdrop on the conversation from SQL Server to ODBC to Jet.

The TraceODBCAPI option produces exactly the same output as the new ODBC DSN option, which can be enabled through the control panel 32-bit ODBC icon. The Control Panel applet enables you to specify how the ODBC driver manager will trace calls to ODBC functions and where the file will be located, so you don't have to go looking for it. On Windows 3.*x* and the Windows on Windows subsystem of Windows NT, the ODBC driver manager traces calls on an all-or-nothing basis—it either traces the calls made by all applications or doesn't trace calls made by any. On Windows NT, the ODBC driver manager traces calls on an application-by-application basis. This Control Panel option can be enabled quite easily and doesn't affect the registry. It also has an auto-shutoff feature. When an application terminates ODBC, the driver manager checks whether tracing has been selected. If so, the driver manager stops tracing calls to ODBC functions and clears the Trace ODBC Calls check box. To start tracing again, you must reselect the Trace ODBC Calls check box and restart your application.

TraceSQLMode, or SQLTraceMode

This option is a summary of the SQL queries submitted to the ODBC driver. It indicates the ODBC API call used and the SQL syntax, as shown in the following example. I created this trace by executing the OpenRecordset method with *"SELECT * from Phones ORDER BY Email."* The first query extracts configuration information; the second performs the data retrieval:

```
SQLExecDirect: SELECT Config, nValue FROM MSysConf
SQLExecDirect: SELECT "First_Name" ,"Last_Name" ,
    "Section" ,"Email" ,"Company" ,"Site" ,"Location" ,
    "Area_Code" ,"Phone" ,"Changed"  FROM "dbo"."Phones"
    ORDER BY "Email"
```

TryJetAuth

When you set up a new Workspace object, you must provide a user ID and password to gate access to secure Jet databases. Once you set the Workspace object user ID and password, however, Jet also uses these values when it attempts to open connections to remote ODBC databases like SQL Server. If these values don't match those intended for the SQL server, you trip a trappable error. To turn off this automatic authentication, simply set the TryJetAuth option to 0, or always provide a user ID and password in your connect strings.

Tuning *MSysConf*

MSysConf is a Jet-specific, server-based configuration table with the structure shown in *Figure 11-2*. This table's existence is purely optional. Immediately after connecting to a server, Jet executes a query to read its contents. If any errors occur, Jet ignores them and assumes that *MSysConf* doesn't exist. And it won't, unless you add it to each database to be accessed by Jet, either directly or via attached tables.

Figure 11-2
The *MSysConf* Server Table

Column Name	Data Type	Description
Config	SmallInt	The number of the configuration option
chValue	VarChar(255)	The text value of the configuration option
nValue	Integer	The integer value of the configuration option
Comments	VarChar(255)	A description of the configuration option

The Visual Basic 4.0 documentation mentions only one Config value, but there are actually several, as shown in *Figure 11-3*. (Online help does list all the values.) The background population options (Config value 102 and Config value 103) allow an administrator to control how fast Jet fetches rows of a query during idle time. When the fetch delay is high, network traffic is reduced but read locks are left on pages longer. With the delay set lower, locking is reduced and the move to the last record in a result set is speeded up, but network traffic increases. The chunk size option provides an ever finer level of control. These options are different from the engine registry entries since they can be set database by database, whereas the registry entries apply to all operations after the engine starts.

Figure 11-3
Config and nValue Settings in the *MSysConf* Table

Config	nValue	Meaning
101	0	Don't allow storing of user ID and password in attachments.
101	1	Allow storing of user ID and password in attachments (the default).
102	D	Jet delays *D* seconds between background chunk fetches (default=10).
103	N	Jet fetches *N* rows on each background chunk fetch (default=100).

Config = 101

This value permits embedded passwords in attached tables. If the corresponding nValue isn't 0, it's ignored. But if the nValue is 0, Jet will never store user ID and password information in tables attached from this database. If you set the dbAttachSavePWD attribute when you attach a table, or if you choose to save the logon ID and password locally when you attach a SQL Server table with Microsoft Access, and if the nValue is True (not 0), the attribute is ignored, as are any embedded user ID and password values. In this case, the user is forced to include a user ID and password when using the attached table for the first time or complying with integrated security restrictions. Jet caches the user ID and password for subsequent access. This option was created to permit database administrators who are concerned about security to eliminate the possibility of unauthorized users gaining access to data by using another person's computer. The query Jet uses to read this table contains the following syntax:

```
SELECT ... FROM MSysConf ...
```

The table must be publicly accessible via this exact syntax, if the table exists at all. (On a server that supports multiple databases, *MSysConf* might or might not exist in a given database.)

Config = 102

This value sets the delay between fetches of background chunks. With this option set, Jet delays *nValue* seconds between background chunk fetches (default = 10) when asynchronous processing is enabled. The Visual Basic Data control uses this option when populating record sets in the background.

Config = 103

This value sets fetch size for chunk data. When this option is set, Jet fetches *nValue* rows on each background chunk fetch. This option is coupled with Config value 102 and asynchronous operations.

12

Chapter

Using
DAO/Jet to
Get Connected

**Jet's Connection
Management Scheme**

Connection Sharing

Connection Caching and Aging

**Managing Connections
on Your Own**

Opening Attached Tables

**Creating an Attached
Table with DAO/Jet Methods**

Connecting: Common Pitfalls

A s we saw earlier, every front-end application needs to establish one or more connections to SQL Server to gain access to data. But getting connected isn't as simple as it might seem on first inspection. Some SQL Server development shops spend considerable time and effort to develop fairly sophisticated connection managers so that their applications won't have to be bothered with making, releasing, and sharing connections. No matter what type of programming model you choose, however, connecting is a task that either your code or Jet has to manage successfully. Jet 3.0 added considerable logic to its connection management code, making it far less consumptive of connection resources and smarter about SQL Server connection issues. For example, the Jet connection manager now supports domain-managed integrated security—if you set the right switches.

To make your life easier, keep these points in mind when you establish connections with Jet:

- Unless you want the ODBC driver manager to take over the connection process and capture missing parameters from the user, you must ensure that all connection arguments are complete before an attempt is made to open a connection. If you don't, the dialog boxes *will* appear, and there is nothing you can do to prevent it—not in DAO/Jet.

- SQL Server connections that are used to populate cursors can't be reused until the population is complete. Jet has no choice in these cases but to open additional connections and then to create additional cursors or perform update operations.

- Reducing the number of rows fetched in creating a cursor to 100 or fewer permits Jet to prefetch all cursor key values and immediately free the connection. If a new record set contains more than 100 rows, Jet might have to open another shareable connection to manage data retrieval, leaving the first cursor open to manage the keyset.

- Jet automatically opens and closes additional connections to perform data fetching and updates or to populate cursors on an as-needed basis.

- Jet holds at least one connection open until the ConnectionTimeout period expires, even after all Database objects are closed, to expedite subsequent use by your application. This is especially troubling because the default timeout is 10 minutes.

- Jet will attempt to share connections whenever the same DSN is referenced, even when user IDs and passwords are different.

One more point before we get into the windy passages of connection management: to make your application more responsive, you can choose to preconnect to your SQL server in the Form_Load event and leave the connection open for the duration of your application. While this practice consumes a connection on the SQL server, it does perform the needed data definition language (DDL) queries. The DAO/Jet Database object opened with this technique can be closed, but Jet doesn't terminate the connection until it hasn't been used for the entire ConnectionTimeout period, which defaults to 10 minutes. Another way to get disconnected is to stop Jet with the following code:

```
Set DBEngine = Nothing
```

TIP When you disconnect with the Close method, you must *still* give Jet a chance to clean up by using the DBEngine.Idle method after the timeout period has expired.

Jet's Connection Management Scheme

Jet devotes quite a bit of code to connection management. Its goals are to reduce the number of connections used at any one time and to hide the connection management details from developers. Jet and Visual Basic 4.0 and 5.0 offer several advanced data access features, many of which require a multiple-connection model:

- *Simultaneous browsing* of multiple tables and queries, including limited background query execution

- *Direct updating of tables and queries* during browsing

- *Data-aware (bound) controls* (list boxes, DBGrid, and so on) that can be based on tables and queries

Because of the way SQL Server implements cursors, your Jet-based application might require multiple connections to implement such features, unless you use server-side cursors. Unfortunately, however, Jet doesn't support server-side cursors. Two server and driver attributes determine when more connections are called for: *active statements* and *cursor commit/rollback behavior*.

Active Statements

When all the rows you want have been fetched from the server, I call the result set *fully populated*. An active statement is a query whose results haven't been completely fetched from the server—the result set isn't fully populated. If there is an active statement on a connection, SQL Server doesn't allow any other statements to be executed on that connection. Jet might use multiple connections in the case of an active statement—for example, when updating a record before the entire result set is fetched. The alternatives—discarding unfetched results or forcing completion of the active statement before allowing updates—are too disruptive to users. And SQL Server does support multiple connections against a database, so Jet can support the creation of updatable Recordset objects—as long as a unique value can be used in building the bookmarks. This unique value can be a SQL Server index, or it can be one or more designated fields that indicate the unique characteristics of the row.

Cursor Commit/Rollback Behavior

Jet maintains several internal cursors in support of updatable record set operations. For efficiency, these cursors are kept in a prepared state. Servers and drivers differ when it comes to how transactions affect all the prepared or active cursors on a connection. Because Jet wraps data modifications in transactions, Jet takes steps to insulate itself from these effects. Jet identifies which cursor behavior to use by analyzing the most limiting behavior of two ODBC information values obtained via SQLGetInfo: SQL_ACTIVE_STATEMENTS and SQL_CURSOR_COMMIT_BEHAVIOR. The contents of these ODBC driver settings are determined when the connection handle is first established. (This doesn't require a connection or query against the server.) SQL Server supports only one active statement per connection, so Jet requires two connections when performing dynaset operations against SQL Server data.

A new optimization in Jet 2.0, carried forward into Jet 3.0, allows updatable Resultset objects with fewer than 100 rows to be processed by means of a single connection. Jet accomplishes this by quickly fetching the first 100 rows before control returns to your application. If this action populates the result set, an additional connection isn't needed to support dynaset operations.

Connection Sharing

Jet shares ODBC connections internally whenever possible. After accounting for transaction effects and the limitations of active statements, Jet shares connections on the basis of connect strings. Two connect strings are considered equal only if *both* of the following criteria are met: the data source name (DSN) values in both connect strings match, and either the Database values in both connect strings match or neither connect string has a Database value. None of this has any bearing on the user ID. Therefore, if you attempt to use two different user IDs but the same DSN, Jet tries to share one connection between the two operations. To ensure that you can open an additional connection with a different user ID, create a separate DSN entry for each user ID.

How many connections might be required for a given query? Well, if you use the DAO interface to open two large SQL Server result sets—greater than 100 rows—a total of three connections is required. The first fetches keys from the first result set. The second fetches keys from the second result set. The third does all the updating and fetching of chunk data from both result sets. As soon as all the keys from either result set are fetched, or as soon as one of the result sets is fully populated, the corresponding connection is released. As long as the cursor is open, at least one connection remains operational. If you open a smaller result set, Jet caches the rows and quickly closes any unneeded connections.

Another interesting scenario involves Jet's ability to perform updates on joined tables. Suppose you have a fairly complex query that joins data from three tables. Because Jet can identify the index or value that makes each table unique, it can perform an update on any of the three tables by means of a single connection.

Connection Caching and Aging

To avoid constant disconnection and reconnection (since it takes so long to reconnect, given the extra overhead that is often needed), Jet maintains connections in a connection pool even when the connections aren't explicitly in use. This feature is invisible to the user but not to the system as a whole.

During idle time, cached connections are aged and eventually closed down, even if record set variables are still using the connections. When a connection is needed again, reconnection is supposed to be silent and automatic. Unfortunately, that's not always the case. Sometimes Jet can't get everything reconnected, requeried, and repositioned after an automatic shutdown. Anyway, all connections are closed down when your application exits. Two conditions prevent a connection from being timed out: an uncommitted transaction on the connection, and a query with unfetched results on the connection.

If you have objects stored in the SQL Server TempDB database, such as temporary tables or procedures or sorted results, these are lost when the connection drops. SQL Server 6.*x* makes extensive use of TempDB-based procedures, so this feature can be quite traumatic for your application. To avoid the loss of objects, take the following actions:

1. Set the ConnectionTimeout engine to 0, to disable the automatic disconnect.

2. Set ConnectionTimeout to a value higher than the number of seconds you intend to keep the TempDB objects open.

3. Keep pumping up the connection; keep activity on the connection with background processing of some kind, and Jet will postpone the automatic closing of connections.

Managing Connections on Your Own

Jet's connection management machine might not really suit your application's needs. If it doesn't, you can do a couple of things to disconnect much of Jet's micromanagement. In some cases, these techniques might be necessary before you can submit action queries against unpopulated result sets:

- *Use a clone DSN*—that is, a DSN identical to another except for its name. When a clone DSN is opened, the Jet connection manager thinks it's a separate server and that it can't be shared.

- *Set the ConnectionTimeout option to 1,* and use the DBEngine.Idle method to get the connection to time out as soon as possible after you close your connection. Be sure to set the DBEngine.INIPath to point to your application's registry entry property before depending on any Jet initialization option settings.

NOTE   When you use an attached table without a stored user ID and password, or if the stored user ID and password are no longer valid, Jet will attempt to log on with the user ID and password that were used to log on to the local Jet database. (This behavior can be disabled by a registry entry.) This can be a convenient feature if local and remote user IDs and passwords are kept consistent. If this logon attempt fails, the user is prompted for a user ID and password by the ODBC driver's logon dialog box, which can't change any other dialog fields. Once the user has logged on to a remote server, however, Jet remembers the user ID and password until the application exits, so the user isn't prompted again every time reconnection is necessary. But if the user connects to another server or database or to a different DSN, he or she will be prompted for the user ID and password that apply there.

There are basically three ways to tell the Jet engine what kind of connection you need:

The Microsoft Jet team hates it when I write about using the OpenDatabase method against a SQL Server database. They hate it because a frequent side effect of using this technique is the perception that Jet performs poorly. It's all my fault.

- Use the OpenDatabase method to open an ODBC data source directly.

- Use the OpenDatabase method to open a Jet MDB database that contains attached SQL Server tables.

- Use the Data control to establish a connection based on its properties.

If the first argument of the OpenDatabase method is the pathname of an MDB file, and if the *Connect* argument doesn't begin with *ODBC*, Jet assumes that you're trying to open an MDB database (or another ISAM database format). Whether or not the Jet database contains attached tables won't be discovered until the engine inspects the individual tables. In fact, Jet won't even try to establish a connection until the attached tables are referenced. If they're never referenced, no connection is ever made.

If Jet decides that you're trying to open an ODBC data source, and if the DSN isn't already open, Jet passes a subset of the arguments that you included in the OpenDatabase method to the SQLDirectConnect ODBC API function. The connect string is really all you need to open an ODBC data source, since it can contain the data source name, the user ID and password, and optional parameters. If the arguments you include in the OpenDatabase method are insufficient to identify a DSN or to get the connection established, the ODBC driver manager exposes one or more dialog boxes to collect the missing pieces—and there is no way to disable this behavior.

The OpenDatabase Connect argument is used to carry most or all of the parameters to the ODBC driver manager. The *DatabaseName* argument can contain the data source name, but it isn't required. The *Connect* argument consists of the keyword *ODBC* followed by a semicolon (;) and all the other arguments. After the keyword, all the other arguments are optional and can be supplied in any order. The connect string is driver-dependent. For SQL Server, it needs a selected subset of the arguments listed in **Figure 12-1**. Some outdated Microsoft documentation shows that a DBQ argument is also an option. You can try it; it's the same as the DATABASE argument. Unfortunately, however, it's not supported and might not work in your driver.

Figure 12-1
Connect String Arguments for SQL Server

Argument	Description	Example
DSN	Specifies the data source name (simply a named entry that contains the driver and server names and anything else about the connection you provide)	DSN=MyDSN;
UID	User ID corresponding to a SQL Server Logon ID	UID=bill;
PWD	Password; matching password for logon ID	PWD=yup;
DATABASE	Overrides SQL Server default database	DATABASE=Farm;
APP	Name of the application calling; by default, set to the name of the current form (optional)	APP=MyAPP
WSID	Workstation ID; by default, set to the workstation computer network name (optional)	WSID=MyComputer
LANGUAGE	National language to be used by SQL Server (optional)	LANGUAGE=English

A completed OpenDatabase function can be coded this way:

```
Dim Db As Database, Connect As String
Connect$ = "ODBC;UID=bill;PWD=yup;DATABASE=Farm;"
Set Db = OpenDatabase("",0,0,Connect$)
```

Remember to code the connect string exactly as shown—don't add extra spaces before or after the =. If you choose to use integrated security, set the *UID* and *PWD* parameters to null:

```
Connect$ = "ODBC;UID=;PWD=;DATABASE=Farm;"
```

This tells the ODBC driver manager that you didn't forget the user ID and password, so it shouldn't prompt for them. This works only against SQL Server systems that support integrated security and on servers where you have rights. When your SQL Server logon account is established, the system administrator sets up a default database for your account. If you provide the name of an override default database, the SQL Server choice switches to the new default database once the connection is established. If you don't have rights to this database, the switch is reversed. If you don't have rights to any databases on the server, the connection is denied and shut down from the SQL Server end.

If you provide no database name argument in the OpenDatabase method or the Data control DatabaseName property, but only the keyword *ODBC* in the connect string, the ODBC driver manager prompts for the correct DSN by permitting a selection from a list of all known (registered) DSNs. Once a DSN is selected, a dialog box for the user ID and password collects valid parameters. When all the parameters have been collected, one way or another, a connection attempt is made. If it's successful, the connection is completed and control returns to Jet and to the application. If the connection doesn't go through, a dialog box explaining the error is exposed. Once the connection is canceled, the user is prompted again for the correct user ID and password. If this dialog box is canceled, a trappable error is returned to the application.

With this scenario, as you can see, the user has the ability to choose from any live DSN and to provide a choice of user ID and password until he or she either gives up or finds a valid pair and gets connected. Once connected, the user has the full rights of the selected logon. You should also consider how Jet shares connections made to the same database and DSN but perhaps not with the same user ID. With connection sharing, the wrong user might get connected to the right server through no fault of yours. If the user plans to connect more than once, especially with different user IDs, a different DSN should be used. This forces Jet to create and manage the second and subsequent connections as separate objects.

One of the neater ways to open an ODBC connection is to avoid using the DSN entry in the Windows registry. It turns out that you can supply *all* the parameters that are needed to identify the SQL Server and the type of driver to use simply by including them in the connect string. Unfortunately, however, "limitations" in some versions of Jet might prevent it from opening a DSN-less connection. If you don't have the bug fix in place—for example, in the version of Jet that shipped with Microsoft Access for Windows 95, or in the version of Jet that was slipped into Visual Basic 4.0—try downloading the latest Jet 3.0 drivers from CompuServe, the Microsoft Network, or wherever else they're being kept nowadays. If you get a GPF, that's a pretty good indication that you don't have the right version of Jet. But just stick this connect string into the OpenDatabase or Connect property of the Data control, and you won't need a DSN at all:

```
Cnct$ = "ODBC;UID=;PWD=;SERVER=SEQUEL;DRIVER=" & _
    "{SQL SERVER};DATABASE=WorkDB;"
```

Opening Attached Tables

When you attach SQL Server tables or views to a Jet database, Jet places connection and DDL information into the Jet database. This means that when you actually access an attached table, the Jet engine doesn't have to refetch anything—it just has to connect. The user ID and password can also be stored in the linkage information, so anyone with access to the Jet database can gain access to the SQL Server data. No, attached tables don't contain *any* data—just DDL and linkage information.

By default, attached tables are named after the SQL Server database table owner and table name. For example, if you use Microsoft Access to attach to the *Pubs.dbo.authors* table, Access names this table *dbo_authors*. This can take some getting used to, so expect it when you write your Jet queries that reference these tables. You can rename the tables after Access attaches them, or you can attach them yourself in code—yes, I also said you can attach SQL Server views, just like other tables. In addition, you can create "fake" Jet indexes on these attached views, so they can be updated just like any other tables. (You can also attach temporary tables, but that's a bit trickier because when the connection gets dropped, so does the temporary table—not good.)

In the summer of 1994, I attended a conference with Drew Fletcher, a program manager in the Microsoft Visual Basic group. One of the vendors at the conference was demonstrating an application that hooked up the ODBC or DB-Library interface so that developers could monitor and compare interface performance. As we watched, the vendor demonstrated a Jet-based SQL Server application that was running especially slow. After a few minutes, I discovered that he was using the attachment without link (AWOL) technique to open a large SQL Server table. With some encouragement from Drew, he changed his demo to use attached tables, which I set up for him. Suddenly the test application just zipped along, and the amount of interface traffic dropped significantly. The vendor said he hadn't known that using attached tables for connecting to SQL Server was even possible. Apparently I didn't stress this enough in the documentation—assuming he read it.

Opening an attached table is no different from opening any other Jet table. You just can't use the Jet table-type Recordset object to do it. Let's just say you have attached the *Pubs* database tables to a Jet database named *JetPubs.MDB*. To create a cursor on a subset of the *Titles* table attached via the local *dbo_titles* table, you could code as follows:

```
Dim Db as Database, Dim SQL as String, Rs as Recordset
Set Db = OpenDatabase("JetPubs.MDB")
SQL$ = "SELECT DISTINCTROW dbo_titles.*, dbo_titles.title" _
    & " FROM dbo_titles WHERE ((dbo_titles.title like 'c*'));"
Set Rs = Db.OpenRecordset(SQL$,dbOpenSnapshot)
```

See any sign of a connect string? It's there, hidden in the TableDef object that describes the *dbo_titles* table.

What happens if the permissions change for the user ID embedded in the TableDef object? Well, either you need to drop and reattach the table with corrected information or you have to go into the TableDef object and change the connect string. If the structure of the underlying table changes, you can use the RefreshLink method against the TableDef object to refresh the linkage information. In any case, you need to use the Refresh method against the TableDefs collection to refresh its structure, too, if the structure changes.

Doesn't this seem like a lot of trouble? I think it does. That's why I always keep Microsoft Access handy to create the Jet database, attach the tables, and create any queries I need. Believe me, it's far, far easier to get Access to do all this setup work and debug the Jet SQL than to try doing it yourself. Note that this example uses Jet syntax to perform the query. Check out the *like* and the table name syntax.

Creating an Attached Table with DAO/Jet Methods

Need to create an attached table on the fly? You must execute a few DAO/Jet methods to add the new table to an existing MDB database. If you need help creating the new table, check out the CreateDatabase method, or use the following example, which creates a Jet 3.0 database that uses typical (English-language) defaults:

```
Dim Ws As Workspace
Dim NewDb As Database
Set Ws = DBEngine.Workspaces(0)
' Create new, unencrypted database
Set NewDB = Ws.CreateDatabase _
    ("NEWDB.MDB", dbLangGeneral, dbVersion30)
```

I'm not suggesting that your application attach to an ODBC table each time it fires up. That's silliness.

Another approach would be to use the CompactDatabase method, which simply makes a compressed copy of an existing Jet database that can then be modified independently of the original.

Once the Jet database is created, you must attach the SQL Server tables and views to it. You can also create Jet QueryDef objects that refer to the SQL Server tables and views and to any Jet tables that you care to add. The Jet database can contain reports, forms, and macros, but these can't be seen or manipulated from Visual Basic. You can use Visual Basic to create and manage referential integrity or security constraints, but these can't involve ODBC SQL Server tables. Remember that attached tables contain *no* data, just DDL information about the SQL Server database tables.

Here is a series of steps used to create a couple of attached tables that link the Jet database to a SQL Server table and view:

1. Create variables for the Database and TableDef objects you are going to modify.

2. Use the OpenDatabase method to open the existing Jet database.

3. Use the CreateTableDef method to create a TableDef object for the external table.

4. Set the TableDef object properties to refer to the attached table.

5. Append the new TableDef object to the TableDefs collection by using the Append method. This is the step that actually creates the linkage object in the Jet database file.

The following code creates a new database and attaches a couple of SQL Server tables:

```
Dim tdf As TableDef, db As Database, ws As Workstation
Set ws = DBEngine.Workspaces(0)
' Create new, unencrypted database.
Set db = ws.CreateDatabase _
    ("NEWDB.MDB", dbLangGeneral, dbVersion30)
Set tdf = db.CreateTableDef("Titles")
tdf.Connect = "ODBC;DSN=SSRVR1;UID=Fred;PWD=RHS;DATABASE=Pubs;"
tdf.SourceTableName = "Titles"
db.TableDefs.Append tdf
Set tdf = db.CreateTableDef("TitleView")
tdf.Connect = "ODBC;DSN=SSRVR1;UID=Fred;PWD=RHS;DATABASE=Pubs;"
tdf.SourceTableName = "TitleView"
db.TableDefs.Append tdf
```

Notice that the TableDef object is reused. If you don't want to embed the password in the table definition this way, you don't have to, but the Jet connection manager and the ODBC driver do have to get the password from somewhere. Note also that you *don't* set the attribute property to dbAttachSavePWD. This is set by Jet when the table is created. When you're using integrated security, the UID or PWD *values* aren't required, just the *keywords*.

```
tdf.Connect = "ODBC;DSN=SSRVR1;UID=;PWD=;DATABASE=Pubs;"
```

Connecting: Common Pitfalls

A number of things can go wrong when you attempt to make a connection. Things are simpler with Windows NT domain-managed security, but connecting can still be tough, for lots of reasons. And the problems are often the same, no matter what programming model you choose:

- *The DSN doesn't exist.* You didn't create one ahead of time, it has been removed, or you spelled it incorrectly.

- *The DSN exists, but it's for 16-bit Visual Basic and you're using 32-bit Visual Basic.* Be sure to install the 32-bit ODBC drivers and convert any existing 16-bit data source names.

- *The DSN exists, but it refers to a missing SQL server.* When the SQL server is down, or if someone stole it in the night and pawned it to feed a Twinkies habit, the driver manager might have some difficulty trying to find it on the net. The ODBC driver help file DRVSSRVR.HLP includes instructions on how to use an ODBC "ping" program that can isolate connection problems. I have seen incorrectly installed SQL servers refuse to respond to the net, even though they worked locally.

- *The user ID and password aren't valid.* You might have to add the user as a member of a Windows NT group *and* add the user as a valid SQL Server logon.

- *The user doesn't have rights to the default database.* You need to make sure that the user has permission to access the default (or chosen) database.

NOTE When I had to change my domain password at the office, the task proved increasingly painful as the day wore on. Each Windows NT server I connected to wanted to know my new password. I also discovered that I couldn't log on to the SQL server unless I created a new logon. I experimented for some time and ended up using the fallback technique of establishing a file share to the server in question. Once I was connected, the Windows NT system running the SQL server asked for a password. When I provided my Windows NT domain password, the SQL server decided I wasn't an interloper after all and granted me access once again.

When you connect to a SQL server, you have to go through several very picky layers of protocol. But keep one thing in mind: what works all over the world in other people's systems should work in yours, too.

If you still can't get connected, try to set up a simple file share on the SQL server. Can you connect to this share? If so, try the connection again. For some reason, I can't always connect to a 4.2 OS/2 server until I establish a connection to a share via the Net Use command. This operation asks for a password, and once I am connected, the system lets me access the IPC$ share needed to do all named pipe work. You can also install ISQL or ISQLW and see whether they can connect. Neither of these programs uses ODBC, so they can be used to eliminate ODBC DSN, network, and rights problems. If these don't work, you probably need to log on to the workstation, or maybe some other basic network layer isn't working. Can you see anything on the net when you use Net View from an MS-DOS prompt? Or check out SQL Server Books Online for a DB-Library "ping" program to test the LAN layers. If you find that you're not being helped by any of these suggestions, fall to your knees and pray—and while you're down there, see if the net cable is plugged in.

TIP If you just can't get connected to a SQL server, remember that you're going through Jet, the ODBC driver manager, the ODBC SQL Server driver, a named-pipe network interface (or its equivalent), a matching network interface on the server, the server's operating system, and a connection manager run by SQL Server itself. When you're debugging this rig, try to bypass one or more layers to eliminate their role in the problem. And make sure the drivers in use are current as well as matched with the other drivers being used.

Getting Connected with Jet: Key Points

- The Jet connection manager keeps a number of connections open long after you close the Database object that opened them. To force termination of the connection, be sure to set the appropriate registry (or INI) entries, and use the DBEngine.Idle method, or shut down Jet by setting the DBEngine value to 0.

- If you use the direct connect (AWOL) technique, every aspect of the Jet-to-SQL Server interface is bogged down with extra DDL queries. In the past, this was the only way to execute Transact-SQL queries using SQL pass-through queries. This is no longer the case now that you can create a SQL pass-through QueryDef object in a Jet database or set the Connect property of the Database object and use the dbSQLPassThrough option.

- If you use attached tables, you have to create or gain read-write (structure) access to a Jet database and attach the SQL Server tables and views.

- Attached table structure remains static, so if the SQL Server table structure changes, you must reattach or use the RefreshLink method to reset the linkage information.

Chapter

Using Jet to Access Data

Understanding Cursors

Creating Cursors

Choosing an Index

Using the ODBC Cache

GetRows and Variant Arrays

Relocating the Current-Row Pointer

Updating Data

Error Handling

The foundation of any front-end application written in Visual Basic is how the application accesses and manipulates data. In most SQL Server shops, data is rarely accessed by SELECT * queries against base tables; rarely is a user even permitted read-write access to the tables at all. Writing an application that merely uses the Data control or the RemoteData control is usually something that can't be done because access via simple cursors simply isn't permitted. SQL Server shops concerned with data integrity and security usually limit access by creating comprehensive sets of stored procedures and views that gate access to vital data and manage changes to the data. As a result, many ISAM-based programming concepts you might have grown used to in the past can't be carried forward to SQL Server front-end applications.

This chapter focuses on the following areas, which form the data access component of any front-end application written in Visual Basic:

- Manipulating data (retrieving, adding, changing, and deleting server data)

- Accessing specific SQL Server features and functions

- Performing administrative operations, such as adding and deleting tables, managing security, and performing DBCC operations (which are used to manage the system and user databases and which let you scan the database structure for trouble and take corrective action)

Understanding Cursors

When you use DAO/Jet to access SQL Server data, you have very little choice about how the data is accessed—you *must* use a cursor of some kind. Jet 1.1 implements the dynaset and Snapshot objects; Jet 2.5 and 3.*x* use the Recordset object for this purpose. There are three types of Recordset objects, but only two of them can be used to access SQL Server data:

- *The dynaset-type Recordset object*. This cursor is created when a *bookmark* is fetched for each row in the query result set. (A bookmark is a variant value that contains enough information for the row to be located if it's ever referenced again.)

- *The snapshot-type Recordset object*. This cursor is created when all the selected data values are fetched for each row in the query result set.

NOTE   The DAO/Jet table-type Recordset object can't be used to access SQL Server data, since it's designed to work with ISAM data, where the index row ID values are directly accessible. Because SQL Server row ID values aren't accessible, there's no easy way to implement table-type Recordset objects.

Let's look a lot more closely at how dynaset- and snapshot-type Recordset objects are created. Generally, you're not thinking about creating a cursor when you're using the Recordset object. You're thinking about executing a query and working with the resulting rows. How the query is phrased plays a significant role in how the result set can be used, its updatability, and the type of cursor created for you. Query phrasing also plays a significant role in query performance. A Jet cursor is created with one of the following techniques, each of which generates a query:

- A table name, which is converted to a SELECT * query

- The name of a DAO/Jet QueryDef object, which contains a stored Jet SQL or Transact-SQL (TSQL) query

- A Jet-syntax SQL query

- A TSQL query, which might simply contain the name of a SQL Server stored procedure, which in turn contains a TSQL query or operation or both

Jet can deal with both Transact-SQL queries and Jet-syntax queries. If you don't specifically indicate otherwise, Jet always assumes Jet query syntax. But don't Jet and SQL Server both use ANSI syntax? Yes—but they both use supersets of the ANSI syntax, and their statements don't always cross-pollinate. For example, a SELECT * FROM AUTHORS statement works on both the Jet and the SQL Server query processor. Nevertheless, consider this common TSQL join:

```
SELECT Title, TNum, Language
FROM Topics T, Languages L
WHERE T.Lang = L.Lang
```

This join is somewhat different in Jet syntax, as you can see at the top of the next page.

```
SELECT DISTINCTROW Topics.Title,
Topics.TNum, Languages.Language

FROM dbo_Topics INNER JOIN dbo_Languages
ON Topics.Lang = Languages.Lang;
```

In the TSQL query, I used table aliasing to refer to the table names in the join, but there is nothing really out of the ordinary in the syntax. In the equivalent Jet query, generated for me by Microsoft Access or by Microsoft Database Tools, the Jet join syntax is different from the syntax in the simpler TSQL form. You can use the TSQL form, but if you do, the Jet query optimizer might not recognize it as a join and might perform a rather clumsy operation to fetch the data. I have invariably used Access to create these queries, and I have unabashedly avoided trying to make my syntax conform to Jet's. Notice, too, that the Jet query ends with a semicolon. I have found that it generally isn't required, since Visual Basic apparently adds it for you if you need it.

With the arrival of SQL 6.0, the rules changed again. SQL Server now supports the ANSI join syntax much in the same way (but not exactly) as Jet. This means that you can (in most cases) simply use Jet SQL syntax for common join operations. Personally, I would prefer to use the old TSQL syntax or simply let Visual Data Tools come up with the right query.

While we're on the subject of Jet syntax, SQL Server table names have the prefix *dbo_* or the table owner's name when Access first attaches the tables to an MDB database. When Jet queries the table names from the server, as when the Data control is used, it also adds the *dbo_* prefix to the table name. This means that when you set up the DataField property of bound controls, you must also follow this convention. Otherwise, you need to go into the MDB database and rename the tables. Do this from Microsoft Access—it's far easier, and Access caused the problem in the first place.

What happens to the query before it gets to SQL Server, since the SQL Server query processor might have problems with Jet syntax? Remember that the ODBC driver manager and the SQL Server driver are also in the execution path. When Jet creates its own syntax (as you use the Data control, or as you supply Jet syntax in a query or a QueryDef), the Jet query processor is forced to convert the query to generic ODBC syntax. The ODBC SQL Server driver then converts *that* syntax to TSQL syntax. Fortunately, ODBC syntax is very similar to the Jet style—another ANSI variation. It's not a cosmic leap, and it doesn't take a lot of CPU cycles, but it does put a pothole in the road now and then.

Jet, working with the ODBC API, makes every attempt to create its own temporary stored procedures, especially when working with parameter queries, to speed up the process of getting the query result sets. This means that your system might end up with quite a few orphaned procedures if your application doesn't give Jet and ODBC a chance to clean them up while working with an application under development. The problem manifests itself as a raft of procedures whose names begin with *ODBC* in your *SysObjects* table. In SQL Server 4.*x*, these procedures are added to your working database. In SQL Server 6.0, however, they are saved in TempDB. This approach means that when your connection gets closed, any orphaned procedures are dropped along with all other instance-owned objects. Swell. The downside of using TempDB space is that *everyone* is using it, regardless of the database. SQL Server 6.0 also uses TempDB space for server-side cursors and all instance-owned temporary objects. Can you see where this is going? Obviously, TempDB space needs to be *much* larger than it was in SQL Server 4.2 installations—especially in 7 × 24 systems.

How do you get rid of the procedures in a SQL Server 4.2 system? You just go into Enterprise Manager, select these procedures, and drop them. Or you could try the following procedure, which we use here at Microsoft to clean up these ODBC droppings:

```
select "drop procedure " + b.name + "."+ a.name + char(13) + 'go'
from sysobjects a, sysusers b
where a.uid = b.uid
    and a.name like "odbc#%"
    and type = "P"
```

Run this script with ISQL (or ISQLQW), using the server administrator's account. Redirect the output into a file, and use the file as another ISQL script—again using the server administrator's account:

```
ISQL /Usa /S /Pmysapw /iCleanUp.SQL > ODBCList.SQL
ISQL /Usa /S /Pmysapw /iODBCList.SQL
```

You don't need this for SQL Server 6.0. It cleans up after errant users, the way a good housekeeper picks up the residents' dirty socks.

NOTE Opening an MDB database that contains one or more attached tables doesn't generate any ODBC activity. When you access the individual tables or run a DAO/Jet QueryDef, Jet executes a number of ODBC functions to retrieve the data. Remember, all the table's data definition language (DDL) information is stored in the TableDef objects in the Jet database.

Once the query arrives at the SQL server, it's executed and the first rows are sent back. Right? Hardly. Let's take a closer look at the traffic passed between Jet, the ODBC driver, and SQL Server. This should give you some idea of the net traffic involved and the amount of processing that must be done by the drivers and by Jet itself. What follows is a condensed version of the ODBC log dump that is generated when I execute the preceding query with attached tables. (The original is on this guide's companion disc for you to examine: SQLLog1.LOG.)

First, you set up the environment. The ODBC API functions you see at the top of the next page establish ODBC environment and connection handles and set up the connect options to be used. (In this case, connect option 103 is logon timeout, set to 20 seconds; 14 is the equivalent hex value.)

```
SQLAllocEnv(phenv436F0000);
SQLAllocConnect(henv436F0000, phdbc4E770000);
SQLSetConnectOption(hdbc4E770000, 103, 00000014);
```

Next, you connect to SQL Server with the connect string embedded in the TableDef for the attached table in question. Note that the user ID and password are embedded here. Note also that anyone can turn on the SQL Trace log and see this information. The SQLGetInfo function returns information about the driver itself. Since a Jet database can be transported to anyone's system, Jet must determine how to approach access problems by polling the driver for its current configuration. All these function calls are made against the ODBC connection handle. This means that the information is probably in the driver, and no query against the server is needed:

```
SQLDriverConnect(hdbc4E770000, hwnd0578, "DSN=Workdb16;UID=;
    PWD=;APP=Microsoft Access;WSID=BETAVP5;DATABASE=workdb",
    72, szConnStrOut, 0, pcbConnStrOut, 0);
SQLGetInfo(hdbc4E770000, 9, rgbInfoValue, 2, pcbInfoValue);
SQLGetInfo(hdbc4E770000, 6, rgbInfoValue, 100, pcbInfoValue);
⋮
SQLSetConnectOption(hdbc4E770000, 101, 00000001);
```

Once the connection has been completed, a statement handle is allocated and its options are retrieved and reset. These two options set the query timeout to 60 (0x3C) seconds and enable asynchronous operations. (Yes, Jet uses asynchronous operations by default—and, no, you can't use any asynchronous features programmatically.) Again, these are driver settings, and we still haven't done anything with the server but open a connection:

```
SQLAllocStmt(hdbc4E770000, phstmt5F870000);
SQLGetStmtOption(hstmt5F870000, 0, pvParam);
SQLSetStmtOption(hstmt5F870000, 0, 0000003C);
SQLGetStmtOption(hstmt5F870000, 4, pvParam);
SQLSetStmtOption(hstmt5F870000, 4, 00000001);
```

Now we're finally ready to send the query, right? Guess again. The following internal ODBC queries pull down options from the *MSysConf* table. Notice that each of the first two lines appears in the log twice. I am told that since Jet has selected the asynchronous mode, these multiple entries are the by-product of Jet polling while the StillExecuting bit is true. Notice that SQLError is invoked twice. This is probably because I don't have an *MSysConf* table in my tiny test database. Once this query is complete, Jet drops the statement handle—only to create another:

```
SQLExecDirect(hstmt5F870000,
    "SELECT Config, nValue FROM MSysConf", -3);
SQLExecDirect(hstmt5F870000,
    "SELECT Config, nValue FROM MSysConf", -3);
SQLError(henv436F0000, hdbc4E770000, hstmt5F870000,
    szSQLState, pfNativeError, szErrorMsg, 8192, pcbErrorMsg);
SQLError(henv436F0000, hdbc4E770000, hstmt5F870000,
    szSQLState, pfNativeError, szErrorMsg, 8102, pcbErrorMsg);
SQLFreeStmt(hstmt5F870000, 1);
```

Are we ready now to do our query? Just about. But first Jet must set up the same statement handle options it set only microseconds ago (but after it dropped the statement handle it used to poll *MSysConf*). Jet now sets the asynchronous mode and query timeout value again. These don't take long; they're just driver options:

```
SQLAllocStmt(hdbc4E770000, phstmt5F870000);
SQLGetStmtOption(hstmt5F870000, 0, pvParam);
SQLSetStmtOption(hstmt5F870000, 0, 0000003C);
SQLGetStmtOption(hstmt5F870000, 4, pvParam);
SQLSetStmtOption(hstmt5F870000, 4, 00000001);
```

Now we really *are* ready to execute the query. By using SQLExecDirect, Jet bypasses creation of a stored procedure to run the query. Notice that Jet has to poll twice before StillExecuting returns False:

```
SQLExecDirect(hstmt5F870000, _
    "SELECT "dbo"."Topics"."TNum" ,"dbo"."Topics"."Title" ,"
    dbo"."Languages"."Language"  FROM"
    dbo"."Topics","dbo"."Languages" WHERE ("
    dbo"."Topics"."Lang" = "dbo"."Languages"."Lang" ) ", -3);

SQLExecDirect(hstmt5F870000, _
    "SELECT "dbo"."Topics"."TNum" ,"dbo"."Topics"."Title" ,"
    dbo"."Languages"."Language"  FROM "dbo"."Topics","
    dbo"."Languages" WHERE ("
    dbo"."Topics"."Lang" = "dbo"."Languages"."Lang" ) ", -3);
```

Once the query is passed to SQL Server and ODBC indicates that the first result set row is available, all that remains is the process of retrieving the data. In this case, Jet executes two ODBC functions: SQLFetch, to get the next row of data; and SQLGetData, for each individual column. This sequence is repeated for each row visited, one row at a time. Only the SQLFetch statement generates network traffic, but there are plenty such statements being executed—and this is where Jet's performance really falls down. When we talked about tuning Jet, we touched on setting the cache size. This permits Jet to make a more intelligent, 100-row fetch in a single operation. You can see how it makes sense to limit both the number of rows and the number of columns returned in a result set:

```
SQLFetch(hstmt5F870000);
SQLGetData(hstmt5F870000, 1, 4, rgbValue, 256, pcbValue);
SQLGetData(hstmt5F870000, 2, 1, rgbValue, 256, pcbValue);
SQLGetData(hstmt5F870000, 3, 1, rgbValue, 256, pcbValue);
SQLFetch(hstmt5F870000);
SQLGetData(hstmt5F870000, 1, 4, rgbValue, 256, pcbValue);
SQLGetData(hstmt5F870000, 2, 1, rgbValue, 256, pcbValue);
SQLGetData(hstmt5F870000, 3, 1, rgbValue, 256, pcbValue);
SQLFetch(hstmt5F870000);
⋮
```

This sequence is repeated for each row and each column in the result set.

Now, why did I bore you with this detail? Because when it comes to figuring out how to tune a Jet application or any ODBC application, including those that use the RDO interface, knowing how to examine SQL trace logs is a must. When you're reporting bugs against ODBC drivers or any of the middleware, it's also a good idea to dump the log as the problem is occurring. This helps both you and the debugging crew.

How do you turn on the log? Easy:

1. Open the Windows Control Panel, and choose either the 16-bit or the 32-bit ODBC setup icon. These are used to manage data source names (DSNs) and can optionally set or disable the trace log.

2. Click on the Options button. This displays the Options dialog box.

3. Select Trace ODBC Calls, and deselect Stop Tracing Automatically. This step is needed because some Jet applications turn off tracing. Be sure to return to this dialog box and disable tracing when you are finished testing.

4. Set the name of the file to receive the trace log in a place where you can find it. Be sure to specify a path, since this file will be tough to find if you let the Windows operating system choose the default path.

5. Click OK to close the ODBC Options dialog box, and then close the Data Sources window. From this point on, all ODBC operations will write to this log. Note that you can (and should) set up separate 16-bit and 32-bit logs.

Another option is to use SQLTrace. This new utility is provided with SQL Server and can help clear up what Jet or any ODBC interface is *really* doing. It's fairly simple to use; you just start it and create a "base" filter. What you see is each operation sent to SQL Server. This differs from ODBC logs, which show what APIs are being executed. SQLTrace shows what commands are being executed by the ODBC driver itself. I showed you one of these SQLTrace logs back in Chapter 2.

Creating Cursors

Now let's look at cursors from the developer's viewpoint. There are two types of DAO/Jet cursors available to the developer accessing ODBC-connected data sources: dynaset-type and snapshot-type Recordset objects. (These are different from the obsolete Dynaset and Snapshot objects supported in Visual Basic 3.0. When I refer to a dynaset or a snapshot in this chapter, I am referring to a type of Recordset object.) When you use the DAO/Jet OpenRecordset method or the Data control, Jet creates a cursor as close as possible to what you specify, though it doesn't always comply exactly with your request. For example, if you request a dynaset-type Recordset object and the underlying table isn't updatable, Jet creates a snapshot-type Recordset object instead.

A dynaset-type Recordset object is a live, updatable view of the data in the underlying tables. Changes to the data in the underlying tables are reflected in the dynaset, and changes to the dynaset data are immediately reflected in the underlying tables. A snapshot-type Recordset object is a read-only, unchanging view of the data in the underlying tables. Dynaset-type Recordset objects are populated differently from snapshot-type Recordset objects.

Coding the OpenRecordset Method

The OpenRecordset method is one of the most frequently used methods, no matter what kind of table or database you are using with Jet. As we saw earlier, the new Jet 2.*x*/3.*x* engine combines several obsolete DAO/Jet methods into one comprehensive method—more specifically, the OpenTable, CreateSnapshot, and CreateDynaset methods and statements are now all replaced by OpenRecordset.

When using the DAO/Jet OpenRecordset method against a SQL Server database, you should use it off the Database object, since creating result sets on result sets is particularly inefficient. I leave the syntax to online help, but I do go over the arguments with special attention to SQL Server access needs. Most of the options shown in *Figure 13-1* on the next page don't apply to DAO/Jet Recordset objects created against ODBC tables, only to Jet-based tables. For example, Recordset parameters in your application can't restrict other SQL Server users' access to base SQL Server tables. The options shown in the figure are set when a combination (or none) of the *Integer* constants specifies characteristics of the new Recordset object, such as restrictions on other users' ability to edit and view it.

Result Set Population

Result set population is a dynamic process that begins when the query is first executed and ends when the last qualifying row is added to the workstation-side result set. Generally, Jet cursor membership isn't closed until population is complete. Membership in the cursor is determined by the query. For example, consider the following query:

```
Select Count(*) from Chickens where eggs > 5
```

This asks how many chickens laid more than five eggs this week. If the query engine froze the entire *Chickens* table, and if the farmer made sure that no eggs were laid while this query was being executed, you could be sure of an accurate count at any one moment. But the mechanics of the query (and chicken biology) don't work that way. Basically, the query processor begins at the first row of the *Chickens* table and tests the criterion established by the WHERE clause. If the row qualifies, it's added to the membership. But if a chicken laid only four eggs this week, its row isn't included in the total. What if the farmer's wife is in the barn choosing chickens for dinner while the query is being populated? If she chooses a chicken that was already counted, or one that would have qualified as a layer of five eggs, the count won't reflect an accurate picture of current egg production. Unless you can ensure that the dynamics of the database remain static, you can't be assured of an accurate count. This principle applies to debits and credits as well as to chickens.

Figure 13-1
Recordset Option Property Settings

Option	Specification
dbDenyWrite	Other users can't modify or add records. Applies only to Jet database cursors.
dbDenyRead	Other users can't view records (table-type Recordset only). Applies only to Jet database cursors.
dbReadOnly	You can only view records; other users can modify them. Opening a Recordset as read-only can significantly improve performance.
dbAppendOnly	You can only append new records (dynaset-type Recordset only). Opening an updatable Recordset as append-only can significantly improve performance.
dbInconsistent	Inconsistent updates are allowed (dynaset-type Recordset only). Applies only to cursors.
dbConsistentOnly	Only consistent updates are allowed (dynaset-type Recordset only). Applies only to heterogeneous cursors.
dbForwardOnly	The Recordset is a forward-only scrolling snapshot. Recordset objects created with this option can't be cloned and support only the MoveNext method for moving through the records.
dbSQLPassThrough	The Microsoft Jet database engine query processor is bypassed. The query specified in the OpenRecordset source argument is passed to an ODBC back-end server for processing.
dbSeeChanges	Generates a run-time error if another user is changing data you are editing. This option is required if your query includes a table with an Identity-type column. For queries that need to access SQL Server 6.0 Identity columns, you must also set the dbSeeChanges option when you are using the OpenRecordset method to perform updates.

Another factor is involved here, too. If a query is so broad that the SQL Server query processor escalates from page locking to table locking, no updates will be possible anywhere in the table until the Recordset object is fully populated. Some chickens might be deleted before or after the count is complete, but none of these changes is reflected in the database until the cursor is fully populated.

The SQL Server query processor approaches this problem by determining which rows are members before the data is extracted—by establishing a share lock on each affected page that contains an affected row. If necessary, the page locks are escalated to one or more table locks. SQL Server then performs the query. All updates to the table pages in use are blocked until the row has been visited as you populate the cursor. That way, an update can take place on any member row but only after it has been counted or included in the membership.

NOTE   All SELECT * FROM *table* queries against ODBC data sources are escalated to table locks, as are queries that simply reference the table by name.

As you can see, it's imperative that you fully populate *all* cursors as quickly as possible. Under no circumstances should you give a user the opportunity to browse through a Recordset object that hasn't been populated in the background or before access to the data has been granted. The problem with prepopulation, however, is that it can take a very long time for large Recordset objects. Again, this means that the Recordset object's size must be limited, especially on multiuser systems with large tables. The point where the SQL server escalates to table locking from page locking is a fixed point determined by the server administrator, so databases with large tables are more likely to cause table-lock escalation than those with small tables.

When the DAO/Jet OpenResultset method is executed, Jet automatically cancels a long-running query after a configurable amount of time. (The default is 60 seconds.) If this happens, it doesn't necessarily mean that the server didn't respond during that time or that you have become disconnected. It simply means that the query didn't return the first row of results in the time allotted.

TIP   If you know that a certain query will take a very long time to execute, increase the QueryTimeout setting. Note that subsequent operations against the Recordset object, like the MoveLast or Find methods, do *not* time out; these can run virtually indefinitely. And once they are started, there's no mechanism exposed in Visual Basic for canceling these operations. You could unplug the system, disconnect the net, or give the application the three-finger salute: Ctrl-Alt-Delete.

A snapshot-type Recordset object is populated via a query that pulls back selected row data meeting the query's criteria. A dynaset, by contrast, is populated by a query that selects only the bookmark (primary key) columns of each qualifying row. In both cases, the result sets are stored in memory (they overflow to disk if they are very large), which allows you to scroll around arbitrarily. Jet doesn't use the Windows swap file; it overflows to the location specified by the TEMP environment variable.

Microsoft Access is optimized to return answers and populate the Recordset object as quickly as possible—as soon as the first screen (about 25 rows) of result data is available, Access paints it. Jet doesn't do this automatically. Access uses Jet's and ODBC's ability to run the population process asynchronously. Visual Basic doesn't offer this luxury with the DAO/Jet interface. The Data control, however, does support asynchronous operations, but only on the DAO/Jet Recordset objects it creates, not on Recordset objects created in code. It also has a somewhat unfortunate problem: when you first refresh the Data control, it begins to populate the Recordset object on its own (so far, so good), but as soon as you push a button on the Data control to move to the next row, the application freezes while the Data control moves to the last row, fully populating the Recordset object. I suppose this problem will be fixed in the future.

In Visual Basic, Jet caches about 50 rows (a *cluster*) at a time, as you can see if you execute a query and examine the Recordset.RecordCount property. I executed the following query:

```
Select * from Animals
```

I discovered that the RecordCount property began at 1 as control returned to my application. When I moved to the second record, it bumped up to 51. It remained on 51 until I reached the 52nd record, where it moved to 101. Apparently, Jet does perform some background processing, even for DAO operations.

When the Jet query processor fully populates a snapshot cursor, it does no further data fetching. Once a dynaset cursor is fully populated, the query processor does no more key fetching but it will continue to fetch clusters of rows on the basis of the bookmarks if you scroll around. If a connection is needed solely for this key-fetching query, it's closed unless either of the following conditions exists:

- It's parameterized. (The connection is maintained to allow fast requery for parameter queries.)

- Closing it would counteract connection caching.

When rows of data are needed, snapshot data is available locally. A dynaset, however, has only keys and must use a separate query to ask the server for the data corresponding to the current row's bookmark. To reduce the querying traffic, Jet asks the server for clusters of rows specified by their bookmarks rather than for rows one at a time. This does reduce the currency of data, though, since the data within the cluster tends to get stale as time goes by. But it greatly speeds movement within a small area.

Snapshot-type and dynaset-type Recordset objects differ in several performance characteristics, given their different methods of retrieving and caching data. Several points are worth noting:

- If your result set is small and you don't need to update data or see changes made by other users, use a snapshot. It's faster to open and scroll through than a dynaset.

- For a larger result set, a dynaset is faster and more efficient. Moving to the end of a snapshot requires the entire result set (including the data) to be downloaded to the client, but a dynaset downloads only the bookmark columns and then fetches the last cluster of data corresponding to those keys when it moves to the last row.

- Dynaset open time and scrolling speed are affected most negatively by the number of columns you select and the number of the query's tables that are output. Select only the columns you need. Requesting all the columns by using *Table.** is more convenient, but it's slower. Sometimes joins are used simply as restrictions and don't need to be output at all.

- As a rule of thumb, it isn't a good idea to include OLE, Text, and Image (binary large object, or BLOB) data type columns in your multi-column snapshot queries. Use a separate query specifying a single row to fetch these columns when the BLOB data is requested. For dynaset-type Recordset queries, Jet fetches BLOB columns only as they are referenced in code. If there is no reference, the data isn't downloaded.

Choosing an Index

In order to update a dynaset-type result set, Jet must be able to locate a unique index on the table. If no such index is found, Jet creates a *snapshot,* which isn't updatable. The key values of a row are also called the row's *bookmark* because they uniquely identify and allow direct access to the row. Remember that SQL Server supports tables that contain duplicate rows—but you can't create a dynaset on this type of table. You can create a snapshot on this type of table or on a query that includes this type of table.

Jet is capable of creating cursors that are based on the result set of either a simple or a fairly complex join. One of its most powerful features is its ability to update this result set. To do so, Jet requires that a unique index be available for each component table. If one or more unique indexes aren't available, the result set won't be updatable.

The Recordset object's Bookmark property contains the bookmark for the current row. Changing the Bookmark to a valid bookmark value resets the current-row pointer to the row with the associated key.

NOTE One of the most common errors is the "Invalid method for this object" error, which simply refers to the fact that the Update method is invalid against a Recordset object whose Updatable property is False. If Jet can't find a unique key or if the dynaset isn't updatable for a litany of other valid (and some not so valid) reasons, you can't execute the Update method on the Recordset object.

When you attach an ODBC table or when Jet opens a table on an ODBC database, Jet chooses the first unique index returned by the ODBC SQLStatistics function to be the *primary index;* its key columns will compose the bookmark. SQLStatistics returns clustered, hashed, and other indexes, in that order, alphabetically within each group. Thus Jet can be forced to elect a particular unique index as primary if you rename the index so that it appears first alphabetically. Jet doesn't call SQLSpecialColumns(SQL_BEST_ROWID), and it makes no attempt to use a server's native record identifier in lieu of a unique index. The longevity of such identifiers varies among servers, and after you insert a new record, there's no efficient, unambiguous way for Jet to receive the new record identifier.

A server view can be attached but will be treated exactly the way an attached table with no indexes is treated. Thus an attached view, and any query based on one, will be a read-only snapshot. Server-based stored procedures can't be attached, because they don't resemble tables and views closely enough. But if you know that certain columns uniquely identify rows in the view (perhaps they comprise a unique index in the underlying table), you can create a "fake" unique index on the attachment itself by using a Jet DDL query such as this one:

```
db.Execute "CREATE UNIQUE INDEX Index1 " _
    & "ON AttachedTable (Column1, Column2)"
```

Don't make this query a SQL pass-through query, since it doesn't create an index on the server's table or view. SQL Server won't let you create an index on a view, but this action query tells Jet which table fields uniquely identify the table's rows, and it allows dynaset functionality, including updating. Note that this "index" isn't really an index at all. It's simply a set of parameters that lets Jet know the columns used for the unique key.

Server-based stored procedures can't be attached, because they don't resemble tables and views closely enough. You can, however, attach temporary tables (#TEMP) and create SQL Server indexes on these. You can also create Jet QueryDef objects that execute stored procedures and treat them as local read-only tables.

Servers vary in how precise they can be when they handle floating-point data, so some precision might be lost. (*Floating-point data,* of course, is numeric data with digits to the right of the decimal point.) Very large or very small floating-point values might lose accuracy when they are being transferred to Jet from some servers. The actual difference is slight enough to be inconsequential, but if the data forms part of a table's bookmark, Jet might think the row has been deleted when Jet asks the server for the row by its key values and no exact match is found. Jet can't distinguish this situation from that of a genuine record deletion by another user. If this occurs and another unique index on the table doesn't involve floating-point data, you should reattach the table and force Jet to elect the other unique index as primary, by renaming it.

Using the ODBC Cache

To improve Jet's performance against ODBC databases, the Jet team added a set of RAM cache management methods. They permit you to set the number of rows to be prefetched when you are populating or browsing cursors. These methods aren't as easy as just opening a Recordset object and executing a MoveNext method, but they do improve performance dramatically.

Basically, a cache is space in local memory that holds the data most recently fetched from the server, on the assumption that the data will probably be requested again while the application is running. Caching improves the performance of any application that retrieves or fetches data from a remote server—assuming, of course, that you have the local memory to devote to caching. If you don't, Windows begins to swap out lower-priority pages in favor of the cache pages, and this can really slow the whole operation down.

When data is requested, Jet checks the cache for the data first rather than fetching it from the server, which would take more time. Instead of waiting for the cache to be filled with records as they are fetched, you can explicitly fill the cache at any time, using the FillCache method. This is a faster way to fill the cache because FillCache fetches several records at once instead of only one at a time. For example, while each screenful of records is being displayed, you can have your application use FillCache to fetch the next screenful of records. Data that doesn't come from an ODBC data source isn't saved in the cache. BLOB data values aren't cached, and a column containing page-based data isn't fetched until its Field is referenced. Jet requests records within the cache range from the cache, and it requests records outside the cache range from the server; you decide on the size of the cache and the starting point.

Any ODBC database accessed with DAO/Jet Recordset objects can have a local cache. To create the cache, open a Recordset object from the remote data source, set the CacheSize and CacheStart properties of the Recordset object, and then use the FillCache method or step through the records by using the Move methods. The CacheSize property setting is usually based on the number of records your application can work with at one time. For example, if you're using a Recordset object as the source of the data to be displayed on the screen, you could set its CacheSize property to 20 to display a screenful of records at one time.

The CacheStart property setting is the bookmark of the first record in the Recordset object to be cached; you can use the bookmark of any record. To set the CacheStart to the current record, just set CacheStart to the Recordset object's Bookmark property.

If you set the FillCache properties to a location in the result set that is partly or wholly outside the range of records specified by the CacheSize and the CacheStart properties, the portion of the record set outside this range is ignored and isn't loaded into the cache. If FillCache requests more records than remain in the remote data source, only the remaining records are fetched and no error occurs.

As always, records fetched from the cache don't reflect changes made concurrently to the source data by other users, so it's up to you to ensure that the cache is updated as necessary. FillCache fetches only those records that aren't already cached. To force an update of all the cached data, take the following steps:

1. Set CacheSize to 0.

2. Set CacheSize to the size of the cache you originally requested.

3. Use FillCache to refresh the cache.

GetRows and Variant Arrays

Another enhancement intended to improve Jet's performance is the GetRows method. GetRows might also be a viable alternative when you can afford to fetch a block of rows at a time. In general, using GetRows is very much like using the ODBC cache except that the cached rows are maintained in a Variant array.

A Variant is a Visual Basic data type that basically morphs to the data passed to it. It can hold strings, binary data, Boolean values, or any other type of data except fixed-length strings and user-defined types. If you don't provide a data type when you declare a variable, it's declared a Variant, and the Variant data type has no type-declaration character. You can determine how the data in a Variant is treated by using the VarType or TypeName functions.

You can use the Variant data type in place of any other data type in order to work with data in a more flexible way. If the contents of a Variant are digits, they could be either the string representation of the digits or their actual value; that depends on the context. Consider this example:

```
Dim MyVar As Variant
MyVar = 98052
```

Here, *MyVar* contains a numeric representation: the actual value 98052. Arithmetic operators work as expected on Variant variables that contain numeric values or string data that can be interpreted as numbers. If you use the + operator to add *MyVar* to another Variant containing a number or to a variable of a numeric data type, the result is an arithmetic sum. If you use the & operator, a Variant variable can be concatenated to another string.

The value Empty denotes a Variant variable that hasn't been initialized (that is, one that hasn't been assigned an initial value). A Variant containing the value Empty is represented as 0 if it's used in a numeric context and as a zero-length string ("") if it's used in a string context. Don't confuse Empty with Null, which indicates the intention that the Variant variable will contain no valid data.

Variants do simplify your code, but at the price of speed. It can take somewhat longer to manipulate Variant values than it takes to manipulate fixed-length or variable-length string variables and integer variables. They are a must, however, because they understand how to deal with Null values. Remember that a SQL Server Null value is *not* the same thing as an empty string.

When you access a field that can contain Null values, either you have to check for the existence of Nulls before you assign the value to an ordinary variable or you have to concatenate an empty string to the Null in order to convert it to an empty string. For example, suppose your query returns a personnel record that contains the value DateMarried. For many people, this is set to Null. Here is how you could move this value from a Recordset field to a variable:

```
DateMarried.Text = "" & rs!DateMarried
```

The GetRows method basically takes the rows from a Recordset object and places them into a Variant array, one block at a time. That way, Jet can reduce network overhead and improve query fetch performance. Once the data is read into the array, you can examine it there instead of in the Recordset object.

Let's look at a code sample. First you need to declare the array:

```
Dim DataCache As Variant
```

You do *not* have to size the array; the GetRows method does that for you dynamically. If you try to fill the array with more rows than there is memory (RAM) to hold them, however, the Windows swapper kicks in and performance plummets.

The next block of code uses the GetRows method to read data from an existing Recordset (named *rsj* in this example). *CacheSizeSetting* is set independently of this procedure; it's simply an integer value. Each time you execute the GetRows method, the current-row pointer moves forward in the Recordset object as if you had performed the MoveNext method the number of times indicated in *CacheSizeSetting*:

```
DataCache = rsj.GetRows(CacheSizeSetting)
```

If you run out of Recordset rows while executing the GetRows method, only the available rows are transferred, GetRows stops, and Jet sets the Recordset object's EOF property to True.

Once *n* rows have been read into *DataCache*, you can use the UBound function to determine how many rows actually were read. In the following example, I loop through all the rows that have been read and simply touch the values. (The code is extracted from DataTest, a sample application provided on this guide's companion disc.)

```
For row = 0 To UBound(DataCache, 2)
    For i = 0 To rsj.Fields.Count - 1
        A = DataCache(i, row)
    Next i
Next row
```

Note that the Variant array is referenced on a *column, row* basis, with 0 as the first column and row. You can assign the contents of the array elements to any variable, not just to another Variant. Basic does the conversion for you. You can also pass the Variant array to another procedure.

One problem you might encounter with this technique is that the number of rows requested might not be the number returned. If an error occurs, you have to retrieve the fields individually before you can determine the cause of the error.

Graphics: Picture and Image Controls

A basic problem in handling graphics is the conversion of raw binary data to a displayable form. Essentially, there are two ways to do this with the Picture and Image controls: you can use the LoadPicture method, which accepts data from a file; or you can bind the Picture or Image control to a Data control. Using a Data control is far easier than managing images yourself with code, especially since the only way to get a Picture or Image control to display a picture is via an external file and the LoadPicture method.

In essence, to add a new picture to the database, you must first save the picture into a file by using one of the graphics formats recognized by Visual Basic. These include bitmap (BMP) files, icon (ICO) files, run-length encoded (RLE) files, and metafile (WMF) files. (For some reason, PCX files are no longer recognized. Unless you convert with a graphics conversion routine—several are supported by Windows 95—you'll have to store your bitmap images in one of these other forms.)

Once the data is in a file, use the AppendChunk method to save the data to the database, chunk by chunk. To display the data, reverse the process: first use the GetChunk method to read the data back into a file, and then use LoadPicture to reformat the file data for the Picture or Image control. The FieldSize method can be used to determine the number of bytes in the specific chunk column.

The AppendChunk and GetChunk methods are used to store text data, too. Instead of using a common TextBox control, use a Rich Text Format (RTF) custom control to manage the data. The RichTextBox control provides a number of properties with which you can apply formatting to any portion of text within the control. To change the formatting of the text, you first must select it;

Relocating the Current-Row Pointer

If the query result set contains any rows, the first row is exposed in the Recordset object. As you know, the one and only row that is visible in the cursor is referred to as the *current row,* where all operations on the underlying data are performed. To extract cursor data or choose a record to be updated or deleted, you must move the current-row pointer from row to row in the Recordset object. As you also know, any rows added to the cursor are appended to the Recordset object, where they remain until the query is reexecuted, at which time they resume their correct positions (if they still qualify).

CAUTION

I was surprised to discover that the default property for the RichTextBox control is the TextRTF property, not the Text property as for the TextBox control. If you don't explicitly indicate which default property to use, all data is saved in RichText format. That's fine, until you save your data to the database and expect to retrieve it as normal text. Be sure to choose the right property for the type of data that will be imported to and exported from this control.

only selected text can be assigned character and paragraph formatting. Using these properties, you can make text bold or italic, change the color, and create superscripts and subscripts. You can adjust paragraph formatting as well, by setting left and right indents and hanging indents.

The RichTextBox also opens and can save files in either the RTF format or regular ASCII text format. You can use the LoadFile and SaveFile methods to read and write files directly, or the SelRTF and TextRTF properties in conjunction with Visual Basic's file input/output statements. You can load the contents of an RTF file into the RichTextBox control simply by dragging the file (from Windows Explorer, for example), or a highlighted portion of a file used in another application (such as Microsoft Word), and dropping the contents directly into the control. You can also set the FileName property to load the contents of an RTF or text file to the control. You can print all or part of the text in a RichTextBox control using the SelPrint method.

Because the RichTextBox is a data-bound control, you can use a Data control to bind it to a Memo field in a Jet database or to a similar large-capacity text field in another database (for example, a Text data type field in SQL Server). The RichTextBox control supports almost all the properties, events, and methods used with the standard TextBox control, many of which are new in Visual Basic 4.0 (including Locked, MaxLength, MultiLine, ScrollBars, SelLength, SelStart, and SelText). Applications that already use TextBox controls can easily be adapted to make use of RichTextBox controls. And the RichTextBox control isn't limited by the 64K-character capacity of the conventional TextBox control; its capacity is basically unlimited.

DAO/Jet 3.x provides a number of methods for repositioning the current record pointer. Many of them are especially helpful to ISAM-oriented developers, since they permit manipulation of the current-row pointer on the basis of row number and allow repositioning of the current-row pointer to specific or relative locations in the result set. Most of these methods also return information about the relative or specific location of the current row:

- The Move method relocates the current-row pointer ahead or back in the record set to a specific row, relative to the current row or a specific bookmark location. You can specify the number of rows to move the pointer. By default, the current-row pointer is relocated relative to the current row, but you can specify a valid bookmark location as a starting point.

- The PercentPosition method relocates the current-row pointer ahead or back in the record set on the basis of a percentage of rows already populated. It returns as well the percentage-based location of the current-row pointer in the Recordset object. The percentage derived from the number of rows processed by Jet includes rows already cached.

- The AbsolutePosition method relocates the current-row pointer ahead or back in the record set to an absolute row. You can position the current-row pointer to any row in the Recordset object that has been populated or read into the cache.

- The Bookmark method relocates the current-row pointer ahead or back in the record set to a recognized key location. This method returns the current row's key value, which can be saved to reposition the current row later.

- The LastModified method returns the bookmark of the last modified record set row.

- The MoveNext and MovePrevious methods move the current-row pointer to the adjacent row, either ahead or back in the record set.

- The MoveLast and MoveFirst methods move the current-row pointer to the end or beginning of the record set.

When you use a method that repositions the current-row pointer beyond the set of the currently populated rows, Jet fetches additional keys or data rows from the SQL server to continue populating the cursor. For example, using the MoveLast method positions the current-row pointer to the last row in the record set, forcing Jet to populate it fully.

NOTE Relational theory denies the existence of row pointers outside the scope of the database engine itself, and it discourages the use of row pointers for locating or manipulating result set rows. But this aspect of programming is involved in virtually all the changes to Jet 3.0 and Visual Basic 4.0 that have to do with relocating the current-row pointer.

Validity of the Current-Row Pointer

At either end of the Recordset object, there is a wall you can cross—but if you do, the current record pointer becomes invalid. If you execute the MovePrevious method and the Beginning of File (BOF) property changes to True, your current record is still valid, but you're touching the wall. If you execute the MovePrevious method *after* the BOF property has changed to True, you go over the wall, and the current record pointer becomes invalid. The End of File (EOF) property works in the same way. As you use the MoveNext or the MoveLast method to move to the end of the Recordset object, the EOF property remains False until you arrive at the last row. The current-row pointer remains valid, but there are no more rows in the Recordset, so you're right up against the wall. Once the EOF property changes to True, you can execute the MoveNext method again, but you'll go over the wall, and the current-row pointer will become invalid. In other cases, you will get a trappable error if you attempt to move farther past either end or use the invalid current-row pointer.

CAUTION

If you choose a forward-only snapshot-type cursor, only the MoveNext method can be used to move the current-row pointer. If you try to use the MoveLast method against an ODBC snapshot-type cursor, an error 3219 ("Invalid operation") will result. This holds true for RDO or ODBC forward-only record sets as well.

A new Data control feature that greatly simplifies record set handling is the EOFAction property. Set to option 2-AddNew, the Data control automatically switches into AddNew mode when the EOF wall is scaled; that is, once the user executes a MoveNext method on the Data control after the EOF property has changed to True, the control automatically starts a new, empty record. This option is also triggered when the Data control is opened on an empty Recordset object.

If you perform any operation that makes the current-row pointer invalid, you can't perform any data access operation that depends on data in the current row. This means that you can't execute the Edit method or access any of the Field properties. You *can* execute the AddNew method to add another row to the dynaset, or you can use one of the repositioning methods to relocate the current-row pointer to a valid row of the record set—if one exists. But if you delete all the rows of the record set, the BOF and EOF property settings change to True and the current-row pointer becomes invalid.

NOTE A data row that has been added to a record set might not qualify for membership if a query is reexecuted, if the Requery method is used, or if the Recordset object is rebuilt. Records added by other users aren't visible to a record set once its membership is frozen, but changes made by anyone to a member row are visible after the current-row pointer has been repositioned to that row. If any change to a row disqualifies it for membership in the record set, that row remains a member of any Recordset objects that exist at the time of the change but it isn't included in any rebuilds of current Recordset objects or in any newly created Recordset objects.

Locating a Specific Row

If you need to have Jet locate a specific row in an existing Recordset object, you can use a number of techniques, including the Find methods. Frankly, I prefer requerying the database to find a specific row, but the Find methods are popular with ISAM developers and work pretty well if there aren't too many rows.

The Find Methods

The FindFirst method is executed against an existing Recordset object and uses a criterion as a search argument. If a match is found, the current-row pointer is relocated to the first matching row. If no match is found, the NoMatch property is set to True; otherwise, it's set to False. When you use the FindLast method, Jet fully populates your record set before beginning the search, if it isn't populated already. Each Find method begins its search from the location and in the direction shown in *Figure 13-2.*

Figure 13-2
Find Methods of Relocation

Find Method	Starting Point	Direction of Search
FindFirst	Beginning of	Toward end of record set
FindLast	End of record set	Toward beginning of record set
FindNext	Current record	Toward end of record set
FindPrevious	Current record	Toward beginning of record set

TIP Using one of the Find methods isn't the same as using a Move method, which simply makes the first or next record current without specifying a condition. You can follow a Find operation with a Move operation.

When you use one of the Find methods with a SQL Server data source, the method is implemented as either *optimized* or *unoptimized*. The optimized version is used only when the table or query is a dynaset-type record set, not a snapshot, and when the column is indexed. The Find restriction must be as follows:

```
column = value
```

or

```
column LIKE value
```

And the *like* string must be as follows:

smith

or

smith*

The optimized Find algorithm first executes a query that takes this form:

```
SELECT bookmark-columns
FROM table
WHERE find-restriction
```

Once this query completes, Jet searches the current Recordset object for a match against the new list of bookmarks. When a match is found in a row, the current-row pointer is repositioned to that row. If no match is found, the NoMatch property is set to True. (This is a significant improvement over the unoptimized Jet 1.1 version of the Find method, which executed a SQL Server query against each individual row in the Recordset object—*very* slow for Recordset objects larger than a few dozen rows.)

The Seek Method

One of the fastest operations Jet performs is the location of records with the Seek method. Ordinarily, the Seek method isn't available to SQL Server users, but I've discovered a way to get around this limitation:

1. Execute a MakeTable query that creates a "permanent" Jet table instead of a cursor. This query can even use SQL pass-through and a TSQL query or stored procedure.

2. Create a new index on the new Jet table, using an action query.

3. Use the Seek method to access the data.

This technique takes slightly longer, but once you've set it up, using the Seek method is at least six times faster than creating a snapshot-type Recordset object and using the Find method—even *with* its enhancements. If you create lookup snapshots from SQL Server data and need to reference them more than a few times, this technique can really pay off. The "permanent" table you create can also be bound with the Data control, which now supports table-type Recordset objects.

Updating Data

You can use two basic strategies to update SQL Server data with DAO/Jet. You can create an updatable cursor, or you can execute a SQL-based action query that updates rows independently of a cursor. The first strategy is popular with some developers, but the second is often dictated by the design of the database. For example, if the only available way to update is via one or more stored procedures, there might be no way to create an updatable cursor, so you must use one of the SQL-based techniques.

NOTE If you have access only to SQL Server views, remember that you can attach a SQL Server view to an MDB database and create one or more Jet indexes on the view, using Jet action queries. This makes the view updatable, at least one table at a time; you can't perform an update that affects more than one table.

Using DAO/Jet Cursors

If you have access to an updatable table or Recordset object, Jet can perform row updates on your data, using the Delete method to drop rows, the Edit method to change existing rows, or the AddNew method to add new rows. When you add a row by using a cursor, the row immediately becomes part of both the cursor and the database. If you use the SQL techniques, the new row or rows don't appear in your open Recordset object and they won't appear until it's rebuilt. Remember that adding, deleting, or modifying rows won't change the membership of existing Recordset objects that have been created by other users, but the changes will appear in these existing dynasets as the current row is positioned over the changed row. And when a database table row changes, it might affect a dynaset that is composed of only part of the changed row (that is, a subset of the columns of the table). A cursor might also be composed of a set of columns drawn from a set of tables. Therefore, a single repositioning or updating operation might require several rows of data to be fetched from several tables before the current row can be rebuilt on the basis of its component parts.

In all cases, Jet can modify the data in cursors or attached server tables that have unique primary keys (bookmarks). When a row is updated or deleted, Jet sends an Update or Delete action query to the server, qualified by a WHERE clause specifying the key values for that row (the bookmark). This query controls exactly which row is changed or dropped and protects against inadvertent multirow changes—assuming that the primary key can identify a specific row.

TIP You can tell whether a result set is updatable by examining the Updatable property. If it's False, you can't use the Update method. If you try anyway, you get a trappable error that complains about an invalid method. There are many reasons why a result set may not be updatable. Often you can get around the restrictions imposed by Jet if you execute an action query that contains an UPDATE SQL statement or the right stored procedure.

Generally, inserting new rows also requires the existence of a bookmark. The dynaset must keep track of newly added records, since they become indistinguishable from existing records. And if the query doesn't return all the columns constituting the bookmark, the insertion of new records isn't allowed. Exceptions to the rule occur, however; Append and MakeTable action queries don't require a unique key on the remote table. An append query is simply a SQL query that contains an INSERT statement; a MakeTable query uses INSERT INTO syntax.

INSERT and UPDATE Statements

When an update or insert is performed, Jet no longer supplies values for every updatable field in the cursor, whether or not the field was explicitly changed or set. The new default behavior sets only those columns touched by the update operation. You can turn this behavior on and off by changing the PreparedInsert and PreparedUpdate registry settings. The PreparedInsert registry setting indicates whether to use a prepared INSERT statement that inserts data in all the columns. Values are 0 (use a custom INSERT statement that inserts only non-Null values) and 1 (use a prepared INSERT statement). The default is 0. Using prepared INSERT statements can cause Nulls to overwrite server defaults and can cause triggers to execute on columns that weren't inserted explicitly. The PreparedUpdate registry setting indicates whether to use a prepared UPDATE statement that updates data in all the columns. Values are 0 (use a custom UPDATE statement that sets only the columns that have changed) and 1 (use a prepared UPDATE statement). The default is 0. Using prepared UPDATE statements can cause triggers to execute on unchanged columns.

This flexibility allows Jet to use a single UPDATE/INSERT statement for all updates and inserts instead of constructing a new statement every time. If you set either of the Prepared settings to 1, however, any of three side effects can occur unexpectedly:

- A trigger that fires when a column is changed might be activated, even if the column is being "changed" to its current value. (You can alter the trigger to do nothing if the old and new values match.)

- Inserts will fail if columns that don't allow null strings aren't included in your query. If you don't supply values for the columns, the Null value that Jet supplies will cause an error.

- Server defaults might be overridden at insertion time by the explicit Null value supplied by Jet.

You can force an updatable query output column to be nonupdatable (and exclude it from UPDATE and INSERT statements) by wrapping it in an expression like one of these:

```
IntegerCol + 0
StringCol & ''
```

If a table has a TimeStamp column, Jet prevents you from updating it manually because SQL Server maintains its value.

Security

Jet neither enforces nor overrides server-based security. Additional client-side security may be set up on attached tables and their queries, but Jet remains strictly ignorant of server security beyond the initial connection-time logon. Security violations caused by Jet queries done in support of dynaset operations can cause ODBC to bring up dialog boxes with server-specific error messages.

Locking, Concurrency, and Transactions

When SQL Server is accessed via the ODBC interface, data page locking is the responsibility of the remote database engine. Jet simply acts as a front end to the database servers; it doesn't control data sharing on back-end database engines. (In some cases, however, you can control how the remote server locks data by using back-end–specific SQL statements or administrative options.) When Jet defers to back-end schemes for page locking, there are a few implications:

- Setting the LockEdits property of the Recordset object has no effect.

- The *exclusive* parameter of the OpenDatabase method is illegal or ignored: you can't open a SQL server exclusively. (You can set the system to run in single-user mode, but only if you are the server administrator.)

- All updates are done with *optimistic* concurrency. Rows aren't locked during editing; they are checked for conflict at update time, when the bookmark-qualified UPDATE statement is further restricted. If a TimeStamp column exists in the table, as reported by SQLSpecial-Columns(SQL_ROWVER), it's qualified with its current value. If not, all columns, excluding the Memo and OLE Object columns, are tested against their former values. (The former method is preferable, especially given the precision-loss problems already described in connection with floating-point data.)

- Attempts to lock the entire table or database by using TSQL syntax can bring the SQL server to its knees, especially in a high-volume transaction environment.

- For maximum throughput and to provide the only reliable way of letting the back-end database engine operate its native locking scheme, sophisticated error handling should be incorporated to react correctly when locking contention occurs.

Jet wraps most data-modifying operations in short transactions, but longer transactions can sometimes occur. (In the case of a large action query, Jet wraps the entire bulk operation within a single transaction.) You are responsible for the length and breadth of your transactions, which can be arbitrarily long and broad. The following caveats should be borne in mind:

- Long-running transactions over large amounts of data can lock out or block other users as SQL Server escalates from page locking to table locking. Try to avoid these transactions when users are connected. Schedule them for hours when their impact won't be felt.

- Automatic idle-time population doesn't apply to Snapshot and Dynaset objects as it does in Microsoft Access, unless they are created by the Data control. If you stop moving through the result set and sit on a row for a long time, the server might hold a lock on that row or page. Because of Jet's buffering schemes, this is no longer a concern once you reach the end of the result set or when you're dealing with smaller result sets. List boxes and combo boxes, when they are bound to large server-based result sets, also don't enjoy background population.

- When performing ORDER BY operations, some servers lock all the data pages or tables involved until the sorting is finished and the results are returned. This behavior is beyond Jet's control.

Some of these caveats are relevant to any client-server environment, regardless of the front-end application. To be a good citizen in such an environment, you should make judicious use of transactions and cursors on result sets of reasonable size and you should be familiar with your server's default locking behavior.

Updating with SQL-Based Action Queries

When you need to update a SQL Server table value, an entire row, or a set of rows, the preferred method involves the use of an action query. You simply send an UPDATE statement with a WHERE clause that reflects the keys of the rows to be changed:

```
db.Execute "UPDATE Animals SET Status = 'Fried' " _
    & " WHERE Animal_ID = 17"
```

This might not be an option, however, since update operations are permitted only through the execution of stored procedures. That doesn't really change this strategy, though; you can still use an action query to perform the update. You just have to submit a different type of query. Whenever you have to execute a stored procedure by using Jet, you must use the dbSQLPassThrough option in the OpenRecordset or Execute methods:

```
db.Execute "ChangeStatus 'Fried', 17", dbSQLPassThrough
```

When you create an UPDATE statement on the fly, you have several design decisions to make. You need to consider how the rules and triggers are going to interact with the process, so you must decide whether the statement will include all the columns or only the ones that are affected. Your code must also be prepared to trap the errors that might be generated by Jet, SQL Server, and the rules and triggers; see "Error Handling," the last section in this chapter.

CAUTION

SQL Server has no mechanism for updating non–SQL Server tables, but you can control your own transactions by submitting SQL pass-through queries containing TSQL transaction statements. Watch out for Jet's connection management, though. If you use this technique, Jet won't know that you're working with transactions, so it might disconnect in the middle of a transaction, causing an immediate rollback. You should consider using Jet's Workspace transaction model instead.

ExecuteSQL? Just Say No

You can use the ExecuteSQL method instead of the Execute method to run action queries, and ExecuteSQL does return the number of rows affected by the operation—but so does the RecordsAffected property of the Database object. Besides, using the ExecuteSQL method has several unfortunate side effects:

- ExecuteSQL doesn't use Jet connection management, so there are complaints about increased connections.

- It forces complete population of the result set before returning control to the user, which encourages the perception of lower performance.

- It uses direct connections to the SQL server, which means that users incur added DDL overhead for no reason, since information is pulled down about the database schema but isn't used.

- The SQL Trace facility doesn't log its operations.

You also have to decide how to handle transactions, since several rows might be affected—in a single table, or in tables spread all over the database. But if you're using Jet to perform heterogeneous joins, your options are very limited: you must let Jet do the update.

Jet's transaction model is built around the Workspace object, and all databases opened under a single Workspace object are in the same transaction scope. If you begin a transaction on two Database objects and subsequently roll back a transaction on either of the two, the rollback applies to both, as far as Jet is concerned, and Jet submits a rollback statement to both. If you need to perform independent transaction operations, create another Workspace object and open the second Database object against the new Workspace:

```
Dim MyWorkspace As Workspace
' Create new Workspace.
Set MyWorkspace = DBEngine.CreateWorkspace("Special", MyUserName, _
    "SpecialPW")
```

NOTE ODBC doesn't support the nesting of transactions to SQL Server, no matter what interface you use, so once you execute the Jet BeginTrans method, subsequent calls are ignored until a matching CommitTrans method or Rollback method is executed.

The Jet 1.1 requirements for sequence of operations have been lifted, and Jet's remote transaction management now allows for seamless use of server transactions in Basic code. BeginTrans now "carries into" opening a dynaset on server data, even if a connection to the server didn't exist before the dynaset was opened. The following code works as expected:

```
BeginTrans
Set ds = d.CreateDynaset(…)
data modifications using ds
ds.Close
CommitTrans/Rollback
```

It's no longer necessary to structure your code as follows (although this code still works):

```
Set ds = d.CreateDynaset(…)
BeginTrans
data modifications using ds
CommitTrans/Rollback
ds.Close
```

If you use the following sequence on remote data, a Rollback isn't sent to the server, as it was in Jet 1.1, and the server transaction remains open until you either explicitly commit it or roll it back or until the application terminates (at which time it will be rolled back):

```
Set ds = d.CreateDynaset(…)
BeginTrans
data modifications using ds
ds.Close
```

These transaction semantics also apply to SQL pass-through queries that modify server data. Explicit transactions within the pass-through queries not only are unnecessary but also could cause problems.

It's now possible to nest several bulk operations in a transaction, as in the following credit/debit–style operation:

```
BeginTrans
d.Execute("UPDATE SavingsAccount
        SET Balance = Balance - 100")
d.Execute("UPDATE CheckingAccount
        SET Balance = Balance + 100")
CommitTrans/Rollback
```

Given the keyset-driven model used by Jet, it's important to note how bulk operations (action queries like Insert, Update, Delete, and MakeTable) are performed. For example, Jet will perform a bulk operation if you use a SELECT statement to drive an INSERT statement or execute an UPDATE statement that uses a WHERE clause referencing more than one row. First the keyset for the affected records is built. Then the appropriate operation is performed for each record in the keyset, one record at a time. This is slower than performing a single qualified bulk operation on the server, but it allows for partially successful bulk queries as well as for bulk queries that can't be executed by the server. When this extra functionality isn't required, it's often faster to use a SQL pass-through query and your own schemes for error management.

A new option has been added for the OpenRecordset method and the Execute method: dbFailOnError. This option permits you to execute bulk operations but still determine whether one of them has failed. For example, if you execute a Jet Update action query that affects a dozen rows, Jet executes each of the 12 operations individually but control normally won't be returned to your application until the operation completes. If any of the 12 individual update operations fails and you haven't set the dbFailOnError option, the process will be stopped but you won't receive any indication that an operation has failed. But if you *do* set the dbFailOnError option, a trappable error is fired if any of the 12 operations fails. (You have no way to tell which of the rows have been updated and which haven't—that's what transaction processing is for.)

Error Handling

SQL Server is an interactive engine that returns a litany of error messages, all of them important to varying degrees. The Jet, ODBC, and network layers also chime in once in a while. Often when a low-importance message arrives, your application doesn't need to be interrupted. But when something significant comes up, your application *will* be interrupted.

Whether the errors are trappable generally depends on your use of the Data control as well as on the operations executed at design time or before the Form_Load event is complete. For all your applications, you must establish an On Error GoTo trap in order to prevent some unexpected timeout from causing the application to crash. And in the case of a general ODBC error, you must be prepared to examine the Errors collection, which maintains an Error object for each error that occurs.

The Error objects were an addition to Visual Basic 4.0. They are especially helpful with ODBC applications, since the error objects give you access to the native error number returned by SQL Server. When you're working with SQL Server and the ODBC drivers, errors are reported in layers. As a low-level operation fails, it reports back to its parent layer, and that layer does the same, all the way up the line. Thus a single error can create three or four Error objects, with the lowest-level error having the most significance. For that reason, the Error(0) object in the Errors collection contains the most valuable information about the root cause of the failure. (The remaining objects rarely contain anything of interest—just the driver name, the server type, and so forth, if that information should interest you.) *Figure 13-3* shows the Visual Basic Error object properties and describes their uses with SQL Server.

CAUTION

Because of the way Jet handles errors for all ODBC clients, any error over a certain level of severity is considered fatal. Unfortunately, a RAISERROR statement is considered to be indicative of a fatal error, so any stored procedures you execute that use a RAISERROR statement to provide a warning message will cause Jet to terminate the operation as if a fatal error had occurred.

Figure 13-3

Property	What It Does
Count	Gives number of Error objects in the Errors collection (0-based)
Description	Gives a short description of the error; displayed to alert the user to an error that you can't or don't want to handle
HelpContext	Returns a context ID, as a string variable, for a topic in a Microsoft Windows help file
HelpFile	Returns a fully qualified path to the help file
Number	Names the error that has occurred (this is the *native* SQL Server error number for ODBC errors)
Source	Represents, by means of a string expression (usually the object's class name or programmatic ID), the object that originally generated the error

The Description property is particularly ugly if it's not reformatted. For example, the following description is returned when you don't provide the right password for the SP_PASSWORD stored procedure: *[Microsoft][ODBC SQL Server Driver][SQL Server] Old (current) password incorrect for use -- password not changed.* One way to reformat the message would be to strip off the preamble. Since you know that your applications always access SQL Server, you can keep everything after the string *[SQL Server]*:

```
E$ = Errors(0).Description
RealError$ = Mid(E$, instr(E$, "[SQL Server]") + 12)
```

14

Chapter

Executing Transact-SQL Queries

**Using SQL
Pass-Through Queries**

**Working with
Stored Procedures**

Handling SQL Server Messages

One aspect of work with a generic interface like ODBC is maximizing the target systems' features. Jet's SQL dialect is similar to the one used by the ODBC driver manager, but it's less comprehensive than Transact-SQL (TSQL), the one used by SQL Server—even though they have evolved toward each other. As you know, TSQL is used to fetch result set rows and to perform all kinds of DBMS maintenance. This chapter covers techniques for executing TSQL queries to get this work done.

Using SQL Pass-Through Queries

SQL pass-through queries can improve performance if you can do without what you lose when you bypass Jet's query processor. Many DAO/Jet applications rely completely on SQL pass-through to perform SQL Server operations. In any case, SQL pass-through should play a major role in any SQL Server front-end application that requires Jet.

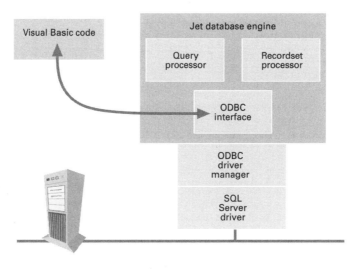

The real problem with using TSQL is the Jet query processor/optimizer, where the syntax provided in the OpenRecordset, Execute, or QueryDef objects is parsed and prepared for execution. For the most part, this rather complex (read convoluted) piece of code just gets in the way and makes your applications run slower than they could if you talked more or less directly to SQL Server. To use any but the simplest TSQL queries, you *must* bypass this portion of Jet (or not use Jet at all—but that's another story). The dbSQLPassThrough option does just this, and it's available on both the OpenRecordset and Execute methods. (You can also use the outdated ExecuteSQL method, which *only* supports ODBC SQL pass-through operations, but ExecuteSQL isn't supported in the 32-bit version of Jet.) One of the most flexible enhancements to Jet is the ability to create a SQL pass-through QueryDef object that contains a reference to a stored procedure. This enhancement permits you to reference the stored procedure result set as a read-only table.

> **NOTE** SQL pass-through was prohibited with the use of attached tables in Visual Basic 3.0 but is now supported. This is one of the innovations that Jet 3.0 has added to improve ODBC.

Typical Applications

Generally, you can use SQL pass-through to perform any of the following operations (each of them requires you to provide a TSQL string and enable the SQL pass-through option):

- Execute a stored procedure and return one or more sets of results and even return values and output parameters

- Run a SQL query, using TSQL syntax, or return one or more sets of results

- Create a new device, database, table, or index on an external server, using TSQL data definition language (DDL) statements

- Create or manage SQL Server triggers, defaults, rules, or stored procedures

- Maintain user accounts or perform other system administrator tasks

- Run maintenance operations, such as Microsoft SQL Server's DBCC

- Execute multiple INSERT or UPDATE statements in a single batch

- Manage transactions independently of Jet

CAUTION

If you use a SQL pass-through action query to send a TSQL BEGIN TRANSACTION statement to the SQL server, that transaction is based on the connection that Jet uses to send it. If the connection closes before you commit, the transaction is automatically rolled back. You don't always have complete control over which connection Jet uses to send queries or how long that connection stays open, so you could be making trouble for yourself. Unless you can somehow keep the specific connection open *and* execute subsequent TSQL SQL pass-through queries through *that* connection, it's *not* a good idea to try to manage connections independently of Jet.

> **NOTE** You can use SQL pass-through to pass single or multiple TSQL commands, stored procedures, or other TSQL statements (such as those involved in administrative functions) to the SQL server for execution. Whenever you specify a SQL pass-through query, the Jet database query processor is bypassed but the Jet *record set* processor is still used to create and manage the result sets that might be generated by your query.

Implementations

The newest way to execute a SQL pass-through query is to have a DAO/Jet QueryDef object store the query. That way, you take advantage of the efficiency of attached tables. Nevertheless, you must create and manage a separate Jet database to hold the QueryDef object, unless you create the database and QueryDef object each time you run the application. I have seen applications that did stranger things.

Although the technique we're about to look at uses the DAO/Jet QueryDef object to store and execute a foreign-language SQL query, you can't set parameters for the query by using the Parameters collection of the QueryDef object. To build SQL queries that are created in code or that require parameters, you need to construct or modify the query in code.

The result set created from a SQL pass-through query is always placed in a snapshot-type Recordset. If *multiple* result sets are generated by your SQL pass-through query, however, Jet can create a separate table-type Recordset object for *each* set of results by using a SELECT INTO query. Jet 2.5 and Jet 3.0 support the use of SQL pass-through by permitting your code to set the SQL property of the QueryDef object to contain non–Jet engine SQL syntax. (You can still place foreign SQL syntax in the SQL argument of the CreateDynaset, CreateSnapshot, or ExecuteSQL methods and use the dbSQLPassThrough option, but this outdated technique isn't recommended.)

> **TIP** If you are *really* considering use of DAO/Jet to execute and manage the result sets from complex multiple result set queries, you should sit down and carefully reconsider your course. Of course, if you are still coding 16-bit applications, this might be your only viable choice, but if RDO or even ODBCDirect are options, they both manage this type of query far more easily.

Creating a SQL Pass-Through QueryDef Object

To create a SQL pass-through QueryDef object, take the following steps:

> **TIP** Folks, don't get ahead of me here and try this with ODBCDirect. It doesn't work the same way. It doesn't even work here if you don't take each of these steps in turn—one by one.

1. Use the CreateQueryDef method to create a DAO/Jet QueryDef object, using *only* a *Name* argument. Don't get too anxious and try to short-circuit this process. If you specify a SQL argument in the CreateQueryDef step, you *can't* use foreign SQL syntax, since the query must comply with Jet engine SQL syntax. To create a temporary QueryDef object that isn't automatically saved in the database, use the CreateQueryDef method without the *Name* argument.

2. Set the Connect property of the QueryDef object to a valid connect string and thereby inform the Jet engine that this is a SQL pass-through query. From this point forward, the Jet engine doesn't attempt to parse the SQL property.

3. Set the SQL property of the QueryDef object to the TSQL statement to be executed. Be sure to use correct TSQL syntax; the syntax isn't checked until the statement is executed by the SQL server for the first time.

4. If you expect your query to return one or more sets of records (rows), set the ReturnsRecords property of the QueryDef object to True and thereby inform the Jet engine to expect records (rows) back from the query. (Otherwise, Jet thinks this is an action query.) Any query that contains a SELECT statement has the potential to return rows. When ReturnsRecords is true, the Jet engine creates a snapshot-type Recordset object for the first set of results. Subsequent result sets are placed in "permanent" tables. If you don't set the ReturnsRecords property to True for a query that returns records, a trappable error results.

CAUTION

Careful now. If you try to shortcut this technique, it won't work. You can't supply the SQL until the Connect property has been set.

Let's look now at the following code, which creates a SQL pass-through QueryDef object that executes a stored procedure that, in turn, returns multiple result sets. In this case, we execute the sp_help *tablename* system stored procedure, which returns several result sets.

```
Private Sub Command1_Click()

Set db = OpenDatabase("C:\attach.mdb")
db.QueryDefs.Delete "MySPHelp"
Set qd = db.CreateQueryDef("MySPHelp")
qd.Connect = "ODBC;dsn=biblio;uid=sa;pwd=;database=biblio;"
qd.SQL = "SP_Help " & (TableDesired)
qd.ReturnsRecords = True
Set rs = qd.OpenRecordset
Debug.Print rs.RecordCount
```

To execute the SQL pass-through QueryDef, use the OpenRecordset method and execute the stored QueryDef so that the first (and only the first) set of results is available:

```
Set Rs = Db.OpenRecordset("MySPHelp", dbOpenSnapshot)
```

To process any *additional* result sets of a SQL pass-through QueryDef, you first create and execute a temporary QueryDef object that executes a Jet SQL MakeTable query, using SELECT INTO syntax. The Jet engine creates one new (permanent) Jet table for each set of results and stores them in your database. (The table need not exist beforehand.) If more than one user on a shared database executes this code at the same time, the multiple applications might generate table-name collisions. The SELECT INTO query doesn't return records, but it builds one or more Jet tables to store the results from the QueryDef. Since a name isn't provided for the CreateQueryDef method, the Jet engine doesn't store a new QueryDef in the database, as you can see in the code at the top of the next page.

```
Set qd = db.CreateQueryDef("")
qd.SQL = "Select [MySPHelp].* Into Result From [MySPHelp];"
qd.Execute
```

Remember, MySPHelp is the query that executes the sp_help stored procedure. Next, you create and process each of the resulting tables (which contain the results of the QueryDef) by using the OpenRecordset method:

```
Set Rs = Db.OpenRecordset("Result")
' Process the results of the query...
```

Repeat this process for each of the result sets. Unless you know how many result set tables were created, you must query the TableDefs collection. Note that the Jet engine numbers the tables sequentially: the table named *Result* contains the first set of results, *Result1* contains the second set, and so on. To deal with this a little more gracefully, I added some code to walk the TableDefs collection, looking for our *Result*n tables. Remember that these are *permanent* tables and *everyone* using this database can see them. It also means that you need to destroy them yourself in code—as quickly as possible.

```
For Each tb In db.TableDefs
    If Left(tb.Name, 6) = "Result" Then
        Set rs = tb.OpenRecordset
        ShowFields rs
        rs.Close
    End If
Next tb
hits = True
Do While hits
    hits = False
    For Each tb In db.TableDefs
        If Left(tb.Name, 6) = "Result" Then
            db.TableDefs.Delete tb.Name
            hits = True
        End If
    Next tb
Loop
```

Notice the somewhat convoluted way I deleted the members of the TableDefs collection. Once you delete a member, all of the other members iterate up, so it takes several passes to get them all. However, if you don't remove these result set tables (*Result* through *Result*n), you won't be able to run the query again—and neither will anyone else.

Using SQL Pass-Through Queries with Attached Tables

You can also use SQL pass-through queries with attached tables. Remember, attached tables are simply linkage entries in a Jet database that point to and describe SQL Server tables. By setting the Connect property of a Database object (after the Jet database is open), you tell Jet that the attached tables should be populated by SQL pass-through queries.

Let's look at some concrete examples of the methods we've already examined. The following sample program, SQL PassThrough test.frm (you can find it on this guide's companion disc), performs the same query in a number of separate ways. Included in this sample is a piece of RDO code to serve as a benchmark—a sanity check, as it were. The first section sets up the global variables, as usual; there is nothing of global importance here:

```
Option Explicit
Dim db As Database
Dim rs As Recordset
Dim rd As rdoResultset
Dim JetQuery As String
Dim TSQLQuery As String
Dim qd As QueryDef
Dim er As Error
```

In the Form_Load procedure, I open a Jet database that serves in four ways:

- It contains a number of attached ODBC tables. These are used in the queries in a variety of ways.

- It contains a Microsoft Access–authored DAO/Jet QueryDef object named JetQuery, which uses the attached tables.

- It serves as a place to build and store the permanent QueryDef object that we are about to create on the fly. (We can't create a temporary QueryDef object for this application.)

- It serves as a conduit for the underlying ODBC database associated with the attached tables.

NOTE While I included a sample of this Jet database on the CD, you will have to reattach the tables once you set up your test database to try it. See Appendix A for instructions on how to set up the test database samples.

The next section of code opens the Jet database. (You have to change the code to point to it, or perhaps create it yourself, if you want to run this test.) We then initialize two strings that contain the Jet syntax query and the TSQL query to be run later. Notice anything strange about the table names? That's right—they don't have the *dbo_*prefix. That's because I went in and removed all those prefixes after building the database:

```
Private Sub Form_Load()
Set DBEngine = Nothing
Set db = OpenDatabase("C:\Attach.mdb")
Open "Jettest.txt" For Output As #1
```

(continued)

```
JetQuery = "SELECT DISTINCTROW Authors.Author, _
    Title_Author.ISBN," _
    & " Titles.Title, Publishers.Company_Name" _
    & " FROM ((Authors INNER JOIN Title_Author " _
    & " ON Authors.Au_ID = Title_Author.Au_ID) " _
    & " INNER JOIN Titles ON Title_Author.ISBN = Titles.ISBN) " _
    & " INNER JOIN Publishers " _
    & " ON Titles.PubID = Publishers.PubID " _
    & " WHERE (((titles.Title) Like '*Hitch*'));"
TSQLQuery = "Select Author, T.ISBN, Title, Company_Name" _
& " From Authors A, Title_Author TA, Titles T, Publishers P " _
& " Where A.Au_ID = TA.Au_ID and " _
& " TA.ISBN = T.ISBN and " _
& " P.PubID = T.PubID and " _
& " T.Title like '%Hitch%' "
End Sub
```

The next seven sections of code are started from command buttons on Form1. These launch the individual tests. The first test is also a benchmark of sorts. It is an example of what *not* to do. It opens the database directly and simply executes *JetQuery* (DAO/Jet QueryDef). Notice the ShowJetResults procedure call near the end. This simply displays the rows of the result set. This application is also designed to create a log of the output and error messages, for debugging purposes:

```
Private Sub JetBaseTest_Click()
Dim db2 As Database
Print #1, "-----------> Starting Plain direct open Jet Test"
Set db2 = OpenDatabase("Biblio", 0, 0, _
    "ODBC;uid=;pwd=;database=Biblio;")
Set rs = db2.OpenRecordset(JetQuery, dbOpenSnapshot)
Print #1, rs.RecordCount
ShowJetResults
rs.Close
End Sub
```

The next test is the RDO benchmark to verify that things are working correctly:

```
Private Sub RDOTest_Click()
Print #1, "-----------------> Starting RDO Test"
Dim cn As New rdoConnection
With cn
    cn.Connect = "dsn=biblio;uid=;pwd=;database=biblio;"
    cn.EstablishConnection rdDriverNoPrompt, True
    Set rd = .OpenResultset(TSQLQuery, rdOpenStatic, _
    rdConcurReadOnly, rdExecDirect)
End With
ShowRDOResults
End Sub
```

Next comes the first of the Jet tests. The strategy here is to run a query through the Jet query processor that uses the attached tables. In this case, we simply execute the DAO/Jet query against the Jet database object and create a snapshot with the resulting rows. The advantage of this approach is that it's easy to code, but it requires a Jet database—one that already has the attached tables. It's not hard to create, however, even in code:

```
Private Sub TestSPT1_Click()
On Error GoTo T1Eh
Print #1, "-----> Starting Jet query against attached tables Test"
' Approach 1 -- Open a Jet query against attached tables.
Set rs = db.OpenRecordset(JetQuery, dbOpenSnapshot)
ShowJetResults
rs.Close
ExitT1:
Exit Sub
T1Eh:
  ShowDAOErrors
  Resume ExitT1
End Sub
```

The next test is slightly more complex to set up and run than the first because it requires a predefined query stored in the Jet database. Once again, I use Microsoft Access or Visual Database Tools to create, tune, and save the query. The test executes a permanent DAO/Jet query that contains the same query we executed in the preceding test:

```
Private Sub JetTest2_Click()
' Approach 2 -- Open Jet query against stored QueryDef object that
' accesses attached tables.
Print #1, "--------> Starting Jet query against Jet QueryDef Test"
Set rs = db.OpenRecordset("JetQuery", dbOpenSnapshot)
ShowJetResults
rs.Close
End Sub
```

Now we start to push the envelope for the Jet/ODBC interface. Here, we send a TSQL query and *bypass* the Jet query processor. Notice that the database that is referenced is a *Jet* database, not an ODBC database opened directly against the SQL server. By setting the Database object's Connect property after it's opened, you can tell Jet to perform SQL pass-through operations by establishing a connection that uses the given connect string:

```
Private Sub TSQLTest1_Click()
Print #1, "------------------> Starting TSQL query" _
    & " against attached tables DB Test"
' Approach 3 -- Execute TSQL query against attached tables.
db.Connect = "ODBC;uid=;pwd=;database=biblio;dsn=biblio;"
Set rs = db.OpenRecordset _
    (TSQLQuery, dbOpenSnapshot, dbSQLPassThrough)
Print #1, rs.RecordCount
ShowJetResults
rs.Close
End Sub
```

The following test shows an even more advanced concept. Here, we create a DAO/Jet QueryDef object in code, set the Connect property, and *then* set the SQL property. Notice that the SQL property is set using TSQL syntax, *not* Jet SQL syntax. This technique creates a true SQL pass-through QueryDef object— a new feature for Jet 2.5 and Jet 3.*x*. We then create a Recordset object against this newly created QueryDef object. Notice that you don't have to set the SQL pass-through bit; that is done for you. This query can also be executed by Microsoft Access or by anyone else who shares this Jet database. You can treat this QueryDef object the way you treat any Jet table. The fact that it gets its information straight from SQL Server and bypasses Jet's query processor is a powerful new feature:

```
Private Sub TSQLTest2_Click()
Print #1, "-------> Starting TSQL query against SPT QueryDef Test"
On Error GoTo TSQLEH1
db.QueryDefs.Delete "TSQLT2"
On Error GoTo 0

Set qd = db.CreateQueryDef(Name:="TSQLT2")
qd.Connect = "ODBC;uid=;pwd=;database=biblio;dsn=biblio;"
qd.SQL = TSQLQuery

Set rs = qd.OpenRecordset(dbOpenSnapshot)
ShowJetResults
rs.Close
db.QueryDefs.Delete "TSQLT2"
Exit Sub
TSQLEH1:
    If Err = 3265 Then Resume Next
    Stop

End Sub
```

The next procedure is similar to the preceding ones, but only a temporary DAO/Jet QueryDef object is created. This technique does eliminate the ability to share the QueryDef object between applications, but it also eliminates the need to delete the QueryDef object each time you run the procedure during development. Notice that we set the ReturnsRecords property to tell Jet that this isn't an action query. Does this mean that you can use SQL pass-through QueryDef objects to execute action queries? It sure does:

```
Private Sub TestSPT3_Click()
Print #1, "--> Starting TSQL query against SPT Temp QueryDef Test"
On Error GoTo SPT3Eh

Set qd = db.CreateQueryDef("")
qd.Connect = "ODBC;uid=;pwd=;database=biblio;dsn=biblio;"
qd.SQL = TSQLQuery
qd.ReturnsRecords = True
Set rs = qd.OpenRecordset(dbOpenSnapshot)
ShowJetResults
SPT3Exit:
```

```
rs.Close
Exit Sub
SPT3Eh:
    For Each er In Errors
        Debug.Print er.Description
    Next
    Resume SPT3Exit
End Sub
```

The following two routines simply dump the result sets to a file and trap any errors that are encountered. The first procedure, ShowRDOResults, is for the RDO query. The second, ShowJetResults, is for the Jet queries:

```
Sub ShowRDOResults()
Dim errdo As rdoError
Dim cl As rdoColumn
On Error GoTo SPTEH:

Print #1, rd.RowCount
Do Until rd.EOF
    For Each cl In rd.rdoColumns
        Print #1, cl,
        Debug.Print cl,
    Next
    Print #1,
    Debug.Print
    rd.MoveNext
Loop
Print #1, rd.RowCount; "  done"
Debug.Print rd.RowCount; "  done"
quit:
Exit Sub
SPTEH:
    Print #1, Error$, Err
    Debug.Print Error$, Err
    For Each errdo In rdoErrors
        Print #1, errdo
        Debug.Print errdo
    Next
    If Err = 3146 Then Resume quit
    Resume Next
End Sub

Sub ShowJetResults()
On Error GoTo SPTEH:
Dim fd As Field
Print #1, rs.RecordCount
Do Until rs.EOF
    For Each fd In rs.Fields
        Print #1, fd,
        Debug.Print fd,
```

(continued)

```
            Next
                Print #1,
                Debug.Print
            rs.MoveNext
Loop
Print #1, rs.RecordCount; "  done"
Debug.Print rs.RecordCount; "  done"
quit:
Exit Sub
SPTEH:
    If Err = 3265 Then Resume Next
    Print #1, Error$, Err
    Debug.Print Error$, Err
    ShowDAOErrors
    If Err = 3146 Then Resume quit
    Resume Next

End Sub

Sub ShowDAOErrors()
    Debug.Print Error$, Err
    For Each er In Errors
        Print #1, er
        Debug.Print er
    Next
End Sub
```

Summary of the Techniques

We've just seen a number of different techniques for executing what is basically the same query against SQL Server. Here the techniques are summarized for you:

- *Open the SQL Server database directly, and use SQL pass-through to create a DAO/Jet Resultset object using a TSQL query string.* This technique is what you probably used in Visual Basic 3.0. It's no longer necessary, nor is it particularly efficient.

- *Execute a string containing a DAO/Jet query against an open Jet database containing attached tables.* The Jet query refers to the attached tables. This technique uses the Jet query processor to execute the query. In this case, SQL pass-through isn't used.

- *Execute a permanent DAO/Jet QueryDef object containing the same Jet SQL query as the first example.* Again, SQL pass-through isn't used.

- *Execute a string containing a TSQL query, but bypass the Jet query processor.* This technique uses a DAO/Jet Database object whose Connect property has been set to connect to the SQL Server database when SQL pass-through is requested, as is done in the OpenRecordset method.

- *Create a permanent DAO/Jet QueryDef object in code so as to make Jet use SQL pass-through to execute it.* The QueryDef object's SQL property contains a TSQL query. This technique also uses a Jet database to store the shareable SQL pass-through QueryDef object.

- *Create and execute a temporary SQL pass-through DAO/QueryDef object that contains a TSQL query, and whose Connect property points to the SQL Server.*

TIP A SQL pass-through query is always created as a snapshot-type Recordset object, so in fetching row data it also fetches page-based data (Text and Image data types), even if that data is never accessed. This can take a long time. But a SQL pass-through query doesn't fetch the page-based data if you don't include page-based columns in the query. If you need to access page-based data, use Jet dynasets against attached tables, since dynasets will fetch page-based columns only when they are accessed. Remember, too, that there is no background population of a Recordset object unless you use the Data control. In code, rows are fetched only when you request them (for example, by using the MoveNext method).

Working with Stored Procedures

It's possible to use DAO/Jet to execute stored procedures from Visual Basic, but it's not possible to retrieve return or output parameters directly without writing specific support queries to retrieve these results and convert them to ordinary row values—that is, ordinary TSQL queries that return the return and output parameter values.

Return Parameters

Besides the result set, the most common parameter returned from a stored procedure is the return status—all stored procedures return it. This integer value can indicate that a procedure has been successfully completed, or it can indicate the degree of success or the reason for failure. SQL Server has a defined set of return values, and you can define your own set. For example, one stored procedure that returns a status is sp_password, which adds or changes a password for a SQL Server logon ID. If the procedure successfully changes the password, it returns 0; otherwise, it returns 1, to indicate failure for some reason. (A descriptive error message is also given.) To execute this procedure and retrieve the return status, you need a TSQL query like the one that follows:

```
declare @rv int
execute @rv = sp_password <old password>, <new password>,
<login ID>
select "Return status"= @rv
```

Notice that you must first declare a TSQL variable, to hold the return status, and use a separate SELECT statement to return the value to your application in the form of a column in a single-row result set. This particular query has two result sets: one for the EXECUTE statement and one for the SELECT statement. It turns out that Jet simply ignores the first result set (because it returns no rows), so coding this is fairly simple.

To execute this query with DAO/Jet, first set up the global variables. To save time, we open an MDB database in the Form_Load event. (Remember to close it when you are done with the application.) This database is simply a placeholder Jet database—hence the use of the same "Attach.MDB" that we used previously.

The code that follows is also provided on this guide's companion disc as "Return Status Stored Procedure."

```
Option Explicit
Dim SQL As String
Dim db As Database
Dim qd As QueryDef
Dim rs As Recordset
Private Sub Form_Load()
Set db = OpenDatabase("c:\Attach.MDB")
End Sub
```

Next, the ChangePassword procedure sets up a query against our *Attach* database. Since there is no way to dynamically insert parameters into this query, we have to concatenate them by using the & operator. Note that an error handler is installed to deal with the anticipated ODBC errors and other unanticipated errors:

```
Private Sub ChangePassword_Click()
On Error GoTo CpEH
ReturnStatus = vbGrayed
SQL$ = "declare @rv int " _
    & " execute @rv = sp_password " & OldPassword & "," _
    & NewPassword
If Len(UserID) > 0 Then SQL$ = SQL$ & "," & UserID
SQL$ = SQL$ & " select 'Return status' = @rv"
```

Next, create a temporary QueryDef object. This technique uses the DAO/Jet Database object but doesn't save anything there. (Remember, you can use a Jet database that contains no tables.) To establish a SQL pass-through QueryDef object, set the Connect property first and the SQL property *second*. (If you set the SQL property first, Jet thinks that the query syntax should be correct for Jet.) Then set the ReturnsRecords property to indicate that the query returns rows—it isn't an action query.

Now we set the Database object's Connect property to contain a connect string pointing to the SQL server. This permits Jet to locate the SQL server when we create the SQL PassThrough result set, in the step that follows this one:

```
Set qd = db.CreateQueryDef("")
qd.Connect = "odbc;dsn=biblio;uid=;pwd=;database=biblio;"
qd.SQL = SQL$
qd.ReturnsRecords = True
```

And now we're ready to execute the query. The OpenRecordset method is used against the temporary QueryDef object. That's where the SQL and connect string information comes from. To execute this query, Jet establishes a connection to the SQL server specified in the QueryDef Connect property, and then Jet passes the query through to the SQL server query processor:

```
Set rs = qd.OpenRecordset(dbOpenSnapshot)
```

NOTE Incidentally, up to this point, most of this code was imported from the Visual Basic version 4.0 CD without modification. Yes, I tuned it up to take advantage of the new Visual Basic version 5.0 features in some cases, and changed the DSN references, but the rest seemed to convert very nicely.

Once the query is executed, the return status from the stored procedure is retrieved when the first member of the Fields collection of the first member of the Recordsets collection is examined. If 0 is returned, it means that the query worked and the password was changed. Otherwise, the query failed and somewhere along the line we got an ODBC error. Since we are done with the Recordset and QueryDef objects, we can toss them out.

An alternative strategy would be to place the CreateQueryDef object in the Form_Load event and simply change the SQL property each time the QueryDef object is executed:

```
If rs(0) Then ReturnStatus = 0 Else ReturnStatus = 1
rs.Close
QuitSub:
qd.Close
Exit Sub
```

When an error occurs, the error handler tests to see whether it is one of the anticipated ODBC errors. Since most ODBC errors return with a value of 3146, I filter out those errors and simply parse the Description property of the Errors collection. This returns a somewhat ugly string full of superfluous information, but the last part of it is usable. If the error is an unanticipated Visual Basic or Jet error, the second part of the handler displays an error message drawn from the Error string returned by Visual Basic. The error handler is fairly simple. It probably should be more sophisticated, but it does the job:

```
CpEH:
    Select Case Err
        Case 3146
            MsgBox Errors(0).Description
            Resume QuitSub
        Case Else
            MsgBox Error$
    End Select
End Sub
```

When the application ends or the user chooses the Exit option on the File menu, the form is unloaded. This approach does a good job of cleaning up the connections and the other Jet objects:

```
Private Sub Form_Unload(Cancel As Integer)
db.Close
End Sub

Private Sub MenuFileExit_Click()
Unload Form1
End Sub
```

Output Parameters

The use of output parameters is common in many shops for returning nonrow data from stored procedures. Getting at these parameters with Jet is a challenge, but it can be done. A stored procedure that returns output parameters specifically marks one or more arguments with the *OUTPUT* keyword. For example, the following TSQL stored procedure has two input arguments and passes back a return status and two output values:

```
CREATE PROCEDURE TestOutputRS
    @LikeTitle  Varchar(128) = '%',
    @LangWanted  Int = 1,
    @MaxTnum  int OUTPUT,
    @MinTnum  int OUTPUT
AS
Select @MaxTnum = max(P.Tnum), @MinTnum = min(P.Tnum)
From Topics T, Tprops P
Where P.Tnum = T.Tnum
and Title like @LikeTitle
and Lang = @LangWanted

if @MaxTnum = NULL Return 0
Return @MaxTnum-@MinTnum
```

To execute this procedure, you need to send a TSQL SQL pass-through query like this one:

```
declare @m1 int
declare @m2 int
declare @rv int
execute @rv = testoutputrs '%r%', 1,@m1 OUT, @m2 OUT
Select 'Return Value' = @rv, 'Max Tnum' = @m1, 'Min Tnum' = @m2
```

But let's say you used named arguments in the query to refer to the first argument of the EXECUTE statement—something like this:

```
execute @rv = testoutputrs @liketitle = 'rd', @m1, @m2
```

This isn't an option, because TSQL syntax insists that *all* the arguments be either named arguments or positional arguments; no mixture is possible.

You must also supply all the output and input arguments if you use the positional syntax. I got an error:

```
Msg 201, Level 16, State 2
Procedure TestOutputRS expects parameter @MinTnum, which was not supplied.
```

The error occurred when I failed to include the second input argument, which I wanted to default. The error message refers to *@MinTnum*—irrelevant in this case.

To execute this query with Jet, use the same method as the one used in the example for the return status. Apparently, Jet simply discards the rowless result set generated by the TSQL EXECUTE statement.

Handling SQL Server Messages

When you submit a query that violates a rule, the violation triggers an error message, which in turn triggers the ODBC error handler. The message that's returned indicates which rule was violated and how the violation occurred. Likewise, if you perform an operation that causes a trigger to fire, the trigger code can execute a PRINT statement that returns a message or a RAISERROR statement that returns a number and an error message. But unless you tell Jet to expect messages, they're simply tossed away. To make matters worse, Jet interprets a RAISERROR statement as indicating a fatal error and stops processing the query that's in progress.

TIP I once executed a query that returned about a dozen rows, followed by a RAISERROR statement. Jet processed the query and began populating the Recordset object. But when Jet had processed the last record, ODBC returned an "ODBC call failed" message, which continued to be returned as long as I tried to execute a MoveNext or MoveLast against the Recordset object. I turned on LogMessages and set up an error handler that dumped the Errors collection, but I still saw no sign of the RAISERROR message or its error number. If any of your procedures use the RAISERROR statement as a warning mechanism, you'll need to rewrite them to take into account this peculiarity of Jet.

CAUTION
If a Null computed value is passed to a RETURN statement, the SQL server resets it to 0 and generates an error message. A TSQL EXECUTE statement doesn't return any values that can be seen by either ODBC or DBLIB; you must include the SELECT statement to expose these values in the form of a result set row. Be sure to include the keyword *OUT* in the final SELECT statement, used to extract the output values, or the value assigned to these variables will be set to Null.

So how do you tell Jet to expect messages? You add a property to a DAO/Jet QueryDef object (and here is one more good reason for creating a "permanent" QueryDef object designed solely as an agent for executing stored procedures). By appending the LogMessages property, as shown in the code on the next page, and working with the permanent Jet tables that are created, you can manage returned messages fairly well. At this point, I wouldn't recommend sharing the Jet database used to hold the QueryDef object (and perhaps some attached SQL Server tables or views); adding multiuser functionality to this interface would be pretty hairy.

To turn on SQL Server message handling, you need to follow these steps. (The help documentation doesn't list all of them.) Start by setting up the global variables. Note that the Database and Recordset objects are declared globally, so they must be closed manually:

```
Option Explicit
Dim SQL As String
Dim db As Database
Dim qd As QueryDef
Dim LmProp As Property
Dim Em As Error
Dim rs As Recordset
Dim tb As TableDef
Dim MsgTable As String
```

Next, open the Attach.MDB database. (This is the same database we used in a previous example, so you'll probably want to make sure that no vestiges of that example are lying around.)

```
Private Sub Form_Load()
Set db = OpenDatabase("Attach.MDB")
End Sub
```

In the next step, the ShowMessages_Click event has the bulk of the code. First, set up the QueryDef object. (It has to be a "permanent" QueryDef object this time because we will be giving it a new property.) In this case, the SQL query to be executed is shown on the form in a text box, to make testing easier. Note that I turn on an error handler to trap the various errors we are bound to get:

```
Private Sub ShowMessages_Click()
On Error GoTo CpEH
Set qd = db.CreateQueryDef("LmQd")
qd.Connect = "odbc;dsn=biblio;uid=;pwd=;database=biblio;"
qd.SQL = Query
qd.ReturnsRecords = True
```

And now we're ready to install the new property on the QueryDef object. When we install the LogMessages property, we'll set its (Boolean) value to True to indicate that any messages this QueryDef object creates should be saved. Note that we use the named-argument Visual Basic syntax to code this function, but you can use the old style or even the Visual Basic 4.0 With syntax. Once the Property object is created, you have to manually append it to the QueryDef properties collection. Use the Refresh method to confirm that the property has been added:

```
Set LmProp = qd.CreateProperty(Name:="LogMessages", _
    Type:=dbBoolean, Value:=True, DDL:=False)
qd.Properties.Append LmProp
qd.Properties.Refresh
```

Now that your QueryDef object is ready, you can execute it and create a snapshot-type Recordset object. After the Recordset object is built, clear out the Messages control and print the resulting rows from the first part of the query:

```
(SELECT * FROM Languages)
```

Note that we haven't seen any sign of the print messages at this point— and we won't until we close the Recordset object. For some reason, the Jet table used to store the messages has been created in Exclusive mode and can't be accessed until the Recordset object that created it is closed:

```
Set rs = qd.OpenRecordset(dbOpenSnapshot)
messages.Cls
Do Until rs.EOF
    messages.Print rs(0), rs(1)
    rs.MoveNext
Loop
```

Once we have finished with the Recordset object and closed it, we can see whether any messages were generated in the course of the query's execution. It's like waiting until we've torn down the barn before checking to see if the horses are inside—but that's the way it works. This routine walks through the TableDefs collection looking for the last (highest) table starting with the name *Admin - .* Each time Jet executes this procedure, it does the same thing and creates another table, using the next name in the sequence. The name used is based on the logged-on user. By default, this is *Admin,* and so *Admin - 00* is the first name generated, *Admin - 01* is next, and so forth:

```
rs.Close                        ' to free Exclusive lock on
                                ' Admin - xx table
MsgTable = ""
For Each tb In db.TableDefs     ' find last Admin - xx table
    If tb.Name Like "Admin -*" Then MsgTable = tb.Name
Next tb
```

If we find a table, the query generated messages, and this routine creates a record set on that table. It contains *all* the print messages generated by the earlier query. Each message occupies one row. Once all the messages are printed, we are ready to clean up the last Recordset object:

```
IfMsgTable <> "" Then
Set rs = db.OpenRecordset(MsgTable, dbOpenTable, dbReadOnly)
Do Until rs.EOF
    Debug.Print rs(0)
    messages.Print Right(rs(0), 30)
    rs.MoveNext
Loop
rs.Close
End If
```

And to make sure we can execute this sample again, we toss out the QueryDef object. This isn't really necessary, since we can use the QueryDef object again later simply by changing the SQL property. I toss the *Admin - xx* table, too, so I don't have to find out what happens when we get to *Admin - 99*. I also refresh the TableDefs collection, just to make sure that Jet knows we deleted some tables:

```
QuitSub:
    db.QueryDefs.Delete "LmQd"
    qd.Close
    db.TableDefs.Delete MsgTable
    db.TableDefs.Refresh
Exit Sub
```

The error handler for this procedure is pretty much like the one in the earlier sample, but in this case I've also added code to deal with early-exit problems that can leave an orphaned QueryDef object:

```
CpEH:
    Select Case Err
        Case 3146
            For Each Em In Errors
                MsgBox Em.Description
            Next
            Resume Next
        Case 3012
                db.QueryDefs.Delete Name:="LmQd"
                Resume
        Case Else
            MsgBox Error$
        End Select
        Resume Next
        Resume QuitSub
End Sub
```

And that's SQL Server message handling, Jet-style. It ain't pretty, but it's better than nothing...almost.

15

Chapter

Using the Jet Data Control

Applying the Data Control

Using the Data Control with SQL Server

Setting Properties

Checking the Properties

Using Bound Controls

hould you use the Data control when accessing SQL Server? My usual advice is, "Just say no." Sometimes, though, that Data control can be tempting when it appears on a lonely highway to pick you up. But once you realize that it loves to strand inexperienced hitchhikers on dead-end streets of frustration, you'll put your thumb back up and wait for a more suitable ride. If you're determined to get picked up anyway, you should make sure you've read the documentation on the Data control and its basic use before you continue reading this chapter.

The real problem with the Data control in previous versions of Visual Basic wasn't performance—not really. You could manage and tune the Data control's performance. And it wasn't really connections. You could control the number of connections if you were careful—very careful. The problem with the Data control was that it required the use of a cursor.

Sometimes you can create cursors against SQL Server base tables. But when it comes time to update a table row, you might not have the luxury of a read-write cursor. Your MIS department might limit SQL Server access to a few choice stored procedures or restricted-access views, so not only can't you update data directly, you also might not be able even to extract it outside the scope of a stored procedure. This made the Data control basically useless unless you had access (at least read-only access) to a base table or view. You could create a Recordset object against a stored procedure's read-only result set, but you couldn't use the Data control to update this data. Besides, Jet always creates a snapshot-type Recordset object against stored-procedure data: neither Jet nor the other programming interfaces can create a keyset-driven cursor against the stored-procedure rows, because they know not whence the data has come.

Now that Visual Basic version 5.0 has arrived, the Data control will get renewed attention—especially now that you can create your own bound controls. But unless you use the RemoteData control, you won't get the neatest feature of all—the ability to trap the WillUpdateRows event, which lets you fire off an appropriate stored procedure instead of depending on an updatable cursor. Has Visual Basic version 5.0 changed the way the Data control works? Not much—other than some bug fixing.

The Visual Basic 5.0 Data control is an improvement over its previous renditions in that it's much more able to deal with common data content scenarios and is a much better ODBC citizen. Simply by pressing Control-Break, you can tell it to cancel the creation of a running query—or you can try to. And yes, you can set up the Data control to run via ODBCDirect, but no, it still doesn't fire the events you see from straight RDO.

Applying the Data Control

Let's assume that you have access to an updatable view or to SQL Server base tables or that you can use the read-only rows from stored procedures and use another update mechanism. The Data control does quite a bit of work for you if you can apply it to your needs, especially if you need to display and update graphics stored in the SQL Server database, since the Data control permits virtually code-free implementation. In general, you can consider the Data control for the following functions:

- *Managing graphics* in bound Picture and Image controls.

- *Managing pick lists* that show valid foreign-key selections. (One common implementation of the Data control fills a bound control from a filtered list of valid part numbers, valid state codes, or valid ship-to addresses.)

- *Managing simple or complex Jet-based Recordset objects* on the basis of simple table-only queries or queries that join, filter, and sort data from a variety of heterogeneous sources.

- *Displaying formatted result set data* in a multirow array, as with the DBGrid control.

Like Microsoft Access, the new Data control is theoretically able to do background population of result sets during idle time. When I execute a query that calls for more than a few hundred rows, however, the Data control's background population doesn't seem to work as I expected it to. For example, I set up a query that pulled back several hundred (OK, 25,000) rows, using a Jet query in the RecordSource property. I also set up a Timer control to monitor the current value of the RecordCount property, which indicates how many rows have been populated. At first, everything went fine. The Data control opened the Recordset object quickly and showed me the first row. The RecordCount property started out at 1, as I had expected it to do. After a few seconds, the timer routine detected that the RecordCount property was inching up 100 rows at a time, which was also what I had expected. The first row was visible in the three bound controls set up to display the current record, so I pressed the Next Row button on the Data control—and the whole application went dead and stayed that way until the Recordset object was fully populated.

The timer control received no further events, but Jet seemed to be busy populating the result set. I could tell it was busy; the Windows System Monitor said the CPU was running at 100 percent, and my hard disk light was steadily flashing—*something* was happening. Visual Basic was locked out the whole time, too, because the form wasn't repainted when it needed to be. When the query was finally finished, the Recordset object was fully populated, as evidenced by the RecordCount property jumping up to the total number of rows in the Recordset object—not good. This isn't what I call background population. I call this the same old "lock up while we do a MoveLast" strategy. So much for background population with the Data control. Perhaps this will be fixed in a later release. As it is, it's another nail in the Data control's tire.

> **NOTE** I thought that this basic problem would be fixed for Visual Basic version 5.0—it isn't. It worked just exactly the same way as it did in Visual Basic 4.0. Sigh. See the test application "Data Control BG Population Test" on the CD if you want to try this yourself.

Using the Data Control with SQL Server

To use the DAO/Jet Data control with any data source, you have several design choices. You can set the Data control properties at design time and have the Data control create a cursor on its own. This technique creates one of two types of DAO/Jet Recordset objects (dynaset or snapshot) against the default Workspaces(0) object. Or you can create a Recordset object by using the OpenRecordset method and then set the Data control's Recordset property to this new result set. This technique is useful for working with independent Recordset objects or with result sets created via parameter queries or QueryDef objects. Another choice is to create a Database object by using the OpenDatabase method. You then set the Data control's Database property to the new Database object. This procedure can be especially useful for working with secondary Workspace objects, since the Data control always assumes that it should use the Workspaces(0) object.

> **NOTE** The Data control does know how to deal with Table objects, but you still can't use them against SQL Server.

When you're working with SQL Server, you still have all three of these basic choices. The only real question is who will create the Recordset object. The Data control can't execute QueryDef objects that require parameters, and it always uses the default Workspace object. If you need to execute parameter queries or have special transaction scope requirements, create an independent Recordset object and pass it into the Data control.

Setting Properties

The DAO/Jet Data control properties that need to be set for accessing SQL Server are shown in *Figure 15-1*. You have several choices when it comes time to set the RecordSource property, and these choices play a big part in the viability of using the Data control with SQL Server. We'll see about using the ODBCDirect version of the Data control a little later.

First, you can set up a valid database name (the DSN) and a connect string and just use the drop-down list of table names. This list is generated by the Data control and Jet when you connect to the SQL server. The Data control and Jet execute an ODBC function that returns the names of selected tables. The list includes views but not stored procedures or system tables. Each table name has the *dbo* prefix. That's the way DAO/Jet passes table names back from ODBC.

CAUTION

Picking a table name from a drop-down list is really easy—and really dangerous. This feature is designed to be used with relatively small ISAM or Jet tables, not with the gargantuan tables often used by SQL Server.

Figure 15-1
Data Control Properties for Accessing SQL Server

Property	Purpose
Connect	This is the connect string. It is coded exactly like the OpenDatabase *Connect* argument. It always begins with *ODBC;* and it can contain a user ID, password, and default SQL Server database name. It can also contain the data source name (DSN) if you don't specify it in the DatabaseName property. After the Data control opens the connection, it contains the connect string that is *actually* used.
DatabaseName	This specifies the DSN unless it is specified in the Connect property (which takes precedence).
RecordSource	This specifies the name of a table (not a good idea) or of a Jet SQL query.[1]
Options	This specifies any needed options.[2]
EOFAction	If this is set to 2, Jet and the Data control handle the empty-result-set case for you by automatically switching to the AddNew mode. I always set this option to 2.
ReadOnly	You can specify a read-only cursor. This can improve performance, since Jet then doesn't have to worry about updating the data.
RecordsetType	This option tells Jet what kind of cursor to create: type 1 (dynaset) or type 2 (snapshot). After the Data control opens the result set, it shows which one was *actually* created.
DefaultCursorType	(ODBCDirect.) Selects type of RDO cursor (not used for DAO/Jet) operation.
DefaultType	This property determines whether the Data control should use Jet (dbUseJet[2]—the default) or ODBCDirect (dbUseODBC[1]).

1. You can use TSQL, but you have to set the SQL pass-through bit in the Options property.
2. You might set the dbReadOnly (4), dbAppendOnly (8), dbSQLPassThrough (64), or dbSeeChanges (512) options. You can't set dbForwardOnly because it returns an "invalid operation" error with no further indication of what is wrong. The problem is that the dbForwardOnly option isn't supported for the Data control.

When you set the RecordSource property by just picking one of the tables, the Data control internally substitutes a SELECT * FROM *table* query. This option brings back *all* the columns from *all* the rows in the table (dumb). Rows and columns are returned in the order in which SQL Server returns them. If you open such a query against a large table, be ready to wait—for a very long time. I recommend writing a carefully worded query that limits the result set to between a few dozen and a few hundred rows and selects only the columns you really need. If SQL Server is using a clustered index on the table, the rows are usually returned in an order that is based on the order in which the rows were added or updated.

Second, you can code a full-blown Jet SQL query in the RecordSource property, with a WHERE clause that limits the number of rows returned. This query can access a single table, pulling back just those columns you need, or a complex multitable or heterogeneous join that includes both Jet-fetched and SQL Server tables. You can also include an ORDER BY clause to sort the rows before they are returned. Remember, though, every column you bring back costs time and resources. A variation on this technique is to reference a Jet QueryDef object. This query could return rows from a stored procedure or any other Jet query.

A third viable choice is to code a TSQL query or stored procedure. If you decide to use TSQL syntax instead of Jet syntax, you should set the Options property to include the dbSQLPassThrough bit. In this case, the result set is always read-only, so you should set the RecordsetType property to dbOpenSnapshot.

Checking the Properties

Once the Data control creates a DAO/Jet Recordset object, the Data control properties reflect what has actually been created. (See **Figure 15-2**.) The Database and Recordset objects created by the Data control can be used just as you would use them if you had created them in DAO code. They support the same methods and properties and manage the same types of result sets.

When you use DAO methods to reposition the current-row pointer (as when you use the MoveNext method), the bound controls are automatically kept in sync with the current row of the result set.

As is true with the DAO interface, you can improve performance against ODBC data sources if you make use of the following choices:

- *Attached tables.*

- *Forward-only snapshots.* (Too bad this option *can't* be used with the Data control; just using a snapshot can help if there aren't too many rows.)

- *The read-only option.* (When the read-only option bit is set, Jet doesn't concern itself with additional overhead to update the result set.)

- *The append-only option.* (When the append-only option bit is set, Jet can optimize the operation, since it has to be concerned only with adding rows, not updating existing rows.)

- *Limited-scope queries* that return only the columns and rows needed.

Figure 15-2
Values of Data Control Properties After Opening

Property	Value
Connect	The Connect property contains the string used to establish the connection. Any missing arguments are filled in.
DatabaseName	This property is unchanged, even if you specify a different DSN in the Connect property.
Database	This is set to the new Database object created when the connection is opened.
Recordset	This is set with the new Recordset object.
ReadOnly	If the data isn't updatable, this property is set to True.
RecordCount	This Recordset property is set to 1 if any rows have resulted from the query. If there were no rows, it's set to 0.
Updatable	This Recordset property is set to True if the underlying data is updatable and if Jet has identified a unique index for the keyset.
RecordsetType	This option tells Jet what kind of cursor was created.

Using Bound Controls

There's nothing special about setting up bound controls against ODBC data sources. You simply set the DataSource property to a chosen Data control, and you set the DataField property to one of the columns returned by the result set. If you do this at design time, the Jet engine populates the TableDefs and Fields collections with the names and descriptions of all possible columns.

TIP If a MaskedEdit control is bound to a Data control, you might get an "Invalid property value" error message whenever you use the AddNew method, which doesn't work if you have specified a mask in any of the bound MaskedEdit fields. To solve this problem, clear the mask, execute the AddNew method, and then reinstate the mask. Something similar can occur when you set the MaxLength property of the TextBox control so that the length of the text entered (either read from the database or pasted in) is too great.

CAUTION
You can use parameter queries and DAO/Jet QueryDef objects with the Data control, but you have to open them independently of the Data control and you must pass in the parameters before you assign the Recordset object to the Data control's Recordset object. Remember, the QueryDef object can't pass parameters to a stored procedure that uses a parameterized query on the SQL server.

Data Control Design Issues: A Few Tips

- When you create an application that uses the Data control against an ODBC data source, you must realize that the first Data control potentially uses two connections. Each additional Data control uses an additional connection, even if it's using the same data source name as the first. All these connections remain open until their result sets are fully populated, when all the connections are released—except the two used to fetch fresh data from a dynaset-type Recordset object and to update rows, as necessary. Two connections remain, even if you have created only a snapshot-type Recordset object.

- The limit to the number of Data controls loaded in your application is set by the number of connections it uses, how long it takes to populate the Data controls' Recordset objects, how much memory you have for storing the keyset or snapshot cursors, and how much patience your user has.

- You can avoid a connection feeding frenzy by not completing all the properties of your Data controls at design time. Instead, complete the Data control properties at run time, one at a time, and use the Refresh method to open the individual controls. This won't help much if you don't fully populate the result sets, however. And be aware that this serial process can make your application take far longer to load.

- Experts tell me that they never permit records to be saved unless the code is bound into some pretty sophisticated error handlers, which verify that the data is correct before, during, and after an update.

- A "Type mismatch" error is generated when a control is bound to a field with an incompatible type, but the Error object isn't populated when it is examined in the Data control Error event. This is a limitation of the Data control in Visual Basic 4.0 because when Jet generates an error, the Error object is cleared.

16 Chapter

Understanding the Jet Query Processor

Many intimate details about how the Jet query processor works with SQL Server are hidden away in obscure white papers or on notes liberally stuck on monitors throughout the land. This chapter compiles as many of those details as I could find for readers who aren't satisfied just to know how to perform day-to-day tasks with the DAO model and Jet. If you're having trouble getting your Jet engine up to flight speed, maybe you'll find some solutions here.

The Microsoft Jet database engine query processor supports such advanced capabilities as heterogeneous joins, queries based on other queries, and arbitrary expressions, including user-defined functions. But because Jet isn't specifically designed for SQL Server, Jet must communicate with a variety of ODBC servers using standard ANSI SQL terms and referring only to functionality and data on each of those specific servers. Jet must determine what portions of any given query can be sent to each server involved in remote processing. The overriding goal is to send as much of the query as possible to the server, but operations that for some reason can't be performed on the server must be performed locally. Don't ignore generic query optimization techniques when you're using attached server tables. Because Jet attempts to send as much of a query as possible to the server for evaluation, you should be familiar with the server's capabilities. (For example, equality and range restrictions should still be done on indexed fields whenever possible.)

The query compiler generates an execution plan for any particular query, in the form of a tree of operations whose leaves are tables and whose root is the final query result set. Jet walks this tree from the bottom up, collapsing subtrees into SQL statements to be sent to a server. The collapsing stops when an operation meets any or all of several criteria. The first criterion is that the operation *joins data from multiple data sources*. The key to query performance on attached server tables is to ensure that little or no data filtering is done on the client machine. Client-side data processing increases network traffic and prevents you from leveraging advanced server hardware; it effectively reduces the client/server system to a file server system. You can optimize performance by being aware of what query operations Jet must evaluate on the client. All

joins spanning multiple data sources must be performed locally. Some servers, such as a SQL server, support multiple databases on a single machine. But because each server is a distinct ODBC data source, Jet won't ask the SQL server or other similar servers to do cross-database joins, only joins within a given database.

The second criterion for Jet's not collapsing subtrees into SQL statements is that the particular operation *would not be expressible in a single SQL statement*. Since Jet queries can be based on other Jet queries, several kinds of operation can be allowed. These include a Group By over a Group By or Distinct operation, a join over one or more Group By or Distinct operations, and complex combinations of inner and outer joins. Jet sends the server as many of these operations as can be expressed in a single standard SQL statement, but it performs the remaining higher-level operations locally.

The third criterion for stopping the collapse of subtrees into SQL statements is that the particular operation *is not supported on the server*. Generally, the SELECT clause of a query has no effect on how much of the query Jet sends the server and how much is processed locally. Jet selects the needed columns from the server and, on that basis, locally evaluates any output expressions. For example, if an output expression (like string concatenation) *can* be evaluated on the server, it's sent to the server for processing.

Constructs That Jet Must Evaluate Locally

Query clauses other than the SELECT clause (WHERE, ORDER BY, and so on) do have a more important effect: the expressions in these clauses determine whether Jet must execute them locally. When expressions are executed locally, this means that Jet must query or download all relevant rows from all data sources involved and do the work on the client machine.

Unsupported Visual Basic Operators and Functions

Visual Basic intrinsically supports many numeric, date/time, statistical, financial, and string functions. Some have server-side equivalents, and some don't. Jet must locally evaluate any function that has no server-side correspondent, using SQLGetInfo to determine what operators or functions are supported on the server by asking the ODBC driver. If these operators and intrinsic functions are supported by the server and driver, Jet sends them to the server for evaluation. *Figure 16-1* on the next page shows these operators and functions.

User-Defined Functions

You can define your own functions in Visual Basic. These never have server-side equivalents, so they are always evaluated locally unless they don't reference any server data. In that case, the function is evaluated and sent to the server.

Figure 16-1

Visual Basic Operators and Functions

General Operators		Numeric Functions	String Functions	Aggregate Functions	Date/Time Functions	
AND	OR	ABS	LCASE	MIN	SECOND	DAY
NOT	LIKE	ATN	LEFT	MAX	MINUTE	MONTH
IN	&	COS	LEN	AVG	HOUR	YEAR
=	+	EXP	INSTR	COUNT	WEEKDAY	
< >	-	INT	LTRIM	SUM	DATEPART ('ddd')	
<	*	LOG	MID		DATEPART('www')	
< =	/	MOD	RIGHT		DATEPART('yyy')	
>	IDIV	RND	RTRIM		DATEPART('mmm')	
=	MOD	SGN	SPACE		DATEPART('qqq')	
BETWEEN		SIN	STRING		DATEPART ('hhh')	
IS [NOT]		SQR	TRIM		DATEPART('nnn')	
NULL		TAN	UCASE		DATEPART('sss')	
					DATEPART('ww')	
					DATEPART('yyyy')	

Miscellaneous Unsupported Functionality

Jet uses SQLGetInfo and SQLGetTypeInfo to ask the ODBC driver whether a particular server supports, among other things, the following functions:

- *Outer joins* (which *are* supported by SQL Server)

- *Expressions in the ORDER BY clause* (which are *not* supported by SQL Server)

- *The LIKE operator in Text and Memo columns* (which is supported by SQL Server)

Miscellaneous Unsupported and Questionable Expressions

These locally evaluated constructs include the following operators and functions:

- *Operations involving incompatible types,* such as *LIKE b + c* (which are *not* supported by SQL Server)

- *Nonstandard LIKE wildcards,* such as the Microsoft Access–specific [and # (which *are* supported by SQL Server)

- *Intrinsic functions,* if arguments have incorrect types

- *Explicit type-conversion functions,* such as CInt and Cdbl (which *are* supported by SQL Server)

- *Nonlogical operators where logical operators should be,* such as *(a > b) AND (c + d),* in which the right side is arithmetic

- *Logical operators where nonlogical operators should be,* such as *a + (b AND c) * d,* using a logical result in an addition

Restriction Splitting

In deciding whether a WHERE or HAVING clause can be sent to the server, Jet dissects the restriction expression into its component conjuncts, separated by ANDs, and locally evaluates only those components that can't be sent. Therefore, if you use restrictions that can't be processed by the server, you should accompany them with restrictions that *can* be processed by the server. For example, suppose you write a Basic function called SomeCalculation. The following query will cause Jet to bring back the entire table and evaluate *SomeCalculation(column1) = 17* locally:

```
SELECT *
FROM huge_table
WHERE SomeCalculation(column1) = 17
```

Note the following query, however:

```
SELECT *
FROM huge_table
WHERE SomeCalculation(column1) = 17 AND
    last_name BETWEEN 'g' AND 'h'
```

The preceding query causes Jet to send the following query to the server, bringing back only those rows that match the restriction:

```
SELECT *
FROM huge_table
WHERE last_name BETWEEN 'g' AND 'h'
```

Jet then locally evaluates the restriction on only those rows:

```
SomeCalculation(column1) = 17
```

Evaluation of Outputs

Although SELECT clause elements are usually evaluated by the server, there are two exceptions to this rule:

- *Queries with the* DISTINCT *keyword.* Provided that all SELECT clause expressions can be evaluated by the server, Jet sends the *DISTINCT* keyword as well. If a SELECT clause expression must be evaluated locally, so must the *DISTINCT* keyword operation.

- *Queries with aggregation.* Jet attempts to do aggregation on the server, since this often drastically reduces the number of rows returned to the client. For example, the query

```
SELECT Sum(column1) FROM huge_table
```

is sent entirely to the server; a single row is returned over the network. But

```
SELECT StdDev(column1) FROM huge_table
```

causes Jet to send *SELECT column1 FROM huge_table* to the server, retrieve every row in the table, and perform the aggregation locally. This happens because StdDev isn't a standard SQL aggregate function.

Removal of Execution of Crosstab Queries

Jet sends some crosstab queries to the server for evaluation, which can mean that far fewer rows are transferred over the network. Jet sends a simpler GROUP BY form of the crosstab and transforms the result set into a true crosstab. This transformation doesn't apply to complex crosstab tables, however. To send the optimal crosstab query to the server, the following criteria must be met. (These apply only to Jet SQL queries, not to TSQL SQL pass-through queries.)

- Row and column headers can't contain aggregates.

- The value must contain only one aggregate.

- There can be no user-defined ORDER BY clause.

All the other reasons for forcing local processing also apply.

Outer Joins

In determining where to perform joins, Jet separates outer joins from inner joins because of ambiguities inherent in mixing the two types. Therefore, any query that Jet sends through the ODBC interface will have a FROM clause containing either of the following:

- Any number of tables, all inner-joined

- Any number of inner joins and one outer join

This means that some complex queries involving inner and outer joins cannot be sent in their entirety to the server, so Jet might perform some of the higher-level joins locally. Another condition that can cause Jet to perform an outer join locally occurs when the join restriction is anything other than an outer join on one column:

```
left_table.column = right_table.column
```

Generating SQL to Send to a Server

The structured query language that Jet sends to the SQL Server ODBC driver is generated according to the SQL grammar defined by ODBC. For the most part, this is standard SQL, but it might contain ODBC-defined canonical escape sequences. The SQL Server ODBC driver is responsible for replacing these escape sequences with SQL Server–specific syntax before passing the SQL along to the server; Jet never uses back-end–specific syntax. For example, most servers support outer joins, but servers differ widely in their outer-join syntax. Jet uses only the ODBC-defined outer-join syntax:

```
SELECT Table1.Col1, Table2.Col1
FROM {oj Table1 LEFT OUTER JOIN Table2 ON
    Table1.Col1 = Table2.Col1}
```

Jet relies on the ODBC driver to translate this to the server-specific outer-join syntax. In the case of SQL Server, this would be the following syntax:

```
SELECT Table1.Col1, Table2.Col1
FROM Table1, Table2
WHERE Table1.Col1 *= Table2.Col1
```

Wildcards for the LIKE Operator

When you use the LIKE operator, you should use the Jet wildcards (? for single-character matching and * for multiple-character matching), not the SQL Server–specific %. Jet translates these wildcards into _ and % before sending the expression to the server. The only exception involves query parameter values: because Jet forwards your parameter values to the server, they must use _ and %.

Owner and Table Prefixing

In generating queries that involve more than a single table, Jet prefixes column names with a table name. In a self-join, Jet generates a correlation name to use as a table name prefix. Jet also supplies an owner name prefix if an owner is associated with the attached table. This owner name (if it exists) is returned by the ODBC driver's SQLTables function at attach time.

Identifier Quoting

Jet calls SQLGetInfo(SQL_IDENTIFIER_QUOTE_CHAR) to determine which identifier-quoting character is supported by the server and driver. If such a character exists, Jet wraps all owner, table, and column names into this character, even if that isn't always strictly necessary. Without knowing the keywords and special characters for a particular server, Jet can't know whether identifier quoting is necessary in any given case.

Chapter

Jet:
A Traveler's
Diary

This chapter is a catchall for a number of fairly random observations about using Jet databases. I accumulated these pearls of wisdom in my wanderings through lonely Air Force bases in East Texas, where old versions of Jet crawl off to die. Much of what I have to say here is particularly focused on client/server architecture, especially on SQL Server–related issues. But some of these observations veer off into ISAM mutterings—not to mention scary recurring dreams.

Allocating Space

MDB database file space allocation is made through MS-DOS—not the Windows 95 and Windows NT operating systems. No preallocation of space is made, which is why the threat is very real that other workstation (or file server) file allocations will rob the database of needed space. This is especially true of locally allocated sort, record set, keyset, and snapshot row-storage space saved on disk in the TEMP directory. Running another application on the workstation that's acting as the database file server will also have a significant impact on the performance of the database.

Jet doesn't actively remove the space that was occupied by records deleted from MDB databases, but it reuses that space if possible. In the course of normal operations, some situations can cause a great deal of unused overhead space to be left behind, so you'll need to compact the MDB file periodically. Compacting is an offline process: the entire database is simply copied to another location, an operation that leaves the dead space behind. You can write an application to compact your database; see the Visual Basic documentation on the CompactDatabase statement. But no matter how you do it, everyone, even that guy from Cleveland who's always logged on, needs to be logged off.

Transaction Loss
and Damage Repair

If your system loses power, you'll want to use the RepairDatabase method against your MDB database, since cached writes might not have completed and the database might have been damaged. If you find errors, you *might* be able to repair them with the RepairDatabase method. In many cases, all the data can be recovered. In others, your database might be hopelessly trashed.

When the database can't be recovered, you must rely on your last backup because there's no transaction log for restoring lost transactions. That's why you should back up mission-critical data by exporting it to other offline or external media. Everyone must be off the database before it can be backed up, but finding out who is still on can be problematic. See the RepairDatabase method in online help for more information.

Losing the Jet database isn't a problem if the only things saved there are attached tables or QueryDef objects, as is commonly the case with front-end applications using Jet to access SQL Server. If you also store data in your MDB database, however, you do need to be careful about shutting down and you must be sensitive to the possibility of lost or incomplete transactions.

Backing Up
Microsoft Access Databases

On the surface, what could be simpler? You just make a copy of the MDB file and the SYSTEM.MDW (formerly SYSTEM.MDA) files. But there's a problem: this strategy won't back up any data at all if the database contains only attached tables (as is typically the case when you are using SQL Server). So you still need to back up the SQL server, which isn't a problem, because the SQL server doesn't have to be brought down in order to be backed up. But a Jet database does. Before you can copy the file as a whole, you need to get at least read-only access to it—but when another user has any object open in the database, the entire database file is locked and can't be read by a file-copy program. Can't you just get everyone else off and back it up? The trouble is, there's no way to tell who is connected, short of using the Windows for Workgroups Net Watch program; there is no sp_who in Microsoft Access or in Visual Basic. Your Jet-format database might also contain linkages to other attached databases: non–SQL Server databases that might not be rigorously backed up.

Does the toolkit for Visual Basic or the one for Microsoft Access include a backup utility? The one for Access does, if you count the Import/Export File feature. Using this method, or writing a program in Visual Basic that dumps to external media, you could back up the data. Doing this wouldn't copy the structure, permissions, referential integrity, forms, reports, or any other Microsoft Access structures built into the database; the data would be safe, although it would be somewhat difficult to restore without a database to write to. For this reason, I recommend that you back up the database again whenever you make any structural changes so that you can restore the data painlessly.

Updating Records

Jet uses a keyset-driven cursor to update rows in SQL Server tables. If for some reason the key values change or can't be determined when it comes time to update a row, Jet reports that the row has been deleted or can't be found. This message might be caused by a trigger in the SQL Server table that assigns the primary key for the new record. If so, Jet loses track of the record, since it isn't aware of the primary-key change made by the trigger, and it shows the record as deleted. There can also be a problem when there are fixed-length string fields in the database and you update values without properly padding them. Try adding a TimeStamp column to the SQL Server table. This seems to help Jet locate records and columns that have changed.

Tidbits

- Apparently, Jet 3.5 now supports SQL Server 6.5 Null-permitted indexes. These weren't supported in Jet 3.0.

- See Q148410 in the Access Knowledge Base for a listing of the Jet 3.0 reserved errors.

- To append a table to a Jet database, open a Jet MDB database and submit the following:

```
Set td = db.CreateTableDef("AttachedAuthors")
td.Connect = "ODBC;uid=;pwd=;Database=Pubs;DSN=MyDSN;"
td.SourceTableName = "authors"
db.TableDefs.Append td
```

- Consider using the SQL Server variable *@@Identity* to determine the last-used identity value when you're adding new rows. This value can be returned from a stored procedure when you use it to insert a new row.

- In DAO 2.5, if you don't close your application (Visual Basic or the EXE) or shut down the Jet engine using *Set DBEngine = Nothing*, the database object never goes out of scope, so its connection is never closed—as in never in a thousand years. Jet 3.0 and 3.5 don't work this way (thank goodness).

- The RecordsAffected property returns 0 or −1 after issuing a SQLPassThrough Execute method. In other words, when using SQL pass-through, Jet isn't passing back the number of rows affected by the last query. You can get this to work by opening the DAO/Jet Database object directly.

PART IV

Using Remote Data Objects and the RemoteData Control

18 Chapter

Using ODBCDirect

n the late fall of 1995, the Dart team was staring at the performance numbers and flexibility of the new RDO ODBC interface. They liked what they saw, but Jet couldn't use any of this technology and neither could DAO because it was heavily intertwined with Jet. While you couldn't say that DAO was married to Jet, you could fairly say they were living in sin. The team had to get the two pieces separated. By January of 1996, the team had accomplished this and DAO 3.1 was sent out as a "free" beta. Using the feedback from this beta, the Dart team finalized the changes incorporated into Microsoft Office 97 and, later, into Visual Basic version 5.0 and Microsoft Visual C++. ODBCDirect was born.

ODBCDirect isn't really DAO, nor RDO, nor even ODBC, although it shares many of the aspects and object names of each. See *Figure 18-1* for a look at its architecture. The Microsoft Office folks need it and want it as an alternative to the ODBC API and DAO programming for reaching back-end ODBC data sources. The merits of ODBCDirect are less obvious to the Visual Basic client/server developer trying to access SQL Server. Look at it this way: if you are a DAO developer, you're working on ISAM, native Jet, or ODBC data sources. In the first two cases, you're bound to be using designs and implementation technology that leverage Jet's exceptional power to deal with this type of database. This means that you're using the Table object with the Seek method, permanent QueryDef objects, and Jet SQL. You don't care about stored procedures, multiple result sets, or remote business classes, and your designs reflect these realities. You have never written a trigger, and you have learned to do without asynchronous operations.

But if you are a DAO developer who works with SQL Server, you have already had to lay off the Table object and the Seek method and you probably don't use the Data control that much. You execute stored procedures but jump through hoops trying to get them to return multiple result sets—or you rewrite your SPs to send back singleton queries. You make heavy use of SQL pass-through, and you might even have figured out how to get Jet QueryDef objects to work with TSQL queries inside. In other words, you've adapted your programming style to deal with the features, power, and limitations of DAO/Jet.

PART IV USING REMOTE DATA OBJECTS AND THE RemoteData CONTROL

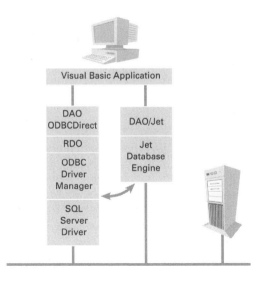

Figure 18-1 *ODBCDirect architecture*

ODBCDirect can't magically make your DAO code work faster and better: only in the simplest of cases will switching to ODBCDirect work without your needing to redesign at least some of your code. While ODBCDirect can make some operations work better, it requires you to recode some parts that no longer work or work differently than they did when you coded to ISAM databases or even ODBC data sources. ODBCDirect doesn't support the concept of permanent QueryDef objects, so many of the strategies we considered in the Jet chapters simply don't map to ODBCDirect. But if you decide to try out ODBCDirect, this chapter aims at making the process of migrating an existing DAO/Jet application over to ODBCDirect—or perhaps straight to RDO—a reasonably straightforward task.

Before you launch yourself on this journey, you really need to ask yourself this question: "Does my current application give me the performance I need?" If it does, don't fix it. If your application doesn't perform well, you need to ask yourself what you're willing to pay to make it faster or easier to code or to make it work better with SQL Server. The cost might be high converting to *anything*—ODBCDirect, RDO, VBSQL, or something else. Will converting to ODBCDirect be any cheaper because you are starting from DAO? It could be, but then again, it depends on how many of the techniques we have examined earlier are ones you use and how many of these will have to be reengineered to work with ODBCDirect. If you are starting from scratch, I don't think that there is a question here—simply use RDO.

Wait! Are we missing a big advantage to ODBCDirect here? Doesn't it work with 16-bit Visual Basic like DAO? Nope, sorry, it doesn't. ODBCDirect directly links to RDO, which is 32-bit only. ODBCDirect *does* have a big advantage, but it's for Microsoft Office 97 users (more 32-bit clients). It means that they can access most of the power and speed of RDO without having to buy a copy of Visual Basic version 5.0 Enterprise Edition.

Understanding ODBCDirect Architecture

ODBCDirect is the second path that DAO 3.5 provides for accessing remote data—the first being through the Microsoft Jet database engine. In previous versions of DAO, if you wanted to access data through ODBC, DAO passed your calls to Jet, which took the query and passed it to its query optimizer, which called ODBC, as needed, to fetch the data. The result sets returned from ODBC were passed back to Jet's cursor builder, which built Resultset objects to pass back to the application. This path, though it got the job done, wasn't always the most efficient way to deal with intelligent remote database engines like SQL Server. Developers using this path soon realized two weaknesses. First, it required loading Microsoft Jet, even though the actual database being accessed wasn't a Microsoft Jet database. Second, it could be slower due to the extra functionality Jet provided and the footprint it required. Yes, applications built this way were far easier to code, but at a price. Even with all of the optimizations turned on, DAO/Jet applications were slower than those that accessed the ODBC APIs more directly. Now, with ODBCDirect, developers have a fairly direct path to ODBC and their data—that is, ODBCDirect provides a direct path to the ODBC API by way of RDO.

ODBCDirect takes far less RAM than DAO/Jet but more than RDO. How much more? Well, someone on the Dart team provided me with this breakdown. Opening a server-side result set against SQL Server and doing a MoveLast cost the following amount of RAM:

- RDO 2.0 took 241,664 KB

- ODBCDirect took 512,000 KB

- DAO/Jet took 643,072 KB

When you choose ODBCDirect over Jet, you give up some of the most powerful aspects of the Jet engine, one being the ability to join data in tables stored in different back ends—for instance, Oracle and Microsoft SQL Server data or SQL Server and native Jet. (You must use Microsoft Jet in this case because it provides heterogeneous joins.) You must also choose to go through Microsoft Jet if you are planning to do a lot of DDL (data definition language), because ODBCDirect doesn't provide table definitions or the ability to create tables through DAO's object model. You can still create tables using ODBCDirect, by executing SQL statements, but it might seem more convenient to use the DAO/Jet TableDef object. OK, that's stretching it a bit, but you get the idea—giving up Jet isn't free.

I don't know how many rows were involved, nor do I know what else the Jet engine had been asked to do up to that point. I do know that DAO/Jet is modularized so that it loads only portions of its functionality as needed—so your mileage may vary.

Most client/server developers simply want to read data in, change it, and write it back to the back end, and they want to do it fast. ODBCDirect can help you do all that. Most client/server developers also want to be able to get at powerful features supplied by remote data servers. For this, I don't think anyone will suggest that you use ODBCDirect if you haven't already been using DAO—unless you don't have a choice (as when working from Microsoft Office).

What *about* Remote Database Objects (RDO), which first shipped with Visual Basic 4.0 Enterprise Edition? Doesn't RDO do all this? Why not use it? There are reasons for using both RDO and DAO with ODBCDirect. But before we get into a tug of war between ODBCDirect and RDO, let me make this clear: these two object models are *not* in competition. They are each designed for different uses and have different heritages that color their approaches to client/server application implementation. ODBCDirect's roots are in DAO, and it expects to be useful *to existing DAO customers* who want a better DAO-like interface to ODBC data sources. RDO is an entirely new interface—born last year outside of the normal DAO development teams to address some of the same client/server issues but with a different approach that didn't pay (much) attention to DAO. Some of the objects have similar names, but in many cases the way they work is very different. The following material walks through the differences between RDO and ODBCDirect so that those trying to figure the costs of one approach or the other can make an informed decision.

NOTE The following analysis was excerpted from a white paper written by Emily Kruglick, Fox Data Access Program Manager, and Peter Tucker, DAO Test Lead at Microsoft. I have edited it quite a bit, so don't blame them for this content. If you want to see the original document, you can find it (or at least I hope that you can find it) at http://www.microsoft.com/accessdev/accwhite/odbcdir.htm.

The basic differences between RDO and ODBCDirect are summarized in *Figure 18-2* on the next page.

In brief, RDO is more specialized and provides more sophisticated functionality than DAO, but RDO requires a license for, and only ships with, Visual Basic Enterprise Edition. DAO is more flexible and portable than RDO, at the cost of some advanced functionality.

Figure 18-2
RDO vs. ODBCDirect

RDO	DAO with ODBCDirect
Available in Visual Basic Enterprise Edition, Visual C++, and Visual J++. May be used in other tools if developer has acquired a license for Enterprise Development Tools.	Available in Visual Basic 5.0 Enterprise Edition and Professional Edition, Microsoft Office 97, Microsoft Excel 97, Microsoft Access 97, and Visual C++ 5.0.
Applications may be redistributed by licensed users of the development tools listed above.	Applications may be redistributed by Enterprise Edition, Visual Basic Professional Edition, Microsoft Office 97 (to other Microsoft Office desktops), or Visual C++ 5.0.
Provides very fast programmatic access to ODBC data, asynchronous processing, and support for events, which eliminates the need to poll for the completion of asynchronous operations. Also supports direct access to underlying ODBC handles for low-level API work, creatable objects for easier coding and more flexibility in object management, and queries as methods.	Provides very fast programmatic access to ODBC data and asynchronous processing. Doesn't support events, creatable objects, or queries as methods. There is no "official" support for underlying ODBC handles—they are there, just hidden.
Supports UserConnection Designer to store permanent queries in the application as UserConnection objects.	Supports the creation of temporary QueryDef objects in code.
Designed for advanced remote database functionality using sophisticated event and offline result set management.	Designed for advanced remote database functionality as well as local database functionality. Applications can be easily modified to switch between local and remote data, thus enabling upsizing to client/server or downsizing for traveling or disconnected scenarios. For more information, see "Tips for Converting Your Application to ODBCDirect" later in this chapter.
Entire object model and most property arguments are enumerated in the typelib, so they show up in IntelliSense coding.	While constants are enumerated, properties are not.
Object model is similar to DAO, but distinct.	Object model is part of DAO. Well, a super-subset of DAO 3.0. Well, actually, it's mapped against RDO.

NOTE At no time should you believe that an existing DAO application can be instantly ported to ODBCDirect or even RDO. While the spelling of the DAO objects is similar for DAO, ODBCDirect, and RDO, the way they are implemented by the underlying layers plays a significant role in how they are used and applied by developers. DAO applications, just like VBSQL applications, have a characteristic design modality. It is this fundamental design that most often must be reengineered to effectively use the interface. It *is* possible to create a single application that can be used to interface both to Jet and ODBC databases using DAO/Jet and ODBCDirect. You have to be careful, but it can be done. See ***Figure 18-3*** for a view of the degree of their overlap.

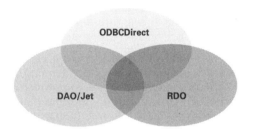

Figure 18-3   *Mapping DAO/Jet to ODBCDirect to RDO functionality*

Activating ODBCDirect

All Data Access Objects are referenced from the base DBEngine object. Once DAO is loaded, your code decides which underlying interface will be used to implement the DAO ODBCDirect objects—Jet or RDO. Basically, a DAO Workspace can be created to access either interface, but it defaults to DAO/ Jet. You can override this default by using the DefaultType property of the DBEngine object. You can have both at the same time by creating additional Workspace objects. This allows you to begin coding an application against a Microsoft Jet Database using a DAO/Jet Workspace and then later convert it to access a remote Microsoft SQL Server database through ODBCDirect by simply opening a new ODBCDirect Workspace. Once a Workspace is created, you can't change its spots (er, type).

You should note, however, that for the conversion of a DAO/Jet to an ODBCDirect application to go smoothly, you must keep in mind what functionality is supported in both Workspaces. We'll look at the specific differences later, and a later section in this chapter will help you convert a DAO application to ODBCDirect. We are back in the "code for both interfaces" business again. That is, you have to write your code so that the objects work pretty much the same no matter which interface you are currently connected to. Of course, if you don't plan to create an application that must work against both types of Workspaces, this isn't a problem.

After you decide to create an ODBCDirect Workspace, you have a couple of choices about how to do it. The most direct way is to create the Workspace using the DBEngine object's CreateWorkspace method. You can't declare a "New" Workspace object the way you can declare objects in RDO. DAO 3.5 implements a new fourth parameter, *Type*, which allows you to specify which type of Workspace to create. You can choose either *dbUseJet* for a Microsoft Jet Workspace or *dbUseODBC* for an ODBCDirect Workspace:

```
Dim wksODBC as Workspace
Dim wksJet as Workspace

    Set wksODBC = DBEngine.CreateWorkspace( _
        "HelloODBCWS", "sa", "", dbUseODBC)

    Set wksJet = DBEngine.CreateWorkspace( _
        "HelloJetWS", "admin", "")
```

Another, less obvious, way to create your choice of Workspace objects is to let DAO do it for you. All you have to do is set the DefaultType property (or don't), and the first reference to the Workspace (even indirectly) forces DAO to load either RDO (for ODBCDirect) or the Jet database engine:

```
Dim wksDefault as Workspace

    DBEngine.DefaultType = dbUseODBC
    ' Since the default type is dbUseODBC, the
    ' default Workspace will be an ODBCDirect
    ' Workspace.
    Set wksDefault = DBEngine.Workspaces(0)
```

To tell the truth, these two objects are identical under the covers. However, some of the new ODBCDirect features were exposed on the Connection object but not on the Database object because the DAO people want you to migrate away from the Database object to the Connection object for future compatibility.

Connecting to Databases

As you'll see when we get to the RDO chapters, RDO doesn't use a Database object to establish a connection—it uses its own unique rdoConnection object. ODBCDirect also uses its own Connection object. For the most part, ODBCDirect's Connection object is very similar to DAO's Database object, although they differ in several functional aspects. We will touch on those differences in a minute.

ODBCDirect and RDO approach the problem of choosing the cursor type a little differently. First RDO supports a global rdoDefaultCursorDriver property on the rdoEngine object. This defines the application-wide default for all rdoEnvironment objects you create. ODBCDirect has a global default that can't be changed—dbUseDefaultCursor, which is equivalent to RDO's rdUseIfNeeded. Both options can be overridden by changing the DBEngine object's DefaultCursorDriver property, changing the rdoEngine object's rdoDefaultCursorDriver property, or by changing the rdoEnvironment object's CursorDriver property. By setting these options before you establish a connection, you can completely disable cursors or choose ODBC client-side, SQL Server server-side, or the new Client Batch cursor libraries. Each has its own advantages and disadvantages—as we'll see in subsequent Part IV chapters.

Because ODBCDirect's default is set to dbUseDefaultCursor, the RDO (or the ODBC driver manager) decides which cursor to use. It will choose SQL Server server-side cursors if they are available. In most cases, if the server doesn't support cursors, local cursors are used. Actually, RDO won't let you select a cursor or cursor driver that's incapable of doing what you ask. The underlying ODBC technology tries to gracefully choose the most appropriate cursor based on the properties and options specified. If the driver is incapable of working under the given parameters, it quietly (and sometimes not so quietly) returns a "Driver not capable" error message and reverts to an operational mode it can handle—if one is available.

ODBCDirect supports RDO's concept of "No Cursor." This is specified by setting the DefaultCursorDriver property to dbUseNoCursor. This sets up a forward-only, read-only Recordset that fetches one record at a time from the server. This Recordset requires the least overhead. It's also the least functional, but it's usually the fastest way to dump data back to the client.

Comparing Database and Connection Objects

Once you have chosen your default cursor, it's time to establish a connection with your data. Remember, once the connection is established, you can't change cursor drivers. With DAO/Jet, you had no choice here—you simply called OpenDatabase and Jet would build a connection for you and manage it for all subclients in your application. ODBCDirect, like RDO, has no connection manager. To maintain DAO code compatibility, ODBCDirect allows you two similar paths to your database, the Database object and the Connection object.

What do you gain by using the Connection object instead of the Database object? Well, the Connection object has the ability to run asynchronous operations and create temporary QueryDef objects (prepared statements, for those of you more familiar with RDO 1.0 or ODBC), while the Database object is more compatible with the Microsoft Jet path. For example, you can't create QueryDef objects from a Database object unless you're working with a Microsoft Jet database. This flies in the face of several of the SQL pass-through techniques I talked about in Part III. This means that you must convert your code to the Connection object to maintain this type of functionality against SQL Server. But wait, before you go off and start ripping up the old roadbed, let's see what other little surprises lie around the bend.

Why use the Database object? If you're writing code that you want to be able to switch easily from one type of Workspace to another because you're planning to change the database back ends (that is, from Microsoft Jet to

Microsoft SQL Server), using Database makes plenty of sense, especially since the Connection object is supported as a property of the Database object. But if your code needs to be able to use QueryDef objects against remote databases or is going to run asynchronous queries, you should use a Connection object—or at least the Connection property of the Database object. So, to cover more contingencies when you open a Connection or a Database object and need the functionality provided by the other object, each has an associated object. That is, the Database object has a Connection property and the Connection object has a Database property. This might come in handy if you have some shared code that uses both types of objects. For instance, you might want to write all your code so that it can run through either Microsoft Jet or ODBCDirect, but then, much later in the code, you might want to run a specific query asynchronously if it is available. By connecting to the database using OpenDatabase, you can use the same code whether or not you're using ODBCDirect. Then, later in the code, you can do a check to see whether you're in ODBCDirect, and, if you are, you can jump on over to the Connection object and execute the statement asynchronously. (See code example 1 later in this chapter.)

Here is sample code that opens both Connection and Database objects:

```
dim dbs as database
dim cnn as connection

    set dbs = OpenDatabase("", _
        dbDriverRequired, false, _
        "ODBC;dsn=DBSer;database=pubs;uid=sa;pwd=pass;")

    set cnn = OpenConnection("", _
        dbDriverNoPrompt, false _
        "ODBC;dsn=DBSer;database=pubs;uid=sa;pwd=pass;")
```

Comparing Connection and rdoConnection Objects

Let's take the time to put these two objects side by side. This comparison bubbles up lots of interesting differences that highlight the different levels of implementation. For the sake of brevity, I've removed all of the entries where both objects provide the same functionality.

You can see from *Figure 18-4* that a few RDO features aren't supported by ODBCDirect or are handled in the following ways:

- *You have to create a new Workspace object* if you need a different cursor driver for a specific connection.

- *The low-level handles you need to execute your own ODBC API functions are hidden and not supported.* They're there, but they won't show up in the object browser and won't be supported by Microsoft.

- *Transactions are managed on the Workspace level,* not on the Connection or Database levels. This is in line with DAO's approach to transactions.

- *Parameter-based queries can be built only against Connection objects,* not against Database objects. (While this is the same as RDO, it took me a while to catch this when writing some samples.)

- *ODBCDirect supports asynchronous operations,* but you have to poll for completion of the operations and you can't change RDO's polling interval.

Figure 18-4
Comparing rdoConnection and ODBCDirect Connection Objects

RDO rdoConnection Object Properties and Methods	DAO ODBCDirect Connection Object Properties and Methods	Notes
AsyncCheckInterval	Not available	Can't change polling interval.
CursorDriver on rdoEnvironment, rdoEngine, Default-CursorDriver	DBEngine object's DefaultCursorDriver	Each Workspace can be assigned its own cursor driver just as each rdoConnection can be assigned its own, but assignments are made via this DBEngine property.
Begin/Commit/RollbackTrans	Only on Workspace	Manage transactions. No Connection-based transaction management.
CreateQuery	CreateQueryDef	Create new temporary client query.
EstablishConnection	Not available	Used with stand-alone rdoConnection objects.
hDbc	Hidden and *not* supported	Exposes underlying ODBC handle.
LastQueryResults	Not available	Used for UserConnection objects.
LoginTimeout	Only on Workspace	Used with creatable Connection objects.
LogMessages	Not available	Points to ODBC trace log.
OpenResultset	OpenRecordset	Create result sets.
rdoQueries	QueryDefs	Contain temporary (local) client-side procedures.
rdoResultsets	Recordsets	Contain open result sets.
rdoTables	Not supported	Exposes base tables.
RowsAffected	RecordsAffected	Record affected by Update/Insert/Delete.
StillConnecting	StillExecuting	Poll for asynchronous connection completion.
Version	Database.Version	
(No equivalent)	Database	Cross-references Database object.

- *ODBCDirect doesn't support stand-alone objects,* but you still can set the Recordset Connection property to Nothing and reset it later to reconnect—just as you can using RDO (well, almost). The real difference is that you can create, connect, and disconnect an rdoConnection object without dropping the object—this is not possible in DAO.

- *Notice that the ODBCDirect connect string still requires the ODBC; prefix.* This isn't required by RDO or the ODBC API.

Executing SQL Queries

Once the Connection (or Database) object has established a connection, you can proceed to submit queries using the chosen cursor driver (as determined by the DBEngine DefaultCursorDriver property). If you want to use another cursor driver, just change the DBEngine DefaultCursorDriver property and the next Connection (or Database) object that gets built will use this new driver. In ODBCDirect, you work with QueryDef objects—but only temporary QueryDefs. If you need to pass parameters to the QueryDef object, then you have to use the CreateQueryDef method against the Connection object—the ODBCDirect Database object doesn't support QueryDef objects. Once the QueryDef is created, you can set its parameters, execute it, reset its parameters, and reexecute it to your heart's content.

Before we look at the process of building cursors and other result sets, let's take a closer look at a couple of objects, starting with the ODBCDirect Recordset object as compared to the RDO rdoResultset implementation.

You can see from ***Figure 18-5*** that a few RDO features aren't supported by ODBCDirect or are handled in the following ways:

- *The CacheSize and CacheStart options are no longer supported* on the ODBCDirect Recordset object. They are implemented via the Query-.RowsetSize property.

- *A consequence of not providing the ClipString method is that you can't pass the data from a result set to a clip-aware control.* Since the (old-fashioned) Grid and the new MSFlexGrid are so equipped, this will mean some more coding when you use ODBCDirect.

- *Again, the internal ODBC handles are hidden and not supported by ODBCDirect.*

- *The UpdateCriteria and UpdateOperation properties are combined* into the UpdateOptions property bits and in additional arguments on the Update method. It's clear that migrating from RDO to ODBCDirect or back won't be easy if you use client batch techniques.

- *The Resync method is also not among the supported RDO subtleties.*

Understanding QueryDef Objects

QueryDef objects created from a Connection object are temporary objects; they aren't saved (permanently) to the data source—unlike the DAO equivalent, which can be stored in a Jet database. QueryDef objects are powerful because they're prepared and optimized statements that can be called again and again. However, their expense isn't outweighed by their benefit if you don't use them more than once—and with the Requery method. Basically, ODBCDirect (and RDO) creates a temporary stored procedure that is kept on the server in

Figure 18-5
Comparing rdoResultset and ODBCDirect Recordset Objects

RDO rdoResultset Object Properties and Methods	DAO ODBCDirect Recordset Object Properties and Methods	Notes
ActiveConnection	Connection	Indicate current connection. Used to work with dissociate Client Batch cursors.
BatchUpdate	Update with option	Used to submit batch operations to server.
BatchCollisionRows	BatchCollisions	Contain an array of bookmarks to rows causing update collisions.
Query.RowsetSize	CacheSize	Implemented on the Query object.
Not applicable	CacheStart	Not supported in ODBCDirect.
CancelBatch	CancelUpdate with option	Used to drop changes in update cache.
GetClipString	Not provided	Used to dump result set contents to "clip-aware" controls like the Grid or MSFlexGrid.
hStmt	Hidden and not supported	Used to gain access to underlying ODBC API.
MoreResults	NextRecordset	Used to move to next result set in a multiple result set query.
Resync	Not supported	Used with Client Batch cursors to refetch original values.
rdoColumns	Fields	Contains data columns.
RowCount	RecordCount	Indicate number of rows in populated result set.
Status	RecordStatus	Indicate success or failure of a client batch operation.
UpdateCriteria	UpdateOptions	Used in client batch updates to build WHERE clause.
UpdateOperation	UpdateOptions	Indicate how client batches should be updated.

TempDB. This means a hit on TempDB, but it can also save time—assuming you use the QueryDef more than a couple of times to amortize the startup expense.

When you touch a QueryDef object's Parameters collection or execute a QueryDef, an instruction is sent to the server to prepare the statement. (ODBC SQLPrepare is executed.) At this time, the temporary stored procedure is created. Then, when you subsequently execute the QueryDef or open a Recordset from the QueryDef, the prepared temporary stored procedure is used by the server. Generally, this temporary procedure remains in place until you close the connection or destroy the QueryDef object. Keep that in mind as you watch TempDB start to grow.

QueryDef objects, like Connection objects, support asynchronous execution through both the Execute and OpenRecordset methods. (See "Running Asynchronous Operations" later in this chapter.) This represents a major difference from QueryDef objects created for Microsoft Jet databases, which were typically saved in the database and could only be executed synchronously.

You can also use the QueryDef object to set up properties of the resulting Recordset, such as the number of records to be cached locally. In ODBCDirect, the CacheStart property and the FillCache method of the Recordset aren't supported; instead, ODBCDirect favors using the CacheSize method of a QueryDef. (See "Handling Recordset Objects.") The Recordset property CacheSize is still supported but is read-only and contains the number of records DAO will cache. An example of how to tell DAO to use a different CacheSize than the default, which is 100 records for ODBCDirect, follows:

```
Dim qdf as QueryDef
Dim rst as Recordset

    set qdf = cnn.CreateQueryDef("tempqd")
    qdf.SQL = "Select author from authors"
    ' The local cache for the Recordset is 200 records.
    qdf.CacheSize = 200
    set rst = qdf.OpenRecordset()
    Debug.Print rst.CacheSize
```

ODBCDirect QueryDef objects can also be used to execute your stored procedures. They are designed to work well with input and output parameters as well as return values. To work with stored procedures, you simply create a QueryDef object whose definition looks very much like an ODBC call to the stored procedure:

```
' Create a simple stored proc.
strSQL$ = "CREATE PROC myproc AS " & _
    "SELECT Title FROM Titles;"
cnn.Execute strSQL$

Set qdf = cnn.CreateQueryDef("q1", _
    "{call myproc()}")
Set rst = qdf.OpenRecordset()
```

Note that you have to code the QueryDef SQL to include the ODBC Call syntax. RDO has moved away from this requirement. You can now create User-

Connection objects that expose queries and stored procedures as methods, no longer requiring the somewhat arcane ODBC API Call syntax. This also means that I haven't given you anywhere near all of the syntax options required to build these call statements. I do talk about them, however, in the next several chapters.

Once you create your QueryDef object, its parameters are managed with the same Parameters collection you are probably familiar with in DAO 3.0. When working with older versions of SQL Server, you also have to set the Direction property that tells the driver whether the parameter is return status, or an input, output, or both. But this isn't required for SQL Server 6.*x* or later. Here's an example of creating a stored procedure with parameters and calling it. Note that this is a *permanent* stored procedure.

```
' Create a simple stored proc
' with a return value.
strSQL$ = "CREATE PROC myproc " & _
    "(@invar int) AS " & _
    "RETURN @invar;"
cnn.Execute stSQL$

' Set up a QueryDef to talk with the
' stored procedure.
Set qdf = cnn.CreateQueryDef("q1", _
    "{? = call myproc(?)}")

' Handle the parameters.
qdf.Parameters(0).Direction = _
    dbParamReturnValue
qdf.Parameters(1) = 10
qdf.Execute

' Read return value.
var = qdf.Parameters(0).Value
```

Now let's take a closer look at the ODBCDirect Query object as compared to the RDO rdoQuery implementation.

Figure 18-6 on the next page shows a few more RDO features that aren't supported by ODBCDirect or that are handled in the following ways:

- When you use OpenResultset in RDO, it's easy to tell the cursor type and concurrency technique by examining the rdoResultset properties. When you use ODBCDirect, it's not clear how you can tell what kind of cursor or concurrency was used to build a cursor after having executed OpenRecordset.

- The BindThreshold property gives an RDO developer a modicum of additional flexibility when it comes to handling BLOBs.

- The Keyset size property is a seldom-used property that few cursor drivers implement—so it's no great loss.

- Again, the internal ODBC handles are hidden and not supported by ODBCDirect.

Figure 18-6
Comparing rdoQuery and ODBCDirect QueryDef Objects

RDO rdoQuery Object Properties and Methods	DAO ODBCDirect QueryDef Object Properties and Methods	Notes
ActiveConnection	Database.Connection, Workspaces.Connections collection	Indicate current connection. Used to work with dissociated Client Batch cursors.
BindThreshold	(Not implemented)	Indicates how large a BLOB should be before the GetChunk method is required.
CursorType	Type	Indicate type of cursor, such as Keyset, Static, Dynamic, and so on, to be created. Used in stand-alone rdoQuery objects.
HStmt	Neither exposed nor supported	ODBC API pointer to statement.
KeysetSize	(Not implemented)	Sets keyset size parameter for certain types of ODBC cursors.
LockType	*LockEdits* argument of OpenRecordset and LockEdits property	Indicate concurrency type of cursor—pessimistic, optimistic, and subtypes thereof—for stand-alone rdoQuery objects.
MaxRows	MaxRecords	Indicate upper cap on number of rows to process—return or update.
Prepared	Prepare	Indicate whether a temporary stored procedure should be created for this query.
QueryTimeout	ODBCTimeout	Indicate how long to wait before giving up the query.
RowsetSize	CacheSize	Indicate how many cursor rows are fetched on each operation.

Handling Recordset Objects

Probably the hardest thing to grasp when dealing with ODBCDirect is the variety of cursors it exposes. When you open an ODBCDirect Recordset, you can specify what type of cursor to open and what type of locking that cursor should use, as you can see in *Figure 18-7*. (Don't get the cursor type and locking confused with the cursor *driver* you must choose before creating the Connection object.) These distinctions lead to many different possibilities, so let's start as simply as possible. There are four different types of Recordset objects (or cursors) that you can open. In addition, you might have already opted for the "cursorless" approach when you chose your cursor driver because not every query result set needs to be returned as a cursor.

Figure 18-7
ODBCDirect Concurrency Types

Cursor Type	Description
dbOpenDynamic	Dynamic cursor
dbOpenDynaset	Keyset cursor
dbOpenSnapshot	Static cursor
dbOpenForwardOnly	Forward-only scrolling cursor
dbOpenTable	Isn't supported for ODBCDirect

You can also choose from five types of locking:

Locking Type	Description
dbOptimistic	Concur row version
dbPessimistic	Concur lock
dbOptimisticValue	Concur values
dbOptimisticBatch	Optimistic batch cursor
dbReadOnly	Read-only

Once you start combining these, you'll find some combinations won't work together, but this situation is entirely dependent on the ODBC driver and remote database server. For instance, against the Microsoft SQL Server 6.0 server-side cursor driver, dbOpenSnapshot supports only dbReadOnly.

The cursor driver you're using also influences what cursors and lock types are supported. DAO ODBCDirect passes the cursor settings to RDO, which passes them directly on to ODBC. This means that the driver controls the world. If it can handle the type of Recordset you're asking for, no problem; if not, it will either fall back to another type of Recordset or it will return an error. If an error occurs, DAO will place the error information in the Errors collection. Some ways to open Recordset objects are shown in the following code:

```
Dim rst as Recordset
    set rst = dbs.OpenRecordset( _
        "select author from authors")
    set rst = dbs.OpenRecordset( _
        "select title from titles" _
        , dbOpenDynaset, 0, dbPessimistic)
    set rst = cnn.OpenRecordset("authors", _
        dbOpenDynamic, 0, dbOptimistic)
```

The first OpenRecordset brings up an interesting question. What are the defaults? In a Microsoft Jet Workspace, the most functional (and often most expensive) Recordset is always opened. In an ODBC Workspace, the default is the (nearly) fastest (and cheapest) Recordset, dbOpenForwardOnly and dbReadOnly. So if you want to edit your data, you need to make sure you supply a lock type other than dbReadOnly, and if you want to be able to scroll around your Recordset, you need to supply a Recordset type other than dbOpenForwardOnly. If you want even better performance, set the cursor's rowset size to 1 (via the CacheSize property) or use the dbUseNoCursor as the DefaultCursorDriver property.

Except for the different types of Recordset objects and record locking, ODBCDirect Recordset objects function roughly the same way they do in DAO 3.0. Just keep in mind that Jet is nowhere to be seen and the way that Jet manages cursors can be really different from the way those created by the simpler (far simpler) ODBC layers are managed. You also won't be able to update nearly as many cursors as you could with Jet because it spends quite a bit of time keeping track of the base tables and update paths for complex joins. More often than not, complex joins won't be updatable with ODBCDirect or RDO cursors. This means that you will probably have to fall back on performing updates via action queries.

Later I will talk about a few more advanced areas, such as running asynchronous queries, working with multiple Recordset objects, and optimistic batch cursors. Other than those, the only change worth mentioning is that Recordset functionality has slimmed down. For instance, ODBCDirect doesn't support most of the ISAM functionality provided by Jet. The Table object and the capacity for selecting indexes to use on the table-type Recordset object and in the Seek function are both left behind. The Find methods FindFirst, FindNext, FindPrevious, and FindLast also aren't supported by RDO—thus ODBCDirect can't perform these operations either. But you know (by now) that to get decent performance going against a remote database, users should allow the back end to navigate the records rather than grab them all and navigate through the records on the client as the Find methods do.

One last change we should talk about is how record caching is handled. The default cache size of Microsoft Jet is one record. The default of ODBCDirect is 100 records. Because Microsoft Jet caches only one record at a time, DAO/Jet provided the FillCache method and the CacheStart and CacheSize properties. These work together so that the user can define what data to cache and then cache it. In ODBCDirect, users can use the 100-record default CacheSize or they can change it by creating a QueryDef and then altering the CacheSize property to dictate how many records should be cached.

Controlling Multiple Recordset Objects

One of the new advanced features ODBCDirect DAO provides is the ability to handle the return of multiple Recordset objects from one SQL call. Note that when you use multiple Recordset objects, you can't plan on updating data through the cursors. You can choose from two ways to get multiple Recordset objects back, and neither allows updating. The first way is to use local (client-side) cursors; they will execute multiple selects and return the data no matter what type of Recordset you request. The second is to use server-side cursors, though you're actually using no cursor at all, just doing simple data fetches under the hood. You do this by setting up a QueryDef with a CacheSize of 1, thus telling the server to give you only one record at a time. Then you open a Recordset as dbOpenForwardOnly and dbReadOnly from the QueryDef. You could also use the dbUseNoCursor option on the Workspace's DefaultCursorDriver property, before opening the connection, to achieve this forward-only, read-only, CacheSize 1 cursor. This tells the server not to bother with cursors, just return one row at a time. In this mode (no cursor mode), SQL Server can handle opening multiple Recordset objects. Without these steps, Microsoft SQL Server simply returns an error when you try to open a multiple Recordset query.

Once you have multiple Recordset objects being returned, you can use DAO to access each Recordset. This is done by using the new NextRecordset method. It throws away the current Recordset and replaces it with the next Recordset. Then you can navigate through it as you would any Recordset. When NextRecordset returns False, you have no further result sets to process—and yes, you have to process them all before beginning another operation or closing the Recordset. (See code example 2 later in this chapter.)

Running Asynchronous Operations

ODBCDirect also exposes the ability to open connections and run queries, both row-returning (select queries) and non-row-returning (action queries), asynchronously. This means that control returns to your application immediately—before the connection has opened or the query has been processed by SQL Server—so you can continue with other operations. Both modes work by passing dbRunAsync to the appropriate methods. Because ODBCDirect doesn't support the RDO event model, you have to poll the StillConnecting or StillExecuting property to check whether the operation is done. As long as these properties return true, the asynchronous operation isn't finished. If you want to abort the operation, simply use the new Cancel method. One thing to note, however, is that canceling in the middle of a bulk operation isn't always a wise thing to do. The operation won't roll back; it just stops updating in the middle. If you think you might cancel a bulk operation, you should wrap it in a transaction so that you can roll back if it isn't completed. (See code examples 3 and 4 later in this chapter.)

Optimistic Batch Updating

ODBCDirect also supports optimistic batch updating. Optimistic batch updating means the data for a given Recordset is cached locally. All changes you make to the Recordset are also cached locally until you specifically tell DAO to flush all changes to the server. Batch updating can really help speed things up because it cuts down on the network traffic between client and server.

Optimistic batch updates are accomplished by creating an ODBCDirect Workspace using the Client Batch cursor library (set DefaultCursorDriver to dbUseClientBatchCursor). This is the only cursor library that supports batch updating. After opening your connection, open a Recordset with a LockType of dbOptimisticBatch, which tells the library that you plan to do batch updates.

At this point, you can use the Recordset as you normally would, reading and updating its data, but the data isn't sent to the server—not yet. The changes are cached on the workstation until you're ready to post the changes to the SQL server. When you've updated all the data you plan to work with, call the Update method on the Recordset by using the dbUpdateBatch option. At this point, all changes are flushed to the server and the updates are made.

How does DAO know which record in the Recordset relates to a particular record in the source? You specify it by using the UpdateOptions property of the Recordset. The default for this is the primary key. But you can override this to use all columns or the time stamp. In addition, you can specify how record updates are executed, either by updating the record in place or by deleting it and adding a new record.

What happens, though, if a collision occurs? (Say the update tries to change a record that has been changed by another source since the process first looked at the records.) In that case, you can use the BatchCollision-Count property to find out how many updates failed and you can use the BatchCollisions property. The BatchCollisions property is an array of bookmarks to your Recordset that points to records that failed. Finally, you can use the VisibleValue and OriginalValue properties of the Field object in conjunction with the Value property to determine how to reconcile the failed updates.

Viewing Errors

The last thing I want to talk about is how to view errors using DAO ODBCDirect. This topic isn't exactly new but is important in ODBCDirect, and it isn't all that well understood. DAO places all incoming messages and errors in its Errors collection as they arrive. Maybe you simply want to check on the status of an operation. Because a single operation can result in many errors (and messages), you want to be sure to check them all if something goes wrong. When something *does* go wrong, DAO ODBCDirect won't volunteer much information. You usually just get a trappable generic "3146: ODBC--call failed." This can be rather annoying. By looking in the Errors collection, you just might find more useful information. The lowest index error usually is the most detailed. Here's some sample code that you can use to print out all the errors from the collection and see exactly what we're talking about:

```
Dim e as Error
Debug.Print Err & ":  " & Error$
For Each e In DBEngine.Errors
    Debug.Print e.Number & ":  " & e.Description
Next e
```

If you tried to open a database to tell the driver not to prompt but you failed to supply the DSN in the connection string, you will get "ODBC--call failed" in *Error$*. If you then look in the Errors collection, you'll find that there were actually two errors returned and that Errors(0) has much more detailed information in it. The errors returned are these:

```
Errors(0).Description =
IM002: [Microsoft][ODBC Driver Manager] Data source name not found
and no default driver specified

Errors(1).Description =
3146:  ODBC--call failed.
```

Examples

To make this new interface a little easier to use, lets look at a few code examples. These walk you through several typical operations that illustrate ODBCDirect's flexibility.

Example 1: Telling Which Workspace Your Database Is Opened In

This routine demonstrates how to tell whether your database is opened in an ODBC Workspace or a Microsoft Jet Workspace. It also shows how to grab the Connection object from a Database object and use it to perform an asynchronous SQL operation.

```
Sub DeleteRecords()
    Dim dbs As Database
    Dim cnn As Connection

    ' This will open a database in the default
    ' Workspace, no matter what type of Workspace it
    ' actually is (ODBC or Microsoft Jet).
    Set dbs = OpenDatabase("", False, False, _
        "ODBC;dsn=DBServer;database=pubs;uid=sa;pwd=;")

    ' Check to see whether it is ODBCDirect.
    fNoError = True
    On Error GoTo ErrorTrap
        Set cnn = dbs.Connection
    On Error GoTo 0

    ' If there was no error, it is ODBCDirect.
    If fNoError Then
        cnn.Execute "delete from authors" _
            , dbRunAsync
        cnn.Close
    Else
        dbs.Execute "delete from authors"
        dbs.Close
    End If
Exit Sub

ErrorTrap:
    fNoError = False
    Resume Next
End Sub
```

Example 2: Getting Multiple Recordset Objects from the Server

This routine demonstrates how to get multiple Recordset objects back from the server and how to walk through them. It has two parts. The first demonstrates forcing local cursors to be used to get multiple Recordset objects. The second demonstrates how to move through multiple Recordset objects in DAO.

```
Sub GetMultipleResults()
    Dim rst As Recordset
    Dim cnn As Connection

    ' Use Local Cursors.
    DefaultType = dbUseODBC
    DBEngine.Workspaces(0).DefaultCursorDriver = _
        dbUseLocalCursor
    ' Now open the connection to the database.
    Set cnn = OpenConnection("", _
        dbDriverNoPrompt, false _
        "ODBC;dsn=DBServer;database=pubs;uid=sa;pwd=")

    strCmd$ = "select * from authors; " & _
        "select * from titles;"

    ' Execute the SQL statement.
    Set rst = cnn.OpenRecordset(strCmd$)
    ViewResults rst
    cnn.Close
End Sub

Sub ViewResults(rst As Recordset)
    Do
        While Not rst.EOF
            ' Loop through each record.
            For Each fld In rst.Fields
                ' Print each field.
                Debug.Print fld.Name & _
                    ":  " & fld.Value
        Next f
        rst.MoveNext
        Wend
    ' Get the next Recordset and stop if we are done.
    Loop Until (rst.NextRecordset() = False)
End Sub
```

Example 3: Canceling a Bulk Operation

The following example illustrates how to cancel a bulk operation. When doing this, you should always wrap the code in a transaction because canceling the operation can leave data in an unknown state.

```
Sub CancelExecute()
    Dim cnn As Connection

    ' By setting this before touching
    ' the default Workspace, the default
    ' Workspace will be created as an
    ' ODBCDirect Workspace.
    DefaultType = dbUseODBC

    ' Open a connection instead of
    ' a database because databases
    ' don't support dbRunAsync.
    Set cnn = OpenConnection("", _
        dbDriverNoPrompt, false _
        "ODBC;dsn=DBServer;database=pubs;uid=sa;pwd=")

    ' Start a transaction to be able
    ' to roll back if you cancel the
    ' operation.
    BeginTrans

    ' Execute your SQL using dbRunAsync.
    cnn.Execute "delete from mytable", dbRunAsync

    ' You should always check that the
    ' query is still running before canceling.
    If cnn.StillExecuting Then
        cnn.Cancel
        ' If you have canceled, roll back
        ' any records that were changed.
        Rollback
    Else
        ' If if completed, go
        ' ahead and commit the changes.
        CommitTrans
    End If

    ' Close the connection to the database.
    cnn.Close
End Sub
```

Example 4: Using dbRunAsync to Open a Recordset

The following routine demonstrates using dbRunAsync to open a Recordset. It should be noted that this can be performed from either a Database object or a Connection object, unlike using dbRunAsync with Execute, which can be performed only from a Connection object.

```
Sub CancelRecordset()
    Dim wks as Workspace
    Dim dbs As Database
    Dim rst As Recordset

    ' Example of how to open a Workspace
    set wks = CreateWorkspace("Space1", "sa", _
        "", dbUseODBC)
    ' Open a database to show you can
    ' use dbRunAsync to OpenRecordset from
    ' the Database object.
    Set dbs = wks.OpenDatabase("", _
        dbDriverNoPrompt, False, _
        "ODBC;dsn=DBServer;database=pubs;uid=sa;pwd=")

    Set rst = dbs.OpenRecordset( _
        "select * from authors", _
        dbOpenDynaset, dbRunAsync)

    ' You should always check that the
    ' query is still running before canceling.
    If rst.StillExecuting Then
        rst.Cancel
    Else
        rst.Close
    End If

    ' Close the database.
    dbs.Close
    wks.close
End Sub
```

Example 5: Working with QueryDef Objects

This routine demonstrates how to work with QueryDef objects. It shows the use of stored procedures and parameters.

```
Sub WorkWithQueryDefs()
    Dim cnn As Connection
    Dim qdf As QueryDef
    Dim rst As Recordset

    ' By setting this before touching
    ' the default Workspace, the default
    ' Workspace will be created as an
```

```
' ODBCDirect Workspace.
DefaultType = dbUseODBC

' Open a connection instead of
' a database because we need
' QueryDef support.
Set cnn = OpenConnection("", _
    dbDriverNoPrompt, false _
    "ODBC;dsn=DBServer;database=pubs;uid=sa;pwd=")

' Create the stored procedure.
' This will usually be done outside the program
' but is done here for clarity's sake.
strCmd$ = "Create proc GetDataFrom" & _
    " (@state char(2))" & _
    " as select * from authors" & _
    " where state = @state"
cnn.Execute strCmd$

' Create a QueryDef with one parameter.
' When the SQL is set, the stored procedure
' is called.
Set qdf = cnn.CreateQueryDef("myquery", _
    "{call GetDataFrom (?)}")
qdf.Parameters(0) = "WA"
qdf.Parameters(0).Direction = dbParamInput

' Get the data.
Set rst = qdf.OpenRecordset()

' Print out the data.
While Not rst.EOF
    Debug.Print rst!au_id
    rst.MoveNext
Wend
rst.Close
qdf.Close

' Close the connection to the database.
cnn.Close
End Sub
```

Tips for Converting Your Application to ODBCDirect

The following are hints for converting existing DAO applications running against DAO/Jet and Microsoft Jet databases so that they hit ODBC data sources instead. It assumes the database has already been placed on the server. I'm also assuming that you want to use only ODBCDirect to communicate with your data on a server.

- **Change the type of Workspaces you are using.** If you don't create any Workspaces, you still need to tell DAO that the default Workspace should be an ODBCDirect Workspace. This is accomplished by setting the DefaultType property of DBEngine to dbUseODBC before executing any operations that will need the default Workspace. Once a Workspace is created, you can't change its type. If you're explicitly creating Workspaces in your application and you have set DefaultType to dbUseODBC, all Workspaces created while DefaultType has this setting will be ODBCDirect Workspaces. But if you want your code to be self-documenting or if you'll be using both Microsoft Jet and ODBCDirect Workspaces, you can pass a fourth parameter to each CreateWorkspace, telling it what type of Workspace to create.

- **Change the database you open.** You need to change the arguments passed to OpenDatabase to represent the new database you're opening. Instead of passing a database name for the first parameter, you will now pass a connection string for the fourth parameter. Note that all connection strings start with the *ODBC;* prefix. You might also decide that you would rather open connections instead of databases; if this is the case, you need to change all your OpenDatabase calls to OpenConnection. Both functions take similar arguments, so this change won't be much work.

- **Choose a way to handle DDL.** ODBCDirect functionality doesn't support the TableDefs collection or Indexes collection. This means that if your application creates new TableDef objects or looks up indexes in the index collection from a TableDef, it will no longer work. If this is a problem, you can choose from two ways to change your code. You can create a Microsoft Jet Workspace and open a second database to the data source, doing all DDL work within it; or you can execute SQL calls to create and find objects. SQL calls are the way to go if you want to keep from loading Microsoft Jet. But if you want to limit the amount of code that changes, the Microsoft Jet path works very well.

- **Change the way you create and use QueryDef objects.** In ODBC-Direct Workspaces, the Database object doesn't support the Create-QueryDef method. That's handled by the Connection object. In your code, you need to change all CreateQueryDef calls so that they are executed on the Connection property of the Database rather than the Database object itself. If you have changed all OpenDatabase calls to OpenConnection calls, you won't have to worry about this. QueryDef objects created in ODBCDirect aren't stored in the database and are lost when the object is closed or goes out of scope.

- **Change the way you open Recordset objects.** ODBCDirect Recordset objects default to the fastest Recordset type rather than to the most functional, as in Microsoft Jet. Typically, this is a Recordset that can't scroll backward and is read-only. If you need more functionality in the Recordset you use, you need to specify that. If you need to scroll backward or if you need bookmarks, choose a different Recordset type, such as dbOpenDynaset. If you need to update the Recordset, choose a locking type, such as dbOptimistic. You can't write code in a Microsoft Jet Workspace that opens a Recordset by providing only the name argument and that intends to edit data in ODBCDirect, unless you change the OpenRecordset to also supply a Recordset type and a locking constant that will allow updating.

- **You can't use parameterized queries.** ODBCDirect doesn't support named parameters. The syntax for a parameter in an SQL statement is a question mark (?) rather than a name as in Microsoft Jet. For example, the Microsoft Jet SQL *SELECT * FROM Employees WHERE LastName = txtName* creates a parameter *txtName*. In ODBCDirect, the SQL would read *SELECT * FROM Employees WHERE LastName = ?* whereas in the Parameters collection, the name of the parameter would be *Parameter1*. It should also be noted that Microsoft Jet allows you to say *Parameters iAuthId Integer; SELECT * from authors where au_id = iAuthId*. Since ODBCDirect doesn't have named parameters, you can't use the *Parameters ...;* part of the previous example.

These tips will get you running quickly using ODBCDirect. But, for best performance, you should always go back over the program and look for optimizations. ODBCDirect offers new and different ways to improve performance, but just getting your program running in an ODBCDirect Workspace may take advantage of all the power available to you.

Working with an ODBCDirect Data Control

It turns out that most, if not all, of the functionality that I have been describing is also exposed by the DAO Data control. It, too, has the needed properties to create ODBCDirect Workspace objects and route its operations through RDO. Check out the Visual Basic version 5.0 Data control—even in the Professional Edition—to discover the new DefaultType and DefaultCursorType properties. Once you set the DefaultType to *1 - UseODBC*, the Data control is switched over to ODBCDirect mode. At this point, you can select a default cursor driver by setting the DefaultCursorType property and everything else works pretty much as I have described. Sure, lots of things don't work as they did with DAO/Jet, but that's the price of this new technology. I think you'll find, however, that you might also want to check out the RemoteData control, which has even more RDO-specific property exposures.

Chapter

Understanding Remote Data Objects

Design Features

Comparing RDO and DAO/Jet

Getting the Latest Information on RDO

Licensing RDO

The Visual Basic version 4.0 team (including myself) first came up with the ideas that evolved into Remote Data Objects and, in accomplishing this, created a new genre, an entirely new way to access data from Visual Basic. About a year later, the new way is wildly popular. How did all of this happen? The team created a body of code that met real developers' needs—it solved real problems—without creating more problems than it solved. For the most part, RDO 1.0 made working around problems easier than did other more complex interfaces that weren't specifically designed for client/server work.

Just for the sake of nostalgia, let's take a look at how we got to where we are with RDO. Suppose you were on the development team for Microsoft Visual Basic 4.0 and you had to make the new product faster, smaller, backward-compatible with Visual Basic 3.0, and usable with the new version of Microsoft SQL Server? What did you need to do?

The Visual Basic 4.0 team knew that we needed to create a clone of the DAO interface and a Data control that didn't need Jet. Our clone had to be faster and smaller, and it had to work with the existing bound controls. Most important of all, it had to leverage all the new SQL Server 6.0 features and still work with other intelligent ODBC-based back ends. It had to be a clone of the DAO interface (or pretty nearly so) to make it easier to transition developers and documentation from DAO to RDO to DAO. We thought developers might need to take existing RDO code and move it back to DAO, but more likely they would need to move existing DAO code to RDO.

The problem was that no one had ever used the new OLE OCX technology to create such a beast. Besides, the current Data control was already an integral part of Visual Basic 4.0 and had never really been cloned. Sure, cloning it was theoretically possible, but so many complex questions remained that we weren't sure it could work.

And then a Microsoft program manager was approached at a conference by a man from New York who said he wanted some help with a new ODBC-based Data control he had written. Our program manager looked at this New Yorker as if the man's coat were lined with hot watches for sale.

PART IV USING REMOTE DATA OBJECTS AND THE RemoteData CONTROL

"Right," the PM said, "an ODBC Data control. Sure."

But gradually the PM realized that this guy held the missing pieces of the puzzle we were trying to assemble. He and his team had indeed created a rudimentary ODBC Data control. They had already solved many of the most complex problems, using nothing but a shaky beta copy of Visual Basic 4.0. (For all I knew, they had bought it from a curbside vendor on Forty-second Street.) And so far, they had done all this work with no help from Redmond.

Over the next six months, this rudimentary product was hammered and polished into a full-blown clone of the Data control and the Data Access Objects. This clone became the RemoteData control (RDC) and the Remote Data Objects (RDO).

Now our team had a plan and a program. After working through hundreds of development glitches in the Remote Data Objects and the RemoteData control, we started to find bugs in the Visual Basic OCX interface, in bound controls, and in the ODBC drivers—bugs we never would have found without our friend from New York. By the time the code was committed to the golden master CDs, the Remote Data Objects and the RemoteData control had become the cornerstone of the new Enterprise edition of Visual Basic 4.0.

NOTE The Remote Data Objects and RemoteData control are features of the Enterprise edition of Visual Basic. In the Professional and Learning editions, you can't use the RDO library or the RemoteData control to develop code. RDO can be used in the Control Creation Edition, but you still need an Enterprise Edition license. You can access the Remote Data Objects from other OLE-aware platforms, but you must have a Visual Basic Enterprise Edition license to distribute the application.

RDO is being pushed along into something altogether different from its original self. It now forms the nucleus of "Active" Data Objects (ADO), a class of objects that will be taking over for DAO and RDO and VBSQL in the years (or months) to come. "Classic" RDO and DAO aren't going away. But as new technologies (new solutions) are developed, the older solutions, no less viable, become less attractive than the new.

Just how fast will ADO take over the world? I expect we will see it mature in 1997 and become a permanent part of Visual Basic in its next major release.

Actually, RDO evolved at least twice in 1996 as Microsoft *quietly* released Visual Basic 4.0a (which included RDO 1.0a) in the first quarter and RDO 1.0b in the second quarter. You can find an article about these releases in the Web directory on this guide's CD.

RDO 2.0 is faster, cleaner, and smarter than RDO—and not much bigger. We didn't want to create another Jet database engine. (Although that wouldn't be so bad if it addressed real client/server needs.) In the past year, the team poured over SQL trace logs and performance comparisons to find where RDO was unnecessarily slowing things down or filling things up. The team made a few changes to the basic architectural assumptions—especially where prepared statements were concerned. Our team also added a significant amount of integration with Visual Basic itself, and this yielded the UserConnection Designer and the ability to express queries and stored procedures as methods. RDO 2.0 also introduces one of the most powerful programming paradigms since the invention of floating-point math—*event driven* data access programming.

Design Features

In case you hadn't noticed, the RemoteData control and the Remote Data Objects are members of the family of client/server programming models—a tribe that hasn't stopped growing since RDO was first built. The RDC/RDO model is implemented via a thin layer of code over the ODBC API and Driver Manager and a specific ODBC driver. The ODBC Driver Manager is what establishes connections, creates result sets and cursors, and executes complex procedures while using minimal workstation resources. Now that RDO 2.0 includes a fairly sophisticated Client Batch cursor library, we will spend some time talking about building updatable batch cursors—something unheard of in RDO 1.0. But RDO doesn't include a cursor engine or query processor to rival Jet's or a complex connection manager. This is an important point to keep in mind when you're trying to diagnose some obscure problem. In most cases, the problem can be narrowed down to how the ODBC API and its drivers are implemented. We have seen most of the problems associated with RDO turn out to be "problems" with the ODBC drivers themselves or with how they were used. Over the past year, they have changed about four times as new versions of SQL Server, Microsoft Access, and other ODBC hosts evolve. Personally, I don't expect this difficulty to ease much.

When the time comes to implement any SQL Server front-end application, you want an easy-to-use programming model that doesn't compromise performance or make excessive demands on system resources. The ideal interface wouldn't be significantly larger than C-based DB-Library, and it would be every bit as fast for sending queries and processing simple result sets. It should be just as easy for you to build a cursorless result set or a complex updatable cursor as it is for you to execute a stored procedure with multiple result sets, with or without output parameters and return values. You should even be able to use SQL server–side cursors as easily as you can use local client cursors. It should also be possible to limit the number of rows returned or updated, and, without compromising the query being executed, you should be able to monitor all the messages and errors generated by the remote data source. This ideal interface should also permit synchronous as well as asynchronous operations, so your application won't be blocked while lengthy queries are being executed. And the asynchronous operations should be manageable via a broad swath of events that let you trap every conceivable aspect of the operations.

Is that too much to ask? Not anymore. For the most part, the RDC/RDO model gives you this ideal interface. It was built with SQL Server (and Oracle) in mind, especially the new features available with SQL Server 6.0. It implements a set of objects for dealing with the special requirements of accessing *remote* data, and it was designed from the outset as an alternative for developers who don't need many of Jet's features and who don't find it productive to program at the API level. The RDC/RDO model can be seen as representing the best of both worlds, in many respects: it comes close to or exceeds the performance of the API tools, but it isn't significantly larger, and you don't lose the flexibility of the API approach. RDO supports the following features:

With the RDC/RDO model, you lose the ability to perform joins on heterogeneous data sources provided by DAO/Jet. You lose Jet's automated connection management schemes, too, as well as the ability to update joined sets of data. But you also get rid of the million or so bytes of code that are used to support those features. And the fact that the RDC/RDO model is also a high-speed interface to Oracle and other ODBC back ends is certainly an added benefit.

- *Direct access to SQL Server stored procedures, including parameters, return status, and output values.* Since many of the more sophisticated data processing shops expose *only* stored procedures or views, it is important that the programming model permit intimate control of access to this query-style data interface paradigm. The RDC/RDO interface is designed with MIS-class security in mind. It supports access to parameters for stored procedures and to query parameters via the rdoParameter object.

- *Complete integration with Visual Basic version 5.0 Enterprise Edition.* This version of Visual Basic includes the UserConnection Designer, which helps build UserConnection objects that expose user-developed queries and stored procedures as methods. Once created, the UserConnection objects can be passed around like any other shared component. They also dramatically reduce the amount of code needed to perform common RDO operations.

- *Complete interpretation of the Visual Database Tools with RDO.* They are implemented with and for RDO 2.0. This means you can develop and share database schemas and an interactive query development tool, and you can even tune web-based designs.

- *Integration of the TSQL Debugger with the IDE.* This means you can test and walk through Transact SQL stored procedures and triggers right from Visual Basic's design environment. For example, when you use the Update method and SQL Server fires a trigger because of the query, the TSQL Debugger fires up and lets you step through the procedure.

- *Sophisticated client-side cursor library.* The new Client Batch cursor library developed by the FoxPro team exposes optimistic batch updates and a faster, more intelligent local cursor library—head and shoulders above the ODBC client-side library. This cursor library also supports dissociate rdoQuery and rdoConnection objects.

- *Complete asynchronous event-driven support.* While RDO supported limited asynchronous operations, RDO 2.0 expands that support to virtually every aspect of the data access paradigm and adds the power of events that fire when the asynchronous operations complete. This means no more indeterminate blockages while the server processes long queries.

- *Events tailored to support read-only result set updatability via stored procedures.* For the first time, you can build cursor (or even noncursor) "nonupdatable" result sets for which you *can* update database rows by trapping the WillUpdateRows event and executing an independent action query to perform the update.

- *Relaxed ODBC Level II compliance requirements.* One of the problems RDO 1.0 developers faced was its fairly rigid compliancy requirements. This often made use of RDO on subcompliant drivers difficult or at least limiting. RDO 2.0 added additional support to take up the slack where suboptimal drivers are used.

- *Redesigned prepared statement methodology.* Another problem faced by RDO 1.0 developers was RDO's overenthusiastic use of prepared statements. This often meant slower performance for some situations and residual stored procedures loitering in TempDB. The RDO 2.0 release changed the defaults and now provides a higher degree of control over the creation and execution of queries. The result is even better performance in some fairly common cases and less stored procedure trash being left on the battlefield.

- *Straight-line access to batched queries.* Many MIS procedures and applications depend on the flexibility of batched queries or complex stored procedures that return one or more result sets. In many cases, batched queries neither return nor affect many rows, but they can dramatically improve performance by lowering the overhead on query submissions.

- *Full Transact-SQL (TSQL) support.* It's vital that the programming interface to SQL Server fully support all aspects of TSQL to permit the broadest possible support for SQL Server functionality. This includes RAISERROR and DBCC support. RDO doesn't parse your SQL code the way DAO/Jet does—every operation is a pass-through query.

- *High-performance data access against remote ODBC data sources, especially SQL Server.* The ability to quickly retrieve results from complex queries is a goal of every data access application. The RDC/RDO interface provides a consistent level of performance rivaled only by the ODBC API and VBSQL API programming models. By leveraging the remote data engine, the RDO model greatly improves response time and user productivity. Because of its size, the RDO interface also loads faster, which in turn improves overall application load time.

- *Management of return codes, input parameters, and output parameters from stored procedures.* Output parameters are used heavily for singleton queries and many administrative functions. In many cases, you can't determine whether a stored procedure has been completed successfully unless you can access the procedure's return value.

- *Management of multiple result sets.* You can make more efficient use of the query processor and system resources if you use a single query that returns several sets of related results. You can also improve performance by running a single query to gather data for filling multiple data-driven list boxes and menus. In addition, by combining a row-count query with a SELECT query, you can accurately set up scroll bars and status bars.

- *Limitation of the number of rows returned.* In situations where a user might select more rows than would be practical to handle, the RDC/RDO model taps the SQL Server query governor that limits the number of rows returned from the server. That way, you can predict query response time and more easily manage the workstation or server resources required to maintain cursor keysets. This feature is implemented against any back end that supports it.

- *Utilization of server-side cursors.* SQL Server 6.*x* supports cursor keysets that are stored on the server rather than on the workstation. Under the right conditions, this type of cursor management can significantly improve system performance and reduce the resource needs of the workstation.

- *Exposure of underlying ODBC handles.* When you need more flexibility or control than is available in the object model, you should have a way of directly accessing the ODBC Driver Manager and the SQL Server driver itself. The RDC/RDO interface provides access to the ODBC environment, connection, and statement handles, so you can set options at the level of the driver and the Driver Manager.

- *Reduction of memory footprint to support "thinner" clients.* In many cases, the workstation has limited RAM and disk capacity. Therefore, it is important that applications designed for this type of system economize on their use of RAM and other resources. The RDC/RDO memory footprint is dramatically smaller than Jet's, and the RDC/RDO model doesn't require local memory or disk space for its lowest-level cursors.

When shops convert from VBSQL or DB-Library, all their code is in TSQL. At best, converting that code into generic SQLSpeak should be unnecessary when you're using RDO. At worst, it should be automatic and painless.

Comparing RDO and DAO/Jet

In many respects, the RDC/RDO and DAO/Jet programming models are very similar, especially at the lowest layers. You use the Remote Data Objects pretty much the way you use the Jet Data Access Objects: you submit a query, create a result set or cursor, and process the results from the query, using database-independent, object-oriented code. Both models let you create cursors against

SQL Server data tables, views, or result sets from stored procedures. Both also let you connect to SQL Server and manage transactions. But how these tasks are accomplished is very different for each model.

Now that DAO has added ODBCDirect, the decision whether or not to use DAO has become more convoluted. Where with DAO/Jet there was little to gain by using DAO, ODBCDirect exposes enough RDO functionality to force many to reconsider this decision.

Figure 19-1 lists the Remote Data Objects and their ODBCDirect and DAO equivalents. Objects labeled *Not implemented* in the RDO column are included in the DAO interface to support ISAM implementations or methodologies that simply aren't needed in a relational model (and require the Jet database engine to implement). Generally, though, most of the DAO methods and properties that you are familiar with are supported by the RDO equivalents. For example, the Move, MoveNext, MoveFirst, MovePrevious, and MoveLast methods are all supported on keyset-type, static-type, and dynamic-type cursors. The PercentPosition, AbsolutePosition, and LastModified properties are also supported. The ISAM-oriented Find and Seek methods are *not* supported by the Remote Data Objects, however, nor are they likely to be in the future. As many of you have already discovered, these methods, used to position the current-row pointer to a specific row in the result set, can be brutally slow. Therefore, developers who work with SQL Server databases have changed strategies and now use targeted queries to address their requirements for row searching. This means that conversion of DAO code to RDO code can be fairly painless, for the most part. It's like putting on a new brand of jeans: there might be a few more pockets, but the zipper is still in the same place. The RDO side of the figure shows a couple of new objects—for example, the forward-only rdoResultset object, used for fetching results on a row-by-row basis. Forward-only rdoResultset objects are simple to create, so they yield the highest possible performance when you're pulling back query results. The rdoQuery object is another newcomer. It maps directly to the ODBC SQLPrepare function, supports the creation of parameter queries, and exposes many of the more sophisticated features of the RDC/RDO programming model.

NOTE Where the DAO model refers to *records* and *fields,* the RDC/RDO model refers, respectively, to *rows* and *columns*. This reflects the lineage of the data models; DAO is an ISAM model while RDO is a relational model.

The RDC/RDO programming model is generally simpler than the DAO model. As such, it should be fairly easy to implement. The real differences between the two have to do with how they expose specific SQL Server features and interfaces. Jet supports the creation and modification of the database schema through DAO methods and properties. The RDC/RDO and ODBCDirect interfaces don't support any type of schema modification because this is fully supported in the tools and utilities provided with SQL Server. Of course, you can still run MakeTable queries and use TSQL statements to execute action queries that create, modify, or delete databases and tables. You can also execute complex stored procedures that manage the database schema, and you can perform maintenance operations that are either very difficult or impossible with the DAO/Jet interface.

CAUTION
The RDC/RDO interface doesn't coddle you as much as the DAO/Jet interface does. It protects you from the complexities of the Visual Basic–to–ODBC API interface, at virtually no cost to the interface's flexibility, but it gives you responsibility for your own destiny: since the ODBC internal handles are exposed, you can scramble ODBC's synapses with the greatest of ease, if that's what you care to do.

Figure 19-1
RDO, DAO, and ODBCDirect Equivalents

RDO	DAO	ODBCDirect
rdoEngine	DBEngine	DBEngine
Not implemented	User, Group	Not implemented
rdoEnvironment	Workspace	Workspace
rdoConnection	Database	Database/Connection
rdoTable	TableDef	TableDef
Not implemented	Index	Index
rdoResultset	Recordset	Recordset
Not implemented	Table-type	Not implemented
Keyset-type	Dynaset-type	Dynaset-type
Static-type	Snapshot-type	Snapshot-type
Dynamic-type	None	Dynamic-type
Forward-only–type	Similar to forward-only snapshot	Forward-only–type
rdoColumn	Field	Field
rdoQuery	QueryDef	QueryDef
rdoParameter	Parameter	Parameter

Getting the Latest Information on RDO

When we shipped Visual Basic version 4.0, the Internet had hardly come to life for Microsoft. Now it forms the core of many of Microsoft's strategies and support services. If you need more information on RDO or any of the topics discussed here, check out the Web directory on the CD that comes with this book. I have downloaded all of the RDO Knowledge Base articles and saved them there on disk. To get more of the same, see *http://www.microsoft.com/support/*.

For years, I lobbied for a programming interface like the RDC/RDO model. It's not everything I would have liked, but it's pretty darn close—and RDO 2.0 is even closer.

Using Other ODBC Drivers

As I have said many times so far, RDO is designed with SQL Server and Oracle in mind. Because of this, a number of things were done to make it work effectively with the types of databases managed by these intelligent, remote database management systems. In addition, since RDO first came out, a number of people have tried to use RDO with other ODBC drivers—many with a great deal of success. But one group seems to be quite frustrated in its attempts to get RDO to work. These are the developers who tried to use the "Brazos" ODBC drivers for Jet. These drivers are designed for Microsoft Office applications—not for those mainstream applications that need access to Jet and SQL Server databases at the same time. These drivers aren't equipped to deal with a variety of ODBC Level II compliance issues, nor will they ever be. Most developers don't realize that these drivers simply load Jet and use it as the interface to the native Jet database being accessed. I can't recommend use of RDO with these or any other ISAM drivers. It's like mounting racing slicks to drive in the snow. There are better tools for the job. Keep in mind that ODBC is a *relational* database interface and not equipped to deal with "seeks" or raw table I/O like its ISAM cousins. That's why Jet is needed to access this type of data source.

Visual Basic version 5.0 also ships with a new set of Oracle drivers. Question: Are these drivers any good? BHOM (Beats the Hell Out of Me). I never tried them. I don't plan to. I do understand that these drivers were developed and tested specifically by Microsoft and have been much more thoroughly tested than the ones previously passed down by Oracle for Visual Basic version 4.0. I certainly hope they work better than the Visual Basic 4.0 versions.

Licensing RDO

RDO is licensed to the Visual Studio suite (Visual Basic version 5.0 Enterprise Edition, IStudio, Visual J++, and Visual C++ Enterprise). Using it in design mode (which VBA in any Office application is always in) requires that you have purchased and installed Visual Basic version 5.0 Enterprise Edition or one of the other host development platforms on the machine. Of course, the registry keys are not hard to find and copy, but *legally* you must have purchased a licensed copy of Visual Basic version 5.0 Enterprise Edition for any machine that is going to use RDO from design mode. This is actually the exact same way that licensed controls (OCX/ActiveX) work, but Microsoft never had any controls that it decided to restrict to only the Enterprise Edition before.

However, there is a nice clean solution to this. Your customers should embrace the services model. Instead of doing all their data access code right in the workbook, you should build Visual Basic ActiveX component servers that do the data access and return data to the calling application. The DLL exposes an interface that encapsulates a bunch of functionality (like gathering all information about sales of a given product from possibly many sources) and is easy to work with at a high level. That DLL can be built in Visual Basic version 5.0 Enterprise Edition and then reused by any Office application or any other automation controller.

Reuse is obviously beneficial, and over time, you'll save your customers the trouble of having to maintain code in lots of workbooks. Also, that same ActiveX component can be used by your customers' other Visual Basic front ends, and therefore all the clients use the same set of business rules regardless of what tool the client was created in. Since the DLL is compiled (and not in design mode), RDO doesn't check for the existence of a license key in the registry and you can freely redistribute it to any client machine.

20 Chapter

Remote Data Objects Up Close

Understanding the RDO Model

The rdoEngine Object

The rdoEnvironment Object

The rdoConnection Object

et's pull off the main highway and take a long, scenic, informative tour of the Remote Data Objects (RDO). There is much to learn here, because much has changed since the last time we passed this way. And once we've crossed this terrain, I hope you'll be able to find your way through it next time on your own.

Understanding the RDO Model

The Remote Data Objects and the RDO collections provide a framework for using code to create and manipulate the components of a remote ODBC database system like SQL Server. Don't get me wrong, though: although the RDO interface was tuned for SQL Server and Oracle, it works with any ODBC back end—and RDO 2.0 is designed to be more tolerant of subcompliant drivers so that the requirement to use an ODBC Level II–compliant driver has been dropped. Objects and collections have properties that describe the characteristics of database components, as well as methods that you use to manipulate them. *Figure 20-1* displays the RDO model.

The RDO objects are like any other Visual Basic objects. In many respects, they behave like Visual Basic controls that have defined properties and methods but no visible representation, such as the Timer control or the VBSQL control. In other words, the RDO objects are simply used to map to one or more ODBC API functions, which in turn permit access to specific back-end result sets or options. A single RDO method or property might be executed as a single ODBC function or as a whole series of functions. Each of the RDO objects, with the exception of the rdoEngine object, is maintained in an associated collection. This means you can examine the properties and execute methods against any created object simply by wading into the right collection. RDO 2.0 also supports the new concept of *stand-alone* objects. These are objects created with the *New* keyword, and they might not be assigned to an associated collection.

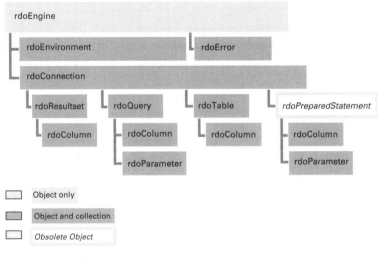

Figure 20-1 *The RDO model*

NOTE If you import existing Visual Basic version 4.0 applications into Visual Basic version 5.0, Visual Basic automatically updates your code to RDO 2.0, including any references to the RemoteData control.

The rdoEngine Object

When the RDO interface is initialized on first access, an instance of the rdoEngine object is automatically created. The rdoEngine object is used to set RDO-wide parameters and options. Unlike applications that use the DAO/Jet DBEngine object, each application that uses RDO gets its own rdoEngine object. When you create new rdoEnvironment, rdoConnection, or rdoResultset objects, the characteristics of the new objects are determined by the default values of the rdoEngine properties unless you override these values with arguments in the rdoCreateEnvironment or OpenResultset methods. What this means is that the rdoEngine object, once it has been created, is referenced only when you address the rdoEnvironments collection. Default values for rdoEngine object properties are shown in *Figure 20-2* on the next page.

The rdoEngine object is predefined, so you can't create additional rdoEngine objects—nor do you need to. All properties and methods executed against the rdoEngine object simply poll the ODBC driver manager for information. Since no specific ODBC driver has been selected, no driver-specific information can be obtained, but internal ODBC handles are automatically allocated to deal with impending connections. These settings determine how subsequent data-related operations are managed—or at least they establish the default values used when rdoEnvironment objects are created.

Figure 20-2
Default Values for rdoEngine Object Properties

Property	What It Specifies	Default Value
rdoDefaultCursorDriver	Cursor driver type (ODBC or server-side)	rdUserIfNeeded
rdoDefaultUser	SQL Server logon ID	"" (empty string)
rdoDefaultPassword	Corresponding SQL Server password	"" (empty string)
rdoDefaultErrorThreshold	Level of severity above which errors are fatal	−1 (disabled)
rdoLocaleID	Determines which language is used for RDO error messages	rdLocaleEnglish
rdoVersion	Returns version of RDO engine DLL	2.0.0000
rdoDefaultLoginTimeout	Time to wait before abandonment of connection attempt	15 seconds

CAUTION

To use the Remote Data Objects, you *must* set a reference to the Microsoft Remote Data Object 2.0 object library in the Visual Basic References dialog box available via the Projects menu. If you don't do this, you will trip a compile error that says your user-defined object is not recognized (or something to that effect). Fortunately, the UserConnection Designer will set this reference for you.

rdoEngine Properties, Events, and Methods

For the most part, you employ the rdoEngine to set parameters used to build the rdoEnvironment objects beneath it. However, there is an important change here for Visual Basic version 5.0—events—and the rdoEngine exposes the first of these. In the following list, I have summarized the various properties, events, and methods exposed by the rdoEngine object.

- *Creating a new rdoEnvironment object with the rdoCreateEnvironment method.* The rdoEnvironment object is used to map alternative users or separate transaction scopes. You don't have to create an rdoEnvironment to get started; the rdoEngine creates a default object for you—rdoEnvironments(0).

- *Using the rdoDefaultCursorDriver property to set or examine the default cursor type.* In some cases, however, the default (server-side cursors) can't implement some of the cursor features you need, so you need to override the default and use one of the other cursor libraries.

- *Using the rdoErrors collection to get details on errors once a connection has been attempted or a cursor has been created.* The rdoErrors collection is used to manage errors generated by the ODBC layers, not by Visual Basic.

- *Using the rdoDefaultLoginTimeout property to set or examine the ODBC logon default timeout value.*

- *Using the rdoDefaultUser and rdoDefaultPassword properties to set the user name and password for opening connections.* You would perform this operation if no specific values have already been supplied. Generally, however, I use domain-managed security, so I leave these values alone.

- *Using the rdoDefaultErrorThreshold property to set or examine the level of severity above which errors are fatal.* A fatal error is one that terminates a query and triggers a trappable Visual Basic error.

- *Using the rdoRegisterDataSource method to create a new DSN entry in the Windows system registry.* I never use this method, and you'll understand why after you've read Chapter 21, which is about using this interface to get connected to SQL Server.

- *Using the InfoMessage event to fire each time an informational message is returned to any open RDO connection.* For those of you familiar with VBSQL, this is virtually identical to the DBLIB message handler. Basically, RDO places any SQL_SUCCESS_WITH_INFO messages into the rdoErrors collection and fires the InfoMessage event to tell you a message (not necessarily an error) has arrived. At this point, you need to scan the rdoErrors collection for the details.

But the rdoDefaultError-Threshold property isn't working as first intended, so I would just steer clear of it.

You can change any of the default values shown in **Figure 20-2** before you create new rdoEnvironment, rdoConnection, or rdoResultset objects. Note, however, that rdoEnvironments(0) is created with the default values shown in the figure because it's created automatically on first reference to the Remote Data Objects or the RemoteData control. Therefore, by the time you get a chance to change any of the defaults, the rdoEngine has already started and the default rdoEnvironment has been created. If the default values aren't appropriate to your application, you can change the properties of rdoEnvironments(0) or the rdoEngine before opening a connection or creating a new rdoEnvironment object.

If you think this is a lot of trouble and you'd just as soon not have to worry about it, check out the UserConnection Designer—it can manage all these details for you.

NOTE Be sure to take advantage of Visual Basic 5.0's new Explorer-like object browser. It makes locating the right object, method, property, or event easy—and help on the selected topic is just an F1 keystroke away. *Figure 20-3* on the next page shows an example of the object browser window for the rdoEngine object. Notice how the events, properties, methods, and collections all have different icons. Visual Basic 5.0's IntelliSense also kicks in here to expose the available objects, methods, properties, and events as you type—so you don't have to look them up.

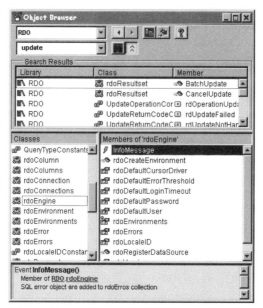

Figure 20-3 *The InfoMessage event of the rdoEngine object as exposed by the Visual Basic 5.0 Object Browser*

The rdoEnvironment Object

Once the RDO interface instantiates the rdoEngine object, it automatically creates the default rdoEnvironment object in rdoEnvironments(0). This default rdoEnvironment object corresponds to the ODBC hEnv handle returned from the SQLAllocEnv function. The underlying ODBC environment is used to determine ODBC driver settings. For example, you can set the type of default cursor via the rdoDefaultCursorDriver property. You can do the same thing by using the rdoEngine object's hEnv property and the ODBC SQLSetConnect-Option function—but why bother? The object property is far easier to use, and you don't have to remember the *SQL_CUR* constants. The point is, you have the *option* of doing it either through the RDO interface or directly through the ODBC API. Most of the time it really doesn't matter—except to the poor soul who has to figure out how to debug your code after you've taken off for Tahiti. (I guess she could just call you up and ask.)

Now that we're beginning to use Microsoft Transaction Server to manage our transactions for us, the need for client-managed transactions might be a thing of the past—like rotary dials on phones and buttonhooks.

RDO 2.0 adds another wrinkle here. Since you can now create a stand-alone rdoConnection object and set its properties before actually connecting, the need for the rdoEnvironment object has been reduced considerably. Sure, you still need it to build independent transaction scopes, but for the most part, you can do without it. It's still useful when you need to trap the transaction events, however.

rdoEnvironment Properties, Events, and Methods

Using the rdoEnvironment object, you can set a number of property options and initiate a number of methods. RDO also fires three events to reflect operations on any rdoConnections established under a specific rdoEnvironment. (As already mentioned, any property options that you set on the rdoEnvironment object will override values set on the rdoEngine object.) Here are some of the operations you can perform:

- *Using the rdoEnvironment object's LoginTimeout property to determine the number of seconds that the ODBC Driver Manager waits for a successful logon operation to complete.* The default value of 15 seconds is usually fine for most local net operations, although it's not nearly enough for some busy networks or RAS connections.

- *Using the rdoEnvironment object's default UserName and Password properties to open connections.* These default values are both "" but they can also be overridden with arguments to the OpenConnection method. Again, I don't use these default values for domain-managed security applications.

- *Opening one or more existing connections.* You use the OpenConnection method to perform this operation. The RDO model provides no automatic connection or disconnection. When you close a connection, it closes—immediately. Actually, now that RDO 2.0 supports the EstablishConnection on the rdoConnection object, I think we will see abandonment of the OpenConnection method.

- *Managing batched transaction processing.* You can use the BeginTrans, CommitTrans, and RollbackTrans methods and the associated events to manage this kind of transaction processing across one or more rdoEnvironment connections. RDO fires events when each of these methods is executed so that you can add additional contingency handling to transaction operations. These events can't be used to derail the transaction.

- *Conducting multiple, simultaneous, independent, and overlapping transactions.* You can use several rdoEnvironment objects to perform these operations. Remember that client-managed transaction scope is based on the rdoEnvironment object.

- *Terminating an environment and the connection and removing them from their respective collections.* Use the Close method to do this.

NOTE ODBC 3.0 has installed a connection pooling mechanism not unlike that used by Jet to help manage limited connection resources. By default, this facility is disabled in RDO because it's really intended for use in Web servers or by remote server-side ActiveX components to handle hundreds (or thousands) of incoming connection requests—not the few dozen to few hundred requests received by a conventional LAN server.

If you are ever inclined to refer to an rdoEnvironment object by name, use the Name property of the rdoEnvironment object or, easier yet, use its ordinal number. The default rdoEnvironments(0) object is named *Default_Environment*— but why you would want to use this instead of the ordinal number 0 is beyond me. The Name property of rdoEnvironment objects is originally set from the *Name* argument passed to the rdoCreateEnvironment method. You can also refer to an rdoEnvironment object by its position in the rdoEnvironments collection, using this syntax (where *n* is the *n*th member of the zero-based rdoEnvironments collection):

```
rdoEngine.rdoEnvironments(n)
```

Or you can do it this way:

```
rdoEnvironments(n)
```

You can't create a stand-alone rdoEnvironment object. You shouldn't find a need to. But how can you tell which objects can be declared as *New*? Well, Visual Basic's IntelliSense will tell you. See what happened when I typed the declare statement in the example shown in Figure 20-4? RDO couldn't find rdoEnvironment as a valid object to be used with the *New* keyword—so Visual Basic won't let you make a mistake—unless you force it to.

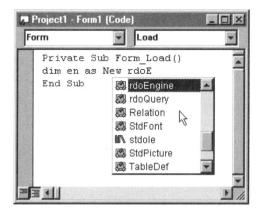

Figure 20-4 *Using Visual Basic 5.0's IntelliSense to help make RDO coding easier*

Transaction Management

If you expect your application to support more than one transaction scope or separate user name and password contexts, you should consider use of the rdoCreateEnvironment method to create a new rdoEnvironment object with specific user-name and password values. This method accepts a unique name for the new object, a user name, and a password. If the name you choose for the new object matches an existing member of the rdoEnvironments collection, a trappable error results. A newly created rdoEnvironment object is automatically appended to the rdoEnvironments collection if you provide a unique name. To create an rdoEnvironment object that is *not* appended to the rdoEnvironments collection, simply provide an empty string for the name. To remove an rdoEnvironment object, use the Close method against it.

NOTE Because of a limitation in the current ODBC drivers, only one hEnv is ever allocated, so it's the same for all rdoEnvironment objects. The RDO interface knows how to deal with this, however, and manages the independent nature of the rdoEnvironment transaction scope on its own.

CAUTION
Implementation of the ODBC driver's transaction management is strictly one level deep. If you execute an RDO BeginTrans method, the ODBC layer simply sets the hDbc connection handle's option for automatic commitment to *off*. But when the CommitTrans is executed, the bit is turned back on, even if it was turned off a dozen times, and the ODBC driver issues the SQLTransact function. This makes it clear to me that you shouldn't try to do any nesting with the transaction methods—at least not by using the rdoEnvironment object.

Additional rdoEnvironment objects are used to manage independent transaction scopes. In this sense, they are very much like the Workspace object in the DAO model. For example, when you use the BeginTrans method against an rdoEnvironment object, all data-altering operations on *all* rdoConnection objects in that environment are considered to be in the same transaction scope. If you roll back a transaction on any one of the common rdoConnection objects, the RDO interface walks through *all* the rdoConnection objects opened on that rdoEnvironment and issues a rollback command. This doesn't mean that the RDO interface and the ODBC driver manager support two-phase commit; they don't. Each operation is an atomic operation—it can succeed or fail on its own. If one of these subtransactions fails, its failure has no effect on previously committed operations. To establish separate transaction scopes, open additional rdoEnvironment objects.

TIP The RDO interface supports fully nested transaction management through use of TSQL transaction statements initiated with the Execute method. For example, on a single connection, you can execute a BEGIN TRANS SQL statement, several UPDATE statements, and another BEGIN TRANS statement. Any operations executed after the second BEGIN TRANS statement can be rolled back independently of the statements executed after the first BEGIN TRANS. To commit the first set of UPDATE statements, you must execute a COMMIT TRANS statement or a ROLLBACK TRANS statement for each BEGIN TRANS executed. You can also use the BEGIN TRANS *name,* SAVETRANS *name,* and ROLLBACK *name* TSQL statements to roll back to specific points in the transaction sequence.

An Alternative Transaction Manager

Another new server has been added to the suite of tools available for RDO developers: Microsoft Transaction Server (MTS). While it is well beyond the scope of this guide to describe how to set up and use MTS, it should be one of the first things you consider as you move your architecture toward implementation of remote business objects, especially when transactions are part of the design. When your design starts to span multiple servers, you often have to expand three-tier design concepts to additional levels. This is where MTS plays a critical support role—performing many complex operations that are, in many cases, simply impossible to perform without its extra help. MTS takes up where SQL Server 6.5's Distributed Transaction Manager leaves off. It not only deals with transaction issues between servers but also manages thread pooling, object brokering, and a dozen other complex functions that you had to code yourself with earlier versions of Visual Basic.

MTS is a key element of Microsoft's Internet and intranet application strategy. The technology is based on proven transaction processing methods, but its importance transcends the domain of transaction processing monitors. It defines a general-purpose programming model for distributed component-based server applications. MTS is specifically designed to allow server applications to scale over a very wide range of users, from small single-user systems to high-volume Internet servers. It provides the robustness and integrity traditionally associated only with high-end transaction processing systems. As you can see, MTS can relieve much of the responsibility involved with the management of the logical business objects we use to build N-tiered applications.

Selecting a Cursor Driver

An rdoEnvironment object isn't used only to set transaction scope. It also determines, among other things, the type of cursor driver to be used in building cursors. I often reset the default driver type and use the Client Batch cursor driver, since it supports multiple result sets, which aren't easily supported by server-side cursors. You can choose the default cursor driver by setting the rdoDefaultCursorDriver property of the rdoEngine or the CursorDriver property of the rdoEnvironment object to one of five constants: *rdUseIfNeeded*, *rdUseOdbc*, *rdUseClientBatch*, *rdUseServer*, or *rdUseNone*.

TIP To execute queries returning multiple result sets against a server-side cursor, set the read-only and forward-only options and set the rowset size to 1.

If you choose *rdUseIfNeeded*, the ODBC Driver Manager chooses the cursor driver on its own. Wherever possible, it uses a server-side cursor, which is the default setting. But unfortunately, the RDO interface has no way of knowing whether you're about to send a multiple result set or logic-constrained query, which might not be supported by a server-side cursor.

If you choose *rdUseOdbc*, it specifies that the ODBC cursor driver is to be used. In this case, cursors are built on the workstation. This driver supports multiple result sets and a variety of other options. But the ODBC cursor driver also consumes workstation resources in order to store the keysets or data rows, as dictated by the type of cursor you specify.

If you choose *rdUseClientBatch*, it specifies that the new FoxPro Client Batch cursor library is to be used. In this case, cursor keysets are also built on the workstation. This driver also supports multiple result sets and a variety of other options, including optimistic batch updates and dissociate Connection objects. Like the ODBC cursor library, the Client Batch library also consumes workstation resources in order to store the keysets or data rows, as dictated by the type of cursor you specify.

If you choose *rdUseServer*, you force the use of server-side cursors (where they are available), an option if you are connected to SQL Server 6.0. In this case, the keysets or data rows are maintained in TempDB space on the SQL server. If the driver reports back that server-side cursors aren't available (as when your application is connected to SQL Server 4.*x*), the ODBC driver simply switches back to the ODBC cursor driver and posts an informational message in the Errors collection. This doesn't trip a trappable error, but it can result in dramatically different performance and operational characteristics. For example, the client will need resources to store the keyset and the network will need to handle the increased load of the returning keys. Not only that, control will be returned to the application before the keyset is populated.

If you choose *rdUseNone*, RDO builds a cursorless result set by setting the read-only and forward-only options and setting the rowset size to 1.

TIP If you ask for a client-side cursor, ODBC stores the temporary keysets you build in RAM and overflows to disk, storing the keys in the TEMP area on disk. The location of this area is set by changing the TEMP environment variable, which is set in AUTOEXEC.BAT. If your drive containing the TEMP space fills up, you are done fetching keys.

Server-side cursors are generally misunderstood, so we need to spend a little more time here. This type of cursor, first implemented on SQL Server (and not implemented on many other systems), saves space on the client system because the cursor keyset is built on the server. That's the good news *and* the bad news. If the cursor contains too many rows, the server's resources get used up instead of the client's. In addition, consider that the cursor is fully populated *before* control returns to your application, unless it exceeds the cursor threshold (which defaults to 100 rows). This means that the RowCount will be accurate and that you can use the same connection again immediately without having to close the cursor. RDO handles fetching the next rowset of data from the server-side cursor as you move down in the keyset. However, RDO will keep only the *current* rowset of rows on the client. (This number is determined by the setting of the RowsetSize property, which defaults to 100.) Whenever you step off this rowset (either forward or backward), RDO calls SQLExtendedFetch to get the next/previous rowset.

Server-side cursors work well for this scenario, provided that you have a fast server. But I've seen server-side cursors perform very badly on servers with limited RAM or slower CPUs or hard drives. Also, you want to make sure TempDB is big enough, since server-side cursor data is stored in TempDB. Remember to allocate enough space in TempDB for *each* application to store its cursor keyset(s). So if you have 500 applications and they each create a 100-row cursor in TempDB, that would mean you would need room to store 500 x 100 (50,000) keyset rows. SQL Server Books Online has a treatise on the subject worth reading. In any case, if you have enough RAM (more then 64 MB), you should consider putting TempDB in RAM—this will make server-side cursors really fly. Of course, you have to realize that server-side cursors do result in more round-trips to the server (which can be offset by using a bigger rowset size), so the speed of the link between the client and the server also comes into play.

You can use sp_configure to set the cursor threshold option in SQL Server, which enables SQL Server to build server-side cursors asynchronously of the client. This means you can return to your application while the server continues to populate the cursor in TempDB. This can really help appearances, and you won't have to wait for the whole cursor to populate before returning control to the client. The option is a threshold setting where you say if the cursor will be over *n* number of rows, populate it asynchronously. You should keep *n* set fairly high because populating a small cursor synchronously will be faster than doing it asynchronously.

NOTE Whenever you set an option or a property that the ODBC driver can't implement, it reverts to a supported option and creates an entry in the rdoErrors collection—but that usually doesn't cause a trappable error.

We haven't talked much about *rdUseNone*. This option tells RDO to forego creation of a cursor when you're building rdoResultset objects. In RDO 1.0, you had to build an rdoPreparedStatement, set its RowsetSize to 1, and build an rdoResultset with the read-only, forward-only options set. With RDO 2.0, this is no longer necessary when you set the *rdUseNone* option. Frankly, this is the "cursor" of choice for me because most of my applications fetch few rows and don't need to scroll around in stale data anyway.

The rdoConnection Object

The rdoConnection object is used to manage a connection with a single SQL Server database. When you coded with RDO 1.0, once you had the rdoEnvironment object set up with the right cursor driver, you were ready to use it to open connections to remote ODBC data sources and create rdoConnection objects with either the RemoteData control or the OpenConnection method of an rdoEnvironment object. With RDO 2.0 and Visual Basic 5.0, you have another, easier-to-code method with which to get connected. First, you can declare rdoConnection objects without using the OpenConnection method—you can use the *New* keyword as follows:

```
Dim Cn as New rdoConnection
```

This instantiates a stand-alone connection object. It's not a member of the rdoConnections collection—not yet. To point to a specific SQL server or a different cursor driver, you need to set the rdoConnection properties. I like to use the *With* keyword to do this; it saves time and makes the code far easier to read:

```
With Cn
    .Connect = "Uid=;Pwd=;Database=Biblio;DSN=MyBiblioDSN;"
    .CursorDriver = rdUseNone      'To set cursor library
    .LoginTimeout = 10             'To set login timeout
End With
```

Notice that we can now reference properties on the rdoConnection object that weren't exposed in RDO 1.0—a number of "parent" properties were added to RDO 2.0 objects to support stand-alone objects. Basically, these "parent" properties can be preset by setting rdoEngine or rdoEnvironment properties, but it's awfully easy to do it here—where we can clearly see what is being done.

At this point, we are ready to make the connection. (We'll look at the details of opening a connection in the next chapter.)

Choosing a Default Database

All of your queries depend on a specific default database—unless you have absolute addressing in everything. In most cases, therefore, you need to set a default database. You can choose from several ways of determining which database you connect to:

- A SQL Server database can be explicitly referenced with the *Connect* argument when the rdoConnection object is opened with the Open-Connection method. For example, if you set the *Connect* argument to *Database= Pubs*, the connection sets the default database to *Pubs*.

- In a similar manner, you can also specify a connect string when using a stand-alone rdoConnection object.

- The default database can be assigned by the SQL Server system administrator when the logon ID is established. This is not always a good idea, though, since the server administrator might assign this database incorrectly or the ID might get changed inadvertently. This setting is the default if you don't specify a Database value in the connect string. Remember that, by default, a login ID is assigned to the Master database, which is a less-than-useful choice when you're building front ends against your own database.

It has become clear to me that the convenience and shareable aspects of the UserConnection Designer make even the reduced code shown here unnecessary. Be sure to spend time checking out this new feature in Visual Basic 5.0. It eliminates much of this drudgery with a simple design-time process.

- The TSQL Use *database* statement can be used to change the currently assigned default database. This works only if you get connected in the first place. If you can't get connected because you haven't specified a permissible database for the logon ID you specified, you're stuck.

NOTE If your user ID doesn't have permission to use the selected database, a trappable ODBC error will be triggered and a proposed change won't be made. This error will usually prevent the connection if you use the Database option in the connect string. Or the connection might be made—but to the wrong database.

Using the rdoConnection Object

When the rdoConnection object is successfully opened using the Open-Connection or EstablishConnection methods, it's automatically appended to the rdoConnections collection. Once a connection is established, you can manipulate a database associated with an rdoConnection object by using the object's methods and properties. The SQL server itself isn't accessed until a connection is established, and once it is, you can use one or more of the following rdoConnection methods:

- *The Execute method, to run an action query or pass an ODBC SQL or TSQL statement to the SQL server for execution.* This technique is useful for UPDATE, INSERT, and DELETE statements or for complex transaction management. It can also be used for DBCC operations or for executing stored procedures (action queries). It's possible to execute a multiple result set query with the Execute method—even if some of the queries return rows. Unlike RDO 1.0, RDO 2.0 doesn't trap action queries that contain SELECT clauses—it assumes you know what you are doing.

- *The OpenResultset method, to create a new rdoResultset cursor object.* And you know, of course, that cursors return a subset of the database information. They can be read-only and updatable and use a variety of fetch options. We look at the rdoResultset and rdoQuery objects in Chapter 24.

- *The CreateQuery method, to create a new rdoQueryobject.* This method is used to create a temporary stored procedure that can take and return parameters and result sets from and to the database.

NOTE The rdoConnection object also supports the now-obsolete CreatePreparedStatement method, but you should convert to the CreateQuery method to enable all of the new features.

- *The BeginTrans, CommitTrans, and RollbackTrans methods, to manage transactions.*

- *The Close method, to close a connection, deallocate the connection handle, and terminate the connection.* As I said before, the RDO interface doesn't cache connections. When you use the Close method, the connection closes.

NOTE When you are done with a connection, you should close it. The RDO interface won't do it for you—remember, there is no connection manager. When you close an rdoConnection object, any open rdoResultset, rdoTable, or rdoQuery objects are automatically closed as well. If the rdoConnection object simply loses scope, however, any open rdoResultset, rdoTable, or rdoQuery objects remain open until the rdoConnection object or the other objects are explicitly closed.

The following rdoConnection object properties determine a number of options that can help manage the result sets you create on the connection:

- *Use the StillConnecting property to see whether your asynchronous connection has been made yet.* This really isn't necessary if you set up a Connect event handler. StillConnecting returns False and the Connect event fires when the connection attempt has completed.

- *Use the Connect property to examine the rdoConnection object's Connect property.* This can be useful when you're cloning the connection.

- *Note that the rdoConnection also exposes the CursorDriver, LoginTimeout, and QueryTimeout properties, which make stand-alone connecting easier.*

- *Use the LastQueryResults property to return the last rdoResultset created against the rdoConnection object.* When we get to Chapter 22 on the UserConnection Designer, you'll see that this is an invaluable property.

- *Use the AsyncCheckInterval property to determine how often RDO polls the interface to see whether your asynchronous operation has completed.* In this case, less might be more—less polling might make the interface less "distracted."

- *Use the RowsAffected property to determine how many rows were affected by the last Execute action query operation.* There is also a RowsAffected property on the rdoPreparedStatement object that is unaffected by Execute method operations.

- *Use the QueryTimeout property to specify how long the ODBC driver manager should wait before abandoning a query.* This property defaults to 0, which indicates that the driver doesn't time out.

- *Use the ODBC API with the hDbc property to determine or set ODBC API connection options—carefully.*

- *Use the Name property setting of an rdoConnection object to refer to that object.* The Name property setting specifies the DSNAME (DSN) parameter used to open the connection. You can refer to the rdoConnection object by using the rdoConnections("*name*") syntax. You can also refer to the object by its ordinal number, using the rdoConnections(0) syntax, which refers to the first member of the rdoConnections collection.

An important change has been made in how RDO handles object instantiation. In RDO 1.0, if you executed the OpenConnection method against a variable that already contained an open rdoConnection object, the existing object was left open and another object was created and added to the rdoConnections collection. Unless you specifically closed the connection, it remained open—even if you assigned another connection to the variable. But in RDO 2.0, this practice was changed. Now, if you use the OpenConnection method against a variable that contains an existing rdoConnection, the current rdoConnection object is dropped and removed from the rdoConnections collection; the new rdoConnection object is now added to the rdoConnections collection. When we examine the rdoResultset object in Chapter 24, you'll discover that it now works the same way. Basically, this change means that if you depended on the persistence of these rdoConnection objects after using the same variable to create new rdoConnection objects, you must now use a different variable when executing the OpenConnection method.

Chapter

Getting Connected with RDO

Locating and Naming the SQL Server

Establishing a Connection

ou don't have a connection manager to worry about when you use the RDO interface. You make and break all connections yourself, whenever you need to. But you're still faced with the same challenges when it comes to managing connections. On the one hand, you don't want to overload the server by making too many. On the other, unless you know how to use server-side cursors, SQL Server doesn't support multiple operations on a single connection, so you often have to open additional connections to update rows or perform other operations. You also have to be concerned about leaving idle connections open while the user decides what to do, but you don't want to slow him down when he finally does figure out what he wants—or comes back from his two-hour lunch. Properly managing connections can mean that an application is scalable to several hundred users or limited to a few dozen.

Locating and Naming the SQL Server

Like other ODBC-based interfaces, RDO connects to your SQL server through the information kept in the ODBC data source name (DSN), a file-based DSN, or from the information you provide in the connect string. Personally, I'm not always in favor of establishing a permanent DSN, since it can be a source of trouble when your application is installed and run in the field. There are several approaches you can take to work around this problem:

- *Use the ODBC registry functions to determine whether a suitable DSN already exists.* This is really a lot of trouble, as far as I'm concerned, so I rarely use this technique. You can use the ODBC API SQLDataSources to list registered DNS entries.

- *Use the rdoRegisterDataSource function to create a new DSN entry.* This is also troublesome, but it's not as bad as using the ODBC registry functions.

PART IV USING REMOTE DATA OBJECTS AND THE RemoteData CONTROL

- *Use an already established DSN.* Most people who use this approach install the DSN themselves or have the user install it when the application is installed. This approach can be risky, though, and it can lead users to phone you in the middle of the night.

- *Launch the ODBC control panel applet directly from your application, and instruct the user on how to set up a DSN.* Yeah, right. Unless your users are a bit more comfortable than mine are with this sort of thing, I don't think this is a very viable option. Letting some users take this route is like turning a four-year-old loose with a 17-blade Swiss Army Knife.

- *Create a file-based DSN.* This new approach is virtually identical to the DSN-less connection technique, except that it requires a file to store the connection information. It should work fine until the file is lost or not installed with the application. It could also lead to security problems because it would be fairly easy to tinker with its ASCII contents.

- *Don't use a DSN entry at all, but include all the driver information in the* Connect *argument of the OpenConnection method.* This approach is far less risky. All it assumes is that the name of the SQL server doesn't change, since you've hard-coded it into the application. It has its drawbacks in that this technique requires that you take all of the default DSN settings (we look at these a little later), but it's the fastest way because it doesn't require a registry hit.

- *Put the name of the SQL server in a registry entry (my preference) or in an INI file, and set this for when the application is run the first time or for when the SQL server can't be located.* (When an OpenConnection method fails, the message that is returned often says that the SQL server couldn't be found—which could mean any of a dozen things.) Generally, the name of the server doesn't change after installation, but if the same application is used to access more than one SQL server, permitting the user to select from a list of valid servers would be an alternative.

- *Use a file-based DSN.* This is the newest option with the ODBC 3.0 drivers. It duplicates the functionality of the DNS-less connection strategy by simply placing all the connection parameters in a file. To use it, you can use the ODBC connection management dialog boxes (launched by the Control Panel) to create the file-based DSN. Then you simply copy the file to the target machine. When you point to this DSN at run time, ODBC fills in the blanks just as it would with a DSN-less connection.

Establishing a Connection

Once you know which SQL server to connect to, you have a couple of options. In RDO 1.0, you could use the OpenConnection method to create an rdoConnection object, which establishes a physical link to the data source. While you can still use this technique in RDO 2.0, now you can also declare a stand-alone rdoConnection object and use the EstablishConnection method to hook it to a selected SQL server. Let's take a look at these two techniques a little more closely.

To establish a connection, you must somehow identify the network location of the data source, as well as the driver type. Your code also provides a number of parameters for logging the user on to the database. By choosing an appropriate *Prompt* argument, you can program the ODBC driver manager to prompt the user for missing arguments and prevent the use of alternate arguments. I feel fairly uncomfortable exposing these dialog boxes, however. On occasion, the previous logon ID is shown, and the next user only has to supply the password. For some applications, this might be just fine. For others, even logon names are secure. For these reasons, I always set the *rdDriverNoPrompt* option to prevent any dialog boxes from appearing. I then must add code to trap the situations in which the user doesn't get logged on.

The OpenConnection method accepts the following arguments. They can be supplied by name, with Visual Basic named argument syntax, or the arguments can be supplied positionally:

- *The* dsName *argument.* This argument indicates the name of the registered data source. If you include this argument, it points to a valid, registered DSN entry (which can include the new file-based DSN). If you supply all the DSN-related parameters in the connect string, you *must* pass an empty string as the *dsName* argument. If supplied, the *dsName* argument value can be used to identify the connection. Since you might connect to the same DSN more than once, however, or simply pass an empty string, you can't really depend on the name to index the rdoConnections collection. You can always use the rdoConnection object's ordinal position in the rdoConnections collection to choose an open rdoConnection object.

- *The* Prompt *argument.* This argument indicates whether the user will be permitted to supply arguments to ODBC connection dialog boxes. If you don't want the user to supply a different data source name, user name, password, or default database, use the *rdDriverNoPrompt* constant as the *Prompt* argument. But if the *Connect* and *dsName* arguments don't lead to a connection (which you have to deal with in code), a trappable error results and the user doesn't see any ODBC-generated dialog boxes to assist with the connection. This feature is unique to RDO (and ODBCDirect) because the DAO/Jet interface defaults to *Prompt if required,* which displays the dialog boxes whenever there is a problem with the logon information or with establishing the connection.

- *The* ReadOnly *argument.* This is set to False if the user expects to update data through the connection. Setting it to True can improve performance because the ODBC drivers can skip code needed to support updatability.

- *The* Connect *argument.* This argument gives the ODBC driver manager either the entire set of ODBC connection parameters or just those parameters not already supplied by the DSN entry. These parameters can include user name, password, default database, DSN (which overrides the value provided in the *dsName* argument), and others as shown in *Figure 21-1*.

Figure 21-1
Valid *Connect* Arguments

Keyword	Description
DSN	The name of the data source, as returned by SQLDataSources. The DSN keyword isn't used if DRIVER is used but must be passed as "" in this case.
DRIVER	The name of the driver, as returned by SQLDrivers. The DRIVER keyword isn't needed if DSN is used. The SQL Server driver name is *{SQL Server}*. Note the use of curly braces.
SERVER	The name of the server on the network where the data source resides. On a Microsoft Windows NT computer, *"(local)"* can be entered as the server, in which case a local copy of SQL Server can be used, even when this isn't a networked version. Note that when the 16-bit SQL Server driver is using *"(local)"* without a network, the Microsoft Loopback Adapter must be installed.
UID	The user logon ID, or an empty string to activate domain-managed security: *UID=;*. In any case, this or the workstation logon name must exist on the SQL server as a valid logon ID.
PWD	The user-specified password, or an empty string to activate domain-managed security: *PWD=;*.
APP	The name of your application (optional).
WSID	The workstation ID. Typically, this is the network name of the computer on which the application resides (optional).
DATABASE	The name of the SQL Server database (optional).
LANGUAGE	The national language to be used by SQL Server (optional).

An important thing to note about this list is what is *missing*. The ODBC DSN maintenance dialog boxes collect several other important values that *can't* be set through these parameters. Among those are (currently) the ones you see in *Figure 21-2* on the next page. The implication here is that if you want to use DSN-less or file-based connections, you must accept these default settings—or create and register a DSN to get connected.

Figure 21-2
DSN-Based Connection Parameters

Parameter	Description
Use Trusted Connection	Should ODBC assume domain-managed security? (Defaults to No.)
Network Address	The address of the SQL Server database management system (DBMS) from which the driver retrieves data. For Microsoft SQL Server, you can usually leave this value set to *(Default)*. This is required for TCP/IP setups.
Network Library	The name of the SQL Server Net-Library DLL that the SQL Server driver uses to communicate with the network software. If the value of this option is *(Default)*, the SQL Server driver uses the client computer's default Net-Library, specified in the Default Network box on the Net-Library tab of the SQL Server Client Configuration Utility. If you create a data source using a Network Library other than *(Default)*, and optionally a Network Address, ODBC SQL Server Setup will create a server name entry that you can see on the Advanced tab in the SQL Server Client Configuration Utility. These server name entries can also be used by DB-Library applications.
Convert OEM to ANSI Characters	If the SQL Server client computer and SQL Server are using the same non-ANSI character set, select this option. For example, if SQL Server uses code page 850 and this client computer uses code page 850 for the OEM code page, selecting this option will ensure that extended characters stored in the database are properly converted to ANSI for use by Windows-based applications. When this option check box is clear and the SQL Server client machine and SQL Server are using different character sets, you must specify a character set translator.
Generate Stored Procedures for Prepared Statements	Stored procedures are created for prepared statements when this option is selected (the default). The SQL Server driver prepares a statement by placing it in a procedure and compiling that procedure. When this option check box is clear, the creation of stored procedures for prepared statements is disabled. In this case, a prepared statement is stored and executed at execution time.
Translation	The description of the current translator. To select a different translator, choose the Select button and select from the list in the Select Translator dialog box.

You can use the code in the following example to establish a connection to a Microsoft SQL Server database with an existing data source name of *MyRemote*:

```
Dim Cn As rdoConnection, En As rdoEnvironment, Conn As String
Set En = rdoEnvironments(0)
Conn = "DSN=MyRemote;UID=Holly;PWD=Huskador;DATABASE=MyDb;"
Set Cn = En.OpenConnection("", rdDriverPrompt, False, Conn)
```

The *dsName* argument of the OpenConnection method can be passed as an empty string. In this case, the data source name is taken from the *Connect* argument (unless you have included the *Driver* and *Server* arguments in an attempt to make a DSN-less connection). Each of the RDO methods will support named arguments, so it is possible to specify each argument of the method by using the *argument:=* syntax. For example, this OpenConnection method could also be coded as follows:

```
Set Cn = En.OpenConnection(prompt:=rdDriverPrompt, _
    readonly:=False,Connect:=Conn)
```

If you choose domain-managed security, you should use empty arguments for the *UID* and *PWD* parameters of the *Connect* argument. This type of security passes your Windows NT logon ID and password to the data source. If your database administrator has implemented integrated or mixed security, this technique should permit you to log on to the data source—assuming that you've been granted permission to do so. Taking the preceding example once again, note that a domain-managed security *Connect* argument is coded as follows:

```
Conn = "DSN=MyRemote;UID=;PWD=;DATABASE=MyDb;"
```

TIP You can use the ODBCPING.EXE program to test the installation of the ODBC drivers and the linkage to a specific SQL server. Just type ODBCPING /S*servername* /U*loginID* /P*password*.

Opening Connections Asynchronously

RDO 2.0 expanded the support for asynchronous operations to include the OpenConnection and EstablishConnection methods. This lets you start the task of opening a connection and continue with other work while ODBC and SQL Server set up the connection. It's easy to request an asynchronous connection: all you have to do is use the *rdAsyncEnable* option as the last argument of the aforementioned methods. When you do, control returns immediately to your application and you can proceed to other tasks. Your connection won't be usable, but you can load forms or perform other operations that don't require use of the connection. To determine when the connection attempt is done, you can poll the rdoConnection object's StillConnecting property or simply wait for the Connect event as I describe below. Actually, I prefer the latter because it doesn't waste cycles polling.

Coding the rdoConnection event handlers

The rdoConnection object exposes several events that are used to help manage both synchronous and asynchronous operations on the connection. These events can be used in lieu of polling the StillConnecting property and to provide a higher degree of control over the connection process. Suppose you wanted to trap all opening connections on the SQL server so that you could initialize global variables or perform some server-side procedure? It's easy now, because if you declare the rdoConnection object WithEvents, you can code the event handlers to do anything you need to do in the BeforeConnect and Connect event handlers. These new events are described in *Figure 21-3*.

Figure 21-3
rdoConnection Event Handlers

Event	Fires
BeforeConnect	Before RDO calls SQLDriverConnect so that you can do your own prompting.
Connect	After a connection operation completes—successfully or not.
Disconnect	After a connection has been closed.

The Connect event handler is passed a Boolean value (*ErrorOccurred*) that indicates whether the attempt to establish the connection succeeded. This way you can expect to have the Connect event fire whether the connection was successfully established, failed to connect, or simply timed out. Whenever an error occurs, the rdoErrors collection is filled in with the details of what went wrong. Remember that the rdoEngine object's InfoMessage event also fires if an informational message is generated by the connection operation. This is fairly common because SQL Server sends back several messages informing the client of the assigned default database and the language chosen.

Working with Stand-Alone rdoConnection Objects

As I mentioned earlier, another connection method is available with RDO 2.0—stand-alone rdoConnection objects. This is where the new EstablishConnection method comes in. This method takes a couple of arguments that are identical to those passed to OpenConnection. But consider that EstablishConnection works against a dormant or stand-alone rdoConnection object—one that has never been opened, or one that was opened, dissociated (disconnected), and is ready to be reopened.

This method also works against the new UserConnection object in much the same way. I talk about this in Chapter 22. Once the connection operation is complete, control returns to your application. But has the connection been made or not? Well, if you trapped the error you would know, but if you coded the Connected event handler, you could simply examine the ErrorOccurred Boolean argument passed back from RDO.

I put together a little sample to illustrate the use of stand-alone rdoConnection objects and coding event handlers:

```
Public WithEvents Eng As rdoEngine
Public WithEvents Cn As rdoConnection

Private Sub Form_Load()
```

```
Set Eng = New rdoEngine
Set Cn = New rdoConnection
With Cn
    .Connect = "Uid=;pwd=;database=pubs;dsn=biblio"
    .LoginTimeout = 5
    .EstablishConnection rdDriverNoPrompt, True, rdAsyncEnable
End With
End Sub
```

The Form_Load procedure sets up the rdoEngine and rdoConnection
objects. Notice that the rdoConnection object is "stand-alone," so we can
address it to assign initial properties. Next come the rdoConnection event
procedures. We use the asynchronous option here so that code passes quickly
out of the Form_Load event. That gets the form loaded quickly but also gives
us a chance to show off our event handler. Next stop, the BeforeConnect event:

```
Private Sub Cn_BeforeConnect(ConnectString As String, _
        Prompt As Variant)
MsgBox "About to open a connection using " & vbCrLf  _
        & ConnectString, vbOKOnly, "Before Connect Event"
End Sub
```

This procedure is fired *before* the connection is established. At this point,
you can't cancel the connection operation without ending the whole program—you have no "cancel" option. You can change the connect string and
Prompt arguments, though, and this might prevent the application from connecting somewhere it shouldn't.

```
Private Sub Cn_Connect(ByVal ErrorOccurred As Boolean)
Dim M As String
If ErrorOccurred Then
    For Each er In rdoErrors
        M = M & er & vbCrLf
    Next
    MsgBox "Connection failed. " & vbCrLf & M
Else
    MsgBox "Connection open..."
    Cn.Execute "use pubs"    ' To test the connection
End If
End Sub
```

This is the post-connect event handler, which is fired after RDO completes trying to connect. If the connection is established, ErrorOccurred will
be set to False. But if something went wrong, ErrorOccurred is set to True and
you will need to check the rdoErrors collection to see what went wrong:

```
Private Sub Eng_InfoMessage()
For Each er In rdoErrors
    Debug.Print er
Next
rdoErrors.Clear
End Sub
```

The last event handler is for the rdoEngine object's InfoMessage event. As I said earlier, this event gets fired when informational messages are returned from SQL Server via ODBC. We generally throw these out as they occur because they're of little consequence. But if you have queries or stored procedures that use the TSQL PRINT statement, these messages cause this event to fire. Yes, all of these messages are appended to the rdoErrors collection whether or not you set up an event handler to fire as they arrive. Notice that the rdoErrors collection has a Clear method, which is ideal for discarding this type of message.

NOTE The code examples that shipped with Visual Basic version 5.0 were written in the summer of 96, long before the code was finalized. Because of a number of important innovations added to RDO event handling, these examples no longer compile. I have included corrected examples on this guide's CD and here in these pages. The code sample shown here is saved as "Connect Event" on the CD.

RDO 2.0 Collection Management

In RDO 1.0, when you executed the following code, you ended up with two separate rdoConnection objects in the rdoConnections collection:

```
Dim cn as rdoConnection
Dim en as rdoEnvironment
Set en = rdoEngine.rdoEnvironments(0)
Set cn = en.OpenConnction("MyDSN",rdDriverNoPrompt, _
    False, "UID=;PWD=;Database=Pubs")
Set cn = en.OpenConnction("MyDSN",rdDriverNoPrompt, _
    False, "UID=;PWD=;Database=Biblio")
```

One of these connections would be established and point to the *Pubs* database, while the other would be established to the *Biblio* database. The *cn* variable would address the second rdoConnection object.

RDO 2.0 changes the way that collections are managed. If the example shown above is executed in RDO 2.0, you end up with only *one* rdoConnection object in the rdoConnections collection—but the variable *cn* still points to the second rdoConnection. While this new technique for handling rdoConnections (and rdoResultsets) is different, it should result in fewer memory leaks. If you don't want to lose an existing rdoConnection as assigned to a variable, you need to use the OpenConnection method against a separate variable.

CAUTION
In many cases, improper Windows NT permissions or group membership configurations prevent users from getting connected. Make sure your Windows NT administrator and server administrator get these set up correctly. (I know I mess it up more often than not.)

Other Connection Parameters

The length of time in seconds that the ODBC Driver Manager waits for the SQL server to begin responding to a request for a connection is determined either by the DBEngine object's rdoDefaultLoginTimeout or by the rdoEnvironment object's LoginTimeout property. RDO 2.0 also includes a LoginTimeout property on stand-alone rdoConnection objects that can be set before you use the

EstablishConnection method. Unless you change it, rdoDefaultLoginTimeout defaults to 15 seconds—which might not be enough for some long-distance or slow-speed connections or when the SQL server is busy, but since most local-net connections begin in under 3 seconds, 15 seconds is a good default. As long as SQL Server *begins* to respond in this length of time, the connection process shouldn't time out.

Connection Problems

You might be unable to establish a connection for a variety of reasons, including lack of permission on the data source, improper network connection or permissions, or a missing or disabled data source. With Microsoft SQL Server or other data sources, the number of simultaneous connections permitted might be limited by license agreements, resource constraints, or database settings. The same problems involved in attempting to connect to SQL Server via Jet also apply to connection attempts made with the RDO interface. Both interfaces use the same ODBC Driver Manager and SQL Server drivers to establish the connection. Check with your server administrator if you suspect that all available connections are allocated or that your logon ID does not have permission to access the server.

CAUTION

RDO connections are never closed unless you explicitly close them—even when the variable used to hold the rdoConnection object goes out of scope—so remember to close the rdoConnection object when you are done with it.

22
Chapter

Using the RDO UserConnection Designer

Understanding Custom UserConnection Objects

Building Custom UserConnection Objects

Executing Queries and Stored Procedures as Methods

Using the UserConnection Object's Events

O ne of the challenges you have to face as a client/server developer is how to leverage the suite of queries built up over the lifetime of your application. Since this code can be deeply buried in an application, it's especially difficult to maintain and keep current. You also have queries, stored procedures, or business objects on the server that must be referenced and maintained. In RDO 1.0, accessing these stored procedures was easier than ever but the procedures still required each application to include fairly complex ODBC call syntax used with balky rdoPreparedStatement objects—hand-coded for each application. To get it all working, you had to build a correct SQL property, make sure all of the rdoParameter objects had the right Direction property setting, and hope that the Type property was set correctly because you couldn't change it if ODBC guessed incorrectly. On top of that, your application was responsible for providing all of the parameters to establish the connection. This meant building a correct connect string as well as setting another half-dozen parameters so that you could consistently get connected. Now that event-driven programming has arrived, connecting is a little easier but it still involves writing and maintaining event procedures to handle the contingencies. And all of this must be repeated for every application you write. Sure, you can use class modules to help perform these operations, but this too can be a challenge because you have to define your own standards for this approach.

With RDO 2.0, this is no longer a problem. While building rdoQueries is easier than it was with RDO 1.0, using the UserConnection Designer makes the process not only easier, it makes the process smarter. For one thing, the UserConnection Designer isolates all of the logic needed to expose these objects in one design-time graphical interface. This means that you can create a custom UserConnection object once and include it in every application your company creates. This way, it can be managed by a central team, and if there are changes, these can be incorporated by recompiling the application. But even recompiling shouldn't be required if the query code is kept server-side in stored procedures. This approach also dramatically reduces the number of lines of code you have to write, test, debug, and maintain. While the User-Connection Designer isn't perfect, it goes a long way toward making team development of applications easier.

Understanding Custom UserConnection Objects

Before we start building our own sample UserConnection object with the UserConnection Designer, we need to take a brief look at what is going on under the hood. The UserConnection Designer accepts a number of parameters through its dialog boxes. These are used to feed a little run-time DLL that performs the following chores:

- *Creates a hidden rdoConnection object* and exposes all of its events as a UserConnection object.

- *Creates a set of hidden rdoQuery objects*—one for each query or stored procedure you specify and exposes them all as methods on the User-Connection object.

- *Exposes the hidden rdoQuery object's rdoParameters collection members as arguments of each method.*

The dialog boxes facilitate the collection of these parameters, but they don't make the decisions for you as to suitability of the options when they are used with one another. It's just as easy (OK, easier) to make a mistake when choosing these options as it was when you had to write code for them all. However, it's also far easier to correct these mistakes later—even *much* later, when the developer has been promoted to management (or marketing) to get him or her out of the trenches.

The process of creating a custom UserConnection object is simple. All you have to do is this:

- Install and start the designer—it's built into Visual Basic version 5.0 Enterprise Edition.

- Fill in the GUI form to provide connection information. This points to your own server and a specific database.

- Choose one or more stored procedures or...

- Tune the arguments used to create the connection and the result sets.

- Provide the syntax for one or more queries. Even this is automated because the UserConnection Designer lets you call Microsoft Query, whose GUI query tool can be used to write the TSQL syntax for you. You can also paste in queries built with Microsoft Database Tools or other query generators.

- Verify or tune the parameters for the queries and stored procedures as required.

That's it. To use your new custom UserConnection object, you have to do this:

- Write one line of code to instantiate it.

- Write a single line of code to establish the connection.

- Write a single line of code to invoke a chosen query by calling it as a method against the UserConnection object. The query parameters are simply passed as arguments to the method.

Each query you add to the control is invoked as a method; this applies to arguments and all. It couldn't be simpler if I sent one of the Visual Basic developers to your office to do it for you.

Building Custom UserConnection Objects

The following section describes step-by-step how to build a typical User-Connection object. We will be using the sample SQL Server *Biblio* database for this example, so you might want to check out Appendix A to get instructions on how to install it. You could also run the example against your own database if installing *Biblio* seems like too much trouble or if you don't have the space to devote to another test database.

1. Start with a new project. For this example, I chose Standard EXE as the template.

2. On the Projects menu, choose Components. In the Components dialog box, choose the Designers tab and select Microsoft User-Connection. Close this tab, and wait a moment while the designer is installed. You won't have to do this again because this designer will be initialized whenever you start Visual Basic from this time forward.

3. Next, from the Project menu, choose Add ActiveX Designer and then Microsoft UserConnection. At this point, a Designers entry should be added to your project tree and the UserConnection1 designer window should be open. On top of that, the designer automatically displays a dialog box to help you choose your data source.

4. At this point, you need to either create a new DSN or use an existing one. My system has a DSN named BIBLIO set up to point to the *Biblio* test database. Later on you can try to set up DSN-less or file-based connections, but for now, just use a "user" DSN.

5. Click the Authentication tab, and fill in a valid User Name and Password. I don't fill these in because I use domain-managed security. Next, set the ODBC Prompt Behavior to Never so that we can trap all of the errors instead of letting our users see the ODBC logon dialog boxes. During development, I like to check the two option boxes to save the connection authentication property settings—you should too.

To alleviate concern about security and password protection, you can choose from two levels of persistence available for the User-Connection object's UserID and Password properties. By default, both levels are turned off so that no caching or persistence of these properties occurs and so no one can dump your code and see these sensitive parameters.

If Save Connection Information For New Run-Mode Class is checked, the user name and password properties are stored in the properties of the actual class and are persistent in the built executable or DLL.

If Save Connection Information For Design Time is checked, the user name and password properties persist only during design time and aren't written into the built EXE or DLL file.

6. Click the Miscellaneous tab, and select Use Client Batch Cursors. You can play with the Login Timeout and Query Timeout settings later if you want to. Leave them alone for now.

7. Click OK at the bottom of the dialog box. At this point, you should be confronted with the basic UserConnection dialog box—ready to accept new queries. It looks like *Figure 22-1*.

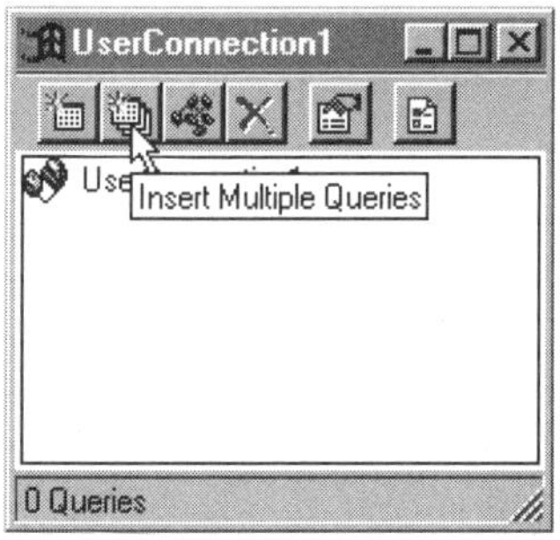

Figure 22-1 *UserConnection dialog box—UserConnection Designer*

8. Click the second toolbar button in the UserConnection1 dialog box—Insert Multiple Queries. At this point, RDO establishes a connection to the SQL server based on the parameters you provided earlier, executes the ODBC API SQLProcedures function that returns all of the stored procedures in the database selected, and populates the list box as shown in *Figure 22-2* on the next page. If you don't get a list of stored procedures that looks like that screen shot, either you don't have a valid DSN set up or the database doesn't have any stored procedures.

Go back and fix this situation before you go on. You should now see something that looks like **Figure 22-2**. (Actually, at this point, I have already selected my TitlesByAuthor stored procedure.)

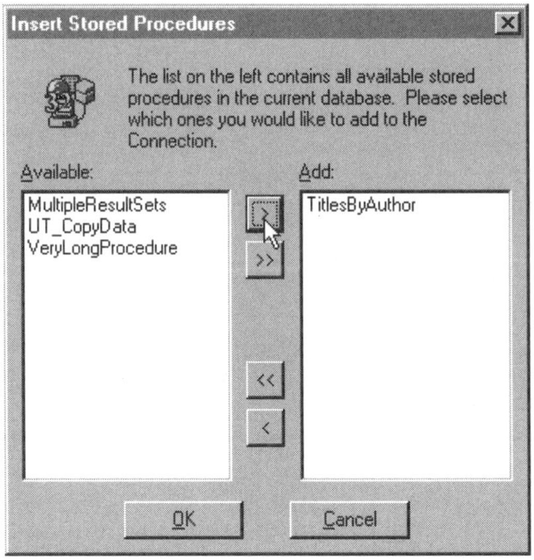

Figure 22-2 Insert Stored Procedures dialog box—UserConnection Designer

9. Sure, the names of your stored procedures might be different than what is shown here in the Available list, but the dialog box should be as shown. Choose one of these queries to test by selecting it and clicking on the right arrow. We will use one of these and write our own query as an example. At this point, the designer queries the database for the details about the chosen query. In my case, I chose the TitlesByAuthor example.

10. We're now ready to explore a little further and check out the query parameters so that we know what to expect. Click OK in the query selection dialog box. Now, I happen to know what this query looks like on the server (because I wrote it):

```
CREATE PROCEDURE TitlesByAuthor @AuthorWanted VARChar(30)
AS  Select Title, Author
From Titles T, Title_Author TA, Authors A
Where T.ISBN = TA.ISBN and
TA.Au_ID = A.Au_ID and
Author like @AuthorWanted
Return @@ROWCOUNT
```

11. Since the query expects one input argument (the Author's name) and returns a return status (the number of rows found), we should expect to see these parameters exposed by the UserConnection Designer. The designer now exposes the properties for our TitlesByAuthor query as shown in **Figure 22-3**. We can select any of the parameters to garner additional details.

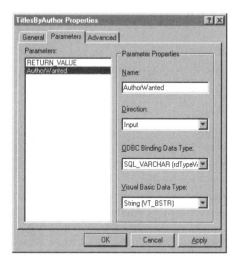

Figure 22-3 *Parameters tab of query parameters dialog box—UserConnection Designer*

Notice that both the *RETURN_VALUE* and the *AuthorWanted* parameters are automatically recognized—by name, direction, ODBC binding data type, and Visual Basic's data type. You didn't have to do anything (this time). But, if the query is a little more complex, you might have to go in and twiddle the data type. For example, if instead of a LIKE expression in the query I used a CHARINDEX expression, the designer might think that the parameter was an integer. That's why you have to double-check to ensure that the right data type is chosen.

12. Next we visit the Advanced tab, as you see in **Figure 22-4** on the next page. This tab lets us set parameters for each query we define. In this case, I know that I don't want to see more than 20 hits from the query, so I set Max Rows to 20. The database is fairly large, but 30 seconds should be plenty of time to get the job done. I don't care about the Bind Threshold because I'm not working with BLOBs in this query. I set the Rowset size to 20 because I know I won't need to scroll around in the keyset. We don't use keyset size. I also deselected Prepare Query Before Execution because this is a stored procedure and it's already "prepared." This option sets the Prepared property on the rdoQuery object that we are creating.

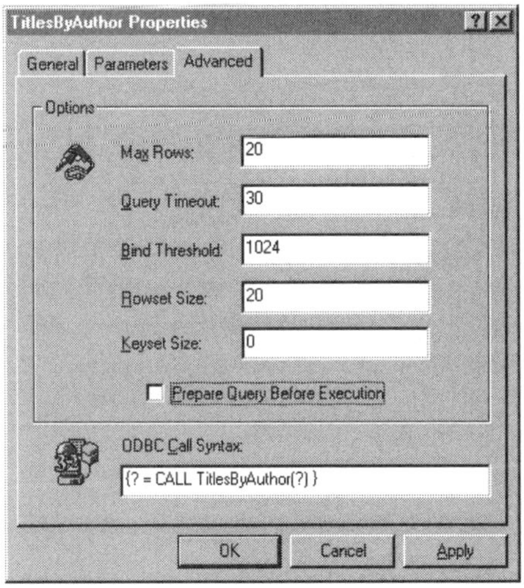

Figure 22-4   *Advanced tab of query definition dialog box—UserConnection Designer*

13. Click OK to close the TitlesByAuthor Properties dialog box. Notice that the query has been added to the designer's window so that we can examine the properties again later if need be.

We are finished with the designer for now, so we can close the designer dialog box. Notice that we now have a UserConnection1 class under the Designers heading in the Project window. You might also discover that the project now includes a reference to RDO 2.0—this was added automatically by the designer. It builds code to handle all of the properties and events associated with the object in RDO. Yes, even the event prototypes are ready to go—all you have to do is supply the code. That's next on the tour.

NOTE   When you build a new table or stored procedure, don't forget to grant permissions for them so that the intended user can access or execute them. While your program might work if you log in as SA, it won't when you log in as a "normal" user. Of course, even the stored procedures that you don't have permission to access are listed by the UserConnection Designer—it's like looking through Tiffany's window at the tiaras.

Executing Queries and Stored Procedures as Methods

Now that the UserConnection object is created, we are ready to take it out for a spin. The first thing we need to do is add some code to instantiate the object from its base class. First, using the *New* keyword, create an instance of the UserConnection object we just built. We also need an rdoResultset object to hold the result set we are about to fetch, unless we use a control that can take an rdoResultset as an argument. I include such a control on the companion CD—my own version of the Grid control customized to accept an rdoResultset.

```
Dim ucTest As New UserConnection1
Dim rs As rdoResultset
```

Next we need to open the connection. You can do this anywhere, but in this case it is a one-time operation, so we put the code in the Form_Load event procedure:

```
Private Sub Form_Load()
ucTest.EstablishConnection
End Sub
```

NOTE If you *don't* want a forward-only, read-only cursor, now is the time to reset rdoQueries(*n*).CursorType to some other type of cursor. In addition, you'll need to set rdoQueries(*n*).LockType to some other type of concurrency—unless you want rdConcurReadOnly. Once the query is executed, it's too late to change it.

At this point, the connection is open—if all is going as planned—and we are ready to try executing the query. Since all of the stored procedures we added with the designer are now exposed as methods on the UserConnection object that we created, they are really easy to code. After we declare the return value variable, start typing the *next* line of code as shown below:

```
Dim lrc As Long
lrc = ucTest.T
```

You should see something like *Figure 22-5*.

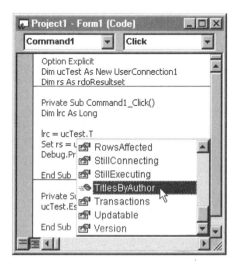

Figure 22-5 *IntelliSense enumerating properties, methods, and events*

Notice that the stored procedure we chose is now in the enumerated list of methods. Now select the TitlesByAuthor method (you can just press the space bar to select it), type the opening parenthesis, and see what happens next. Part of Visual Basic 5.0's IntelliSense knows that this method takes a single input argument (a String) and returns an integer (Long). Because of this, Visual Basic can help you write the code for the method by exposing this, as you see in *Figure 22-6*.

```
lrc = ucTest.TitlesByAuthor (|
Set rs = ucTest.LastQueryRes  TitlesByAuthor(AuthorWanted As String) As Long
```

Figure 22-6 *IntelliSense exposing method arguments*

We complete the line by filling in the argument to pass to our TitlesBy-Author query. For our example, I am simply hard-coding the parameter. You would probably pass in a parameter via a TextBox or other control.

```
lrc = ucTest.TitlesByAuthor("%Vaughn%")
```

When this line executes, it runs the query and, if the query is available, returns the return status value and result set rows as described in the User-Connection properties. A word of caution: I have seen a number of strange instances where I trip an Invalid Use Of NULL error when using the syntax shown above. Apparently, some of the cursor drivers don't provide the return status value until the query is fully populated—they return NULL until that value is available. Well, you can choose from a number of ways around this. Here are two:

- First you can code the call *without* the return value:

```
ucTest.TitlesByAuthor "%Vaughn%"
```

and fetch it later when the rdoResultset is at EOF. At this point, the rdoQuery object under the UserConnection object contains the return status value:

```
lrc = ucTest.rdoQueries(0).rdoParameters(0)
```

- You can also capture the return value as shown below but declare the variable to capture the value as a variant. In this case, you must test for NULL in case the stored procedure doesn't return the status value until later.

```
Dim vRetVal As Variant
vRetVal = ucTest.TitlesByAuthor("%Vaughn%")
```

Referencing the New rdoResultset

To access the result set, you *must* address the rdoResultset object just created, which is passed in the LastQueryResults property as shown—

Stop right there. Don't move a muscle. There's something nasty in that bush over to your right. If you know it's there and what to do, you'll be fine—

just don't make any sudden movements. I was recently mauled by this creature and spent about 10 hours trying to figure out why. After the developers and I had a weeklong e-mail conversation, we came to the conclusion that this "feature" is a necessary evil that has some very unusual characteristics. This beast calls itself LastQueryResults. At first, the LastQueryResults property might *look* like an rdoResultset—but it's not. It's unusually shy: if you touch it or even look at it, it disappears. Sure, you get to look at it once—but once you reference the LastQueryResults property, no matter how you do it, it's gone.

Let's look at the implications of this paradox. Assume that you have created and executed a UserConnection object (*ucTest*) and you're ready to fetch the results of the query. That's where we were in our walk-through, anyway. Before you simply set a variable declared as rdoResultset to LastQueryResults, consider this: if you have a valid rdoResultset addressed by the variable (*rs* in our example), you might not have addressability after the assignment—if the LastQueryResults returns NULL. So it would be a good idea to assign LastQueryResults to a temporary variable first. Then you can test the temporary variable and be assured of using the result set if it is available. No, you *can't* combine this into a single step like this:

```
If ucTest.LastQueryResults is Nothing Then
Else
Set rs = ucTest.LastQueryResults
```

If you try, the phantom LastQueryResults object will be gone by the time you try to assign it to *rs*. You *can* do this:

```
Set tRs = ucTest.LastQueryResults
If tRs is Nothing Then Else Set rs = tRs
```

Once the rdoResultset addressed by LastQueryResults is captured into another variable, it's safe. At that point, Visual Basic and RDO add it to the list of "referenced" objects and it starts to behave like other RDO objects. Here are a few other tips that you need to keep in mind when you're working with this property:

- You shouldn't set a watchpoint to LastQueryResults. If you do, the watchpoint will work the first time but the underlying result set will be lost from that point forward.

- You shouldn't use a Debug reference or any other break-mode references either—except to capture the rdoResultset into another variable.

- You shouldn't let the cursor accidentally stray over the LastQueryResults property when you are in Break mode at run time. If you do, Visual Basic fetches the contents of the property and destroys it in the process.

- You can't expect to be able to use any of the LastQueryResults methods or properties more than once. Yes, LastQueryResults exposes all of the underlying rdoResultset properties and methods—but again, once they are touched, the object is history and returns Nothing.

Once you assign the LastQueryResults property to a variable declared as rdoResultset or pass it on to another control, you can treat it just like any other rdoResultset object, just as if you had created it with an OpenResultset—all of the same rules and techniques apply. The result set might not be fully populated, so you will want to do a MoveLast on it as soon as possible—but remember that RDO and the Client Batch cursor library might do this for you. You can't use the MoveLast method or the UserConnection again without first dealing with the result set you just created. This means that you have to use the Close method on the rdoResultset. You can't use the Close method on the LastQueryResults property—it's gone. To see what ReturnStatus was sent back, we can examine the variable we used when executing the method (*lrc*). Notice that the RowCount property returns a –1 because it is not (yet) available:

```
Debug.Print rs.RowCount, lrc
```

NOTE In some cases, the return status isn't available when the cursor is first opened and won't be available until you fetch the last row. It works this way in VBSQL, and in the ODBC API as well, so you might already understand this limitation. In these cases, you have to wait until after the result set is populated to be able to access the value. If you try to fetch it too early, you will get an Invalid Use Of NULL error as RDO attempts to pass the NULL return status to your Long variable. You can simply declare the Long variable as a variant to accommodate this reality, if you have a mind to, but you still need to check for NULL.

Wait a minute! There's something missing here. When I create a result set, I like to choose the *type* of cursor. For some situations, I use cursorless result sets, but other times I need a keyset, static, forward-only, or if I have gone completely bonkers, I use a dynamic cursor. (Actually, that's a lie. I have never been crazy enough to use a dynamic cursor.) You can set the type of cursor that the UserConnection method is to create by changing the CursorType property of the rdoQuery that the UserConnection object creates for the chosen stored procedure. RDO and Visual Basic will help you choose one because Visual Basic enumerates your choices when you address this property, as you see in *Figure 22-7.*

ucTest.rdoQueries!TitlesByAuthor.CursorType=

Figure 22-7 *DataTips exposing enumerated* CursorType *constants*

While this isn't as easy as clicking on a tab and selecting a cursor type from the UserConnection Designer dialog boxes, it isn't that hard to do in code. Notice that I have addressed the rdoQuery object using the bang (!) syntax. This causes an "early" binding of the rdoQueries collection member and speeds up your code (a tad). I wouldn't like to reference this member by its ordinal number, because the code would break if I added another stored procedure or query ahead of it.

I have provided a couple of examples for the UserConnection Designer. These are located on the companion CD in the UserConnection Designer Examples directory. A simple Base example and a fleshed-out applet are there as well. I put the applications I generated for VBits here, too.

Building Your Own Queries

Generally, I recommend that any queries your two-tiered application executes should be in the form of stored procedures. In cases where this isn't possible, you can use the UserConnection Designer's ability to manage queries *you* provide in the form of TSQL queries. Since Microsoft Query is cross-connected to the UserConnection Designer, it can be used to help you build your custom queries interactively through a graphical interface. You might also consider using the new Microsoft Visual Database Tools to build your queries. Frankly, I prefer the latter as it has a much better, albeit more complex, interface.

NOTE We'll see how to create and execute RDO parameter queries in Chapter 24.

The steps you need to take to get to the Microsoft Query window are fairly straightforward. Let's step through them to make sure you are ready to use this interface when the time comes to build a complex query. Incidentally, after your query has been developed and tested, it would be a good idea to move it over to SQL Server as a stored procedure. To try out this interface, let's create a variation on our previous query, but this time let's add the *Publishers* table. Since we already have a UserConnection object created, we can go right to the designer's main form.

1. Click the first toolbar button, Insert Query, to build a new query. Again, a connection to SQL Server is established to populate the list of stored procedures—which we won't be using this time.

2. Type in the name of the new query. Call it TitlesPubsByAuthor. This is a Visual Basic method name, so it can't have embedded spaces. At this point, you should see something like *Figure 22-8* on the next page.

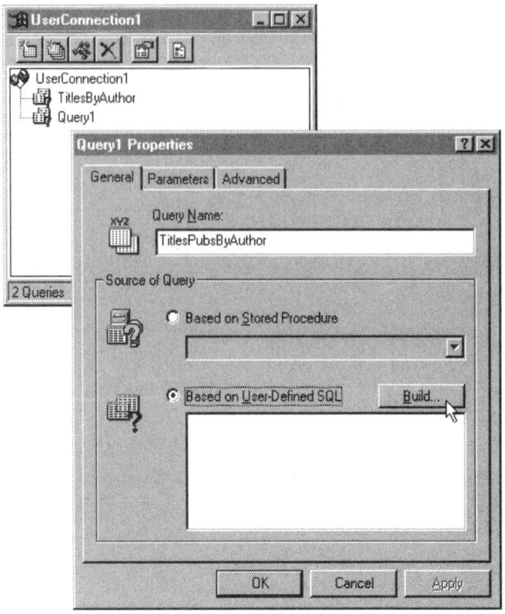

Figure 22-8 *Defining your own SQL for a user-defined UserConnection object*

3. Wait! Don't just click the Build button. This launches Microsoft Query (MSQ), but we aren't ready to do that just yet. For some reason, MSQ expects something to be entered into the Text box at the bottom of the dialog box. If you don't enter anything, it returns an Unable To Start error. For now, just enter *Select * From Authors* so we can get into MSQ.

4. *Now* click the Build button. At this point, the designer launches MSQ but it also executes the query right away. So we have just locked up the entire *Authors* table. Not good. We need to either get out of this immediately or populate the result set to free locks on the table. By default, there is no upper limit on the number of rows that MSQ pulls down, but you can set this limit by going into MSQ's Options dialog box and setting the number of rows to 10 or so. Do this now so that we don't have to worry about this again. What MSQ lacks in features it makes up for in lack of client/server awareness—but I digress. Let's move on.

5. Use the interactive dialog boxes to add the *Titles*, *Publishers*, and *Title_Authors* tables to the already present *Authors* table. Use the Add Tables command on the Tables menu for this, or click the Add Table(s) toolbar button. Unfortunately, as you add the tables, MSQ merrily tries to join them all—whether or not they're related. It gets silly after a while as MSQ constantly complains that all of the rows can't be shown. It would probably work better if you added the tables in order. That is, first *Title_Authors* because it has a link to the *Authors* table. Next add *Titles* and then *Publishers* so that MSQ can attempt to figure out the relationships more easily. Once you are finished adding tables, you should have a screen that looks like **Figure 22-9**. (I rearranged the table dialog boxes so that their relationship lines could be seen.)

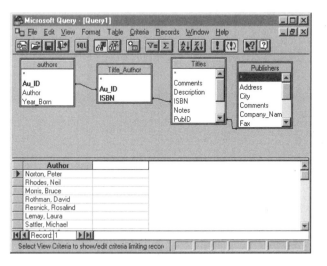

Figure 22-9   *Using Microsoft Query to define your SQL—choosing the tables*

6. We're now ready to choose the columns to appear in our query, but before we take this next step, go to the Records menu and deselect the Automatic Query option. This prevents MSQ from attempting to execute the query we're building as we work on it. It's almost as if the people developing this application weren't aware that these tables could be used in production and that doing random queries isn't such a good idea.

7. Using the drag and drop techniques you learned when using Microsoft Access, drag the ISBN, Title, and Company_Name columns to the columns area at the bottom of the query window—where you see the Author column now. At this point, you should have something on your screen that looks like **Figure 22-10** on the next page.

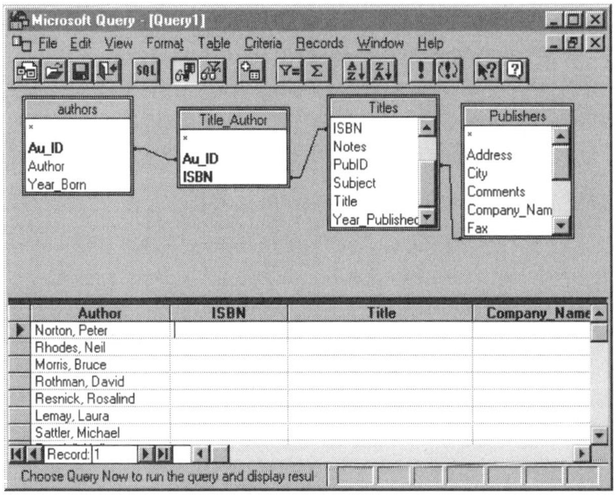

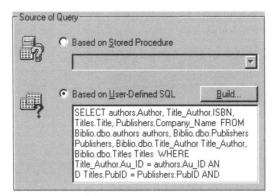

Figure 22-10 *Using Microsoft Query to define your SQL—choosing the columns*

8. If you want to, you can add sort criteria, change the way the joins work, or preview the SQL, but for now, let's just keep it simple and exit back to Visual Basic and the UserConnection Designer. What you might do before you leave is test the query by clicking the ! button. I did, and the query ran, but it returned another Can't Show All Records error for some reason. Let's just click the little door icon and get back to Visual Basic.

9. When we return to Visual Basic, MSQ has passed back the SQL needed to execute our query. (See *Figure 22-11*.) There's no vertical scroll bar, so you just have to walk the cursor down with the arrow keys to see the bottom of the query.

Figure 22-11 *User-defined SQL query built by Microsoft Query*

10. While MSQ doesn't seem to have a way to add parameters to our user-written queries, we can add them fairly easily by editing the SQL that MSQ generated. As with RDO 1.0, we can insert a question mark (?)

where we want RDO and ODBC to insert and manage a query parameter for us. These parameters can be only input type; return value, output, or input/output parameters aren't supported.

Let's try to add a parameter and see what happens. Edit the SQL shown in the dialog box in *Figure 22-11*, and add *WHERE Author = ?* to the end. Select the Parameters tab when you are finished editing the SQL.

You should now see something like *Figure 22-12*.

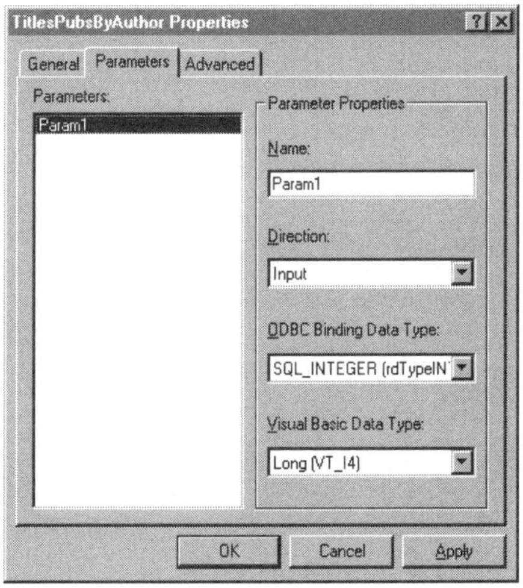

Figure 22-12   *Tuning query parameters using the UserConnection Designer*

Now follow these steps:

1. Notice that this Parameters dialog box isn't filled in nearly as intelligently as the one we saw earlier (*Figure 22-3*). That's because the designer and RDO have no way to tell what the question mark is supposed to mean. The designer simply guessed that the question mark was meant to represent an integer. However, in our case, we'll be providing a string, so we have to go in and change the settings.

2. Change the Name to *AuthorWanted*. This value will show up when we code the method. Change the ODBC Binding Data Type to *SQL_VARCHAR*. Change the Visual Basic Data Type to *String*. We don't have to change the Direction; it is already set at Input. Once these values are set, our query is ready to save. It hasn't been saved and won't be until we click OK or Apply. Click OK.

3. Click the View Code button in the designer. Notice that the event handlers are already filled in. Remember that these handlers apply to all the queries you define on this connection. You might also want to visit the Advanced tab to set some of the other properties. I didn't bother this time because we won't test this new query. That's something else you might want to do on your own.

You know that SELECT queries aren't the only kind of queries in use today—far from it. While fetching rows is important, many of our client/server front-end operations use action queries, too. I don't think the interactive query development strategy used in MSQ would be much good for this type of work. However, there is nothing to stop you from creating your own action queries and adding them to your user connection. Visual Database Tools might also be helpful here.

Tips on Using Your Own SQL and Parameters

You can include your own queries instead of pointing to a stored procedure. You can even code queries that contain parameters. I often take this back-road approach when I am developing a new application—before I commit the query to a stored procedure. There are a few chuckholes here that you need to watch out for:

- To create a parameter query, simply insert a *?* where the parameters go. For example, do this:

```
Select * From Authors Where Name Like ?
```

  The UserConnection Designer will detect this parameter marker and let you choose a data type for it.

- If you write your own procedure, you can mark the parameters only as *Input*. Return value, input/output, and output parameters are accessible only on stored procedure queries.

- Be sure to recheck these settings if you tune the SQL query because the UserConnection Designer overrides your changes whenever the SQL is altered.

- If you need to insert a carriage return into your query, press Ctrl-Return. Remember to include space between operators—especially on new lines.

- Make sure you know what you are asking for when you make a parameter a CHAR as opposed to a VARCHAR. Remember that CHAR expressions are fixed length and VARCHAR is variable length. This means if the length of the parameter you are passing changes, you should be using a VARCHAR.

Using the UserConnection Object's Events

The UserConnection object exposes an entire set of events that can help you fine-tune your custom UserConnection object for special circumstances. The events exposed are the same as for the rdoConnection object plus the Terminate event, which is always associated with user-created objects.

At a minimum, I would also add an error handling routine to deal with the stuff that happens when we work with SQL Server. Since the UserConnection object exposes all of the rdoConnection events, you can simply add some code to the QueryComplete event handler. Remember that this error handler becomes part of the UserConnection object and is carried around in the DSR file. This means other developers can use your custom UserConnection object and get all of the error handling code as well.

```
Private Sub UserConnection_QueryComplete _
   (ByVal Query As RDO.rdoQuery, _
   ByVal ErrorOccurred As Boolean)
Dim er As rdoError
Dim m As String
If ErrorOccurred Then
    For Each er In rdoErrors
        m = m & er & vbCrLf
    Next er
    MsgBox "Something went wrong with the query" & vbCrLf & m
End If
```

Chapter

Using the Transact-SQL Debugger

Setting Up the Server and Visual Basic

Invoking the TSQL Debugger Interactively

Invoking the TSQL Debugger from RDO Code

Debugging the TSQL Debugger

ave you noticed that I keep encouraging you to move more and more of your query logic to the server? For many of you, that has meant creation of stored procedures—often by the hundreds. Some servers manage an avalanche of stored procedures developed by people long since departed. Some of these could have been lying around since I first started lecturing on SQL Server six years ago. Until now, debugging these procedures was expensive. It meant putting extra code into the procedures to dump the time, exposing variable states and logic flow, building stored procedures up in small, testable pieces, and a litany of other tricks of the trade that remain the closely guarded secrets of the stored-procedure development teams. When a stored procedure breaks, you have to deal with the logic very much in the way we used to have to deal with COBOL programs run off 80-column cards in the IBM 360 days. It's a real pain.

SQL Server 6.5 added support for a feedback mechanism to help take some of this burden off your shoulders. After having talked with some friends over in our MIS department, I think that the TSQL Debugger (TSQLD) in SQL Server 6.5 will help these professional stored-procedure developers to some extent, but it's not a complete solution. However, it *will* go a long way to help all of us learn to use stored procedures more efficiently and get a feel for how they interact with the front-end applications we write.

SQL Server 6.5 uses SDI.DLL and either Remote Automation (Windows 95/Windows NT 3.51) or DCOM (Windows NT 4.0) to set up a back link to the applications being tested. Basically, these routines pass back the current line number and other essential information so that the TSQL Debugger can display the stored-procedure text and current line number. TSQL Debugger opens an additional connection to fetch SQL system tables, SQL stored-procedure text, and global variables. This shouldn't affect your maximum user count, but it will affect how much performance you can expect out of your server. While the SDI DLL might not bring the system to its knees, it must have an impact on overall system performance. It will *certainly* impact the performance of a running stored procedure while it is being watched.

TIP   Most of the problems I have setting up and running TSQL debugging have been caused by balky Remote Automation connections and problems with setting up the correct accounts to manage these intersystem connections. Pay close attention to these setup details. One tip that might get you through a number of these problems will be to run the SQL Server in "console" mode by using the *-c* option to start it.

The TSQLD works interactively as a stand-alone program, or it can be launched from Visual Basic when you are debugging your own code as your code launches a stored procedure via RDO. Visual Basic also invokes TSQLD to walk through your triggers if you perform an action query that causes one to fire on the server. The TSQL Debugger supports the following features:

- *Displaying the Transact SQL call stack, global variables, local variables, and parameters for the SQL stored procedure.* When a procedure calls a procedure, as when a trigger calls a procedure, you'll be able to tell how you got into the current pothole. You'll also be able to examine any of the selected global variables or the parameters for the stored procedure being executed.

- *Setting and managing breakpoints in stored procedure code.* You can stop execution at a chosen point to examine the stored procedure state.

- *Viewing and manipulating local variables.* You can also examine the variables declared within the stored procedure and change their values as needed.

- *Creating your own stored procedures interactively, using an edit window.*

Setting Up the Server and Visual Basic

Depending on the SQL Server and Windows NT release you are running, TSQL Debugger (TSQLD) setup can be fairly complicated or an even more complex multistep manual process. The TSQL debugger code and interface libraries are located in the TOOLS directory on the Visual Basic version 5.0 Enterprise Edition CD under TSQL. You'll find two directories here, one that contains the SQL Server service pack 2 (SP2), which you should prudently install, and the SRVSETUP directory that contains additional code especially for Windows NT 3.51 systems. As I understand it, Windows NT 4.0 comes with some of this stuff already installed.

TIP   Find and follow the late-breaking instructions found in the README.TXT file supplied with the Transact SQL Debugger code in the \TOOLS\TSQL directory. It does *not* get installed automatically on your hard disk—it doesn't need to be.

Client-Side Setup

You need to do a few things on the client side—on your development workstation—to start using TSQLD. You have to make sure T-SQL Debugger is selected in the custom options window. Once you are in the design mode, go to the Add-Ins menu and choose Add-In Manager. Next, check the VB T-SQL Debugger add-in. After an initialization dialog box, you can then use the TSQLD interactively or you can have it launched automatically as you execute stored procedures.

Server-Side Setup

On the server side, you must be using SQL Server 6.5 with SP1 or later. This is when support for the new debugging interface was added. If you haven't yet installed 6.5, skip to the next chapter and come back here when you upgrade. You must follow these steps to get TSQL debugging installed on your server.

- If you simply haven't installed the SP1 or SP2 code, you need to do this before going on. SP2 is on the Visual Basic version 5.0 Enterprise Edition CD in the TOOLS\TSQL directory.

- Next, make sure that SQL Server is installed so that it doesn't start up with a "system" account. It must be changed via the Control Panel settings option to specify a Windows NT logon account with sufficient permission to access the SDI automation interface. You can do this by creating a separate account that doesn't expire.

- Next, make sure that the Remote Procedure Call (RPC) Service and Locator are set to Automatic so that they start when the system boots.

- Finally, you must install and register the SQL Debugging interface and Remote Automation components. This is described in the next sections for Windows NT 4.0 and 3.51.

Windows NT 4.0 setup

If you are using Windows NT 4.0, this setup process is automatic because it's handled by the SDI_NT4.EXE program as supplied in the \TOOLS\SRVSETUP directory. When this application runs, it guesses the location of your SQL Server installation directory, prompts you with this guess, and asks for verification. This is where you told SQL Server to install itself; it's usually C:\MSSQL\BINN. Just type *MSSQL*, and the setup program knows to copy the files to the \BINN directory. If this process doesn't seem to work, fall back 10 yards and punt— or try the Windows NT 3.51 manual setup instructions. You might also check the Windows NT event log because any errors encountered will be logged by Windows NT.

Windows NT 3.51 setup

The setup process on Windows NT 3.51 isn't automated (at least not yet), so here are the manual steps you need to perform to install TSQLD. You might need to fall back on these steps if your Windows NT 4.0 install doesn't seem to take:

1. Copy SDI.DLL to your SQL Server BINN directory. It is usually located on C:\MSSQL. Notice we are talking about the BINN directory here, not the BIN directory.

2. Copy the Remote Automation Proxy and Manager files to your 32-bit system directory. This is usually C:\WINNT\SYSTEM32. Folks, this is dangerous because the process might overlay more recent copies of these files. I recommend that you check the version of each of the source and target files to ensure that you are *not* overlaying any newer versions. Do *not* call me if this doesn't work—you're on your own. After you are certain that the copy process won't overlay more recent files, you can do this:

   ```
   Copy aut???32.* C:\WINNT\SYSTEM32
   ```

3. Next, you need to register all of these files and start the Remote Automation Manager for the first time. To do this, use the REGSVR32.EXE, which is also provided in the Visual Basic 5.0 Enterprise Edition Tools directory:

   ```
   REGSVR32 C:\MSSQL\BINN\SDI.DLL
   REGSVR32 C:\WINTN\SYSTEM32\AUTPRX32.DLL
   C:\WINNT\SYSTEM32\AUTMGR32.EXE
   ```

TIP In case you didn't know, the REGSVR32 program can also *un*register a DLL. Simply run the application just shown and add */U* at the end of the command line.

That's it. Once all of these files have been installed, your SQL server should be able to communicate back to your applications through Remote Automation. We are now ready to test a typical stored procedure from Visual Basic. However, in my experience with lots of systems and lots of complaints from fellow workers, this process doesn't always work as planned. For best results, be sure to follow the steps carefully and watch the Web for white papers and Knowledge Base articles on how to make this process easier.

Invoking the TSQL Debugger Interactively

If you simply want to walk through the execution of a stored procedure, you can launch TSQLD via the Visual Basic version 5.0 Enterprise Edition User Interface at design time. Drop down the Add-Ins menu, and click on the little lightning bolt next to the T-SQL Debugger command. If you don't see the entry here, go back and reselect the Add-Ins menu and make sure VB T-SQL Debugger is checked.

If everything is installed right, you should get the virgin Batch T-SQL Debugger screen.

Notice that the Stored Procedure and Batch Query tabs aren't active. They won't be until you choose a DSN. Let's do that now. Because we are running interactively, the TSQLD needs to connect to your server before it can pull down the list of available stored procedures. The Register DSN button can be clicked to launch the ODBC dialog boxes used to build and register new DSNs. Once the connection is open, you can click on the Stored Procedures tab and choose from the drop-down list a stored procedure to work with. You can enter the name of a stored procedure, but if your server can't find it, you won't be able to continue.

Select from the list sp_helpdb, which is a fairly harmless stored procedure. It accepts a single parameter (the database name to display). Type *Pubs* in the Value text box and click Execute.

After the TSQLD establishes the connection and launches the stored procedure, you see a dialog box containing the stored-procedure code ready to be stepped into. Press F8 at this point to start running the stored procedure.

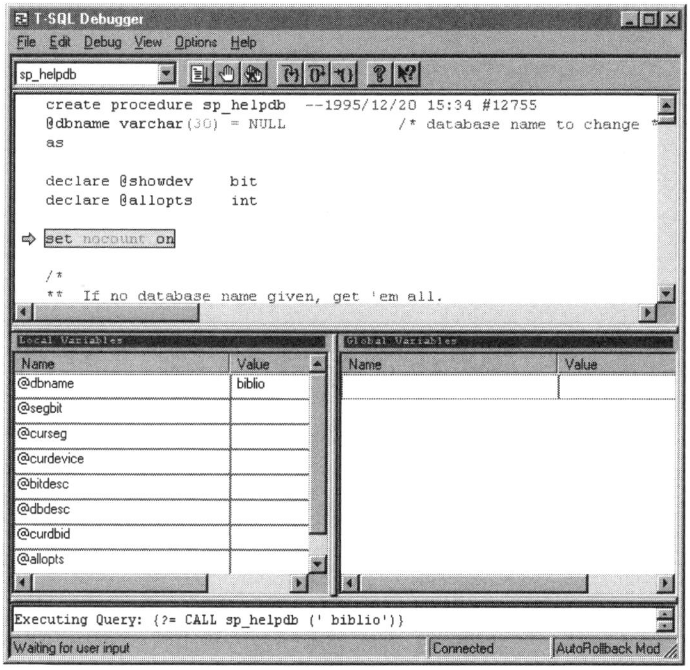

Try this yourself and step through the whole procedure. Notice how the local variables change as you go. You can choose from a number of options on the toolbar buttons and on the Debug menu. These options are listed in *Figure 23-1*.

Figure 23-1
TSQL Debugger Options

TSQL Debugger Operation	What It Does
Go	Same as the Run button or the F5 key in Visual Basic. Runs until the next breakpoint or the end of the stored procedure.
Set and clear breakpoints	Same as the F9 key. Toggles a breakpoint on the current line.
Step	Same as the F8 key. Executes the current line and break.
Step into subexpression	Same as the F8 key, but follows execution into procedure.
Step over subexpression	Same as the Shift-F8 key combination. Does not follow trace into procedure.
Run to cursor	Executes all code without stopping until the trace reaches the selected line.
Stop debugging	Continues execution to the end of the procedure.
Restart	Starts the procedure from the beginning.

Managing global variables

If you want to take a peek at the global variables, click under Name in the Global Variables window and type in one of the valid global variables. Remember, all of these begin with @@. While some global variables apply to the system as a whole, some are connection-specific because their contents apply only to the current connection. *Figure 23-2* lists a number of interesting connection-specific global variables.

Figure 23-2
Some Connection-Specific Global Variables

Global Variable	What It Does
@@CURSOR_ROWS	Specifies the number of qualifying rows in the last-opened cursor. *@@CURSOR_ROWS* returns the following: $-m$ If the cursor is being populated asynchronously. The value returned $(-m)$ refers to the number of rows currently in the keyset. n If the cursor is fully populated. The value returned (n) refers to the number of rows. 0 If no cursors have been opened or the last opened cursor has been closed or deallocated.
@@ERROR	Specifies the last error number generated by the system for the user connection. The *@@ERROR* global variable is commonly used to check the error status (success or failure) of the most recently executed statement. It contains 0 if the last statement succeeded. Using *@@ERROR* with control-of-flow statements is advantageous for handling errors. The statement *IF @@ERROR <> 0 RETURN* exits if an error is returned.
@@IDENTITY	Saves the last-inserted IDENTITY value. The *@@IDENTITY* variable is updated specifically for each user when an INSERT or SELECT INTO statement or a bulk copy insertion into a table occurs.
@@NESTLEVEL	Specifies the nesting level of the current execution (initially 0). Each time a stored procedure calls another stored procedure, the nesting level is incremented. If the maximum of 16 is exceeded, the transaction is terminated.
@@ROWCOUNT	Specifies the number of rows affected by the last statement. This variable is set to 0 by any statement that doesn't return rows, such as an IF statement.
@@TRANCOUNT	Specifies the number of currently active transactions for the current user.

Invoking the TSQL Debugger from RDO Code

Now that you have a feel for how a stored procedure can be debugged interactively, let's try to do the same thing from Visual Basic RDO code. (This doesn't work from ODBCDirect code.) The TSQLD is tightly integrated with the UserConnection Designer. This means that you don't really have to do anything special besides setting the TSQLD option that says to step into your stored procedures as they are encountered in code. You can find the option on the Tools menu. You should have a T-SQL Debugging Options item on this menu if TSQLD is installed.

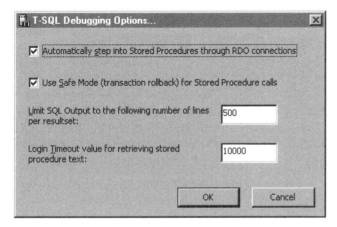

This dialog box informs Visual Basic to watch out for stored-procedure invocations so that if your code happens to trip a stored procedure, even when executing an Update method that invokes a trigger, the next screen you see (after a 10- to 30-second wait) is the TSQLD window, waiting for you to step through the code. You can also set the Safe Mode option that makes sure the operations you perform in the stored procedure are rolled back when you exit. There is also a cap to limit the number of rows sent back by the procedure and a cap on the time that the TSQLD waits while trying to get the SQL server to wake up and return status information. In this dialog box, the timeout limit is 10,000. However, 10,000 seconds seems like a *very* long time—that's about 2.8 hours, if the unit of measure is indeed seconds. (Actually, it's *milli*seconds, which puts the delay time at 10 seconds. Either delay should be long enough.)

Once you have selected the Automatically Step Into Stored Procedures Through RDO Connections check box and if you step into (F8) a line of code that executes an RDO method that invokes a stored procedure, the debugger automatically starts. You can then step through the stored procedure and continue debugging your Visual Basic code. You can also debug a stored procedure from within a Visual Basic UserConnection object if the need presents itself— just right-click on the Query object and select Debug Stored Procedure from the menu to start a debug session for the stored procedure in that query.

Debugging the TSQL Debugger

When something goes wrong with the TSQLD, the fault can often be found on the server end of the wire. Check the SQL Server and Windows NT event log. If SDI gets into trouble, it records its woes in the log in the application section. Use the Event Viewer to examine the log. You might also find reports from the Remote Automation components there because COM or DCOM might log events that can tell you what went wrong. Watch out for a few more hazards:

- If you are using TCP/IP, make sure that the two machines are on speaking terms. You can use the Ping application to test this interface. Just type this:

  `Ping servername`

  If this fails, there is no way that TSQLD can work.

- Make sure the file SDI.DLL resides in the same directory as SQLSERVR.EXE. This will be in the BINN subdirectory under the main SQL Server directory. The default is C:\MSSQL\BINN.

- Ensure that the Remote Procedure Call (RPC) services are started on your SQL server. You do this by opening the Control Panel on the Windows NT server, starting the Services application, and checking to be sure the Remote Procedure Call (RPC) Service and Remote Procedure Call Locator are running and set to start automatically. This should have been set up when the TSQLD was installed, but sometimes this can be turned off by those not familiar with what's needed and what's extra baggage.

- Ensure that SQL Server isn't set to log on using the system account. You do this by opening the Control Panel, starting the Services application, and double-clicking on the MSSQLServer service. If the service is set to run using the system account, change this so the server will log on to a specific account that is valid to the domain that you're in.

If debugging still fails, make sure that the SQL Server account has sufficient rights to launch an Automation server on the client machine. (If you don't have access to a domain controller, you might have to run the SQL server in console mode.)

- If you see COM error 80080005 in the event log, make sure that you didn't start Remote Automation (AUTMGR32) from the command prompt. AUTMGR32.EXE should be running *only* in the winstation of the account on which SQL Server logged in. Any other winstation will cause problems because it doesn't have sufficient permission to perform global operations. If this is the case, close down AUTMGR32.EXE via the Task Manager and let SDI.DLL and AUTPRX32.DLL load AUTMGR32 via COM.

- Make sure Remote Automation is successfully installed on the server *and* client machine if neither the client nor server have Distributed COM (DCOM) installed and loaded.

- If your client is running Windows NT version 4.0 or later, run DCOMCNFG and make sure that everyone has launch and access permission for VBSDICLI.EXE.

24

Chapter

Building
Result Sets
with RDO

So far, we've been touring the outskirts of the RDO interface, and so we haven't seen any real signs of how data is retrieved. But now that we know how to use RDO to get connected to SQL Server and how to create UserConnection objects, we're ready to take a leisurely ride through the streets and alleys of the model's data-fetching aspects. When we're done with this part of the tour, you will know how, when, and why to build a cursor—*and* when not to.

RDO cursors are created either by the cursor driver included with the ODBC driver manager or by the SQL Server driver itself, which is capable of creating and managing server-side cursors on SQL Server 6.0 and later versions. (Which means that if you access SQL Server 4.*x*, you can't use server-side cursors.) And with RDO 2.0, the Client Batch cursor library has been added to replace, or at least supplement, the ODBC cursor library. You can choose from four basic types of cursors that the OpenResultset method can create and manage using the rdoResultset object:

- Forward-only result sets

- Static cursors

- Keyset cursors

- Dynamic cursors

These cursor types were described in Chapter 5, in case you need to review their basic construction. If you decide that you need the functionality provided by a cursor, you can select a specific type of rdoResultset cursor by setting the RemoteData control's ResultsetType property or the *Type* argument of the OpenResultset method to one of the constants shown in *Figure 24-1.*

Figure 24-1
Types of RDO Cursors

Cursor Type	Constant
Forward-only	rdOpenForwardOnly
Static	rdOpenStatic
Keyset	rdOpenKeyset (default)
Dynamic	rdOpenDynamic

NOTE Be sure you understand that the forward-only, read-only, single-row (*RowsetSize=1*) result set isn't really a cursor at all. (I guess you could call it an *uncursor*.) All of the drivers support this form of data retrieval, since it's the simplest of the four to implement, but it's read-only when created by the ODBC driver library. Moreover, you can't move backward through the result set or even jump to the end with this form of data retrieval. This unique type of result set is created when you specify rdUseNone as the cursor type.

Each of these cursor types is implemented by the chosen cursor *driver* or, as it's sometimes called, the chosen cursor library. Not every cursor type can be created by every cursor library. *Figure 24-2* on page 431 is a capabilities chart that shows the options—basically, which type works with which driver. The RDO CursorDriver options are as follows:

- *rdUseODBC:* Forces use of the ODBC cursor library, which works against any version of Microsoft SQL Server, including SQL Server 6.*x*.

- *rdUseServer:* Forces use of the SQL Server 6.0 cursor driver, which is the only driver that supports server-side cursors.

- *rdUseClientBatch:* Uses the Client Batch client-side cursor library. For the most part, this library is intended to replace the ODBC library and should be used in its place wherever possible.

- *rdUseIfNeeded:* Lets RDO choose the type of cursor library—RDO always chooses server-side cursors if they are available. In most cases, this is the default type.

- *rdUseNone:* Sets up a "cursorless" result set. This forces forward-only, read-only, *RowsetSize=1* for all result sets.

Remember, we are talking about SQL Server here. Yes, there are ODBC drivers that can connect to other back-end systems—even to Jet. Do they work the same way as the SQL Server drivers? Nope. Are they similar? Yep. But don't take any cosmic leaps (based on your experience connecting to SQL Server) by trying to perform the same operations on every ODBC driver.

You choose the cursor *driver* by setting up the rdoEnvironment object before the rdoConnection object is made or RDO defaults to a chosen type—as when you create a stand-alone rdoConnection object. All operations under a single connection use the selected cursor driver. But as I have said on any number of occasions, *don't use a cursor unless you need its features.* If you simply want to fetch the data as quickly as possible, use something cheaper—and faster. To make this option easier, RDO 2.0 includes the rdUseNone option when creating rdoConnection objects.

NOTE The rdoPreparedStatement object has been replaced in RDO 2.0 by the rdoQuery object. The old rdoPreparedStatement is still there (although hidden) so that your old code works, but you should convert to the rdoQuery object.

You can choose from several Remote Data Objects to retrieve data from SQL Server base tables:

- *The rdoResultset object, RDO's basic cursor object.* Like the DAO Recordset object, the rdoResultset object can be used to manage any of the cursors or cursorless result sets. You create the rdoResultset object by using the OpenResultset method against the rdoConnection object or the rdoQuery object. Executing a method against the UserConnection object also exposes the LastQueryResults property, which points to an rdoResultset object. You can still use the rdoPreparedStatement statement in RDO 2.0, but it's now obsolete.

- *The rdoQuery object, a query definition similar to a DAO QueryDef.* This object doesn't persist after your application ends, however. You create the rdoQuery object by using the CreatePreparedStatement method against the rdoConnection object or indirectly by creating a User-Connection object. The rdoQuery object maps directly to the ODBC SQLPrepare function.

- *The UserConnection object.* This is a new object for RDO 2.0, which creates an rdoConnection object and one or more rdoQuery objects to expose stored procedures or user-written queries. Use the User-Connection Designer.

- *The rdoTable object, an addition to the RDO model.* This object permits you to expose all the rows of a chosen SQL Server table. The rdoTable object is simply a member of the rdoTables collection. You can create an rdoResultset object against the rdoTable object, but I wouldn't recommend it.

CAUTION
If you use the RemoteData control and don't specify a type of result set, the Remote-Data control creates a keyset-type rdoResultset object. With the OpenResultset method, the default type is now a forward-only result set.

The first three objects are fairly easy to understand and deal with. When you're working with data, the fourth object is about as useful as a set of snow skis on a beach in the Bahamas, but it's as vital as a good sunblock on the same beach when you're trying to map a table's schema. All of these objects are used, directly or indirectly, to access result set data. (The Value property of the Column object in the rdoColumns collection of the rdoResultset object contains the data from the SQL table in the query.) Since most of these properties are defaulted, you can easily reference the data once you build an rdoResultset object.

TIP Decide whether your query is going to be executed once and then forgotten, or whether it will be executed several times. If you plan to execute your query repeatedly, you need to use one of the techniques that uses stored procedures to execute the code. This saves having to recompile the code each time the query is run. As I've said before, you can execute stored procedures using a couple of techniques—using temporary or permanent stored procedures. Since the rdExecDirect option on the OpenResultset and Execute methods is now "on" by default, you don't need to specify it in code. The Prepared property also exposes this functionality when you define an rdoQuery object. These options instruct RDO to create a temporary stored procedure to execute your query.

Choosing a Cursor—or Not

The choice of cursor for your application can significantly affect performance and resource management. All four cursor types are implemented by the ODBC driver manager and the selected driver. There is nothing extra in the RDO interface (unless you count the new Client Batch cursor library as being part of RDO) that creates or manages these cursors; it just calls ODBC functions to set options and request result sets according to the methods you execute and the properties you set or examine. Unlike the Microsoft Jet database engine, which has its own cursor processor on top of the selected ODBC cursor library, the RDO interface and the ODBC cursor library don't always support updatable joins—especially for complex SQL products—so you shouldn't always expect to be able to update a cursor generated from a join or against a result set returned by a stored procedure that includes a join. Stored procedures that don't join two or more tables can be updatable, however. In general, only single-table queries are updatable, so you should plan on opening an additional connection to execute update statements. By using the Execute method right off the existing connection, the RDO interface handles all this for you—but only if your result set is fully populated. The rows you add to the database won't always appear in your cursor's membership, even if you do create an updatable cursor; that's the nature of some ODBC cursors.

That said, a number of factors should play a role in your choice. To start with, ask yourself a few questions, like those on the next page, about the design of your application and your intended use of cursors.

CAUTION
Some RDO cursors are populated automatically, so you have to be careful about how you describe result sets and about which cursor you choose for which job.

- *How many rows do you intend to access?* Do you need all the rows of a table, or just a selected few? If you expect to scale your application, it had better be the latter.

- *Can you afford to wait until the cursor is built,* or does the user object to staring at an hourglass pointer?

- *Do you have the necessary client or server resources* to store the cursor you are specifying?

- *How do you expect to navigate through the result set?* Do you need to move the current-row pointer randomly from point to point in the cursor, or do you need to move just once down through the rows?

- *How should cursor membership be determined?* Are you concerned with the changes you and others make to the rows included in the cursor?

- *How do you intend to update the data?* Do you need to update the data at all? Do you intend to update through the cursor, via the Execute method, or through a stored procedure?

- *How should the cursor be populated?* Will you need access to the rows before they are all populated?

The rdOpenForwardOnly-Type Resultset Object

A forward-only cursor fetches one or more rows of data—not just the keys as with a keyset or dynamic cursor. It supports no scrolling so that the data can be fetched more quickly. Only one row is exposed at a time from the RowsetSize set of rows. These rows are stored on the client or, if you opt for a server-side cursor, on the server. In addition, only the MoveNext method is supported—executing a MoveLast would simply flush the cursor, so it makes no sense. In most cases, you won't be able to use the RowCount property until you reach the last row in the result set: until then, it returns –1. You can, however, use the GetRows or GetClipString methods to stream data from rdoResultSet objects. Both these methods can dramatically improve result set fetch performance.

As you ought to know by now, I'm not a cursor man. I like to feel the wind in my face and see the data streaming by at the speed of light. With a read-only, forward-only, single-row result set, no cursor keyset is created and data values aren't updated as they change on the SQL server. The forward-only result set is so efficient that it's often faster to rebuild one than to create and maintain a keyset-type rdoResultset object. This type of "firehose" cursor is built when you choose rdUseNone as the cursor driver.

The rdOpenStatic-Type rdoResultset Object

Just as with a forward-only cursor, a static cursor contains the chosen data rows—not just the keys, as in a keyset or dynamic cursor. Unlike the forward-only cursor, a static cursor is fully scrollable. These rows are stored either on the client or, if you choose server-side cursors, on the server. The static-type rdoResultset object is similar to the Jet snapshot-type Recordset object, although a static cursor isn't necessarily read-only like a DAO/Jet snapshot. A static cursor's order and membership are frozen once it's populated, so the static cursor might not *appear* to change as rows are added. But even though a static result set seems not to be changing, it can actually move farther and farther away from reality as time goes on, as the underlying data is changed.

Data downloaded to the workstation is like raw chicken taken out of the refrigerator: after sitting out awhile on a warm kitchen counter, it's hardly worth consuming. In a multiuser database management system, static cursors are for static data: information that can sit out overnight without losing any of its accuracy.

Wait a minute. Why all these ambiguities—why is this not more definitive? Well, it turns out that the way each of the cursor drivers is implemented significantly impacts the membership and data validity properties. For example, the ODBC cursor library does *not* support updatable static cursors at all, but the Client Batch cursor library not only supports them, it keeps track of changes to membership made by the application. This means that depending on the cursor driver chosen, you might have to dramatically change the techniques you use when working with a cursor.

However, as a rule of thumb, don't use a static cursor for dynamic data. A list of valid state codes or other relatively unchanging foreign-key lookup values would be ideal for this type of cursor. (I usually populate a small ListBox control or a local array with values like these, so I generally use a forward-only result set for such values.)

The rdOpenKeyset-Type rdoResultset Object

The keyset cursor doesn't build a set of data rows but builds instead a fully scrollable set of pointers to the member rows. The keyset-type rdoResultset object is similar to the Jet dynaset-type Recordset object. A key is built and saved for each row in the result set and is stored either on the client workstation or on the server machine. As you access each row, the saved key is used to fetch the current data values from SQL Server data tables. In a keyset-driven cursor, membership is frozen once the keyset is fully populated. Therefore, additions or updates that affect membership might not be made part of the cursor until it's rebuilt.

With some cursor drivers, modifications or additions made directly to keyset cursors with the AddNew and Edit methods are included in the result set, but additions or modifications made with the Execute method don't affect the cursor; consult your server manual for details. To build a keyset-driven cursor, you must provide enough resources on the client or the server to hold the keys and a block of buffered data rows.

The rdOpenDynamic-Type rdoResultset Object

The dynamic-type rdoResultset object is identical to a keyset-driven cursor except, by definition, its membership is *not* frozen. Because the RDO interface checks constantly to see that all qualified rows are included in the cursor's membership, this type of cursor carries the largest overhead. A dynamic cursor may be faster to initiate than a keyset cursor, however, because the keyset cursor carries the overhead of building the initial keyset. After that, the dynamic cursor is likely to be the slowest to fetch and update data and to place the greatest load on the client, network, and server.

Building Cursorless Result Sets

When you specify the rdUseNone option as the cursor driver, RDO permits you to specify only a firehose cursor. You can specify this type of rdoResultset by setting the read-only, forward-only properties to True and setting the RowsetSize property to 1. The *Programming ODBC for SQL Server* manual in the SQL Server Books Online calls these *Type A cursors* and calls server-side cursors *Type B cursors*. Kyle Geiger's book *Inside ODBC* calls them *firehose cursors* and *badminton cursors*. Whatever name you use, the effect is the same—high-speed, nonscrolling, read-only result sets. To get a firehose cursor in RDO, you have to use the rdoQuery object for your query and set the RowsetSize property to 1 before calling OpenResultset, or simply use the rdUseNone option for your CursorDriver. If you change your program to use firehose cursors instead of ODBC Cursor Library cursors (both flavors of client-side cursors), my test shows you can fetch 500-row result sets approximately 2.5 times faster.

A couple more tidbits that can help you make the *right* cursor decision: For a singleton select from a stored procedure, it is even more efficient to use output parameters for the result column values than to open a firehose cursor and fetch a single-row result set. I found output parameters to be about 30 percent faster for a singleton select. (I'm not sure why this is so—it might be RDO, the ODBC driver, or the network efficiencies helping out, or all of these.) Second, I found that setting the MaxRows property of the rdoQuery object to 0 prior to calling OpenResultset saves an additional round-trip SET ROWCOUNT command being sent to the server.

Deciding Between Client-Side and Server-Side Cursors

An important aspect of keyset or dynamic cursors involves *where* the keyset is created. If you are connecting to SQL Server 6.*x*, you can specify that the cursor keyset be created and maintained on the server. If you use client-side cursors, supported on all versions of SQL Server, cursor keysets are downloaded to the workstation and stored in local memory. Server-side cursors expose a number of important benefits:

- *They support multiple active result sets on a single connection.* Client cursors can have only one active (unfetched) result set on a SQL Server connection.

- *They support more efficient updatability than client-side cursors.* This is because the server knows which tables and primary keys are involved, while a client cursor must figure this out in order to formulate SQL update statements.

- *They don't hold locks at the server on large unfetched result sets.* Client cursors hold share locks at the server until the result set is either fetched to the end or canceled. This is an especially serious problem if the application waits for user input before it finishes fetching—MSQuery does this. The user might go to lunch, holding the share locks for a long time and so preventing other users from updating their data. Some client-side cursor implementations (such as Jet) avoid this by fetching data automatically on a background thread, spooling the result set off into local memory or onto disk. This is OK as far as the server is concerned but can be a waste if you decide that you didn't really want all the millions of rows you asked for. RDO does no automatic background fetching—that's all up to your code.

In exchange for these benefits, server-side cursors incur some cost and have some limitations:

- *Opening a server-side cursor is more expensive.* Server-side cursors take longer to parse, compile, and execute, and they use more TempDB resources than just streaming a result set back to the client would. Not only that, but it appears that your query runs to completion and the cursor is fully populated *before* control is returned to your application. Keep this in mind when doing performance tests against unpopulated cursors, which amortize the population costs as the rows are fetched. The additional cost of a server-side cursor varies by query (as with single table versus join) and type of cursor (as with forward-only/ dynamic versus keyset versus static).

- *Fetching from a server-side cursor requires one round-trip from client to server to open the cursor, and one round-trip per RowsetSize rows.* (In ODBC terms, this is one round-trip per call to SQLExtendedFetch.) On the other hand, fetching data from a client-side cursor just moves rows from the local network buffers into local program memory. Requesting and receiving the result set is one round-trip to the server.

- *Server-side cursors can't be opened on some SQL batches or stored procedures,* such as those that return multiple result sets or involve conditional logic—not unless you disable the scrolling by using a forward-only, read-only, single-row cursor.

How do you know whether you are going to need the benefits of server-side cursors for a given result set? You probably know whether the result set needs to be updatable; if it does, a server-side cursor is usually best, although I'm told that RDO 2.0 has better updatability strategies on client cursors, so this trade-off may change. If you don't know how big the result set is going to be and aren't inclined to fetch the whole cursor (by means of a query tool like MSQuery), use a server-side cursor. If you know in advance that the result set is going to be small, use a firehose cursor and fetch all the result rows immediately into program variables. Many times you do know in advance that the result set is going to be exactly one row. In this case, you should definitely use a firehose cursor and fetch immediately after the execute.

As you can see, in *many* cases, using server-side cursors can improve performance. Consider, however, that the server must have the resources to store the cursor keyset. For example, if you build a cursor keyset that has 20 bytes per row and includes 200 rows, it requires about 4 KB of data space—only two data pages. This is not too bad, even if you have to multiply that figure by 100 users, when the data load becomes 400 KB. This is a manageable number as far as data space is concerned, although it might take up most of the data cache on a small system. But what if your typical 100-user cursor is 2000 rows? You now have 4 MB of space dedicated to the cursor keysets. That would exhaust your data cache completely, unless you tossed another 32 MB of RAM into the box.

What about CPU load? If you are using a P5 or P6 processor clocked at 100 MHz, you should have enough spare CPU ticks to handle the extra load, but you won't if you are running a low-powered server. Many of my tests have been done on my "po' folks" server running with 16 MB of RAM but dedicated to SQL Server (there is no UI). All these tests show the server-side cursors to be slower than workstation-based cursors—although not dramatically so. And consider that I have a 60-MHz P5 with 24 MB of RAM, which seems to be able to manage the keysets faster than the 486SX server. I also ran a number of similar tests on podium systems and found dramatically different results. Considering that these systems, used for demos at VBits and the like, are often 200-MHz P6 systems with 64 MB of RAM and a 16-MB RAM TempDB, you can see how the results would vary.

So why bother with server-side cursors at all? Well, in a *normal* installation, the P5 is the dedicated server and the 486SX (or less) is the workstation. The workstation often doesn't have the resources to build a local cursor. Server-side cursors give you the option of choosing where the keyset gets built. I'm still convinced that it's usually possible to create systems where server-side cursors can have a significantly positive impact on overall performance.

Tuning the Cursor Rowset Size

The RowsetSize property determines how big a bite the ODBC driver takes out of the data when it fetches rows. Instead of making a round-trip for a single row, the cursor library fetches RowsetSize rows and works on these rows in memory until your code steps outside of that subset by changing the position of the current-row pointer—as when you use the MoveNext, MoveLast, or AbsolutePosition properties. At that point, the ODBC driver goes out and fetches the next, previous, or selected RowsetSize rows. You can change the responsiveness of queries by bumping up the RowsetSize property, but remember that data kept on the workstation gets stale pretty fast.

TIP If RowsetSize is set to 1, you'll find it far easier to update records in the cursor without imposing exclusive locks on other pages. The default RowsetSize is 100 rows, which tends to span several (if not dozens of) pages.

We have also seen that by changing the RowsetSize to 1, we can *partially* disable the cursor processor. But if you don't set the forward-only and read-only options as well, you can create a fairly inefficient cursor—one that fetches a single row each time you position to a new row. But then again, you might need this strategy for some pessimistic locking situations.

The default RowsetSize in RDO is 100 when you use the server-side CursorDriver options, which always results in a Type B cursor. If you use the ODBC driver, the default RowsetSize in the ODBC driver is 1. As you can see, setting the rowset size has a dramatic effect on the behavior of the cursor you get back, but it was done that way for backward compatibility reasons back in the SQL Server 6.0 days and because the ODBC standard doesn't have an official way to distinguish between firehose and server-side cursors.

CAUTION

As you can see in the following tables, the RDO cursor types aren't all implemented in the same way. Different aspects of the cursors are enabled according to the driver chosen. For example, static cursors are updatable against the SQL Server 4.2 ODBC driver but not against the server-side cursor driver. If you choose a cursor type that the driver can't support, you get a trappable run-time error: 40002, Driver Not Capable.

Support for rdoResultset Cursors

Figure 24-2 summarizes the features and capabilities of the four types of rdoResultset cursors. In addition to the restrictions shown in the figure, we should note that not all SQL Server data sources support every type of cursor. In some cases, the ODBC cursor library, rdUseODBC, has to be used in lieu of a server-side cursor, rdUseServer. This need puts limits on the types of cursors supported by SQL Server data sources. *Figure 24-3* summarizes the types of cursors that are supported by several typical data sources and by the Remote-Data control. *Figure 24-4* on the next page summarizes the capabilities of cursor types according to drivers and options you're using.

Figure 24-2
Attributes of RDO Cursors

Attribute	Forward-Only	Static	Keyset	Dynamic
Updatable	Yes (*SS*) [1] No (*CL*)	No (*SS*) Yes (*CL*)	Yes	Yes
Membership	Fixed	Fixed	Fixed	Dynamic
Visibility	One row	Cursor	Cursor	Cursor
Movement of current row	Via MoveNext method only	Anywhere	Anywhere	Anywhere

1. *SS* indicates support by the SQL Server 6.*x* server-side library. *CL* indicates support by the ODBC cursor library.

Figure 24-3
Support for RDO Cursors by Typical Data Sources

Data Source	Forward-Only	Static	Keyset	Dynamic
SQL Server 4.2	Yes	Yes (*CL*) [1]	No	No
SQL Server 6.*x*	Yes	Yes	Yes	Yes
RemoteData control	No	Yes	Yes	No

1. *CL* indicates support by the ODBC cursor library.

Figure 24-4
Cursor Capability by Driver and Option

Driver	Cursor Type	Concurrency	Status	Updatable/ Populated?	
rdUseODBC	rdOpenForwardOnly	rdConcurReadOnly	OK	False	No
		rdConcurLock	* (3)		
		rdConcurRowver	* (3)		
		rdConcurValues	* (3)		
		rdConcurBatch	* (1)		
	rdOpenKeyset	rdConcurReadOnly	OK	False	Yes
		rdConcurLock	* (3)		
		rdConcurRowver	OK	True	Yes
		rdConcurValues	OK	True	Yes
		rdConcurBatch	* (1)		
	rdOpenDynamic	rdConcurReadOnly	OK	False	Yes
		rdConcurLock	* (3)		
		rdConcurRowver	OK	True	Yes
		rdConcurValues	OK	True	Yes
		rdConcurBatch	* (1)		
	rdOpenStatic	rdConcurReadOnly	OK	False	Yes
		rdConcurLock	* (3)		
		rdConcurRowver	OK	True	Yes
		rdConcurValues	OK	True	Yes
		rdConcurBatch	* (1)		
rdUseServer * (5)	rdOpenForwardOnly	rdConcurReadOnly	OK	False	No
		rdConcurLock	OK	True	No
		rdConcurRowver	OK	True	No
		rdConcurValues	OK	True	No
		rdConcurBatch	* (1)		
	rdOpenKeyset	rdConcurReadOnly	OK	False	Yes
		rdConcurLock	OK	True	Yes
		rdConcurRowver	OK	True	Yes
		rdConcurValues	OK	True	Yes
		rdConcurBatch	* (1)		
	rdOpenDynamic	rdConcurReadOnly	OK	False	No
		rdConcurLock	OK	True	No
		rdConcurRowver	OK	True	No

Driver	Cursor Type	Concurrency	Status	Updatable/	Populated?
		rdConcurValues	OK	True	No
		rdConcurBatch	* (1)		
	rdOpenStatic	rdConcurReadOnly	OK	False	Yes
		rdConcurLock	* (2)		
		rdConcurRowver	* (2)		
		rdConcurValues	* (2)		
		rdConcurBatch	* (1)		
	rdOpenForwardOnly	rdConcurReadOnly	OK	False	No
		rdConcurLock	OK	True	No
		rdConcurRowver	OK	True	No
		rdConcurValues	OK	True	No
		rdConcurBatch	OK	True	No
	rdOpenKeyset	rdConcurReadOnly	OK	False	Yes
		rdConcurLock	OK	True	Yes
		rdConcurRowver	OK	True	Yes
		rdConcurValues	OK	True	Yes
		rdConcurBatch	OK	True	Yes
	rdOpenDynamic	rdConcurReadOnly	OK	False	Yes
		rdConcurLock	OK	True	Yes
		rdConcurRowver	OK	True	Yes
		rdConcurValues	OK	True	Yes
		rdConcurBatch	OK	True	Yes
	rdOpenStatic	rdConcurReadOnly	OK	False	Yes
		rdConcurLock	OK	True	Yes
		rdConcurRowver	OK	True	Yes
		rdConcurValues	OK	True	Yes
		rdConcurBatch	OK	True	Yes
rdUseNone * (4)	rdOpenForwardOnly	rdConcurReadOnly	OK	False	No

* (1)—Only the rdUseClientBatch cursor driver can support.
* (2)—Driver not capable.
* (3)—Cursor library not capable.
* (4)—Cursor type should be rdOpenForwardOnly, rdConcurReadOnly, *RowsetSize=1*. This library doesn't permit any modes other than the one shown.
* (5)—rdUseIfNeeded always chooses rdUseServer, so their settings are the same.

Where Populated is Yes, the RowCount property returns the number of rows in the result set. Where Populated is No, the RowCount property returns –1 to indicate that the number of result set rows wasn't (yet) available.

To make things even more difficult, not all of the four cursors support all types of concurrency. Static server-side cursors with rdConcurLock aren't supported, for example, but forward-only server side cursors with rdConcurLock are. Confused? Me, too. And when you consider that driver types, cursor types, and locking options changed as the technology improved with RDO 2.0 or that they might be different if connections are made to a non-Microsoft SQL server (like a Sybase SQL server), you have a right to be confused. To generate *Figure 24-4,* I wrote a program that uses each type of cursor driver, cursor, and concurrency mechanism. The program is included on this guide's companion disc as one of the samples (Cursor Map.vbp); I encourage you to try it yourself. The figure was created against SQL Server 6.5. The query I used was a simple one-table fetch that returned about 585 rows from a table with a unique index.

Page Locking

RDO doesn't make any explicit locking or unlocking calls—all locking is handled by the ODBC driver and the remote query engine, if there is one. In any case, make sure you don't use rdConcurLock for your concurrency type—this tells the driver that you want it to lock *all* the rows in the current rowset (based on the current RowsetSize property setting). You'll find very few times that you'd really want to do this anyway. If you don't plan on updating the data, use rdConcurReadOnly for your locking type; if you want to edit the data, use something like rdConcurValues to do optimistic updates using old values of the columns. If you want some scrolling ability (MovePrevious), use a static cursor type (rdOpenStatic).

When you open an RDO cursor, SQL Server applies a share lock to all pages in the data set containing rows of the result set, as it also does with Jet cursors. If too many rows are locked, SQL Server escalates to table locks, and it can lock any number of tables if a query is complex enough. Only after the SQL server is convinced that the rows are no longer needed does it release the pages to other users. Regardless of the type of cursor you choose to open, you need to consider its impact on the SQL server and on other users who are sharing the data. Other users can read the rows while pages are locked, but no changes are permitted on these shared pages. It's important to practice safe sharing: move to the end of your cursor as quickly as possible. Either do it in the background, as the user peruses the first 20 rows or so, or execute a MoveLast method (if you can) before the user gets any rows at all. I prefer the latter technique. Although it can be slow, it's fairly simple to implement and it's generally foolproof.

If you choose a server-side cursor, the strategy is somewhat different. In this case, the type of lock chosen is held for the duration of the cursor. Fortunately, when you use SQL Server 6.*x*, you can specify a number of locking strategies right in the SELECT statement. That way, you can request dirty reads (except in some states in the South), where no locks of any kind are placed on the rows.

In any case, having to fall back on a MoveLast method is an expensive proposition if the cursor is too large. But you know better than to create a cursor with more than a couple of hundred rows—don't you?

By setting one of the four types of concurrency control options as the *LockType* argument of the OpenResultset method, you can specify how and when SQL Server pages are locked as the rows in the rdoResultset object are edited and updated. If you don't specify a lock type, rdConcurReadOnly is assumed; use one of the Integer constants shown in **Figure 24-5** to define the lock type of the new rdoResultset object.

Remember that users are the slowest component of the system. Never, never depend on users to move quickly through the data on their own. That's like depending on the cable TV guy to arrive and finish his work before you have to leave the house and pick up the kids from school.

Figure 24-5
Integer Constants for Setting the *LockType* Argument

Lock Type	Concurrency Option
rdConcurBatch	Optimistic concurrency with Client Batch cursors
rdConcurReadOnly	Read-only (default)
rdConcurLock	Pessimistic concurrency
rdConcurRowver	Optimistic concurrency based on a TimeStamp column
rdConcurValues	Optimistic concurrency based on row values

The RDO interface uses the ODBC SQLSetScrollOptions function to set values for the various types of concurrency management, but these are *not* the same strategies as those you might have seen before in DAO/Jet and other relational systems. They are, however, identical to the locking strategies used in other ODBC API implementations. Note that DAO/Jet does *not* support pessimistic concurrency because it's so different from the DAO/Jet pessimistic approach.

In RDO (and ODBC API) *pessimistic* locking, the pages containing the rows in the rowset are locked exclusively and are unavailable to other users as soon as you create the cursor. These locks aren't imposed when the Edit or AddNew method is used, to be released when the Update method is executed—instead, they are imposed when the cursor is first opened and remain in place as long as the cursor is open. This is very different from the way that Jet/DAO manages pessimistic locking: as you reposition the current row to various points within the result set, the locks propagate with the rowset window. (Remember that the RowsetSize property determines the size of the rowset.) Pessimistic locking is the easier type to code but can be the more demanding of system resources because it's capable of locking down one or more pages for considerable (infinite) lengths of time. If you *must* use pessimistic locking, be sure to reduce the RowsetSize property to lock only a single page. This might mean 5, 25, or 250 rows, depending on how many rows fit on a data page.

In *optimistic* locking, the page containing the row being edited is also locked exclusively but is unavailable to other users only while the Update method is being executed. This is very similar to the DAO/Jet approach. Optimistic locking assumes that the other users aren't likely to be editing the row being updated. It also requires more complex error management, since your code must be prepared for update failures caused by changes made to the record after the Edit mode is entered.

The ODBC driver detects changes on the basis of either a TimeStamp column or a comparison between the actual data values on the old row before editing and the existing SQL Server row. Your error-recovery routine must decide what to do with the three different rows: the unedited version and the two changed versions (the workstation version and the server version).

Disconnecting rdoResultset Objects

When stand-alone objects were added to RDO 2.0, another unique RDO feature was added: the ability to "dissociate" the rdoConnection object from an rdoResultset object—as long as it was created with the Client Batch cursor library. This means that you can do the following:

1. Open a connection to SQL Server using a stand-alone rdoConnection object, the UserConnection object, or the OpenConnection method— just remember to use the rdUseClientBatch cursor library.

2. Create a static updatable rdoResultset using the OpenResultset method with the rdConcurBatch option.

3. Set the rdoResultset object's ActiveConnection to Nothing. This dissociates the rdoResultset from the connection used to create it but, unlike the Close method, doesn't destroy the object.

4. At this point, you can continue to extract data from the rdoResultset and even make changes—adding, deleting, or changing existing rows. The Client Batch cursor library maintains the current state in local RAM (and disk) and records all of the changes in its own log.

5. When you are ready, you can associate the rdoResultset to a valid rdoConnection object and use the BatchUpdate method to post the changes made to the rdoResultset to the database. If a collision occurs, RDO and the Client Batch cursor library create an array of bookmarks pointing to the rows in the rdoResultset that didn't update for whatever reason.

One of the first questions you might want to ask is, "Can I just create a stand-alone rdoResultset and associate it with an rdo-Connection later?" Nope, sorry, this feature isn't implemented. It was considered but didn't make the final cut. It is implemented in ADO.

Specifying the Source of the Result Set

Every rdoResultset object you create must have a SQL statement behind it somewhere. This SQL statement is written either in TSQL or in ODBC SQL. Basically, it tells the SQL server which rows from which tables should be included in the result set. You pass this SQL statement either in the *Source* argument of the OpenResultset method or in the rdoQuery from which the rdoResultset is created.

Using an ODBC-syntax SQL statement is the easiest. RDO expects to see an ODBC-syntax SQL statement anyway, so you don't really need to set any other options in this case.

Using a TSQL-syntax SQL statement is also fairly easy, but you have to make sure that the ODBC driver doesn't choke on the statement when it creates a temporary stored procedure to execute the query. To make sure, set the SQLExecDirect option or the Prepared property. These options tell the ODBC driver to forego the creation of a temporary stored procedure. While this is a NOOP whenever SQL Server discovers you are simply executing a stored procedure, there are any number of situations where you don't want the extra overhead of creating a stored procedure to perform a one-of-a-kind operation. Consider, however, that if you are rolling your own queries for repetitive operations, it's often much more efficient to go ahead and create a parameter query, with an associated temporary stored procedure to do the job. And RDO can do virtually all of the work for you, if you give it half a chance.

Using the name of a stored procedure that returns rows is also fairly easy. If the RDO interface can't figure out that the *Source* argument is one of the other options, it assumes that it's a stored procedure. In RDO 1.0, when you execute a stored procedure, you should use the ODBC Call syntax, since it helps the RDO interface and the ODBC driver execute the stored procedure more efficiently. But in RDO 2.0, you should use the UserConnection object to expose your stored procedures as methods. I talked about the UserConnection Designer, which is used to build custom UserConnection objects, in Chapter 22, in case you missed it. You can still use the ODBC call syntax if you want to, but it's like using that old country road to cross the backcountry when a new freeway gets you there four hours sooner. I'll also talk about building parameter queries a little later.

Referencing the rdoQuery object by its name is a technique I don't usually go for, since I use the OpenResultset method off the rdoQuery when I want to reference an rdoQuery. But this is also cool, and it does the same thing. In this case, the SQL statement is a property of the rdoQuery. But as I said earlier, this is old technology and should be replaced with the User-Connection object.

Using the name of a SQL Server table is a little tricky—and mostly pointless. Keep in mind that if you're manipulating tables directly, you could be building in limits to scalability. It seems that the RDO interface knows nothing about the schema of your database and will figure that this string (which you know is a table name) is the name of a stored procedure. To get the RDO interface to recognize your table names, you first have to populate the rdoTables collection. To do this, simply execute an rdoTables.Refresh method or reference one of its members by its ordinal number. For example, referencing rdoTables(0) will populate the entire collection. Of course, this means an overhead hit while the RDO interface queries the SQL server for the names of the tables, and so forth. And now that you've gone to the trouble of getting *all* the database table names through a separate query, your only option is to get *all* the rows—not so clever, if there are more than a few. You might as well just code *Select * from \<table\>*.

CAUTION

If users enter their own SQL syntax and you just pass it up to SQL Server for execution, that can really put the brakes on your application—and compromise system security. What happens when someone types *Drop Table Customers*? All he wanted to do was find the customers who bought drop-leaf tables....

Managing Asynchronous Operations

Among the more powerful features of the RDO programming model is its ability to open connections and execute, populate, and rebuild queries asynchronously. Asynchronous operations, you will recall, permit you to start an RDO operation without having to pass control to the RDO interface while you wait for the operation to complete. Instead, you can pass control back to your application, to the line of code directly after the asynchronous operation. In the case of the OpenResultset method, asynchronously means that the rdoResultset object isn't all there yet. As a matter of fact, the only things working are the StillExecuting property and the Close and Cancel methods. The StillExecuting property remains True until the first row of data has returned. Once StillExecuting changes to False, the rest of the rdoResultset properties and methods are activated. If you decide to give up waiting, you can simply use the Close or Cancel methods to stop the operation. To turn on asynchronous operations, set the rdAsyncEnable option when you use the OpenResultset method. If you choose to use the StillExecuting property to wait for an asynchronous operation to complete, you need to periodically poll the StillExecuting or StillConnecting property and then execute DoEvents to pass control back to Windows and Visual Basic to permit other portions of your application to execute. For example, the following code creates an rdoResultset asynchronously and polls until it is open.

```
Set rs = CnMyConnection.OpenResultset ( _
    name:= "Select * From Authors Where Year_Born = 1947", _
    options:= rdAsyncEnable)
While rs.StillExecuting
    DoEvents
Loop
```

Actually, polling this often won't make things run any faster because the real polling is being done by the ODBC driver. You can adjust the frequency of ODBC's polling by changing the AsyncCheckInterval property of the rdoConnection object. Polling too frequently adversely affects system performance and too infrequently results in your application not being notified immediately that the query has completed.

If you choose to stop waiting for an asynchronous operation to complete, you can execute the Cancel or Close methods, but this might not be such a great idea if you are in the middle of an Update or other data modification operation. Keep in mind that, with RDO 2.0, you don't have to poll at all—you can use RDO events to determine when your asynchronous operations are complete.

RDO 2.0 Asynchronous Enhancements

RDO 2.0 brings a new depth and dimension to asynchronous operations. First, asynchronous operations have been expanded to include the following methods:

- *OpenConnection and EstablishConnection:* to deal with more complex connections that don't open immediately or to use when you want to overlap processing with the connection operation. For example, you can finish painting the initial forms while the connection is opening.

- *OpenResultset:* as I've mentioned, this method can be used to start the creation of an rdoResultset while you continue other work—perhaps preparing the form to display the pending contents.

- *Requery:* when you reexecute a query, you're essentially repeating the process used to build it in the first place.

- *MoveLast:* to fully populate a result set, this method can also take quite a bit of time to execute. Using the asynchronous option, you can continue other work while the rows are fetched.

- *Execute:* because many of the queries we execute are action queries, including Update and Delete operations that can span many rows, using the asynchronous option means that users are no longer blocked while the operation progresses.

These additions mean that virtually all aspects of result set management can be executed asynchronously. It remains true that the MoveNext, MovePrevious, and MoveFirst methods do *not* support asynchronous operations, and, yes, these can take quite a bit of time to execute for complex result sets. Perhaps these will be added at a later time.

RDO 2.0 Events

RDO 2.0 has also implemented event-driven programming. This means that both asynchronous and synchronous (nonasynchronous) operations can be managed using a bevy of events. You can still use the StillConnecting and StillExecuting properties, but if you code an event handler for the Connected and QueryComplete events, you have no need of them. The real benefit here is that you don't have to use the DoEvents operator.

Using events to handle asynchronous operations makes a lot more sense. These are listed in *Figure 24-6* on the next page. Let's take a closer look at the events associated with creating result sets. Some of the most important events are on the rdoResultset object's parent rdoConnection object, because these events fire for *all* result sets created on the connection.

Every time the use of DoEvents is mentioned in front of one of the Visual Basic developers, a strange look comes over the developer's face—as if he had just bitten a lemon. Apparently, DoEvents exposes your application and Visual Basic to a number of potential problems.

Figure 24-6
rdoConnection Object Asynchronous Query Events

Event	Fires
QueryComplete	After a query completes—successfully or not.
QueryTimeout	When the QueryTimeout time has elapsed and the query hasn't yet completed.
WillExecute	Before the query is run. This allows the developer to prohibit the query from running or to make last-minute adjustments to the SQL.

A number of events fire against specific rdoConnection objects as well. (See *Figure 24-7*.) These are used to track when the rdoResultset is associated or dissociated from its parent rdoConnection and as your code traverses from one result set to another or from one row to another.

Figure 24-7
rdoResultset Object Asynchronous Events

Event	Fires
Associate	After a new connection is associated with the object.
Dissociate	After the connection is set to Nothing.
ResultsChange	After current rowset is changed (multiple result sets).
RowCurrencyChange	After the current-row pointer has changed. This tracks the AbsolutePosition property. This can fire on an insert, delete, or update as the current row gets changed.
RowStatusChange	After the state of the current row has changed from unmodified to modified or to deleted (due to an edit, delete, or insert). Basically, this event tracks the rdoColumn Status property.
WillAssociate	Before a new connection is associated with the object—developer can override or cancel the operation.
WillDissociate	Before the connection is set to Nothing—developer can override or cancel the operation.
WillUpdateRows	Before an update to the server occurs—developer can override or cancel the operation.

In the next chapter, we'll see how to temporarily disconnect (or dissociate) an rdoResultset from its connection. This doesn't destroy the rdoResultset *if* it is created with the Client Batch cursor library. This means that you can create a cursor, dissociate it from its connection, perform operations on it, associate it with an active rdoConnection object, and execute a BatchUpdate operation on it. Four separate events relate to this technique, as shown in *Figure 24-7.*

A couple of events can also be exposed on selected rdoColumn objects, as you can see in *Figure 24-8.* These fire both before and after the column data has changed. To verify the column's data, you can examine the current state of the rdoColumn object's data by examining the Value property. While it's possible to change the Value property in the WillChangeData event procedure or even cancel the pending operation, the data has already been committed once the DataChanged event has fired.

Figure 24-8
rdoColumn Object Asynchronous Events

Event	Fires
DataChanged	When the value of the column has changed.
WillChangeData	Before data is changed in the column. This allows the developer to cancel.

Performance Tuning rdoResultset Operations

The following sections highlight a few performance tips and techniques as passed down from the developers both here at Microsoft and in the field.

Managing Temporary Stored Procedures

A rather significant change has been made to RDO 2.0 in the way that the rdExecDirect option is used. For one thing, it's now "on" by default. If you have never heard of this option, don't feel bad. It didn't make it into the printed documentation. Basically, the rdExecDirect option bit is used to tell RDO whether it should have ODBC create a temporary stored procedure to execute your query or, if the option is set, to execute the statement directly. Before the ODBC driver sends a SQL statement out to be executed, RDO checks this option (and the Prepared property) to determine whether it should have ODBC create one or more temporary stored procedures on the SQL server—unless you are executing a stored procedure in the first place, in which case it simply executes the procedure. These temporary procedures contain the SQL statement specified in the rdoQuery object or in the OpenResultset method and are designed to accept any parameters that might be specified for the statement.

This means that if you have code that *won't* work with the rdExecDirect option, you have to take steps to turn it off. When you execute the Open-Resultset or Execute methods or set the Option property of the RemoteData control, the rules used internally by RDO to enable or disable the rdExecDirect option are listed at the top of the next page.

- *If your code supplies an option value* (as either an integer or a long), RDO accepts this as a mask for the option bits. That is, if the bit is set, the option selected is enabled.

- *If your code does* not *supply an option value,* rdExecDirect is assumed enabled by default.

- *If your code supplies a bogus value,* rdExecDirect is assumed enabled by default—no error is generated.

However, the rdExecDirect option is *not* set by default on the rdoQuery object, and the Prepared property *does* default to True—so unless you specify otherwise, RDO *will* create a stored procedure to execute your query. So in cases where your code *can't* run with the rdExecDirect option, you have to turn it off by passing 0 as the option or choose one of the other options.

In SQL Server 6.*x*, these procedures are created in TempDB space. In SQL Server 4.*x*, they are created in the current database. In some cases, several stored procedures can be created for a single statement. Generally, these procedures aren't released until you close the connection or end the application. Ending the application in Design mode doesn't necessarily clear these statements; only ending Visual Basic or your compiled EXE flushes the temporary procedures. If the ODBC driver doesn't get a chance to clear these out, they are orphaned—forever. On SQL Server 4.*x* systems, they can be quite a nuisance. On SQL Server 6.*x* systems, they're dropped as soon as the hStmt that created them is closed. To avoid the creation of these procedures in the first place, specify the rdExecDirect option when you use the OpenResultset or Execute method:

```
Set rs = cn.OpenResultset("Select * from Authors", _
    rdOpenStatic, rdConcurValues, rdExecDirect)
```

> **TIP** When you use the rdExecDirect option, the ODBC interface doesn't create a temporary procedure that is then used to run the SQL statement. This can save some time—but only if the statement is used infrequently. For example, if the rdExecDirect option is used with a query that is executed only once, your application's performance can be improved. If your queries can be worded to accept parameters, however, it is better to let temporary stored procedures take up some of the preprocessing that must be done whenever a new query is executed.

In RDO 2.0, the default for OpenResultset is rdExecDirect, but you can also set the Prepared property on an rdoQuery or UserConnection object. This indicates that the query is to be prepared before execution.

Using the OpenResultset Options

The OpenResultset method was originally created with only a single option: rdAsyncEnable. Just before RDO shipped, the team discovered that without the rdExecDirect option, users were going to be stuck with a lot of needlessly prepared

SQL statements. It seems that a couple of last-minute enhancements have been added to RDO 2.0 as well—one of which forced the rdExecDirect option on by default. Let's take a look at each of the *Options* arguments listed in **Figure 24-9.** Note that these are binary values, so you can use them in any combination (that makes sense) by adding/ANDing their values together:

Figure 24-9
OpenResultset Options

Option	Value	Used to
rdAsyncEnable	32 (&H20)	Enable asynchronous operations.
rdExecDirect	64 (&H40)	Bypass creation of a stored procedure to execute the query by using SQLExecDirect instead of SQLPrepare and SQLExecute. See the Prepared property, as it provides similar functionality. This option is on by default, so it must be specifically disabled (see text). Pass 0 for *Options* if you wish to prepare the query (disable rdExecDirect).
rdFetchLongColumns	128 (&H80)	If set, the Client Batch cursor library fetches BLOB data along with the other columns instead of deferring this operation until the BLOB column is referenced. This might be needed if you can't scroll back to the row later to get the data—as in a forward-only cursor or after the connection has been dissociated.
rdBackgroundFetch	256 (&H100)	Create a separate thread to complete result set population for Client Batch cursor library result sets. This can help alleviate nagging locking problems on larger result sets.

NOTE If you supply *any* of these options and you want to use rdExecDirect, you *must* include the rdExecDirect option in the list of options you choose. If you don't, rdExecDirect will be disabled and your statement *will* be prepared.

Let's look a little more closely at the two newest options because they didn't make it into the documentation. Both these options enable features on the new Client Batch cursor library—and don't apply to the other libraries.

rdFetchLongColumns

If specified, the RDO client cursor fetches BLOB (Binary Large Object) data, together with fixed-length data, as part of the initial population of static cursors. BLOB data here refers to the ODBC data types LONGVARCHAR and LONGVARBINARY, which, for Client Batch cursors, are temporarily stored in a separate file. The advantage to you is that you download all the data that you decide you need up front. In addition, you don't need update properties on the cursor. The drawbacks are that your fetch time is longer and you might fill your disk with data you'll never use.

By default, Client Batch cursors don't fetch BLOB data until specifically referenced. In order to fetch BLOB values as needed, the cursor needs a primary key and the SourceTable and SourceColumn properties must be filled in for the BLOB field. The fetch requires one trip to the server for each BLOB value and, for SQL Server, can be performed only after the cursor has been fully populated. This is due to the limitation of a single pending result set per connection.

rdBackgroundFetch

If specified, the Client Batch cursor library uses a second (background) thread to fetch the data. The advantage is that all data is eventually fetched, regardless of the actual usage of the client cursor. Because client cursors use ODBC firehose cursors to fetch data, this background fetch option guarantees for SQL Server that all the data is eventually fetched and no locks will be held on the server. The disadvantage of background fetching, as opposed to the default "fetch as needed", is that you lose control over the fetch process, and the fetched data might unnecessarily fill all available disk space. The Cancel and Move methods are synchronized with the background fetch, as expected.

The rdoResultset Object

The rdoResultset object is RDO's one and only interface to the result sets you create—be they cursors of one kind or another or simple cursorless sets of rows. You can create rdoResultset objects in a number of ways, including these:

- *Using the OpenResultset method off the rdoConnection object.* This technique is used to pass hard-coded SQL statements to the server for execution—especially those that you don't intend to execute more than once or those that don't have parameters. This method forces the RowsetSize to 100 and doesn't process parameter markers (?) in the SQL statement.

- *Using the OpenResultset method off the rdoQuery object.* This technique is used to execute parameter queries or stored procedures—especially where you need to specify additional limitations on the operation.

- *Using methods of UserConnection objects that expose queries as methods.* The UserConnection object returns a LastQueryResults property that points to an rdoResultset object. This technique is used to construct prefabricated queries that can be exposed and executed using far less code and that can be maintained independently of other code.

The following sections examine the inner workings of the rdoResultset object and how to work with its properties, methods, and events.

RDO 2.0 Collection Management

RDO 2.0 fundamentally changes the way that the rdoResultsets and rdo-Connections collections are managed. In RDO 1.0, when you executed the following code, you ended up with two separate rdoResultset objects in the rdoResultsets collection:

```
Dim cn as rdoConnection
Dim en as rdoEnvironment
Dim rs as rdoResultset
Set en = rdoEngine.rdoEnvironments(0)
Set cn = en.OpenConnection("MyDSN",rdDriverNoPrompt, _
    False, "UID=;PWD=;Database=Pubs")
Set rs = cn.OpenResultset("Select * from Authors")
Set rs = cn.OpenResultset("Select * from Titles")
```

One of these rdoResultset objects would be established against the *Authors* table, while the other would be established against the *Titles* table. The *rs* variable would address the second rdoResultset object.

But RDO 2.0 is different. When the example code just shown is executed in RDO 2.0, only *one* rdoResultset object remains in the rdoResultsets collection—but the variable *cn* points to the *Titles* rdoResultset, the last result set created against the variable. While this new technique for handling rdoResultset (and rdoConnection) objects and collections is different from earlier RDO versions, it now conforms to the way that collections are managed in DAO and it should result in fewer memory leaks. If you don't want to lose an existing rdoResultset as assigned to a variable, you need to use the OpenResultset method against a separate variable.

NOTE If you create an rdoResultset object and then use this new object to set the RemoteData control's Resultset property, the ResultsetType property of the RemoteData control is set to the Type property of the new rdoResultset object.

Exploring rdoResultset Methods and Properties

You can use the methods and properties of the rdoResultset object to manipulate data and navigate the rows of a result set. For example, you can perform the following actions.

CAUTION
On SQL Server 6.*x* systems, an hStmt is created by the ODBC driver when an rdo-Resultset object is created. If the client application's system is then hit by a beer truck, which breaks your connection and kills your application, any remaining temporary procedures stored in TempDB space are also dropped.

- *Use the ActiveConnection property* to determine the rdoConnection used to build, refresh, or update the result set. This property can be set to Nothing to dissociate the rdoResultset object from its connection and can be set back to a valid rdoConnection object as needed to requery, refresh, or execute additional queries.

- *Use the Status property* to determine whether the current row has been changed since the result set was first built. This property is also set when RDO performs an update on the row using either the Update or BatchUpdate methods.

- *Use the BatchCollisionRows and BatchCollisionCount properties* to help manage collisions that occur when you use the BatchUpdate method.

- *Use the UpdateCriteria and UpdateOperation properties* to determine how the BatchUpdate method builds its update statements.

- *Use the BatchSize property and the BatchUpdate and Resync methods* with batch mode operations. All of these batch properties and methods are reviewed in Chapter 25.

- *Use the RowCount property* to determine how many rows were returned by the query. This property isn't valid until the result set has been fully populated, so behind the scenes, RDO executes a MoveLast for you when RowCount is referenced—at least on those rdoResultset objects that support it. If you create a forward-only result set, this is a NOOP, so RowCount won't be valid (and returns a –1) until you reach EOF.

- *Use the GetClipString property* to fetch *n* rows of an rdoResultset into a delimited string. This can make filling a grid control a snap. Actually, any control that accepts a delimited string or supports the Clip method can accept the string generated by this method.

- *Use the Type property* to indicate the type of rdoResultset object created. For an rdoTable object, the Type property indicates the type of SQL Server table.

- *Use the Updatable property* to see whether you can change the rdo-Resultset rows. There are reasons why the Updatable property is set to True when the rdoResultset object is *not* updatable—but those are ODBC shortcomings. For example, sometimes when you create an rdoResultset object from a SQL join, the result might not be updatable. While you used to be able to update similar queries with DAO/Jet, you might not be able to do it with RDO. You can always resort to a SQL UPDATE statement, but that might require another connection.

- *Use the EditMode property* to determine whether the AddNew or Edit methods have been invoked against this rdoResultset object.

- *Use the BOF and EOF properties* to see whether the current-row pointer is positioned beyond either end of the rdoResultset object. When you move through the rows in the result set one by one, you can safely loop until EOF changes to True, but once either BOF or EOF is true, there is *no* current row, so you must reposition the current-row pointer to a valid row.

- *Use the Move, MoveNext, MovePrevious, MoveFirst, and MoveLast methods* to reposition the current row. These repositioning methods work in all but forward-only rdoResultset objects, where *only* the MoveNext method can be used.

- *Use the PercentPosition property* to indicate or change the approximate position of the current row in an rdoResultset object. If you use the PercentPosition property *before* fully populating the rdoResultset object, the amount of movement is relative to the number of rows accessed, as indicated by the RowCount property. This property can be handy when you're working with scroll bars on result set windows. Again, this property works only against scrollable result sets.

- *Use the AbsolutePosition property* to position the current-row pointer to a specific row on the basis of the row's ordinal position in a keyset, dynamic, or static-type rdoResultset object. You can also determine the current row number by checking the AbsolutePosition property setting. Note that this property might not be particularly accurate. For example, with one row in the result set, repositioning the current-row pointer can make the AbsolutePosition property return a value of 2. The AbsolutePosition property isn't available on forward-only–type rdoResultset objects. The AbsolutePosition property can also be used to position deleted rows in the result set. Unlike the MoveNext or other Move methods, it doesn't step over deleted rows. This property works only against scrollable result sets.

- *Use the Bookmark property,* which contains a pointer to the current row and can be set to the bookmark of any other row in the rdoResultset object. This action immediately moves the current record pointer to that row. Again, this property works only against scrollable result sets.

- *Use the Bookmarkable and Transactions properties* to determine whether the rdoResultset object supports bookmarks or transactions.

- *Avoid the Restartable property;* it's really a degenerate vestige of its DAO/Jet cousin. As such, it shouldn't be depended on to determine the restartability of any query.

- *Use the LastModified property* to return the bookmark for the last row changed for *some* of the cursors—those that add new rows to the keyset. Let's look at the individual cursor types one by one:

  - Keyset server-side cursors add the new row to the cursor membership, so you should be able to use LastModified to arrive at the position of that row.

CAUTION

Using the PercentPosition property to move the current row to a specific row in an rdoResultset object isn't recommended. The Bookmark property or AbsolutePosition property would be better suited to this task.

CAUTION

The AbsolutePosition property isn't intended to be used as a surrogate row number, and there's no guarantee that a row will have the same absolute position when the rdoResultset is re-created. That's guaranteed only when the rdoResultset is created with a SQL statement using an ORDER BY clause—and even then, if a member is added or removed, the ordinal numbers are completely different. Bookmarks are still the best way to retain and return to a given position.

- Static cursors on ODBC client cursors don't add the row to the membership; thus the value is undefined if this is the first edit, or it should be the bookmark for the last updated row if there were updates before the AddNew method. Server-side static cursors are read-only, so this property doesn't apply.

- Dynamic and forward-only cursors never support bookmarks (Bookmarkable returns False), so the value of LastModified is irrelevant.

- For Client Batch static cursors, newly added rows *do* get added to the membership, so the LastModified property should contain a bookmark to that newly added row.

- *Use the LockEdits property* to check the type of locking used for updating the rdoResultset. This property checks the ODBC SQLSetScrollOptions function to determine how concurrency control is carried out.

- *Use the AddNew, Edit, Update, and Delete methods* to add new rows or otherwise modify updatable rdoResultset objects. (To cancel a pending edit, you can use the CancelUpdate method.) These methods work pretty much the way the corresponding DAO methods do.

- *Use the Requery method* to restart the query used to create an rdoResultset object. This method can also be used to reexecute an rdoQuery query.

- *Use the MoreResults method* to complete processing of the current rdoResultset object and begin processing the next result set generated from a query.

- *Use the Cancel or Close method* to terminate processing of an rdoResultset object query.

Managing rdoResultset Events

RDO 2.0 exposed a comprehensive set of events to help manage rdoResultset objects. These events fire for both asynchronous *and* synchronous operations and for a number of other operations including many batch mode tasks:

- *The WillDissociate and Dissociate events* fire when the ActiveConnection property is dissociated with its connection.

- *The WillAssociate and Associate events* fire when you reassociate the ActiveConnection property with a connection.

- *The RowStatusChange event* fires when the Status property changes. Examples of such changes are when you use the Edit or AddNew method followed by the Update method or the Delete method.

- *The RowCurrencyChange event* fires when the current-row pointer is moved. This can be caused by an AddNew method or any other move method that changes the current-row pointer.

Only the WillAssociate and WillDissociate events support the *Cancel* argument, which can be set to True to derail the operation in progress. I talk about all of the batch events in Chapter 25.

Some of the events you would expect to be exposed on the rdoResultset aren't. For example, I first expected the QueryComplete and QueryTimeout events to be handled on a rdoResultset basis—they're not. These events are synced to the rdoConnection object where the event handler is passed a pointer to the rdoQuery that caused the event, along with an *ErrorOccurred* Boolean value.

Handling Query-Related rdoConnection Events

The rdoConnection object is also the sync point for any queries executed against it. These events aren't exposed on the individual rdoQuery objects or even on the rdoResultset object cursors where you might expect them. Here is a brief description of each of these events:

- *QueryComplete:* This event occurs after the query of an rdoResultset returns the *first* result set, so you can use this event as a notification that the result set is ready for processing or that an error occurred while processing the query. The QueryComplete event should be used instead of polling the StillExecuting property to test for completion of OpenResultset or Execute method queries. This event returns an *ErrorOccurred* Boolean value that indicates whether there was an error while the query was executing. If this flag is True, you should check the rdoErrors collection for more information.

- *QueryTimeout:* Occurs when the query execution time has exceeded the value set in the QueryTimeout property—in other words, the query took longer to execute than expected. Unlike other interfaces (except VBSQL), RDO can continue processing the query if you return False in the *Cancel* argument. In this case, the query continues for another *n* seconds as determined by the QueryTimeout property. You can't change the timeout value after the query has started. If left alone or set to True, the Cancel property tells RDO to give up waiting for the query to complete. You can use this event to display a message box to users, asking them if they want to cancel their query or continue to wait another *n* seconds.

- *WillExecute:* This event is fired before the execution of any query. You can trap this event to disallow the execution of certain queries or to make last-minute adjustments to the rdoQuery object's SQL string. The *Cancel* argument allows you to disallow the query—just set it to True and RDO generates a trappable error indicating that the query was canceled. For example, you can prescreen the query to make sure the WHERE clause doesn't contain a prohibited operation. Thus, by setting the *Cancel* argument to True, you can prohibit users from executing damaging DML or DDL queries.

These events are fired for *all* queries executed on each rdoConnection—that is, any rdoConnection declared using the WithEvents syntax. This includes both asynchronous and synchronous queries and includes those queries executed via the OpenResultset or Execute methods as well as those executed from an associated rdoQuery object. The *Query* argument is an object reference indicating which query was executed and caused the event. Using this argument, you can write a single event handler for all queries on the connection but still customize the handler for specific queries. When executing queries against the rdoConnection object itself, RDO creates an rdoQuery object internally and a reference to this internal rdoQuery is passed as the *Query* argument.

Managing rdoResultsets

When you create an rdoResultset object, the current-row pointer is initially positioned to the first row (if there are any rows) of the result set. The RowCount property isn't applicable to dynamic cursors, in which the number of rows can change, or to forward-only result sets that expose only one row—at least not until the last row is fetched. If there are no rows, the RowCount property returns 0, and the BOF and EOF property settings are both True. If there *are* rows, the BOF and EOF settings are both False and the RowCount property setting returns a nonzero value. If the number of member rows has already been determined, the RowCount property is set to that number; otherwise, it is updated as cursor rows are populated. If the cursor can't determine the row count, RDO returns –1.

Even if you request an updatable rdoResultset object, the result set might not be updatable for a litany of reasons:

- No primary keys are specified for the tables in the query. This is, by far, the most common reason for read-only result sets based on simple queries.

- The underlying database, table, or column isn't updatable based on server-side database settings.

- The cursor doesn't support updatability on the selected cursor.

- You opened the rdoConnection or rdoResultset object as read-only.

- Your user doesn't have update permission on the table or columns selected.

- The join is too complex for ODBC to figure out the SourceTable and SourceColumn.

In any case, you can examine the Updatable property of the rdoConnection, rdoResultset, and rdoColumn objects to determine whether your code can change the rows. But even when this property is True, you might still have problems updating the result set rows without using an update query.

Sequencing operations

If there is an unpopulated rdoResultset object pending on a SQL Server data source, you can't create additional rdoQuery or rdoResultset objects, nor can you use the Refresh method on the rdoTable object, until the rdoResultset object is flushed, closed, or fully populated. When you're working with server-side cursors, however, you can execute additional commands against the connection before the last row is fetched, since the RDO interface, independent of any needed update operations, references the cursor that is on the server. You will have to fetch all of the result sets generated by a query before you can execute another query against the connection. This means that you have to poll the MoreResults property until it returns False or until you simply close the rdoResultset.

Positioning the current-row pointer

At any one time, only one row in an rdoResultset object is exposed for data retrieval or modification: the row addressed by the current-row pointer. Remember that forward-only or cursorless result sets are *not* scrollable—their current-row pointer can be repositioned forward only one row at a time with the MoveNext method. You can reposition the current-row pointer of a scrollable cursor by using any of the Move methods or the AbsolutePosition and PercentPosition properties; they work the same way the DAO methods do. The rdoResultset object supports bookmarks, which can be used to save the current location in a *Variant* variable. You can subsequently position back to a saved location in the rdoResultset object by setting the Bookmark property with a valid bookmark. If you modify data in the rdoResultset object and want to reposition to the last row that was changed, set the Bookmark property to the bookmark returned in the LastModified property. In most cases, RDO skips over rows that have been deleted since the rdoResultset was created—with the exception of those rows retrieved with a bookmark or the AbsolutePosition property. In this case, you might position to a deleted row, in which case a trappable error is triggered.

TIP When you position the current-row pointer, it's possible to position it past either end of the result set or to a row that has been deleted. The RDO interface may also *leave* the current-row pointer positioned over an invalid row, as when a row is deleted. Be sure to check the EOF and BOF properties to determine whether the current row is positioned beyond the end or the beginning of the result set. If you're using the Bookmark property to reposition the current row, you can reposition it to a row that has been deleted by another user. If so, a trappable error results.

Using GetRows

It's time to remember what I said about the GetRows method in Chapter 13. Or did you skip Chapter 13 to get here? If so, I recommend that you go back and take a look. The GetRows method has also been implemented by the RDO interface and can greatly increase the performance of this interface, just as it helps Jet. In a nutshell, GetRows lets you set up a Variant array and fetch data into it right off the wire. Once the data is in the array, you can move to any particular row or column and extract data as needed.

When you're working with RDO in an ActiveX control running on a remote system (perhaps managed by Microsoft Transaction Server), consider using GetRows and a Variant array to return the results from your result set. You can't simply pass back an rdoResultset; RDO is incapable of dealing with it once it arrives from a remote component. But you can move the Variant array into a display control.

The rdoColumn Object

The rdoColumn object is roughly equivalent to the DAO Field object. Its Value property contains the column data returned from the query. It also provides a way to read and set values in the rdoResultset object's current row.

The rdoColumns collection of an rdoResultset object contains all the rdoColumn objects of an rdoResultset, an rdoQuery, or an rdoTable object—one for each column of the result set. An rdoColumn object's name is set from the table's column name or from the name assigned to the object in the SQL query that was used to create the rdoResultset. For example, the following query returns two columns, one named *Pigs* and the other *PigAge*:

```
Select Pigs, Avg(Age) PigAge from Animals
```

Whenever you execute a query that includes an aggregate or computed column, you should provide an alias name for the column, as shown in the preceding code. If you don't, the rdoColumn object's Name property is set to a null string—which can't be used to reference the rdoColumn object in code.

rdoColumn Properties

The rdoColumn object supports a variety of properties that can fully describe the characteristics of a result set column. Generally, you'll find that these properties are designed to be as close as possible to their DAO counterparts. You can extract information about the rdoColumn in the following ways:

- *Use the Attributes property* to determine many of the base characteristics of a column by using the bit flags shown in *Figure 24-10* on page 454.

- *Use the SourceColumn and SourceTable property settings* to locate the original source of the data. For example, you can use these properties to determine the table and column name of a query column whose name is unrelated to either the name of the column in the underlying table or the names of columns and tables used to define the query. Unless these properties are filled in, the BatchUpdate method can't execute and returns a trappable error, so in some cases you might have to supply these values using your own code.

- *Use the Type property settings* to get the column data type. (See online help for valid data types.) Generally, valid RDO data types map one to one to the ODBC data types.

- *Use the Size property* to determine the length of the data if it is an rdTypeChar. For chunk data types, use the ColumnSize method.

- *Use the OriginalValue property* to return a Variant containing the value of the column as first fetched from the database. When working with optimistic batch update operations, you might need to resolve update conflicts by comparing the column values as originally returned by RDO with the value as supplied by the user. The OriginalValue property provides this value as first fetched from the database.

- *Use the Status property* to determine whether and how a column has been changed.

- *Use the BatchConflictValue property* to determine the value of the column as currently stored in the database. During an optimistic batch update, a collision might occur where a second client modified the same column and row between the time the first client fetched the data and the update attempt. When this happens, the value that the second client set will be accessible through the BatchConflictValue property.

- *Use the OrdinalPosition property* to get presentation order of the rdoColumn objects in an rdoColumns collection.

- *Use the AllowZeroLength property setting* to get the zero-length string-handling setting. If AllowZeroLength is False for a column, you must use Null to represent "unknown" states; you can't use empty strings.

- *Use the Required property settings* to determine whether Nulls are permitted in the column. You can use the Required property, along with the AllowZeroLength property, to determine the validity of the Value property setting for any particular rdoColumn object. If the Required property is set to False, the column can contain Null values as well as values that meet the conditions specified by the AllowZeroLength property setting.

- *Use the BindThreshold property* to set the maximum number of bytes that RDO will bind to. When RDO peruses the rdoResultset object's rdo-Column objects, it binds to each column whose type it recognizes. Ordinarily, RDO won't bind to BLOB columns, but RDO 2.0 now lets you decide. If the size of the column return is below the BindThreshold value, RDO treats the column just like any other character or binary value.

- *Use the ChunkRequired property* to determine whether you need to use the Chunk methods to fetch the column. This property is gated by the BindThreshold property. Those columns whose data size exceeds the rdoQuery object's BindThreshold value set the ChunkRequired property to True.

- *Use the AppendChunk, GetChunk, and ColumnSize methods* to manipulate BLOB columns if the ChunkRequired property is True.

- *Use the Updatable property* to see whether a column can be changed. SQL Server can restrict permissions right down to the column level, so if your user has permission for the table but not for the column, the Updatable property is set to False. See the rdoResultset property for the reasons why a column's Updatable property would be false.

Figure 24-10
Bit Flags for Determining Base Characteristics of Columns

Constant	Value	Description
rdFixedColumn	1	The column size is fixed (default for numeric columns).
rdVariableColumn	2	The column size is variable (text columns only).
rdAutoIncrColumn	16	The column value for new rows is automatically incremented to a unique Long integer that can't be changed.
rdUpdatableColumn	32	The column value can be changed.
rdTimeStampColumn	64	The column is designated as a server-managed TimeStamp for Client Batch cursors.

Addressing Column Data

The Value property is the one you might reference the most but never actually use in code. If you use the default collection and property settings, it's very easy to get at the data from an rdoResultset column. Remember, Visual Basic has already done all the needed data type binding, so when you have to convert incoming data, simply assign the data from the Value property to the program variable of your choice. For example, let's extract data from a simple rdoResultset but do it in a variety of equivalent ways:

```
Dim rs As rdoResultsets
Set rd = cn.OpenResultset _
    ("Select PigName from Pigs", rdOpenStatic)
print rd(0)         ' This returns data from the
                    ' first column "PigName"
print rd!PigName    ' So does this
print rd("PigName") ' So does this
A$ = "PigName"
print rd(A$)        ' And so does this
```

Mapping Database Schema

Only the rdoTable object's rdoColumns collection contains specifications for the data columns of a database table. If you need to examine a table's schema, use the rdoColumn object in an rdoTable to map a base table's column structure. The RDO interface, unlike the DAO model, doesn't include built-in mechanisms for changing the database schema, but nothing will stop you from using TSQL statements and the Execute method to make whatever changes you choose. Once these changes are made, however, you'll have to refresh the rdoTables collection if you expect it to contain valid schema information. But I think you'll find few mapping requirements that can't be solved by directly addressing SQL Server's *sysobjects* table.

25

Chapter

Optimistic Batch Updates

Optimistic Batch Updates—An Overview

Using RDO to Perform Optimistic Batch Updates

hen you enable the Client Batch cursor library by using the rdUseClientBatch option for your Cursor-Driver, you expose an entirely new concurrency handling paradigm. To bring this technology to life, the FoxPro team was approached with a challenge: create a cursor library that duplicated the functionality of the ODBC cursor library and still support the concept of optimistic batch concurrency as already provided by FoxPro. The result is the Client Batch cursor library as implemented in RDO 2.0. This cursor library provides a number of features that significantly increase the flexibility of the RDO interface well beyond that provided by RDO by itself. This cursor library includes some of the additional functionality left behind when you choose not to use DAO/Jet, although it takes up more RAM than the ODBC cursor library. The Client Batch cursor library makes up for these extra resource demands with better (far better) performance than the ODBC cursor library that it is intended to replace. This new cursor library is also very closely integrated with Visual Basic because it was originally developed specifically for Visual Basic. Let's go over the features of this technology one by one to better understand how to best implement them.

NOTE The optimistic batch updates feature is also accessible from ODBCDirect. The event side of the technology isn't implemented, but you should be able to use most, if not all, of the other methods and properties. You still can't build stand-alone Connection objects in ODBCDirect, but you can dissociate and reassociate them once they are created.

Optimistic Batch Updates—An Overview

In many situations, your client application must deal with sets of rows that can (or should) be updated as a set or whose changes can (or should) be deferred until later. Consider a situation where you have a set of rows that can be fetched, operated on, and returned later without much chance of other applications attempting to perform the same task. For example, the Lake Washington Youth Soccer Association could use a method like this to manage team rosters. The coaches could query their teams' member records from the database—often from home and over a RAS connection. The records could be updated off line and later posted back to the database as a batch. Since no other team in the league has access to the individuals on any particular coach's team, there's little chance that there would be a conflict over access. If there is a conflict, the coach would certainly want to know about it.

Users shouldn't be forced to make this kind of decision. Not only does it exacerbate the problem, it can also be a pathway to corrupted data.

Unfortunately, the concept of optimistic batch updates doesn't work very well in situations where the data being worked on is under constant assault from various clients. The Client Batch library is prepared to deal with "collisions," where changes made to one or more of the rows in the batch conflict with changes already made by other users. But these situations make the operation fairly complex as you (or your user) try to decide which update to accept—the current operation or the one already made.

Consider the case where a user is forced to choose between three conflicting values:

- The data as first fetched and as returned in rdoResultset.rdo-Columns(*n*).OriginalValue.

- The data as modified via the Update statement as in rdoResultset.rdo-Columns(*n*).Value.

- The data as modified via the *other* user's changes as returned in rdo-Resultset.rdoColumns(*n*).BatchConflictValue.

By the time the user might have made a decision, another few changes might have taken place, making the user's decision moot. Even if a user responds within a few seconds, or your code does the job, the complexity of the code to support this decision-making process can be both overwhelming and tough to support.

The concept of optimistic batch updates is *not* designed nor recommended for situations where data is constantly changing. That's not to say that there aren't plenty of applications for optimistic batch updates. You just have to be careful when choosing these situations and avoid those that require too much collision handling.

Using RDO to Perform Optimistic Batch Updates

The steps involved in setting up an optimistic batch update are fairly simple when taken individually, but the whole collection of steps gives you plenty of room to stray. Let's walk through the steps—we have to cross over that rope bridge up ahead, so don't look down.

Establish a Connection

The first step is to set up your connection. This is the interface to the selected server. (While you can use DCOM for this operation, we won't be talking about that here.) You can use the UserConnection Designer to build a UserConnection object that includes specifications for your connection. But be sure to perform these tasks:

- Specify the Client Batch cursor library for the connection (rdUse-ClientBatch). This must be done *before* you establish the connection—after that, it's too late to say what library you want.

- Grant access to the underlying table or stored procedures for the specified user.

You can roll your own connection object using stand-alone connections, or you can even use the OpenConnection method against the rdoEnvironment object, but the same caveats apply. These older techniques don't really buy you anything, but they are a little faster to work with because you don't have to wander around in the UserConnection Designer to set properties—it's simply done in code. On the other hand, connection objects made this way are harder to maintain later, and it's tougher to share the code later.

Create an rdoQuery Object

I'm not thrilled about providing this information in code. I would prefer some way to get this metadata from the server. Executing a stored procedure loses quite a bit of its luster if you have to hard-code SourceTable or SourceColumn information.

While this step isn't absolutely necessary, it can make handling the query parameters and other properties a lot easier. In some cases, some of the properties you might need are exposed *only* on the rdoQuery object. At this point, you need to make a decision that makes a big impact on how your code must approach the update process. RDO must identify the source table and column for each column in the result set. Depending on how you build your query, this information can be determined automatically by ODBC. If ODBC doesn't provide this information, you must provide it in code.

Consider the following scenarios:

- *If you build a query that references a stored procedure or a business object and you plan to use the BatchUpdate method,* you most likely have to fill in the SourceTable and SourceColumn properties for each rdoColumn object in the rdoResultset object. Basically, it works like this: when you execute a stored procedure, RDO retrieves the rows but doesn't ask from whence they came. In other words, RDO can access the data and even build a WHERE clause to update the rows later, but it doesn't know where the individual columns came from. This Metadata *can* be fetched by a number of techniques, but it's expensive code to run and for most cases, it isn't needed. The bottom line? If you choose to fetch data via a stored procedure, plan to fill in the SourceColumn for each column in the result set you intend to update—*if* you want to use the BatchUpdate method.

- *If you build a query based on hard-coded SQL and use the BatchUpdate method,* ODBC should be able to determine the SourceColumn rows—at least if the query isn't too complicated. In some cases, however, you *still* might have to provide this information.

- *If you don't plan to use the BatchUpdate method,* you needn't worry about the SourceTable and SourceColumn properties. No matter how the rows are fetched, you can perform the update through other means while still using most of the optimistic batch update technology. You can plan to use the WillUpdateRows event or scan the rdoResultset object's Status property for rows that need updating and roll your own updates using stored procedures or your own update queries—even those defined by the UserConnection Designer.

In any case, you have to decide whether or not to use stored procedures or hard-coded queries. No matter which technique you choose, the resultant rdoResultset still might not be updatable—either because it is too complex or because it's simply not permitted. This all-too-common scenario means that your update strategy will have to be adapted somewhat. We'll get to the update strategy options in a minute.

Choose the Right CursorType Option

Once the connection is open, but before you attempt to execute the query, you must specify the cursor type—unless you can use rdForwardOnly, the read-only cursor built by the UserConnection Designer by default. If you are rolling your own connection and query, you still must set the OpenResultset options to match your approach to updatability. Depending on how you intend to manage the result set when it arrives, you might not need anything other than a forward-only, read-only result set. You might want to settle for a nonscrolling read-only cursor if you have to update via a stored procedure, but remember that only a scrollable cursor permits you to peruse the rdoResultset Status property that indicates when individual rows and columns need updating.

Choose the Right Concurrency Options

Before you build the result set, you need to specify rdConcurBatch as the LockType concurrency option. This is set against the UserConnection object's rdoQuery object, or it's set when you execute the OpenResultset method against your rdoConnection object. Once you enable this option, RDO and the Client Batch cursor library know that you intend to defer updates until the BatchUpdate method is executed. Sure, you can override this decision, but I'll get to that later. You want to populate your result set as soon as possible, so you might consider using the rdBackgroundFetch option when you're creating the rdoResultset. Depending on how you plan to deal with BLOB columns, you might consider setting the rdFetchLongColumns property to ensure that

I would make every attempt to use the UserConnection Designer to build this connection/query interface object before I tried to do this in code. Being able to use the query-as-methods feature should make it worthwhile and a lot easier to share with your development team.

the BLOB columns are fetched along with the other data. This is a requirement if you plan to dissociate the connection or use a forward-only cursor.

Execute the Row Retrieval Query

Once the connection is open, your CursorDriver choice is cast in stone. You have to tear down your rdoConnection or UserConnection object to change this option. You *can* change the CursorType and LockType as required—whenever you rebuild the cursor. So, once the cursor type and concurrency options are set, you're finally ready to open (or establish) the connection and fetch the rows. This query can be in the form of a SQL statement passed to the OpenRecordset object or built into an rdoQuery or UserConnection object. It can be a stored procedure or a hard-coded SQL statement—I prefer the former, but if you use stored procedures, your ability to use the BatchUpdate statement will be limited unless you provide the SourceTable and SourceColumn properties later on. If you plan to use the BatchUpdate method, you can create a simple but updatable rdoResultset. If you don't plan to use the BatchUpdate method, you might still want to create a scrollable result set because you'll want to make a pass over the rows to check the Status property for rows that need updating when the time comes. Remember that if you code this correctly, you have to follow the preceding setup steps only once. After that, you can reexecute the query with different parameters as many times as you need to.

Retrieve the Rows

If your query returns rows, you can display them in a grid (as illustrated in the example on the book's companion CD) or simply maintain the rdoResultset in local memory. Consider using the GetClipString method to fill the grid. Note that you can choose from a number of important rdoResultset and rdoColumn properties that can be used to manage the data and facilitate the update process. Let's take a look at the most important and newest of these.

rdoResultset properties

AbsolutePosition You need this property to step through your rdoResultset when it comes time to check the Status property for changes—if you don't intend to use the BatchUpdate method to make the changes yourself. Remember that AbsolutePosition does *not* step over deleted rows, so be prepared for the errors that result—errors indicate that the underlying row was deleted since the rdoResultset was built.

ActiveConnection This property points to the rdoConnection object used to build the rdoResultset object. Once the result set has been populated, you can set this property to Nothing to dissociate from the connection and set this property to an active rdoConnection object to reassociate it with a remote server.

BatchCollisionCount This contains the number of rows that failed to update for some reason. It's set by the BatchUpdate method. This property can be checked to see whether any rows have been affected by the updates or have caused collisions.

BatchCollisionRows This is a collection of bookmarks—one for each row in the rdoResultset that failed to update when you executed the BatchUpdate method. If you create a scrollable result set, you can use this set of bookmarks to reposition to each row that failed to update. At that point, you can check the rdoColumn status property to see which column caused the failure.

BatchSize RDO and the Client Batch cursor library do *not* try to update the whole result set at once—they use the BatchSize property to set how many update statements are batched up in the command buffer. The default is 15 statements. You can set BatchSize to 1 in cases when you want to update on a row-by-row basis.

Status This property serves double duty as it indicates whether the row has been "touched" by an edit, update, or delete operation, or whether the BatchUpdate operation accepted this row. Its setting also indicates whether and how this row will (or should) be involved in the next optimistic batch update. You can set the status property of individual rows (or columns) in code, or expect the status to be changed for you when you use the Edit, Delete, or Update methods against the rows. (See *Figure 25-1* on the next page.)

For example, suppose you're working with an unbound Grid control filled with rows from a query. The user selects one of the rows, and you detect that a change has been made in the row. At this point, you can mark this row for updating by setting the Status property of the associated rdoResultset to *rdRowModified*. Similarly, if a row is added or deleted, you can use the appropriate Status property setting to indicate this change. When you use the BatchUpdate method, RDO submits an appropriate operation to the remote server for each row, based on its Status property. You could also use the Edit, AddNew, and Delete methods followed by the Update method against your result set to set the Status flags for you.

Once the BatchUpdate operation is complete, you can examine the Status property of each row to determine whether the update is successful because RDO and the Client Batch cursor library post the success or failure of each update to this property. If the Status property value doesn't return *rdRowUnmodified* after the BatchUpdate, the operation to update the row couldn't be completed. In this case, you should check the rdoErrors collection and the BatchCollisionRows property for bookmarks that point to the rows that failed to update. Better yet, you should check the BatchCollisionCount property to see how many collisions occurred, and then visit each row affected, using the bookmarks in the BatchCollisionRows array.

Figure 25-1
Status Property Values

Constant	Value	Prepared Property Setting
rdRowUnmodified	0	(Default) The row hasn't been modified or has been updated successfully.
rdRowModified	1	The row has been modified and *not* updated in the database—usually because you haven't executed BatchUpdate yet.
rdRowNew	2	The row has been inserted with the AddNew method but not yet inserted in the database.
rdRowDeleted	3	The row has been deleted but not yet deleted in the database.
rdRowDBDeleted	4	The row has been deleted locally and in the database.

The Status property can play an important role when it comes time to build a DML update query to post changes made to the batch—especially if you have to call a stored procedure for each change. For example, if you can't use the BatchUpdate method to perform the update, you can still scan the result set yourself and perform the updates for each row that has the status set to a value other than *rdRowUnmodified*. One approach would be to code a Case statement that executed a different stored procedure or SQL query for each type of change—adds, deletes, and updates. To implement this, you would loop through the modified rdoResultset and where the Status property of a selected row was *not* the value *rdRowUnmodified*, you could walk the rdoColumns collection to see which columns were changed—again checking the rdoColumn object's Status property. Your code would then build an UPDATE statement or an appropriate stored procedure to perform the needed update, insert, or delete operations.

UpdateCriteria When a batch mode operation is executed, RDO and the Client Batch cursor library create a series of DELETE, UPDATE, or INSERT statements to make the needed changes. A SQL WHERE clause is created for each update to isolate the rows that are marked as changed (by the Status property). Because some remote servers use triggers or other ways to enforce referential integrity, it's often important to limit the columns being updated to just those affected by the change. This way, only the absolute minimum amount of trigger code is executed. As a result, the update operation is executed more quickly and with fewer potential errors. You should set the UpdateCriteria property to rdKey when BLOB columns are included in the result set. Setting this property to a value other than the ones listed here results in a run-time error.

The UpdateCriteria property has the settings you see in *Figure 25-2*.

Figure 25-2
UpdateCriteria Property Values

Constant	Value	rdoResultset Type
rdCriteriaKey	0	(Default) Uses just the key column(s) in the WHERE clause.
rdCriteriaAllCols	1	Uses the key column(s) and all updated columns in the WHERE clause.
rdCriteriaUpdCols	2	Uses the key column(s) and all the columns in the WHERE clause.
rdCriteriaTimeStamp	3	Uses just the TimeStamp column if available (generates a run-time error if no TimeStamp column is in the result set).

UpdateOperation This property determines whether the optimistic batch update cursor library uses an UPDATE statement or a pair of DELETE and INSERT statements when sending modifications back to the database server. In the latter case, two separate operations are required to update the row. In some cases, especially where the remote system implements delete, insert, and update triggers, choosing the correct UpdateOperation property can significantly impact performance. Newly added rows will always generate INSERT statements and deleted rows will always generate DELETE statements, so this property applies only to how the cursor library updates modified rows. See *Figure 25-3*.

Figure 25-3
UpdateOperation Types

Constant	Value	UpdateOperation Type
rdUpdate	0	(Default) Executes an Update statement for each modified row.
rdInsertDelete	1	Executes a pair of Delete and Insert statements for each modified row.

TIP Be sure to check out the new GetClipString method against the rdoResultset object to extract the result set rows into a delimited string. It can make putting rows in a grid control a simple process. I included an example of this in this section's sample. It's also in my version of the RDOGrid control, which you can find on the companion CD.

rdoColumn object properties

BatchConflictValue If a collision occurs during an optimistic batch update, this property contains the value retrieved from the database for the chosen column. That is, it's the value (just fetched from the database) that some other user saved there since the last time you fetched this column. You can use this value to help decide which column value to accept—your new value, the value someone else wrote to the database, or the original value. I don't expect that you will find a BLOB-type column value here.

OriginalValue This is the value of the column when it was first fetched from the database when you created the rdoResultset. If you change the Value property, you can revert back to the original value by accessing this property. It can also be used to help decide which of the three values to accept. I don't expect that the BLOB database columns are maintained here, either.

SourceColumn and SourceTable This pair of properties points back to the original source of the data. That is, when you perform a SELECT query or a join to build the result set, these columns must point back to the table and column from whence the chosen column draws its data. This information isn't filled in if you are using stored procedures because the ODBC layers can't be expected to parse the SQL query to figure it out. So in many cases, you'll have to provide it in code—especially if you expect the BatchUpdate method to work.

Status The Status property of the rdoColumn object reflects pretty much the same information as the Status property on the rdoResultset object. In this case, however, the Status property shows, on a column-by-column basis, whether or not the column has been changed or needs to be. This property can be checked when you are building up your own SQL DML query to update the database. It works pretty much the same way and with the same values we saw earlier, in the section titled "rdoResultset Properties."

TIP In many cases, it's not a good idea to simply send all columns to the database when updating a row. This can cause unnecessary trigger firing and overhead that might complicate a simple operation. If you consider that some columns being updated might not be in the same tables, you can see how this practice can greatly increase DBMS thrashing.

Dissociate from the Connection

When your result set is fully populated, you can choose to disconnect from the server. This might not be such a bad idea if your user plans to stare at the rows for any length of time. But, if your query contains BLOB data and you choose not to pull down these columns (the default), you won't be able to reference these columns after you disconnect. You will be able to scroll through the result set (assuming you have populated it) and make as many changes as you care to using the Edit, AddNew, Delete, and Update methods. To drop the connection but keep the rdoResultset object, set the ActiveConnection property to Nothing. This fires the WillDissociate event (before the operation is complete), and if you set the *Cancel* argument to True, you can stop the disconnect from taking place. Sure, you can stay connected if you want to—but keep scalability in mind if you choose to stay connected.

What happens if the application ends or you close the rdoResultset before you post the changes? Any changes you have made will be lost. This leads to the obvious question, "Can I save the rows in the rdoResultset, rebuild an rdoResultset later, and associate it with a connection to post the changes?" Nope. This isn't implemented in RDO, but I expect it will be someday.

Make the Changes

Once you have built your rdoResultset, making the changes is easy. You can use the Edit, AddNew, Delete, and Update methods just as you normally do, constrained by all of the same rules—except for one. When the Update method is executed, the local copy of the rdoResultset data being managed by the Client Batch cursor library is changed and the Status property is modified to indicate that the row has been altered.

Reassociate with a Connection

When you are ready to post the changes, you must reconnect (reassociate) to an active rdoConnection object. To do this, you can use any one of these strategies:

- Create a new object by using the OpenConnection method.

- Use the *Dim cn As New rdoConnection* technique, and also use the EstablishConnection method.

- Use an existing UserConnection object's rdoConnection object.

- Reference an existing rdoConnection object.

No matter where the rdoConnection object comes from, you reconnect to it by setting the ActiveConnection property to this rdoConnection object. Does the connection have to point to the same SQL server as was used to fetch the rows? Nope, it can point to any SQL server as long as the same tables, permissions, and schema (for the most part) exist there too. This opens up some interesting possibilities. Don't expect the update to work if the user ID and password you provide for the connection don't have permission to make changes to the database.

Perform the Update

By this time, you have chosen one of the update strategies and you are ready to update the database with the changes made to your rdoResultset. As you've seen already, you can choose from a number of strategies to work with the

Client Batch cursor library and optimistic batch updates. The best choice of these hinges on whether you intend to use business objects, stored procedures, or user-written queries. If your system design uses stored procedures, you'll find it difficult, if not impossible, to execute a BatchUpdate—unless the SourceTable and SourceColumn properties are filled in first. So let's look at your choices.

Using the BatchUpdate method

If you can, use the BatchUpdate method to post the changes to the database. Since it performs so many functions behind the scenes, it's a shame if you can't take advantage of this technology. When BatchUpdate executes, it performs the following operations:

- Scans the provided rdoResultset, checking the Status property for any rows *not* marked with *rdRowUnmodified*.

- For each of these "modified" rows, builds an INSERT, DELETE, or UPDATE statement based on the UpdateCriteria and UpdateOperation properties.

- Groups these statements together in batches based on the BatchSize property and submits them to the connection indicated by the AssociatedConnection property.

- Fires the WillUpdateRows event for each event handler registered for the rdoResultset—there might be several.

- Manages any update collisions generated either by the server or by the WillUpdateRows event by capturing the error row's bookmark in the BatchCollisionRows array, and tallies the number of collisions in the BatchCollisionRows property.

- Sets each rdoResultset row Status property to indicate either the reason for the collision or the success of the update, which is indicated by a setting of *rdRowUnmodified*.

- Sets each rdoColumn object's Status property to indicate the reason for a collision, and records server-side column data in the BatchConflictValue property.

- Repeats the operation for every row in the batch.

- Returns a trappable error to the method in case of errors generated by the WillUpdateRows event.

Unless you want to duplicate some or all of this code, using the BatchUpdate method can be the easiest way to get your changes posted to the server—if you can get it to work. One of the reasons it might not work could be that while you can access rows from the database by whatever means, you *must* use a stored procedure to update the rows. Well, all is not lost even in this case, because you can use the WillUpdateRows event to trap the update operation and substitute stored procedures or your own update code.

Using the WillUpdateRows event

Let's take a closer look at this event handler. The WillUpdateRows event is raised *before* updated, new, and deleted rows are committed to the server—that is, before the chosen cursor library sends the appropriate UPDATE, INSERT, or DELETE statements to the server. This event fires even if you aren't using the Client Batch cursor library. The most important feature of this event is its ability to override the cursor library's update behavior. In other words, you can tell the cursor library that the event handler performed the update and how it was done—even if it didn't do anything. You can do this by coding an event handler, performing your own updates using stored procedures (or any other mechanism you choose), and passing back a *ReturnCode* argument that indicates how your code handled the operation.

If the result set is using optimistic batch concurrency, this event is raised *only* when the BatchUpdate method is called—*not* when the Update method is fired. In this case, the entire set of changes is about to be transmitted to the server, so your code is responsible for dealing with *all* rows in the rdoResultset that need updating. If the result set isn't in a batch mode, the WillUpdateRows event is raised for each call to the Update method, because the changes for that row are immediately sent to the server.

The event procedure should deal with *every* row in the rdoResultset that needs updating. This means you have to scan the rdoResultset, checking the Status property for rows that require updates. Once you find a row that needs to be updated, you need to take whatever steps are necessary to update the row. One approach would be to execute singleton queries that perform the operations one at a time. While this would make the error handling easier, it would take longer to perform than an approach that batches up the operations.

TIP Another approach you could take is to create your own array of bookmarks for those rows that require changes. This can be built by installing a handler for the RowStatusChange event. Each time this event fires, the Status property of the current row indicates what change must be made to the row. If you record the bookmark in your own collection or array, your array can be used later to determine which rows need to be posted to the server and what operation needs to occur.

When you have dealt with all of the rows in the rdoResultset that need updating, you need to set the event handler's *ReturnCode* argument to tell the Client Batch cursor library what you did. Let's look at the options:

- *rdUpdateSuccessful:* RDO assumes that your code successfully handled the update. RDO won't send this event to any additional clients (if there is more than one handler of this event), and the status for the rows and their columns is set to *rdRowUnmodified* and *rdColUnmodified*, respectively.

- *rdUpdateWithCollisions:* RDO assumes that you have successfully handled the update, but some rows caused collisions. Your code is responsible for setting the column status flags during the handling of this event. The option *rdUpdateWithCollisions* would be used only if you're using optimistic batch concurrency and you wanted to check for and handle collisions in code.

- *rdUpdateFailed:* RDO assumes that your code attempted to handle the update but encountered an error while doing so. RDO generates a trappable run-time error to the specific Update or BatchUpdate method causing the WillUpdateRows event to fire.

- *rdUpdateNotHandled:* RDO assumes that your code didn't handle the update, and RDO will continue to raise this event to all remaining clients (if there was more than one handler of this event). If all clients return *rdUpdateNotHandled*, RDO will perform the update itself, according to the normal rules.

The default value for the *ReturnCode* parameter is *rdUpdateNotHandled*, so if no client sinks the event or no client changes the value of *ReturnCode*, RDO will perform the update.

Check for Errors and Resolve the Collisions

If something goes wrong during the BatchUpdate, the rdoErrors collection will be posted with ODBC errors and a trappable error will occur on the BatchUpdate method that started the operation. The Client Batch cursor library doesn't know how to resolve the collision problems you might be faced with if your optimistic approach to the data was squashed by the reality of others using the data. Maybe someone was trying to steal one of your key players. In any case, you have to resubmit the BatchUpdate command after having set the Force option to force the changes through, or you must simply skip the row in question.

Using the CancelBatch method

You can also use the rdoResultset object's CancelBatch method to cancel an asynchronous batch operation. This method cancels all uncommitted changes in the local cursor (used in batch mode) and returns the data to the state it was when originally fetched from the database. Note that this method doesn't refresh the data by requerying the server as the Refresh method does—instead, it discards changes made in the local cursor that haven't already been sent in a batch update operation. When you use the CancelUpdate method, only the current row's changes are rolled back to the state prior to execution of the last Update method.

Using the Resync method

When a collision occurs or you simply want to avoid collisions because you haven't recently fetched data from the server, consider using the Resync method to capture the current state of the cursor's data. Resync resynchronizes the columns in the current row in the cursor library with the current data on the server (visible to your transaction). If you haven't modified the row, this method changes the Value and OriginalValue properties to match what is currently on the server. If you have modified the row, this method adjusts only the OriginalValue property so as not to loose your edits. This second case is useful when you want to avoid an optimistic concurrency conflict.

Another situation in which you might want to use this method is when you're dealing with a row that you attempted to update using BatchUpdate but a conflict occurred because the concurrency check failed. In this case, this method adjusts the BatchConflictValue to reflect the most recent version of the column on the server. The Resync method is valid only when you're using Client Batch cursors.

Chapter

26

Taking RDO Off Road

The rdoQuery Object

Working with
Parameter Queries

Executing Stored Procedures

Managing Multiple Result Sets

Working with
Page-Based Data Types

Face to Face
with the rdoTable Object

e've already been down the RDO main highways, so now it's time to hit a few of the less traveled back roads. I hope you packed your wet-weather gear and a pair of hip boots—in this neck of the woods, we might have to abandon the vehicle and tangle with some of the wilder, hairier aspects of the RDO interface. Get out your binoculars, too, so that you can spy on such flora and fauna as the rdoQuery object, the rdoParameters collection, multiple result sets, and page-based data types. You can also expect to meet up with a rare and endangered species: the rdoTable object.

The rdoQuery Object

The rdoQuery object should be fairly familiar by now, because we've looked at it in passing when talking about the UserConnection Designer and when working with rdoResultset objects created against it. Unlike the (obsolete) RDO 1.0 rdoPreparedStatement object, which maps directly to the ODBC SQLPrepare function, the rdoQuery object does *not*, by default, create a SQL Server temporary stored procedure to execute its queries. While this strategy makes sense for many application situations, as when you're executing repeated queries or parameter queries, including parameter-based SQL Server stored procedures, creating temporary stored procedures isn't always the best approach. So the rdoQuery object now defaults to the rdExecDirect mode. But, if you want RDO to build a temporary stored procedure for you, you can simply set the Prepared property to True on the rdoQuery object or when you're building your UserConnection object.

TIP Temporary stored procedures for executing queries are stored in TempDB space on SQL Server 6.*x* systems or in your current database on SQL Server 4.2 systems. Be sure to make room for these stored procedures while developing your application.

When prebuilding temporary stored procedures is necessary, using the SQLPrepare function behind the scenes saves the RDO interface (and you) time by precompiling SQL queries and storing them in anticipation of their execution. This is the same strategy that is often used in developing SQL Server applications when queries are created off line and left in the SQL server as stored procedures, to be used by the entire team. Your rdoQuery stored queries can't be shared, but they can call shared stored procedures. Another important benefit of using the rdoQuery to execute stored procedures is the RDO interface's ability to directly manage the stored procedure return status and output parameters. But, as I said before, be sure to use this technology the way it was intended. We have seen too many cases where the process of creating the rdoPreparedStatement objects was put in a loop to test RDO's performance. The CreateQuery method shouldn't be executed more than once in your application. After the rdoQuery object is created, you can use it to execute its query as many times as needed using the Requery method—even *with* parameters.

Creating rdoQuery Objects

The rdoQuery object can be created in one of three ways, as shown below. This means you have more flexibility than ever when instantiating these objects.

- Use the rdoConnection object's CreateQuery method.

- Use the statement *Dim qy As New rdoQuery*. Yes, the rdoQuery object can be created as a stand-alone object.

- Use the UserConnection Designer (my favorite technique).

When you create an rdoQuery object by using any of these techniques, the SQL server is referenced as soon as the rdoParameters collection is referenced—but not before. At this time, RDO and the ODBC layers need to determine the number and characteristics of the parameters used in the query. In the case of hard-coded SQL, ODBC can figure this out on its own. But when you execute a stored procedure, it must ask the remote server to decode it and describe the parameters. Because of this, you must be able to connect to the server so that a valid connection is available to perform this query. Many problems, in addition to connection difficulties, could surface at this point. For example, if the SQL syntax is incorrect or your user doesn't have sufficient permission to access the procedure or the objects it references, RDO won't be able to instantiate the rdoParameters collection. The error that results from this failure indicates the inability to reference this nonexistent object.

If you use the stand-alone creation technique to create your rdoQuery, it isn't appended to the rdoQueries collection—in all other cases, this is done automatically. The temporary stored procedure is created only when the query is first executed. At this point, the hStmt is created to address the underlying ODBC "statement"—your rdoResultset.

The rdoQuery object's Name property is set when you create the object using the CreateQuery method, but since there are other techniques at work, name collisions can occur. If you want to add the rdoQuery to the rdoQueries collection, you can't append rdoQuery objects that have duplicate names without running the risk of getting an error message like this: "This environment name already exists in the collection." If you need to create another version of an existing object, you have a couple of choices:

- Drop the existing rdoQuery object by using the Close method against it.

- Change the properties of the existing rdoQuery object to match your new requirements.

The rdoQuery object can execute simple parameterless queries, but it's really designed to create queries that require one or more parameters. If you don't choose to use the UserConnection Designer, creating a new rdoQuery object that contains a parameter query can be a little challenging at first—especially if you are calling a stored procedure. This is because RDO and ODBC require you to use ODBC SQL syntax to identify the *gazintas* and the *gazoutas* (those arguments going *into* the query and those coming *from* the query). You can still use rdoQuery objects to build parameterless queries, and this makes sense if you plan to execute the same query more than a couple of times over the course of your application. In this case, it's perfectly OK to use TSQL syntax in your queries.

OK, let's take a look at some of this theory implemented in code. First we need to set up some objects. We'll start with an rdoConnection, an rdoQuery, an rdoResultset, and a string to hold the SQL. Notice that both the rdoConnection and the rdoQuery are created as stand-alone objects. You also might notice that the archaic rdoEnvironment object is nowhere to be found:

```
Dim cn As New rdoConnection
Dim qy As New rdoQuery
Dim rs As rdoResultset
Dim SQL As String
```

Notice that I didn't bother to set up these objects with event handlers. Unless you declare these objects to be instantiated WithEvents, no event handlers are exposed.

Next we set up these stand-alone objects in the Form_Load event so that we can use them elsewhere in the application:

NOTE This application is named "rdoQuery Examples" on the companion CD.

```
Private Sub Form_Load()
With cn
    .Connect = "uid=;pwd=;dsn=biblio"
    .EstablishConnection rdDriverNoPrompt, True
End With
```

At this point, the rdoConnection is open against our *Biblio* DSN and the *Biblio* test database.

Now I'm ready to show you how to work with a stand-alone rdoQuery object. Step-by-step, we set each property starting with the SQL property:

```
Qy.SQL = "select * from authors where author like ?"
```

Next we point to the rdoConnection object we just opened and set the one parameter—marked in the SQL query with a question mark (?). (When we get to the section "Creating Parameter Queries," I'll show you a number of ways to pass parameters in code.)

```
Set Qy.ActiveConnection = cn
Qy.rdoParameters(0) = "%Vaughn%"
```

Next we set the cursor's rowset size to 1 to disable the cursor and execute the query:

```
Qy.RowsetSize = 1
Set rs = Qy.OpenResultset()
```

As a final step, we simply loop through the rows and dump the first and second columns sent back from the rdoResultset. Since this is a forward-only rdoResultset, we can use only the MoveNext method to step through the rows:

```
    Do Until rs.EOF
        Debug.Print rs(0), rs(1)
        rs.MoveNext
    Loop
End With
```

> **NOTE** This whole exercise is for those who feel the need to code all of this by hand—despite the fact that the UserConnection Designer does most, if not all of this, for us.

Now that we have the stage set, we're ready to look at a few typical queries and how they're coded. First we'll submit a very simple query using the OpenResultset method off the rdoConnection we created earlier:

```
Set rs = cn.OpenResultset("Select Title from Titles")
```

This query is unremarkable, but it returns too many rows, so we need to add a WHERE clause that filters out all but the rows we need. Let's recode this to be more efficient—after all, there are over 20,000 titles in the database and we don't need to see nearly all of them.

```
Set rs = cn.OpenResultset("Select Title from Titles" _
    & "Where Charindex('Hitch', Title) > 0")
```

This is fine as far as it goes—it narrows down our search to just book titles that have the string "Hitch" therein, but it doesn't deal with our need to set the Title filter in our application. We also need to deal with cases that involve titles other than our own. This time, let's create an rdoQuery to manage a parameter query. The next few lines of code set up a new rdoQuery object that can be used as many times as need be throughout the application. (In the example, I placed this code in the Form_Load event.) The code creates a query that returns from the *Titles* table all titles that contain the string "Hitch"—just like the earlier example.

```
SQL = "Select Title from Titles " _
    & " Where Charindex(?, Title) > 0"
Set qy = cn.CreateQuery("Qy1", SQL)
qy(0).Type = rdTypeVARCHAR
```

Now when the user fills in the TextBox control with the title string we want, we can execute this query with only the two following lines of code. RDO does the rest for us.

```
qy(0) = SearchForString.Text
Set rs = qy.OpenResultset
```

It's that easy. Notice how we set the first parameter (actually the *only* parameter) to the value in the *SearchForString* TextBox and ran the query. If you need to change the parameter to another value, just use the Requery method, like this:

```
ps.rdoParameters(0) = SearchForString
rs.Requery
```

When you're working with result sets generated from rdoQuery objects, you use the Requery method to ensure that an rdoResultset object contains the most recent data. When you use Requery, all changes made by you and other users to the data in the underlying table are returned in the rdoResultset object, and the first row in the rdoResultset object becomes the current row. If the rdoParameter objects have changed, their new values are used in the query to generate the new rdoResultset object.

NOTE Once the Requery method has been executed, all previously stored rdoResultset bookmarks are invalid. You can't use the Requery method on rdoResultset objects whose Restartable property is set to False.

Personally, I prefer the TSQL CHARINDEX function to the LIKE operator because it's easier to code and more tolerant of my mistakes. But whenever I use CHARINDEX with a parameter, the ODBC functions used to determine the parameter data types don't figure out that while the CHARINDEX function does indeed *return* an Integer, I am passing in a *VarChar* string as a parameter. Because of this, I have to force the parameter data type to return *rdTypeVARCHAR* as shown at the top of this page. This is a new RDO 2.0 feature that makes executing complex ODBC queries far easier.

Exploring rdoQuery Properties

Once the rdoQuery object has been created (by whatever means), you can manipulate its properties to determine how the ODBC Driver Manager will control the query and to set limits on the size and complexity of the rdoResultset. Since the rdoQuery object can now be created as a stand-alone object, RDO 2.0 had to add a number of properties that were previously available only on the rdoQuery object's parent rdoConnection object. Here is some of what you can do:

- *Use the ActiveConnection property* just as you did with the rdoResultset object to set the current rdoConnection object. The events supported on the rdoResultset to watch the associations aren't exposed here. If you create a stand-alone rdoConnection object, be sure to set the ActiveConnection to a valid rdoConnection—you won't go far without one.

- *Use the CursorType property* just as you would on the rdoResultset object to determine the type of cursor the rdoResultset objects built from this rdoQuery. The cursor *driver* you use is still set on the parent rdoConnection object.

- *Use the LockType property* to set the concurrency option used by the rdoResultset objects built from this rdoQuery. This can be overridden by the OpenResultset method LockType option, but if you set the LockType property, you won't have to specify it on the OpenResultset later.

- *Use the Prepared property* to determine whether the ODBC layers use SQLPrepare or simply SQLExecute for the queries being executed. This defaults to True. If you set it to False, some of the parameter queries you might have been able to execute won't work anymore. That's because if you need to execute parameter queries, you must use ODBC call syntax or otherwise prepare the statement for execution, unless you substitute the values into the query yourself.

- *Use the StillExecuting property* to determine whether the query is still running—if you're using asynchronous operations. This works just as it does on the rdoResultset object. But it's really better to use the QueryComplete event from the rdoConnection object.

- *Use the RowsetSize property* to determine how many rows are buffered internally when you build a cursor. Tuning this property can affect performance and the amount of memory required to maintain the keyset buffer. Larger rowsets store more rows and reduce concurrency; smaller rowsets reduce performance due to increased LAN traffic and server thrashing. This property must be set *before* an rdoResultset object is created. The size of the rowset is determined by the SQL Server ODBC driver—but, just between you and me, its size is virtually unlimited. (The lower limit for this value is 1, and the default value is 100, but the *practical* limit is a function of how much memory you have available.) This limit is set internally, when the RDO interface calls the ODBC SQLSetStmtOption function. Remember, when you want to set up a firehose cursor, set RowsetSize to 1.

- *Use the QueryTimeout property* to indicate how long the driver manager should wait before abandoning a query. This value defaults to 0 (no timeout), but it should be set if you don't expect the query to take a considerable length of time. When this period of time has expired, the rdoConnection object's QueryTimeout event will fire. If you don't set up an event handler (you should), you get a trappable error.

- *Use the BindThreshold property* to indicate the largest column to be bound automatically. This property is important when you're working with chunk data, since it sets the size of the largest chunk to be handled automatically.

- *Use the MaxRows property* to indicate the maximum number of rows to be processed by a query. You should do this with extreme caution, however, since this property can also affect the number of rows updated, inserted, or deleted. Why? Because when the SQL_MAX_ROWS ODBC statement option is set to a nonzero value, the maximum number of rows processed for any reason is limited to *n* rows. This means that only *n* rows are returned by a query, or only *n* rows are inserted, updated, or deleted by an action query. SQL_MAX_ROWS is set indirectly, via the rdoQuery object's MaxRows property. If you share the hStmt created for an rdoQuery object that has the MaxRows property set, the operations executed against the hStmt are also affected by the limit that SQL_MAX_ROWS imposes on the number of rows returned from a query and on the number of rows processed in an action query.

- *Use the RowsAffected property* to indicate how many rows will be affected by an action query. SQL Server, right after it executes an UPDATE statement, returns a Rows Affected value. This property exposes that value. The RowsAffected property also appears on the rdoConnection object, which is unaffected by rdoQuery operations. If you execute a multiple result set query that contains embedded action queries, these execute normally, but the RowsAffected property remains unaffected. Note that this property isn't exposed until all the rows of a result set are processed, so you might have to loop through all of the rows to get this filled in by ODBC.

- *Use the Updatable property* to see whether the result set generated by an rdoQuery can be updated. Ah, if it were so. This property *sometimes* tells if the rdoQuery is updatable—but not always.

- *Use the LogMessages property* to activate ODBC tracing. Basically, this property points to a file used by the ODBC driver to record ODBC traffic for debugging purposes. This is *not* the same as the LogMessages property in the DAO model. In the RDO interface, all SQL Server messages are delivered to the Errors collection, but not every message trips a trappable error. You must check for a message every time you expect one. If a message arrives asynchronously, it could be dropped when the next set of errors arrives. This is one of those features that is *not* exposed in ODBCDirect.

- *Use the hStmt property* to access ODBC API functions that control the aspects of this statement. Remember, this is a "use at your own risk" property.

TIP Use the Close method to terminate an rdoQuery query and release its resources. This also removes it from the rdoQueries collection. And use the Execute method to run an action query with SQL and other rdoQuery properties. These properties will include any values specified in the rdoParameters collection.

NOTE Remember that the rdoQuery object is also built when you create a UserConnection object with the UserConnection Designer. You can manipulate this rdoQuery object's properties just like any other rdoQuery object. You simply have to address the object relative to its parent UserConnection object.

Working with Parameter Queries

Do you ever need to send the same query more than once? Most of my applications do. If yours do too, you might be able to use a parameter query to send it. Parameter queries generally save processing time on the workstation and on SQL Server. In front-end applications, many situations call for parameter queries—especially in cases where the user provides a value for your application to locate or you have to perform other repetitive operations.

Every query you execute, whether it's a parameter query or not, goes through a compilation step. This takes time and server resources. Queries that you generate on the fly in code—even parameter queries—can't be shared by other applications. But if the query you generate invokes a stored procedure and passes arguments to it as parameters, you can benefit from shared code in the SQL Server procedure cache and the ability to share with other developers use of the common stored procedure. In addition, if you define your queries as UserConnection objects, they can be invoked as methods and you can simply pass the parameters as arguments of the method calls. These UserConnection objects can also be shared among developers working on programs that perform similar operations.

When executing queries whose parameters change in the course of the application, use the rdoQuery object to create the result sets instead of using the OpenResultset directly against the rdoConnection object. Or simply use a UserConnection object. The rdoQuery object (which is also created as a component of all UserConnection objects) is the most efficient way to supply input parameters to a query. When you provide parameters in "roll-your-own" queries by concatenating parameters to the SQL query string and call OpenResultset directly on the connection, RDO can't treat the operation as a parameterized query—just as raw SQL. In addition, wherever possible, build a UserConnection object to avoid having to use ODBC canonical syntax. If you insist on coding this yourself, be sure to read through this entire section carefully and don't venture off into those fields on the right—they are mined.

For best performance and resource utilization, your application needs to reexecute the stored procedures you reference rather than drop the rdoQuery and create a new one for each iteration. When you create an rdoQuery object, it creates a temporary stored procedure to execute. When you use the Requery method, this query is referenced again and again to eliminate the need to recompile the procedure. To reexecute a query that doesn't return a result set, you simply need to call Execute on the rdoQuery object. To reexecute a row-returning query, you need to first call OpenResultset on the rdoQuery object and subsequently use the Requery method against the rdoResultset object you just created. In either case, you can reset parameter values before each execution.

NOTE If you want RDO to manage your query's parameters, you *must* tell RDO to prepare the query. This means that you can't use the rdExecDirect option nor set the Prepared property to False. By default, an rdoQuery object is set up to prepare all queries that it runs. In contrast, by default, the OpenResultset and Execute methods are set up to bypass the ODBC preparation steps. This also means that if you roll your own queries, you can't expect RDO to manage any output parameters for you.

If you don't use the Requery method on an existing rdoResultset, you burden the server with heavy TempDB activity caused by creating and dropping stored procedures for each iteration. This rates very poorly with lots of clients. You must develop a strategy that leverages the Requery method to simply change the parameters of an existing query and resubmit it, if you expect to gain anything out of this technology.

Creating Parameter Queries

The process of coding parameters queries has always been one the toughest parts of working with RDO and is a source of a high number of support calls. Nevertheless, building parameter queries is only slightly different from building other queries, except in this case, you must tell RDO where the parameters should be placed in the query. The rules regarding what can and can't be replaced by a parameter are defined by SQL Server in its rules for building and coding stored procedures and TSQL statements. When you code the queries yourself, you *must* use the ODBC Call syntax, which lays out the parameters using a carefully orchestrated regimen—that is, if you want RDO to manage the queries and their parameters (both input and output) for you. RDO gives you lots of rules to follow—and while breaking or simply bending the rules doesn't always result in immediate failure of the query, it can result in inconsistent results, to say the least. On the other hand, if you create a UserConnection object with the UserConnection Designer, you are notified at once that something is amiss, often while you're still in the context of the Designer. This makes it much easier to figure out what went wrong and to develop work-the-first time queries.

> **NOTE** Once the rdoParameters collection has been built, it contains an rdoParameter object for each parameter marker in the SQL statement passed to the rdoQuery. These parameter markers are simply question marks—one for each parameter. You can't append objects to or delete objects from the rdoParameters collection; the collection is managed automatically by the RDO interface. But if something goes wrong as ODBC and SQL Server parse your query, this collection isn't built and RDO quietly fails.

Providing parameters

Your query's parameters can be provided using a variety of techniques, each of which has advantages and drawbacks that include (or don't include) the ability to leverage your procedures and scale your applications. You can pass your parameters in these ways:

- *As hard-coded arguments in an SQL query string,* as you see in the following code. In this case, RDO can't really help manage the parameters for you—and other people can't use the query either, even if they are performing the same search. The real disadvantage here is that to change the query, you have to recode, recompile, retest, and redeploy your application.

  ```
  " Select Publisher from Publishers Where State = 'CA' "
  ```

- *As concatenated text or numeric values extracted* from TextBox, Label, or other controls. This is another example of a "roll-your-own" query, popular because it lets the user choose the parameters. It's easy to code and can be used to build fairly complex queries. It causes problems, though, in that it doesn't deal with embedded quotes or invalid arguments. Unfortunately, RDO still can't help manage the parameters, nor can you share the query—and you still have to deal with embedded quotes in the query and any needed framing quotes:

  ```
  " Select Publisher from Publishers Where State =   '" _
      & StateWanted.Text & "'"
  ```

- *Using an ODBC question mark (?) parameter placeholder in an SQL statement.* In this case, you begin to enable RDO's ability to manage the parameters for you. Simply setting an rdoQuery object's SQL property to this string gives enough information to RDO to build a parameters collection. However, we really haven't reached a point where we can leverage this query—no one else can share it. But your code doesn't have to deal with embedded quotes in the parameters passed or any framing quotes because RDO and ODBC handle these for you:

```
" Select Publisher from Publishers Where State =  ?"
```

- *As the question mark (?) parameter placeholders in a stored procedure call* that accepts input, output, or return status arguments. We have now reached the next (but not the highest) level of sophistication when building parameter queries. When you execute a stored procedure, you *must* use this ODBC Call syntax so that RDO can manage the query and its parameters for you. Because we're executing a server-side procedure, people on your team can address it, although they can't easily share the code you wrote to access it. Because ODBC is handling the parameters for you, you don't need to worry about embedded or framing quotes:

```
"{Call GetPublisherByState (?)}"
```

NOTE Stored procedure invocations that use the Call syntax (as shown above) are executed in their "native" format, so they don't require parsing and data conversion by the ODBC Driver Manager. Because of this, the Call syntax can be executed somewhat faster than other syntaxes.

The ODBC Call Syntax: A Summary

This table summarizes the ODBC Call syntax that you will have to include in your queries unless you use the UserConnection Designer, which creates this Call syntax for you.

Query Parameter Configuration	ODBC Call Syntax
No parameters	{Call My_sp}
All parameters marked—input, output, both	{Call My_sp (?, ?)}
Some parameters marked	{Call My_sp (?, 'Y')}
With just a return status argument	{? = Call My_sp}
With the works	{? = Call My_sp (?, ?, 'Y')}

- *As the question mark (?) parameter placeholders in a UserConnection object.* You can also build parameter queries using the UserConnection Designer. This performs most of the complex tasks you would have to duplicate in code and also provides a shareable way to build the fairly complex SQL statements required by parameter queries. That is, once you create a UserConnection object that references a stored procedure (or other query), you can share it among the other developers on your team who also need access to this query.

When to mark parameters

The only time you *must* use parameter markers is when executing stored procedures that require output or return status arguments. If the stored procedure requires only input arguments, these can be provided in line as embedded values concatenated into the query (as shown below). You *can* use parameter markers for any parameter query whenever you want RDO to manage the parameters for you.

When the rdoParameters collection is first referenced (but not before), RDO and the ODBC interface preprocess the query, create an rdoParameter object for each marked parameter, and add it to the rdoParameters collection. You can also create queries with multiple parameters, and in this case, you can mark some parameters and provide the others by hard-coding or concatenation—in any combination. But, all marked parameters *must* appear to the left of all other parameters. If they don't, a trappable error occurs indicating "Wrong number of parameters."

NOTE   Because of the extra overhead in creating and managing rdoQuery objects and their rdoParameters collection, you shouldn't use parameter queries for SQL statements that don't change from execution to execution—especially those that are executed only once or infrequently.

How to mark parameters

Each query parameter that you want to have RDO manage must be indicated by a question mark (?) in the text of the SQL statement and must correspond to an rdoParameter object referenced either by its ordinal number (counting from zero—left to right) or by its name. To execute a query that takes a single input parameter, your SQL statement would look something like this:

```
" Select Publisher from Publishers Where State =  ? "
```

Multiple parameters can be salted throughout the query, as required. You need to follow a few rules, though, and we'll get to those in a minute. But you can pass queries to several queries at once when building multiple result set queries. For example, you could provide the SQL statement on the next page to an rdoQuery for execution and expect it to manage all three parameters.

```
" Select Title from Titles " _
& " Where Description between ? and ? " _
& "Select Author from Authors where Author Like ? "
```

The ODBC syntax for the parameter query uses question marks as place-holders for both the input and output parameters. ODBC syntax requires Call, rather than the commonly used SQL Server EXECUTE keyword. Stored procedure calls should be surrounded by braces ({}), as shown in the code fragment on page 482. Failure to use correct syntax might not prevent the procedure from being executed, but the ODBC driver might not be able to identify the parameter positions or markers. Some early versions of the ODBC driver also give you a GPF when the syntax isn't to their liking.

Acceptable parameters

Not all types of data are acceptable as parameters. For example, you can't always use a TEXT or IMAGE data type as an output parameter—although the newer drivers are more tolerant of this option. In addition, if your query doesn't require parameters or has no parameters in a specific invocation of the query, you can't use parentheses in the query. For example, for a stored procedure that does *not* require parameters, you can code this way:

```
"{ ? = Call MySP }"
```

In this case, we're still building the rdoParameters collection but using it to capture the return value parameter.

Here are the rules I mentioned earlier having to do with what, when, and where parameters can be used:

- When you submit queries that return output parameters, these parameters must appear at the end of the list of your query's parameters.

- While it is possible to provide both marked and unmarked (inline) parameters, your output parameters must still appear at the end of the list of parameters. This means that your stored procedure must be coded to place all output parameters at the end of the parameter list.

- ODBC still doesn't support named parameters for stored procedures—so RDO doesn't either. You can use named parameters when calling stored procedures. It's just that RDO can't manage them for you.

- All inline parameters must be placed to the *right* of marked parameters. If this isn't the case, RDO returns an error indicating "Wrong number of parameters." An inline parameter is one that you hard-code or provide yourself, in lieu of using a parameter marker.

- RDO 2.0 supports BLOB data types as parameters, and you also can use the AppendChunk method against the rdoParameter object to pass TEXT or IMAGE data types as parameters into a procedure.

Identifying the parameter's data type

When your parameter query is processed by ODBC, it attempts to identify the data type of each parameter by executing ODBC functions that ask the remote server for specific information about the query. In some cases, the data type can't be correctly determined. In these cases, use the Type property to force the correct data type or create a custom query by using the UserConnection Designer.

NOTE   You don't have to surround text parameters with quotes because this is handled automatically by the ODBC API interface.

Handling output and return status arguments

In some cases, a stored procedure returns an output or return status argument instead of or in addition to any rows returned by a SELECT statement. If you want to capture these values, each of these parameters must also be marked in the SQL statement with a question mark and you might have to set the Direction property as well—at least for some SQL servers. Using this technique, you can mark the position of (almost) any number of parameters in your SQL query, including input, output, or input/output parameters.

Whenever your query returns output or return status arguments, you *must* use the ODBC Call syntax when setting the SQL property of the rdoQuery object. In this case, a typical stored procedure call would look like this:

```
Dim qd as rdoQuery, rd as rdoResultset, SQL as String
SQL = "{ ? = Call master..sp_password (?, ?) }"
Set qd = db.CreateQuery ("SetPassword", SQL)
qd.rdoParameters(0).Direction = rdParamReturnValue
qd(1) = "Fred"        ' The old password
qd(2) = "George"      ' The new password
set rd = qd.Execute
if qd(0) <> 0 then MsgBox "Operation failed"
```

TIP   Be sure to specifically address stored procedures that don't reside in the current (default) database. In this example, the default database isn't Master where the sp_password procedure is maintained, so this procedure is specifically addressed in the Master database.

When control returns to your application after the procedure is executed, the rdoParameter objects designated as rdParamReturnValue, rdParamOutput, or rdParamInputOutput contain the returned argument values. In the code example shown above, the return status is available by examining *qd(0)* after the query is executed.

Before we move on, let's look at a little larger example and take a closer look at capturing parameters that are returned to our application. As I have said before, many stored procedures return nonrowset information in the form of output argument values. The following example executes a stored procedure that expects two input parameters and returns two output parameters along with a return status argument:

```
Dim SQL As String, MyOutputVal1 As Variant
Dim MyOutputVal2 As Variant, MyRetVal As Variant
Dim Cn As New rdoConnection, rs As rdoResultset
Dim Qy As New rdoQuery
Cn.CursorDriver = rdUseOdbc
Cn.Connect = "UID=;PWD=;DSN=BIBLIO"
Cn.EstablishConnection rdDriverNoPrompt
Set Qy.ActiveConnection = Cn
' Use ODBC parameter argument syntax.
Qy.SQL = "{ ? = call MyProcName (?, ?, ?, ?) }"
' Set Parameter "direction" types for each parameter,
' both input and output.
' No, this isn't necessary. It's for illustration only.
Qy(0).Direction = rdParamReturnValue
Qy(1).Direction = rdParamInput
Qy(2).Direction = rdParamInput
Qy(3).Direction = rdParamOutput
Qy(4).Direction = rdParamOutput

' Set the input argument values. Yes, this is necessary.
' Note that we are addressing the
' default rdoParameters collection.
Qy(1) = "Test"
Qy(2) = 1

' Create the result set and populate the Qy values.
Set rs = Qy.OpenResultset()
MyRetVal = Qy(0)          ' Contains the return value argument
MyOutputVal1 = Qy(3)      ' Contains the first output parameter
MyOutputVal2 = Qy(4)      ' Contains the second output parameter
```

Executing parameter queries

You have a number of choices here, too—depending on whether or not your query returns rows and you want to retrieve them.

- If your query doesn't return rows or parameters or you simply don't want to retrieve them (ever), use the Execute method against the rdoQuery object.

- If you want to fetch the rows from your query, use the OpenRecordset method.

- If you have created a UserConnection object, simply execute the query as a method against the UserConnection object.

- When you want to change parameters and run the query again, use the Requery method against the rdoResultset.

How to pass parameters for the *n*th time

It doesn't do any good to simply execute a parameter query once—especially if you go to the trouble of having RDO and ODBC construct elaborate mechanisms to handle the parameters. When it's time to execute your parameter for the second through the nth time, you simply need to place the new input (or input/output) parameters in the rdoParameters collection—wherever it might be—and use the Requery method. Let's look at some common scenarios. First, when you create the rdoQuery object in code:

```
rs.rdoParameters(1) = "New parameter of some kind"
rs.(2) = 14  ' Another value passed to 3rd member of rdoParameters
rs!Parameter3 = 23  ' Addressing by name
rs("Parameter4") = "Also addressing by name"  ' "Late" binding
```

Or when you need to access the parameters of a UserConnection object's query:

```
MyUc.rdoQueries(0).rdoParameters(1) = "New Param"
```

or

```
Dim Parm as rdoQuery ' Declare a holder object
Set Parm = UserConnction1.rdoQueries("MyQuery")
Parm.rdoParameters(n) = "the nth parameter"
```

Once the parameters are set, you can use the Requery method to reexecute the query using the newly set parameters. As a result, the rdoResultset object is rebuilt from the beginning with the new data:

```
rs.Requery
```

The Requery method also supports the rdAsyncEnable option, so you don't have to block when ODBC is away building your result set.

You also have another option—simply reexecute the rdoQuery as a UserConnection object method with the new parameters. If you choose to take this course, RDO and ODBC reuse the rdoQuery object's temporary stored procedure and pass in the new parameters. This option is slightly slower because the rdoResultset object is torn down and reinstantiated instead of being reused.

Using other rdoParameter object properties

Using the properties of an rdoParameter object, you can set a query parameter that can be changed before the query is run. You have these choices:

- *Use the Name property* to identify the individual query parameters. Note that the names are built automatically and are set to Parameter*n*, where *n* is the ordinal number plus one. You can assign your own names with the UserConnection Designer or by setting the Name property of the rdoParameter object before the query is executed. RDO and ODBC don't support named parameters passed to queries.

- *Use the Direction property* to set the parameter's function: input, output, or input/output, or a return value. In RDO 2.0, the Direction property is usually set automatically, so it's unnecessary to set this value. It's also unnecessary to set it for an input parameter—which is the default value.

- *Use the Type property* to determine the data type of the rdoParameter. Data types are identical to those specified by the rdoColumn.Type property. In some cases, ODBC might not be able to determine the correct parameter data type. In these cases, you can force a specific data type by setting the Type property. Be careful when you're setting the data type—the wrong one can keep you up nights finding strange problems. Don't choose CHAR when you really mean VARCHAR.

- *Use the Value property* (the default property of an rdoParameter) to pass values to the SQL queries containing parameter markers used in the rdoQuery.Execute or rdoQuery.OpenResultset methods.

NOTE RDO 1.0 required that your ODBC driver support a number of Level II compliant options and support the SQLNumParams, SQLProcedureColumns, and SQLDescribeParam ODBC API functions in order to be able to create the rdoParameters collection and parse parameter markers in SQL statements. While some drivers could be used to create and execute queries, if your driver didn't support creation of the rdoParameters collection, RDO failed quietly and simply didn't create the collection. As a result, any reference to the collection resulted in a trappable error. RDO 2.0, on the other hand, is far more tolerant of noncompliant drivers. When using the Client Batch cursor library, RDO 2.0 can often make up for the shortcomings of lightweight ODBC drivers.

Addressing the parameters

By default, members of the rdoParameters collection are named Parameter*n*, where *n* is the rdoParameter object's ordinal number plus one. For example, if an rdoParameters collection has two members, they are named Parameter1 and Parameter2.

But if you use the User Connection Designer, you can specify names for specific parameters. Because the rdoParameters collection is the default collection for the rdoQuery object, addressing parameters is easy. Assuming you have created an rdoQuery object referenced by *rdoQo*, you can refer to the Value property of its rdoParameter objects by choosing either of these strategies:

- Reference the Name property setting using this syntax:

```
' Refers to PubDate parameter
rdoQo("PubDate")
```

or

```
' Refers to PubDate parameter
rdoQo!PubDate
```

- Reference its ordinal position in the rdoParameters collection using this syntax:

```
' Refers to the first parameter marker
rdoQo(0)
```

A common mistake here is to refer to the right parameter with the wrong ordinal. I know, because I do it all the time. Remember that the return value is always the first member of the rdoParameters collection (*rdoQo(0)*)—if it's requested. If you didn't put the *? =* at the front of your Call statement, it won't be extracted. In this case, the first parameter encountered after the parenthesis in the Call statement is the first parameter in the collection—addressed as *rdoQo(0)*.

NOTE When your query specifies a return value parameter, you might not be able to reference it until *after* the entire result set has been populated—that is, not until you reach the last row. This isn't RDO's fault, it's just that SQL Server doesn't return a value for this parameter until the procedure ends. So, depending on an *@@ROWCOUNT* value placed in the return status in order to see how many rows qualified for the result set isn't a reasonable strategy.

The rdoParameters collection

Basically, the rdoParameters collection is used to expose the parameters marked in the SQL property of the parent rdoQuery object. In RDO 1.0, you had to tell RDO the direction for each parameter—return status, input, output, or both input and output. This is generally unnecessary with SQL Server because its driver is capable of reporting the configuration of each query parameter. But some other database drivers might need a little help, so you have to set the Direction property of each rdoParameter object before the rdoQuery is executed. The Direction property can be set to any of the values shown in *Figure 26-1*.

For most situations, you don't need to set the rdoParameter object's Type property before the query is sent, but I have already shown you a case

CAUTION

Warning: Watch out for the automatic naming of the parameters. RDO automatically assigns a name to each rdoParameter object in the rdoParameters collection, but it starts naming at 1, not 0 as you would expect. This means that the first (ordinal 0) rdoParameter object is named Parameter1, *not* Parameter0. And note that the names assigned to the members of the rdoParameters collection are *not* Param1, Param2, and so on. The documentation is wrong!

Figure 26-1
Values for Setting the Direction Property

Constant	Value	Description
rdParamInput	0	(Default) The parameter is used to pass information *to* the procedure.
rdParamInputOutput	1	The parameter is used to pass information *both to and from* the procedure.
rdParamOutput	2	The parameter is used to return information *from* the procedure, as in a SQL output parameter.
rdParamReturnValue	3	The parameter is used to *fetch* the return status from a SQL procedure.

or two where it *was* necessary to manually set the parameter data type. Remember when we tried to pass a parameter to the first argument of the TSQL CHARINDEX function? You *do* need to set the Value property (the default property) to the value to be passed for each SQL parameter. Once the parent rdoQuery has been executed, the rdoParameter object can be examined for the input or the returned parameter values and the data type of the returned value. The data types are identical to those specified by the rdoColumn object's Type property.

When you successfully define an rdoQuery in code, then, and only then, is an rdoParameters collection created. If the syntax used in the SQL property is incorrect as far as the parameters are concerned, the ODBC driver manager does *not* permit the RDO interface to create the rdoParameters collection. Since no error is generated when this process fails, the first indication that something has gone wrong is error 40002, which complains about the syntax or permissions associated with the collection. The parameter syntax isn't especially picky, but I have encountered a number of errors while experimenting and doing things that I thought were fairly intuitive.

Working with ODBC Query Syntax

In particular cases, you *must* use special ODBC query syntax to get the job done. ODBC defines extensions to the ANSI SQL syntax when you're dealing with any of the following:

- Date, time, and TimeStamp column data
- Scalar functions, such as numeric, string, and data type conversion functions
- LIKE predicate escape characters
- Outer joins
- Procedures

When the ODBC interface executes a SQL statement, it creates one or more stored procedures on the server. These procedures contain the SQL statement specified in the rdoQuery object or in the OpenResultset method and are designed to accept any parameters that might be specified for the statement. The procedures are created either in the current database or in the SQL Server TempDB database; it depends on which version of the server you're using. In some cases, several stored procedures can be created for a single statement. Generally, these procedures aren't released until you close the hStmt (rdoResultset), the hDbc (rdoConnection), the hEnv (rdoEnvironment), or end the application. Ending the application in Design mode doesn't always clear these statements; so in some cases, ending Visual Basic is the only way to clear out these temporary procedures. To avoid creating these procedures in the first place, specify the rdExecDirect option when you're using the OpenResultset method:

```
Set rs = cn.OpenResultset("Select * from Authors", _
    rdOpenStatic, rdConcurValues, rdExecDirect)
```

When you specify the rdExecDirect option, the ODBC interface does *not* create a procedure that is then used to run the SQL statement. Having the ODBC interface create such a procedure and run the statement can be faster, but only if the statement is used infrequently.

NOTE You don't usually have to use special ODBC query syntax if you don't care about application portability. All the standard TSQL functions and operators work just as they always have. These functions are needed only in special cases when you want the ODBC driver to help pass parameters or assist in some other obscure applications.

Let's look at some practical examples of using this special ODBC query syntax. We've already examined one case in which it's used: executing a stored procedure that needs one or more parameters. Remember the *?* placeholder? It's part of the ODBC SQL syntax extensions. The formal syntax for these extensions looks like this:

```
{[?=] call procedure-name [([parameter][,[parameter]]…)]}
```

When you apply it to one of the queries passed to an rdoQuery object, it looks like this:

```
SQL$ = {?= call MarryPig ('Miss Piggy', ?)}
```

In this example, the *MarryPig* (or is it *MerryPig*?) procedure is designed to pass back a return status and accept two parameters. We supply one of those in the code and expect another to be passed as a parameter at run time.

SQL syntax extensions with date values

When you're working with date, time, and TimeStamp column data, you must enclose the values in curly braces, like this:

```
UPDATE Pigs
Set DateOfBirth = {d '1995-01-31'}
```

The three date values are coded as follows:

```
{d 'date value'}
{t 'time value'}
{ts 'timestamp value'}
```

Note that I left off the special encoding of the *Date* argument when I created my earlier *AddPig* test, and it made no difference. The date made it to the server just fine.

SQL syntax extensions with scalar functions

The scalar functions are used to manage string length, absolute value, or current date values. These functions can be used on columns of a result set and on columns that restrict rows of a result set. The syntax is fairly simple. For example, here is how we return the uppercase value of a column:

```
SELECT {fn UCASE(NAME)} FROM Pigs
```

NOTE If this stored procedure isn't in the local database, you must fully qualify its name this way: *mydb..myproc*.

Executing Stored Procedures

Stored procedures are only slightly more difficult to access than parameter queries, and I've set out most of these details already. But here are a few tips that can make accessing stored procedures easier.

Stored procedures aren't always located in the default database, and while SQL Server is capable of locating them, you might not be able to execute the procedure you want unless you are logged in to a specific database. You can execute the TSQL Use statement to switch to another database—it's fast and painless. But it can't always be concatenated to the front of your SQL statement. You also don't need to prepare a stored procedure invocation. You don't need to create a temporary stored procedure to execute a stored procedure. RDO and the ODBC layers should prevent this from happening anyway.

Be sure to grant permission to your intended users to access the stored procedures you create. If they don't have permission to execute the procedures, users aren't going to get much out of them. You can prohibit access to the underlying tables and still grant access to stored procedures that reference the protected tables. Consider that stored procedures live in a world of their own. Because of this, the temporary objects they create belong to them and disappear when they end. This is the reason that when you execute a SELECT INTO statement as you execute a stored procedure, the table can't be seen when the stored procedure has ended. However, your users can see tables if you use SELECT INTO on a permanent table (where you need to have the SELECT INTO BULK COPY mode turned on) or on a semipermanent ##Temp table. You can't open a server-side cursor on the contents of a temporary table unless that table is created *outside* a stored procedure. When a temporary table is created *inside* a stored procedure, the table is automatically dropped by SQL Server when the procedure ends. Thus, if you select data from the temporary table at the end of your procedure, the server tries to create a server-side cursor on the table. But as soon as the procedure exits, the base table is gone, making the cursor unable to function.

If you use the OpenResultset method to execute action queries to do things like CREATE TABLE and INSERT INTO, you're asking SQL Server to create a server-side cursor based on the results of these statements (of which there aren't any). When running procedures like these, which don't return rows, simply use the Execute method instead of the OpenResultset method. Using OpenResultset inappropriately causes SQL Server to do a boatload of extra and meaningless work.

Although you might not be explicitly calling a stored procedure, remember that when you ask the SQL Server driver to prepare a statement, it creates a temporary stored procedure on the server and, when executing that statement, executes the temporary procedure. Thus when executing a prepared statement, you're executing a stored procedure, and the situation I describe above happens. So don't open a server-side cursor on a table that's going to be dropped. You can use the ODBC cursor library in this case, since it simply streams the data down from the server and builds a static cursor on the client side. The ODBC cursor library couldn't care less whether the temp table was dropped, but if it's dropped, you obviously won't be able to perform updates against it.

Managing Multiple Result Sets

Many of the production programs I have written include the use of TSQL queries or stored procedures that return several distinct but related sets of result data. Some of these result sets contain rows, but not all of them do. Only queries containing the SELECT statement return zero or more rows. An UPDATE or other data modification query returns a result set but no row sets. Any SQL statement can include multiple SELECT statements or invoke stored procedures that execute one or more SELECT statements. Since stored procedures can execute other procedures, it might not always be easy to tell how many sets of results a chosen query will return. Each SELECT statement generates a result set that *must* be processed by your code or discarded before the RDO resources are released and the next result set is made available. How do you manage these multiple sets of results with the RDO interface? It turns out that the RDO interface and the ODBC API are designed to deal (at least to some extent) with this contingency by implementing the rdoResultset object's MoreResults method.

NOTE The server-side cursor driver will balk if you try to send it a query that it even *thinks* has more than one SELECT statement (or is otherwise too complex). There are two ways around this. If you must create multiple *scrollable* result sets, you have to use one of the other cursor libraries. But you *can* use a server-side cursor library if you disable the cursor.

Action queries also generate rowless result sets, which must also be processed, but the ODBC drivers and the RDO interface basically ignore embedded action queries included in SELECT statements. For example, if you submit a query that includes (1) four SELECT queries for populating four local ListBox controls and (2) a stored procedure that updates a table, your code has to deal with only four result sets. But you might not know how many result sets can be generated by a stored procedure, so your code must be prepared to process *n* sets of results.

For example, some system stored procedures generate a result set for each column in a table or each table in a database—you generally don't know ahead of time how many to expect. Executing queries that return multiple result sets is done no differently from the way you execute other queries. Not really. If you use the rdoQuery object, however, you can't depend on the RowsAffected property to determine the number of rows affected by action queries, since embedded action queries are ignored and don't set the RowsAffected property. It's possible to execute a multiple result set query by using the Execute method but not possible to retrieve the affected rows from individual statements, and a trappable error results if any of the queries returns rows.

The following steps lead you through the process of creating and managing the results of a multiple result set TSQL procedure:

1. Set up an rdoResultset object, using whatever means you choose. You might create an rdoQuery object or simply execute an OpenResultset with a TSQL query. The SQL query itself contains more than one statement—a batch. Although you can include an action query in a SELECT statement, you can't examine the RowsAffected property of the action query: its result set is basically ignored by the RDO interface. To retrieve RowsAffected from an action query, execute the action queries singly, in rdoQuery objects, or with Execute statements. You can also pass back the *@@ROWCOUNT* value from the stored procedure as a return status or additional output parameter. The rdoQuery

CAUTION

Not every combination of TSQL statements can be included in a batch. If you don't know what constitutes a correct batch, consult the TSQL documentation.

object's RowsAffected property is used in the first case; in the second, the rdoConnection object's RowsAffected property is used.

2. Use whatever means you want to move through the rdoResultset rows. The first result set containing a SELECT statement is made available as soon as the rdoResultset returns control to your application, as soon as StillExecuting returns False when running with the rdAsyncEnable option, or as soon as the QueryComplete event fires—and before the QueryTimeout event fires.

3. When you are through with the first result set, even if you haven't moved to the last row, you can use the MoreResults method to flush the first result set and move on to the next. MoreResults returns True if there are more result sets to process. Once you execute MoreResults, the previous result set is no longer available.

4. Once you execute MoreResults, the next *row-returning* result set is available. There is no way to tell how many result sets an arbitrary query can produce, unless you write it yourself.

> **NOTE** A row-returning result set is generated by the SELECT statement. Not all SELECT statements return rows—some simply return values. But these are treated like rowsets by RDO.

5. If you decide to abandon the entire batch, execute the rdoResultset object's Cancel method, or simply close the rdoResultset object using the Close method.

> **TIP** If you use a forward-only cursor to move through the rows of the result set, you won't be able to examine the RowCount property to see whether the query returned any rows—not, at least, until the result set is fully populated. You can also check the EOF (end of file) property instead. If it's True, the query didn't return rows.

Here is a step-by-step procedure that demonstrates how to execute a multiple result set query by using the rdoQuery object:

1. Create your SQL statement and place it in a string variable—for instance, *MySQL*. For SQL Server, multiple statements must be separated by semicolons:

```
MySQL = "Select Author from Authors; " _
 & " Select City from Publishers; " _
 & " Update MyTable Set Age = 18 " _
 & " Where Name = 'Fred' "
```

2. Use an existing rdoQuery object from the rdoQueries collection, or create a new rdoQuery object, and set a variable declared as *rdoQuery* and multiple result sets to this object (in this case, *MyQy*). The

example assumes an rdoConnection object (*Cn*) already exists. You can pass the SQL statement to the CreateQuery method, but this example sets the SQL property after creating an instance of the object. This technique can also be used if the rdoQuery object has already been created and is referenced by its name or ordinal number in the rdoQueries collection:

```
Dim MyQy As New rdoQuery      ' Create a stand-alone rdoQuery
MyQy.ActiveConnection = Cn    ' rdoConnection created earlier
MyQy.SQL = MySQL
```

3. Execute the query by using the OpenResultset method against the rdoQuery object. If you don't need the extra properties or the ability to pass parameters to the query, just use the OpenResultset method directly against the rdoConnection object. The arguments you use here affect all result sets fetched from this query. For example, if you need to use a cursor on the second result set, you must specify a cursor type (like rdOpenKeyset) when the first result set is opened:

```
Dim MyRs As rdoResultset
Set MyRs = MyPs.OpenResultset _
    (rdOpenForwardOnly, rdConcurReadOnly)
```

4. You are now ready to process the first result set. Note that the Options argument *rdAsyncEnable* wasn't set, and so control is *not* returned to the application until the first row of the first result set is ready for processing. Even if the current rdoResultset contains rows, the RowCount property is set to –1 because the forward-only snapshot doesn't update the RowCount until after the rdoResultset is fully populated. If there are no rows, the EOF property returns True. If you use any other type of cursor, the RowCount property returns 1, indicating that the first row has been populated (there are rows to process), or 0, indicating that no rows were returned by the rdoResultset.

    The following example fills a ListBox control named *NameList1* with the results of the query:

```
Do Until MyRs.EOF               ' Loop through all rows
    NameList1.AddItem = MyRs(0)  ' Use the first column
    MyRs.MoveNext                ' Position to the next row
                                 ' in the result set
Loop
```

5. The first result set is now at the EOF position. At this point, you can use either the MoreResults method to activate the next result set or the Cancel method to abandon processing of the rdoResultset—even if it's running in Asynchronous mode. Once you execute MoreResults, the previous set of rows is no longer available, even if you used one of the cursor options to create it:

```
' Activate the next set of results.
If (MyRs.MoreResults) Then…
```

6. Now you're ready to process the second result set. This example uses only the first few names and discards the remaining rows:

```
' Loop through some rows
Do While Not MyRs.EOF and MyRs(0) < "B"
' Use the first column
  NameList1.AddItem = MyRs(0)
  MyRs.MoveNext
Loop
' Activate the next set of results and discard remaining rows
If (MyRs.MoreResults) Then…
```

7. And now you can process the last set of results. Because this is an UPDATE statement, there are no rows to be returned and the RDO interface ignores the result set that is generated. The action query was executed, but you have no way of knowing whether it returned rows. The MoreResults method is used for the last time to release all resources connected with this query:

```
' Activate the next set of results.
If (MyRs.MoreResults) Then…
```

8. When you use the MoreResults method against the last result set, it should return False, and other resources required to process the query should be released. At this point, the rdoQuery object can be reused. If you use the Close method against the rdoPreparedStatement, the rdoQuery is removed from the rdoQueries collection. If you intend to reuse it later by passing it different parameters or simply by changing its SQL property, you can leave the rdoQuery open.

CAUTION
You will get a trappable error if you try to use the MoveLast method on an rdoResultset that has no rows or can't be scrolled. Check the EOF property first.

Working with Page-Based Data Types

Before we venture into the next town, I need to get something off my chest. In my opinion (which is certainly not shared by everyone), before you commit to putting TEXT and IMAGE (BLOB) columns in your database, you need to take a *big* step back and think again. I haven't heard of very many implementations (OK, I've heard of *one*) where putting BLOBs in the database ended up making sense. I came to this conclusion over the years by listening to countless cries of help from developers and their managers who had waded off into the BLOB swamp and needed rescuing. In virtually all cases, we were able to find faster, easier, and more supportable ways to access BLOB data—and none of them involved using the Chunk methods or storing the BLOB data in the database. Sure, it can be done, and you can deliver pizza with a pregnant camel, but it's not something I would wish on most people.

So why not? Let's look at the facts. The TEXT and IMAGE SQL Server data types are stored on a linked set of 2-KB data pages. Therefore, they're called *page-based data types*. The Visual Basic documentation also refers to them as *binary large object* (BLOB) or *chunk* data. These types are used to store extremely large columns, such as graphics or "memo"-type data. It's entirely possible to use the Chunk methods in working with page-based OLE objects and graphics, but I think you might find it far easier to use the RemoteData control for this purpose.

Basically, the RDO interface works the same way Jet does in this respect—just faster. If and when you store a byte in a BLOB column, SQL Server allocates a 2 KB page to store it on. It keeps using this page until you get up to a little less than 2 KB of data, when it allocates another page. This continues as the data is uploaded to the server. Compared to saving a file to disk, this process is extremely inefficient and can take quite a bit of system resources to process. When it comes time to back up the database (as you do once a week or so), these BLOB pages get saved just like any other page—even though they haven't changed since you put them on the system last spring. This means more tape, longer backup cycles, and sometimes fewer backups. It also means larger transaction logs because the operations used to upload the data from ODBC are logged. In some cases, this means disrupting the normal transaction log cycles to accommodate the BLOB transfers. When it comes time to fetch the data, it can be located only by some fairly crude techniques because you can't just write code that says *select * From Authors Where MyBlob like '%some string%'*. You can do this with Microsoft Word documents but not with SQL Server BLOB types—at least not without a text-search package. And look at the hoops you have to jump through to deal with the BLOB data types. The Chunk methods are some of the least understood and most finicky around. They're no joy to use, and if you don't play your cards right, they won't return what you expect at all—at least not very fast. And what about displaying, editing, or manipulating this data? In most cases, the data stored isn't ASCII text at all but complex ActiveX objects or graphics structures that can be viewed only with a control designed specifically for the data type. And how do those controls take the data? Well, if you don't use the RemoteData control, you have to save the data to a file and use a LoadPicture method against the Picture control or save the data to a file and set up an ActiveX link to Word or Microsoft Excel (or whatever was used to create the file) and pass the file reference to the link.

So what's the solution? It has become pretty clear to me that BLOB data belongs in files, such as Word DOC files, Microsoft Excel XLS files, or other native format files used to hold the data—not in databases. This means that picture data lives in BMP, GIF, or PCS files in their native formats. But how do you locate and retrieve the data? That's easy. That's what the database is for. When you record the row that would contain the BLOB column, store a pointer to the file instead. You could also store the owner, check-out status, date created, size, type, and anything else that makes sense in the database, where this type of data belongs. You could go so far as to store a set of keywords that *can* be searched with a SELECT statement. Since BLOB data is often read only, you can store the data anywhere—even on the client's system. Make your clients take out that Doom CD and put in your data CD containing the current edition of your files and images. The database can then fetch pathnames relative to the location of the CD. And what if the files change suddenly? The database could be loaded with a URL pointing to the new file or image out on the Web. If the files change all the time, you simply use the net to download the data. It's not as fast as local disk or CD access, but far faster and easier on the net than using the Chunk methods. When it's time to display the data, you might still have to launch an ActiveX-driven version of Word or another custom application to display the text (unless you can use RTF, in which case the RichText control will do the trick). If you need only to load pictures, simply point to the file with the Picture or Image control (or your favorite alternative) and use the LoadPicture method. My tests show this technique yields a performance at least six times better than what you can achieve using BLOB methods. This also means that not all clients need to be connected by means of a LAN to get the retrieval performance they need because the data can be stored locally and retrieved locally on demand. Some very experienced people have commented that "real" BLOB management solutions cache the data using one mechanism or another to improve performance. Yes, I expect that's true. But it seems to me that solution adds even more complexity and system resource expense to the design.

And now for an opposing point of view. When I expressed these opinions over e-mail, I received a dozen or so replies supporting my position. But I did hear an experienced voice say that my approach didn't lead to a bed of roses. To summarize, the opposition said that maintenance, security, error handling, and referential integrity were nightmares when using the file-based approach—at least for his application. In addition, overall features didn't work well because of the synchronization that was required. When his team designed their new system to store its BLOB in the database, all the previous problems were handled. Although a few more surfaced. In this person's opinion (and I share *some* but not all of his views), the following points are advantages to the BLOB-in-the-database approach:

- It's easier to keep data in sync (referential integrity) when storing the BLOB data in the database.

- Error handling and resource management (space) are better with a database than with a database and a file system.

- Database dumps, maintenance of the application data (including BLOB), reporting, and moving data from one source to another are easier from an infrastructure point of view when the BLOB is stored in the image data of the database.

- You don't have overall maintenance requirements for a second storage system (file system), which is big.

- Security, implementation, and maintenance are much better when the BLOB data is stored in the database.

The opposing e-mail voice conceded the following points as arguments *against* storing BLOBs in the database:

- Database size is much bigger with BLOB data stored in the database. Database DBCC, dumps, and other maintenance tasks take more time and effort.

- ODBC didn't work well, so his team used DBLIB. They gained additional speed by using a bigger packet size (4 KB to 8 KB). Default packet size is 512 bytes.

- Coding in DBLIB was more complex than DAO.

For performance reasons, they placed the BLOB (image data) in its own table so that queries searching for information wouldn't be involved in reading or dealing in some other way with the BLOB data. This would also help the backup situation because you could engineer a selective table backup. Only when you wanted to read, update, or delete the BLOB data would you reference the table.

I think that the points made in opposition to my file system were for the most part valid. While I don't agree with all of the assessments, the arguments show the complexity of the solutions. For that team's particular situation, storing BLOBs in the database was more attractive because of the large number and relatively small size of that application's data chunks. They were usually under 50 KB (but grew to over 20 MB) and averaged 5 KB—and there were bazillions of rows. That application also had no static data.

OK, I'm done. For those of you determined to use the Chunk methods, here are a few paragraphs and some sample code that should make this daunting task a little easier. But I feel like I'm throwing a can of soda to someone stuck in quicksand.

Using the Chunk Methods to Fetch Page-Based Data

The ColumnSize property of the rdoColumn object returns the actual length of the data in a BLOB column. When you're using the ODBC cursor library, this value is always −1, which indicates that the data length isn't available. When you're using server-side cursors or the Client Batch cursor library, the ColumnSize property always returns the actual data length of a BLOB column.

To retrieve the data from a BLOB column by using the Chunk methods, you have to use the GetChunk method, specifically, which takes as an argument the number of bytes to retrieve. That way, you can decide how many bytes to buffer per fetch. When you're using server-side cursors, you can pass the value of the ColumnSize property as the number of bytes to retrieve to get all the data at once. Since the ColumnSize property isn't available when you use the ODBC cursor library, you should call GetChunk repeatedly until no more data is returned. Here is code for how to do this. First, create an rdoResultset that contains the primary key and the BLOB column:

```
Dim s As String
Dim sTemp As String
Dim lColSize As Long
lColSize = MyResultset!MyBLOBColumn.ColumnSize
If lColSize = -1 Then
    ' Column size is not available.
    ' Loop getting chunks until no more data.
    sTemp = MyResultset!MyBLOBColumn.GetChunk(50)
    Do
        s = s & sTemp
        sTemp = MyResultset!MyBLOBColumn.GetChunk(50)
    Loop While Len(sTemp) > 0
Else
' Get all of it.
    If lColSize > 0 Then
        s = MyResultset!MyBLOBColumn.GetChunk(lColSize)
    End If
End If
```

When you use the ODBC cursor library and the BLOB data types, you must also select at least one non-BLOB column in the result set so that the RDO interface can use SQLExtendedFetch to retrieve the data. This is what would usually happen anyway, since you need to include a key field in the result set if you want to update the data.

Tips and Techniques When Accessing BLOBs

It's tough to fetch BLOB data with a stored procedure because the ODBC cursor library doesn't bind to the BLOB columns and needs to be able to know a source table name in order to go back and retrieve the image data when it's requested. Since the source of the query was just a stored procedure call, it has no way of knowing how to do this. You can use the Client Batch cursor library instead—but make sure the SourceTable is filled in.

One problem still remains: you'll notice when you try the GetChunk method that you might get an Invalid Cursor Position error from the ODBC SQL Server driver. This happens because RDO attempts to call SQLSetPos to position to the current row so that the subsequent SQLGetData call will begin reading data from the beginning of the column. (This is in case you called Move 0 and then did a GetChunk loop again, expecting to reset the reading position to the beginning of the column.) Technically, this isn't allowed in ODBC, and the SQL Server driver returns an error. The good news is that this error is totally harmless and can be ignored. Since it's just the SQLSetPos call that generated the error, the SQLGetData calls (produced by the GetChunk method) work just fine. All you need to do is trap the error in an On Error trap and call Resume to ignore the error. The error will happen only on the first GetChunk call for a row, so it falls into the error trap only once.

If you examine the data buffer returned from GetChunk, Visual Basic attempts to convert it to a string and display it in the debug window or watch window. The result is binary trash. The good news is that you can tell Visual Basic to print that data buffer in hexadecimal instead of as a string so that you can validate that the correct data is coming back—assuming you know what you are looking for.

The GetChunk and AppendChunk methods work with the LongVarChar and LongVarBinary column types, also known as TEXT and IMAGE columns, in Microsoft SQL Server. To identify these column types in RDO, use the rdoColumn object's Type property, which returns the constants *rdLongVarChar* or *rdLongVarBinary*, or you can use the rdoColumn object's ChunkRequired property to determine whether you need to use the Get/AppendChunk methods to access the column.

Random BLOB Musings

The following items were extracted from a popular Web page on handling BLOBs, but brought up to date—code and all.

- When selecting a result set containing BLOB columns, you should place the BLOB columns at the end of the select list. If you usually use the *Select * from table* syntax, you should change this to *Select char1, text1, image1 from table* to explicitly reference each column and place the BLOB columns at the end.

- When editing a BLOB column using the AppendChunk method, you should select at least one other editable non-BLOB column in your result set and edit the non-BLOB column as well as the BLOB column. If you don't edit the non-BLOB column, RDO won't raise an error but the data might not be saved back to the base table.

- In RDO 1.0, you couldn't bind a BLOB value to a parameter marker because the AppendChunk method wasn't available on the rdo-Parameter object. If you wanted to pass a BLOB as an input parameter to a stored procedure, you had to utilize the ODBC handle from RDO to process this through ODBC API calls. AppendChunk has now been implemented on the rdoColumn *and* rdoParameter objects in RDO 2.0.

- If you are trying to display a bitmap image in a Picture control that's stored in a LongVarBinary column, keep in mind that the Picture control in Visual Basic can't accept a stream of bits via Visual Basic code. The only way to place a picture into, or get the bits back out of, a Picture control through code is through use of a disk file. You can also use the RDC and bind the Picture box to the BLOB column. This works well for reads (displaying the Picture), but updates are unstable in Visual Basic 4.0 because of problems in Visual Basic's binding manager. To perform updates, you should use code rather than the Visual Basic version 4.0 RDC. The jury is still out on the Visual Basic version 5.0 RemoteData control.

- With the ODBC cursor library, you can't use the GetChunk or AppendChunk methods on a result set returned by a stored procedure. This is because the BLOB data doesn't come across the pipe with the rest of the result set. RDO has to go back and use the SQLGetData or SQLPutData ODBC API functions on the column when you request it with the RDO GetChunk or AppendChunk methods. Without reference to the SourceTable, refetching data isn't possible.

- If you're using server-side cursors, you can get at your BLOB data. The server-side cursor knows the content of the stored procedure and can thus get at the base table. A limitation of this is that you can't create a server-side cursor based on a stored procedure that has anything more than one single SELECT statement in it (a SQL Server restriction), so it's limiting and doubtful that you would be able to use this as your primary technique.

- The fact that users want to update their BLOB column demands that they expose their base tables and create the cursor by using a standard SELECT statement from that base table. This would be true even if you were coding directly to ODBC (not an RDO thing), as well as to DBLIB. If you use Jet, you can't update cursors based on stored procedures at all because they are always read-only.

A BLOB Example

The following example code is divided into three separate procedures: Command1_Click, ColumnToFile, and FileToColumn. ColumnToFile and FileToColumn are two self-contained procedures that you should be able to paste directly into your code if you're moving BLOB data back and forth from your table to files on disk. Each of the procedures accepts parameters that can be provided by your application. Form_Load contains the example code that makes the connection to your database and creates the table *chunktable* if it doesn't exist; FetchButton_Click calls the ColumnToFile and FileToColumn procedures with the proper parameters.

NOTE You'll find this code on the companion CD. See "BLOB Example."

```
Option Explicit

    Dim cn As New rdoConnection
    Dim rs As rdoResultset, TempRs As rdoResultset
    Dim SQL As String
    Dim CurRec As Integer
```

(continued)

```
Private Sub Form_Load()
    cn.Connect = "Driver={SQL Server}; " _
      & " Server=Betav1;Database=pubs;" _
      & " Uid=;Pwd="
      SQL = "Select int1, char1, text1, image1 from chunktable"

    cn.CursorDriver = rdUseServer
    cn.EstablishConnection rdDriverNoPrompt
    On Error Resume Next

    If cn.rdoTables("chunktable").Updatable Then Else
    If Err > 0 Then
        On Error GoTo 0
        Debug.Print "Creating new table…"
        cn.Execute "Create table chunktable " _
            "(int1 int identity, " & _
            "char1 char(30), text1 text, image1 image)"
        cn.Execute "create unique index int1index on " _
            & " chunktable(int1)"
    End If

End Sub

Private Sub BuildAndSave_Click()
BuildAndSave.Enabled = False
MousePointer = vbHourglass
On Error GoTo 0
Set rs = cn.OpenResultset(Name:=SQL, _
    Type:=rdOpenDynamic, _
    LockType:=rdConcurRowVer)

If rs.EOF Then
    rs.AddNew
    rs("char1") = Now
    rs.Update
    rs.Requery
End If
CurRec = rs("int1")
rs.Edit
FileToColumn rs.rdoColumns("text1"), _
    App.Path & "\README.TXT", 102400
FileToColumn rs.rdoColumns("image1"), _
    App.Path & "\SETUP.BMP", 102400
rs("char1") = Now
' Need to update at least one non-BLOB column
    rs.Update
    FetchButton.Enabled = True
    MousePointer = vbNormal
End Sub

Sub FetchButton_Click()
    ' This code gets the column size of each column.
```

```
        Dim text1_len As Long, image1_len As Long
        Set rs = cn.OpenResultset(Name:=SQL, _
            Type:=rdOpenDynamic, _
            LockType:=rdConcurRowVer)
        If rs("text1").ColumnSize = -1 Then
            ' The function Datalength is SQL Server-specific,
            ' so you might have to change this for your database.
            SQL = "Select Datalength(text1) As text1_len, " _
                & "Datalength(image1) As image1_len from chunktable " _
                & "Where int1=" & CurRec
            Set TempRs = cn.OpenResultset(Name:=SQL, _
                Type:=rdOpenStatic, _
                LockType:=rdConcurReadOnly)
            text1_len = TempRs("text1_len")
            image1_len = TempRs("image1_len")
            TempRs.Close
        Else
            text1_len = rs("text1").ColumnSize
            image1_len = rs("image1").ColumnSize
        End If

        ColumnToFile rs.rdoColumns("text1"), _
            & App.Path & "\text1.txt", _
            102400, text1_len
        ColumnToFile rs.rdoColumns("image1"), _
            & App.Path & "\image1.bmp", _
            102400, image1_len
        Set Image1 = LoadPicture(App.Path & "\image1.bmp")
        RichTextBox1.filename = App.Path & "\text1.txt"
        MousePointer = vbNormal
End Sub

Sub ColumnToFile(Col As rdoColumn, ByVal DiskFile As String,
    BlockSize As Long, ColSize As Long)
    Dim NumBlocks As Integer
    Dim LeftOver As Long
    Dim byteData() As Byte      ' Byte array for LongVarBinary
    Dim strData As String       ' String for LongVarChar
    Dim DestFileNum As Integer, i As Integer

    ' Remove any existing destination file.
    If Len(Dir$(DiskFile)) > 0 Then
        Kill DiskFile
    End If
    DestFileNum = FreeFile
    Open DiskFile For Binary As DestFileNum
    NumBlocks = ColSize \ BlockSize
    LeftOver = ColSize Mod BlockSize
    Select Case Col.Type
        Case rdTypeLONGVARBINARY
        byteData() = Col.GetChunk(LeftOver)
```

(continued)

```
                Put DestFileNum, , byteData()
                For i = 1 To NumBlocks
                    byteData() = Col.GetChunk(BlockSize)
                    Put DestFileNum, , byteData()
                Next i
            Case rdTypeLONGVARCHAR
                For i = 1 To NumBlocks
                    strData = String(BlockSize, 32)
                    strData = Col.GetChunk(BlockSize)
                    Put DestFileNum, , strData
                Next i
                strData = String(LeftOver, 32)
                strData = Col.GetChunk(LeftOver)
                Put DestFileNum, , strData
            Case Else
                MsgBox "Not a ChunkRequired column."
            End Select
            Close DestFileNum
    End Sub

    Sub FileToColumn(Col As rdoColumn, _
        DiskFile As String, BlockSize As Long)
    ' Moves a disk file to a ChunkRequired column in the table.
    ' A Byte array is used to avoid a Unicode string.
        Dim byteData() As Byte    ' Byte array for LongVarBinary
        Dim strData As String     ' String for LongVarChar
        Dim NumBlocks As Integer
        Dim filelength As Long
        Dim LeftOver As Long
        Dim SourceFile As Integer
        Dim i As Integer
        SourceFile = FreeFile
        Open DiskFile For Binary Access Read As SourceFile
        filelength = LOF(SourceFile) ' Get the length of the file
        If filelength = 0 Then
            Close SourceFile
            MsgBox DiskFile & " empty or not found."
        Else
            ' Calculate number of blocks to read and leftover bytes.
            NumBlocks = filelength \ BlockSize
            LeftOver = filelength Mod BlockSize
            Col.AppendChunk Null

            Select Case Col.Type
            Case rdTypeLONGVARCHAR
                ' Read the 'leftover' amount of LONGVARCHAR data.
                strData = String(LeftOver, " ")
                Get SourceFile, , strData
                Col.AppendChunk strData
                strData = String(BlockSize, " ")
                For i = 1 To NumBlocks
                    Get SourceFile, , strData
```

```
                 Col.AppendChunk strData
            Next i
            Close SourceFile
        Case rdTypeLONGVARBINARY
            ' Read the leftover amount of LONGVARBINARY data.
            ReDim byteData(LeftOver)
            Get SourceFile, , byteData()
            Col.AppendChunk byteData()
            ReDim byteData(BlockSize)
            For i = 1 To NumBlocks
                Get SourceFile, , byteData()
                Col.AppendChunk byteData()
            Next i
            Close SourceFile
        Case Else
            MsgBox "Not a ChunkRequired column."
        End Select
    End If
End Sub
```

You will need to change the Server, Database, UID, and PWD values in the connect string in order to connect to your database.

The code in the FetchButton_Click event expects to find two files, README.TXT and SETUP.BMP, in the current directory. These files are usually found in the Windows directory. You can either move these files to your current directory or change the path to match another bitmap and text file on your hard drive.

Face to Face with the rdoTable Object

OK, I promised, and here we are—staring down that rare and endangered wild thing known as the rdoTable object. To turn this object on, you simply access it in code:

```
Dim tb As rdoTable
For Each tb In rdoTables
    ListOfTables.AddItem tb.Name
Next
```

The rdoTables collection isn't automatically populated, because doing that is very expensive, especially since this functionality is almost never used. Therefore, until you reference the rdoTables collection and the rdoTable object, they are *not* populated. Indirect or internal references can't succeed until the rdoTables collection is populated.

Once the rdoTables collection is populated with *all* the tables in the current SQL Server database, you can examine the column properties of any table. (But you can't change any of these properties—they are all read-only.)

Very few of my production programs examine the schema of a working database, but when I do need to take a drive through the schema, I just run SQL Enterprise Manager, right from Windows 95. Since the RDO interface doesn't support changing the database's schema, you must resort to an external utility: TSQL statements, executed with the Execute method, or—heaven forbid—the Jet/DAO model. I don't believe I just said that.

Here are three steps for getting acquainted with this exotic beast:

1. Use the OpenResultset method to create an rdoResultset object based on *all* the rows of the base table. When you do this, you essentially execute a SELECT * FROM *table* query. (By the way, if the table has more than a few hundred rows, this is a great way to bring your workstation to its knees.)

2. Use the Name property to determine the name of the table or view.

3. Use the Type property to determine the type of table. The ODBC data source driver determines the supported table type as a string. With SQL Server, the possible settings for the rdoTable Type property are *Table, View, System Table, Global Temporary, Local Temporary, Alias,* and *Synonym*. Somewhere along the line, however, it seems that the SQL Server system tables were ignored—they don't appear in the list of known tables. All I've seen are *Table-* and *View-*type tables.

NOTE The documentation says to use the RowCount property when you want to determine the number of rows in a table or view. It also says that for base tables the RowCount property contains the number of rows in the specified database table. That's true for Jet tables, but you can't determine the number of rows in a SQL Server table unless you run an all-inclusive query against it. Therefore, RowCount for an rdoTable object is 0 until you create an rdoResultset against the rdoTable object. What else does the documentation say? It says you can use the Updatable property to determine whether a table supports changes to its data. Wrong again: this is an rdoTable object, so the Updatable property is always False.

I wrote a little program to verify these factoids. Let's take a ride through the code and pick up the nuances along the way. I use a common grid to show the column properties, so I set this up in Form_Load:

```
Option Explicit
Dim en As rdoEnvironment
Dim cn As rdoConnection
Dim cl As rdoColumn
Dim tb As rdoTable
Dim i As Integer
Private Sub Form_Load()
Grid1.Row = 0
For i = 0 To 8
    Grid1.Cols = i + 1
    Grid1.Col = i
    Grid1.ColWidth(i) = TextWidth("MMMMMMyy")
    Grid1 = Choose(i + 1, "Type", "Size", "AllowZeroLength", _
        "Attributes", "ChunkRequired", "OrdinalPosition", _
        "Required", "SourceColumn", "SourceTable")
Next i
```

Now we're ready to open up the connection to our test database. It has about a dozen tables, so there are plenty of examples to show. I populate a list box with all the table names. (Note that the system tables aren't included.)

```
Private Sub Populate_Click()
Set en = rdoEngine.rdoEnvironments(0)
Set cn = en.OpenConnection(dsname:="BIBLIO", Connect:="uid=;pwd=")
For Each tb In cn.rdoTables
    TableList.AddItem tb.Name
Next
TableList.ListIndex = 0
End Sub
```

To discover the details on a chosen table, we grab the indicated table by name. You have to dereference the TableList object in order to get its Text property. Next, we create a list of columns for the chosen table:

```
Private Sub TableList_Click()
ColumnList.Clear
Set tb = cn.rdoTables((TableList))
Rows = tb.RowCount
Updatable = tb.Updatable
TType = tb.Type
For Each cl In tb.rdoColumns
    ColumnList.AddItem cl.Name
Next
ColumnList.ListIndex = 0
End Sub
```

Once a column is selected, we simply enumerate all the properties and dump the value returned into the DBGrid. Notice the dereferencing when we choose a column name on the basis of the chosen ColumnList value:

```
Private Sub ColumnList_Click()
Grid1.Row = 1
Set cl = tb.rdoColumns((ColumnList))
For i = 0 To Grid1.Cols - 1
    Grid1.Row = 1
    Grid1.Col = i
    Select Case i
        Case 0: Grid1 = cl.Type
        Case 1: Grid1 = cl.Size
        Case 2: Grid1 = cl.AllowZeroLength
        Case 3: Grid1 = cl.Attributes
        Case 4: Grid1 = cl.ChunkRequired
        Case 5: Grid1 = cl.OrdinalPosition
        Case 6: Grid1 = cl.Required
        Case 7: Grid1 = cl.SourceColumn
        Case 8: Grid1 = cl.SourceTable
    End Select
Next
End Sub
```

Assigning Column Data to Visual Basic Controls

In Visual Basic 3.0, the process of taking data from Recordset fields was fairly straightforward. In later versions of Visual Basic, the task is somewhat more difficult, only because there are so many more field types to deal with. I have a few suggestions that might save you some time late at night:

- When you're working with TextBox controls, simply assign the value returned from the rdoResultset to the Text property. This is the default property of the control.

- When you work with the Microsoft RichText control, you can do the same thing, but in this case the default property is the RTFText property, which is very different from the Text property. Be sure to choose the right property when you want to assign and extract data from the control.

- When you're working with a control that is associated with a special-format column, you must be aware of the format as you attempt to update. If there is a problem with the data content of the control, the Update method fails—usually with Error 40060.

- You handle Picture and Image controls with the RDO interface virtually the same way you handle them with the Jet/DAO method. Basically, the controls' data must be loaded by means of the LoadPicture method.

- Remember to concatenate an empty string to a column that might contain a Null value like this:

```
A = "" & MyRS(0)
```

Chapter 27

Maintaining Data with the RDO Interface

Options for Data Modification

Adding Data

Updating Data

Deleting Data

When Things Go Wrong

From time to time, almost any database system has to have rows added, updated, or deleted—that is, the database needs to be *maintained*. You already know, after reading the previous chapters in Part IV, how to retrieve data. This chapter is about using the RDO interface to maintain data.

Options for Data Modification

When you use the RDO interface (as when you use the Microsoft Jet database engine), you have basically two choices for modifying the database: you can use a read-write cursor (if you want to modify base tables directly), or you can use the Execute method. The problem with cursors is that they are inherently evil—especially for developers trying to create scalable applications. Unless you are very clever, persistent cursors can't be used for server-side components because they require your remote component to maintain a state that can lock out other users. Cursors can be used for client-side data access because it's fairly easy to maintain state, but they still lock out other users trying to share the database. Sure, it's possible to create cursors that don't lock down lots of pages, and this is what you will have to do if you choose this approach. But it's very easy to get carried away and create broad-scope cursors that lock entire regions of the database—for indeterminate lengths of time. Stateless update strategies are the most scalable. That is, the update operation doesn't depend on the row being locked while the application decides what to do and it doesn't have to "remember" which rows were being worked on. That's where the Execute method comes in.

As we migrate to server-side components, you'll eventually migrate to stateless techniques that don't depend on cursors but on strategies that depend on more robust contingency handlers, which deal with the realities of heavily contested database resources. ADO will take us closer toward that reality as it implements more and more sophisticated server-side functionality to make this type of architecture easier to implement and more efficient.

NOTE The RDO interface supports only two basic methods for modifying data in the database, but there are several others you should consider. For example, when data must be imported into or exported from the database, consider using the SQL Transfer Manager or BCP. And don't forget about the RemoteData control (the topic of the next chapter).

As Visual Basic matures, it seems to be gaining power and features exponentially. Many of the more mature techniques described here are for two-tiered applications. While this is a viable architecture, these techniques don't always play well in three-tiered distributed component architectures.

Read-Write Cursors

Assume, if you will, that we are working with a more traditional two-tiered client application. In this case, if you decide on an RDO cursor, you must choose a cursor driver, a cursor type, and a locking mechanism that can yield a read-write rdoResultset cursor against a single table while still meeting your requirements for performance and the user interface. Remember, the RDO interface can't update queries generated from joined tables, views, or stored procedures. This means that you will often have to execute several update operations if more than one table is involved in the change.

Once your rdoResultset cursor is open, you can use the AddNew method against it. At this point, you shouldn't expect an error unless you forgot to check the Updatable property: if it returns False, go back and try again; you probably did something wrong. The rdoResultset object's AddNew method does two things:

- It saves the current-row pointer, so RDO can reposition to the current row's bookmark.

- It creates a new, empty row and provides addressability to it through your rdoResultset object.

After you've executed the AddNew method, all you have to do is assign new values to each of the columns in the row. At the minimum, you must provide data for all columns that can't accept Null values and have no defaults. Unless you are adding rows to a table that uses the new Identity column, you're going to need to provide a unique key value for the index columns. You must use the AppendChunk method to add data to binary large object (BLOB) data columns.

NOTE The RDO interface doesn't automatically fill in default values, the way Jet does. That's something SQL Server can do for you if your database system is set up to include defaults.

Once the row is ready to save, use the rdoResultset object's Update method to save the row in the database. Errors can and do occur at this point. (See the section of this chapter named "When Things Go Wrong.") So be careful. After the insert takes place, don't expect the new row to suddenly become a member of your rdoResultset object. Some ODBC cursors support this feature, but most don't. If you need to ensure that the new row is a member of the rdoResultset, use the Refresh method to repopulate the result set.

The Execute Method

Almost every RDO-based application will end up using the Execute method for most, if not all, operations that involve data modification. Adding records with this technique is fairly simple. Basically, you create a TSQL INSERT statement containing the data for the new row, place it in a string, and execute it with the Execute method. If you use the Execute method against an rdoQuery, you can examine the RowsAffected property after the insert to verify that the operation has taken place. This technique can be used to add more than one row at a time, and it can affect several tables in a single operation. You can also include TSQL transaction processing around the multiple-statement operation to maintain referential integrity. The operation might include DELETE or UPDATE statements as well, all bound together with BEGIN TRANSACTION and COMMIT TRANSACTION TSQL statements. You can write a stored procedure to do all of this and simply pass the new columns as parameters. Using the UserConnection object to create an UpdateRow method would also be possible and fairly easy to implement. In any case, you need to be prepared to roll back partially completed operations—especially in cases where more than one table is involved. Of course, that's where Microsoft Transaction Server comes in handy. It can handle all of these operations for you—automatically.

Adding Data

When you want to add data to the database, keep the following questions in mind:

- *Are you adding a row that other users might also be trying to add?* Be prepared for unique key violations as other users add rows to the same tables. To avoid this, have SQL Server build an Identity column for you.

- *Do you have read-write access to the base table(s)?* You need permission on at least one SQL Server database level, not to mention permission to log on to the server itself. For example, your system administrator needs to grant you or your logon group Execute permission on any stored procedures or updatable views or on the underlying tables.

- *Do you have to use a stored procedure to make the changes?* If so, do you have permission to use this procedure? It's entirely possible to have access to stored procedures but not to the underlying tables.

- *Are you prepared for errors, including those that might be generated by SQL Server rules and triggers?* When you add records, a variety of things can go wrong and your code had best be ready.

- *Does the new record meet all the criteria set up for referential integrity, business rules, and validation of data columns?* Have you already edited the data? Preediting the data reduces (but doesn't eliminate) the chance that one or more fields will fail column or row validation.

- *Are you prepared for duplicate-row errors?* Most relational tables require unique row identifiers, and these are often enforced by SQL Server unique indexes.

Updating Data

For update operations, you should ask yourself the same questions as for adding data. You update existing data in much the same way as you add data, but there are a number of additional considerations.

Updating is a challenge in itself. When you're adding rows, you aren't nearly as concerned with having to block other users as you are when you're making changes to data that others are working with. You might already have a copy of the row to be changed on your workstation, or you could be making a blind update. If you have a copy of the row, it probably has been sitting on the screen for some time, so the data is probably growing stale. As other users modify the rows in the database, the likelihood is high that some other user will change or delete the row you're working on. And don't forget about the possibility that a page you're using is in contention. In any case, you need to have error handlers in place that are prepared for more problems than you'll have when you're adding rows.

Any update operation has to deal with three versions of the row:

1. The row as read from the database, before the user changed it

2. The row as modified by the user

3. The row as modified by some other user whose changes were completed first

Each of these versions of the row plays a part in the locking mechanism you choose and in the decision you make when you discover that an update has failed. As we saw in Chapter 24, the RDO interface supports two types of optimistic locking (rdConcurValues and rdConcurRowver) as well as one type of pessimistic locking (rdConcurLock), with rdConcurReadOnly as the default. But in most cases, pessimistic locking is neither practical nor prudent.

The first question you have to ask is, "What should I do with the changes my user has made?" If you think your user will have to choose among the three versions of the row, you must program a mechanism for reviewing changes made (or proposed) by other users. And consider that while the user ponders this decision, other changes to version 3 of the row might be under way, which compounds the problem. One approach might be to change locking schemes. You have basically the same two choices when you're updating existing data as you do when you're adding data: a read-write cursor or the Execute method. That is, unless you decide to use server-side components to perform the operations.

CAUTION
No matter how much you like them, you don't always have the luxury of using read-write cursors. Sometimes you can't create an updatable cursor against the database because you have only query access to stored procedures or read-only views, or you don't have permission to modify tables, or the RDO interface just won't let you do it on the basis of a SQL join. The use of stored procedures to gate access to underlying data is a fundamental SQL Server feature, so you'll probably have to deal with this limitation sooner or later.

For systems that have to scale beyond a few dozen users, this choice seems to be emerging as the most reasonable.

Positioning the Current-Row Pointer Post Update

Keep in mind that after you call the Update method on an updatable cursor, RDO (and DAO works the same way) repositions to the row you were on before the AddNew method was called. RDO does this mostly because this is the way DAO handles it, and the RDO team wanted to follow their lead. It also makes sense when you think about it—newly added records are appended to the result set, and it would be disconcerting to lose the user's current position in the result set and just leave him hanging out at the end. To provide an easy way to jump back to the newly added row, both DAO and RDO have the LastModified property, which is a bookmark. You can use it to jump back to the last modified row in the result set.

Updating with a Read-Only Cursor

You can choose from a number of ways to update database rows with RDO 2.0. It's nice if you know the key of the row to update, although in many cases you don't have access to the tables at all. You *should* have access to stored procedures or remote business objects that not only know how to perform the updates but have permission to do so. RDO 2.0 makes this easier than ever—now that the WillUpdateRows event has been implemented. This event fires whenever the Update method is executed, which gives you the opportunity to trap the operation and issue your own update operations. At this point, you can execute one or more stored procedures, call a business object or two, or do anything else that the situation demands.

You *can* still update rows directly with RDO, and the following list itemizes the procedure. If you choose an rdoResultset to locate the row you want to change, follow these steps:

1. Use the rdoResultset method to position the current-row pointer to the row to be changed. This becomes version 1 of the row.

2. Execute the Edit method. If you are using optimistic locking, you shouldn't expect an error at this point. If you are using pessimistic locking, you might be denied exclusive access to the page containing the target row. If so, you must trap the resulting error and try again later.

3. Once the Edit method succeeds, post your changes to the affected columns. This becomes version 2 of the row. Be sure to follow the formatting rules. If you change the primary key, you might set off a variety of conditions, including the same kinds of errors that can be generated when you add a new row. Never permit your user to provide data at this stage: every instant of waiting, from the time version 1 of the row is read to the time the update is completed, increases the chances of an error.

4. When the changes are complete, use the Update method. This submits version 2 to the server. If you selected optimistic locking, this is the point where you discover whether version 2 of the row matches version 1. If this test fails, you must decide how to deal with the updated version 3 as read back from the server. If you selected pessimistic locking, your update should succeed without problems—but we rarely use pessimistic locking.

Once the Update succeeds, the page containing the row is unlocked and released to all the other users who are attempting to read or write to rows on the page. If you move your cursor's current-row pointer to another row before using the Update method, any changes are lost. You can also abandon an edit and refresh the current row by using the Move method with a *0* argument or by using the CancelUpdate method. After a successful edit, the current-row pointer is positioned to the row that has been modified—and that could be at the end of the rdoResultset cursor. To revisit the row that was just changed, use the bookmark provided in the LastModified property. If you use the BeginTrans method before beginning your data alterations, any changes are deferred until you use the CommitTrans method to save the changes or the RollbackTrans method to discard them.

Updating with the Execute Method

Another approach is to create an UPDATE statement in TSQL and use the Execute method. As when you're adding rows, you have the option of performing several related operations at once.

TIP As a general rule, don't update columns that haven't changed because doing this could set off triggers that don't need to be executed.

One technique for making update or insert operations more efficient has been suggested by the Microsoft Consulting Services developers who created the RDO interface. This technique uses an rdoQuery object to perform repeated updates. That way, you set up a TSQL update statement only once, passing the column data and WHERE clause qualifier in as parameters. Now you can use the rdoQuery repeatedly and gain significant performance benefits. For this chapter, I wrote sample code that uses this technique two different ways. The first is the old way, in which we create an rdoQuery object against the rdo-Connection object. The second is the new way, in which I simply put the SQL UPDATE statement in a UserConnection object and execute the query as a method—passing the parameters as arguments to the method.

The following first section of code sets up both techniques. We instantiate the UserConnection object and the rdoQuery and rdoConnection objects. Notice that the rdoQuery object is set up to contain a hard-coded query. Consider what would have to be done to this code if the database schema changes.

```
Dim Uc As New UserConnection1
Dim Qy As New rdoQuery
Dim Cn As New rdoConnection
Private Sub Form_Load()
Uc.EstablishConnection
Cn.Connect = "uid=;pwd=;dsn=biblio;database=biblio"
Cn.EstablishConnection rdDriverNoPrompt
Qy.Name = "UpdateTitles"
Set Qy.ActiveConnection = Cn
Qy.SQL = "Update Titles Set " _
    & " PubID = ? ," _
    & " Description = ?, " _
    & " Year_Published = ?," _
    & " Notes = ?" _
    & " Where ISBN = ? "
Qy.rdoParameters(0).Name = "PubID"
End Sub
```

Okay, we're now ready to try the old way. In this case, we have to set up each of the rdoParameter objects to pass in the query parameters one by one and then execute the query. Of course, you would probably pass in the parameters from user-filled-in controls instead of hard-coding the parameters. Notice that we can reference the first parameter by name because we named it when we built the query:

```
Private Sub UpdateTitlesButton_Click()
With Cn.rdoQueries!UpdateTitles
    .rdoParameters!PubID = 264      ' PubID
    .rdoParameters(1) = "My new description"
    .rdoParameters(2) = "1997"
    .rdoParameters(3) = "Some notes..."
    .rdoParameters(4) = "1-57231-567-9" ' ISBN
    .Execute
End With

End Sub
```

Compare the old way I just showed you with the following code. We can replace nine lines of code with one line. And it performs the same ODBC and SQL Server operations:

```
Private Sub Query1Button_Click()
Uc.Query1 264, "My Query1 Description", _
    1997, "Some notes", "1-57231-567-9"
End Sub
```

NOTE This sample code is on the companion CD as "Update Test."

These same strategies can be used to execute stored procedures that do the updating for you. In many cases, that's the only way you can update data in a secure database. This is also an easy way to set up an update or insert operation that affects more than one table.

Deleting Data

Deleting rows isn't nearly as difficult as adding or updating them: either a delete operation completes or it doesn't. It's still possible to time out while you're trying to delete a row on a locked page, but you shouldn't have much trouble setting up an error handler to deal with the contingencies.

As before, you have the same two choices: a read-only cursor or the Execute method. A cursor can delete only the current row in the rdoResultset, but the Execute method can execute a SQL query to delete one row or a whole set of rows. It can also simply truncate the entire table, stripping out all the data rows. There are only a few real concerns:

- *The delete operation might be blocked by someone changing one of the rows on the target row's page.* All you can do is wait and retry—or get out your wire cutters.

- *The delete operation might drop the last row in the rdoResultset.* If this is possible, check for a RowCount of 0 after the Delete method. (I *would* say check for BOF equal to True and EOF equal to True, but these won't change state until you try to cross the "wall" at the end of the rdo-Resultset.) Since your deletes affect other users who are sharing these rows, their rdoResultset objects might also turn up empty or they just might not be able to access populated rows.

- *If you attempt an rdoResultset operation after the Delete, make sure before you do that there is a current row.* Otherwise, you might trip a trappable error.

- *Be prepared for trigger violations.* For example, you might violate one or more referential integrity constraints if you delete a foreign-key row. If this happens, you have to make a decision: Should the rows using foreign keys be updated? Deleted? Or should you just ignore the problem? (If you do, there goes your database's referential integrity.)

When Things Go Wrong

As errors are generated, they are placed in the rdoErrors collection. You can examine the individual members of the rdoErrors collection for details on what caused an error. Visual Basic also produces a trappable error whenever an error occurs. In your On Error handler, you can examine the rdoErrors collection and determine what action to take. To change the threshold of severity for tripping a fatal error, set the rdoDefaultErrorThreshold or the ErrorThreshold properties.

Any application that expects to be taken seriously should include handlers for a variety of errors, as well as contingency plans for dealing with them. And try not to show the user raw error messages generated from the server or ODBC drivers; the user shouldn't be bothered with the gritty details. Your application should just decide what it needs to do and then do it—quickly, quietly, and efficiently.

At any rate, your code is bound to encounter problems from time to time. For example, you should expect problems if you execute the Update method after using the Edit or AddNew methods. An error can also be generated whenever the ODBC driver manager is used to carry out an RDO request. Make sure you're prepared for the laundry list of errors that can occur in the following situations:

- *An added or updated row violates one of the database's validation rules.* You didn't follow the formatting requirements closely enough, or they changed since you last compiled your program. The error message that SQL Server generates is very clear about which rule and column are affected. And note that the error generated might not be in the rdoErrors(0) collection; it might be in rdoErrors(1) or higher. (See the section "Creating a Virtual Application" in Chapter 5.)

- *An added or updated row violates the unique key established for the row.* This problem can be caused when another user adds a row that matches your self-generated key and that user's row arrives before your record is added. When you generate your own keys, you must include transaction processing that prevents this type of failure.

- *The table's Insert trigger finds an error and rolls back the transaction.* Such an error might involve referential integrity or business rules, among other things. The Insert trigger might also have issued a RAISERROR message, which should show up in the rdoErrors collection.

- *One or more database pages are locked.* When this happens, your operation hangs until the QueryTimeout period elapses. Your only recourse is to retry or abandon the operation.

- *The SQL server times out.* This can happen because your QueryTimeout value isn't high enough to account for network traffic, periodic maintenance, or other conditions that slow the server down. The server might also be broken or up to its armpits in somebody else's tough query. Just retry your operation and hope for the best—or find the guy with the tough query and cut his LAN cable.

- *The SQL server enfolds your operation in a deadly embrace.* In these gruesome circumstances, you need to reevaluate your sequence of operations in order to avoid this embrace's lethal clutches in the future. (See "Distributed-Engine Performance," in Chapter 3, if you're lucky enough not to know what a deadly embrace is.)

- *A connection error or other modal error brings the interface down.* Or maybe this time *you're* the one whose LAN cable got cut.

Chapter

Using the RemoteData Control

What's Different About the RemoteData Control?

RemoteData Control Methods and Events

Getting Started

The RemoteData control is a fairly complex piece of code that binds ActiveX-based data-aware controls to the RDO interface. For you to have realized all the advantages of RDO 1.0's features, the RemoteData control would have had to support a read-write cursor against a stored procedure—but it didn't. That's why it was so unappealing to developers who couldn't work with a read-only, data-bound control. To add to this particular limitation, the RemoteData control was plagued with bugs. Soon after Visual Basic version 4.0 was on the shelves, 4.0a was shipped to replace it in an attempt to address many of those troubles.

Visual Basic version 5.0 and RDO 2.0 bring new versions of the RemoteData control, but possibly more important, they bring the ODBCDirect version of the Data control. More important even than that event, the new Advanced Data Connector (ADC) and ADO promise a much more reasonable way to access data from remote data components. But that's a story for another book. When you consider that bound controls have grown considerably in sophistication, this innovation seems even more attractive. Visual Basic version 5.0 now supports the DataBindings collection that lets you choose not one but several columns of an rdoResultset to bind to. (Check out the DataBindings collection.) If you add to that the ability to roll your own bound controls or make your own ActiveX controls data aware, the rationale behind using a "Data Access" control becomes easier to justify.

Don't get me wrong: there *are* applications that can gain from the quick development paradigm offered by the RemoteData control. For example, if you have to work with graphics or ActiveX objects, the RemoteData control solves a few complex problems that really don't have other solutions. Let's look at some potential uses for this control, with SQL Server systems in mind—that is, SQL Server systems that restrict access to data through stored procedures for queries and updates. Here is some of what you can do with the RemoteData control:

- *Fill a DBList control with all valid state codes.* The user can choose from this list instead of entering an incorrect code. The list of valid states hasn't changed since 1959 though, so this list is pretty well set. Anyway, you don't need more than about three lines of code to fill the DBList control, so the RemoteData control is overkill for a static list.

- *Fill a DBCombo control with a selected set of suppliers on the basis of a limited-scope query.* Users choose from this list when they want vendors of particular parts. But why use the RemoteData control? You don't need to update the list, and even if you did, you would do it on a form that exposes the whole row and perhaps more. Again, the updating features of the RemoteData control aren't needed.

- *Bind a set of TextBox controls to the columns in a limited-scope result set.* This seems like a reasonable thing to do. You still have to validate the data being sent from the control to the database, however, and you don't save much with a read-only result set. The RemoteData control does fill the bound controls for you, but you still have to use your custom stored procedure to update the data. If you were to use a custom stored procedure to save these rows in a read-write temporary table uploaded to the main database, this mechanism might have some possibilities.

- *Display the picture of a selected employee on the basis of a one-row query.* This is more like it. If you don't change the picture too often, the RemoteData control can really make this kind of display easy. But I don't recommend putting BLOB data into the database. In this case, you don't need the RDC to fetch or update the data.

As you can see, not many problems cry out for the RemoteData control (or the Data control, either, for that matter). But let's move on to a closer look at this control and how it is implemented. And who knows, you might even find a use for it after all.

What's Different About the RemoteData Control?

The absence of the Microsoft Jet database engine is the biggest difference between the RemoteData control and the Data control. (True, now that there's an ODBCDirect version of the DAO/Jet Data control, the RemoteData control's singular mission is really clouded.) The RemoteData control exposes a number of familiar properties, as well as some that are unique when compared to the DAO/Jet Data control. In virtually all cases, these properties work differently from the corresponding DAO/Jet Data control properties, so you have to pay attention to how you implement the RemoteData control. The ODBCDirect Data control does incorporate many of the same interfaces (although not nearly all), which makes it easier to use with RDO.

The ODBCDirect version might be a better alternative for many developers who require access to data-aware bound controls. At this point, the RemoteData control is totally unproven as far as I am concerned. Until it has shown a lot more reliability than it has in the past, I can't, in all good conscience, endorse it.

With the RemoteData control, you can open a cursor against a stored procedure but you can't do an update. It's a stretch to think of how read-only data-bound controls can help in many SQL Server situations that depend on stored procedures. If your server administrator allows direct access to base tables, you can make better use of the RemoteData control. But it would be a shame to create applications that are dependent on this functionality only to have to dump it when a new SA restricts access.

Figure 28-1 shows the data-related properties for the RemoteData control, the ODBCDirect Data control, and the DAO/Jet Data control. Those that are virtually identical in purpose and functionality are marked with an asterisk in the column labeled "Notes." Most of the data access properties of the RemoteData control simply expose arguments of the underlying RDO methods and object properties. By the way, activating the ODBCDirect implementation of the Data control is very easy—you simply set the DefaultType property to 1-Use ODBC.

The following sections discuss the RemoteData control properties and how to set them.

Setting rdoEnvironment Properties

The Environment property exposes the current rdoEnvironment object. The following rdoEnvironment properties determine how the default rdoEnvironment properties are set:

- *The CursorDriver property* lets you choose the type of cursor driver to use—server-side or ODBC cursor library. This is an rdoEnvironment property.

- *The LogMessages property* lets you enable ODBC tracing and is ordinarily an rdoQuery property.

- *The Version property* lets you see the rdoEngine version number. This maps to the rdoEngine Version property.

Setting rdoConnection Properties

The Connection property exposes a new rdoConnection object. The following rdoConnection properties determine how this object is created:

- *The Connect property* specifies the ODBC connect string. This is an *OpenConnection* argument.

- *The DataSourceName property* specifies the name of an ODBC DSN if you are using one. This is the same as the *OpenConnection* argument.

- *The LoginTimeout property* specifies the length of time that elapses before the user's attempt to log on times out.

- *The UserName and Password properties* specify the SQL Server logon ID and password, unless they are already in the connect string.

- *The Prompt property* specifies how the ODBC driver manager should prompt you at logon time. This is the same as the *OpenConnection* argument.

- *The ReadOnly property* tells the ODBC driver that this is a read-only connection. This is also an *OpenConnection* argument.

Figure 28-1
RemoteData Control and Data Control Properties

RemoteData Control	ODBCDirect Data Control	DAO/Jet Data Control	Notes
BOFAction	BOFAction	BOFAction	*
Connection	Database	Database	Both identify the connection.
Connect	Connect	Connect	Connect string. RDO has no *ODBC;* prefix.
CursorDriver	DefaultCursorType	——	Jet gives no choice of cursor driver.
DataSourceName	DatabaseName	DatabaseName	Both determine the DSN.
EditMode	EditMode	EditMode	*
Environment	——		Exposes the ODBC hEnv.
EOFAction	EOFAction	EOFAction	Supposed to work the same.
ErrorThreshold	——	——	No Jet equivalent.
——	N/A	Exclusive	Can't open SQL Server in exclusive mode.
KeysetSize	——	——	No Jet equivalent.
LoginTimeout	——	——	Set with Jet DBEngine property.
LogMessages	——	——	Points to ODBC log file.
MaxRows	——	——	No Jet equivalent.
Options	Options	Options	Different constants, different options.
Password	——	——	Set with Jet connect string or Workspace options.
Prompt	——	——	No Jet equivalent.
QueryTimeout	——	——	Set with Database option.
ReadOnly	ReadOnly	ReadOnly	*
Resultset	Recordset	Recordset	Different result set objects.
ResultsetType	RecordsetType	RecordsetType	Different cursor types.
RowsetSize	——	——	No Jet equivalent.
SQL	RecordSource	RecordSource	Very similar.
StillExecuting	——	——	No Jet equivalent.
Transactions	——	——	Supports transactions in Jet Recordset Transactions property.
UserName	——	——	Set with Jet connect string or Workspace options.
Version	——	——	Returns Jet DBEngine version or RDO database driver version.

Setting rdoResultset Properties

The Resultset property exposes a new rdoResultset object. Most of the remaining properties determine how the new rdoResultset object is created or managed:

- *The BOFAction property* determines how the RemoteData control behaves when the BOF property returns True.

  - rdMoveFirst (default): this keeps the first row as the current row.

  - rdBOF: moving past the beginning of an rdoResultset object triggers the RemoteData control's Validate event on the first row, followed by a Reposition event on the invalid (BOF) row. At this point, the Move Previous button on the RemoteData control is disabled.

- *The EditMode property* indicates whether the AddNew or Edit methods are active, just as with the Jet Data control.

- *The EOFAction property* is supposed to help when you are working with empty rdoResultset objects or are near the end of the result set, by automatically switching to AddNew mode when the result set is empty.

  - rdMoveLast (default): this keeps the last row as the current row.

  - rdEOF: moving past the end of an rdoResultset object triggers the RemoteData control's Validation event on the last row, followed by a Reposition event on the invalid (EOF) row. At this point, the Move Next button on the RemoteData control is disabled.

  - rdAddNew: moving past the last row triggers the RemoteData control's Validation event on the current row, followed by an automatic AddNew, followed by a Reposition event on the new row.

- *The MaxRows property* maps to the rdoQuery MaxRows property and can set an upper limit on the number of rows retrieved, inserted, deleted, or updated when you're using the control.

- *The Options property* maps to the OpenResultset options, rdAsyncEnable and rdExecDirect. This means that you can create an rdoResultset object asynchronously. If the rdAsyncEnable bit is on, the RemoteData control creates the rdoResultset object in the background and trips the QueryCompleted event when it's done.

- *The QueryTimeout property* maps to the rdoQuery QueryTimeout property.

- *The ResultsetType property* exposes the type of rdoResultset object that is to be created or that has been created. You can open only two of the four types of cursors with the RemoteData control: rdOpenStatic opens a static-type rdoResultset object, and rdOpenKeyset opens a keyset-type rdoResultset object. This property maps to the OpenResultset method *Type* argument.

- *The RowsetSize property* maps to the same property of the rdoQuery object.

- *The SQL property* maps to the same property of the rdoQuery object. It's used in much the same way as the RecordSource property of the Data control; just don't plan on sticking a table name here unless you are prepared for the consequences.

- *The StillExecuting property* maps to the same property of the rdoResultset object. It indicates whether the asynchronous query is done.

- *The Transactions property* has the same function as the Jet Recordset object Transactions property. It simply says that the server supports transactions. In the case of SQL Server, this is always True.

RemoteData Control Methods and Events

As well as the methods exposed by the underlying Connection (rdoConnection), Environment (rdoEnvironment), and Resultset (rdoResultset) objects, the RemoteData control supports a number of methods on its own. These are displayed in *Figure 28-2.*

The RemoteData control has only three data-oriented events, which are shown in *Figure 28-3* on the next page. In general, these events are used to keep invalid data from reaching the SQL Server rules.

The Validate event is fairly powerful. It can undo what the user has done, preventing data from reaching the SQL server. It occurs before a different row becomes the current row but also before the Update method (except when

Figure 28-2
RemoteData Control Methods

Method	Note
BeginTrans, CommitTrans, RollbackTrans	These transaction methods map to the rdoConnection object.
Cancel	This method stops an asynchronous query.
Refresh	This method rebuilds the rdoResultset object on the basis of current properties.
UpdateControls	This method gets the current row from a RemoteData control's rdoResultset object and displays the data in the bound controls.
UpdateRow	This method saves the current values of bound controls to the database.

data is saved with the UpdateRow method) and before a Delete, Unload, or Close operation. In the Validate event procedure, you get a chance to take an action on the basis of whatever criterion you choose. You can execute another query (on another connection) to check out the data, or you can simply perform a reality check on the data.

You have two arguments at your disposal when the Validate event occurs. The first is the *Action* argument, an integer or constant that initially indicates the operation that is causing the Validate event to occur. For example, if the *Action* argument is rdActionMoveLast, the operation that tried to move the current-row pointer is the MoveLast method. Once you know what has caused the reposition, you can do something about it; all you have to do before exiting the Validate event procedure is set the *Action* argument to some other value. For instance, you can change the operation from a MoveNext (rdActionMoveNext) to an AddNew (rdActionAddNew). You can also change the various Move methods and the AddNew method, which can be freely exchanged (any Move into AddNew, AddNew into any Move, and any Move into any other Move). An attempt to change AddNew or one of the Move methods into any others besides these either is ignored or produces a trappable error. You can stop any action by setting the *Action* argument to rdAction-Cancel. In this case, no further action takes place, and the current-row pointer remains where it was before the operation that tried to reposition it. You can't use any methods (such as MoveNext) on the underlying rdoResultset object during the Validate event. *Figure 28-4* shows the *Action* arguments to the Validate event. It also shows that for some reason the argument names have

Figure 28-3
RemoteData Control Events

Events	Notes
QueryCompleted	The asynchronous query has completed. Note that this event is different from the Query-Complete event fired by the rdoConnection.
Reposition	When a RemoteData control is loaded, the first row in the rdoResultset object becomes the current row, causing the Reposition event. Whenever a user clicks any button on the RemoteData control (moving from row to row or using one of the Move methods, such as MoveNext, or any other property or method that changes the current row), the Reposition event occurs after each row becomes current.
Validate	The Validate event occurs *before* the move to a different row. You can use this event to perform calculations based on data in the current row or to change the form in response to data in the current row.

changed. I don't know why, but they have been shortened somewhat, so you'll have to recode. Don't pay any attention to the help topic that lists these—it doesn't match the ODL, so it's wrong.

The second argument at your disposal in the Validate event procedure is the *Save* argument. This argument greatly simplifies your validation routine. It's a Boolean expression that specifies whether bound data has changed. *Save* is True if the bound data has changed since the current row was last repositioned. *Save* is False if the data has not changed. Although the *Save* argument initially indicates whether bound data has changed, the argument can be False even if data in the copy buffer actually has changed. If *Save* is True when the Validate event procedure exits, the Edit and UpdateRow methods are invoked. If you set the *Save* argument to False, the data isn't written to the SQL server.

CAUTION

The Validate event action constants given in the documentation are *still* wrong. See Figure 28-4 or the object browser for the correct values.

Figure 28-4
Action Arguments to the Validate Event

RDO 1.0 Constants	New RDO 2.0 Constants	Value	Description
rdDataActionCancel	rdActionCancel	0	Cancels operation when subroutine exits
rdDataActionMoveFirst	rdActionMoveFirst	1	MoveFirst method
rdDataActionMovePrevious	rdActionMovePrevious	2	MovePrevious method
rdDataActionMoveNext	rdActionMoveNext	3	MoveNext method
rdDataActionMoveLast	rdActionMoveLast	4	MoveLast method
rdDataActionAddNew	rdActionAddNew	5	AddNew method
rdDataActionUpdate	rdActionUpdate	6	Update operation (not UpdateRow)
rdDataActionDelete	rdActionDelete	7	Delete method
rdDataActionFind	rdActionFind	8	Not used, but reserved
rdDataActionBookmark	rdActionBookmark	9	Bookmark property set
rdDataActionClose	rdActionClose	10	Close method
rdDataActionUnload	rdActionUnload	11	Form being unloaded
	rdActionUpdateAddNew	12	Update for AddNew
	rdActionUpdateModified	13	Update operation for Edit
	rdActionRefresh	14	Refresh method
	rdActionCancelUpdate	15	CancelUpdate method
	rdActionBeginTransact	16	BeginTrans method
	rdActionCommitTransact	17	CommitTrans method
	rdActionRollbackTransact	18	RollbackTrans method
	rdActionNewParameters	19	New parameters
	rdActionNewSQL	20	New SQL statement

The Validate event occurs even if no changes have been made to data in bound controls and even if no bound controls exist. You can use this event to change values and update data. You can also save data, or you can stop whatever action is causing the Validate event and substitute a different action. In your code for this event, you can check the data in each bound control where *DataChanged* is True. You can then set *DataChanged* to False to avoid saving that data in the database.

Getting Started

To establish a connection to the SQL server and set up one or more bound controls, you can follow these steps:

1. Set the Connect property with a valid connect string. If you are used to working with the Data control, be aware that the connect string doesn't have an *ODBC;* prefix, nor does it support the LoginTimeout as an argument. If you put the data source name (DSN) here, it doesn't need to go in the DataSourceName property. You can also include the *UID* (UserName) and *PWD* (Password) arguments here, instead of in their properties. You can still use *UID=;PWD=;* for Windows NT domain security.

2. Set the DataSourceName property (if you didn't include it in the connect string).

3. Set the UserName and Password properties (if they aren't in the connect string).

4. Set the SQL property. This is coded in the same way as the rdoQuery object's SQL property. Generally, this is a SELECT statement that returns the desired columns exposed by the bound controls. Be sure to limit the scope of the result set with a WHERE clause, or set the MaxRows property to 100 or so.

The RemoteData control is ready to go. You might want to set some additional properties: CursorDriver or ResultsetType, for example, to return a more suitable cursor, or the Options property, to run in asynchronous mode.

You're now ready to add one or more bound controls to your form. Choose controls that match the data type of the column being queried. For example, choose the RichText control for binary large object (BLOB) text or the TextBox control for Char or VarChar columns. You can also use the MaskedEdit control for numeric types, but the TextBox or Label controls also work for these. If you don't want the user to change the data, simply choose a Label control or set the Locked property on the control to True. Once you have chosen your control and placed it on the form, follow the next two steps to bind it to the RemoteData control:

1. Set the bound control's DataSource property to point to MSRDC1 or to the name of your RemoteData control. Repeat this step for each control bound to the RemoteData control.

2. Set the bound control's DataField property to the name of the rdoResultset column that will be exposed and managed.

That's it. Note that you can select both the DataSource and DataField property values from drop-down lists generated from all available data-like controls and from the rdoColumns collection of the rdoResultset that is created. You do this on the basis of the RemoteData control properties you set.

When the program starts, the RemoteData control and the RDO interface populate the bound controls with column data from the first row (if there are any rows) of the rdoResultset object. The RemoteData control doesn't automatically populate the rdoResultset object unless you set the rdAsyncEnable option bit in the Options property. After the rdoResultset object is fully populated, the QueryCompleted event is fired.

TIP To avoid setting focus to the bound controls if there's no current row, put all bound controls on a frame and disable the frame until the Resultset.RowCount property is greater than 0. If you delete a row, check for no rows and again disable the frame.

Without a RemoteData control, a Data control, or their equivalent, data-aware (bound) controls on a form can't automatically access data. You can put data in bound controls manually and independently of the RemoteData control. You can also perform most remote data access operations with the RemoteData control and not write any code at all. Data-aware controls bound to a RemoteData control automatically display data from one or more columns for the current row—or, in some cases, for a set of rows on either side of the current row.

If the RemoteData control is instructed to move to a different row, all bound controls automatically pass any changes to the RemoteData control, so they can be saved to the SQL server. The RemoteData control then moves to the requested row and passes back data from the current row to the bound controls, where it's displayed.

CAUTION
The RemoteData control performs all operations on the current row—assuming there is one. If there are no rows in the result set, there's no current row, so the RemoteData control binds your controls to a non-current row. If you then set focus to one of these bound controls, you get a No Current Row error. (Isn't *that* special!)

NOTE You can use the mouse to manipulate the RemoteData control, moving from row to row of the result set or to the beginning or end. But you can't use the mouse to move off either end of the rdoResultset object or set focus to the RemoteData control.

The RemoteData control automatically handles a number of contingencies, including empty result sets (at least it's *supposed* to do that), adding new rows, editing and updating existing rows, and dealing with some types of errors. In more sophisticated applications, however, you need to trap some error conditions that the RemoteData control can't handle. For example, if the remote server has a problem accessing the data source, if the user doesn't have permission, or if the query can't be executed as coded, a trappable error results. If the error occurs before your application starts or as a result of some internal error, the Error event is triggered.

If you alter the RemoteData control properties after the result set has been created, use the Refresh method to rebuild the underlying rdoResultset object on the basis of the new property settings. You can also use the objects created by the RemoteData control to create additional rdoConnection, rdoResultset, or rdoQuery objects. In addition, you can set the RemoteData control Resultset property to an rdoResultset object created independently of the control. If you do this, the RemoteData control properties are reset on the basis of the new rdoResultset and rdoConnection objects.

The Validate event is triggered before each reposition of the current-row pointer. You can choose to accept the changes made to bound controls, or you can cancel the operation by using the Validate event's *Action* argument. These work like the Jet Data control's Validate event and *Action* arguments.

After the RemoteData control starts, the Connect property contains a fully populated connect string. The Resultset property contains the rdoResultset object that has been created, and the ResultsetType property indicates its type. You can also use any of the rdoResultset methods against the RemoteData control's Resultset property, just as if it were an rdoResultset object. For example, the MoveNext method of an rdoResultset object moves you from the current row to the next row in the rdoResultset object. To invoke this method with an rdoResultset object created by a RemoteData control, you can use the following code:

```
RemoteData1.Resultset.MoveNext
```

NOTE To execute a parameter query with the RemoteData control, you have to create an independent rdoResultset object with an rdoQuery query. Or you can concatenate the query parameters yourself, place the resulting query in the SQL property, and use the Refresh method.

PART V

The Visual Basic
Library for SQL Server

Chapter

29

Getting Ready for the VBSQL Interface

Starting a Dialog with SQL Server

Establishing a Development Strategy

Error and Message Handling

Yup, it's still hanging in there—the Visual Basic Library for SQL Server is still supported out there in the trenches—even in SQL 6.5. This API-interface to DB-Library, also known as VBSQL, was Visual Basic's first native interface to SQL Server. But this interface is still an API interface. It doesn't share the features afforded by the new object-oriented development paradigms. Sure, it's been "VB-ized" so that many of the complex binding and interface issues have been taken care of, but because it's still an API call interface, you won't see support for more sophisticated object-management techniques.

DB-Library is the API used by all non-ODBC applications to communicate with SQL Server. It's one of the oldest interfaces to SQL Server, and for Microsoft SQL Server it's still one of the most efficient. Despite rumors of its demise, DB-Library keeps working its way back to the forefront, at least for many power developers. But we won't be seeing any more improvements to the API in future SQL Server releases as we transition to RDO and ADO over the next couple of years.

Several years ago, an industrywide power shift affected how you approached VBSQL application development. Basically, Microsoft and Sybase parted company. The result of this split is two separate Visual Basic–to–SQL Server development paradigms, one for Sybase and the other for Microsoft. Microsoft still supports DB-Library, but Sybase doesn't; you have to use Sybase's proprietary interfaces. The Visual Basic ODBC drivers work against Microsoft SQL Server but not against Sybase; you have to use Sybase's proprietary CT-LIB or ODBC drivers. The SQL Server team at Microsoft has also completely rewritten the SQL Server database engine to support the Windows NT multitasking, multithreaded platform, but Sybase is still based on a UNIX or OS/2 platform, which basically uses Sybase's established technology. This means that if you plan to write a front-end application using VBSQL, you had better not plan on having it work with newer Sybase SQL Server systems. The RDO interface is a better idea for Sybase systems—as long as you can get hold of Sybase's ODBC drivers.

PART V   THE VISUAL BASIC LIBRARY FOR SQL SERVER

VBSQL is now in its fourth (and probably last) major release, so in this section of this guide I attempt to note differences between versions of the VBSQL functions, especially when these changes might have an adverse impact on the development cycle. The new versions of Microsoft SQL Server have implemented a number of innovative functions and features. These include DB-Library–based cursors, server-side cursors, and improved management of remote stored procedures.

NOTE The original Windows NT version of SQL Server is basically a complete rewrite of the Sybase SQL Server 4.2 engine. It has a significantly better platform with Windows NT and significantly more capacity, but it uses the same DBLIB calls as the older SQL Server 4.2 versions. SQL Server 6.0 is a big step beyond the Sybase implementation in that it implements a sophisticated multithreaded architecture.

As we have noted in earlier chapters, many problems associated with the creation of front ends to SQL Server are due to the inability of a development language to interact adequately with the SQL server during the development cycle. In many ways, Transact-SQL is an interactive, two-way language. The server expects to be told what to do in specific terms, and it will respond in a fairly deterministic way. Visual Basic's interactive development mode is an efficient and relatively trouble-free way to get a front-end application to hear what the server says back.

DB-Library functions do for C developers what the VBSQL functions do for Visual Basic developers. Not all the DBLIB functions are supported by VBSQL. Fortunately, however, not all of them are needed. For example, C developers spend a significant amount of time dealing with fairly involved "binding" of SQL arguments to C variables, but this is completely unnecessary in Visual Basic since virtually all arguments are returned in the form of string (BSTR) variables, which can be converted as necessary with built-in Visual Basic functions or simple assignment statements.

NOTE In many cases, VBSQL functions are merely linkages to the C-based DBLIB functions; there are no objects, methods, or properties to deal with. There are a number of Visual Basic functions that have no equivalents in C, such as the SQLOpenConnection function. This VBSQL "utility" function is provided to perform a series of C calls that are normally sent together. These utility functions make VBSQL programming even easier.

This chapter takes you through the first few steps toward designing a successful VBSQL application. While many of these steps seem somewhat complicated, they really aren't—much of the detail here is due to the wide variety of VBSQL options and the copious SQL Server features. As you read, you will learn about the following areas:

- The overall philosophy and architecture of a VBSQL application

- Establishing a workable VBSQL development strategy

- Setting up error and message handlers and managing query timeouts

NOTE Sure, VBSQL isn't an object library in the ActiveX sense—even though it's implemented as OCX. You can, however, take advantage of Visual Basic version 5.0's IntelliSense features as soon as you load the API declare files. This makes coding almost as easy as working with RDO or one of the object-oriented programming models.

Starting a Dialog with SQL Server

Writing programs that converse with other programs isn't difficult. Anyone who has worked with a highly intelligent but extremely literal child knows how to get that child to do what is wanted. Or maybe SQL Server isn't *that* hard to work with—but you do need to be prepared for some degree of obstinacy and what may appear to be willful acts of destruction. Generally, your code must be prepared for any eventuality, even the sudden death of the other entity in the conversation. The SQL server sometimes refuses to execute one or more instructions, and it stamps its foot for emphasis. Just as when you're guiding a two-year-old who has a will of her own, you must be prepared to be told "*No!*"

Creating a State Machine

For those of you who haven't worked with process control, I will outline here what that discipline refers to as a *state machine*. (I talked about this earlier in this guide, in Chapter 5, when I covered overall front-end design.) A state machine is what the interactive SQL interface expects you to set up so that it can communicate with you.

Figure 29-1 shows the outline of the simple SQL state machine you will be expected to set up. It shows what questions can be asked at each level and the points where you can ask for data. This is your road map for traveling in and around VBSQL. Once your state machine is set up and you understand that you can't ask another question before you have exhausted all the answers to previous questions, the job of creating a VBSQL application (or any other kind of SQL application, for that matter) is easy. At this point, we need to look at the remaining aspects of a VBSQL application's architecture, with a focus on coding, development strategy, and setting expectations.

Using Utility Functions and DLLs

When you write any Visual Basic application, you're presented with a number of choices. You'll have to decide at every level whether to write new code or clone existing code. DLLs generally take less space and run more quickly than interpreted Visual Basic code. (Visual Basic code is compiled p-code that's examined by the Visual Basic run-time engine. Each Visual Basic p-code instruction triggers a corresponding procedure to perform the actual operation. Generally, interpreted systems are slower to execute by comparison with languages that compile down to machine code.) There is a degree of overhead involved whenever you call any external module (a Far call is involved), but once there, you work closer to CPU speed to perform the function. VBSQL.VBX, VBSQL.OCX, and the SQL DLLs are all written in C or assembly language and have already been tuned for the highest possible performance.

You should leverage existing code whenever possible. This does *not* mean breaking into your competitors' offices at night and walking off with their solutions to your toughest problems. It *does* mean using custom controls and C-based dynamic-link libraries (DLLs) whenever possible— even if you have to write them yourself.

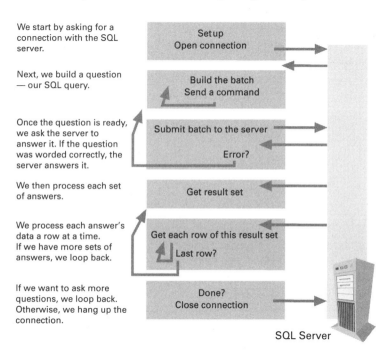

We start by asking for a connection with the SQL server.

Next, we build a question — our SQL query.

Once the question is ready, we ask the server to answer it. If the question was worded correctly, the server answers it.

We then process each set of answers.

We process each answer's data a row at a time. If we have more sets of answers, we loop back.

If we want to ask more questions, we loop back. Otherwise, we hang up the connection.

Setup
Open connection

Build the batch
Send a command

Submit batch to the server

Error?

Get result set

Get each row of this result set

Last row?

Done?
Close connection

SQL Server

Figure 29-1 *A SQL state machine*

You don't have a choice about whether to use the SQL DLLs, OCXs, and VBXs, but you do have a choice for both your own Visual Basic code and for some of the low-level VBSQL calls. In the case of your own code, you might be able to convert a more intensive subroutine to a C DLL and streamline your program that way. Microsoft has already done this for a number of the common utility functions that all VBSQL applications use. I encourage you to design around these functions whenever possible. ***Figure 29-2*** on the next page shows some of these functions. When you use these utility functions, you save not only the overhead of individual calls but also the code for checking results between steps. Generally, I use the SQLOpenConnection and SQLSendCmd functions for all my normal setup and query operations.

Using Cursors

"Cursors? VBSQL has cursors?"

VBSQL has had cursors for years.

"But they can't get to server-side cursors, right?"

Wrong. VBSQL began supporting server-side cursors the day SQL Server 6.0 shipped. In fact, VBSQL supports four types of cursors, most of them supported in turn by server-side implementations. VBSQL also supports at least three noncursor data access strategies.

Figure 29-2
VBSQL Utility Functions

Utility Function	Purpose	Calls
SQLBCPColumnFormat	Sets up column information for a bulk copy	2 +
SQLGetAltColInfo	Fills in AltColumnData structure from current results	4 +
SQLGetColumnInfo	Fills in ColumnData structure from current results	3 +
SQLOpenConnection	Sets up connection	6 +
SQLSendCmd	Sends query to server	3 +
SQLTextUpdate1Row	Updates Text columns	3 +
SQLTextUpdateManyRows	Updates all rows of results in Text/Image column	3 +
SQLTsUpdate	Updates the TimeStamp column in a table	2 +

The question is, do cursors *always* make sense? You know they don't. With VBSQL, you get to choose from a variety of data retrieval mechanisms:

- *The default,* which is a single-row, forward-only Resultset object that handles single or multiple result sets. As we saw with the other models, this is often the most efficient.

- *Row buffering,* a buffered *n*-row cache that supports random scrolling within the cache. This is considerably more sophisticated than a scrollable cursor and far more efficient.

- *Browse mode row buffering,* which returns a bookmark for each row so that the row can be updated as you want. This is also not supported elsewhere and can be very handy for many situations.

- *Static, keyset, dynamic, or mixed cursors*

Can you create a cursor on the result set returned from a stored procedure? Yes, though updating the rows isn't as easy as a query that you submit yourself—but it can be done.

Establishing a Development Strategy

At this point, I'll call your attention to several important outlooks on developing and debugging VBSQL programs. I imagine that you'll be using Visual Basic's interactive development mode almost exclusively, so you need to be aware of a couple of pitfalls often encountered with this technique.

Handling Connections

One of the more serious problems associated with interactive programming environments is that the Visual Basic interpreter (VBRUNn00.EXE) is managing resources as an *agent* of the application being executed (or debugged) in Design mode. When you execute your application compiled into its own EXE, it takes over responsibility and ownership of the resources it allocates. For example, if an application instructs Visual Basic to close a file or SQL connection handle, Visual Basic will do so. As is sometimes the case during VBSQL development, however, if the interpreted code crashes, or if you simply push the Stop button and don't subsequently execute SQLWinExit, SQLExit, or at least SQLClose, the connection established by SQLOpen or SQLOpenConnection remains open as far as Windows and SQL Server are concerned. In addition, the instance of the DB-Library interface created for you when you executed SQLInit continues to live. This creates what is called an orphaned process handle. Like zombies roaming the park at night, these aren't good to have hanging around.

Orphaned process handles usually pose no immediate problem, since there are probably enough handles and RAM to have several connections open at once on both the Windows workstation and the SQL server. When I set up my SQL server, however, I limit the number of users or connections to five. That way, I can test situations where additional connections are really *not* available. I also save a little RAM on the server—but things fall apart sooner than on systems where there are more connections available.

NOTE There is an upper limit on handles in 16-bit Windows. The downside here is that you might not be able to save your work if Windows can't open a new file handle for your save file(s). If you end your application abnormally (or just early), open the Debug window and execute SQLExit:SQLWinExit to clean up your act. If you don't properly clean up your open connections each time, the next time you execute SQLInit it returns a "NULL DbProcess encountered" error.

What should you do if you fear that there are too many open handles? You can start by seeing how many orphaned processes are on the server. Execute an sp_who on the server. This will show you the current connections. If you have a dedicated server, there should be only a couple of overhead processes active. Next, you can run SQL Enterprise Manager from a Windows 95 or Windows NT workstation—or on the server. Check out the User Activity tab. If there are open connections that can't be accounted for, you know that these are your orphaned pipe connections. You can try to close the pipes at the server end, using the KILL process TSQL command, but this might not solve the Windows resource problem. The only sure way to close all open connections is to shut Visual Basic down and restart it. You might be lucky enough to still have enough handles for Windows to save your work before you go down.

One of the changes implemented in the latest VBSQL.OCX is the way SQLExit handles orphaned processes: it automatically closes all of them. This greatly simplifies development, since you no longer have to worry about more than a few orphans. Simply typing *SQLExit* periodically in the Debug window effectively cleans out unused procedures.

Step-Through Debugging

There are several important debugging features that you should keep in mind when you're developing a VBSQL application. Because of the interactive nature of the SQL server, you might not be completely sure about whether the hard-coded query submitted to the server is syntactically correct or about how many result sets are generated by the query. For this reason, I've found it easiest to develop queries one piece at a time, letting the code loop through the SQLSendCmd statement until the syntax is correct for each case. This is especially necessary because many of the queries I send are generated on the fly, iteratively using concatenation and user-supplied arguments. To do this, you can use the F8 key to step through the code line by line, correcting code and TSQL syntax as you go. If a query doesn't pass muster, simply use the right mouse button to point to the next line to execute, even if it's several lines back in the procedure, and reexecute SQLExec or SQLSendCmd. If the SQL server decides it can't understand the query, it automatically resets its state (from confusion) to prepare for another query. I also use this feature to examine the properties of the returned data. For example, you can ask DBLIB if any rows are returned. (Unfortunately, it won't tell you *how many* rows are in the result set.) For each of those rows, DBLIB can be queried about the content and description of the columns.

Error and Message Handling

Every single VBSQL application you create should have error and message handlers—every single last one. If you don't have error and message handlers established *before* you attempt to use SQLOpen, there's no way to know whether something went wrong in the connection process.

NOTE The SQL Server group made a number of changes to the VBSQL interface in the error and message handlers that will affect your conversion process. To deal with these changes, rip out your existing 16-bit VBSQL1_Error and VBSQL1_Message procedure prototypes (the first line of the event procedure that describes the procedure arguments) and replace them with code from the VBSQL.OCX control. These prototype lines are generated automatically when you populate an empty event handler.

CAUTION
Coding an application without establishing error and message handlers is like crossing the street with your eyes closed and cotton in your ears. Your application works because when you add the VBSQL custom control, the linkages are automatically established. But if you don't add code to the error and message handlers, they simply throw away all the Error and Message events—and you get yourself run over the first time you wander into a busy intersection.

Establishing Callback Entry Points

The DBLIB architecture depends on two additional entry points in your application to permit SQL Server to talk back to your application—to tell it when things go wrong or to pass information back to your code. The programmer coding in C calls an appropriate DBLIB API, which indicates the entry points of the C message and error handler subroutines. In VBSQL, connecting the callback handlers is made as painless as possible. In this case, the developer must drag the VBSQL.VBX or VBSQL.OCX icon over to a form that will remain in memory (loaded) during all VBSQL operations. This establishes what are referred to as *callback entry points*. That's it—it's that simple. What you end up with on the form is a single control that can neither accept the focus nor accept any user input. It has no methods, only a few properties that you don't set at run time, and only two very important events—one for errors and one for messages.

NOTE The VBSQL.OCX might *look* like it has a number of new events, but it doesn't implement them.

The following error and message handler prototype statements show each of the arguments passed to your application. Note the *OSErrorNum* and *OSErrorStr* error arguments and the *ServerNameStr* and *Line* arguments added for the 32-bit OCX version. These were dropped when VBSQL made the transition from the QuickBasic implementation to the first Visual Basic VBX. This shouldn't affect existing programs but should make for an easier transition from C-based code to Visual Basic:

```
Private Sub VBSQL1_Error(ByVal SQLConn As Long, _
    ByVal Severity As Long, ByVal ErrorNum As Long, _
    ByVal ErrorStr As String, ByVal OSErrorNum As Long, _
    ByVal OSErrorStr As String, RetCode As Long)

Private Sub VBSQL1_Message(ByVal SQLConn As Long, _
    ByVal Message As Long, ByVal State As Long, _
    ByVal Severity As Long, ByVal MsgStr As String, _
    ByVal ServerNameStr As String, ByVal ProcNameStr As String, _
    ByVal Line As Long)
```

Some of the SQL Server group's changes to the VBSQL interface bring you more information than ever. Others just make your life difficult.

Although the new SQL Server 6.0 version of DB-Library now supports multiple error and message handlers—one for each connection—VBSQL doesn't implement this feature. Both error and message handlers are passed the connection that triggered the error or message, just as in previous versions. It is up to your error and message routines to decide how to split up handling for each connection you establish. Generally, this doesn't have to be a problem. For one thing, *you* create all connections. For another, you need only a few connections. I usually use one or two at most, which simplifies the application logic and the handlers.

When the SQL server reports an error to the DB-Library interface, the VBSQL control fires one or both of the event handlers. The same thing happens when DB-Library or SQL Server generates a message, but messages usually fire only the Message event. Many "errors" reported to the error handler are due to problems with the DBLIB interface—the body of code that creates the Tabular Data Stream (TDS) sent to the SQL server and interprets the metadata coming back. When an error occurs, your application's error handler can do very little but acknowledge the error or inform the user that the error has occurred. In most cases, your mainstream logic, which made the VBSQL/DBLIB call that caused the error, must deal with the originating problem. For many of the more common (and expected) errors that occur, I usually place an informational Visual Basic message box in the handler to explain the error and offer courses of action. These suggestions could just as easily be placed in the mainline code. It's fairly common for the SQL engine to send a series of messages or errors to your application (all in response to a single VBSQL function), so your application code might choose to ignore several messages or errors (which can be identified by their message or error codes). In all but one case, your VBSQL Error event procedure must return a 0 as it exits. If you do nothing, a 0 will be returned by default in the Error event's *RetCode* argument.

Skeleton Error and Message Handlers

As I said earlier, you need to establish at least a bare-bones handler to deal with the *listening* side of the front-end client to a SQL Server conversation. The following code is what I use for my event procedures—at least this is the skeleton version of it. Note that I use Case statements to filter the events by message or error number. For example, I always toss the 10007 error, which says that a message was sent, as well as the 5701 message, which says that the default database changed. (It always does, and I rarely care.)

```
Private Sub VBSQL1_Error(ByVal SQLConn As Long, _
    ByVal Severity As Long, ByVal ErrorNum As Long, _
    ByVal ErrorStr As String, ByVal OSErrorNum As Long, _
```

```
        ByVal OSErrorStr As String, RetCode As Long)
        Select Case ErrorNum
            Case 10007
            Case Else
                MsgBox ("VBSQL Error: Sev:" & Severity & _
                    "Error:" & ErrorNum & " - " & ErrorStr)
        End Select
End Sub

Private Sub VBSQL1_Message(ByVal SQLConn As Long, _
    ByVal Message As Long, ByVal State As Long, _
    ByVal Severity As Long, ByVal MsgStr As String, _
    ByVal ServerNameStr As String, ByVal ProcNameStr As String, _
    ByVal Line As Long)
    Select Case Message
        Case 5701:
        Case Else
            MsgBox ("Msg:" & MsgStr & " - State:" & State & _
                " - Severity:" & Severity & " : " & Message)
    End Select
End Sub
```

Managing Query Timeouts

Once an error occurs, SQL Server or DB-Library informs your Error and Message event handlers of that fact. If your query times out, VBSQL is the one and only interface that lets you respond to this error; neither the RDO interface nor the Jet DAO model gives you this ability.

A SQL query timeout can be set by calling the SQLSetTime function, which sets the number of seconds that DBLIB will wait for the SQL server to complete a SQL command. When your error handler gets *ErrorNum SQLETIME*, you can tell the SQL server to continue working on the query or simply give up and toss the results. *SQLETIME* is the *only* error that recognizes a return code. By default, the query timeout duration is infinite, so this error shouldn't occur unless your application changes the amount of time that DBLIB waits.

It's perfectly normal for SQL Server to take a long time to carry out some instructions. For example, it's not unusual for a bulk copy operation, a complex query, or a DBCC operation to take hours (or at least several minutes). A typical update might also take several minutes or several hours, depending on the scope of the query and lots of other factors outside your control. Obviously, it wouldn't be in the best interest of productivity to stop one of these necessary but time-consuming operations before it had less than a *reasonable* amount of time to complete. It's up to your application to indicate a reasonable time for a query to run, and it's the error handler's job to decide what to do once the DBLIB interface reports that the allotted time is up. Some strategies that have worked for me in the past are described on the next page.

- *Setting the timeout value to a fairly low value (five seconds or so)*. That way, the user can be presented with an animated figure (say, the ticks of a clock's second hand) to indicate that the system is still working during each timeout handler call. The handler can keep track of the total time taken and execute the "SQL Server is not coming back" code when the clock's second hand has ticked too many times.

- *Setting the timeout value to infinity (or a very long time)*. Use the SQLSend, SQLOK, and SQLResults commands instead of SQLExec, and poll the SQL server for completion of the command, using an animated figure similar to the one just described.

- *Setting the timeout value for each specific class of command*. For example, a simple query should execute much faster than a complex update. In any case, the speed of the LAN interface should be taken into account. I have also discovered that the time needed to update or insert a row in a table can vary from seconds to over a minute (or more), according to how much work the SQL server must do to allocate space, write to disk, update the data, and index pages. Apparently, the amount of work needed to do a specific operation can vary quite a bit from row to row. Decide what's reasonable on the basis of numerous field tests conducted on a loaded machine. Then add a comfort factor and proceed from there.

Using *INTCONTINUE*

If your handler decides that you should wait another *n* seconds, the error handler needs to return a 1 (*INTCONTINUE*). Otherwise, DBLIB informs the SQL server that your application can no longer wait for the current operation to complete and that it should be canceled. Control returns, with a *FAIL* return code, to the mainline VBSQL function that started the operation. Your mainline code should then decide what to do. In any case, I never leave the timeout value at infinity. That would remove any control I might have over a SQL server trying to accomplish an impossible task.

Using *INTCANCEL*

If you want to cancel the current query from inside the error handler (you can't do this from inside the message handler), return *INTCANCEL* in the *RetCode* argument. This will cause DB-Library to send an Attention to the server, which should then release all locks, return as much data as it has, clean up the result set, and put you back into nonbusy mode.

In any case, your application error handler may pass only one of three values back to DB-Library as your error handler exits:

- 0 (*INTEXIT*). This is treated as *INTCANCEL*.

- 1 (*INTCONTINUE*). (Return to DBLIB and continue to wait.) This should be used only in cases where the error *SQLETIME* has occurred and your handler desires to wait another *n* seconds (as set by SQLSetTime).

- 2 (*INTCANCEL*). (Returns *FAIL* from the DB-Library for the Visual Basic function that caused the error.) For timeout errors (*SQLETIME*) only, DB-Library calls SQLCancel in an attempt to cancel the current command batch and flush any pending results. If this SQLCancel attempt also times out, the connection is broken.

Dealing with specific cases

Generally, the Message event handler deals with SQL Server–generated events, but some of these can be construed as errors. Let's say your application tried to insert a duplicate row into an indexed table or was chosen as the victim of a deadly embrace. When these events occur, the message handler doesn't usually contain the logic to deal with them. For example, a "duplicate row" error (2601) could be triggered from any of the SQL UPDATE statements in your application. Only that logic context (that section of code) should be programmed to deal with this specific instance of this condition.

The message handler has no built-in facility for passing a return code back to the logic. When specific message-spawning events occur, the command that caused the error *might* be passed a *FAIL* return code. Dealing with these specific events is the challenge. One approach would be to pass the error code returned from the SQL server to your main logic via a global variable, such as *ErrorReceived*. That way, your application can test for the reason for a failed update, by examining the *ErrorReceived* variable. Here is what you might see in the message handler:

```
Select Case Message
    ...
    Case 2601 : ErrorReceived = Message
    ...
```

And here is what you might see in the main logic:

```
Q$ = "Update Pubs..authors set au_id = '172-32-1176' " _
    & " where au_id = '213-46-8915' "
r = SQLSendCmd(SQLConn, Q$)
If r <> SUCCEED Then
    Select Case ErrorReceived
        Case 2601: Msgbox _
            "An author with this id is already on file..."
...
```

The sequence of handler events triggered by this improper update is as follows:

1. The Message event fires with message number 2601, "Attempt to insert duplicate key row in object 'authors' with unique index 'auidind'." (Note that the string provided by the SQL server specifies *exactly* what table and key are involved.) This string might be suitable for presentation to the user if he or she knows that a SQL update is being attempted. The fact that this message has arrived is recorded and passed back to the calling procedure.

2. The Message event fires with message number 3621, "Command has been aborted." (This is our indication that the SQL server didn't execute the transaction.) Generally, I ignore this message—or at least take no specific action.

3. The Error event fires with error number 10007, "General SQL Server error: Check messages from the SQL Server." (In this case, the error handler is informed that an error has occurred.) It doesn't say which error or why it has occurred, only that the message handler was informed of an error. I usually ignore this message, too.

Informational messages

As you can see from the preceding points, some messages can be safely ignored. For example, message 5701, generated by the SQL server, indicates that the default database has changed; the message text will indicate the name of that database. All such messages are stored in SysMessages.

Handling PRINT and RAISERROR statements

Message handlers also process TSQL statements that return informational messages as part of their functions:

- The PRINT statement is used in TSQL procedures to pass ASCII text back to the front end. PRINT statements are used to transmit warnings, send informational text, or pass error codes back to the application without triggering an error in the interface. The new SQL Server 6.0 TSQL syntax has greatly expanded the PRINT statement's functionality, so you're likely to see quite a few additional uses for this statement.

- The TSQL RAISERROR statement is used in TSQL procedures to return a message *and* trip an error that is passed back to the VBSQL Error event handler. You don't have to worry about how RAISERROR interacts with the rows that return from a query. In VBSQL, this functionality is completely supported; in fact, VBSQL is the only programming interface that does support it.

Suppose the following code is executed by a TSQL procedure:

```
RAISERROR 20001, "Important stuff happened"
```

In this case, the message handler receives message number 20001, with the message text (a separate parameter passed back from the SQL server by DBLIB) "Important stuff happened." Next, the error handler gets a *SQLESMSG*, which merely tells the developer that the message handler received an error message. If you are going to use RAISERROR to send error codes and messages to yourself (a very useful tool), you need to include logic for these message codes in the Message event procedure.

Generally, when a RAISERROR is executed, it is included in a SQL trigger executed when an update, insert, or delete operation is attempted. It is the responsibility of your message and error handlers to prepare for and deal with these very common occurrences. RAISERROR is also commonly used in stored procedures, in a variety of ways. You must prepare for each of these implementations. To do this, however, you would actually have to converse with the developer who includes the RAISERROR or PRINT statement in a TSQL procedure, to see how the error would best be handled.

Other responsibilities of the message handler

Besides handling PRINT and RAISERROR messages, the message handler has several other responsibilities. One is to deal with messages that come back from successful queries that violate SQL Server rules. For example, when you add a row with a duplicate key, a message is generated and your message handler and logic have to deal with it. Your message handler must also know what to do when your query is chosen as the victim of a deadly embrace and when your SQL server or DB-Library senses a fatal error (one with a severity level greater than 18).

Error and Message Handler Interaction

Note that in many cases the Message and Error events are both fired, in sequence. This permits your application to treat "messages" that are really errors (like a message about failing to complete a transaction) as errors, if need be. *Figure 29-3* shows this sequence and how the two handlers interact.

Figure 29-3
Interaction of Errors and Messages

Error or Message	Message Handler Called?	Error Handler Called?	What Handler Should Do
SQL syntax error (SQLSendCmd)	Yes	Yes (SQLESMSG)	Ignore
SQL PRINT statement	Yes	No	
SQL RAISERROR statement	Yes	Yes (SQLESMSG)	Ignore
SQL server dies	No	Yes (SQLESEOF)	Exit the program or rebuild the connection
Timeout from SQL server	No	Yes (SQLETIME)	Note and decide whether to continue
Logon fails (SQLOpen)	Yes	Yes (SQLEPWD)	Exit the program or get a valid password
SQL USE DATABASE statement	Yes	No	
Improper sequence of DBLIB calls	No	Yes (SQLERPND)	Ignore
Fatal SQL Server error (severity > 18)	Yes	Yes (SQLESMSG)	Inform user, exit application

Dealing with Common Errors

Figure 29-4 shows the errors that you are most likely to encounter with virtually any VBSQL application. The figure indicates when each error is likely to occur and suggests how to deal with it. (See Appendix B for a complete listing of SQL Server errors.)

Figure 29-4
Most Common VBSQL Errors

Error	Constant Name	What It Really Means	When It Occurs	What to Do
10000	SQLEMEM	Unable to allocate RAM.	During row buffering, opening a new connection, reading in data	Back off this query until Windows can free more RAM.
10001	SQLENULL	Connection is dead or not open.	While ending applications without SQLExit, SQLClose, etc.; while using any VBSQL function with invalid DbProcess handle	If handle is OK, ignore, but close properly next time. (There might be an orphaned handle.)
10003	SQLEPWD	Password has failed.	During SQLOpen, SQLOpenConnection	Make sure logon ID and password are registered in server.
10004	SQLECONN	Search on LAN for server has failed, server down, or LAN permissions resources will not allow connection.	During SQLOpen, SQLOpenConnection	Make sure server is up and user doesn't have too many LAN resources in use (NET USEs).
10005	SQLEDDNE	SQL server connection has died.	Almost anytime after SQLOpen	Check LAN connection.
10007	SQLESMSG	Something has triggered an error message.	During SQLSendCmd, SQLExec, etc.	Check message handler, or ignore.
10024	SQLETIME	Your query has timed out; request took longer than SQLSetTime seconds.	During SQLSendCmd, SQLExec	Reset SQLSetTime to a higher number. Retry *n* times and quit.
10025	SQLEWRIT	Write to SQL server has failed; all SQL server connections in use.	With SQLOpen, SQLOpenConnection	Back off and try again later. Increase number of connections on the SQL server. Inform user.

Error	Constant Name	What It Really Means	When It Occurs	What to Do
10029	SQLEDBPS	Your application cannot open any more SQL connections.	With SQLOpen, SQLOpenConnection	Bump number of possible connections with SQLSetMax-Procs, or close some connections.
10037	SQLESEOF	Probably no additional user connections on the SQL server.	With SQLOpen, SQLOpenConnection	Back off and try again later. Increase number of connections on the SQL server. Inform user.
10037	SQLESEOF	LAN has dropped your share or connection.	After SQLOpen	Reestablish connection.
10038	SQLERPND	Attempt has been made to start a new query without dealing with result set from previous query.	During SQLSendCmd, SQLExec	If you want to start a new query, prefix it with SQLCancel, etc.
10040	SQLENONET	LAN error of some kind; not a SQL error.	During SQLOpen, SQLOpenConnection	Check user permissions on LAN and number of users on LAN server.
(Bogus)	SQLESQLPS	Maximum number of SQL server connections already allocated.	During SQLOpen, SQLOpenConnection	Back off and try again later. Increase number of connections on the SQL server. Inform user. (Not otherwise documented.)

30

Chapter

Getting Connected with VBSQL

n this chapter, we begin a fairly easy expedition into well-charted territory, where we see how to perform the following actions:

- Install the VBSQL custom control and get it registered
- Set up the DBLIB interface
- Set up a LoginRec structure to handle DBLIB initialization
- Gather parameters from passing users
- Open a connection to the SQL server

Setting Up a VBSQL Application

We are now ready to go through the steps of installing the VBSQL custom control and setting up your Error and Message event procedures. Error and message handlers deal with the bulk of the communications that come back from the server when things don't go exactly as planned. The steps that follow show how to set up VBSQL with Visual Basic version 4.0 or version 5.0, but many of these procedures can be done in Visual Basic version 3.0 as well.

Installing the VBSQL Custom Control

Before you can begin your VBSQL application, you will have to install VBSQL. Generally, this means running the Setup program provided with the SQL Server Programmer's Toolkit.

NOTE   VBSQL includes one of the only remaining 16-bit data access implementations. Since Visual Basic version 5.0 comes in only 32-bit flavors (if you don't count 16-bit DAO), I will stick with the 32-bit implementations here. Previous editions of my book covered the 16-bit platforms pretty well.

After you've installed VBSQL, adding VBSQL functionality to your Visual Basic application will require the following steps:

1. Launch Visual Basic. (You don't *need* the Enterprise edition, but you might wish you had it.)

2. Register the VBSQL custom control using the Tools/Custom Controls dialog box. Visual Basic 5.0 requires you to use the Components dialog box (available via the Project menu) to load and register the VBSQL custom control. You might have to use the Browse button to go looking for the control if it's not listed. You must use VBSQL.VBX for 16-bit applications and VBSQL.OCX for 32-bit applications. The first time you do this, you must use the Browse button to point to the appropriate file. You should load the VBSQL custom control in the WINDOWS\SYSTEM directory along with all other custom controls to make this process easier and to avoid loading an incorrect version.

3. After you register the control, or if the control is already registered, use the Custom Controls dialog box to include it in your application. Its entry in the list of registered custom controls should be checked. You shouldn't have to use the References dialog box, since the control is automatically registered for the application when you check it off in the custom controls list.

4. Load the VBSQL.BAS module, using the Add File command on the File menu (the Project menu in Visual Basic 5.0). You no longer have to load a constants file, as you did in earlier versions. The VBSQL.BAS module contains all the function declarations and constants you need. For 16-bit applications, load the VBSQL.BI file.

5. When these steps have been completed, the VBSQL custom control should be in the Toolbox. The 16-bit VBSQL.VBX looks like this:

   The new 32-bit VBSQL.OCX looks like this:

6. Drag the VBSQL control from the toolbox over to a form that will be loaded whenever you perform SQL operations. The form also contains the Message and Error event procedures. This action creates an icon on the form that looks like the one shown here:

   (OK, it might not look like this, but it doesn't matter because you aren't going to see it anyway.)

7. If you are using VBSQL.VBX for 16-bit applications, click on the new VBSQL icon, press F4 to open the Properties window, and set the Visible property to False. The control supports no user-initiated events.

8. Install basic Error and Message event procedures. Double-click the VBSQL control on the form. This opens the code window for the VBSQL1 control you have just created. The first handler presented is the Error event procedure. On the basis of your application's needs,

add as much error code here as you feel is appropriate for this stage of development. I usually add a debug line and a MsgBox statement that dumps the errors as they occur. Repeat this action for the message handler. Without these basic handlers, you will not see most of the developmental errors that occur during the early stages of an application's life cycle.

At this point, you are ready to start coding.

TIP The VBSQL custom control *must* be placed on a form that is *loaded* at all times to maintain addressability to the Error and Message event procedures. It does not have to be visible, just loaded. For example, if you put the VBSQL custom control on a logon form, you can set the form's Visible property to False but you cannot use the Unload method on the form.

The Support Libraries

In the early days of VBSQL, it was fairly easy to install all of the needed libraries. You just copied VBSQL.VBX, W3DBLIB.DLL, and your choice of network library to the WINDOWS\SYSTEM directory. Now there are many more choices and combinations. All of these libraries still should be installed in the WINDOWS\SYSTEM directory. Partly because of the split-up with Sybase and partly because of the transition to Microsoft Windows NT–based and 32-bit platforms, the names of the VBSQL and DBLIB support libraries have changed. *Figure 30-1* shows the required libraries for 16-bit and 32-bit platforms. If you don't use named pipes to connect to SQL Server, you can choose from one of the alternate network libraries shown in *Figure 30-2*.

One of the most common problems I've seen while debugging supposedly strange or inexplicable VBSQL problems is caused by mismatched libraries. If you have the component files scattered all over the system and one application loads one of these libraries—which are also used by non-VBSQL applications—and your application then loads another library, the chances for

Figure 30-1
Libraries Required for 16-Bit and 32-Bit Platforms

Platform	Custom Control	Support Library	Other Files for Named-Pipe Support
16-bit Windows	VBSQL.VBX	W3DBLIB.DLL or MSDBLIB3.DLL	DBNMP3.DLL
32-bit Microsoft Windows 95 or Windows NT	VBSQL.OCX	NTWDBLIB.DLL	DBNMPNTW.DLL

Figure 30-2
Alternate Network Libraries

Network	Win16	Win32
TCP/IP	DBMSSOC3.DLL	DBMSSOCN.DLL
Multiprotocol (RPC)	DBMSRPC3.DLL	DBMSRPCN.DLL
IPX/SPX	DBMSSPX3.DLL	DBMSSPXN.DLL
Vines	DBMSVIN3.DLL	DBMSVINN.DLL
DECNet		DBMSDECN.DLL
ADSP		DBMSADSN.DLL

a mismatched set are very good. Make sure that there is only one matched set on your system.

Initializing the VBSQL Interface

One of the most common mistakes a VBSQL programmer can make is to forget or miscode the SQLInit function. This function establishes the callback entry points for the DBLIB interface, initializes the VBSQL DLLs, and creates an instance data segment for your application. This memory allocation remains in place until you use SQLWinExit to free it.

SQLInit returns, in the form of a string, the version number of the DBLIB interface you've loaded. If your application needs a particular revision of the DBLIB DLLs to work, you can parse this string and test for proper values. If your program gets a GPF or otherwise fails as soon as you use your first VBSQL function, it's likely that SQLInit hasn't been executed properly. Here's an example of using SQLInit correctly:

```
' Initialize VBSQL
A$ = SQLInit$()
If A$ = "" Then
    MsgBox "Like… there is no VBSQL DLL present!"
Else
    MsgBox "You are currently running version " & A$ & _
        " of VBSQL."
End If
```

You don't have to tell your user which version is running unless you're worried about DLL version problems. But you do need at least the following code:

```
If SQLInit$() = "" Then Form1_Unload : End
```

Or you can do this:

```
A$ = SQLInit()
```

Making the Connection

Now that the interface is established, you need to connect to the SQL server. The server's name is the same as the name of the Windows NT host server. Remember, you must establish a valid logon and password on the target SQL server before you try to log on. If you don't log on as server administrator, you must make sure that the user name you provide has the correct SQL server permissions to use the database.

Setting Logon Timeout

Before logging on, you should set a reasonable amount of time to wait before deciding that the connection isn't going to complete. On a fairly busy network, a connection should take between 0.5 second and 5 seconds to complete. A logon timeout of 10 seconds or so is completely reasonable in this case. If you connect over RAS, however, it can take somewhat longer— 5 to 50 seconds.

The default timeout value for SQLOpen or SQLOpenConnection is 60 seconds. This means that if you pass an incorrect or misspelled server name, or if the server is unavailable (down), you will have to wait for a full minute before control will be returned to your application. Most servers on a LAN (as opposed to a WAN or RAS) will respond in a few seconds. I usually set the timeout value for a LAN to about 15 seconds to accommodate fully loaded networks. Perhaps you should use an option flag for those sites that are on remote servers and need more time. Use SQLSetLoginTime before you call SQLOpen to set the number of seconds DBLIB should wait for a response from the selected SQL server:

```
r& = SQLSetLoginTime(15)          ' Wait 15 seconds before giving up
```

Opening the First Time

As is true also for the Microsoft Jet interface, the time to complete the process is far longer (by about 50 percent) the *first* time a workstation opens a connection to a server than subsequent times, even if the application ends and another begins. I can only account for this extra time as the time required to load and initialize the VBSQL DLLs and LAN overhead, which isn't needed after the initial connection is established. This extra time is considered a component of the SQLSetLoginTime value; it should *not* be considered when you are devising a strategy for managing logons.

The User Interface: Getting Parameters

When you design your VBSQL application, you should consider the following ideas, which concern how the user interface is built. This early in the process, we need to consider how the logon dialog boxes are presented.

Getting the password and user name

When you need to capture the user's name and password, you will have to create a dialog box that doesn't echo the password as it is being typed. Fortunately, Visual Basic provides this feature as a property of its TextBox control. Just set the Password property to * to echo an asterisk when letters are typed into the control.

Getting the server name

When the SQL server name *must* be entered by the user, present a list of valid servers instead of permitting the user to fill in a TextBox control. For such a list to be presented, the network must be polled for all visible SQL servers. In 16-bit VBSQL, you can use the SQLServerEnum function (see the next section). In the 32-bit version, however, this function is no longer supported because of restrictions in the way the network exposes SQL servers.

If these controls or the code is unavailable, it's possible to set up a call to the Microsoft LAN Manager API NETSERVENUM2, documented in the *SQL Server Programmer's Reference for C*. But this API is functional only against Microsoft networks, not against Novell or other topologies.

TIP   More and more, I hear of problems associated with the "visibility" of SQL servers. Don't be alarmed if your SQL server isn't on a list of valid servers as presented by any application that depends on this function. For reasons that aren't particularly clear, any number of situations can permit you to connect to a server that doesn't appear on such a list. The SQL server might also be marked as not visible, and this too can cause the same aberration.

Using SQLServerEnum

For the 16-bit version of VBSQL, the SQL Server team added a new function that lists the SQL servers visible on the net: SQLServerEnum. This function searches either on the local system (assuming you are running Windows NT) or across the net and returns a string containing a delimited list of server names. Each name returned is separated from the text by a zero byte: *Chr$(0)*. The end of the list is designated by two zeroes. If there are more names than will fit the length of the buffer you have provided, the call returns *MOREDATA* to indicate that there are more names, which aren't included in the list. Because of the design of named-pipe servers, all systems with SQL Server installed are listed, even if the particular SQL server isn't running. In my tests, the call took almost 25 seconds to return meaningful results. Syntax for the call is as follows:

```
Result = SQLServerEnum(SearchMode, ServerBuf$, NumEntries)
```

SearchMode can be *LOCSEARCH* (1) or *NETSEARCH* (2). If you ask for *LOCSEARCH*, the function will simply enumerate the server list already kept in the WIN.INI, as shown at the top of the next page.

CAUTION
If you haven't installed the latest 16-bit DBNMP3.DLL, you might get a "Procedure not found" when you try to call SQLServerEnum.

```
[SQLSERVER]
Work=dbnmp3,\\VOFFICE\PIPE\SQL\QUERY
Default=dbnmp3,\\VOFFICE\PIPE\SQL\QUERY
Hemingway=dbnmp3,\\hemingway\PIPE\SQL\QUERY
University=dbnmp3,\\University\PIPE\SQL\QUERY
AutoAnsiToOem=off
DSQUERY=DBNMP3
```

NOTE The 32-bit version of VBSQL doesn't support the SQLServerEnum function in Windows 95 because the 32-bit version has no facility for returning a list of valid servers, and so you get a *NETNOTAVAIL* error. It does work in Windows NT, but the function itself returns a Long return code and NumEntries value, and it takes a Long *SearchMode* argument. All these arguments are Integers in the 16-bit version of VBSQL.

If you ask for *NETSEARCH*, SQLServerEnum searches the net for any and all visible SQL servers. The function's scope is limited to the network domain, however, so servers outside the domain might not show up. If your user knows the server name, it should be added to the SQLSERVER section of the WIN.INI so that it will be visible later.

TIP SQLServerEnum still does not always return a complete list of servers. The function apparently listens to the net for a length of time and simply records any servers that happen to be broadcasting. If the server in question is busy and does not broadcast its identity and type while you're listening, its name will not show up on your list.

ServerBuf is the buffer that stores the list of names returned. As with most other API-style calls, you must prefill and pass a fixed-length string for this parameter. For example, the following code will save space for 4096 characters of names:

```
Dim ServerList as String * 4097
```

NumEntries is a parameter returned from the call that indicates the number of entries in the list; Result returns one of the following values:

ENUMSUCCESS = 0	OUTOFMEMORY = 4
MOREDATA = 1	NOTSUPPORTED = 8
NETNOTAVAIL = 2	ENUMINVALIDPARAM = 16 (Undocumented)

A zero-delimited string is passed back from SQLServerEnum. This list can be parsed, as shown in the following code example. The code in this example polls the system for server names and then places them in a ListBox control. It also pulls server names both from the local list kept in WIN.INI and from the network:

```
Public Sub GetServers()
Dim A As String, j As Integer
Dim Servers As String * 4097
Dim Msg As String

#If Win16 Then
    Dim i As Integer, r As Integer, Entries As Integer
#Else
    Dim i As Long, r As Long, Entries As Long
#End If
r = SQLServerEnum(NETSEARCH + LOCSEARCH, Servers, Entries)
If r = ENUMSUCCESS Then
    i = 1
    Do While Entries > 0
        j = InStr(i, Servers, Chr$(0))    ' Find the end of name
        Serverlist.AddItem Mid$(Servers, i, j - 1)
        i = j + 1
        Entries = Entries - 1
    Loop
    Serverlist.ListIndex = 0
Else
    Select Case r
        Case MOREDATA: Msg = "Too many servers to list all…"
        Case NETNOTAVAIL: Msg = "Could not access the net."
        Case OUTOFMEMORY: Msg = "Not enough resources to list."
        Case NOTSUPPORTED: Msg = "This version does not support" _
                                & " a server list."
    End Select
    MsgBox Msg
End If
End Sub
```

Connection Strategies

Available SQL Server connections constitute one of the most important resources that your application and all other competing applications must
conserve. Each connection requires 40–45 KB on the SQL server. This RAM
is preallocated when the SQL server starts, and it can't be dynamically increased (or decreased) as the load on the SQL server changes. This isn't a lot
of memory for larger systems, but it can have quite an impact on smaller SQL
servers. I figure that 10 user connections will cost only about 450 KB, and
the more typical configuration of 50 users will require 2.25 MB of RAM dedicated just to connections, used or not. This RAM, taken from the system pool,
could be better utilized as data or procedure cache space to increase system
performance dramatically.

SQL Server's RAM isn't swapped out by Windows NT during normal
operations, and the SQL server itself doesn't use disk as a swap area for its
overhead needs. For this reason, it's vitally important to keep the amount of
RAM allocated to the connections at a minimum and thereby free RAM for use

The single most important
contributor to SQL Server
performance is RAM. It can
cure more sloppy design
and poor performance than
a month's work by a consultant on the database schema.
Since Windows NT can eas-
ily address many gigabytes
of RAM and SQL Server can
use all of it, putting a large
number of pages in RAM is
a surefire way to get everything running faster.

by the caches. To this end, many of my applications use an intelligent "just in time" strategy for their connection operations. This strategy boils down to the following points:

- *Don't establish the connection until just before the query needs it.* This causes a performance hit for the first open, but it seems that subsequent SQLOpenConnection functions don't take nearly as long as the first.

- *Close the connection when it isn't in use.* This means that if your logic doesn't lead immediately to another query (or to the continued extraction of data from the current query), you should close the connection.

- *Close the connection after the operator walks away.* Like a screen saver, your "connection saver" timer would time out and drop the connection if the operator didn't respond to a prompt. Although this is more complicated to implement, it can save not only connections but also locked data rows when a pending share lock doesn't permit an update operation.

NOTE When a Select or other read-only operation takes place, the SQL server places a share lock on the rows involved. This prevents an update operation from disturbing the rows while the data is being examined by your application. Share locks can be extended in time and scope with the SELECT HOLDLOCK statement.

To implement this strategy, you can use one or more of the following techniques to provide more active connections to the server by eliminating or at least reducing the number of idle connections (those that are between requests for the server).

Opening Just in Time

With the exception of the first SQLOpen, most SQL connections take only a second or less to complete. Many applications use a "just in time" SQLOpen technique to increase the number of simultaneous users. This method slows the workstation somewhat, but it can be an effective way to increase the number of users capable of accessing the SQL server at any one time. This strategy calls for the application to close the connection as soon as it's clear that the user has paused and that the logic path won't lead to another query, at least not anytime within the next *n* seconds.

Using Watchdog Timer Disconnect

Another recommended technique drops connections that aren't being actively used (and that don't have active queries pending). This technique uses conventional logic but sets up a watchdog timer to monitor activity that resets the wait time. Once the time has expired, the timer routine closes the connection. Of course, the next VBSQL access fails because of a null connection. In this case, the error handler reopens the connection and passes control back to the requesting call.

Using a Connection Manager

Remember how Jet manages connections for you? There is nothing to stop you from creating a connection "object" with properties, methods, and all the trappings to manage connections for an entire application. A procedure could use this VBSQLConnection object to return a valid DbProcess handle—the result of a successful connection. The manager could automatically cut off connections that it sensed were idle and could perform many of the automated functions performed by the Jet connection manager.

Choosing an Open Connection Function

You have two choices when it comes to connecting with the SQL server. You can build and set up a LoginRec structure, call SQLOpen, and free up the LoginRec structure (about six to nine functions); or you can use the SQLOpenConnection utility function that performs about 50 percent of the same operations with a single call. Things have changed, though; and those familiar with VBSQL need to take note. To enable many SQL Server version 6.0 features, you *must* use the LoginRec structure and SQLOpen approach. Don't believe me? Check out the SQLSetLVersion function. This function enables many of the SQL Server 6.0 data types. That one feature makes it necessary, in many cases, to forego the ease of use of SQLOpenConnection.

Using Application-Specific Logons

For many of the applications I write, the user need not enter *any* logon or password information for a variety of reasons. And now that Windows NT supports domain-managed security, the need to ask users for a logon ID and password has been reduced even more. Integrating SQL Server security with Windows NT makes it even more important to limit access to the SQL server by limiting access to the workstation and the LAN.

A variation on this approach leverages the Windows NT logon ID and password but embeds a special SQL Server logon ID and password in the application. In this case, the logon name is known only to the developer (me), the application (where it's hard-coded), and the SQL administrator who sets up an account for it. The user gains access to the application EXE and the SQL server by entering a valid Windows NT user name and password. Since the application can't be used to gain access to any but the hard-coded tables built into the application, and then only via the queries hard-coded into the application, the chance of losing data integrity is no greater than if the user had logged on with a specific SQL logon ID; but this technique can make the fact that SQL operations are taking place totally transparent to the user.

Using LoginRec Initialization Parameters

If you decide to use SQLOpen instead of SQLOpenConnection, you have to use a number of other VBSQL functions designed to create and fill in the LoginRec structure. These functions specify a litany of parameters used to tune and customize the connection for your specific needs. (Note that there have been several additions to this list since the SQL Server 4.*x* days.) Once the connection is open, you can free the LoginRec structure with SQLFreeLogin unless you plan to make additional connections. In this case, you can set one or more parameters and then reuse the structure. The functions that create, alter, and free the LoginRec structure are shown in *Figure 30-3.*

Each of these SQLSet functions requires a handle to a valid LoginRec structure, as provided by the SQLLogin function. Only the logon name and password are required. These functions will fail only if the LoginRec structure isn't created first or if the parameters are too long. For example, to set the user ID, use the following code:

```
Dim LoginRec As Long
LoginRec = SQLLogin()
R = SQLSetLUser(LoginRec, "sa")
R = SQLSetLPwd(LoginRec, "")
SQLConn = SQLOpen(LoginRec, "BetaV486")
```

The purpose of many of these LoginRec options is self-evident, but a few options need a little more explanation, especially those new to SQL Server 6.0.

Figure 30-3
Functions for Creating, Altering,
and Freeing the LoginRec Structure

Logon Record Function	Purpose
SQLLogin	Creates and initializes a LoginRec structure. Returns handle to structure.
SQLSetLUser	Indicates the SQL Server logon name.
SQLSetLPwd	Indicates the SQL Server password for this logon name. The logon/password pair must exist in *SysLogins* for the SQLOpen to succeed. No test is made when this function is called.
SQLSetLHost	Indicates the host name (up to 30 characters). This appears in sp_who as *Host name* and is stored as *host* in *SysProcesses*. This is called "workstation" in the documentation.
SQLSetLApp	Indicates the application name (up to 30 characters). Stored as *program_name* in *SysProcesses*.
SQLBCPSetL	Enables bulk copy operations.
SQLSetLNatLang	Indicates the national language to be used. The value used must be one of the names listed in *SysLanguages*. (SQL Server always recognizes U.S. English.)
SQLSetLPacket	Sets the Tabular Data Stream (TDS) packet size (new in SQL Server 6.0).
SQLSetLSecure	Requests a secure connection (new in SQL Server 6.0).
SQLSetLVersion	Sets DBLIB version 6.0 behavior (new in SQL Server 6.0).
SQLFreeLogin	Frees the LoginRec structure. Call this function after the SQLOpen unless you want to use the LoginRec structure again in another SQLOpen.

Tuning the TDS Packet Size

Tabular Data Stream (TDS) is an application protocol used for the transfer of requests and request results between clients and the SQL server. TDS data is sent in fixed-size chunks called *packets*. The default packet size is set by SQL Server. If an application does bulk copy operations or if it sends or receives large amounts of text or image data, a packet size larger than the default might improve efficiency since it results in fewer network reads and writes. For large data transfers, a packet size between 4092 and 8192 bytes is usually best; larger sizes can degrade performance.

You can examine the current packet size by using the SQLGetPacket function, which returns either the packet size or 0 (if the function fails for some reason). If you don't set the packet size before the connection is opened, you miss your chance because the only way an application can change the TDS packet size is by using the SQLSetLPacket *and* the SQLOpen functions: if you use the SQLOpenConnection function, SQL Server uses its default packet size, which is set by the server administrator. To determine the packet size that the server has set, call SQLGetPacket. Each connection you make to the SQL server can use a different SQL Server packet size. The SQLSetLPacket function sets the TDS packet size in a SQL Server logon record. The packet size requested is expressed in bytes (0–65535). The server sets the actual packet size to a value less than or equal to the requested size.

SQLSetLSecure sets the secure connection flag in a SQL Server logon record. By setting the secure connection flag, the application requests a secure or trusted connection to SQL Server. This means that SQL Server uses integrated logon security to establish connections made (via SQLOpen) with the specified logon record, regardless of the current logon security mode at the server. Any logon ID or password supplied by SQLSetLUser or SQLSetLPwd is ignored. SQLSetLSecure enables trusted connections even when the server is in standard logon security mode.

TIP   To use SQLSetLSecure and trusted connections, you must first use *XP_GRANTLOGIN* or SQL Security Manager to grant SQL Server system administrator or user privilege to the appropriate Windows NT–based groups or users. Use *XP_REVOKELOGIN* or SQL Security Manager to revoke SQL Server privileges and stop a user or group from using a trusted connection.

SQLSetLVersion determines how SQL Server treats this client connection, whether it's a SQL Server 4.2 client or as a SQL Server 6.0 client, by specifying one of two constants: *SQLVER60* (to set DBLIB 6.0 behavior) or *SQLVER42* (to set DBLIB 4.2 behavior). If this function is *not* called, the default is DB-Library 4.2 behavior. *SQLVER60* is not required to use SQL Server 6.0 server cursors. Using the *SQLVER60* value means that SQL Server treats any connection with the specified LoginRec structure as a DBLIB 6.0 client in every way. In this case, SQL Server returns decimal and numeric data values and returns complete column information (including identity column information) to DBLIB and SQLColInfo.

Using the *SQLVER42* value (or not calling SQLSetLVersion for the logon record) means that SQL Server will treat that connection as a DBLIB 4.2x client. In this case, SQL Server converts decimal and numeric data values to float before returning them to the client and returns limited, DBLIB 4.2 column information (not including identity column information) to DBLIB and SQLColInfo.

Opening a Connection with SQLOpen

This strategy requires the creation of a LoginRec structure that can be used as many times as needed. After you've set up the LoginRec structure with at least the logon name and password, you can call the SQLOpen function, which performs the following actions:

- Opens the communication channel with the network (for example, the named-pipe connection)

- Logs on to the SQL server using the name and password in the LoginRec structure

- Initializes the national language and default database

- Returns the SQL connection handle needed by virtually every other function

Figure 30-4 shows the SQLOpen parameters.

Figure 30-4
SQLOpen Parameters

SQLOpen Parameter	Description
LoginRec	The result of a SQLLogin call. The structure created is modified by the SQLSet... functions.
ServerName$	The name of the SQL server. This is the LAN Manager server name.

The following code uses the SQLSet... functions with SQLOpen. Notice the use of the new Visual Basic conditional compilation to change the declarations so that they accommodate both the 16-bit and the 32-bit versions. This way, the same code can be used with either version:

```
Sub MenuSQLOpen_Click ()
#If Win16 Then
    Dim LoginRec As Integer, r As Integer, SQLConn As Integer
#Else
    Dim LoginRec As Long, r As Long, SQLConn As Long
#End If
Dim A As String
A = SQLInit()
LoginRec = SQLLogin()
r = SQLSetLUser(LoginRec, "SA")
r = SQLSetLPwd(LoginRec, "gizerinplatz")
r = SQLSetLApp(LoginRec, "My Application Name")
r = SQLSetLHost(LoginRec, "My Workstation Name")
r = SQLSetLNatLang(LoginRec, "U.S. ENGLISH")
r = SQLSetLoginTime(15)
SQLConn = SQLOpen(LoginRec, "Voffice")
End Sub
```

Using SQLOpenConnection

An alternative to SQLOpen is the SQLOpenConnection function, which takes as parameters some of the same arguments set into the LoginRec structure and performs the same sequence of functions needed to establish a connection and free the LoginRec structure. The LoginRec structure isn't used in this case, however; any settings made to the LoginRec structure have no effect on this connection. *Figure 30-5* shows the SQLOpenConnection parameters.

Figure 30-5
SQLOpenConnection Parameters

Parameter	Description
ServerName$	The name of the SQL server. This is the LAN Manager server name.
LoginName$	Indicates the SQL Server logon name. This is not a logon identification number.
Password$	Indicates the SQL Server password for this logon name. The logon-password pair must exist in *SysLogins* for the SQLOpenConnection to succeed.
HostName$	Indicates the host name (up to 30 characters). The name appears in sp_who as *Host name* and is stored as *host* in *SysProcesses*. The host name is called "workstation" in the documentation.
ApplicationName$	Indicates the application name (up to 30 characters). Stored as *program_name* in *SysProcesses*.

> **NOTE** You can't choose the national language with the SQLOpen Connection function nor can you set the SQL Server 6.0 behavior or packet-size options. You have to either depend on the system defaults for these options or use the SQLOpen function with a properly initialized LoginRec structure.

The following code uses the SQLOpenConnection function:

```
SQLConn = SQLOpenConnection("Voffice", "SA", "gizerinplatz", _
                            "Workstation Name", _
                            "Application Name")
```

Now, doesn't this look a little more manageable than the SQLOpen function? That's why I use it most of the time.

The Payoff: An Open Connection Handle

If the SQLOpen or SQLOpenConnection function succeeds, it returns a valid connection handle (which I refer to as the *SQLConn*). The variable you use to hold *SQLConn* must remain in scope for it to be maintained by Visual Basic. If you declare the variable in the procedure that performs the open, you must pass the variable back in the form of a function return value—if you don't, the connection handle is lost.

> **NOTE** For 16-bit VBSQL applications, the connection handle is an Integer. In the 32-bit version of VBSQL, however, the connection handle is returned as a Long. This is one of the biggest changes in porting VBSQL to 32-bit Visual Basic.

The *SQLConn* is used in virtually every VBSQL function executed from this point onward to refer to this specific connection. You can open as many connections as you need to, but each one must have its own variable to store the *SQLConn*. Both the Error and Message event handlers are passed to the *SQLConn* so that you can tell which connection caused the error or sent the message. If you want to open another connection, you can reuse the LoginRec structure from the SQLOpen function, but you need to establish another variable to hold the connection handle. If the SQLOpen or SQLOpenConnection operation fails for some reason, the function returns a 0 and the Error event procedure is fired with an error code that reflects the problem.

You can close a connection at any almost any time. This doesn't affect the variable holding the *SQLConn* value, however. The only way to tell if a *SQLConn* value refers to a valid connection handle is to use the SQLDead function, which returns *SUCCEED* if the connection is good and *FAIL* if it's not. It does *not* return True if it's dead, regardless of what the documentation says. Visual Basic and DBLIB don't use the same variables for True, so don't get confused.

Note that the default database isn't a parameter here. To change to a chosen database, use the SQLUse function after the connection has been established. A default database is already set for you when you connect, however; the system administrator set one up for you. I usually set it myself, though, just to be safe.

CAUTION

VBSQL online help mentions UserSQLErrorHandler, but this function is meaningless in the context of telling which connection has caused an error. It appears to be a documentation artifact from Microsoft QuickBasic.

Opening More Connections

It's possible to open additional connections, but remember what your parents told you: "Take as many as you want, dear, but no more than you need." When you're deciding whether to use another connection or trying to reuse the current connection, keep in mind that the number of *users* on a SQL server is a function of the number of *connections* required per application. When an application requires more connections to get its work done, fewer systemwide instances of that application are able to run at any one time.

You also need to remember to store the resulting *SQLConn* in a separate variable. Treat this variable just like the Jet Database object or the rdoConnection object—it must be kept in scope to be valid. Once Visual Basic drops it out of scope, it's gone. (Yes, you can keep your *SQLConn* variables in an array or collection and reference the nth connection in the array.)

What Can Go Wrong?

Failure to connect can be due to a seemingly endless number of factors, not all of which are caused by the application, SQL Server, or the phase of the moon. The following errors are typical of the conditions your application should be prepared for. Generally, the application should have a fallback plan for each of these contingencies; at least users should be told what they can do about a problem. Most of these errors have specific error codes that are returned. In some cases, however, the indication of the error isn't so clear. A significant number of the errors in the following list are LAN-related; generally, I deal with far more LAN-related problems than SQL Server–related problems when supporting VBSQL applications. The Windows network can't access the SQL server in the following circumstances:

- The user hasn't logged on to the LAN with a password. (A password might not have been necessary before this application.) This problem is especially prevalent in user-level or domain-based security environments.

- The user is running Microsoft Windows version 3.1 with persistent connections, and a large number of remote drives are connected (and might not even be in use). The total number of LAN connections is limited. Generally, with the default settings, if a user has more than four or five remote drives connected, he or she might experience problems running VBSQL applications.

- The Windows NT maximum users (MAXUSERS) limit has been reached on the LAN long before the maximum number of SQL connections is reached. Both Windows NT and SQL Server are sold in limited-user configurations. Once this limit is reached, no additional users will be permitted to log on. (This restriction shouldn't apply to a share-level security system as far as SQL Server connections are concerned.)

- The net is down. You might be surprised to get two calls from a user: the first to tell you that his or her e-mail is down (you explain that the net is down), and the second to tell you that his or her VBSQL application is also down for some reason—or is *really* slow.

- For older 16-bit VBSQL implementations, an improper share has been established for IPC$ (named pipes). The STARTUP.CMD on the OS/2 host server must contain a NET SHARE IPC$ statement if LAN Manager is running share-level security. With user-level security, permissions to access the IPC$ share are set on a user-by-user basis by the LAN administrator. It might also happen that improper permissions were assigned in user-level security, that there is an invalid LAN domain configuration, or that the LAN or a bridge to the OS/2 host server is down.

- SQL Server isn't running, which might be caused by any of the following events or circumstances:

  - The host server has been damaged or is in a trap state.

  - The host Windows NT server doesn't include a command to start the SQL server.

  - There is a corrupt or otherwise damaged database.

  - There is a shortage of disk or RAM space on the host server.

- SQL Server might be improperly configured. For example, SQL Server might be in single-user mode, or the server administrator might be doing maintenance work. There might also be too few SQL Server user connections to meet current demand.

- An improper SQL logon ID or password has been entered by the user. Maybe the user doesn't have permission to use this SQL server, or maybe an attempt was made to move or restore a database (or just a table), and the permissions, logon IDs, and passwords weren't properly restored or ended up being assigned to the wrong databases.

TIP One of the more successful fallback plans I have used involves the use of INI files (or registry entries). If the SQL server name is recorded in WIN.INI, a replacement server can be specified more easily (in case the original server is being repaired) if that contingency is ever needed.

Exhausting SQL Server Connections

Another not so unusual error is generated when the SQL server runs out of user connections. You should always test your application to see how it behaves in this situation. The number of connections on any SQL server can be easily changed by an administrator who is trying to free additional cache RAM because each connection consumes about 40 KB of system RAM, which could be allocated to additional procedure or data cache space.

The message string that is returned to the Message event handler when the number of connections is exhausted is technically correct—but hardly indicative of the root cause. SQL Server versions 1.0 and 1.1 return a message that indicates the server has unexpectedly lost the named-pipe interface. Apparently, the LAN layer opens a named pipe to the SQL server but is unable to add another connection. SQL Server responds by closing the named pipe at the SQL server end—thus the "unexpected EOF" from the server.

In versions of SQL Server earlier than version 6.0, when the sixth instance of an application is started and the SQL server has been set to permit five user connections, DBLIB reports: "Write to SQL Server failed. This error number is unused" (*SQLEWRIT*). At this point, the application might become toast. Only by ending the sixth and one other instance of the application have I been able to reach the SQL server. With Visual Basic SQL, DBLIB returns this *SQLEWRIT* error message; but it also sends a *SQLECONN* message, which indicates some sort of LAN failure. In SQL Server 6.0, this condition is handled much better. Now the message handler is fired with this message: "Unable to connect. The maximum number of *n*-configured user connections are already connected. System Administrator can configure to a higher value with sp_configure." This message text includes the reason for the error and the configured number of connections, so you can tell how many connections are available.

CAUTION
The error code *SQLESQLPS* (which is supposed to indicate that the maximum number of connections is already allocated) is *not* defined in VBSQL.BI nor in the DBLIB C documentation.

Unfortunately, the VBSQL Error event is also fired in this case. It returns an error indicating that the logon has failed. The point is that what happens when various error conditions occur might vary according to the version of SQL Server you're running. You'll probably want to test for a number of possible errors during the SQLOpen or SQLOpenConnection functions.

The application and host (workstation) name parameters are useful to you and your application, so include them in the SQLOpen or SQLOpenConnection function. Both parameters appear in the *sp_who* dump and can be queried from the system via an *sp_who* query. This makes it easy to see which applications are doing what and locking what, and it helps identify them to the system administrator. The *sp_who* utility and the Current Activity button of the SQL Enterprise Manager return the following information:

```
spid  status    loginame  hostname    blk dbname  cmd
-----------------------------------------------------------------
1     runnable  sa        BILLVAHOME  0   master  SELECT
2     sleeping  sa                    0   master  NETWORK HANDLER
3     sleeping  sa                    0   master  MIRROR HANDLER
4     sleeping  sa                    0   master  CHECKPOINT SLEEP
5     sleeping  sa        Workstatio  0   master  AWAITING COMMAND
```

Note row 5 under *spid*. The host name used in the SQLOpen (or SQL-OpenConnection) function is shown under *hostname* in the fourth column. To get more detail, you can also execute a query (or use the Details button in the SQL Enterprise Manager Current Activity dialog box):

```
Select spid, hostname, program_name from sysprocesses
```

The following information is returned:

```
spid   hostname    program_name
-----------------------------------------------
1      BILLVAHOME  SQL Administrator
2
3
4
5      Workstatio  Application
```

Again, note row 5 under *spid*. Here, *hostname* and *program_name* can be seen.

What do you use these parameters for? One of the utility applications I developed keeps a running log of who has logged on when and who is doing what at any given time, using queries on *SysProcedures*. It's especially helpful to have the name of the program spelled out when you're running this application. You might also want to set the *hostname* string to reflect the current time of logon or such additional user-specific information as the purpose of the connection.

Disconnecting from the Server

When the data access aspects of your application are complete, it's imperative that you tell DBLIB and the SQL server that you want to disconnect from the server. If you don't, you might not have any outward sign that anything is wrong until some other application can't get connected. If your application is in executable form, the file handles are freed automatically when the application ends. In rare cases, this doesn't work, however, and the connection handles are orphaned. When you're finished with your connection (even for the short term), you should use one or more of the following functions:

- *SQLClose (SQLConn),* to close the specified *SQLConn* connection. (This leaves all other connections open.)

- *SQLExit,* to close *all* open connections.

- *SQLWinExit,* when you are done with the DBLIB interface at the end of your application.

NOTE SQLExit and SQLWinExit are subroutines. They take no arguments or empty parentheses, and they return no result code. You can restart your SQL connection after using SQLWinExit, but only after calling SQLInit( ) again, to restart the DBLIB interface.

A Look Back

Your VBSQL application is set up and connected, your message handler has returned a few messages, and perhaps the Error event handler got fired a few times. Let's look at the code for this cornerstone application. It can serve as the starting point for every VBSQL application you write from now on. Note that the code includes conditional compilation code for both the 16-bit and the 32-bit versions of VBSQL:

```
Option Explicit
#If Win16 Then
    Dim SQLConn As Integer, R As Integer
#Else
    Dim SQLConn As Long, R As Long
#End If
Dim i As Integer
Const Server = "BetaV486"
Dim row As Long
Private Sub OpenConnection_Click()
SQLConn = SQLOpenConnection(Server, "", "", "Ws" & i, "app")
End Sub
```

(continued)

```
Private Sub Form_Load()
Dim A$
A$ = SQLInit()
End Sub

Private Sub Form_QueryUnload(Cancel As Integer, _
                             UnloadMode As Integer)
SQLExit
SQLWinExit
End Sub

Private Sub VBSQL1_Error(ByVal SQLConn As Long, _
                         ByVal Severity As Long, _
                         ByVal ErrorNum As Long, _
                         ByVal ErrorStr As String, _
                         RetCode As Long)
Select Case ErrorNum
    Case 10007
    Case Else
        MsgBox ("VBSQL Error: Sev:" & Severity & "Error:" _
                & ErrorNum & " - " & ErrorStr)
End Select
End Sub

Private Sub VBSQL1_Message(ByVal SQLConn As Long, _
                           ByVal Msg As Long, _
                           ByVal State As Long, _
                           ByVal Severity As Long, _
                           ByVal Message As String)
  Select Case Msg
    Case 5701:
    Case Else
        MsgBox ("Msg:" & Msg & " - State:" & State _
                & " - Severity:" _
                & Severity & " : " & Message)
End Select
End Sub
```

31
Chapter

Accessing
Data with
VBSQL

Setting the Default Database

Building and Submitting Queries

Sending the Query

**Five Phases of VBSQL
Operations: A Quick Review**

Dealing with Contingencies

Executing Stored Procedures

You have just witnessed the construction of the foundations for most of your VBSQL applications, and now we are ready to get into some tougher territory—working with data. But just relax—there isn't an object, property, or method in sight. You will, however, find that the IntelliSense features of Microsoft Visual Basic version 5.0 are activated as you work with the API calls.

The real purpose of any SQL Server front-end application isn't to open connections but to fetch data. Much of the groundwork is already done, and you're now ready to start a conversation with your chosen SQL server.

The server has already called your Message event handler to tell your application that it set your default database and national language, and you probably threw those messages away. At this point, we are ready to set the default database again (if we need to), build a query, send it to the server, and process the results.

Setting the Default Database

A SQL administrator who sets up a user account specifies the default database that the system assigns to this user. Whenever this user logs on, the SQL server changes the database from *Master* to the default database. DB-Library is notified of the change via a message. The same holds true for the national language option.

It's important for an application to have the default database set correctly, or the queries run by the application won't function properly (if at all)—not unless you qualify every database reference in your TSQL queries. Since the administrator can arbitrarily change the default database, it's wise to set this yourself as one of the first things your application does. To set the default database, simply call the following VBSQL function, using the name of the default database in place of the *"MyDefaultDB"* string:

```
Database$ = "MyDefaultDB"
r = SQLUse(SQLConn, Database$)
```

Once you request a change in the default database, your Message event procedure receives notification from the server, informing you of the change. Note, however, that this default database setting applies just to the specified connection, isn't inherited by subsequent connections, and doesn't affect the settings of other connections or the default database setting established by the system administrator. To change this logon ID setting, you have to submit a query to the SQL server—but unless you're a system administrator, you can affect only the current logon ID's default database setting:

```
sp_defaultdb MyLoginID, NewDefaultDB
```

NOTE   You can change the default database as often as you like and at almost any time results aren't pending on the connection.

Building and Submitting Queries

Now that you've set the default database, you're ready to build and submit your queries to the SQL server. Before we see how to send a query, however, we need to consider what constitutes a query and how to build a query that the server will be able to understand and process.

SQL Command Batches

All of your SQL queries will be in the form of Transact-SQL command *batches*. As a refresher, let's review the rules about batches so that you'll have no surprises when you send batches to the SQL server. A batch, you recall, is one or more Transact-SQL commands sent at one time. If you send an improper batch for processing to the SQL server, you'll be greeted with a TSQL syntax error, the batch will be canceled, and you'll be sent to bed without supper.

Building Batches

The rules and regulations that govern the creation of batches are summarized as follows:

- *CREATE PROCEDURE, CREATE RULE, CREATE DEFAULT, CREATE TRIGGER, and CREATE VIEW must be sent to the SQL server alone.* They can't be combined with any other TSQL statements. Doing so will cause a SQL syntax error.

- *CREATE DATABASE, CREATE TABLE, and CREATE INDEX can be combined with other Transact-SQL statements in a batch.*

- *Rules and defaults can't be bound to columns and used during the same batch.* The sp_bindrule and sp_bindefault system procedures can't be in the same batch as INSERT statements that invoke the rule or default.

- *The SQL Server version 6.x CHECK constraints follow the same rules as TSQL rules and defaults.* A table created with CHECK constraints cannot enforce those constraints in the same batch as the definition.

- *When you change the default database with the SQLUse function or send the TSQL USE command in SQL Server 4.2, the change doesn't take effect until after the batch has been completed.* In SQL Server 6.x, however, the batch is executed in the specified database if the TSQL USE command is contained within a batch. The database context switch is immediate.

- *You can't drop an object and then reference it or reuse it in the same batch.*

- *You can't alter a table and then reference the new columns in the same batch.*

- *Any options changed with a SET statement take effect at the end of the batch.* You can combine SET statements and queries in the same batch, but the SET options won't apply to the queries in that batch.

CAUTION

Some memory is required for a query's execution plan, so the limit on the number of explicit data values you can insert or update in a single batch is actually somewhat less than the SQL Server batch size of 128 KB. You might be able to insert or update one column of 124 KB or two columns of 62 KB each.

Batch Limits

There are also a few limits that apply to batches. The SQL Server batch size of 128 KB limits the maximum number of explicit data values that can be inserted or updated in a single batch. This limit doesn't apply to page-based data, such as Text or Image, that is inserted or updated through the WRITETEXT or UPDATETEXT statements. It also doesn't apply to data inserted with the BCP command-line utility, data inserted from another table, or data passed from remote procedure calls.

Sending Multiple Batches

In ISQL or SAF (or ISQLW or SQL Enterprise Manager), you seem to send several batches (scripts) to the SQL server at once. Actually, though, only one batch is processed at a time. The term GO is *not* a TSQL statement or operator; it's simply a batch separator for SQL Server utilities that know how to execute multiple batches. The SQL server can't execute more than one batch of commands at any one time unless you open another connection and then use the new connection to execute another batch. You must process all the results of each batch after it has been processed by the SQL server before you can submit another batch to process.

Working with Batch Results

When you process batches, you need to keep in mind that not every TSQL statement returns rows but each statement's result set must be processed by your application. There's a one-to-one correspondence between the number of statements sent to the SQL server and the number of result sets that have to be processed. When you do a 5500-row update (which you can do with a single UPDATE statement), no rows are returned to the application; but the statement *does* generate a result set that must be processed before the next statement in the batch can be processed or before a new batch can be sent.

Fixed queries

You will probably start by sending what I call a *fixed query*. This is a hard-coded TSQL batch with just one TSQL statement. Many of my production applications have a few of these fixed batches. I use them to ask simple questions, and I expect simple, low-row-count answers. The problem with using fixed batches that send more than a few simple commands is that they can tend to slow the SQL server down. They don't place much extra load on the LAN (they're typically shorter than a dozen lines), but they do consume time and CPU power on the SQL server, which has to compile these batches.

On-the-fly queries

The most common queries used in my applications are generated automatically by the application. The user, via menu or CheckBox selections, decides what subset of the data is desired, and the program logic creates an appropriate query to fetch the data. These queries aren't readily adapted to stored procedures, at least not on the surface. Later we'll see how it's entirely possible to send parameters to a procedure (and get parameters back); but you may not pass object names that are unknown to the procedure during the query's compilation—not unless you use the compile-on-the-fly feature of SQL Server 6.*x*.

Using Drop-Down Lists

The following illustration shows a user selection form that is designed to accept the parameters for a fairly complex query. The idea here is to avoid the use of *ad hoc* queries—those that require the user to type in the SELECT statement. This screen could be expanded to include selections for the columns (or views) wanted, sort orders, or formatting options. Note the use of drop-down combo box lists. These lists are built either as the form is loaded or as the user selects them. In either case, a query is made to the SQL server to determine all valid choices. None of the options are hard-coded into the application.

The following code segment is used to create the SQL query WHERE clause that will be used to extract the data from the *FarmAnimals* database. (Some of the code has been removed for the sake of brevity.) During debug, and whenever I want the user to learn how to make SQL queries, I display the query either alongside the form or in a pop-up form:

```
Sub BuildWhere ()
Where = ""
If Search(BirthDay).Value = VbChecked _
    And Argument(Birthday).Text <> "" Then
    Where = " Birth like '" & Argument(Birthday).Text & "' and "
End If
If Search(Animal_Type).Value = VbChecked _
    And Argument(Animal_Type).Text <> "" Then
    Where = Where & " Animal_type like '" & _
        Argument(Animal_Type).Text & "' and "
End If
⋮
' Strip off last 'and'.
If Right$(Where, 5) = " and " Then
    Where = " WHERE " & Left$(Where, Len(Where) - 5)
End If
End Sub
```

NOTE No, the *FarmAnimals* database is not on the companion CD-ROM. It doesn't exist outside my lab. These examples have served for years as just that—examples. I'm sure you can transmogrify them to your own test databases.

Converting Queries to Stored Procedures

Any production application should evolve toward using stored procedures almost exclusively. It's perfectly all right to use large fixed batches during development. After the application is stable, however, the developer should go back and replace large fixed batches with stored procedures.

Whenever possible, fixed queries and on-the-fly queries should be converted to SQL Server–based, compiled stored procedures, especially with applications that have more than a few users or when additional SQL Server speed is needed. With the addition of stored procedures that can return parameters, developers should make themselves aware of all of the new opportunities for improving performance. As a rule, my development procedure builds the prototype and first release of the application without referencing user-written stored procedures. Once the application is stable, I reexamine the application for likely stored-procedure candidates, convert the queries as necessary, and retest the application.

Quoted identifiers contain as many as 31 characters. The delimited string can contain any combination of characters represented by the current code page except double quotation marks. To enforce or remove quoted identifier and string constant resolution at the session level, use the SET statement. This causes the current session to differentiate between single and double quotation marks when evaluating an expression. When QUOTED_IDENTIFIER is turned on, strings in double quotation marks (") will not be evaluated or checked against keywords. If you use a keyword for an object name or for a portion of an object name, the QUOTED_IDENTIFIER option must be set when you create that object and when you access it.

NOTE Some of the examples provided in Visual Basic include "smart" quotes. These *won't* substitute for normal double or single quotes—you'll have to replace them before trying the examples.

Quoting Strings

The TSQL language doesn't care what kind of quotes you use to denote strings. (Well, it didn't mind.) Support for quoted identifiers has been added to SQL Server 6.*x*. According to ANSI syntax, you must now use double quotation marks (") to delimit keywords (quoted identifiers) and single quotation marks (') to delimit string constants. This resolves the conflict between quoted identifiers and string constants during expression evaluation at the parser level and provides ANSI compatibility for delimited identifiers. Keywords specified within double quotation marks can now be used as object names, though this practice isn't recommended. If you want to use object names and if the object names you want are keywords, reserved words, database technology terms, or names that could cause conflict with future keywords, you should first attempt to resolve possible conflicts by choosing other words for the object names. When this isn't possible, use quoted identifiers.

TIP If an object name or part of an object name (for example, a column) is created from a keyword when the SET QUOTED_IDENTIFIER option is turned on, all subsequent references to that object must be made with the SET QUOTED_IDENTIFIER option on. In general, of course, it's best to avoid using keywords as object names.

Visual Basic cares what kind of quotes you use to delineate strings, and it uses the single quote to indicate the beginning of a comment. Therefore, you *must* surround your SQL command batches with double quotes and delineate the quoted strings, dates, and so forth in the SQL commands with single quotes. Don't worry about the use of single quotes. As long as you include them in the double-quoted strings, they're considered part of the string, not comments. This means, however, that you'll have to parse any string typed by a user and passed to you; if it has embedded single or double quotes, make sure your string still has matched sets of quotes for Visual Basic and TSQL. For example, the following string will have problems being parsed by TSQL:

```
Bob's wife was quoted as saying, "Gee, he's a great guy!"
```

If your application permits users to enter text of this nature, you'll have to modify your string parser to accommodate the embedded possessives and quoted strings. I also find it somewhat irritating when an application requires me to do the quoting myself during data entry. If the user is permitted to specify arguments that will be used to build a query, the application should include the quotes wherever they're needed during the actual creation of the query.

Sending the Query

Once you have created the query in the Transact-SQL language, it's time to send it to DB-Library, where it's formatted into TDS and transmitted to SQL Server. Sending a command involves filling the DB-Library command buffer with a query and telling DB-Library to send the buffer to the SQL server. This section describes a number of techniques for accomplishing that step.

The Long Way

There are at least two ways to send a query to the SQL server. We'll start with the long way, which involves these three steps:

1. Loading the command buffer with one or more calls to SQLCmd

2. Sending the command with SQLExec

3. Requesting the first result set with SQLResults

Building the command buffer

With either method, you first have to build the TSQL command buffer, which is the holding area for all queries sent to the SQL server. DB-Library creates the command buffer and manages all aspects of it. To make things easier to develop, it would be helpful if you could see the query in its completed stage before it goes to the SQL server. (Unfortunately, this isn't particularly easy *after* the data has been sent to the command buffer.) I have never felt a compelling need to do so, however. Instead, I make a single call to SQLCmd once I have a string ready to submit because it's far simpler, more flexible, easier to debug, and somewhat faster to execute.

Using multiple calls to SQLCmd

It's possible to send the query one piece at a time to DB-Library by using the SQLCmd function. Each time you call SQLCmd, it takes the string you pass and concatenates it to any string that was previously sent. Old batches are automatically deleted when you start a new query. A common problem with this method is the inclusion of white space between SQL statements. For example, the following set of function calls results in a SQL syntax error:

```
r = SQLCmd(SQLConn, "Select * from")
r = SQLCmd(SQLConn, "Animals where")
r = SQLCmd(SQLConn, "Name = 'Miss Piggy'")
```

The command buffer after all these calls would read this way:

```
Select * fromAnimals whereName = 'Miss Piggy'
```

This is obviously wrong. The SQLCmd function doesn't care what is sent to the command buffer. No syntax, object, or any other kind of checking takes place before the command is sent to the SQL server—not even checks for potentially damaging binary data (or politically offensive words).

CAUTION
You could send your spouse's recipe for brine-soaked chicken gizzards to the SQL server, and SQLCmd, which does no checking of any kind, would return a *SUCCEED*.

Using a single call to SQLCmd

When using this method, I create a single string (*q$*) that contains the TSQL query and pass the string to the SQLCmd function. The SQLCmd function, like virtually all the other VBSQL functions, takes the connection handle *SQLConn* as its first argument. Yes, that means that *each* connection has its own independent command buffer. The example below shows how this is done. (Note the use of the new Visual Basic line-continuation character to break up the string.)

```
q$ = " Select * " _
    & " FROM Authors " _
    & " WHERE au_id = '172-32-1176'"
R = SQLCmd(SQLConn, q$)
debug.print q$
```

The only time you really need to worry about the return code is when you expect to overflow the 128-KB command buffer or available memory. Remember, SQLCmd couldn't care less about the content of the string.

> **NOTE**   Just because a query fits in the 128-KB buffer doesn't mean that it won't be too complex to execute. A number of other resource limitations could keep the query from executing.

Executing the query

The SQLExec function instructs DB-Library to convert the command buffer into a TDS packet and send it to the server. In many cases, SQL Server takes less than a second to *begin* replying to a request. But some applications process and retrieve all results before showing you any resulting rows, so the delay is multiplied by the number of rows returned. ISQL queries give you a better idea of SQL Server response time—ISQL dumps all returning rows to the screen as they arrive.

If the query succeeds, SQL Server processes only enough rows to fill a 4-KB buffer and signals DB-Library that the results are ready. If your application stops accepting rows, the server stops writing packets after 4 KB is buffered, until your application asks for more rows. If the results are being built incrementally by the SQL server, a share lock is left on the current working page for each table in the query. If the results are being built from a work table, no locks are held. No further processing of the command takes place until your application requests more rows from DB-Library.

CAUTION
Make sure your strings aren't contaminated with binary trash, as can often happen with fixed-length strings in Visual Basic—I have seen binary data actually crash the server. In one particular case, Microsoft Word for Windows had passed Visual Basic a string ending with a binary 0. When it was made part of the query, this embedded 0 was invisible to Visual Basic but it caused DB-Library to ignore everything that came after it.

What can go wrong?

If the query causes an error, your Error or Message event procedure (or both) will be called before DB-Library returns to the SQLExec function. Depending on the success or failure of the TSQL statement, DB-Library passes either *SUCCEED* (1) or *FAIL* (0) to the SQLExec function. Note that these are *not* True or False. The most specific information regarding any errors is in the parameters passed to your Error and Message event procedures. This is the primary reason why it's so important to have Error and Message event handlers.

If the query fails, you can safely send a new command; the previous command buffer is automatically cleared when you make your next SQLCmd call. Any of the following can cause SQLExec to return *FAIL*:

- The command buffer contains a TSQL syntax error.

- At least one of the statements has caused a permissions violation.

- You didn't complete processing of the previous query.

- The command buffer is empty.

- The command buffer contains binary trash.

If SQLExec returns *SUCCEED*, you know that at least one of the TSQL statements in the batch executed successfully and that all the statements are syntactically correct.

Getting the results

For each statement in your batch, you need to ask DB-Library to prepare the pending result sets by using the SQLResults function to fetch the first and all subsequent result sets. SQLResults doesn't fetch any data. It merely tells DB-

Library that you're ready to process the data from the result set specified by the connection handle, *SQLConn*. Remember, you must request a result set from each command in your batch, even though you don't expect rows to be returned. The SQLResults function returns one of the following constants to indicate whether there are more results or whether the batch has been completely processed:

- *SUCCEED (1)*. There is a result set to process. (This doesn't necessarily mean that there are rows to process, just that a result set is active.)

- *FAIL (0)*. Something went wrong. (The most common reason for failure is an invalid SQL Server connection.)

- *NOMORERESULTS (2)*. There are no further result sets to process. (The connection is now free to be used again.)

- *NOMORERPCRESULTS (3)*. This is returned when stored-procedure return information is available from one stored procedure in a batch of multiple stored procedures.

TIP SQLResults doesn't return control to the application until the server sends the required response. The application can be blocked for a considerable time if the server is waiting for a lock or is processing a large sort. If this is unacceptable, always call SQLDataReady before SQLResults and set the DB-Library timeout to regain control periodically.

A simple VBSQL function sequence using SQLResults (with the long method) looks like this:

```
' Put the statement into the command buffer...the long way
R = SQLCmd(SQLConn, "SELECT * from Pubs..authors")
' Send the statement to SQL Server and start execution
R = SQLExec(SQLConn)
If R = SUCCEED Then
    Do Until R = NOMORERESULTS
        R = SQLResults(SQLConn)
        ' Retrieve the data for each row
    Loop
Else
    ' Deal with the failed SQLExec statement
End If
```

Remember, you *can't* use SQLExec with this *SQLConn* handle to send another batch until SQLResults returns *NOMORERESULTS*.

The Easy Way

The easy way to send a query to the SQL server is to use the SQLSendCmd utility function. It won't do everything that the long method does, but it will perform 90 percent of the work with a single command. That's why it's become the *de facto* standard way to send commands to the SQL server with VBSQL—at least for quick synchronous queries.

SQLSendCmd takes the connection handle *SQLConn* and a Visual Basic string that contains a TSQL command batch. This string can contain a single TSQL statement or a set of commands that constitute the batch. You call SQLSendCmd only once, so you need to make sure the string sent contains the *entire* batch of commands you need to send.

SQLSendCmd makes internal (C-based) DB-Library calls to SQLCmd and SQLExec, as well as the first call to SQLResults. It passes the return code from each step out to its own return code—*SUCCEED* (1) or *FAIL* (0). If any underlying command fails, SQLSendCmd returns *FAIL*. By using a C-based interface, Visual Basic can execute the same code faster and do it with less application overhead. Coding what we did before with SQLSendCmd looks like this:

```
' Send the command...the short way
R = SQLSendCmd(SQLConn, "SELECT * from Pubs..authors")
If R = SUCCEED Then
    Do
        ' Retrieve the data for the first row
    Loop Until SQLResults(SQLConn) = NOMORERESULTS
Else
    ' Deal with the failed SQLExec statement
End If
```

It's that easy. Note that the program logic is now ready to process the first set of rows.

Fetching Result Set Data Rows

Once your program logic is in the processing loop that prepares each result set (triggered by SQLResults), you're ready to fetch the first and subsequent data rows with the SQLNextRow function. SQLNextRow instructs DB-Library to make one row available to your program variables from the pending result set, on the basis of the specified *SQLConn* connection. (It does *not* place anything in the variables, the way C does, but you're blessed in that you don't have to do any of the variable binding that the C developers do.) Once so instructed, DB-Library asks the server for the requested row and parses it for your use.

The SQLNextRow function returns one of three constants, which either indicates the type of row fetched or indicates that there are no more rows in the result set:

- MOREROWS *(–1) indicates that this is a normal (regular) data row, not a row created with the COMPUTE BY statement.* (This was REGROW in earlier versions of VBSQL, and REGROW is still supported.)

- NOMOREROWS *(–2) is what you get if there are no more rows to be processed or there were none to begin with.* This is equivalent to having the result set EOF property set to True. For example, you can loop until you see this:

```
SQLNextRow(SQLConn) = NOMOREROWS
```

- **FAIL** *(0) is returned if the call is unsuccessful.* Generally, failure is caused by a DB-Library linkage failure: the connection was dropped, or a packet was scrambled.

There are also some result values that apply to result sets. Here are two that we haven't considered yet:

- **BUFFULL** *(-3), when you're using row buffers, is the return value that indicates the buffer is filled before this row is read.* No new row is read.

- *A COMPUTE clause's identification number is sent when the application has included a COMPUTE clause in the command batch.*

Once you have used SQLNextRow to ask DB-Library to prepare the result set row for processing, you can use the SQLData function to ask DB-Library to move the data from its buffers to your program variables. SQLData passes the data from the rows one column at a time, in the form of a string, regardless of the data type. You can do the conversions later, or Visual Basic can do them for you as it copies the data to program variables more appropriate to the data type.

NOTE SQLData returns the string data type for all data types except Binary (not *bit*), VarBinary, and Image. For these data types, the result is still in string form but the contents are (you guessed it) in binary.

SQLData accepts the connection handle *SQLConn* and the column number to fetch as arguments. Column 1 is the first column. The column number to be fetched is a function of the TSQL query and has no bearing on the order of the data in the table, unless the query didn't specify a particular column—but all columns (as in SELECT *). Look at the following code example for SQLData:

```
q$ = "Select name, age, status from dogs where breed = 'Beagle'"
r = SQLSendCmd(SQLConn, q$)
If r = SUCCEED Then
    r = SQLNextRow(SQLConn)
    Do                                    ' Get the first and
                                          ' subsequent rows
        dog_name$ = SQLData$(SQLConn, 1)   ' Data from the 1st col.
        dog_age = Val(SQLData$(SQLConn, 2) ' Data from the 2nd col.
        dog_status$ = SQLData$(SQLConn, 3) ' Data from the 3rd col.
        Print "Row:"; n;
        Print " - Name:"; dog_name$;
        Print ", age:"; dog_age;
        Print " status:"; dog_status$
    Loop Until SQLNextRow(SQLConn) = NOMOREROWS
Do
Until SQLResults(SQLConn) = NOMORERESULTS
```

NOTE When you execute a procedure that contains a RAISERROR statement (as when you perform an update that includes a trigger), unless you call the SQLResults function, you might have to wait until *NOMORERESULTS* is returned before you can see the error generated by RAISERROR.

Five Phases of VBSQL Operations: A Quick Review

At this point, let's review the entire sequence of commands, from logon to processing rows. This sequence is used for virtually every VBSQL application that works with synchronous (or nonasynchronous) queries. *Figure 31-1* shows that the workstation process has five major phases, or states.

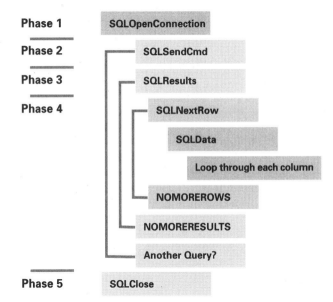

Figure 31-1 *Five phases of a VBSQL operation*

Phase 1 initializes the interface and makes a connection with the SQL server. We use SQLInit, SQLLogin, and associated commands, or we use SQLOpenConnection. Each phase after the first is implemented as a loop.

Phase 2 builds the command buffer. We can usually do this in one step, by submitting a single string to SQLCmd or looping through multiple calls to SQLCmd, as needed, to build up the command buffer. The end of this phase is signaled by submission of the batch to the SQL server for processing. We use SQLExec to do this. Up to this point, the server knows of our existence but it's done no real work for us. Once the query is submitted, however, the SQL server compiles the query, decides on a plan of attack, and fetches the data—

assuming that the query is syntactically correct and that the user has permission to access the data.

In phase 3, the SQL server notifies us that the query either has failed or has executed successfully (or at least, that part of it has). At this point, we must parse the results (if any) from this query. We begin by using SQLResults to request each result set. We now begin an internal loop that marks the beginning of phase 4. Phase 3 ends when SQLResults returns *NOMORERESULTS*. We can then loop back to phase 2 and submit another query, or we can terminate the connection.

In phase 4, we ask DB-Library to fetch each row of the current result set from the SQL server. We use SQLNextRow for the first row and each subsequent row of data. Next we process each column of data, using SQLData. When SQLNextRow returns *NOMOREROWS*, the current result set is empty and we proceed to the next result set—and loop back to phase 3.

Phase 5 begins and ends with the termination of the SQL server connection. Once the connection is dropped (for whatever reason), you need to re-open it before you attempt to send data to the server; the current connection handle is no longer of any use.

CAUTION
If you don't fully process each result set—that is, if SQLNextRow hasn't returned *NOMOREROWS*—you get an error message (*SQLERPND*) from DBLIB.

Dealing with Contingencies

If your application isn't prepared for the inevitable glitch, it won't last long in a production environment. Here is how to design in some additional error handling, to keep your user conscious—and contented.

Setting Processing Time

When you use the SQLExec or SQLSendCmd functions to submit your query, DB-Library blocks. It doesn't yield to the Microsoft Windows operating system, and other operations can't take place on the workstation while the query is being processed by the SQL server. In 16-bit Windows, this is a real concern, since the whole system seems to hang in suspended animation while the query is being processed. With Microsoft Windows NT or Microsoft Windows 95, however, the rest of Windows continues to work using what's left of the available CPU time. (The particular application still freezes, but other applications can continue to run.) In most cases, this time is very short (a few hundredths of a second), so the waiting time is of no real consequence. But when you submit a broad-scope UPDATE or DELETE statement or try to create a large cursor, you might have to wait more than a few seconds for the query to complete. In this case, you're faced with a new problem: timeouts.

DB-Library doesn't return control to your application before the time (in seconds) specified by the last call to SQLSetTime or before the *user* times out and tries to reboot the system. Whatever else happens, you don't want the user to reset the computer or try to kill the application while there's a query pending. In fact, you don't want the user *ever* to reboot. A few things you can do to keep this from happening are described on the next page.

- *Use a short timeout (five seconds or so), and keep track of total query processing time in the application.* After DB-Library times out, you can animate a "still working" icon and pass DB-Library an *INTCONTINUE* to indicate that you want to continue waiting. That way, the user knows the application is still working correctly (if slowly) and is in control of the situation.

- *Let the user decide, after an extended period, not to wait any longer.* At this point, you can pass DB-Library an *INTCANCEL*, which will terminate the query and pass a *FAIL* return code back to the function making the query.

- *Use the asynchronous SQLSend, SQLReady, and SQLOK functions.* These functions are somewhat more complex to use, but they don't block while waiting for the SQL server to return. (We'll examine these functions in Chapter 35.)

CAUTION

SQLCancel tells DB-Library to discard all TDS data in the outbound named pipe, so any work not yet started by SQL Server is tossed. DB-Library then tries to get SQL Server to stop working on the current batch. But it's difficult to know just where SQL Server is in the batch it's currently working on, so the SQLCancel command can yield unpredictable results if the batch is long and contains several statements. If you intend to use SQLCancel, keep your batches simple. Don't send batches that have more than one transaction, and don't spread transactions over more than one batch.

Completing the Query

It's important to complete processing of each result set that the SQL server *returns*. Note that I didn't say each result set for each command *submitted*. If you invoke a batch that includes stored procedures, even indirectly, you don't know how many result sets are going to be returned. Therefore, you must code sufficient logic to deal with *all* result sets as they're returned—regardless of origin.

It's not unusual to abandon processing of the rows once your question is answered. I often send queries that return only a single row, which indicates whether it's necessary to submit further queries. In these cases, I have several options:

- *Use SQLCancel to cancel the execution of all statements submitted, as well as statements still in the command buffer that haven't been processed.* (This returns me to phase 2, where I can safely submit another query.) SQLCancel essentially kills the batch.

- *Use SQLCanQuery to cancel any rows pending from the current (only the current) statement.* (This returns me to the top of phase 3.) I can continue to process result sets from other, previously submitted batch commands.

- *To flush the current command, I can use a loop to call SQLNextRow until NOMOREROWS is returned.* This can be time-consuming and resource-intensive. I don't use this option unless I need the data from the remaining rows.

- *I can use a loop to call SQLResults until NOMORERESULTS is returned.* Note that an inner loop calling SQLNextRow to process each row will be needed to flush individual rows. The same caveat applies to this option as to looping with SQLNextRow.

Neither of the last two looping options is really recommended, since both force the SQL server to fetch data rows and pass the results over the net to your workstation. The SQLCancel and SQLCanQuery functions simply inform the SQL server that you don't want to complete the query, which saves significant processing time on your workstation and on the SQL server.

Handling Errors

One of your application's principal functions is to handle the errors that DB-Library and SQL Server generate. Fortunately, the VBSQL interface gives your application the opportunity to deal intelligently with the entire range of errors. Higher-level interfaces often bury DB-Library and SQL Server errors in generalized error codes that don't permit any flexibility in your approach.

SQLExec and SQLSendCmd return immediately if your query contains any syntax errors. If there are such errors, the query is never successfully compiled and is never executed. Once your query is executed, you have to be prepared for several contingencies:

- *Your query might have exhausted available RAM or other resources, either on the workstation or on the SQL server.* For example, your recordset buffer couldn't hold the string or the image that the SQL query requested.

- *The net connection or SQL Server connection might have failed.* Perhaps the server crashed.

- *The query might have attempted to access SQL Server resources outside the scope of its permissions.*

- *The transaction log might have been full.* This is fairly common when planning has not taken into account the transaction volume between transaction log dumps.

- *TempDB might have been full.* Since the default size of TempDB is 2 MB, this is a fairly common problem, especially when you use ORDER BY clauses or server-side cursors.

- *Your query might have requested an update that violated the uniqueness of a primary key.*

- *Your query might have failed because of a rule violation or a trigger violation.*

CAUTION
In Transact-SQL, a rule is a set of conditions (written in TSQL) that establishes certain criteria for each data element or table. Rules and triggers are used to ensure that minimum requirements are met. If the requirements aren't met, data can't be accepted into the elements or tables to which the rules or triggers are attached.

TIP Not all transactions affect the size of the transaction log. Only transactions that change the database are recorded in the log. For example, UPDATE, DELETE, and INSERT statements are recorded in the log, but SELECT statements are not.

When a trigger fails to pass the query, there is a particularly interesting problem: SQL Server doesn't consider the successful execution of TSQL trigger code to be an error, even if the trigger rolls back (or rejects) the transaction. Whenever an UPDATE, INSERT, or DELETE statement is executed against a table having an assigned trigger, a stored procedure executes code that tests for the validity of that operation. For example, a trigger might test to see if the row chosen for deletion can properly be deleted.

NOTE   A well-known trigger routine was built into the robot in the film *Robocop*. The TSQL trigger prevented the "deletion" of any executive listed in the *Current Executives* table. But once the villain had been dropped from the company payroll, the robot was able to "delete" his row with his trigger, so to speak.

Your application is *not* notified if the requested operation is incomplete unless the code in the trigger passes back a message. One of the only ways to tell the application that the query didn't succeed is through the RAISERROR statement. That way, your application can pass back a code to your Message event procedure. Even if your trigger code accepts and commits the query, it's possible to send a message to that effect back to the application; the server won't pass back any other indication that the query has succeeded.

Microsoft SQL Server is designed to give you high performance by executing precompiled modules. It optimizes queries automatically as they arrive from command batches. Other SQL Servers don't have this kind of intelligent query optimization. They depend on the developer or user to tune the query—presumably by exercising his or her powers of precognition in order to take advantage of indexes and "know" just which transaction approach will yield the highest performance at the time the query is submitted.

Executing Stored Procedures

If your application is to wring the best possible performance out of SQL Server, it will have to use stored procedures. I encourage all my students and clients to write their applications with eventual conversion to stored procedures in mind. SQL Server's query optimizer makes a number of complex decisions during compilation of a query. If storing the results of that decision-making process and reusing them later can save the time required for those decisions, the system will be much faster. Stored procedures do save that time.

Stored procedures also add something to your design: they permit the developer to write code that an entire staff of other developers can leverage. Stored procedures are global subroutines for making queries or simply for shielding the user from underlying data tables. Remember, too, that protection schemes can be based on access to stored procedures, just as the master database tables are shielded from user damage by system stored procedures.

Stored Procedures: An Overview

Essentially, stored procedures are compiled, linked, optimized query "executables" stored in your database. Once they have been compiled, SQL Server stores their execution plans so that the plans don't have to be re-created when the time comes to run the query. This precompilation strategy has its downside, however; when a procedure is compiled, the query optimizer bases a number of decisions on the status of the database at the time. It inspects the keys and key "statistics" to see which keys (if any) will be useful in this particular query.

TIP If a key's statistics don't reflect the state of the data when a stored procedure is executed, the procedure might not run efficiently. When the dynamics of a database are constantly changing, it might make sense to force recompilation of critical stored procedures as they're executed.

Sharing code for stored procedures

Stored procedures are shared by multiple users on the database, but they aren't shared in the same way programs or DLLs are shared in the Windows or OS/2 platforms. When another user wants a stored procedure, SQL Server loads an *additional* copy of the procedure, even if there is one already in memory. Once a stored procedure has completed and is no longer active, it's marked for deletion but not purged. If another user requests this procedure, it's reactivated, which saves the cost of disk access for reloading it. If another stored procedure is called up and SQL Server needs procedure queue space to store it, the oldest (least frequently used) procedure cache pages are given over to the new procedure.

Using the latest features

Starting with SQL Server 4.2, procedures on one server could be run by workstations connected to another server. These are called *remote stored procedures*. They come as close as Microsoft SQL Server gets to global sharing of data. To permit the operation of remote stored procedures, remote (and local) servers must be specially configured. This configuration includes the establishment of remote logons to the remote server, so that applications like the ones we'll be writing don't have to log on twice to get to the remote procedures. The remote procedures will be able to return rows from tables on a local server as if they were a part of the local server's database. The user can also write triggers on the local server that execute remote stored procedures for synchronizing multiple servers. The EXECUTE command now has a new variation in its syntax to support the execution of remote stored procedures:

```
declare @r int
execute @r = SOMEOTHER.AnimalDB.DBO.FindSkunkName "George"
```

Another SQL Server 4.2 feature, of significantly more importance, is the ability of stored procedures to return parameters. Before SQL Server 4.2, stored procedures could return rows in only one or more sets of results. Now that stored procedures can return data in the form of arguments, handling these procedures has grown in complexity, by an order of magnitude. Many of the VBSQL functions we work with deal with parameterizing these returning pieces of information. Incidentally, one feature of the VBSQL interface not matched by many of the other types of interfaces is its ability to handle multiple result sets, such as those typically returned by stored procedures.

Calling Stored Procedures

If you have absorbed anything up to this point, you already know how to call stored procedures. You merely have to include a command to execute the stored procedure or procedures in your command batch. (Remember, a batch is simply a set of commands that can be sent together.)

> **NOTE** SQL Server has a number of prewritten stored procedures, which are used to configure and administer the SQL server. All of these procedures have the prefix sp_, which distinguishes them from user- or application-written stored procedures.

You have to remember only one rule when calling stored procedures: if the stored procedure isn't called as the first command in the batch, precede it with the EXECUTE (or EXEC) command. For example, just set a string to one of the following, and send it to the server via SQLSendCmd:

```
sp_setopt work, 'Select', true
```

Or do this:

```
sp_helpdb MyTable
Execute sp_helpdb MyOtherTable
Execute sp_helpdb MyStillAnother
```

Handling Results from Stored Procedures

As you can see, executing stored procedures isn't that tough. Getting back the results is a little trickier. Remember, a stored procedure might—just might—return one or more result sets. Many system stored procedures are meant to act as database administrative tools, and the result sets aren't particularly easy to parse.

> **NOTE** Stored procedures are kept in the database (either the master database or your own) in source-code form. Unless you're using the new encrypted-procedures option, you can examine any of the procedures saved in the system. You can also do a quick SELECT on the system table *SysComments*. After having perused these procedures, you'll agree that they are more like full-blown applets than you might have expected. Another possibility is to use SQLOLE functions or SQL Enterprise Manager to dump a specific procedure.

If your procedure doesn't return parameters (and it's perfectly rational to create procedures that don't), your parsing job is fairly straightforward. Just set up the usual loop that tests for multiple result sets and multiple rows within those sets:

```
Sub Send_Parse_Proc (Proc$)
Dim r
Dim i, Row
Form2.Show ' This is just a blank form to dump the output to
r = SQLCancel(SQLConn)              ' Flush the command buffer
r = SQLSendCmd(SQLConn, Proc$)      ' Send the query and call
                                    ' SQLResults

If r <> FAIL Then
    Do
        Select Case r
        Case FAIL
        'MsgBox ("Results failed on stored procedure")
        Debug.Print "FAIL"
        Case SUCCEED
        Row = 0
        Do                    ' Loop through the rows
            r = SQLNextRow(SQLConn)    ' SQLSendCmd does not call
                                       ' this!

            Select Case r
            Case FAIL
                MsgBox ("Failed to get row from procedure")
            Case REGROW
                Row = Row + 1
                If Row = 1 Then
                    For i = 1 To SQLNumCols(SQLConn)
                        Form2.Print SQLColName$(SQLConn, i)
                    Next i
                    Form2.Print
                End If
                For i = 1 To SQLNumCols(SQLConn)
                    Form2.Print SQLData$(SQLConn, i)
                Next i
                Form2.Print
            Case NOMOREROWS
                Exit Do
            Case Else          ' Must be a COMPUTEid
                               ' code to deparse any compute rows...

            End Select
        Loop
        Case NOMORERESULTS
        Exit Do
        End Select
        r = SQLResults(SQLConn)
    Loop
End If

End Sub
```

Dealing with Stored-Procedure Parameters

If you choose to call stored procedures that implement SQL Server return parameter values, you need some additional code to parse them. There are seven new functions to work with—SQLHasRetStat, SQLNumRets, SQLRetData$, SQLRetLen&, SQLRetName$, SQLRetStatus&, and SQLRetType—plus four functions that deal specifically with remote stored procedures. These are displayed in *Figure 31-2*.

Figure 31-2
VBSQL Functions for Handling Stored Procedures

Function	Purpose
SQLHasRetStat	Indicates whether the current statement has a return status number
SQLNumRets	Indicates how many parameter values were generated by the procedure
SQLRetData$	Returns data from the procedure
SQLRetLen&	Indicates length of the data that was returned
SQLRetName$	Indicates the name of the parameter for a chosen return value
SQLRetStatus&	Indicates the procedure status number for the current procedure
SQLRetType	Indicates the data type of the chosen return value
SQLRpcExec	Executes a single stored procedure, a single remote stored procedure, or a batch of stored procedures or remote stored procedures on the SQL server
SQLRpcInit	Initializes a stored or a remote stored procedure
SQLRpcParam	Adds a parameter to a stored procedure or a remote stored procedure
SQLRpcSend	Sends a single stored procedure, a single remote stored procedure, or batch of stored procedures or remote stored procedures to the SQL server to be executed

Procedure status numbers

All stored procedures (since SQL Server 4.2) return a status number, or return status. This number indicates the overall success or failure of a procedure. If the procedure succeeds, the return status is 0. Unfortunately, this is also the value for most failed operations. I recommend using the manifest constant *ProcRetSucceed* (see *Figure 31-3*) in testing for SQL Server–generated errors.

A stored procedure created by you or someone else with access to your database might also generate the return value. Any number lower than −99 is reserved for user-written stored procedures. In any case, the return status is stored by DBLIB and is retrievable via SQLRetStatus&. A whole set of status (error) codes might be returned, and all of them are listed in the documentation for the SQLRetStatus& function. No manifest constants are listed for these errors in VBSQL.BAS, however, so I have suggested some in *Figure 31-3*. You are welcome to use them, but they're totally unsupported beyond the audience of this guide's readers, so you'll have to include them in your own CONSTANTS.BAS or add them to VBSQL.BAS.

TIP The procedure return status is available only after *all* the procedure's result sets and *all* its rows have been processed. To acquire the status code, you *must* loop through all of the result sets and their rows; you can't just send a SQLCanQuery once you have the data rows that you want.

Figure 31-3
Suggested Manifest Constants for SQLRetStatus& Errors

Suggested Manifest Constant	Decimal/Hex Value	What It Indicates
ProcRetSucceed	0 / 0	Procedure successful
ProcRetFail	−1 / 0xFFFF	SQLRetLen& failed; return number out of range
ProcRetMissing	−1 / 0xFFFF	Missing object
ProcRetDataType	−2 / 0xFFFE	Data type error
ProcRetProcess	−3 / 0xFFFD	Process chosen as dead-lock victim
ProcRetPermission	−4 / 0xFFFC	Permissions error
ProcRetSyntax	−5 / 0xFFFB	Syntax error
ProcRetMisc	−6 / 0xFFFA	Miscellaneous user error
ProcRetResource	−7 / 0xFFF9	Resource error, such as lack of space
ProcRetInternal	−8 / 0xFFF8	Nonfatal internal error
ProcRetSysLimit	−9 / 0xFFF7	System limit reached
ProcRetFatalInter10	−10 / 0xFFF6	Fatal internal inconsistency
ProcRetFatalInter11	−11 / 0xFFF5	Fatal internal inconsistency
ProcRetBadTableIndex	−12 / 0xFFF4	Corrupt table or index
ProcRetBadDatabase	−13 / 0xFFF3	Corrupt database
ProcRetHardware	−14 / 0xFFF2	Hardware error
Undefined	−15 through −99	Reserved for SQL Server
Reserved for user errors	−100 through −2,147,483,648	Reserved for user-written stored procedures (Long)

Transact-SQL procedures can return the value of chosen parameters. Once one of these parameters is changed, the new value can be returned to DBLIB. Since not all SQL servers support parameters or status codes, VBSQL provides a call to test the availability of the status code: SQLHasRetStat.

When a stored procedure is programmed to return arguments (declared as OUT), these parameters have to be identified when DB-Library and your VBSQL application parse the set of returned parameters. You have to check out the original CREATE PROCEDURE statement to determine the exact order of the parameters returned. Count only those parameters that return values. Specifically, the output parameters are returned in the order in which they were created, starting with 1. The return value number is used in several functions, which return the output argument data (SQLRetData$), the parameter name (SQLRetName$), and the parameter data type (SQLRetType).

Processing before access to return values

After the stored procedure has been fully executed, SQL Server returns the results of any parameter changes to DBLIB. As with the preceding calls, all result sets must be fully processed with SQLResults and SQLNextRow. If the stored procedure is executed with the EXECUTE statement, the return parameters use local variables, not constants. This caveat applies to all of the following procedure parameter functions. Let's look now at how individual functions allow you to describe the components of a stored procedure.

SQLHasRetStat This Boolean function tests to see whether a procedure has generated a return status. If the procedure is running on an older version of SQL Server, such as SQL Server 1.0, it doesn't have a procedure status number. This function can't be used until all result sets and their rows have been processed with SQLResults and SQLNextRow calls. The current batch must also contain a call to either a local or a remote stored procedure. This function takes the connection handle (*SQLConn*) as its sole parameter and returns either *SUCCEED* (1), if a pending procedure has a return code, or *FAIL* (0).

SQLRetStatus& The status number indicates whether the most current procedure has succeeded or failed. The status number is 0 if the procedure hasn't generated any errors; otherwise, it's 1. This function works until *all* result sets and their rows have been processed with SQLResults and SQLNextRow calls. The current batch must also contain a call to either a local or a remote stored procedure. This function takes the connection handle (*SQLConn*) as its sole parameter and returns a Long status number.

SQLNumRets This function is useful when you're setting a loop count as you process each returned parameter. Return parameters can be declared only in stored procedures (either local or remote). After the stored procedure has been fully executed, SQL Server returns the results of any parameter changes to DBLIB. This function takes the connection handle (*SQLConn*) as its sole parameter and returns an Integer that indicates the number of parameters available for processing.

SQLRetLen& This function takes the connection handle (*SQLConn*) as its sole parameter and returns a Long value that indicates the length of the chosen parameters available for processing, or it returns –1 (*ProcRetFail*) if the number is out of range (that is, greater than SQLNumRets). It's unclear how a parameter passed back from a procedure can be longer than 255 bytes, since Text and Image data types can't be passed via returned parameters.

SQLRetName$ This function returns the name of a specified return value parameter. Its parameters are the connection handle (*SQLConn*) and the return value number (an Integer) of the specific parameter desired. This number can range from 1 through SQLNumRets. This function returns the name (a string) of the specific parameter desired. This name is based on the name established during CREATE PROCEDURE compilation, but if the number is out of range (that is, greater than SQLNumRets), this name is a null string ("").

SQLRetData$ This function returns data from the procedure arguments. Its parameters are the connection handle (*SQLConn*) and an Integer that indicates which parameter to access.

SQLRetType This function returns the data type of a specified return value parameter. Its parameters are the connection handle (*SQLConn*) and the return value number (an Integer) of the specific parameter desired. This number can range from 1 through SQLNumRets. This function returns either an Integer number (token), which indicates the data type of the chosen parameters available for processing, or –1 (*ProcRetFail*) if the number is out of range (that is, greater than SQLNumRets). You might want to convert the token returned into a readable string by using the SQLPrType function. A list of these data types and functions appears in the VBSQL documentation under the SQLPrType function.

Using SQLRpcInit Instead of EXECUTE

Your application can execute a single stored procedure by using the EXECUTE TSQL statement. If you have to retrieve the status number and parameter values from the procedure, however, you must use SQLRpcInit. Using SQLRpcInit and the other associated VBSQL functions to invoke a stored procedure causes DB-Library to pass parameters in their native data types. Using an EXECUTE statement passes them as ASCII characters. Calling stored procedures with these special VBSQL functions works faster and is usually more efficient than using an EXECUTE statement because the server isn't required to convert native data types into their ASCII equivalents. This technique also accommodates return parameters for stored procedures more quickly because the return parameters are always available to the application via a call to SQLRetData.

NOTE A return parameter must be specified as such when it's added to a stored procedure for the first time via SQLRpcParam.

When a stored procedure is called with an EXECUTE statement, the return parameter values are available only if the command batch containing the EXECUTE statement uses local variables, rather than constants, as the return parameters. This involves additional parsing each time the command batch is executed.

The client application can also use VBSQL functions to issue a stored-procedure call directly to an Open Data Services server application that detects this request as a remote stored procedure. The Open Data Services server application isn't required to parse the language buffer in order to find out what the client is requesting.

SQLRpcInit sets up the sequence of VBSQL functions needed to execute a stored procedure. This function takes three parameters: *SQLConn* (the SQL Server connection handle), *rpcName* (the name of the stored procedure to be invoked), and *Option* (a 2-byte bitmask of stored-procedure options). Specify 0 to indicate no options. The available options are SQLRPCRECOMPILE, which recompiles a stored procedure before it's executed, and SQLRPCRESET, which cancels a single stored procedure or a batch of stored procedures. If *rpcName* is specified, that new stored procedure is initialized after the cancel is complete.

Using VBSQL functions instead of EXECUTE isn't all that difficult. To execute a single stored procedure or a batch of stored procedures with DB-Library functions, follow these steps:

1. Call SQLRpcInit once to initialize a new stored procedure.

2. Call SQLRpcParam for each *parameter* of the stored procedure that does not have a default value. Repeat steps 1 and 2 for each *stored procedure* in the batch.

3. Call SQLRpcSend or SQLRpcExec to send the entire stored procedure batch to SQL Server.

4. Call SQLOK to wait for SQL Server to start returning results.

5. Call SQLResults to process the results from each stored procedure. If SQLResults returns *SUCCEED*, call SQLNextRow until it returns *NOMOREROWS*, to process the normal results from the stored procedure. If SQLResults returns *NOMORERPCRESULTS* and you want to retrieve information on the status number and what is returned by the stored procedure, repeat this step until SQLResults returns *NOMORERESULTS*. If you want to retrieve information on the status number and what is returned by the last stored procedure in the batch, go on to step 6.

CAUTION

Stored procedures executed with the *SqlConn* handle on a *local* SQL server participate in transactions normally and can be rolled back. Stored procedures executed on a *remote* SQL server can't be rolled back—unless you use the new Distributed Transaction Controller mechanism.

6. After SQLResults returns *NOMORERPCRESULTS* (for all stored procedures in a batch except the last one) or *NOMORERESULTS* (for a single stored procedure or for the last stored procedure in a batch), you can retrieve the status number and return parameter information for a stored procedure. To retrieve the return status number, Call SQLRetStatus and SQLHasRetStat. To determine the number of return parameters, call SQLNumRets. To retrieve information for each return parameter, call SQLRetData, SQLRetType, SQLRetLen, and SQLRetName.

Examples

In a moment, we'll walk through some examples of parsing a stored procedure that has parameters. First, though, let's look at the process of creating a stored procedure that returns values via its parameters.

Creating stored procedures

Assuming that your system administrator or database owner has given you permission to create stored procedures, you'll be able to create procedures on the local SQL server. To create procedures on a remote SQL server, you'll need to log on to an account on that server or get one of its users or its system administrator to create the procedure for you. Your procedure, once created, has its name stored in *SysObjects*, its execution plan in *SysProcedures*, and its text in *SysComments*. (These are system tables in your database.) From this point on, the procedures will be visible to users of your database.

When you create a stored procedure, you have basically three options for deciding how to return the completion status to your user or developer: you can pass result sets (just include a SELECT that returns a set of rows), pass a return status (set a value from –100 through –2,147,483,648), or return a parameter argument. Both the return status and returned parameter arguments can be tested by other procedures, so it's now possible (with SQL Server 4.2) to pass values from procedures called from procedures (such as functions in Visual Basic). Now let's look at some examples.

Creating a return status procedure

The following procedure counts up all the animals that have put themselves on the sick list. It returns a count of those slackers—and defaults to horses, since they're the ones most likely to pull this kind of trick:

```
create procedure CountSick @type_in char(10) = 'Horse'
as
declare @cnt int
select @cnt = count(*) from Animals where type = @type_in and
    Health like "sick"
return @cnt
```

Note that all you need to do in order to pass back a return code is assign a value to the RETURN TSQL statement. To get this parameter back in a TSQL statement that calls the procedure, use this code:

```
declare @cnt int
exec @cnt = countsick "pig"
select @cnt
```

Accessing the return status with VBSQL

I declared a local variable to hold the return value. When you write your VBSQL program, you might want to do the same. If you code the query as we just did, your job is easy: just look for the row generated by the SELECT statement, using conventional query techniques (SQLData$). To access the return code via VBSQL, you have to code as follows. (I've included annotations.)

`Sub ParseProcReturn ()`	
`Dim q$, r`	
`q$ = "exec work..countsick 'pig'"`	Use the fully qualified name, so I don't have to use *work*.
`r = SQLSendCmd(SQLConn, q$)`	Send the query.
`If r <> FAIL Then`	Test SQLResults for *FAIL*.
`  Do`	Loop through all results and rows.
`    Do While SQLNextRow(SQLConn) _`	
`        <> NOMOREROWS`	
`    Loop`	
`  Loop While SQLResults(SQLConn) _`	
`        <> NOMORERESULTS`	
`End If`	
`r = SQLHasRetStat(SQLConn)`	Test to see whether a return status exists.
`If r = SUCCEED Then`	If so...
`  form2.Show`	show the output form...
`  form2.Cls`	and clear it.
`  form2.Print "Number of returns:";`	Display the number of return
`  form2.print SQLNumRets(SQLConn)`	arguments (there are none).
`  form2.Print "Return status:";`	Display the return status
	(number of sick animals).
`  form2.print SQLRetStatus&(SQLConn)`	
`End If`	

If you get message 2821, "Stored procedure not found," it might mean that your procedure isn't in the specified database (the default database, if you didn't specify another one). You might also get message 229, "Permission denied on procedure," if your database owner has not assigned you specific permission to execute this procedure. Note that these are *messages,* not errors, which once again shows the importance of having a message handler in your code.

Creating a return parameter procedure

Building a procedure that passes back more than one Long value is somewhat more difficult—but not exceedingly so. There are two different ways that the SQL server handles returned parameters:

- *Pass by reference.* If the Output option is included in both the EXECUTE and CREATE PROCEDURE statements, the value of the parameter(s) can be returned to the caller; changes to the parameter caused by the procedure are retained by the calling procedure.

- *Pass by value.* If the Output option isn't included, only a copy of the parameter is passed back to the caller. In this case, changes to the parameter have no effect on the local value of the parameter.

To pass values out of a procedure, you must execute a CREATE PROCEDURE statement with the *OUTPUT* parameter:

```
create procedure CountAllSick

    @type_in char(10) = 'Horse'
    @cnt int OUTPUT
    @cnt2 int OUTPUT
as
select @cnt = count(*) from Animals
where type = @type_in and Health like "sick"
select @cnt2 = count(*) from Animals
where type = @type_in and Health like "not"
return 0
```

In this case, I don't have to declare the local variables *@cnt* or *@cnt2*, since they are contained in the list of output parameters. The *@cnt* and *@cnt2* values are assigned with the SELECT statements. Here, we are returning the results of two queries. We'll also pass a return value back (0) to indicate that the procedure was successful.

We can call this procedure *without* asking for the returned parameter, so to call this procedure and get the returned parameter, we must code as follows:

```
declare @retval int
declare @cnt int

exec @retval = countsick "pig", @cnt OUTPUT
select @cnt
```

Notice that the parameter to be passed back must be declared and included in the EXEC line as an *OUTPUT* parameter. Here is an expansion of the basic procedure that returns two *OUTPUT* parameters and a return value:

```
create procedure CountAllSick @type_in char(10) = 'Horse' ,
@cnt int OUTPUT, @cnt2 int OUTPUT
as
```

(continued)

```
select @cnt = count(*) from work..Animals
    where type = @type_in and Health like "sick"
select @cnt2 = count(*) from work..Animals
    where type = @type_in and Health like "not"
return 0
```

The following code can be used from a TSQL query to return a row that contains the two *OUTPUT* parameters:

```
declare @mycnt1 int
declare @mycnt2 int
exec CountAllSick "pig", @mycnt1 output, @mycnt2 output
select @mycnt1 Sick, @mycnt2 Not_Well
```

The VBSQL code for parsing this procedure is shown here:

`Sub ParseProcReturn ()`	
`Dim q$, r`	
`q$ = "exec work..countsick 'pig'"`	Use the fully qualified name, so I don't have to use *work*.
`r = SQLSendCmd(SQLConn, q$)`	Send the query.
`If r <> FAIL Then`	Test SQLResults for *FAIL*.
`  Do`	Loop through all results
`    Do While SQLNextRow(SQLConn) _`	and rows.
`        <> NOMOREROWS`	
`    Loop`	
`  Loop While SQLResults(SQLConn) _`	
`        <> NOMORERESULTS`	
`End If`	
	Test to see whether a
	return status exists.
`r = SQLHasRetStat(SQLConn)`	If so...
`If r = SUCCEED Then`	
`    form2.Show`	show the output form...
`    form2.Cls`	and clear it.
`    form2.Print "Number of returns:";`	Display the number of return
`    form2.Print SQLNumRets(SQLConn)`	arguments (there are none).
`    form2.Print "Return status:";`	Display the return status
	(number of sick animals).
`    form2.print SQLRetStatus&(SQLConn)`	
`End If`	

32

Chapter

Using VBSQL
Row Buffers

**Accessing More
Than One Row**

**Inserting, Updating,
and Deleting Rows**

C

ongratulations! You have sent your first query and read back your first row of data. Guess what—many of you can now get back to work because, for many applications, the techniques you've learned so far are more than enough to get you through the challenges of real-world SQL Server front-end development. As for those of you who need to do more, such as work with multiple-row buffers and cursors, fasten your seat belts and let's move on.

VBSQL provides a plethora of techniques for accessing data. By far the fastest (with a little help from a generous TDS packet setting) is the single-row fetch. Although we have already covered this, in some situations you have to either fetch and manage data rows in blocks or build a full-blown updatable cursor. Let's take a look at some other options for VBSQL data access:

- *Default result set:* single-row, forward-only result set; updatable via separate connection and independent UPDATE statement

- *Row buffers:* multiple-row result set; scrollable within *n* rows, but forward-only; updatable via separate connection and independent UPDATE statement

- *Browse mode query:* applicable to either of the above; exposes additional metadata to return a qualified WHERE clause and permit single-row update

- *DB-Library cursors:* any of four types (static, keyset, dynamic, or mixed), all scrollable and updatable; also support server-side cursors

- *TSQL-based cursors:* not highly recommended

Personally, I have found some use for several of these options (such as the single-row, forward-only result set). Frankly, though, most of my applications use less intensive techniques.

Accessing More Than One Row

In this section, we deal with the challenges of fetching and processing more than one row of results at a time. This technique is important for those of you who want to display a screenful of data or want to let users simply scroll back and forth in a result set. Generally, these techniques involve moving data from the fixed disk and cache queues on the SQL server to temporary tables on the SQL server or to local workstation RAM. Just how much data gets downloaded into local RAM is up to you and your schemes for storing (or buffering) the data locally. These techniques can be (and often are) replaced by application-managed arrays that move data from the result set into memory allocated and addressed by the application.

The Whys and Why Nots of Local Buffering

Before we get started, it's important to consider the implications of buffered data. Whenever an application pulls data rows from any real-time multiuser data source, the data extracted almost immediately becomes stale, as we learned earlier. Using VBSQL doesn't change the hazards of keeping copies of data in local RAM.

One of the problems that VBSQL application developers try to solve with these buffering schemes is quick (instant) access to the next set of rows above or below the currently fetched block of rows. They simply don't want their users to wait as the application scrolls up or down in the data. To address this problem more directly, and before row buffering is implemented, consider using more specific key-driven queries to fetch a specific range of rows. By building appropriate table indexes for tables that are to be browsed, you might be able to forego large row buffers or cursors and depend on the speed of the server instead. *Figure 32-1* on the next page shows the costs and benefits of workstation-buffered data.

Browse Mode

Browse mode is a variation on row buffering that lets the SQL server and DB-Library help in the management of stale data sitting around on your workstation. You don't *need* to use row buffers to use Browse mode, but you will usually want to.

Browse mode requires that the tables have a column called TimeStamp. When Browse mode result set rows are passed to the workstation's buffer(s), any changes made by other applications to the SQL Server–based data are noted with a change to the TimeStamp column. Basically, when you ask for Browse mode, DB-Library creates a fully qualified WHERE clause that includes the TimeStamp value fetched when the data is retrieved, along with enough key information to identify a specific row.

When it's time to update your data, SQL Server compares the TimeStamp value in the WHERE clause with the value you provide in the UPDATE statement. If the TimeStamp columns are different, someone changed the row, and

CAUTION
Make sure that the Time-Stamp column is called TimeStamp—not Author-TableTimeStamp or some such. Otherwise, it simply won't work. The TimeStamp column is updated automatically. You won't be permitted to provide a value for this column or alter it, since DB-Library and SQL Server manage TimeStamp columns automatically.

Figure 32-1
Cost-Benefit Breakdown of Local Buffering

Method	Benefit	Server Costs and Benefits	Workstation Costs
Application-managed buffering	Total control of what's kept or discarded. Faster access to a subset of the resultset. Strategy can depend on program logic.	Higher overhead in maintaining current data. Possibility of medium-term table locks. Higher cost of concurrent operations.	Uses much more RAM. Probably will have to use virtual RAM to swap data if result set gets too large. Increased time to fetch swapped data from local fixed disk. First and all subsequent forward fetches still take time.
Row buffering with three screens (one above, one below)	Faster access to next or previous screen.	Low overhead in maintaining current data. Low loss of concurrency.	Local RAM (enough for three pages). Application more complex and error-prone. Background processing to anticipate fetch while user is working with current screen. Slower access to areas beyond anticipated result set and to rows below the currently buffered set.
Row buffering (entire result set)	Faster access to all subsequent or previous screens.	Higher overhead in maintaining current data. Possibility of medium-term table locks. Higher loss of concurrent operations. Higher TempDB space requirements.	Dramatically more RAM. Probably will have to use virtual RAM to swap data. Increased time to fetch swapped data from local fixed disk. First and all subsequent forward fetches still take time.
Cursor-based queries	Same access time for most screens. Fewer rows fetched, so faster access.	Need to build and maintain a per-connection keyset. Higher number of queries. Higher TempDB space requirements. Greater LAN traffic.	Limit of 64 KB space for keysets limits number of rows fetchable with this method. Application much more complex. Incompatible with Sybase.

your code has to deal with this contingency. At this point, you'll have to decide what to do about the locally generated changes—whether to start over and let the user decide, or override the changed row on the SQL server. We'll see how to implement Browse mode in code a little later in this chapter; for now, start thinking about it as part of an overall scheme for row buffering.

Enabling Row Buffers

You have decided that you must buffer some or all of a result set. You have read all of the warning labels and are satisfied that aging data isn't a problem. To turn on row buffering at your workstation, you have to execute the following function:

```
SQLSetOpt (SQLConn, SQLBUFFER, "24")
```

For one of my applications, I wanted to pass a variable number of rows to the function so that I could test buffers that varied in size from run to run. To do this, you need to strip off the leading space, since DB-Library can't figure out that " 24" is the same as "24"—I guess it never made it past third grade. This is coded as follows:

```
BuffersWanted$ = Ltrim$(Str$(Buffers))
SQLSetOpt(SQLConn, SQLBUFFER, BuffersWanted$)
```

That's all there is to setting up row buffering. You don't have to allocate memory or tell DBLIB the size and shape of the rows or columns to be buffered, only the number of rows you want to keep in your workstation's memory. DB-Library dynamically computes all of this for you and manages the space automatically.

CAUTION
Your code must deal with the result set generated by the SQLSetOpt function in your *next* query, so you have to call SQLResults one more time. If you miscode the SQLSetOpt function or use the SET ROWCOUNT operation improperly, you won't know what happened until your first query is sent and you test the results with SQLResults.

> **TIP** You might run out of RAM when DB-Library tries to find room for the data after you use SQLNextRow, so you need to be prepared for this possibility. You might also run out of room on the SQL server when you use row buffering. When you send your row-buffered query, SQL Server creates a snapshot of your data in TempDB space. Remember that any space used in TempDB is multiplied by the number of concurrent users doing the same operation.

Once you have decided that you are done with the result set and won't be making another row-buffered query, it's a good idea to turn off row buffering and free up the memory allocated to your buffer. To turn off row buffering, just send a query to the SQL server that contains the following code:

```
SET ROWCOUNT 0
```

This action query frees up any RAM allocated for your buffers and reverts back to single-row buffering. Remember that you need to be prepared for the "results" of this query, so you need to include an extra SQLResults.

Processing the Buffered Rows

Working with row buffers is a lot like working with any of the other cursors we've already considered, but let's look at the technique a little more closely.

The query

As far as the query is concerned, there's nothing different about processing data with row buffering. I like to set up a query that doesn't pull the entire database down into the workstation; I prefer to leave data management to the SQL server. Remember that data not brought over the net to the workstation is still shareable. Unless you specifically or accidentally lock it, SQL Server continues to manage it for you and other users. My buffers are usually a screen or two in size—about 50 rows. This also means that I don't have to worry about filling up TempDB space.

The buffer

When you make a query with row buffering turned on, DB-Library creates a "window" into the result set. This window is not unlike some of the windows in old apartment buildings—it goes down but not up. If you are keeping all the result set rows in your workstation's local memory, by doing your own row buffering you can access all of the data as you need it. But if you are depending on DB-Library's copy of the data (kept in the TempDB row buffers) and if the entire result set doesn't fit into the buffer, you have to free up space in the buffer by dropping rows before additional rows can be read in from the SQL server. In other words, once the data has been passed to your local variables or screen and you delete the rows from the buffer, these result set rows are no longer accessible via this query.

TIP Think of a row buffer as a type of cursor for which *you* decide the keyset size and manage the range of rows that are members.

To move backward in the buffered result set, such as when the user requests a previous page of data no longer in the buffer, your only recourse is to cancel and resubmit the original query and then step forward in the data to the desired row—and possibly eliminate some of the performance gains you achieved by buffering. At this point, alternative key methods and cursors begin to look more viable.

It's also possible to make an intelligent query when you have to step backward. For example, suppose you know that the result set is in a certain key sequence, such as *city*. By keeping bookmarks at strategic points, you might be able to create an intelligent query that steps deep into the result set and starts returning rows closer to the point desired by the user. Let's say that the current screen is showing cities between Everett and Kirkland. Your bookmark for the desired page says it started with Bremerton. Your query would look something like this:

```
SELECT * From Address Where City >= "Bremerton"
```

Figure 32-2 shows how a row buffer that is smaller than the result set (all rows that would be returned from this query) reflects the contents of a subset of the result set. If you can't buffer all of the desired rows in a result set, your code is far more complex than it would be if you knew the buffer could hold all possible result rows.

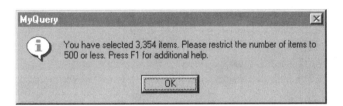

213-46-8915	Green	Majorie
238-95-7766	Carson	Cheryl
267-41-2394	OLeary	Martin
274-80-9391	Straiht	Dean
841-22-1782	Smith	Meander
409-56-7008	Bennet	Adrian
427-17-2319	Dell	Ann
472-27-2349	Gringegsy	Bill
648-92-1786	Locksley	Chanene
527-72-3248	Greene	Morningstar
648-92-1872	Biochet-Marie	Reginstar
672-71-3249	Tokomota	Akiko
490-23-1784	Karsen	Lydia
568-23-9034	Ringer	Anno
568-23-9532	Ringer	Burt
684-56-5634	Wille	Jordan
298-51-3856	Parterry	Sylvia
290-24-6511	Forester	Richard
117-94-3829	Ogren	Weston
408-31-1196	Williams	Harold

Figure 32-2 *Row buffering as a "window" on the result set*

Generally, I try to build queries that will return as few rows as possible. This makes management of the row buffer far easier and also makes the user happier, since the data is presented faster. You will have to accommodate the rows that don't fit in the buffer if you can't limit the number of queried rows with messages, as shown here:

MyQuery

> You have selected 3,354 items. Please restrict the number of items to 500 or less. Press F1 for additional help.

[OK]

Fetching Buffered Rows

Once the query completes, you still need to use SQLNextRow to fetch the result set rows, except that SQLNextRow passes back two additional return codes: *NOMOREROWS* (–2) and *BUFFULL* (–3). According to your interactive strategy, you might want to display the rows as they are moved to the buffer or simply store them in a local array until you're ready. The SQLNextRow call still moves data from the SQL server to the buffer and makes that single row visible to SQLData. In any case, only *one* row of the buffer is visible to SQLData at any time, just as with any other cursor. When you are working with a row buffer, there's a current-row pointer that references the data in a single buffered row of the result set. There are also situations in which there is no current row, and so the current-row pointer is invalid—just as with Microsoft Jet or RDO cursors.

You reposition the current-row pointer with the VBSQL functions shown in *Figure 32-3* before the buffer fills, after the buffer fills (as indicated by a return code of *BUFFULL* from SQLNextRow), or after the number of rows in the result set is exhausted (as indicated by a return code of *NOMOREROWS*). Only the current row is visible to SQLData. As long as DB-Library has returned at least one result set row and SQLNextRow succeeds, SQLData points to a valid row.

Figure 32-3
VBSQL Functions for Repositioning the Current-Row Pointer

Command	Function	Notes
SQLCurRow	Returns the number of the current row, as set by SQLGetRow or SQLNextRow.	Save this value, to return to this row later.
SQLFirstRow	Returns the number of the oldest (first) row of the result set in the buffer.	The first row returned from the SQL server is 1.
SQLLastRow	Returns the number of the youngest (last) row of the result set in the buffer.	Returns result set row most recently read from the SQL server.
SQLNextRow	Moves the next row from the result set into the next empty space in the buffer or positions the current-row pointer to the next row.	Changes behavior, depending on the state of the buffer.
SQLGetRow	Moves the buffer current-row pointer to the specified row.	Returns *REGROW*, *ComputeID*, *NOMOREROWS* (if row is not between SQLFirstRow and SQLLastRow), or *FAIL*.

A Hands-On Example

The indexing method used in a DB-Library row buffer can be somewhat confusing at first. The pointer returned from the DB-Library "row" commands, as shown in *Figure 32-3*, refers to the row number *of the result set*. For example, SQLLastRow returns the number of the most recent (newest) result set row that SQLNextRow has moved into the buffer. SQLFirstRow returns the row number of the oldest row in the buffer—the row that SQLNextRow placed in the buffer before all the other rows. As rows are deleted from the buffer (with SQLClrBuf), the buffer "window" moves forward in the result set, making space at the bottom of the buffer. The oldest row (as pointed to by SQLFirstRow) is *always* deleted first. You can't delete an arbitrary row of the buffer, and you can't delete the last row of the buffer; DBLIB won't let you.

The following series of examples shows how the current row is positioned within the confines of the row buffer. It also shows the contents of the buffer as additional rows are added and deleted. To start with, assume that row buffering is enabled and that this small result set is the rows returned from the query. All of our row buffer functions are executed against these result set rows.

Row	Row Contents		
1	172-32-1176	White	Johnson
2	213-46-8915	Green	Marjorie
3	238-95-7766	Carson	Cheryl
4	267-41-2394	O'Leary	Michael
5	274-80-9391	Straight	Dean
6	341-22-1782	Smith	Meander
7	409-56-7008	Bennet	Abraham
8	427-17-2319	Dull	Ann
9	472-27-2349	Gringlesby	Burt
10	486-29-1786	Locksley	Charlene
11	527-72-3246	Greene	Morningstar
12	648-92-1872	Blotchet-Halls	Reginald
13	672-71-3249	Yokomoto	Akiko
14	712-45-1867	del Castillo	Innes
15	722-51-5454	DeFrance	Michel
16	724-08-9931	Stringer	Dirk

First we execute the SQLNextRow function three times, with the following results. Note that the first three rows of the result set are placed in the local buffer. There are two rows remaining because we set the row buffer size to five rows.

Operation	Row	Row Buffer Contents		
First SQLNextRow(SQLConn)	1	172-32-1176	White	Johnson
Second SQLNextRow(SQLConn)	2	213-46-8915	Green	Marjorie
Third SQLNextRow(SQLConn)	3	238-95-7766	Carson	Cheryl
		Empty row		
		Empty row		

After the first three SQLNextRow calls, the other row buffer functions return the values shown at the top of the next page.

Row Buffer Function	Returns
SQLCurRow	3
SQLFirstRow	1
SQLLastRow	3
SQLData(SQLConn, 2)	"White"

Note that two additional spaces in the buffer can't yet be accessed. You can do anything you want to with the rows as they are read into the buffer with SQLNextRow. To access the current rows' data, use SQLData. For example, you can use SQLData to move the data elements into a Grid control or a local array managed independently of the row buffer.

TIP It's a good idea to provide a way for the user to abort a query. Keep in mind that users might have already changed their minds by the time the first row appears on the screen, and be prepared for a change in plans that negates current processing.

The next command repositions the current-row pointer to a specific row in the row buffer:

```
SQLGetRow(SQLConn,2)
```

This command changes the values returned by the row buffer functions, as shown in the following example, but it doesn't change the contents of the buffer or bring back any additional rows from the SQL server.

Row Buffer Function	Returns
SQLCurRow	2
SQLFirstRow	1
SQLLastRow	3
SQLData(SQLConn, 2)	"Green"

Valid arguments for SQLGetRow, on the basis of the data read so far, are 1, 2, or 3 (any number from SQLFirstRow to SQLLastRow). After you reposition the current-row pointer, SQLData can fetch the data from the newly selected row. Using SQLGetRow with a value higher than SQLLastRow or lower than SQLFirstRow results in a *NOMOREROWS* error. Once you reposition to a row with a value lower than SQLLastRow, SQLNextRow moves the buffer row pointer to the next row in the buffer, if there are rows remaining in the result set. (It doesn't get another row from the SQL server.) If the buffer isn't full and you position to SQLLastRow and execute SQLNextRow, the next row from the result set is moved into the free buffer slot from the SQL server.

Next we use SQLNextRow three more times. After the first two calls to SQLNextRow, the buffer is filled with data drawn from the SQL server. The third call to SQLNextRow returns *BUFFULL*, and nothing is returned from the SQL server. Note the location of the first, last, and current pointers. Remember that SQLData always fetches data from the current row (SQLCurRow).

Row Buffer Function	Returns
SQLCurRow	5
SQLFirstRow	1
SQLLastRow	5
SQLData(SQLConn, 2)	"Straight"

Take a look at the row buffer after these operations:

Operation	Row	Row Buffer Contents		
Fourth SQLNextRow(SQLConn)	1	172-32-1176	White	Johnson
Fifth SQLNextRow(SQLConn)	2	213-46-8915	Green	Marjorie
Sixth SQLNextRow(SQLConn)	3	238-95-7766	Carson	Cheryl
	4	267-41-2394	O'Leary	Michael
	5	274-80-9391	Straight	Dean

Next we need to clear the oldest row from the buffer, making a space at the bottom of the buffer for another row of SQL Server data. All the buffer rows seem to slide up, leaving space at the bottom.

```
SQLClrBuf(SQLConn, 1)
```

The oldest row is *always* dropped first. SQLClrBuf can also remove a series of rows from the buffer, starting with the oldest row and working toward the newest. Note that the current-row pointer is unchanged. If the current row is 1 when the SQLClrBuf command is sent, the current row becomes 2—the next row. Also note that the rows in the buffer are always referred to by their *result set* row numbers. Take a look at the results of row buffer functions and the row buffer after this operation:

Row Buffer Function	Returns
SQLCurRow(SQLConn)	5
SQLFirstRow(SQLConn)	2
SQLLastRow(SQLConn)	5
SQLData(SQLConn, 2)	"Straight"

Operation	Row	Row Buffer Contents		
SQLClrBuf(SQLConn,1)	2	213-46-8915	Green	Marjorie
	3	238-95-7766	Carson	Cheryl
	4	267-41-2394	O'Leary	Michael
	5	274-80-9391	Straight	Dean

The next set of operations moves the sixth row from the result set to the row buffer and repositions the current buffer pointer to the fourth row of the row buffer. (Note that this is in the third buffer slot.) The final call to SQLNextRow moves the current buffer pointer to the fifth row in the result set. Yes, *BUFFULL* is returned, but that merely means that the row returned by SQLNextRow comes from the buffer, not from the SQL Server result set. Take a look at the results of row buffer functions and the row buffer after this operation:

Row Buffer Function	Returns
SQLCurRow	4
SQLFirstRow	2
SQLLastRow	6
SQLData(SQLConn, 2)	"Straight"

Operation	Row	Row Buffer Contents		
SQLNextRow(SQLConn)	2	213-46-8915	Green	Marjorie
SQLGetRow(SQLConn, 4)	3	238-95-7766	Carson	Cheryl
SQLNextRow(SQLConn)	4	267-41-2394	O'Leary	Michael
	5	274-80-9391	Straight	Dean
	6	341-22-1782	Smith	Meander

This sequence of operations should have given you a pretty good idea about how the various row buffering functions work. Now let's look at some subtler points.

Using SQLNextRow with Row Buffering

CAUTION
SqlNextRow behaves differently once the buffer is full.

You'll find one of the more complex aspects of row buffering is the behavior of SQLNextRow. *Figure 32-4* shows its peculiar deportment when row buffering is enabled. As you can see, SQLNextRow changes its behavior quite a bit according to the state of the buffer and the result set. For this reason, using SQLNextRow to step down through a buffer isn't particularly easy. I prefer to use the following code:

```
' Move current-row pointer down one row
r = SQLGetRow(SQLConn, SQLCurRow(SQLConn) + 1)
```

This method might seem a little convoluted, but it *always* works. SQLNextRow works only when the result set isn't depleted.

Figure 32-4
Behavior of SQLNextRow with Row Buffering

State of the Buffer	Result of a Call to SQLNextRow
Room for another row.	Returns *REGROW* or *ComputeID*. Moves the next row from the SQL server result set into the current +1 (next) row of the buffer.
Full, but more results are available in the result set.	Returns *BUFFULL*. No data is moved from the SQL server. If current-row pointer is lower than SQLLastRow, DBLIB moves the current-row pointer to the current row +1.
Full, with no more rows available.	Returns *NOMOREROWS*. Current-row pointer isn't affected.

Inserting, Updating, and Deleting Rows

Once you've made a query, the next step is often dealing with a request to add (more), change, or remove the data. At this point, you have several decisions to make. One of the things you do *not* want to do is throw away the current result set, but this is exactly what must happen if you try to send another query by using the current unpopulated result set's connection.

We've already touched on Browse mode. Remember that the data in the row buffers is a copy (perhaps a somewhat stale, moldy copy) of the data kept in the database. Since multiuser or single-user multitasking systems exacerbate this problem, you spend more time dealing with stale data in these systems, especially if you choose to buffer more than a few rows. Browse mode can dramatically reduce the work of identifying the specific row you want to delete or update. A Browse mode query uses optimistic concurrency control, which basically "hopes" that no conflicts will occur before an update is required. It establishes and holds no locks while the data is being accessed.

Enabling TSQL Browse Mode

When a SELECT...FOR BROWSE is made, SQL Server places a copy of the result set into TempDB space. The impact of this action is obvious: you can't select more than TempDB can hold divided by the number of simultaneous users trying to do the same thing. The data stored in the Browse mode buffers in TempDB isn't updatable. The only way to change this data is to submit a separate UPDATE statement against the row to be changed, which still resides on the server. You usually do this by opening an additional connection.

Setup and Operation

To make Browse mode work for your query (whether it is buffered or not), you have to do the following:

- Ensure that the table to be updated has a TimeStamp column.

- Make sure that the queried table or view has a *unique* key. If DB-Library does not have a way to identify specific rows, how are you going to choose a particular row to update or delete?

- The query must not have any GROUP BY clauses, any "computed" columns such as MAX(sales), or COMPUTE BY clauses.

- Build your query, and add FOR BROWSE. For example,

```
SELECT * from FarmAnimals WHERE type = 'Cow' FOR BROWSE
```

    returns all of the cows from the *FarmAnimals* table (well, at least their rows) and permits DB-Library to create and store a WHERE clause that retrieves this row when it is needed. Your query should not contain any GROUP BY or DISTINCT clauses.

- Fetch your row(s) or build your row buffer by processing the results of your query one row at a time. For the current row, you can build an appropriate WHERE clause by using the SQLQual function. SQLQual is usually called just after SQLNextRow or SQLGetRow. Generally, I build an array of captured WHERE clauses for each row displayed to the user. That way, I can quickly access the data once the user chooses a row to delete or update.

- When the user chooses a row to change (or delete), concatenate the stored WHERE clause generated by the SQLQual statement to an appropriate UPDATE or DELETE statement. The WHERE clause is used to isolate the specific row.

- Use an additional short-term connection to submit the query. Be prepared for the UPDATE to fail (SQLResults returns *FAIL*). DB-Library will inform you if the row is no longer current. (The TimeStamp columns will not match if the row was updated or deleted by another user while your user was deciding what to do.)

- If the UPDATE fails, you get SQL message 532—"The TimeStamp (changed to ...) shows that the row was updated by another user"— and you must decide what to do about it. Inform the user that the data presented before this change didn't reflect the current state of the rows. You might want to use your second connection to fetch the current row data.

Tactics of Browsing

Now that you know the basics of Browse mode, let's look at several data access scenarios and application tactics for dealing with each one. All these scenarios involve using a second (short-term) connection. Multiple connections are needed, since you usually don't want to abandon the current-row buffer just to update one of its rows.

As you buffer the rows, you might have to save the WHERE clause that will be used to update or delete the rows later. Keep in mind that the data is getting stale the second you put it into your buffer, so you need to move quickly—avoid long user-interactive sessions. If you have a heavily used SQL server, your buffering strategy must deal with collision problems caused by trying to update data with stale contents. You also want to refresh the WHERE clause (with its fresh TimeStamp) after you update your rows. I keep a parallel array of the WHERE clauses for each row so that I can easily modify the rows later.

Inserting a new row

This is perhaps the easiest scenario to deal with. Open a second connection, insert the new row using an INSERT statement, and make appropriate changes to the records displayed. Be prepared for duplicate-key errors, since some other user might have added an identical row while your data got stale. Of course, you might also get rule or trigger violations if the data doesn't meet minimum referential or data integrity constraints. Close the connection when you have successfully added the row. (Your current result set won't contain the added row; if you require that level of functionality, you should consider the use of a true cursor.) You can include the new row on the screen in the correct place, but you can't place it into the DB-Library row buffer without resubmitting a query that includes this row in the result set.

> **NOTE** One of the problems involved in trying to insert rows that have a TimeStamp is the contents of that column. Remember, you should *not* have to provide any data for this column. I find it easier to define the TimeStamp column as *permitting* Nulls. That way, DB-Library doesn't bother with a value until it is supplied by the SQL server, as appropriate.

Deleting an existing row

As with the INSERT, open a second connection and drop the row by creating a DELETE statement using a WHERE clause that identifies the specific row. (Remember, creating the correct WHERE clause is the job of the DB-Library Browse mode.) You should use SQLQual to generate the WHERE clause. Make appropriate changes to the records displayed. Again, you might get rule or trigger violations if the data doesn't meet minimum referential or data integrity constraints. Close the connection when you have successfully deleted the row. Note that your current result set will *still contain* the deleted row. Again, if you require this type of functionality, you should consider the use of true cursors. You can drop the deleted row from the screen, but you can't affect the DB-Library row buffer without resubmitting a query that no longer includes this row in the result set.

Updating an existing row

This gets a little more complex. As with the INSERT operation, open a second connection and set up a change for the row with an UPDATE statement using a SQLQual-generated WHERE clause that points to the specific row. Make appropriate changes to the records displayed. You might get rule or trigger violations if the data doesn't meet minimum referential or data integrity constraints. If the row to be updated has been changed since you originally fetched the data, the UPDATE fails. In this case, inform the user and, if necessary, resubmit the query. Close the connection when you have successfully changed the row. Note that your current result set *still contains* the old (not updated) data row. You can drop the deleted row from the screen, but you can't affect the DB-Library row buffer without submitting a query that no longer includes this row in the result set.

TIP If you plan to do several edits, you might consider keeping the connection open.

Using SQLTsNewVal

Once you have made a successful update, a new TimeStamp value is created for you. To get DB-Library to return this value, call SQLTsNewVal, which returns a string containing the new value. SQLTsNewVal returns a null string if the update didn't work. (Perhaps you didn't have a SQLQual-generated WHERE clause, or perhaps some other user changed the record while you were waiting to update it.)

Using SQLTsPut

SQLTsPut is used to update a TimeStamp value in the *current* Browse mode row, as set by SQLGetRow or SQLNextRow. Its parameters are as follows:

- The connection handle (*SQLConn*).

- The current TimeStamp value (as supplied by SQLTsNewVal).

- The current TimeStamp length (as supplied by SQLTsNewLen).

- The table number of the browsable table. (You can use SQLTabBrowse to see if the table is browsable; if you set the table number to –1, DB-Library uses the table name, specified next, to determine the table.)

- The table name or a null string (if you want to identify the table by the table number).

SQLTsPut fails if you try to update the TimeStamp column of a nonexistent row, update the TimeStamp column with a Null value (which can happen on new rows that have no TimeStamp value assigned), or browse a table that isn't browsable.

Using SQLQual

If you have set up a correctly phrased Browse mode query, you can ask DB-Library to re-create the string containing the WHERE clause that can reaccess each row. As each row becomes the current row (just after SQLNextRow and SQLGetRow), you can call SQLQual to build its WHERE clause. I usually keep a parallel array that holds the SQLQual-generated WHERE clause for each row. That way, I can easily step down to each buffered row and do any deletes or updates as needed. This WHERE clause also includes the TimeStamp value fetched when the row is first browsed. A typical call to SQLQual contains *SQLConn*, which identifies the specific connection, and *TableNumber*, which identifies the table that the query is referring to. If the value is –1, the table name is expected to be in the *TableName* argument:

```
SELECT Chickens.EggCount, Hens.FeatherCount
FROM Chickens, Hens
WHERE Chicken_Name = Hens_Name and
    Chicken.Color = 'Brown'
```

Here, *SQLQual(SQLConn, 2, "")* refers to the *Hens* table. The call to SQLQual typically also contains *TableName*, which identifies the name of the table to which the query is referring. If this value is Null (""), the *TableNumber* argument is used:

```
SELECT Chickens.EggCount, Hens.FeatherCount
FROM Chickens, Hens
WHERE Chicken_Name = Hens_Name and
    Chicken.Color = 'Brown'
```

SQLQual$(SQLConn, –1, "Hens") refers to the *Hens* table.

Managing Browse Mode TimeStamps

A number of other VBSQL functions are needed to help manage the TimeStamp values used in managing Browse mode rows. When Browse mode operations are executed, you can use the SQLQual function to return a WHERE clause for the current row that contains the row's TimeStamp value, along with a fully qualified key for the buffered row. When you update a data row in the database, a new TimeStamp value is inserted by the SQL server. If other processes have also read this row and are using the TimeStamp value to test validity of their updates, their update processes fail because the TimeStamp values no longer match. If you want to extract or resave this new TimeStamp value, you must use the functions described on the next page.

- *SQLTsNewVal, which returns the new TimeStamp value from the current row in a row buffer.* It has only one parameter, *SQLConn* (the current connection handle). It returns an empty string if the row was not a Browse mode row (did not contain a WHERE clause returned by SQLQual).

- *SQLTsNewLen, which returns the length of the new TimeStamp value after a Browse mode operation.* If −1 is returned, the TimeStamp is invalid for the same reasons that SQLTsNewVal fails.

- *SQLTsPut, which places a newly fetched TimeStamp value back into a specified table's current row in the row buffer.* In this case, you have to specify exactly where to find the row. The parameters are as follows:

  - *SQLConn* (the valid connection handle)

  - *New TimeStamp* (as fetched by SQLTsNewVal)

  - *New TimeStamp length* (as fetched by SQLTsNewLen)

  - *TableNumber* (the number of the table, beginning with 1 or −1, to indicate the table via the *TABLENAME* parameter used to identify the table)

  - *TableName* (the name of the table, or "", to use the *TABLENUMBER* parameter to identify the table)

33
Chapter

Using
VBSQL Cursors

Why Cursors (and Why Not)?

Using Cursors to
Get Individual Rows

The VBSQL-Supported
Cursor API

Implementing a
Cursor-Based Application

Converting 16-Bit
VBSQL Applications

nlike hierarchical (flat) file structures, in which the application or the database engine manages individual records, relational databases are based on data stored in tables and don't lend themselves to the fetching of individual records. There's no concept of the "next" or "previous" row except in the set of rows resulting from a SQL query. As far as the user is concerned, physical rows bear no relationship to one another except that they're accidentally adjacent to each other in the result set. There's no guarantee that they'll have the same physical relationships the next time the result set is fetched unless changes are made in the ORDER BY or GROUP BY clauses. Our workstation applications need to process result set rows one at a time and present them to the user in small blocks. The SQL cursor acts like the CRT's cursor in that it permits the result set data to be tracked one row at a time by the user and the application. This section deals specifically with the Microsoft SQL Server implementation of cursors via DB-Library. The entire API has been implemented in the Microsoft Visual Basic SQL function set.

NOTE In the mainframe days, I spent many an hour accessing sequential, index-sequential, and "random"-access data files. Many databases today are still built around card-format databases created over the last 30 years, and many mainframe companies still mount hundreds of reels of card-image tape every night to process Medicare claims.

Why Cursors (and Why Not)?

A number of important changes have been made to SQL Server recently and to how it supports cursors. SQL Server now has not only server-side cursors but also extensions to the Transact-SQL dialect for supporting cursors. Even with these enhancements, however, I'm not convinced that server-side cursors or cursors of any other kind are a universal solution. Lower-impact approaches are often totally adequate for my applications. But let's look anyway at the advantages of using SQL Server version 6.*x* server-based cursors:

- *Performance.* If you're going to access a small fraction of the data in the cursor (as you typically would in many browsing applications), server-based cursors give you a performance boost, since only the required data (and not the entire result set) is sent over the network.

- *Range.* Keyset and dynamic cursor types are available only with server-based cursors. The normal VBSQL cursor library supports only forward-only cursors, with read-only concurrency, and static cursors, with read-only optimistic concurrency. Server-based cursors give you the full range of concurrency values with the different cursor types.

- *Cleaner semantics.* The normal cursor library simulates cursor updates by generating a SQL SEARCHED UPDATE statement, which can sometimes lead to unintended updates.

- *Memory use.* With server-based cursors, the client doesn't need to cache large amounts of data or maintain information about the cursor position. The server provides that functionality.

- *Multitasking.* When server-based cursors are in use, the connection between the client and the server doesn't remain busy between cursor operations, so you can have multiple cursors active at the same time.

A cursor is often about as helpful as a drinking straw is to a man crawling out of the desert, dying of thirst.

Cursors provide a way to work with relational sets and are implemented here in much the same way they're implemented in the RDO interface. Many of the RDO design considerations also apply here. Cursors can go a long way toward making complex row buffering easier to manage. Let's look now at the advantages of cursors for capturing and updating specific rows of a result set:

- *Single-connection operation.* All the SQL CURSOR operations described here require only one additional connection to implement.

- *Bidirectional scrolling.* This permits you to fetch the first row of the result set as easily (and as quickly) as the last. Any and all rows can be fetched at any time, and additional queries are handled automatically.

- *Virtually random access to results.* The result set is built around pre-fetched keys, so access to any row of the result set, in any order, is relatively easy.

- *Sensitivity to volatility.* By selecting appropriate options, developers can tell when other users have changed the result set. Data in the result set can also be locked from updates by other users or opened to change, as the situation demands.

- *Additional concurrency control.* Access to the values, order, and membership of each result set can be restricted or permitted, as necessary.

CAUTION

Be sure to test SQL Server 6.*x* server-side cursors on a full-blown production machine, not on some wimpy 486/33 with 16 MB of RAM, as I did. Apparently, without the extra CPU horsepower, they run slower than client-side cursors.

Using Cursors to Get Individual Rows

Here in Redmond, Washington (Microsoft's home), we are blessed with an active and prolific SQL user group. Their members, with the help of a number of talented SQL experts at Microsoft, have made a number of suggestions about accessing individual rows. One SQL developer, for example, has found that in some applications it's beneficial for the table rows to be numbered so that fetches can be made by row number. (Remember, though, that unless the table itself or each row of the result set has a system-generated unique row number, this isn't possible.) To use this developer's technique, you have to add row numbers to the result set as seen at one point in time.

The technique involves setting up a WHILE loop with an embedded SELECT statement that fetches the key that comes after the key fetched previously. We use a MIN aggregate to force the retrieval of a single row instead of an entire set. Basically, we fetch the lowest ID (in this case, *Store_ID* from the *Stores* table in the *Pubs* sample database) that is higher than the key previously fetched. We've also added a RowID column to the *Stores* table for the code presented below. This approach is more reasonable than ever now that you can easily create and maintain a row number or unique row identifier using the new Identity TSQL data type.

```
DECLARE
@key Char(4),                          Set up program variables.
@rid INT,
@cnt INT
  BEGIN TRAN                           Do everything or nothing.
  SELECT @rid=0,@key="",
    @cnt=COUNT(*)                      Find total number of rows in the
                                       result set.

  FROM stores HOLDLOCK                 Use HOLDLOCK to prevent changes
                                       to the result set while we insert
                                       computed row numbers.

  WHILE @rid < @cnt                    Select each row in turn.
  BEGIN
    SELECT @rid = @rid+1,
      @key=MIN(storid)
    FROM stores
    WHERE storid > @key
    UPDATE stores
      SET rowid = @rid                 Set the new RowID column to the
                                       current computed RowID.

      WHERE storid=@key

  END
COMMIT TRAN                            Release the locks.
```

Note that the code freezes the result set by using SELECT...HOLDLOCK, which prevents any share locks on the data rows. This means other users won't be able to get access, not even read-only access, to the rows that constitute the result set. This lock might be expanded to the entire table—or even to all tables mentioned in the SELECT, if the query optimizer decides that too many rows are affected by the lock and escalates the individual row locks to table locks. The length of time the HOLDLOCK is in effect and its impact on system concurrency are functions of the number of rows to be indexed in the result set. A unique key of some kind is needed for this technique to work, and having a SQL index on this key will dramatically improve performance.

Dave Durant, former trainer and SQL relational authority at Microsoft, once proposed five possible methods for scrolling through data. One benefit of cursors is that they provide an easy way to accomplish any of the first three methods, as shown in *Figure 33-1* on the next page.

CAUTION
A number of problems have been traced to misunderstandings about cursors. They can have a significant impact on overall application and server performance, so be sure to test your cursor tactics carefully before committing yourself to a long-term strategy.

The VBSQL-Supported Cursor API

The VBSQL DB-Library cursor engine supports several types of cursors whose operation varies according to concurrency and the data's sensitivity to change. Depending on what cursor options you choose, the cursor engine either locks down the data or permits fairly free access to the rows of the result set. As more concurrent access is permitted, it takes DBLIB longer to fetch and update the data.

TIP One of the most difficult operations to perform with the VBSQL cursor API seems to be backward movement in a cursor result set. Any number of options will let you move anywhere *within* a keyset, but you can move to *previous* keysets only by moving to the first keyset and then moving forward to the desired location.

Cursor Setup

To use this new "cursor" API, you must have SQL Server create a unique index on the table(s) that you want to access. (I think you'll find that the requirement to create unique indexes is also true for virtually all the other access methods besides VBSQL.) Generally, this requirement is based on the problem of accessing the individual rows of the result set. Without unique indexes, the cursor API can't create the keysets needed for choosing and updating specific rows. Both the new Microsoft Access DBMS and Visual Basic 2.0's ODBC also require unique table indexes for individual row access. But you don't need to set up a TimeStamp column or a second connection as you do in Browse mode.

CAUTION
You should limit the scope of your query as much as possible to keep the cursor result set within range of easy repositioning—entirely within the keyset.

Figure 33-1
Techniques for Scrolling Through Data

Method	Implementation	Advantages	Disadvantages
Brute force	Submit a SELECT statement and walk through result set, as needed. Send SQLNextRow as user scrolls down. If user scrolls up, resubmit and start over.	No buffering required. Simple, generic, and easy to implement. Fine for small result sets. No strain on RAM.	Often unacceptably slow for long scrolls (especially up). Impossible to hold lock when data is not static. Connection must remain open to maintain result set.
Row buffering	Submit a SELECT statement and buffer rows on the workstation. Scroll through buffer.	Easy if the buffer size is the size of the number of rows in the result set. Reduces server load. Fast scrolling after data is buffered.	Might require a SELECT COUNT(*) to be practical. Not much better than brute force if too many rows. RAM use unpredictable. Building big buffers slow—better to limit rows to fixed value: SET ROWCOUNT=n.
Primary key buffering	Submit SELECT PK1, PK2. Buffer the primary keys (PK) on the workstation. Retrieve a windowful of rows based on ranges of PKs.	Good response. (Submit one SELECT statement per scroll.) Smaller RAM use. (You buffer just the keys.) Can close connection between SELECT statements.	Key values subject to change and might not be valid. Difficult to deal with a constantly updated result set. Tough to deal with adds and deletes of rows and keys.
Presequencing the rows	Add a sequence number to all rows. Keep sequence number updated with triggers. Use one sequence per sort order on a table. To get a window of rows, select rows with a sequence number between current and desired position.	Very fast response time, even on the largest tables. Can close connection between queries. Reduced server load. Can pivot rows about a pinned row. Can have a number of predetermined sort orders.	Must have static data. Read-only, with no locks. Difficult to renumber the rows quickly.
Using a smart stored procedure	Stored procedure will deliver the next n rows, in x sequence, starting at row y. Needs a TimeStamp column.	Very fast response time; data subject to change.	Index required on each sequence by column. Separate stored procedure required per sequence because each is optimized when compiled. Least generic of all five solutions.

SQL Server 6.x Cursor Support

I waded into the VBSQL and C documentation while writing this section and had to be pulled out of a deep sinkhole by one of my associates. It seems that there are a number of new terms used in the documentation that are not really defined anywhere. The documentation refers to cursors in four different ways:

- *Client cursors*. This is the term for the type of cursors available before server-side cursors were available with SQL 6.x. Basically, these cursors are built by code running on the client and create keysets on the client system. Microsoft Jet, RDO, and ODBC also support client cursors, very much as DB-Library and VBSQL do.

- *Server-side cursors*. These cursors are available only on SQL Server 6.0 systems and are created by code running on the SQL server. They create keysets in TempDB on the server. RDO and ODBC also support server-side cursors, very much as DB-Library and VBSQL do.

- *Transparent server cursors*. These server-side cursors are supposed to behave exactly like the old client-side cursors and are provided mainly for backward compatibility. This type of server-side cursor automatically emulates client-side cursor behavior if you use the SQLCursorFetch function after the cursor is opened.

- *Explicit server-side cursors*. These have some significant differences and are recommended for those creating new applications. For one thing, the *FTC_ENDOFRESULTS* flag, set in the status array when the end of the array is reached in transparent and client-side cursors, has been done away with in server-side cursors. *FTC_ENDOFKEYSET* would also be set for keyset cursors, and these are gone, too, with server-side cursors. Another difference is that server-side cursors let you vary the number of rows fetched for each fetch. With client-side and transparent cursors, fetch buffer size is fixed when the cursor is first opened.

If you're using the VBSQL 6.x custom control and connect to a SQL Server 6.x server, DB-Library uses server-side cursors, which are supposed to be faster and more efficient. Basically, this is transparent to the application. You can also use server-side cursors explicitly now with the SQLCursorFetchEx function, which takes a couple of extra parameters and gives more power and flexibility.

You can force SQL Server 6.x to use client-side cursors if you set the SQLClientCursors option with SQLSetOpt or if you set the SQLClientCursors option in the registry. (No, *DBCLIENTCURSORS* isn't the right constant—it's for DB-Library.) This option can also be enabled for a client running 16-bit Windows if you place the line *UseClientCursors= ON* in the [SQLSERVER] section of WIN.INI. You can enable this option for a client running Microsoft

Windows NT or Microsoft Windows 95 by setting the value UseClientCursors to ON (UseClientCursors : REG_SZ : ON) in the following Windows registry key:

```
HKEY_LOCAL_MACHINE\
    SOFTWARE\
        Microsoft\
            MSSQLServer\
                Client\
                    DB-Lib
```

This option is provided for those who are extremely sensitive and paranoid, wanting nothing to do with server-side cursors and happy only with the bulky and memory-hogging client-side stuff, or for those who are highly unstrung about compatibility issues.

The type of server cursor (explicit or transparent) that you'll get is determined when you execute the first fetch function against the open cursor: SQLCursorFetchEx or SQLCursorFetch, respectively. The two calls can't be mixed on the same cursor; you can't use the SQLCursorFetchEx function on a cursor once you've used a SQLCursorFetch function on it, and vice versa. **Figure 33-2** shows a summary of the new types of cursors.

Figure 33-2
New Types of Cursors

DBLIB	Type of SQL Server	Type of Cursor You Get
4.21	4.21	Client-side
4.21	6.x	Client-side
6.x	4.21	Client-side
6.x	6.x	Transparent (if SQLCursorFetch used)
6.x	6.x	Client-side (if SQLCursorFetch used and SQLClientCursor set with SQLSetOpt)
6.x	6.x	Server-side (if SQLCursorFetchEx used)

Supported Cursor Types

Now that you have a general idea of how to open a cursor, you might find it useful to know which cursors best meet the immediate needs of your application. VBSQL and SQL Server support several types of cursors. (See **Figure 33-3**.) These cursor types are basically the same as those implemented in the other three programming models.

Figure 33-3
Cursors Supported by VBSQL and SQL Server

Cursor Type	Values	Order	Membership
Static	Fixed	Fixed	Fixed
Keyset-driven	Changeable	Fixed	Fixed
Partial keyset	Changeable	Fixed	Fixed
Dynamic	Changeable	Changeable	Changeable

Static Cursors

Static cursors aren't supported in DB-Library by specific Cursor APIs. The documentation encourages you to use the "snapshot" approach to static cursors by "pre-fetching" data into TempDB via SELECT ... INTO and browsing the temporary table with the Cursor API. Of course, changes made to the temporary table have no effect on the actual table(s), and concurrency isn't a problem—except for the fact that others are free to change the data in the real tables at will. (You might run out of space in TempDB if too many rows are included or if too many users request these snapshots at the same time.) If you want to maintain control of the data, you must use the HOLDLOCK keyword to ensure that the result set generated by the SELECT statement isn't altered by others. Row buffering might be the best solution when you're trying to implement static cursors.

CAUTION
Static cursors are fastest—for *your* user's instance of the application. But since they depend on HOLDLOCK, they can slow down or block *other* users.

Keyset-driven cursors

Keyset-driven cursors fix the membership and order of the result set once the cursor is opened. The DB-Library layer creates a table of keys that point to a desired result set in the database. Because of this, you can't change the membership of the result set once the cursor is open. Other users can get access to the database rows, and you can see their changes (once you refresh your cursor). But if some other user (or something you do) makes a row no longer qualify for the result set, that row *does* remain in your keyset—and therefore in your result set, until you close the cursor and reopen it (which rebuilds the keyset). You can tell when you access a row that has been deleted or its key has been updated, because DB-Library fires an Error event.

This type of cursor is a close approximation of the dynaset-type Recordset object created by the DAO interface. If you force creation of client-side cursors, all keys are kept "locally" in your workstation RAM. You also need a unique index to build this type of cursor. Basically, the data fetched into your workstation is a collection of the unique index keys. When the cursor is first constructed, the order of the rows is fixed by the index or the ORDER BY clause. When you access the rows using the cursor, you are making only indirect reference to the underlying data rows. Changes in the data that affect the order of the rows have no effect on the keyset. Note that the keyset is large enough (in this case) to hold the entire result set, as shown in **Figure 33-4.**

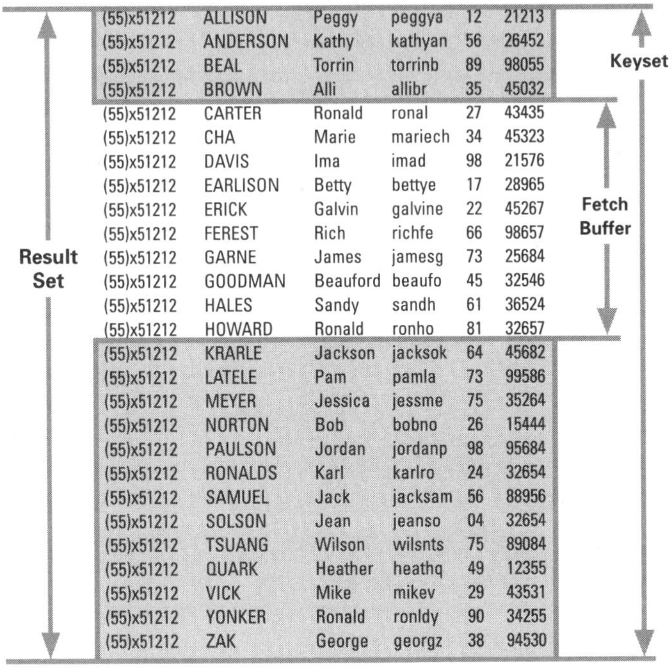

(55)x51212	ALLISON	Peggy	peggya	12	21213	Keyset
(55)x51212	ANDERSON	Kathy	kathyan	56	26452	
(55)x51212	BEAL	Torrin	torrinb	89	98055	
(55)x51212	BROWN	Alli	allibr	35	45032	
(55)x51212	CARTER	Ronald	ronal	27	43435	
(55)x51212	CHA	Marie	mariech	34	45323	
(55)x51212	DAVIS	Ima	imad	98	21576	
(55)x51212	EARLISON	Betty	bettye	17	28965	
(55)x51212	ERICK	Galvin	galvine	22	45267	Fetch Buffer
(55)x51212	FEREST	Rich	richfe	66	98657	
(55)x51212	GARNE	James	jamesg	73	25684	
(55)x51212	GOODMAN	Beauford	beaufo	45	32546	
(55)x51212	HALES	Sandy	sandh	61	36524	
(55)x51212	HOWARD	Ronald	ronho	81	32657	
(55)x51212	KRARLE	Jackson	jacksok	64	45682	
(55)x51212	LATELE	Pam	pamla	73	99586	
(55)x51212	MEYER	Jessica	jessme	75	35264	
(55)x51212	NORTON	Bob	bobno	26	15444	
(55)x51212	PAULSON	Jordan	jordanp	98	95684	
(55)x51212	RONALDS	Karl	karlro	24	32654	
(55)x51212	SAMUEL	Jack	jacksam	56	88956	
(55)x51212	SOLSON	Jean	jeanso	04	32654	
(55)x51212	TSUANG	Wilson	wilsnts	75	89084	
(55)x51212	QUARK	Heather	heathq	49	12355	
(55)x51212	VICK	Mike	mikev	29	43531	
(55)x51212	YONKER	Ronald	ronldy	90	34255	
(55)x51212	ZAK	George	georgz	38	94530	

(Result Set spans the full table)

Figure 33-4   *A keyset-driven cursor*

In some cases, the result set is too large to fit in local memory. If this is the case, I recommend that you first rethink your strategy. Try a query with fewer rows. If this isn't possible, set the keyset size to a more reasonable value, and buffer fewer rows.

When you can't (or don't want to) fit the keyset into local workstation RAM, set the keyset size to the maximum number of keyed rows to be buffered, as shown in **Figure 33-5.** Generally, it would make sense to set the keyset large enough to hold several screens of data. Scrolling within the keyset using both absolute and relative row accessing is fast. The interface has to do a fetch only on a specific row, on the basis of the selected keyset. When the cursor is asked to move outside the keyset, performance decreases as the out-of-bounds keys are fetched.

Dynamic cursors

The most flexible of the cursor types is the dynamic cursor, an example of which is shown in **Figure 33-6.**

(55)x51212	ALLISON	Peggy	peggya	12	21213
(55)x51212	ANDERSON	Kathy	kathyan	56	26452
(55)x51212	BEAL	Torrin	torrinb	89	98055
(55)x51212	BROWN	Alli	allibr	35	45032
(55)x51212	CARTER	Ronald	ronal	27	43435
(55)x51212	CHA	Marie	mariech	34	45323
(55)x51212	DAVIS	Ima	imad	98	21576
(55)x51212	EARLISON	Betty	bettye	17	28965
(55)x51212	ERICK	Galvin	galvine	22	45267
(55)x51212	FEREST	Rich	richfe	66	98657
(55)x51212	GARNE	James	jamesg	73	25684
(55)x51212	GOODMAN	Beauford	beaufo	45	32546
(55)x51212	HALES	Sandy	sandh	61	36524
(55)x51212	HOWARD	Ronald	ronho	81	32657
(55)x51212	KRARLE	Jackson	jacksok	64	45682
(55)x51212	LATELE	Pam	pamla	73	99586
(55)x51212	MEYER	Jessica	jessme	75	35264
(55)x51212	NORTON	Bob	bobno	26	15444
(55)x51212	PAULSON	Jordan	jordanp	98	95684
(55)x51212	RONALDS	Karl	karlro	24	32654
(55)x51212	SAMUEL	Jack	jacksam	56	88956
(55)x51212	SOLSON	Jean	jeanso	04	32654
(55)x51212	TSUANG	Wilson	wilsnts	75	89084
(55)x51212	QUARK	Heather	heathq	49	12355
(55)x51212	VICK	Mike	mikev	29	43531
(55)x51212	YONKER	Ronald	ronldy	90	34255
(55)x51212	ZAK	George	georgz	38	94530

Result Set, Keyset, Fetch Buffer

Figure 33-5 *A partial keyset cursor*

(55)x51212	ALLISON	Peggy	peggya	12	21213
(55)x51212	ANDERSON	Kathy	kathyan	56	26452
(55)x51212	BEAL	Torrin	torrinb	89	98055
(55)x51212	BROWN	Alli	allibr	35	45032
(55)x51212	CARTER	Ronald	ronal	27	43435
(55)x51212	CHA	Marie	mariech	34	45323
(55)x51212	DAVIS	Ima	imad	98	21576
(55)x51212	EARLISON	Betty	bettye	17	28965
(55)x51212	ERICK	Galvin	galvine	22	45267
(55)x51212	FEREST	Rich	richfe	66	98657
(55)x51212	GARNE	James	jamesg	73	25684
(55)x51212	GOODMAN	Beauford	beaufo	45	32546
(55)x51212	HALES	Sandy	sandh	61	36524
(55)x51212	HOWARD	Ronald	ronho	81	32657
(55)x51212	KRARLE	Jackson	jacksok	64	45682
(55)x51212	LATELE	Pam	pamla	73	99586
(55)x51212	MEYER	Jessica	jessme	75	35264
(55)x51212	NORTON	Bob	bobno	26	15444
(55)x51212	PAULSON	Jordan	jordanp	98	95684
(55)x51212	RONALDS	Karl	karlro	24	32654
(55)x51212	SAMUEL	Jack	jacksam	56	88956
(55)x51212	SOLSON	Jean	jeanso	04	32654
(55)x51212	TSUANG	Wilson	wilsnts	75	89084
(55)x51212	QUARK	Heather	heathq	49	12355
(55)x51212	VICK	Mike	mikev	29	43531
(55)x51212	YONKER	Ronald	ronldy	90	34255
(55)x51212	ZAK	George	georgz	38	94530

Result Set, Keyset, Fetch Buffer

Figure 33-6 *A dynamic cursor*

The dynamic cursor permits any other user to fetch and change rows from the cursor result set *and* make these changes visible to the cursor owner. Once a row is deleted or the membership state is changed, the row is no longer included in the cursor result set. Dynamic cursors aren't permitted to include an ORDER BY clause in their queries unless you're using server-side cursors.

By setting the keyset value to –1, you set the cursor to the size of the fetch buffer. Using more than a couple dozen rows will slow the process down significantly. Within the cursor, scrolling forward will be fairly fast (as in work with common row buffers). Moving backward in the cursor set, however, is possible but slower, since unbuffered keys need to be fetched. This cursor's performance decreases in direct proportion to the number of rows buffered.

Mixed cursors

This option, shown in *Figure 33-7*, lets you create a cursor that is a cross between the keyset-driven and dynamic cursors.

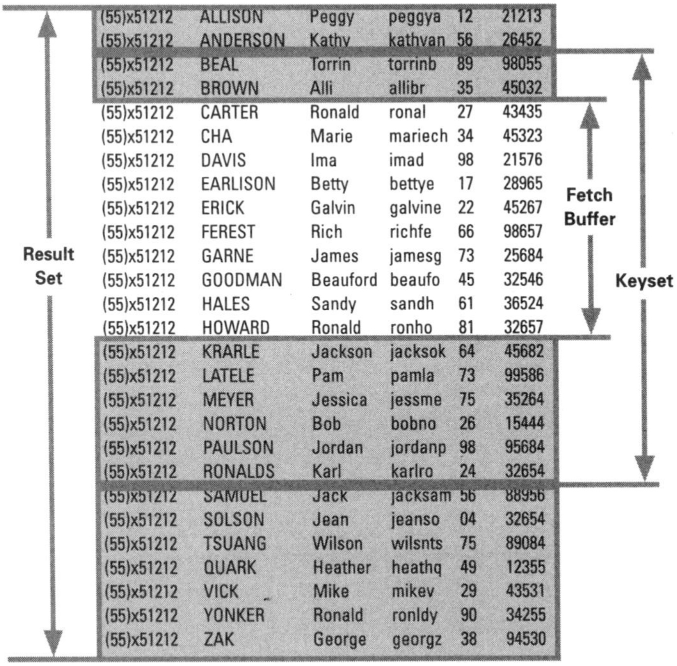

Figure 33-7 *A mixed cursor*

Set the *ScrollOpt(n)* parameter in the SQLCursorOpen call to the number of blocks needed for the keyset. The API sets up a keyset-driven cursor within *n*numrows* (where *numrows* is the number of rows in the fetch buffer) and a dynamic cursor outside that keyset.

Cursor Buffer Definitions

All these terms for describing cursor data structures can seem confusing. Let's define a few of them:

- *Fetch buffer.* This is the number of rows retrieved from the SQL server with a single fetch. The size of the fetch buffer is also referred to as the *width* of the cursor. Its size is set by the SQLCursorOpen parameter *nrows* when you are using client-side or transparent cursors. With server-side cursors, the *nfetchrows* parameter of SQLCursorFetchEx sets the number of rows fetched—the fetch buffer's size. Only rows in the fetch buffer are active. References to rows outside the fetch buffer require SQL Server interaction. Indexing of the rows in the fetch buffer starts at 1 and ends at *nrows*, as set by SQLCursorOpen.

- *Keyset.* This is the set of keys required to fetch the individual rows of a cursor result set. Keysets are limited by RAM (64 KB) in keyset-driven cursors. In a keyset-driven cursor, all result set rows are in the keyset. In a mixed or dynamic cursor, only a subset of the keys is in the keyset.

- *Cursor result set.* This consists of all the rows that match the conditions of the WHERE clause in SQLCursorOpen.

- *Transaction block.* This is the set of rows touched by a fetch (as the term is used in SQLCursorOpen). All these rows might be locked (via the *CURLOCKCC* option).

- *Row status array.* This is an array of 32-bit values that is filled by SQLCursorFetch. This array is indexed, starting at 0 and ending at *nrows* (one for each row in the fetch buffer). The Visual Basic program is responsible for the creation of the status array. (The row status array is *not* implemented in the 32-bit VBSQL.OCX, however.)

CAUTION
The 16-bit VBSQL cursor functions are different when they're ported to the 32-bit OCX, so watch out for changes—some radical, some subtle.

NOTE The "fetch buffer" mentioned in the SQLCursorOpen documentation is the same as the "block of rows" specified in the SQLCursorFetch documentation.

Cursor Strategies

How do you choose the right type of cursor? There's no simple answer, but I can offer a few guidelines. For a small result set, set the keyset to a value larger than the number of rows and use a static or keyset-driven cursor. For a large result set, set the keyset to 1 (which tells DB-Library to make the keyset the same size as the fetch buffer [20–30 rows]) and use a dynamic cursor. When the result set is very large, set the keyset to a value that equals the maximum number of rows to be buffered (this value will depend on system load and workstation capacity) and use a mixed cursor.

The Cursor API Up Close

These specific functions are used to implement your cursor-based application:

- SQLCursorOpen returns a cursor handle to a new cursor based on a SELECT statement and the size of the fetch buffer and keyset. This function also sets the options for concurrency control.

- SQLCursorFetch moves the fetch buffer within the cursor result set by using the cursor handle just created.

- SQLCursorFetchEx fetches a block of rows from an explicit server-side cursor and makes the rows available via SQLCursorData.

- SQLCursorData extracts data from a specified row and column in the fetch buffer.

- SQLCursor updates, deletes, inserts, and refreshes rows of the fetch buffer.

- SQLCursorColInfo returns information about specified columns.

- SQLCursorInfo returns the number of columns and rows in the keyset once the end of the keyset is reached.

- SQLCursorClose releases the resources for the cursor.

A perusal of the error documentation yields these caveats:

- Aggregate functions and table aliases, as well as COMPUTE, UNION, FOR BROWSE, and SELECT INTO clauses, aren't allowed in client-side cursor SELECT statements, but the restriction against Union operations and aggregate functions and table aliases is lifted for the use of server-side cursors.

- Row buffering shouldn't be turned on when Cursor API calls are being used. This applies only to the connection used in SQLCursorOpen.

- All pending commands should be complete (as evidenced by *SQLNextRow = NOMOREROWS* and *SQLResults = NOMORERESULTS*) before cursor functions are called.

- Cursor SELECT statements (in SQLCursorOpen) must generate at least one row.

- Update or delete (SQLCursor) operations must affect at least one row.

- Not all servers support the Cursor API. Note that only Microsoft SQL Server version 4.2 and later versions of SQL Server support the Cursor API.

Implementing a Cursor-Based Application

Now that we've gone through all these terms and definitions, let's take a close look at the basic functions that any implementation will need.

SQLCursorOpen

The SQLCursorOpen function defines how the cursor is built as well as most of its characteristics, including membership, concurrency, and how it can be manipulated in code. The function's *SQLConn* argument points to the desired SQL Server connection. The next argument is a SQL query that defines the cursor. Restrictions on how the SQL statement is phrased depend on where that cursor is to be implemented—on the client or on the SQL server.

For a client-side cursor, the SQL query must be a single SELECT statement. (This does *not* imply that you can substitute a stored procedure, even if it returns a single result set.) Any table included in the query's FROM clause must have a unique index.

The SELECT statement can't contain aggregate functions, table aliases, or any of the following clauses:

- INTO

- FOR BROWSE

- COMPUTE

- UNION

- COMPUTE BY

If you're opening a keyset-type cursor (*ScrollOpt = CURKEYSET*), the SELECT statement can contain the following keywords:

- ORDER BY

- HAVING

- GROUP BY

If the SELECT statement includes a view, the FROM clause must include only a single view (no other tables or views). Any base table included in the FROM clause of the view definition must have a unique index, and the select list must include all of the unique index columns of the base tables.

For any type of server-side cursor, with either a transparent server or an explicit server, the SQL query can be a single SELECT statement or the name of a stored procedure that contains only a single SELECT statement. If a stored procedure is used, any input parameters must be constants; declared variables can't be used. Any output parameters or return values from the stored procedure are ignored. The SELECT statement (alone or in a stored procedure) can't contain any of the following keywords:

- INTO

- FOR BROWSE

- COMPUTE

The SELECT statement *can* contain an ORDER BY clause. If the columns in the ORDER BY clause match the columns of the unique indexes used by the cursor, the cursor uses the *ScrollOpt* requested. If they don't match, SQL Server must generate a temporary table, and a *CURKEYSET* cursor is used if a *ScrollOpt* of *CURFORWARD* or *CURDYNAMIC* is requested. This also occurs if the SELECT contains a subquery.

The cursor is automatically opened with a *ScrollOpt* of *CURINSENSITIVE* and a *ConcurOpt* of *CURREADONLY* if the SELECT statement contains any of the following:

- A table with no unique index

- UNION

- DISTINCT

- GROUP BY

- HAVING

- An aggregate function

- An outer join

The *ScrollOpt* argument of the SQLCursorOpen function sets cursor behavior. *ScrollOpt* also limits which fetch type is supported when you fetch rows with SQLCursorFetch or SQLCursorFetchEx. *ScrollOpt* can be set to one of the constants in **Figure 33-8**. *ConcurOpt* determines what type of locking (if any) is used with the cursor, as shown in **Figure 33-9** (page 640).

The method used to create the server-side or client-side cursor is determined automatically unless you force client-side cursors through initialization settings or use the SQLCursorFetchEx function (which implies server-side cursors). *ScrollOpt* simply sets one of four types of cursor management.

Figure 33-8
ScrollOpt Settings

ScrollOpt	Transparent Client-Side Cursor Behavior	Explicit Server-Side Cursor Behavior
Dynamic cursor (*CURDYNAMIC*)	SQLCursorFetch function allows only a fetch type of *FETCHFIRST*, *FETCHNEXT*, or *FETCHPREV*.	*Explicit server-side cursor:* the SQLCursorFetchEx function allows all fetch type values except *FETCHRANDOM*.
Forward-only dynamic cursor (*CURFORWARD*)	SQLCursorFetch function allows only a fetch type of *FETCHFIRST* or *FETCHNEXT*.	*Explicit server-side cursor:* SQLCursorFetchEx function allows only a fetch type of *FETCHFIRST, FETCHNEXT*, or *FETCHRELATIVE* with a positive *rownum*.
Keyset cursor (*CURKEYSET*)	SQLCursorFetch and SQLCursorFetchEx functions allow all fetch type values.	SQLCursorFetch and SQLCursorFetchEx functions allow all fetch type values.
Insensitive keyset cursor (*CURINSENSITIVE*)	*Client cursor:* not supported. *Transparent server-side cursor:* use a *ConcurOpt* of *CURREADONLY*. SQL Server generates a temporary table. Changes made to the rows by others will not be visible through the cursor. SQLCursorFetch and SQLCursorFetchEx functions allow all fetch type values.	Use a *ConcurOpt* of *CURREADONLY*. SQL Server generates a temporary table. Changes made to the rows by others will not be visible through the cursor. SQLCursorFetch and SQLCursorFetchEx functions allow all fetch type values.
"Mixed" cursor $n > 1$	*Client cursor:* for backward compatibility with "mixed" client cursors. *Transparent server-side cursor:* mapped to a *CURKEYSET* cursor.	Mapped to a *CURKEYSET* cursor.

What is returned

SQLCursorOpen returns the handle to your cursor if the open succeeds. You use this handle in all subsequent SQLCursor calls. *FAIL* (0) is returned if something goes wrong.

CAUTION

Watch out for indexing on the row status array (*pstatus*) versus indexing on the SQL-CursorData rows. SQLCursor-Data rows start at 1; the *pstatus* array starts at 0. For more information on the *nrows* and *pstatus&()* parameters with SQLCursor-Open, see the note at the end of the section on SQL-CursorFetchEx (page 645).

Figure 33-9
ConcurOpt Settings

ConcurOpt	Description
Read-only cursor (*CURREADONLY*)	You can't modify rows in the cursor result set.
Intent to update locking (*CURLOCKCC*)	*Client-side cursor:* places an exclusive lock on the data page that contains each row as the row is fetched. The locks are maintained only if they are inside an open transaction block defined by BEGIN TRANSACTION; the locks are released when the transaction is closed by a COMMIT TRANSACTION or ROLLBACK TRANSACTION statement.
	Server-side cursor: places an update-intent lock on the data page that contains each row as the row is fetched. If the rows aren't inside an open transaction, the locks are released when the next fetch is performed. If the rows are inside an open transaction, the locks are released when the transaction is closed.
Optimistic concurrency control, using TimeStamp or values (*CUROPTCC*)	Changes to a row through the cursor succeed only if the row remains unchanged since the last fetch. If TimeStamp is not available, it reverts to *CUROPTCCVAL*.
Optimistic concurrency control, using values (*CUROPTCCVAL*)	Changes to a row through the cursor succeed only if the row remains unchanged since the last fetch. Changes are detected through comparison of all nontext, non-image values.

What can go wrong?

With as many parameters as this function has, lots of things can go wrong. Unfortunately, some of these errors will return 0 (zero) instead of the handle to the cursor.

NOTE   The row status array is created but accessed differently in the 32-bit OCX cursor implementations.

Check your code for the following problems:

- *Your row status array isn't large enough to hold all the entries specified by the* numrows *parameter.* This error can manifest itself as almost anything, since it overlays Visual Basic memory. I got a protection violation on the *next* SQLCursor statement in W3DBLIB.DLL (35:2298). Both Visual Basic and Windows were toasted.

- *Memory is exhausted.* Perhaps the scope of your query is too wide—it returned too many rows. I created a keyset-driven cursor with 50 rows and an open-ended query on a table with about 14,000 rows. The SQLCursorOpen returned a SQLCRSMEM error indicating that there wasn't enough workstation RAM to create the keyset—not a likely scenario on a workstation running Windows. Remember that the size of a client-side keyset can't exceed a single 64-KB segment. The SQL-CursorOpen *numrows* sets the size of the fetch buffer, not the size of the keyset. You could get the SQL server to limit the number of rows to be returned by setting *MAXROWS* to an appropriate value. Computing the correct value will be tricky, since you have to multiply the amount of data stored for each row fetched into the keyset buffer. One other manifestation of this condition generates the 10080 error (SQLCRSORD, "Only fully keyset-driven cursors can have ORDER BY, GROUP BY...") if the SELECT statement has an ORDER BY clause and too many rows are selected in the cursor result set.

- *Indexes aren't correctly set up for the chosen columns.* This generates error 10077, "One of the tables involved in the cursor statement did not have a unique index"(SQLCRSNOIND). Each specified table or view must be indexed. Each column of a view index must be included in the view to be used in the SQLCursorOpen.

- *The SELECT statement has a syntax error.* This generates error 10075, "Invalid cursor statement" (SQLCRSINV).

- *There are rows pending on the connection.* To open the cursor, DB-Library first makes a number of queries behind the scenes to find out whether all required indexes are in place (in both the referenced tables and views). Before DB-Library can do this, the connection must be ready to accept another command. Perhaps a SQLCancel would be appropriate just before the SQLCursorOpen, if you aren't sure. I tested this condition, and all I got back was a return code of 0 (zero) from the SQLCursorOpen.

Examples

Take a look at the following code for a 16-bit application:

```
'
' Set up a keyset-driven cursor.
' We compute the expected row count of the cursor result set.
' We use that value to set up the size of the status array and the
' number of rows in the keyset.
'
Dim CurSelect As String
Dim MyPStatus() As Long
Dim ExpectedRowCount As Integer
Dim RowsInCursor As Integer
```

(continued)

```
ExpectedRowCount = 100                   ' We expect as many as 100 rows
RowsInCursor = 100                       ' We want to fetch entire
                                         ' cursor result set

ReDim MyPStatus&(ExpectedRowCount) ' Dimension status array to
                                   ' hold 'n' rows

CurSelect$ = "Select * from Animals where type = 'alive' "
AnimalCursor = SQLCursorOpen(SQLConn, CurSelect$, CURKEYSET, _
                       CURREADONLY, RowsInCursor, _
                       MyPstatus&(0))
```

The 32-bit VBSQL implementation has changed in only a few ways from the 16-bit implementation, but one of those ways involves SQLCursorOpen. The *pstatus* array couldn't be handled in the new VBSQL.OCX the way it was handled in the 16-bit VBSQL.VBX, so this array, which indicated individual row status, has been dropped from the function. It's still created, but it's now built and managed automatically by a new function: SQLCursorRowStatus. There's little or no documentation on this function, but it should return the same row status values as described below:

```
Declare Function SQLCursorRowStatus Lib "VBSQL.OCX" _
    (SQLCursor As Long, ByVal Row As Long, _
     ByRef Status As Long) As Long
```

This function accepts the SQL cursor value as generated by SQLCursorOpen and the row in question. In the third argument, it returns the row status as described below. If the function doesn't recognize the cursor or row, it returns *FAIL*.

The status of each row copied into the fetch buffer is returned by the SQLCursorFetch function, as shown here:

Constant	Meaning
FTCSUCCEED	The row was successfully copied. If this flag isn't set, the row wasn't fetched.
FTCMISSING	The row is missing.
FTCENDOFKEYSET	The end of the keyset. The remaining rows aren't used.
FTCENDOFRESULTS	The end of the result set. The remaining rows aren't used.

Since the 32-bit implementation is so different, here's a sample of code used with the VBSQL.OCX:

```
' Set up a 32-bit Keyset-driven cursor.
' We no longer have to build a PStatus array with the
' expected row count of the cursor result set because
' the array is built for us by the OCX.
```

```
Dim CurSelect As String
Dim RowsInCursor As Long

RowsInCursor = 100

CurSelect$ = "Select * from Animals where type = 'alive' "
AnimalCursor = SQLCursorOpen(SQLConn, CurSelect$, CURKEYSET, _
                            CURREADONLY, RowsInCursor)
```

SQLCursorFetch

Once you have a valid cursor handle (from SQLCursorOpen), you can walk through the keyset and get your data. SQLCursorFetch does just that—it fetches a block of rows (filling the fetch buffer) from the SQL server. The number of rows in that block is set by the SQLCursorOpen function's *nrows* parameter.

SQLCursorFetch instructs DB-Library to fetch *n* rows from the SQL server, using a single SELECT for each row. The WHERE clause is constructed from qualifiers built when the cursor was opened. These are stored in workstation RAM. Just how these rows are fetched is a function of several parameters:

- *The Cursor Handle argument* is created by SQLCursorOpen and identifies this specific cursor.

- *The Fetch Type argument* tells DB-Library where to start fetching rows. The fetch type flags and their meanings are as follows:

  - *FETCHFIRST*. This positions the cursor to the first row of the result set and moves the first block of rows (the first keyset) from the SQL server into the fetch buffer. For a cursor opened as *CURFORWARD* (forward-fetching only), this is the best way to reposition to the top of the result set.

  - *FETCHNEXT*. Like SQLNextRow, this fetch option gets the next *nrows* from the SQL server into the fetch buffer unless this is the first fetch on a new cursor, in which case it behaves like *FETCHFIRST*. The complicated part here is what happens when the result set is larger than the keyset size and you have been using one of the *FETCHRANDOM* or *FETCHRELATIVE* options. For example, your query has returned 100 rows into the result set. You decide that your keyset should be 20 rows, since that's all you can show on the screen at any one time. If you request *FETCHNEXT*, you'll get the next block of 20 rows. If you use one of the *FETCHRELATIVE* or *FETCHRANDOM* calls, however, the buffer pointer might not be sitting at the top of the buffer. It will span across the keyset boundary, and you might not get all 20 rows. The *next* SQLCursorFetch shifts down the keyset window and gets you the next full set of rows.

  - *FETCHPREV*. This is used to reposition to the *previous* fetch buffer. Only rows within the keyset are returned. This option is not available if you opened the cursor with the *CURFORWARD* option. *FETCHPREV* won't change the keyset, so you won't be able to scroll backward outside the keyset. This isn't a problem in a keyset-driven cursor, where the entire cursor result set fits in the keyset. If the result set isn't very large, set the keyset to be larger than the anticipated result set size. This permits relative or absolute row access, without the problems associated with moving backward outside the range of the keyset.

- *FETCHRANDOM.* This is not used to fetch a randomly selected set of rows from the result set; only keyset-driven cursors can use this option. It is used to get a selected block of rows *from the keyset,* starting at the row specified by the *rownum* parameter. Note that this option does not fetch rows outside the keyset—if the end of the keyset is reached, the fetch buffer will not be filled. You will need to use *FETCHNEXT* to reposition the keyset within the cursor result set.

- *FETCHRELATIVE.* This is used to fetch a block of rows *from the keyset,* starting from the first row of the previous fetch. Only keyset-driven cursors can use this option. This call can't fetch rows outside the keyset—if the end of the keyset is reached, the fetch buffer won't be filled.

- *FETCHLAST.* This fetches the last block of rows. This option is available *only* with totally keyset-driven cursors (not mixed cursors).

- *Rownum:* With *FETCHRANDOM* or *FETCHRELATIVE,* this indicates the buffer row where filling should begin. The *rownum* is the specified random or relative row number to use as the first row of the new fetch buffer. Use *rownum* only with a fetch type of *FETCHRANDOM* or *FETCHRELATIVE.* Specify 0 (zero) for any other fetch type. When the fetch type is *FETCHRANDOM,* the first row of the new fetch buffer is the *rownum* row (counting forward from the beginning) of the keyset cursor result set. The *rownum* must be positive. When the fetch type is *FETCHRELATIVE,* the following conditions apply:

  - A positive *rownum* means that the first row of the new fetch buffer is *rownum* rows after the first row of the current fetch buffer.

  - A negative *rownum* means that the first row of the new fetch buffer is *rownum* rows before the first row of the current fetch buffer.

  - A *rownum* of 0 (zero) means that all rows in the fetch buffer are refreshed with current data from SQL Server, without the need to move the current cursor position. This is identical to calling SQL-Cursor with *OpType* set to *CRSREFRESH.*

What is returned

SQLCursorFetch returns *SUCCEED* (1) or *FAIL* (0). If *SUCCEED* is returned, the status array (as defined by SQLCursorOpen) is filled with a status code for each row fetched from the SQL server. Once the fetch succeeds, you'll be able to use SQLCursorData to access individual rows of the fetch buffer. These status indicators can be tested for each row in the fetch buffer once SQLCursorFetch completes. (See *Figure 33-10*.) Note that if the row couldn't be fetched, the *FTCSUCCEED* flag isn't set (to 1). You'll have to use binary logic to test for each of these flags. For example, the following would test for the presence of *FTCENDOFKEYSET*:

```
If (MyPStat(Row) And FTCENDOFKEYSET <> 0) Then
'We are at the end of the keyset.
```

In 16-bit applications, test the status array (*pstatus*) bit flags for each row as it is referenced. In 32-bit applications, use the new SQLCursorRowStatus function, as described in the section on SQLCursorOpen. These flags will be updated as the API moves the data to and from the SQL server. If the row was deleted after you opened your cursor, you'll find that the *FTCMISSING* bit is set.

Figure 33-10
Status Indicators for Rows in Fetch Buffer

Manifest Constant	Value	Description
FTCSUCCEED	&H1	Row successfully fetched from the server
FTCMISSING	&H2	Row missing
FTCENDOFKEYSET	&H4	End of keyset reached
FTCENDOFRESULTS	&H8	End of result set reached

What can go wrong

If *FAIL* is returned by SQLCursorFetch, one of the following things has happened:

- *You ignored the* pstatus *value of the last row fetched* (which should have the *FTCENDOFKEYSET* bit set). Check each *pstatus* value for the rows as they are processed.

- *You did not use a keyset-driven cursor* when using the *FETCHRANDOM*, *FETCHRELATIVE*, or *FETCHLAST* options.

- *You used an option other than* FETCHFIRST *or* FETCHNEXT on forward-only scrolling cursors.

- *DB-Library failed to complete the transaction* because of a connection loss, a timeout, or insufficient memory. The problem might be with the SQL server or with the DB-Library interface itself.

CAUTION
When DB-Library is checking to see whether data has changed, it does no checking for Image and Text data type columns.

NOTE To tell whether the data has changed, DB-Library performs several tests. If you've included a TimeStamp column in the SELECT, it's used. Otherwise, a mechanism will be set up to save row data to be used as a basis for comparison, and this mechanism will be tested just before an update. In other words, DB-Library does another fetch of the row and compares (on a column-by-column basis) the current values with those saved when the SQLCursorFetch returned its data. If there are differences, DB-Library knows that some other process has changed the data since it was last read. (This can take extra time and RAM.)

SQLCursorFetchEx

This is a new function specifically added to address the features and power of SQL Server 6.x server-side cursors. If you use this function instead of SQL-CursorFetch against an open cursor, DB-Library assumes that the cursor is a full-blown "explicit" server-side cursor. If you've already used the SQLCursor-Fetch function against the cursor, however, you can't use SQLCursorFetchEx. Once you have a valid cursor handle (from SQLCursorOpen), you can walk through the keyset and get your data. SQLCursorFetchEx does just that—it fetches a block of rows (filling the fetch buffer) from an explicit server-side cursor and makes the rows available via SQLCursorData. The number of rows in that block is set by the SQLCursorOpen function's *nrows* parameter.

> **NOTE** The block of rows retrieved by a fetch is called the *fetch buffer*. The number of rows in the fetch buffer is determined by the *nfetchrows* parameter. For a forward-only dynamic cursor (*ScrollOpt* is CURFORWARD in SQLCursorOpen), you can use only the *FETCHFIRST*, *FETCHNEXT*, or *FETCHRELATIVE* (with a positive *rownum*) types.

SQLCursorFetchEx instructs DB-Library to fetch *nrows* from the SQL server, using a single SELECT statement for each row. The WHERE clause is constructed from qualifiers built when the cursor was opened. These are stored in workstation RAM. Just how those rows are fetched is a function of several parameters:

- *The* CursorHandle *argument* refers to an explicit server-side cursor handle returned by SQLCursorOpen. All cursors opened against SQL Server 6.x are explicit server-side cursors unless you specifically force client-side cursors or use the SQLCursorFetch function, which prevents the use of SQLCursorFetchEx and changes to transparent server-side cursors.

- *The* Fetchtype *argument* specifies the type of fetch to execute, changing the position of the fetch buffer within the cursor result set. ***Figure 33-11*** (page 648) shows the different fetch type values.

- *The* rownum *argument* is the specified random or relative row number to use as the first row of the new fetch buffer. If *rownum* is set to 0 (zero), DB-Library updates, deletes, or refreshes all rows in the current fetch buffer. Use *rownum* only with a fetchtype of *FETCHRANDOM* or *FETCHRELATIVE*. Specify 0 for any other fetch type. When the fetch type is *FETCHRANDOM*, the following conditions apply:

  - A positive *rownum* means that the first row of the new fetch buffer is the *rownum* row (counting forward from the beginning) of the cursor result set.

  - A negative *rownum* means that the first row of the new fetch buffer is *rownum* rows backward from the end of the cursor result set. Given *n* rows in the cursor result set, the first row of the new fetch buffer is row $n + 1 + rownum$ of the cursor result set. For example, a *rownum* of −1 means the first row of the new fetch buffer is row n ($n + 1 − 1$), or the last row, of the current result set. A rownum of $−n$ means the first row of the new fetch buffer is row 1 ($n + 1 − n$), or the first row, of the current result set.

- A *rownum* of 0 (zero) means that the first row of the new fetch buffer is before the beginning (first row) of the cursor result set.

When the fetch type is *FETCHRELATIVE*, the following conditions apply:

- A positive *rownum* means that the first row of the new fetch buffer is *rownum* rows after the first row of the current fetch buffer. For dynamic cursors, if the first row in the current fetch buffer is deleted before a relative fetch, the current cursor position becomes invalid. Let D be the number of contiguous rows, including the first row, deleted from the beginning of the current fetch buffer. Before a relative fetch is executed, the current cursor position is set to before the first nondeleted row (row $D + 1$) in the current fetch buffer. In this case, when a relative fetch is performed with a positive *rownum*, the first row of the new fetch buffer is row $rownum + D$ of the current fetch buffer.

- A negative *rownum* means that the first row of the new fetch buffer is *rownum* rows before the first row of the current fetch buffer.

- For a dynamic cursor, a *rownum* of 0 (zero) means that all the rows in the current fetch buffer are fetched again without any changes in the current cursor position. This is different from a Refresh operation because the rows in the new fetch buffer can differ from the rows in the current fetch buffer. New rows can appear, and old rows can disappear. After D contiguous rows have been deleted from the beginning of the current fetch buffer, when a relative fetch is performed with a *rownum* of 0, the first row of the new fetch buffer is the first nondeleted row (row $D + 1$) of the current fetch buffer. For keyset cursors, a *rownum* of 0 means that the current fetch buffer is refreshed with current data from SQL Server with no change in the current cursor position. This is identical to calling SQLCursor with *OpType* set to *CRSREFRESH*.

- *The* nfetchrows *argument* refers to the number of rows in the new fetch buffer. This value must be less than or equal to the *nrows* parameter specified for this cursor in SQLCursorOpen. When the fetch type is *FETCHFIRST*, an *nfetchrows* value of 0 (zero) means that the new cursor position is set to before the beginning (first row) of the cursor result set. When the fetch type is *FETCHLAST*, an *nfetchrows* value of 0 means that the new cursor position is set to after the end (last row) of the cursor result set.

- *The* reserved& *argument* should be set to 0.

CAUTION

Sometimes you have to watch out for the warnings you're given. For example, both the printed documentation and online books caution you about dbCursorBind—but this C API doesn't play any role when you're working with VBSQL cursors. Binding is unnecessary.

Figure 33-11
Values for Fetch Types

Value	Description
FETCHFIRST	Fetches the first block of rows from a dynamic or keyset cursor. The first row of the new fetch buffer is the first row in the cursor result set.
FETCHNEXT	Fetches the next block of rows from a dynamic or keyset cursor. The first row of the new fetch buffer is the row after the last row of the current fetch buffer. If this is the first fetch with a new cursor, it behaves the same as *FETCHFIRST*.
FETCHPREV	Fetches the previous block of rows from a fully dynamic or keyset cursor. The first row of the new fetch buffer is *nrows* (specified in SQLCursorOpen) before the first row of the current fetch buffer.
FETCHRANDOM	Fetches a block of rows from a keyset cursor. The first row of the new fetch buffer is the specified *rownum* row in the cursor result set.
FETCHRELATIVE	Fetches a block of rows from a dynamic or keyset cursor. The first row of the new fetch buffer is *rownum* rows before or after the first row of the current fetch buffer.
FETCHLAST	Fetches the last block of rows from a dynamic or keyset cursor. The last row of the new fetch buffer is the last row of the cursor result set.

What is returned

SUCCEED (1) is returned if every row was fetched successfully. *FAIL* (0) is returned if at least one of the following is true:

- A fetch type of *FETCHRANDOM* was used on a dynamic cursor.
- A fetch type other than *FETCHFIRST*, *FETCHNEXT*, or *FETCHRELATIVE* (with a positive *rownum*) was used on a forward-only dynamic cursor.
- The SQL Server connection was broken or timed out.
- DB-Library is out of memory.

NOTE For a keyset cursor, a fetch that results in a missing row won't cause SQLCursorFetchEx to return *FAIL* (0).

In a 32-bit application, the elements of the array of row status indicators (*pstatus&()* in SQLCursorOpen) are filled with row status values after the fetch, one for each row in the fetch buffer. In 32-bit applications, the row status is returned via the SQLCursorRowStatus function. Each row status value is a series of fetch status values ORed together. **Figure 33-12** shows the meaning of each row status value. A row status indicator of 0 means that the row is invalid, and SQLCursorData can't return valid data. This happens when the current-row pointer is positioned before the beginning (first row) or after the end (last row) of the cursor result set.

Figure 33-12
Status Indicators for Rows

Fetch Status	Description
FTCSUCCEED	The row was fetched successfully. SQLCursorData returns valid data for the row.
FTCMISSING	The row has been deleted, or a unique index column of the row has been changed. Don't use the values returned by SQLCursorData for the row. For a keyset cursor, this fetch status can appear at any time. For a dynamic cursor, this fetch status can appear only after the current fetch buffer is refreshed.

Once you get a *SUCCEED* from SQLCursorFetchEx, you can use SQL-CursorData to retrieve the column data only for those columns where the *FTSUCCEED* bit is set in the *pstatus* array. If no fetches have been performed on a cursor, the current cursor position is located before the beginning (first row) of the cursor result set. After a fetch completes, the new server cursor position is one of the following:

- The first row of the new fetch buffer, as specified under fetch type, if the first row of the new fetch buffer stayed within the cursor result set

- Adjusted to the first row of the cursor result set, if the first row of the new fetch buffer would have been before the first row of the cursor result set and if the last row of the new fetch buffer would have stayed within the cursor result set

- Before the beginning of the cursor result set, if all rows of the new fetch buffer are before the first row of the cursor result set or if any backward fetch (*FETCHPREV* or *FETCHRELATIVE* with a negative *rownum*) is performed when the first row of the current fetch buffer is the first row of the cursor result set

- After the end of the cursor result set, if the first row (and therefore all other rows) of the new fetch buffer is after the last row of the cursor result set

When the current cursor position is before the beginning of the cursor, a *FETCHNEXT* operation is identical to a *FETCHFIRST* operation. When the current cursor position is after the end of the cursor, a *FETCHPREV* operation is identical to a *FETCHLAST* operation. Each call to SQLCursorFetch leaves the connection available for use, with no pending results.

What can go wrong

SQLCursorFetch and SQLCursorFetchEx can't be used with the same server cursor handle. After either of these functions is used on a specific cursor handle, any attempt to use the other function will return *FAIL* (0).

> **NOTE** For client-side cursors or transparent server-side cursors, *nrows* is the number of rows in the fetch buffer filled by calls to SQLCursorFetch. For explicit server-side cursors, *nrows* is the maximum number of rows in the fetch buffer. The *nfetchrows* parameter of SQLCursorFetchEx must be less than or equal to this value. In 16-bit applications, the *pstatus* array must contain *n* rows of Long integer elements. When you pass a *pstatus&()* parameter to SQLCursorOpen, pass the first element of the array—for example, *mypstatus&(0)*. Each row in the fetch buffer has a corresponding row status indicator. After a fetch, the status of every row in the fetch buffer is returned in the corresponding element of this array. In 32-bit applications, use the new SQLCursorRowStatus function to fetch individual row status values.

SQLCursorData

Once you've created a cursor and positioned it to one of the fetch buffers, you're ready to get column data from the selected rows. You'll need to provide SQLCursorData with the following parameters to extract the data:

- *The cursor handle*. Remember the value passed back from SQLCursor-Open? It goes here. You can have lots of open cursors. Use the appropriate handle here.

- *The row number*. This integer is used to select the fetch buffer row desired. Fetch buffer row numbers range from 1 to *nrows* (as set by SQL-CursorOpen). You'll have to keep track of these numbers yourself.

- *The column identifier*. This integer is used to select the column as specified by the SQLCursorOpen SELECT clause. The first column is 1.

What is returned

SQLCursorData returns a string containing the value of the data specified by the row and column parameters. If the column value is Null, a null string is returned. This is Visual Basic, so converting strings to numbers is easy: just use VAL to convert the string into the target data type. Visual Basic will do the correct conversion for you.

What can go wrong

If one of the row or column values is incorrect, a null string is returned.

SQLCursor

If you decide to modify data on the SQL server on the basis of values in the fetch buffer, you'll need to use the SQLCursor call. The SQLCursor function inserts, updates, deletes, locks, or refreshes a chosen row in the fetch buffer.

If you update a row's key, the row might be disqualified from the keyset. Depending on the type of cursor you use, rows might seem to disappear from the keyset as changes are made by your application and others. You'll need to provide SQLCursor with the following parameters to modify the data:

- *The cursor handle.* The value passed back from SQLCursorOpen goes here.

- *The operation type.* This parameter must be one of the following:

  - *CRSUPDATE:* Update the data in a specified row according to information provided in the *VALUE* parameter.

  - *CRSDELETE:* Delete the row specified.

  - *CRSINSERT:* Add a new row to a table and the fetch buffer.

  - *CRSREFRESH:* Rebuild the data columns for the chosen row from the SQL Server database.

  - *CRSLOCKCC:* Refresh a specified row, and lock the data if it's inside a transaction block. (The lock is released once the application commits or ends the transaction.)

- *The selected row.* This integer is used to select the row in the fetch buffer to operate on. If you want to refresh all of the rows in the fetch buffer, use a 0 (zero) here. The first row in the buffer is 1. (In 32-bit applications, this integer is a Long, as are all other integer arguments.)

- *The selected table.* This string is needed only if the SQLCursorOpen SELECT statement referred to more than one table or view or to a view with more than one table. If needed, this is the name of the specific table to operate on.

- *The new value.* This string contains the replacement values for update operations or the new values for insert operations.

What is returned

SQLCursor returns *SUCCEED* (0) if the operation was successful. *FAIL* (0) is returned if the operation fails.

What can go wrong

This is another fairly complex function, and lots of things can go wrong:

- You tried to do an update operation on a cursor opened with the *CURREADONLY* option.

- Your user name does not have permission to update or change the database.

- One of the triggers on a targeted table went off; and the lock, insert, or update operation failed.

- DB-Library couldn't complete the operation because of insufficient memory, loss of connection, or timeout.

- You're using optimistic concurrency control, and someone else has already modified one or more rows.

SQLCursorCollnfo

When you need to know the details of a chosen column in a query (if your code doesn't generate them directly), SQLCursorCollnfo is one answer. (You can use SQLCollnfo instead—in fact, SQLCollnfo returns more information about the cursor columns. SQLCursorCollnfo is mentioned here only for backward compatibility: your code might already include it.) SQLCursorCollnfo gives you the name, data type, length, and user-defined type (if any) for a chosen column of the cursor. You'll need to provide SQLCursorCollnfo with the following parameters:

- The cursor handle created by SQLCursorOpen.

- The cursor column number. (Column numbers range from 1 to the number of columns you submitted in your SQLCursorOpen SELECT statement; don't confuse this with the *pstatus&* array index, which is zero-relative.)

Call SQLCursorCollnfo after SQLCursorOpen returns a valid cursor handle. The SQLCollnfo function can return additional detailed information about a cursor column.

What is returned

SQLCursorCollnfo returns *SUCCEED* (0) if the operation is successful. *FAIL* (0) is returned if the operation fails. SQLCursorCollnfo also returns the following values:

- *colname$:* a program variable string, where the column name is returned. Use a variable-length string for this argument.

- *collen&:* a program variable, where the maximum length of the column in bytes is returned. If *collen&* is set to –1, the maximum column length isn't returned. This is the *capacity* of the specified column. It doesn't reflect the size of the data in the column—just how much it will hold. Note that this is a Long integer large enough to hold the length of Text and Image data types.

- *usertype:* a program variable, where the user-defined data type of the column is returned. If *usertype* is set to –1, the column's user-defined data type is not returned. If there's a user-defined data type defined for this column, this integer returns the value.

- *coltype:* a program variable where the data type token of the column is returned. If *coltype* is set to –1, the column data type isn't returned. *Figure 33-13* is a summary of the column data types and the VBSQL constants that are used to expose them.

Figure 33-13
Column Data Types and VBSQL Constants

Data Type	Constant	Decimal Value	Hex Value	Notes
Image	SQLIMAGE	34	22H	Image
Text	SQLTEXT	35	23H	Text
Array	SQLARRAY	36	24H	1 byte/variable length
VarBinary	SQLVARBINARY	37	25H	VarBinary
TinyInt, SmallInt, or Int	SQLINTN	38	26H	Null values allowed
VarChar	SQLVARCHAR	39	27H	VarChar
Binary	SQLBINARY	45	2DH	Binary
Char	SQLCHAR	47	2FH	Char
TinyInt	SQLINT1	48	30H	1 byte TinyInt
Bit	SQLBIT	50	32H	Bit
SmallInt	SQLINT2	52	34H	2 byte
Int	SQLINT4	56	38H	4 byte
SmallDateTime	SQLDATETIM4	58	3AH	4 byte
Real	SQLFLT4	59	3BH	4 byte
Money	SQLMONEY	60	3CH	8 byte Money
DateTime	SQLDATETIME	61	3DH	8 byte
Float	SQLFLT8	62	3EH	8 byte
Decimal	SQLDECIMAL	106	6AH	
Numeric	SQLNUMERIC	108	6CH	
Float or Real	SQLFLTN	109	6DH	Null values allowed
Money or SmallMoney	SQLMONEYN	110	6EH	Null values allowed
DateTime or SmallDateTime	SQLDATETIMN	111	6FH	Null values allowed
SmallMoney	SQLMONEY4	122	7AH	4 byte

TIP I often use the data length (SQLDatLen) function when I am building data-sensitive screens. This function isn't accessible when you use cursors. I suggest using the Visual Basic LEN function to act as a substitute. Of course, this will work fine for VarChar and Char data type columns. It isn't at all clear that it will work for Text or Image data types.

What can go wrong

This is a very simple function that returns a *FAIL* (0) only if one of the parameters is wrong (improper column or cursor handle). No interaction with the SQL server is needed.

SQLCursorInfo

SQLCursorInfo gives you the number of columns and rows in the keyset. (The documentation would lead you to believe that these values aren't available until you reach the end of the keyset.) After you open a keyset-driven cursor and a single *FETCHFIRST*, the data seems valid. You can also use SQLCursorInfoEx to get a more detailed description of server-side cursors. All you need to pass to the function is the cursor handle (the value passed back from SQLCursorOpen).

What is returned

SQLCursorInfo returns *SUCCEED* (0) if the operation is successful. It also returns *ncols* (the number of columns in this cursor keyset) and *nrows* (–1, or the number of rows in the result set after population). This is very much like the RowCount property in the RDO interface. The *nrows* value is based on the conditions listed in *Figure 33-14*. *FAIL* (0) is returned if the function fails.

Figure 33-14
Conditions for SQLCursorInfo

Cursor Type	What *nrows* Returns
Client	
Completely keyset-driven	Number of rows in keyset
Dynamic or mixed before last row read	–1
Dynamic or mixed after last row read	Number of rows in keyset
Server	
Dynamic	–1
Keyset before population complete	Rows populated
Keyset after population complete	Total rows in cursor

What can go wrong

SQLCursorInfo simply returns *FAIL* (0) if you pass an invalid cursor handle.

SQLCursorInfoEx

This function gives you information about a client-side cursor, a transparent server-side cursor, or an explicit server cursor. It requires you to declare a VBSQL structure before the call to hold the information returned. All you pass to this function is the cursor handle, which is returned by SQLCursorOpen for the cursor in question, and *CursorInfo*, a program variable that points to a SQLCursorInfo structure that DB-Library fills with information about the specified cursor.

What is returned

This function returns *SUCCEED* (1) or *FAIL* (0) and a filled SQLCursorInfo structure. You don't need to bother with setting any SizeOfStruct fields before calling SQLCursorInfoEx. The SQLCursorInfo fields are shown in **Figure 33-15** on the next page. The SQLCursorInfo structure is defined as follows:

```
Type SQLCursorInfo
    TotCols As Long
    TotRows As Long
    CurRow As Long
    TotRowsFetched As Long
    CursorType As Long
    Status As Long
End Type
```

What can go wrong

SQLCursorInfoEx simply returns *FAIL* (0) if you pass an invalid cursor handle.

SQLCursorClose

When you're done with a cursor and need to release its resources (which can be considerable), SQLCursorClose releases the memory tied up with its RAM-based keysets. All data associated with the cursor is also released (if it was locked). When you close the connection, all cursors associated with it are closed as well. Only the cursor handle (of an open cursor) needs to be passed to the subroutine for the cursor to be closed.

What is returned

Nothing. This is a subroutine, not a function.

What can go wrong

You could pass a handle to a cursor that isn't open or to one that is contaminated (and therefore no longer valid).

Figure 33-15
SQLCursorInfo Fields

Field	Description
TotCols	Total number of columns in the cursor.
TotRows	Total number of rows in the cursor result set.
	Client-side cursor: For a keyset cursor, this number is always valid. For a dynamic cursor, this number is valid only if the current fetch buffer contains the last row in the cursor results set; otherwise, –1 is returned.
	Transparent server-side cursor, explicit server-side cursor: For a dynamic cursor, –1 is returned. For a keyset cursor, when the status field is *CU_FILLING*, the asynchronous population of the cursor result set is incomplete; *TotRows* indicates the number of rows populated. When the status field is *CU_FILLED*, the cursor result set is completely populated; *TotRows* indicates the total number of rows in the cursor result set.
CurRow	Row number in the cursor result set of the current cursor position (first row of the fetch buffer). The first row of the cursor results set is 1.
	Client-side cursor: This value is 0.
	Transparent server-side cursor, explicit server-side cursor: For a keyset cursor, this value is always valid. For a dynamic cursor, this value is 1 when the current position is within the cursor result set, 0 if the current position is before the beginning of the cursor, or –1 if the current position is after the end of the cursor.
TotRowsFetched	Total number of valid rows in the current fetch buffer.
Type	Bitmap of cursor type, scroll option, and concurrency control information. It is a series of the following values ORed together. *Type* indicates client-side or server-side cursor type: *CU_CLIENT* (client-side cursor) or *CU_SERVER* (transparent or explicit server-side cursor). *Scroll option* indicates *CU_DYNAMIC* (dynamic cursor), *CU_FORWARD* (forward-only dynamic cursor), *CU_KEYSET* (keyset cursor), *CU_INSENSITIVE* (insensitive keyset cursor), or *CU_MIXED* (mixed-mode cursor, provided for backward compatibility only). *Concurrency control* indicates *CU_READONLY* (read-only concurrency), *CU_LOCKCC* (intent to update concurrency), *CU_OPTCC* (optimistic concurrency based on TimeStamp or values), *CU_OPTCCVAL* (optimistic concurrency based on values).
Status	Bitmap of status information. It's a series of the following values ORed together:
	Client cursor: CU_FILLED (all cursors).
	Transparent server cursor, explicit server cursor:
	CU_FILLING (Asynchronous population of a keyset transparent server cursor or keyset explicit server cursor result set is incomplete.)
	CU_FILLED (Asynchronous population of a keyset transparent server cursor or keyset explicit server cursor result set is complete, or the cursor is a dynamic cursor.)

Converting 16-Bit VBSQL Applications

Here's a brief summary of how to convert your existing 16-bit applications to 32-bit VBSQL:

1. Load your 16-bit VBSQL project into 32-bit Visual Basic. You're sure to get a number of errors—but just keep loading. The VBSQL.VBX might be loaded as a Picture control. If this happens, just delete it from the project. Don't worry: your Error and Message event handler code won't be affected.

2. Use the Custom Controls dialog box to load the VBSQL.OCX. You might have to browse for it; it's not always installed in the WINDOWS\ SYSTEM directory. Just between you and me, though, this is not such a good idea. For safety's sake, use Windows Explorer to move it there yourself. The DLLs should already be there.

3. Replace the 16-bit VBSQL.BI file with the new VBSQL.BAS file provided with the control. If you don't do this, all kinds of strange errors will stack up (so to speak).

4. Remove all Integer type-declaration characters (%) from your VBSQL code. If you aren't sure about the arguments of a specific function, consult the VBSQL.BAS file. Remember not to remove any % signs that appear in SQL queries (as in LIKE expressions). This will force you to formally declare all variables.

5. Change all VBSQL function parameters, arguments, and return values to be formally dimensioned as Long. Remember, this is a 32-bit control, so Integers are now 4 bytes:

```
Dim SQLConn% becomes Dim SQLConn As Long
Dim retVal As Integer becomes Dim retVal As Long
```

6. Convert the Error and Message event prototype statements to reflect the 32-bit VBSQL.OCX control's events. The Message and Error event prototypes have both changed dramatically. You might want to beef up your Error and Message event handlers to reflect the additional information that is now returned.

7. Remove the last (*pstatus*) argument from any SQLOpenCursor function calls. This is handled internally in the 32-bit OCX.

8. Change all references to the *pstatus* array to use the new SQLCursor-RowStatus function.

Chapter

Taking
the VBSQL
Interface
Off Road

Dealing with Ad Hoc Queries

**Managing Database and
Query-Processing Operations**

Asynchronous Operations

orking with Microsoft SQL Server is more than using cursors to access characters and a few numbers. Data is often saved in more complex forms, like binary images and large blocks of text. In many MIS shops, you might find it virtually impossible to access data in the base tables, since it's closely guarded by a phalanx of stored procedures. When you're faced with importing or exporting dozens or millions of rows of data, you can't always depend on the ability of a cursor-based or even a fast row-based routine to transport the data. Solutions to all of these problems are discussed in this chapter, which leads you off the beaten path of client/server development.

Dealing with Ad Hoc Queries

An ad hoc query contains a SQL statement that's either fully or partially written by the user. Most of the VBSQL applications I write don't permit the user to submit ad hoc queries—it's simply too dangerous. Although I now depend somewhat on SQL Server protection schemes to keep users from accidentally sending a DROP TABLE statement or doing other damage, intended or not, I still don't permit users to enter random SQL statements and execute them. In my applications, the program logic is what generates the query, submits it to the SQL server, and parses the results. When the application needs to permit the user to choose the scope, the search criteria, and the sort order, I usually create a query generator, which produces a correctly worded query. Keeping all of this in mind, I include this discussion for those of you who still need to think about the following issues:

- Letting users send Transact-SQL commands that they write themselves, for the most part

- Creating routines that parse the results of SQL queries, when the results might not be particularly predictable

- Creating general-purpose result parsers

- Gathering information about the query sent and the result set returned

Processing Results

Most of the work involved with sending an ad hoc query isn't in the sending. That's easy. The problem is parsing what comes back. Since you don't know the name, length, or data type of the columns, or even how many columns (if any) are in the result set, you'll need to ask DB-Library some questions before you can deal with the result set data.

Generally, these functions are very simple and intuitive, but they're not very useful if you don't know they're there. These functions answer questions about the most recent query; obviously, they can't be used before DB-Library knows the answers. In no case is DB-Library required to send an additional query to the SQL server. All the answers you need are already in the structures created by DB-Library as it fetches your data. Your call to SQLResults or SQLNextRow sets up these structures.

Almost all the columns in a result set can be described with the same functions, so you have to check on the query description only once. The one exception is a query that contains a COMPUTE clause; this type of query has its own set of support functions. The answers you get back from these functions apply only to the current result set or row, however, and a query can generate virtually any number of result sets. So for each call to SQLResults, you have to retest the values.

Asking About the Query

Let's look at the questions you can ask DB-Library, how to ask them, and how DB-Library answers. There are exceptions, but usually you must call SQLResults and SQLNextRow first to get most of these to work. The most common questions are shown in *Figure 34-1* (on pages 662–663).

NOTE One of the most asked-about functions is SQLCount, whose purpose is to return the number of rows in a populated result set. SQL-Count doesn't return the number of rows in the result set until SQLNext-Row returns *NOMOREROWS*.

Figure 34-2 (page 664) shows the values returned by various functions after the following query has been submitted:

```
Select Feet, Ears, Birth_Date, Name Animal_Name, Notes, Pen_No
From Animals, Pens
Where Animals.Name=Pen.Name
Order by Pen.Name, Pen_No
```

Figure 34-1
Questions and Answers for Query Description

Question	How to Ask	Answer
Can this statement return rows?	SQLCmdRow	*SUCCEED* (yes) or *FAIL* (no) to indicate whether the statement being processed is capable of returning rows—not necessarily that it did return rows. Only TSQL SELECT statements can return rows. (Some stored procedures contain SELECT statements, so they would return *SUCCEED*.)
Did this statement return rows?	SQLRows	*SUCCEED* (yes, at least 1 row was returned) or *FAIL* (no rows were returned). (You must call SQLRows *before* you call SQLNextRow.)
I submitted a batch with several statements. Which statement in the command buffer is currently being processed?	SQLCurCmd	Value (starting with 1) indicating which command is being processed. This is bumped each time SQLResults is called—even if it failed. It's reset when SQLExec or SQLSend is called.
How many columns were returned in the current result set?	SQLNumCols	Value indicating number of columns in the query. SQLData will accept from 1 to this number as valid columns.
What's the name of a chosen column?	SQLColName$	String containing name of chosen column. (This isn't necessarily the database column name if the query aliased the column.)
What's the data type of a chosen column?	SQLColType	Tells you what is supposed to be in the column, on the basis of the SQL Server table description. (Data in all columns is converted to a string before you get it.)
What's the defined length of a chosen column?	SQLColLen	Returns the size of the column, which is based on the length specified in the database table. (This isn't how much data *is* in this column, just how much data *could* be there. For Text and Image types, this function returns 4096.)
Did the chosen row or column (element) value contain a Null value? What's the maximum printable width of the data in this row for a chosen column?	SQLDatLen&	Returns *FAIL* (0) if the element is a Null or a zero-length string.
What's the name of the data type (in string form)?	SQLPrType$	Returns a string that contains the name of the data type.

Question	How to Ask	Answer
Given the number of a result column, what's the name of the database column that was the source of the query?	SQLColSource$	Returns the database column name. This is helpful if the name is hidden in an alias. This also permits an update to the database column, regardless of how it was queried.
How many tables were involved in the query?	SQLTabCount	A value containing the number of tables in the query.
Given the table number, what's its name?	SQLTabName$	Used when your code needs to ferret out the names of the tables in the query.
What are the name and number of the table used to derive the indicated column?	SQLTabSource$	Returns a table name and places the table number into a value passed as an argument. This table number is used in Browse mode. This function can be used to determine where a result column was drawn from.
Given the table number, can this table be used in a Browse mode procedure?	SQLTabBrowse	*SUCCEED* (1) (yes, the table has the needed indexes and TimeStamp column for Browse mode) or *FAIL* (0) (no, it isn't suitable).
Did this statement return rows?	SQLRows	*SUCCEED* (1) (yes, the statement returned rows) or *FAIL* (0) (no rows were returned). (You must call SQLRows *before* you call SQLNextRow.)
How many rows were affected by the latest query?	SQLCount&	Returns the number of rows affected as a Long after SQLNextRow returns *NOMOREROWS*. (This doesn't work before you've processed all of the result set's rows.)
Is the value returned by SQLCount a real value?	SQLIsCount	Called after SQLCount and indicates whether the SQL command did or didn't affect rows. Returns *SUCCEED* (1) if the count returned by SQLCount is the correct value. *FAIL* (0) says this command didn't affect any rows.
What is the current row number, based on this result set?	SQLCurRow&	A number from 1 to the number of rows in the result set. When all rows have been read, this number will equal SQLCount&.
How many columns are specified in the ORDER BY clause of the current SELECT statement?	SQLNumOrders	Value showing how many columns were used to sort the data.
What data was returned at a chosen row and column?	SQLData$	String containing the data from the chosen row or column element. SQLData returns a string, regardless of the data type defined, so it's up to you to test for Null, using SQLDatLen, and deal with binary data types.

NOTE The SQLDatLen& function looks at the *data*, not at the SQL Server column definition. In C, you have the ability to differentiate Null elements from zero-length strings. Regrettably, the VBSQL implementation doesn't make this distinction. In the case of strings, it's easy; SQLDatLen returns the length of the data string. In the case of numbers, SQLDatLen returns the number of bytes that would be needed to store the value. Since SQLData returns a string, this value isn't likely to be the length of the data returned. Just use Len(SQLData$(SQLConn, *column*)) to be sure.

Figure 34-2
Using VBSQL Functions to Describe a Typical Query

Function	Returns	Reason
SQLCmdRow(SQLConn)	1 (*SUCCEED*)	The query *can* return rows. It's a SELECT statement.
SQLRows(SQLConn)	1 (*SUCCEED*)	The query *did* return rows.
SQLCurCmd(SQLConn)	1	This statement is the first (and only) statement in this batch.
SQLNumCols(SQLConn)	6	The SELECT returns 6 columns.
SQLColName$(SQLConn, 4)	*Animal_Name*	The fourth column, *Name*, is aliased.
SQLColType(SQLConn, 2)	48	(SQLINT1) A TinyInt. (How many ears *can* an animal have?)
SQLColLen(SQLConn, 2)	3	Column 2 is a TinyInt.
SQLColLen(SQLConn, 5)	4096	Column 5 is Text data type. The actual length that Text columns can hold is far larger; this shows default buffer size.
SQLDatLen(SQLConn, 5)	4	The string returned by SQLData$(SQLConn, 5) is 4 bytes long.
SQLPrType$(SQLConn, 5)	Text	The data type of the fifth column is SQLText.
SQLData$(SQLConn, 5)	"A dead duck"	SQLData returns the first 4 KB of data from a Text column.
SQLTabCount(SQLConn)	2	Only two tables are used in this query.
SQLColSource$(SQLConn, 1)	*Name*	*Animal_Name* is derived from SQL column name.
SQLTabSource$(SQLConn, 6, t)	*Pens*, 2	Column 6 is drawn from table 2 (*Pens*).
SQLCount(SQLConn)	23	There are 23 rows in the result set (after reaching SQLNextRow = *NOMOREROWS*).
SQLNumOrders(SQLConn)	2	There are two columns involved with the sort: *Name* and *Pen_No*.
SQLData$(SQLConn, 4)	"Daffy"	Data in the fourth column of the current row.

Dealing with COMPUTE Rows

If your query happens to contain a COMPUTE clause, as in the following example, you have to deal with the special result set rows that are generated, and you do this by using a special set of functions. Let's take a look at a typical query that includes the COMPUTE clause, so we can break it down with the use of these special functions.

```
Select type, ears, feet From animals
Where type = "bovine"
Order by type, ears
Compute sum(ears), sum(feet) by type
```

Again, these functions can be used only after you've called SQLResults and SQLNextRow (which returns the *ComputeID* needed in all these calls). Note that most of these functions refer to the COMPUTE columns as ALT, or alternate. This differentiates the regular row from the COMPUTE row functions. *Figure 35-3* on the next page describes the COMPUTE clause functions. (Note references to the preceding example.)

What Is a ByList?

When you submit a query with a COMPUTE BY clause, part of the syntax requires a ByList. This is the list of columns that determine the breakpoints (when the subtotals are to be produced). A ByList is returned as a variable-length binary string that contains a list of the columns from the SELECT list that appear in the COMPUTE BY clause's list. Consider the following statement:

```
Select department, last_name, year sales from employee
Order By dept, last_name, year
Compute Count(last_name) by dept, last_name
```

It produces the 2-byte binary string 0x0102 because there are two statements in the ByList, and they're columns 1 and 2 from the SELECT list. The following program fragment shows how to convert a binary value to an Integer to get the number of a column position:

```
ByList$ = SQLByList$(SQLConn, ComputeID)
Dim ByListNumber(LEN(ByList$)) As Integer
For x = 1 to Len(ByList$)
    ByListNumber(x) = Asc(Mid$(ByList$, x, 1))
Next x
```

Figure 34-3
Questions and Answers for Handling COMPUTE Rows

Question	How to Ask	Answer
How many COMPUTE columns were returned for this *ComputeID* in the current result set?	SQLNumAlts	Number of columns for the chosen *ComputeID* as returned by SQLNextRow. The example has two, for *sum(ears)* and *sum(feet)*.
How many COMPUTE clauses are in the current result set?	SQLNumCompute	Number of COMPUTE clauses in the current result set. In the example, only one is used.
What is the data type of a chosen (for this *ComputeID*) COMPUTE column?	SQLAltType	Data type of chosen column (based on *ComputeID* and column number). In the example, all columns return *sqlint1* because that's the way they were originally defined in the database.
What is the maximum length defined for a selected (for this *ComputeID*) COMPUTE column?	SQLAltLen	Returns the size of the column on the basis of the defined SQL Server database length. (This is not how much data *is* in this column, just how much data *could be* in this column.)
What is the length of the data in a chosen (for this *ComputeID*) COMPUTE column?	SQLADLen&	Returns a 0 if the element is a Null or a zero-length string.
What is the type of aggregate function for a selected COMPUTE column?	SQLAltOp$	Returns a string that defines the type of aggregate for the chosen COMPUTE column.
Which column in the SELECT statement corresponds to the chosen (by *ComputeID*) COMPUTE column?	SQLAltColId	Shows what column in the SELECT statement matches up with a chosen column in the COMPUTE clause. In the code, COMPUTE column 2's *ComputeID* is 3.
What is the ByList for the chosen (by *ComputeID*) COMPUTE column?	SQLByList$	Returns a string that has the column positions for the ByList in the SELECT statement.
What data was returned at a chosen row and column?	SQLAData$	String containing the data from the chosen row or column element. (SQLAData returns a string, regardless of the data type defined.)

The SQLAltOp$ Function

The SQLAltOp$ function has the following defined values:

Valid Aggregate Operator	Hex/Decimal Value	Aggregate Function Type
SUM	&H4D/77	SQLAOPSUM
COUNT	&H4E/78	SQLAOPCNT
AVG	&H4F/79	SQLAOPAVG
MIN	&H51/81	SQLAOPMIN
MAX	&H52/82	SQLAOPMAX
ANY	&H53/83	SQLAOPANY
NOOP	&H7A/122	SQLAOPNOOP (not documented)

NOTE The SQLADLen& function looks at the *data,* not at the SQL Server column definition. In C, you have the ability to differentiate Null elements from zero-length strings. Regrettably, the VBSQL implementation doesn't make this distinction. SQLADLen& returns the number of bytes needed to store the (numeric) value. Since SQLAData returns a string, this value isn't likely to be the length of the data returned. Just use Len(SQLAData$(SQLConn, *column*)) to be sure. You also need to be prepared for a 0 (zero) return here if the row or column value is Null— however unlikely that might be.

Gathering Other Information

There are a number of other questions you can ask regarding the operation of your application or an individual query, as outlined in *Figure 34-4* on the next page.

TIP When a TSQL function returns a numeric value, it's most often an integer, declared as an Integer (2 bytes) in 16-bit Visual Basic and as a Long (4 bytes) in 32-bit Visual Basic.

Figure 34-4
Questions and Answers for Determining Connection Status

Question	How to Ask	Answer
If the default database has changed, what's the new name?	SQLChange$	String containing the name of the current database—but only if it has changed for the current result set. If no change has occurred, a null string is returned.
Is the current SQL connection dead?	SQLDead	*SUCCEED* (1) (yes, the connection is dead) or *FAIL* (0) (no, the connection is still alive).
What's the maximum number of connections I can open at once?	SQLGetMaxProcs	Current maximum number of simultaneously open *SQLConn* connections.
How many seconds will DB-Library wait before timing out?	SQLGetTime	Number of seconds; 0 indicates that DB-Library won't time out, so the maximum is 32,768 seconds, or about 9.1 hours. Change this value with SQLSetTime.
Is the connection available for general use? (Is some other application task using the connection?)	SQLIsAvail	*SUCCEED* (1) (yes, the connection is available) or *FAIL* (0) (no, some other task is using it). Useful when several parts of an application try to share a connection.
Are there more statements in the command buffer to be processed?	SQLMoreCmds	*SUCCEED* (1) (yes, there are more commands to process) or *FAIL* (0) (no, SQLResults will return *NOMORERESULTS*).
What is the name of the current database?	SQLName$	Name of the current default database (result of system administrator–assigned commands or USE DATABASE commands).
How many parameters were returned by the most recently executed stored procedure?	SQLNumRets	Number. Works only *after* you have processed all results from the query. Results from stored procedures are returned last.

Trying to Get a Date: SQLDateCrack

This function is designed to let you break down the date components of the binary date format returned by the SQL server, since this data type is virtually useless without some means of getting the dates into a reasonable format. One workaround is to phrase your query to return the individual date/time components using the TSQL DatePart or Convert statements. If this isn't possible or if you want to offload some of the work from the server, the SQL-DateCrack function can help. (No, the Visual Basic Format$ command can't decode this format.)

SQLDateCrack uses three arguments: *SQLConn*, the current connection handle; a DateInfo structure, provided for you in VBSQL.BAS; and the date to be converted into string form. The 16-bit VBSQL DateInfo structure uses Integer variables instead of Long variables. The DateInfo structure for 32-bit VBSQL looks like this:

```
' User-defined data type for SQLDateCrack (32-bit)
Type DateInfo
    Year As Long
    Quarter As Long
    Month As Long
    DayOfYear As Long
    Day As Long
    Week As Long
    WeekDay As Long
    Hour As Long
    Minute As Long
    Second As Long
    Millisecond As Long
End Type
```

Once you make the SQLDateCrack call, you can pick out the pieces of the date that you need. Here's an example of using the function:

```
r = SQLSendCmd(SQLConn,"Select Date_of_birth " _
    & " From Animals Where Name = 'Donald'" )
If r = SUCCEED Then
    r = SQLResults(SQLConn)
    If r = SUCCEED Then
        r = SQLNextRow(SQLConn)
            While r <> NOMOREROWS
                Birthday$ = SQLDateCrack(SQLConn, _
                                         DateInfo(), _
                                         SQLData$(SQLConn, 1))
            Print Birthday$
            r = SQLNextRow(SQLConn)
        Wend
    End If
Else
    Print "What Donald?"
End If
```

Managing Database and Query-Processing Operations

One of the less-obvious jobs your application has to do is set, reset, and test for various query-processing options. These options control how DB-Library and SQL Server deal with various operations, buffer sizes, and the number of rows returned by the query.

Query Options

The options that can be set are listed in *Figure 34-5*. Setting them is a little tricky for a couple of reasons. Some of the options have different parameter limits for Visual Basic according to the particular memory constraints at the time the interface is written. Some options don't affect the SQL server; they merely set parameters in DBLIB. Some have parameters, and some don't. Some aren't documented.

Setting TextSize and TextLimit

To change the amount of data the Text/Image (page-based) data type processing routines are permitted to handle, you have to set both TextSize and Text-Limit. TextSize is an option on the SQL server; it sets the maximum amount of page-based data that will be returned on any SELECT statement from a particular workstation. TextLimit sets the amount of data passed to the application from DB-Library. Setting TextSize to a value larger than its default size of 4096 won't suffice to permit the application to process ("see") more than 4 KB of data from a Text or Image column.

Setting query options

Once you've decided to alter an option that isn't to your liking, you'll need to set it. You do this with the SQLSetOpt function. The function has three arguments, as follows:

```
r = SQLSetOpt(SQLConn, Option, Optional_Parameter$)
```

SQLConn is the current connection handle. *Option* is the manifest constant of the option to be set. If the query option takes a parameter (*Optional_Parameter$*)— many don't—you have to pass it in the form of a string. This means that if you convert a number to a string, you'll also have to strip off any leading (or trailing) spaces. If the query option doesn't take a parameter, pass a null string ("") as the parameter.

Let's say you've called the SQLSetOpt function. This function is fairly insidious in that it doesn't do anything until you send another query to the SQL server. You also have to call SQLResults for this extra command (which was placed in the buffer but *not* sent). This extra command appears in the buffer at the point where you call SQLSetOpt. If you are in the middle of building up a batch using SQLCmd, you might discover that your batch isn't what you intended. I prefer to send these options at the front of a cleared buffer and be prepared for the extra SQLResults at the front of the query-processing loop. If you hard-code the results parser to look for row results after the first call to SQLResults, you could spend an entire Sunday evening figuring it out. You could also get radical and change the options with the TSQL SET command.

Figure 34-5
Options for Processing Queries

Option	Purpose	Hex/Decimal Value	Range/ Default	TSQL SET
SQLANSItoOEM	Converts DOS character sets to Windows ANSI format.	0E/14	On[1]	No
SQLARITHABORT	Aborts query on divide-by-0 or overflow errors.	6/6	Off[2]	No
SQLARITHIGNORE	Defeats error message on divide-by-0 or overflow errors.	7/7	Off	No
SQLBUFFER	Sets number of rows buffered.	0/0	Integer (not 1)/0	No
SQLCLIENTCURSORS	Forces use of client cursors.	0F/15	Off	No
SQLNOAUTOFREE	Deactivates automatic clearing of command buffer (SQLCmd) between SQLSendCmd, SQLExec, and SQLSend calls.	8/8	Off	No
SQLNOCOUNT	Deactivates row-count information return.	9/9	Off	No
SQLNOEXEC	Compiles but does not execute commands.	0A/10	Off	No
SQLOFFSET	Chooses type of statement to search for in the command buffer.	1/1	(Special)[3]/ Off	Yes
SQLPARSEONLY	Checks syntax only and does not execute command.	0B/11	Off	No
SQLROWCOUNT	Shows maximum non-COMPUTE rows returned.	2/2	Long/ 0 (off)	Yes
SQLSHOWPLAN	Returns processing plan and executes.	C/12	Off	No
SQLSTAT	Returns performance statistics.	3/3	IO or Time/Off	Yes
SQLSTORPROCID	Sends stored procedure ProcID before sending rows from procedure.	D/13	Off	No
SQLTEXTLIMIT (DBLIB option)	Overrides maximum size limit of Text/Image columns. Maximum size DBLIB "shows."	4/4	Integer/ 4096	No
SQLTEXTSIZE (SQL Server option)	Overrides maximum size of Text/Image columns returned with a SELECT.	5/5	Integer/ 4096	Yes

1. The SQLANSItoOEM option seems to be missing from the list of known Visual Basic constants. We might be able to assume that it defaults to ON for the Visual Basic environment.
2. SQLARITHABORT and SQLARITHIGNORE can't both be on at the same time.
3. The offsets are specified in the documentation. Basically, there's one option for each part of the statement (SELECT, FROM, ORDER, and so on).

If SQLSetOpt works, you get *SUCCEED* in the return code. Typically, SQLSetOpt does succeed, but it causes the command batch to fail later on if there's a TSQL syntax error—especially if you don't specify the option identifier or the parameter string correctly.

The following examples should make your life easier by getting you through some of the typical situations for setting options. To turn on row buffering, code as follows:

```
r = SQLSetOpt (SQLConn, SQLBUFFER, "200")
```

or

```
Buffers$ = LTrim$(Str$(MyBuffers))
r = SQLSetOpt(SQLconn, SQLBUFFER, Buffers$)
```

To set the NOEXEC option (which takes no parameters), code as follows:

```
r = SQLSetOpt(SQLConn, SQLNOEXEC, "")
```

To set the STATISTICS IO option, code as follows:

```
r = SQLSetOpt(SQLConn, SQLSTAT, "IO")
```

Easy? Sure. Just remember to call SQLResults for this extra command, which was just added to your current SQLCmd batch.

TIP If you call SQLSetOpt more than once before you call SQLExec, you'll have to call SQLResults for *each* SQLSetOpt call. You can test each of these SQLResults for rows by calling SQLRows, which returns *SUCCEED* when there are rows to process.

Clearing and testing query options

Once you understand how to set the various options, clearing and testing for them is easy. You have to use the SQLClrOpt or SQLIsOpt functions. These use the same parameters as SQLSetOpt, but they ignore all optional parameter strings (except the SQLSTAT IO and Time options).

Using the TSQL SET command

You can use the TSQL SET command to change most of the query options. However, SQLBUFFER, SQLNOAUTOFREE, and SQLTEXTLIMIT *can't* be set via the TSQL SET command. To use the SET option to change one or more query options at the same time, just build up a query like this one:

```
Cmd$ = "Set Showplan on Set Statistics IO on Set TextSize 8192"
r = SQLSendCmd(SQLConn, Cmd$)
```

Undocumented Query Options

While researching this section, I discovered a number of undocumented but valid options in the current version of SQL Server. These can't be set, tested, or cleared with SQLSetOpt, SQLIsOpt, or SQLClrOpt because there are no manifest constants assigned to them in Visual Basic (or C). They can be manipulated only with the TSQL SET command. These options are listed in *Figure 34-6*. Valid DATEFORMAT options are mdy, dmy, ymd, ydm, myd, and dym. The default in U.S. English is mdy.

Figure 34-6
Undocumented but Valid SQL Server Options

Option	Purpose	Range/Default	TSQL SET
DATEFIRST	Sets first day of the week for date processing.	1–7/7 (Sat.)	Only
DATEFORMAT	Sets default month, day, and year order for date parts.	Various/mdy	Only
LANGUAGE	Sets national language used in system messages. Must be supported (installed).	Various/U.S. English	Only
FORCEPLAN	Defeats optimizer.	Off	Only

Setting Database Options

Several TSQL commands require you to set one or more SQL Server database options before they're accepted. Basically, you must ask permission to perform some operations. If you're going to administer your server from your application (I sometimes do), you must be able to set and reset these database options. When you set these options, the entire database and all users connected to it might be affected, not just your specific connection or workstation. Generally, I set these options only after carefully considering their impact, and I quickly set them back to normal when the transaction is completed. Here's a listing of the database options that can be set:

- *ANSI Null Default* allows the user to control the database default nullability. When not explicitly defined, a user-defined data type or a column definition will use the default setting for nullability. With this option set to TRUE, all user-defined data types or columns not explicitly defined as NOT NULL during a CREATE TABLE or ALTER TABLE statement will default to allowing Nulls.

- *DBO Use Only* sets a database for use only by the database owner. Active users of the database can continue to access the database, but no new users are allowed. When active users disconnect or change database context (with the USE statement), they won't be allowed access to this database again unless this option has been set to FALSE.

- *No Chkpt On Recovery* defines whether a checkpoint record is added to the database after it's recovered during a SQL Server startup. If this option is off (FALSE, the default), a checkpoint record is added.

CAUTION
It's really easy to toast the database while setting database options—trust me.

- *Offline* allows a database to be placed on line (when set to FALSE, the database is ready to be used) or off line (when set to TRUE, the database is unavailable and can't be used). This option is used primarily on databases with removable media devices, but it can be used on any database. (A database can't be placed off line if it has an active user.)

- *Published* allows the database to be published for replication. This option doesn't publish a database—it *permits* the tables of a database to be published. When set to TRUE, this option enables publishing and adds the user *repl_subscriber* to the database. When set to FALSE, it disables publishing, drops all publications, unmarks all transactions that were marked for replication in the transaction log, and removes the database user *repl_subscriber*.

- *Read Only* defines a read-only database. This option means that users can retrieve data from the database but can't modify anything. Because a read-only database doesn't allow data modification, automatic recovery is skipped at system startup.

- *Select Into/Bulk Copy* allows a database to accept nonlogged operations, which include using the UPDATETEXT or WRITETEXT statements, using SELECT INTO into a permanent table, using fast bulk copy (BCP), or performing a table load. This option need not be set to run BCP on a table that has indexes because tables with indexes are always copied with the slower version of BCP and are logged. Once all nonlogged operations are completed, turn off Select Into/Bulk Copy and issue the DUMP DATABASE statement. (Because SELECT is a keyword, you must enclose Select Into/Bulk Copy in quotation marks to avoid a syntax error.)

- *Single User* restricts database access to a single user. A user already accessing the database when this option is set to TRUE can continue to use the database.

- *Subscribed* allows the database to be subscribed for replication.

- *Trunc Log On Chkpt* causes the transaction log to be truncated (committed transactions are removed) every time the CHECKPOINT process occurs (usually once each minute).

If your application has to do quite a bit of this kind of work, you have to work out a reasonable strategy. Generally, use the Select Into/Bulk Copy option to enable Text/Image handling, BCP, and SELECT INTO permanent tables.

NOTE All the database options require you to be logged on as system administrator or database owner. If you're not the database owner or don't have access to the system administrator password, you simply won't be able to perform any of the more sophisticated functions that require run-time modification of the database options.

To set or reset the database options, you'll have to execute a system stored procedure: sp_dboption. To get this procedure to work, here is what you'll have to do:

1. Have *Master* as the default database.

2. Execute sp_dboption.

3. Run a Checkpoint operation against the affected database. (Nothing takes effect until you do.)

This stored procedure has three parameters: *DBName*, the database name where the changes are to be made; *OptName*, the database option to be changed; and *TRUE* or *FALSE*, to turn the option on or off. (These are string values passed to the stored procedure, not Boolean values.) You should pass the *OptName* option as a quoted string—it's easier. With the *OptName* option, you only need to use enough of the option name to make it unique. (Just the first word is enough.)

To turn on (set) the Select Into/Bulk Copy option, you'll have to code as follows:

CAUTION

Dump your database before you turn off the Select Into/Bulk Copy option. If you've inserted unlogged data into your database (which happens if you use the BCP, WRITETEXT, or SELECT INTO commands) and then try to perform a DUMP TRANSACTION before a DUMP DATABASE, you can't recover your data—not good! SQL Server is supposed to send you a warning if you try this.

`Db$=SQLName$(SQLConn)`	To find the current database name
`r=SQLUse(SQLConn, "Master")`	To set *Master* as default database
`r=SQLSendCmd("exec sp_dboption mydatabase,`	
`'select', true")`	To set the option
`r=SQLResults(SQLConn)`	Parse the results
`r=SQLUse(SQLConn, "MyDatabase")`	To set working database as default
`r=SQLSendCmd("Checkpoint")`	Checkpoint that database
`r=SQLResults(SQLConn)`	Parse the results
`r=SQLUse(SQLConn,DB$)`	Change back to the current database

NOTE You have to call SQLResults, even though you know that no results are possible from the preceding commands. You'll probably want to test for results after running sp_dboption, to make sure that your syntax is correct and that you really do have database owner or system administrator permission.

Other Administrative Operations

You'll probably want to perform any number of other SQL administrative functions from your application or write your own administrative applications tuned to your special needs. You have to be a system administrator or database owner to perform these operations, but that doesn't mean all your users have to have access to these passwords. Your application can log on behind the scenes as a system administrator or database owner to prepare the database for your operations.

You might want to (and you had better) back up the database between BULK COPY, SELECT INTO, and WRITETEXT operations that are not logged (and most are not). As another example, when your application (coupled with all the others running out there) fills up the transaction log, you can't continue until the log has been cleaned out. You'll have to dump the transaction log, if you can, to an incremental log—one created new each time. (All the versions are used in turn to recover the database at rebuild time.) If this isn't possible, you *must* dump the transaction log to the bit bucket (*dump transaction <mydb> with truncate_only*) and then, without fail, dump the database to a dump device. (At this point, the incremental transaction logs are not much good; they're based on the previous database dump.)

For my applications, I depend on the system administrator or automated procedures or both to perform periodic transaction-log dumps (or just daily database dumps). The new SQL Server Enterprise Manager can do these for you automatically. Get your system administrator to help you set these up. And heaven help you if you took the system administrator's password without permission.

Asynchronous Operations

The 16-bit Microsoft Windows operating system is a nonpreemptive, multitasking (but single-threaded) system. Unlike Microsoft Windows 95 or Microsoft Windows NT, it doesn't share the processor's time by passing control from thread to thread or process to process using the system clock. It can't preempt other tasks because 16-bit Windows programs are written so that they control how much CPU time they get and how much they share. Unless a 16-bit Windows application is written to share the processor time with others, those other applications can suffer whenever it runs.

Unfortunately, many applications, especially DB-Library applications, are written without regard for users' desire to do some other productive work while the SQL server crunches up their queries. That's when your users begin to say, "Can't you let us do other work while some of the longer queries are running? Our systems seem to lock up for minutes at a time. We can't seem to print or use the word processor or anything." At this point, you start to debug your code, looking for places where the workstation seems to lock up for long periods. Sooner or later, you're bound to discover that the culprit is SQLSendCmd or SQLExec (which SQLSendCmd uses internally). Can anything be done? How else can you send a query to DB-Library and get a response back from the SQL server?

How SQLExec Wastes Time

When you execute SQLSendCmd or SQLExec, DB-Library carries out the following operations:

- It takes a query string you provide (through SQLCmd or as a parameter to SQLSendCmd), builds a TDS packet, and sends it to the SQL server.

- It goes into a processing loop as it waits for a signal from the SQL server that your results are ready.

- It returns control to your application when the first result set is ready.

As **Figure 34-7** shows, your application doesn't get any CPU cycles from the time SQLExec starts until the first set of results from the SQL server is ready to process. This could take less than a second or up to the timeout value you set before you sent the query. (Your VBSQL error handler gets control if DB-Library decides, on the basis of the SQLSetTime value you set, that it has waited long enough.)

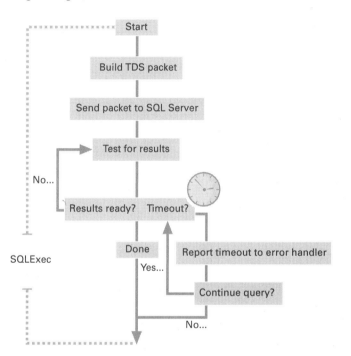

Figure 34-7   *Using SQLExec*

One approach to this problem is to remove the SQLSendCmd function declaration in your code and replace it with your own Visual Basic function (or C function) to do the same thing, only better. Don't try to just replace SQLExec and expect SQLSendCmd to use your function instead. SQLSendCmd is written in C and doesn't call the SQLExec entry point in your program; it calls the SQLExec entry point in the VBSQL support DLLs. But the first thing you have to do is decide which of your queries need this treatment. I don't recommend using this method for all of your VBSQL operations—many of them take so little time that there's no need to go to the trouble of coding them to be more user-sensitive.

Post/Wait logic

Never heard of it? Neither had I before I got involved with mainframe computers in the early 1970s. This term refers to applications that set up a two-part logic set, which begins (posts) a task and then blocks (waits) until it is complete. In real multitasking systems like Windows NT, you can program your application to block (go to sleep) on an event that the operating system waits for. When the event occurs, your application is reawakened by the OS. In 16-bit Windows, there is no such facility, so you have to fake it in your code. Terminology aside, we're really talking about asynchronous operations.

Remember that the problem with SQLExec is that it doesn't yield any CPU time while waiting for the SQL server to return the first set of results. What we need to do is send the query and get control back immediately. With that done, we can do more productive work locally or just give control back (yield) to Windows in case there is work to be done in other applications.

Using the SQLSend command

All you really have to do is use the SQLSend command (and its associated cousins) instead of SQLExec. SQLSend transmits a query string to the SQL server (which begins to process it at once) but returns control directly to your application. In contrast to SQLSendCmd, you *must* send the query to the DB-Library command buffer via the SQLCmd function. Its syntax looks like this:

```
Dim Query$
Dim R

Query$ = "Select * from pigfarmers where legs != 'dirty' "

R = SQLCmd(SQLConn, Query$)
R = SQLSend(SQLConn)
```

This query might take some time. As anyone could tell you, pig farmers' legs aren't indexed, so the SQL server must do a row scan and search every row in the table.

Once you have sent your command, you can exit the subroutine and not test for the results until the following conditions exist:

- The user selects another control.
- Your Timer event goes off.
- The cows come home in a 1946 Plymouth.

If your query has a syntax error, such as when you misspell SELECT or leave off a quote, SQLSend won't tell you. As far as I can see, the only thing that could cause SQLSend to fail is a bad connection handle or an unforeseen problem on the server end. We don't get an indication that the query has bad syntax or other errors until you execute SQLOK.

Using SQLDataReady

Once you have submitted your query, you can test for the readiness of the query results by calling SQLDataReady, which also returns immediately if the SQL server has not completed the query—but with *FAIL* as the return code.

SQLDataReady returns *SUCCEED* if there is even as little as a single byte of data ready from your query. The SQL server might not have finished your query, but some of the data is ready to come back. For example, consider the following query:

```
WAITFOR DELAY '00:90:00'
```

SQLDataReady does not return *SUCCEED* for 90 minutes—after the WAITFOR is complete.

NOTE SQL Server won't return anything until the connection cache is full or the query completes.

Now look at this query:

```
SELECT * from PIGS
WAITFOR DELAY '00:90:00'
```

The SQL server will return results almost immediately, but the query won't complete itself for another 90 minutes, and the application will be blocked until it is.

TIP Your application can reduce the chance of locking up by using SQLDataReady *before* any calls are made to SQLResults and SQLNextRow. But if you call SQLDataReady before SQLResults is going to return *NO_MORE_RESULTS*, SQLDataReady will *never* return *SUCCEED*. Use SQLMoreCmds to test for more pending result sets. When SQLMoreCmds returns *SUCCEED*, you can safely call SQLResults.

Knowing when to poll

The timing of when you poll for results can have a significant impact on the performance of your workstation and also on the server's performance. If you ask DB-Library to poll the SQL server too often, you waste your workstation's time and interrupt the server. Another method is to open another connection to the server, examine the *SysProcesses* table, and look for the status of your query. When it falls asleep, you have a completed query.

Fishing for results

I placed a SQLDataReady in a Timer event that was set to go off about once every two seconds. That way, the first test for completion didn't occur for two seconds after the SQLSend. Should you also do a SQLDataReady immediately

When the server is spending more time saying "Not yet!" than processing queries, it is being polled far too often. That kind of constant polling is one sign of an incorrectly written DB-Library application.

upon sending the query (with SQLSend) to see if there was a syntax error? "Immediately" might be too soon. I would still give the server at least 0.5 to 2 seconds before testing for successful compilation. Most of my queries have either executed or failed by then. If you use the timer method, the 2 seconds go by soon enough. Remember, we're using this method for queries that are more complex and usually take quite a bit of clock time to get results. Waiting an extra second shouldn't perceptibly change any application. The timer interval you set should be a function of the query. See how long it usually takes, and after a first, fairly quick test, don't check again until you have reached a point that is within 80 percent of the completion time, and then not again until 90 percent of the time has passed. Of course, you'll want to try altering the logic to meet the needs of your individual query.

Here's a code segment that can be used to substitute for SQLSendCmd (which I have been encouraging you to use up to this point). Notice the third parameter, which indicates whether the logic is supposed to block and wait for the query to complete (use SQLExec) or let the Timer1 timer poll for the results. (This timer routine doesn't have sophisticated, staggered timing.)

```
Function SQLSendNow(SQLConn, Query$, SendNow) As Integer
Dim R
If SendNow = TRUE Then
R = SQLSendCmd(SQLConn, Query$)
Else
    R = SQLCmd (SQLConn, Query$)
    R = SQLSend(SQLConn)                ' Send the query off for
                                        ' processing

    MyTimeOut = 0                       ' Clear the timeout value
    Timer1.Duration = 2000              ' Don't poll for two
                                        ' seconds
If R = SUCCEED Then Timer1.Enabled = TRUE
' If it didn't go, don't enable timer.
End If
SQLSendNow = R                          ' Pass back the return
                                        ' code...

End Sub


Sub Timer1_Timer()
Dim R

MyTimeout = MyTimeout&Timer1.Duration   ' Keep track of how long we
                                        ' do this
If MyTimeout > MaxWaitTime Then
    R = TimeOutConst                    ' Tell mainline that the
                                        ' query timed out
Else
    If SQLDataReady(SQLconn) = SUCCEED Then
        R = SQLOK(SQLConn)
        Timer1.Enabled = False
```

```
        If R = SUCCEED Then
            FillGridButton.Enabled = True
        Else
            FillGridButton.Enabled = False
            ' If it didn't come back in 2 seconds,
            ' don't check for another 4 seconds.
            Timer1.Duration = 4000
        End If
    End If
End If

GlobalReturnCode = R                    ' Save result of query;
                                        ' it might have failed

End Sub
```

One of the most serious things that can go wrong with any query is its failure to complete—ever. That the query might have been submitted with SQLSend has nothing to do with its potential for success. If the SQL server finds that it can't resolve a deadlock situation, the connection fails, the net fails, or some other global component fails, and you might never get a *SUCCEED* from SQLDataReady. If you sent the query with SQLSendCmd or SQLExec, your workstation is hopelessly locked—forever. In this case, the only recourse is to put the workstation out of its misery with a warm boot (unless you can get Windows to terminate the DB-Library application—good luck).

Fortunately, your application is in control if you used SQLSend *and did not call* SQLOK. If so, you have lots of choices. Your application can time out locally, but it won't time out on the basis of the SQLSetTime value. DB-Library timeouts are apparently disabled if you use SQLSend. Once you've decided that your application has waited long enough, you can ask your user if she wants to continue waiting or give up the query. At this point, you might open an additional connection to test the viability of the SQL server. If it's still out there, there's a possibility that your query is involved in a locking condition that can't be resolved or is just taking longer than expected because of the workload. If you submit a SQLCancel or SQLCanQuery, the SQL server might free up resources held by your application, thus giving the system a chance to clear up the deadlock. And then again, it might not.

Using SQLOK

After SQLDataReady returns *SUCCEED*, you *must* call SQLOK to get DB-Library to pull over the first set of results from the SQL server. Once you call SQLOK, the API works just as when you use SQLSendCmd or SQLExec. You might also use SQLOK before SQLDataReady returns *SUCCEED*.

SQLOK returns *SUCCEED* if the query compiled, "linked," and ran. Its return code can be *FAIL* for the same reasons that SQLSendCmd or SQLExec fails (usually TSQL syntax errors).

Another Look

Let's look at the program flow once more, this time with SQLCmd, SQLSend, SQLDataReady, and SQLOK instead of SQLSendCmd. (See *Figure 34-8*.) This design is a little more complicated, but it enables a significant amount of functionality, which is simply turned off if your application uses SQLSendCmd or SQLExec.

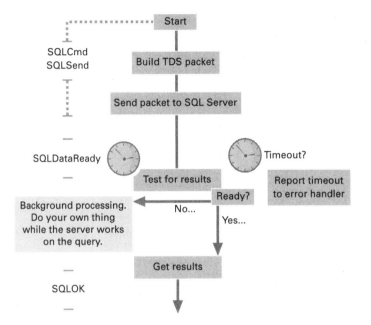

Figure 34-8   *Program flow without SQLSendCmd*

35 Chapter

Managing Page-Based Data

Accessing Text
and Image Data Types

Allocating Space for the Data

TSQL Support for
Saving Page-Based Data

Using VBSQL to Save
and Retrieve Page-Based Data

Using VBSQL
Page-Based Functions

Inserting Page-Based
Data with VBSQL

ome time ago, I spoke with a company in Houston that wanted advice on accessing medical imagery to be stored in a SQL Server database. After a while, I discovered that the data changed only infrequently, since these images showed examples and X rays of typical medical conditions. "Why keep these images in the database?" I asked. "Can't they be recorded on CDs and then accessed like files? That way, a database search could locate the right image and just pass the filename to Visual Basic and Visual Basic could use the LoadPicture function with an Image control to display the image."

The moral of the story is that SQL Server is perfectly capable of saving large blocks of page-based data, but this might not be the best idea. When the data you are managing is relatively static or when it already requires special applications so that it can be managed, it might be a better idea to use the database for storing pointers to the data rather than storing the data itself.

Accessing Text and Image Data Types

SQL Server treats both Text and Image data columns as special cases that need customized sets of functions. In almost all cases, the functions that work with the Text data type also work with the Image data type. I call both Text and Image data types *page-based data types,* since they are managed by SQL Server in 2-KB data pages.

Two notable features of Microsoft SQL Server 6.*x* are its ability to pass page-based data types as parameters to stored procedures and its addition of the UPDATETEXT TSQL statement. When you append new data to a string in an existing column, you can now pass the Text value via a stored procedure to a routine that uses the UPDATETEXT statement to concatenate the passed value to the existing Text column's value. This strategy is faster than the old method of reading the entire Text value, concatenating the new string, and sending back the newly created composite string.

Allocating Space for the Data

SQL Server treats the Text and Image (page-based) data types differently from the other data types. The server doesn't allocate database space in the row until there's actually some data to store. This saves room in the database, since the SQL server defers allocating space until the first insert or update affects the page-based element. When you store the first byte of data in a page-based column, SQL Server allocates a 2-KB page to hold it. The element stored in the data row column is really a pointer to the first 2-KB page holding the actual data. This first 2-KB page also contains a TimeStamp value for the element and a pointer to the next page in the chain (if there is one). Each subsequent 2-KB page also contains a pointer to the next page, so we have a linked list of pages. The first page pointer is needed whenever we want to access data from later pages. Once allocated, the first 2-KB space is never deallocated, regardless of the length of the data. The only way to eliminate this remaining overhead is to delete the entire row.

TSQL Support for Saving Page-Based Data

You can choose from an entire set of TSQL commands to support the Text and Image data types. Both are treated as virtually identical and really differ only in the types of conversions permitted. SQL Server 4.2 and later versions support the search for Text and Image data types with PATINDEX, and Text is permitted as an argument in LIKE expressions. You can also use the SETTEXTSIZE function to set (limit) the amount of page-based data that SELECT statements return. But you can't use the Text (or Image) data field in the following ways:

- *In a WHERE clause, except with the keyword* like. The following query *is* permitted with the Text column History:

```
Select * from Animals
where History like 'kicks' or History like 'bucks'
```

- *As an argument passed to a stored procedure or as a parameter in a stored procedure.*

- *As a declared local variable.*

- *In an ORDER BY, COMPUTE, or GROUP BY clause.*

- *In an index.*

Using VBSQL to Save and Retrieve Page-Based Data

Up to a point, using page-based data can be as easy as using the Char data type. Nothing really needs to be done differently unless you intend to *retrieve* more than the first 4192 characters (4 KB) of a long page-based string. In other words, you can treat a page-based column the way you treat a simple string.

To save a long page-based string (up to the capacity of the DB-Library command buffer—about 128 KB—or Visual Basic's ability to handle long strings), just concatenate your data string to the INSERT or UPDATE statement:

```
Dim A As String * 32768
Get #1,,A$     ' Pretend we are reading the string from a file…
r = SQLSendCmd$(SQLConn, "UPDATE Animals Set Story = ' "& A$ & "'"
```

This method works fine right up to the point where the string (*A$*) has an embedded single quote (*'*), because we framed our page-based string with single quotes. There are several alternative approaches we can use to solve this problem:

- *Replace all instances of the single quote (') with two single quotes ('').*

- *Replace the outer framing quotes with double quotes (") and all instances of embedded double quotes with pairs of double quotes ("").*

- *Remove all embedded quotes that match the framing quotes.*

- *Punt.*

This seems like a somewhat time-consuming job to do for every page-based column you want to save. If you have data too long to fit in the command buffer or too long for Visual Basic to handle easily, or if you don't want to munge the quotes, you'll have to use the SQLWriteText method.

Using VBSQL Page-Based Functions

To get shorter strings back from the SQL server, all you need to do is call the SQLData function to retrieve page-based columns, just as you do with any other type of column. If you want to pull back more than 4 KB of data, however, you have to use the page-based functions.

Several low-level API functions have been designed to handle the peculiar problems of large page-based data types. There are also a number of utility functions that can compress the time to program (and run) these operations.

SQLTxPtr$

To work with a long string, you have to ask DB-Library to fetch a pointer to the chosen string element. This pointer is different for each page-based column in every row (each element). Note that this pointer isn't returned from the SQL server as a 16-byte VarBinary number; it's returned by VBSQL as a string. It's perfectly safe to save this identifier in an array or another variable. We use this identifier string with the SQLWriteText command.

> **NOTE** The value returned by SQLTxPtr becomes invalid if you execute a new query on the *SQLConn* that retrieved it or if you use SQLCancel or SQLCanQuery.

How can you update or insert a page-based element without putting the whole page-based string in the command buffer? Isn't that what we are using the APIs for? Because nothing is really stored in the SQL server until something is assigned to the column, what you need to do is set up a query that assigns something—in this case, a dummy placeholder—to the target element, so that this structure is built on the SQL server. It's not a good idea to do this to all the rows in the table as a way of saving time; it will cost a minimum of 2 KB of database space per element changed. With this structure set up for the chosen row, you can fetch the page-based pointer for that row with a subsequent call.

> **TIP** The page-based data pointer is kept internally in the SQL server as a VarBinary. If you're fetching a pointer to a page-based element where there was none before, you have to create it first. In other words, if there's no data in the page-based column of the row in question before you try to get a pointer to it, you'll have to execute an INSERT or UPDATE against the element to activate it. You can't get a valid pointer from a page-based element that hasn't had data written to it—the page simply doesn't exist. You can execute a SQLTxPtr function against the element to see if there is a valid Text pointer available.

Here's some code that you might want to clone (put in the name of your own table and columns) if you need to insert a new row with a page-based column. There's nothing magic about it; you simply use the TSQL INSERT statement. What we are doing is getting the SQL server to initialize the page-based pointer and build the first 2-KB data page. If the row has already been initialized (the page-based element isn't null) and if you merely want to update the contents of the page-based column, skip this first step. (Note that *History* is stored with a Text data type in our fictitious *Animals* table.)

```
r = SQLSendCmd(SQLConn, "INSERT Animals (History) " _
    & " Values ( ' a placeholder ' ) " _
    & " Where Name = 'Bossie' ")
r = SQLResults(SQLConn)
' … test for success - There can be no rows -
' No need to do a SQLNextRow…
```

Now that the page-based column of the selected row has been initialized, we can fetch the Text pointer to that element's first data page. (Note that we're also pulling back a TimeStamp value in this routine, which is used later to see if the page-based column was changed by some other user while we were busy getting ready to update it.)

```
r = SQLSendCmd(SQLConn, "Select History From Animals " _
    & " where Name = 'Bossie' ")
Do While SQLResults(SQLConn) <> NOMORERESULTS
    Do While SQLNextRow(SQLConn) <> NOMOREROWS
        TextPointer$ = SQLTxPtr$ (SQLConn, 1)
        RowTimeStamp$ = SQLTxTimeStamp$(SQLConn, 1)
    Loop
Loop
```

Of course, this routine *should* get only one row back. If it gets more, only the *last* row is referenced by the Text pointer—better tighten up your table's keys or the WHERE clause. Remember, you still have to do the SQLResults and SQLNextRow to get DB-Library to recognize the row (even if there is only one). There's no reason why you can't do a SQLSend, SQLDataReady, SQLOK sequence on this command, but if it affects only one row, there's little need for it; we haven't sent the bulk of the page-based data yet.

SQLWriteText and SQLTimeStamp

At this point, we're almost ready to update the row and column specified by the *TextPointer$* identifier with the bulk of the page-based data. The SQLWriteText function sets up (but doesn't complete) this update for us. Note the SQLTxpLen argument, which must always be used (until DB-Library supports more than 16 *somethings*).

We also include the TimeStamp value we acquired earlier. If the data's changed since we obtained the TimeStamp value, the SQLWriteText function fails. When the page-based data element changes, its associated TimeStamp value is updated by the SQL server. Only SQLWriteText has tested for a change in this value, comparing it to the value fetched by the previous INSERT or UPDATE query. When SQLWriteText is finished, it makes the new TimeStamp value for the Text column available to DB-Library. If we're using row buffering, we have to store that value in the buffer with the page-based data. Then, if we want to do another SQLWriteText from the buffer, the value will be available.

In addition, we include the length of the data to be sent in the form of a Long. The new Len function in Visual Basic supports strings of virtually any length. We also have to tell the SQLWriteText function whether the operation is to be logged. All queries that change the database are recorded on the database's transaction log.

CAUTION

The VBSQL documentation says that you can invoke SqlWriteText with or without logging on. I don't think so! I assume the documentation is referring to the Log option, which turns transaction logging on or off. (After all these years, this bug is still in the documentation and has been propagated to online help and Books Online.)

NOTE In a few cases, the system administrator can tell SQL Server to bypass logging. These cases assume the logging operation deals with imported data that can easily be reconstructed if something goes wrong.

If you don't want to log the transaction (for example, if you're afraid of filling up the transaction log with a couple of Text inserts), you must first turn on the Select Into/Bulk Copy option. (Use *SP_DBOPTION <database>, "select", True* while logged on to the *Master* database—but only if you have system administrator or database owner permission.) You should also back up the database after the bulk update of page-based data columns. The DUMP DATABASE (backup) command saves the database image in case a recovery is needed later.

Even if you log the SQLWriteText operation, you might still want to back up the database and truncate the transaction log to free the inactive portion. Here are typical TSQL commands used by the system administrator or database owner to back up a database to an existing dump device, *Animal_Dump*:

```
Dump Database Animals to Animal_Dump
Dump Transaction Animals with Truncate_only
```

One other concern comes up at this point: Visual Basic 3.0 strings have a length limit of approximately 65,500 bytes. This is no longer a problem in the 32-bit versions of Visual Basic, but it continues to be a concern for the 16-bit versions. This string length is far shorter than the maximum length of a page-based data element ($2^{31} - 1$ or 2,147,483,647 bytes). String lengths in excess of 64 KB are problematic. (Actually, strings longer than 32 KB are tough to handle unless you create them ahead of time and don't try to concatenate two strings together to arrive at a string length greater than 32 KB.) If you declare a string in a procedure to hold anything larger than the capacity of the stack, you're forced to create the string in a global module. (With Visual Basic 2.0 and later versions, all modules are global.) It's best to create this string as a fixed-length string so that you won't have to deal with the problems of concatenation. Try this in a module (instead of in one of the form declaration areas):

```
Global My_String as String * 65000
```

Once you have created a string to hold the data, the next question you'll have to answer is where these long strings come from. If you're reading data from a file, you can pass the data buffers directly to SQLWriteText, or to SQLMoreText if the data is larger. In either case, you'll still have to deal with blocks of data less than 64 KB long. If the data is coming from a data collection source (data entry from the user or from something like a modem), just watch out for concatenating the data into pieces too large for Visual Basic to handle. Be sure to use Long (&) pointers in dealing with these strings, since Integer pointers will be able to cover only the first half of the string (unless you do some fancy footwork with negative numbers).

Establishing Permission to Bypass Logging

The WriteTextToServer function first checks to see whether the database has permission to avoid logging the transaction. A user with system administrator or database owner permissions can make the needed changes to the database options. If the user doesn't have either of these permissions, the routines fail with appropriate errors.

It's best to send larger blocks of data (in the range of 8–20 KB) to the SQL server. If a shared server has to thrash around too much to add your new data, this might have an adverse impact on other workstations' performance. It might also affect your own workstation's performance. And if you're logging the operation (I wouldn't), your impact on system performance is almost doubled. You should pare down the size of the procedure cache to the point whoro you'll havo onough data cache to get your operation through in the shortest possible time.

You can get error 3505—"Only DBO of database may perform a CHECK-POINT"—if a non-DBO user attempts to do the Checkpoint operation, which is required after the SP_DBOPTION procedure is used to change the Select Into/Bulk Copy option. You don't get these permission errors until you try to run the Checkpoint, since none of the changes take place until then.

Coding SQLWriteText and SQLMoreText

We won't send the actual data with SQLWriteText. We'll do that with SQLMoreText commands that follow directly afterward, since we have to concatenate the Text string to the command. This routine expects that the string to be printed will be passed *by reference,* not on the stack. When you use this combination of APIs, the SQL server locks the row involved to prevent any other updates from conflicting with the transaction. No other application can select or update the data while this lock is in place.

If you don't use SQLMoreText, the SQLWriteText call does everything, including calling SQLOK and SQLResults. Setting the *Text$* argument in SQLWriteText to a null string ("") requests the SQLMoreText method:

```
Option Explicit
Function WriteTextToServer(SQLConn, A$, TextPointer$, _
    RowTimeStamp$) As Integer
Const FAIL1 = 1            ' SQLWriteText failed
Const FAIL2 = 2            ' SQLWriteMoreText failed
Const FAIL3 = 3            ' Final SQLResults failed
Dim r, i, Db$, Logged, Tlen&, ChunkSize&, Chunk$

Tlen& = Len(A$)
Db$=SQLName$( SQLConn)   ' Fetch the name of the current database

r = CheckForPermission(SQLConn, DB$)

' Do we have permission to do nonlogged ops?
If r = FAIL Then
    r = SetSelectIntoPermission(SQLConn, DB$, "TRUE")

    if r = FAIL then Logged = TRUE else Logged = FALSE
End If

If Tlen > 8192 Then ChunkSize = 8192 Else ChunkSize = Tlen
r = SQLWriteText(SQLConn, "Text_table.Text_col", TextPointer$, _
    SQLTXPLEN, RowTimeStamp$, Logged, Tlen, "")
If r <> FAIL Then
    i = 1
    Do  ' Break the Text into ChunkSize pieces
        Chunk$ = Mid$(A$, i, ChunkSize)
        r = SQLMoreText(SQLConn, ChunkSize, Chunk$)
        If r <> SUCCEED Then Exit Do
        i = i & ChunkSize
```

```
        If i & ChunkSize > Tlen Then ChunkSize = Tlen - i & 1
    Loop While i < Tlen And ChunkSize > 0

    If r <> SUCCEED Then
        MsgBox ("The attempt to write a block of Text to the" _
                & " server failed.")
        WriteTextToServer = FAIL2
        Exit Function

    End If
Else
    MsgBox ("The attempt to start writing a block of Text" _
            & " to the server failed.")
    WriteTextToServer = FAIL1
    Exit Function
End If
r = SQLOK(SQLConn)

r = r & SQLResults(SQLConn)
If r = SUCCEED & SUCCEED Then
    WriteTextToServer = SUCCEED
    Exit Function
Else
    MsgBox ("The attempt to complete writing a block of Text" _
            & " to the server failed. Suspect invalid server" _
            & " permissions")
    WriteTextToServer = FAIL3
End If
End Function

Function CheckForPermission(SQLConn, DB$) As Integer
Dim Query$, Options$
Dim r
Static OneShot

If OneShot <> 0 Then CheckForPermission = True
OneShot = 1
Screen.MousePointer = HOURGLASS
CheckForPermission = FAIL
r = SQLSendCmd(SQLConn, "Sp_helpdb " & DB$)
If R = SUCCEED Then
    Do
        Do While SQLNextRow(SQLConn) <> NOMOREROWS
            If SQLNumCols(SQLConn) >= 6 Then _
                If SQLColName$(SQLConn, 6) = "status" Then _
                Options$ = SQLData$(SQLConn, 6)
        Loop
    Loop While SQLResults(SQLConn) <> NOMORERESULTS
End If
If Options$ = "" Then
```

(continued)

```
        MsgBox "Could not test for permissions on " & DB$ & _
            " database"
        GoTo CheckExit
    End If
    If InStr(Options$, "select") Then CheckForPermission = SUCCEED
    CheckExit:
    Screen.MousePointer = DEFAULT
    r = SQLCancel(SQLConn)
    End Function


    Function SetSelectIntoPermission(SQLConn, DB$, State$)
    Dim Query$, CurrentDb$, r
    SetSelectIntoPermission = FAIL
    CurrentDb$ = SQLName$(SQLConn)
    r = SQLUse(SQLConn, "Master")
    r = SQLSendCmd(SQLConn, "Sp_dboption " & DB$ & ", 'select', " _
                    & State$)
    If r = FAIL Then
        MsgBox "Could not change system option to permit" _
            & " unlogged Text operation on " & DB$ & " database."
        GoTo ExitGetSelect
    End If
    SetSelectIntoPermission = True
    ExitGetSelect:
    r = SQLUse(SQLConn, CurrentDb$)
    r = SQLSendCmd(SQLConn, "Checkpoint")
    End Function
```

What Can Go Wrong?

With a set of commands as complicated as these, lots of things can go wrong. One surprising aspect of such failures is their timing. When you use the method just shown (with SQLWriteText sending a null string and SQLMore-Text sending the bulk of the page-based data), you won't see an error until the SQLOK or SQLResults at the end if there is a problem with logging or the transaction. If you don't send the number of bytes specified in the SQLWriteText command before sending SQLOK, you get an error. These errors trigger events in the error and message handlers. Remember that the Text pointer created can point to only one row at a time. TextPtr returns the *last* row that matches the WHERE clause—it can point to only one element.

CAUTION
The procedure sp_help is notoriously slow in executing. I have brought down perfectly functional networks when this stored procedure forced a timeout.

Inserting Page-Based Data with VBSQL

As *Figure 35-1* shows, writing page-based data is only slightly more complex than writing normal rows to the database. Remember that you are working with a special pointer to the data page, one that has to be created before you start adding information.

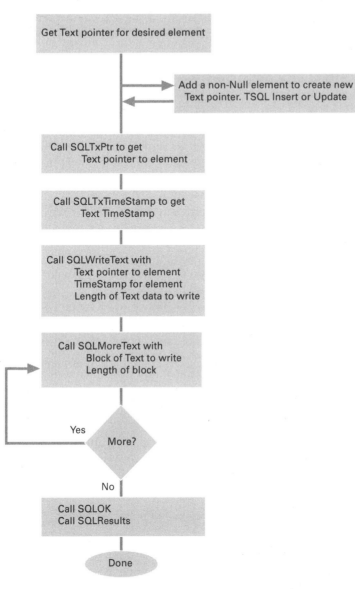

Figure 35-1   *Using SQLWriteText and SQLMoreText*

Another alternative to using individual commands for updating a chosen row in a table is to use the C-based utility functions SQLTextUpdate1Row and SQLTextUpdateManyRows. These VBSQL functions, added to the DLL, combine the functions used to perform the most common of the Text operations—updating one row and updating multiple rows.

Coding SQLTextUpdate1Row and SQLTextUpdateManyRows

Using SQLTextUpdate1Row is the equivalent of calling SQLTxPtr to retrieve the page-based data pointer, SQLTxTsPut to update the TimeStamp value, and SQLWriteText to write the page-based data to the server. To use SQLText-Update1Row, set up a pending query on the desired row. After you have called SQLNextRow, SQLTextUpdate1Row is ready to update the current row. Note that the Text passed to the function is limited to one Visual Basic string. The parameters for SQLTextUpdate1Row are *SQLConn* (to indicate the connection), *DatabaseName.Tablename* (to identify which table is to be updated), *Column-Number* (to identify which column is to be updated—column numbers start at 1), and *DataValue* (to identify the page-based data to be placed in the selected column). SQLTextUpdate1Row returns *SUCCEED* (1) or *FAIL* (0).

As you can see, SQLTextUpdate1Row is far easier to implement than the fairly complex set of commands surrounding SQLWriteText, but it might be overkill as opposed to just sending out an UPDATE command with the page-based data string attached.

Coding SQLTextUpdateManyRows

This function works in conjunction with a pending query. Unlike any other command in the VBSQL library, this command requires use of a second live connection. You have to open an additional connection before calling the function, or you need an available unused connection that has no results pending. This function is also unusual in that it updates *all* rows of a table, starting from the current row (as determined by SQLNextRow).

Setup is fairly easy. First, execute a query on a table, followed by a call to SQLResults. If you want to update the entire table, don't call SQLNextRow. If you want to skip down first, call SQLNextRow as many times as needed or phrase the query to start deeper in the table. Once SQLTextUpdateManyRows takes off, it places a fixed Text value in each row after that point. This could be very costly, since it appears to be a logged operation and creates a new 2-KB data page for every row affected that did not already have one. Of course, if the Text value was Null, all but the first data page are freed. The parameters for this function are *SQLConn* (to indicate the connection), *SQLConn#2* (to indicate a second connection with no results pending), *DatabaseName.Table-Name* (to identify which table is to be updated), *ColumnNumber* (to identify which column is to be updated—column numbers start at 1), and *DataValue* (to indicate the page-based data to be placed in the selected column in all subsequent rows, starting at the current position). SQLTextUpdateManyRows returns *SUCCEED* (1) or *FAIL* (0).

Retrieving Page-Based Data

Now that we've saved some page-based data, we must deal with getting it back out of the SQL server. Generally, there are no specific VBSQL functions used to extract page-based data from the server. You should set one or more system options again to set or limit the amount of data returned by the SELECT statement. Set the Set TextSize *nn* option (or SQLTextSize) to an appropriate value before you make a query on the page-based column of your choice. SQLTextLimit *also* needs to be set to a value between 0 and 32767 to tell DB-Library to set or limit the size of the longest page-based string passed back to your application.

We fetch the page-based Text pointer for the element desired by using the page-based TSQL command TextPtr. This 16-byte VarBinary value is needed later on, in the TSQL READTEXT statement. READTEXT is used to fetch the data, one chunk at a time. Note that the Text pointer returns the *last* row that matches the WHERE clause—it can point to only one element.

READTEXT takes the following arguments: the table and column names (to identify the source of the page-based data), a valid page-based Text pointer, as created with TextPtr (to indicate the elements to be fetched), an offset, which is a value between 0 and the length of the element −1 (to indicate the number of bytes to skip before fetching), and the number of bytes to be read, or 0, which returns 4096 bytes (4 KB).

On the next page, you'll find a list of the TSQL statements you must submit to fetch a section of the page-based data in the database. The list also includes descriptions of the various statements to walk you through them. There are no sneaky tricks here. You might want to add logic to fetch only a specific-length piece at the end to accommodate the actual length of the data in the column.

Managing TimeStamps

A number of other VBSQL functions are needed to help manage the TimeStamp values used in the management of page-based data rows. These functions are similar to the TimeStamp management functions used in Browse mode, but they're designed to work on the current page-based data rows. Remember that each modification to a page-based data element (not just to the row) changes its TimeStamp value. If you want to fetch or change this value, you'll need to use the functions SQLTxTimeStamp, SQLTxTsNewVal, and SQLTxTsPut.

SQLTxTimeStamp

This function returns a TimeStamp for a chosen column in the *current* row (as determined by SQLNextRow). If there's no TimeStamp (for an uninitialized page-based element), a null string is returned. This function takes two parameters: *SQLConn*, a valid connection handle; and *Column*, the number (starting with 1) of the page-based column.

SQLTxTsNewVal

After you call SQLWriteText, the TimeStamp value you might have fetched before with SQLTxTimeStamp is no longer valid, since the SQL server has replaced it with the time of the update (if it was successful). To fetch this new value, use the SQLTxTsNewVal function. It takes only one parameter: *SQLConn*, a valid connection handle.

`Send:(SQLSendCmd)`	Gets the length of the data desired.
`Select datalength(Text_col)`	
`    from Text_table`	
`    where … …`	
`r = SQLResults(SQLConn)`	Fetches the results of the query.
`r = SQLNextRow(SQLConn)`	
`TextLen& = Val(SQLData(SQLConn,1))`	Gets the answer to the query. (Note the Long data type.) We now know the length of the page-based data in the desired column.
`Buffer (SQLCmd): Set TextSize = 8192`	We'll limit any return to 8 KB.
`Buffer (SQLCmd):`	Holds the page-based Text pointer.
`Declare @TP varbinary (16)`	Queries for the data itself, using the Text pointer provided for the chosen column.
`    Select @TP = TextPtr(Text_col)`	
`    from Text_table`	
`    where …`	
`Buffer(SQLCmd):`	
`READText Text_table.Text_col`	Indicates the table and column…
`    @val`	the Text pointer…
`    0`	the offset…
`    8192`	and says we want to read the first 8 KB.
`Repeat READText for each block desired`	Gives instructions to bump offset block size (8192) each time.
`Buffer(SQLCmd):`	
`READText Text_table.Text_col`	Indicates the table and column…
`    @val`	the Text pointer…
`    8192`	the offset for the next block…
`    8192`	and says we want to read the second 8 KB.
`r=SQLExec(SQLConn)`	Executes the command buffer (you can use SQLSend instead).
`r = SQLResults(SQLConn)`	Gets the result set.
`r = SQLNextRow(SQLConn)`	Gets the row(s). Each READTEXT passes back a row.
`TextData$ = TextData$ &`	Builds up the result set (32 KB, or 4 rows, is the limit, unless you use another strategy).
`SQLData$(SQLConn,1)`	

SQLTxTsPut

The SQLTxTsPut function changes the TimeStamp column in the current row, as held by DB-Library. When a successful update takes place, the TimeStamp value is changed on the first page in the database but not in the current row kept in memory by DB-Library. If you want to update the row again, you must have the latest TimeStamp value in the current row. Note that you need to run SQLQual$ again to build a new WHERE clause for Browse mode operations. The parameters are *SQLConn* (a valid connection handle), a new TimeStamp value (as returned from SQLTxTsNewVal), and *Column*, the number (starting with 1) of the page-based column.

36
Chapter

Running Bulk Copy via API

Understanding Bulk Copy

BCP: The Executable

Establishing Permission to Use BCP

Alternatives to the BCP API

A Bird's-Eye View of the Bulk Copy API

Bulk copy is generally misunderstood. For the most part, it gains its reputation from the BCP command-line utility that many of us have learned to love—and hate. This chapter discusses how to use the little-known Visual Basic BCP functions. Although these functions are also available in C, I would hesitate to recommend that approach.

Understanding Bulk Copy

The Visual Basic SQL Library contains a set of functions whose sole purpose is to facilitate the exporting and importing of bulk table data. Included with the SQL Server Programmer's Toolkit applications is a program that implements these functions in C—namely, BCP.EXE. So that you'll understand what your options are, I'll outline the features and functionality of the executable. One of the Microsoft SQL Server version 6.*x* enhancements is the ability to execute multiple BCP sessions; this wasn't possible with SQL Server 4.2.

One of the most common problems with BCP is the failure to properly initialize the LoginRec *before* opening the BCP connection. Remember to hardcode a value of 1 (one), not *True*, when setting up the LoginRec BCP enable flag with SQLBCPSetL:

```
Dim LoginRec as Integer
LoginRec = SQLLogin()
I = SQLBCPSetL(LoginRec, 1)     ' Set the enable property to "True"
```

BCP: The Executable

BCP.EXE is designed to perform the following operations:

- Copy a chosen table's data from SQL Server to a file.
- Copy a file to a chosen SQL Server table.

- Copy data from one SQL server to another.
- Select and format data being copied, using a format file.

BCP converses in ASCII. It can read or write almost any flat-file format—as long as you can define the format. BCP expects to see delimited fields in a record and identically formatted records. It can't read other database files, such as dBASE or Microsoft Jet files.

BCP appends data (via an INSERT) to the chosen table. It can't access more than one table at a time, but the database might have triggers enabled that can affect other tables. Data copied *out* of the SQL server with BCP overwrites the output file; it doesn't append to the file.

Establishing Permission to Use BCP

Not everyone will have permission to run BCP, since it accesses the *SysObjects*, *SysColumns*, and *SysIndexes* tables in addition to the target table. You also have to take into account how the Select Into/Bulk Copy option is set.

If the target table has indexes, BCP automatically uses the—well, "not fast" mode. If you're the system administrator or database owner, you can set this option with the following ISQL script:

```
Use Master
go
sp_dboption my_database, "select", true
go
Use my_database
Checkpoint
```

The "Fast" Mode

If the table doesn't have indexes, you have no choice; you'll have to use the "fast" version of BCP. All you really need to do to enable "fast" mode is access a table that doesn't have indexes. If the table had indexes before the upload operation, it *might* make sense to drop them first instead of having the SQL server update the indexes for each row as the server appends to the table. If the Create Index operation took most of last week to run, however, you might want to reconsider dropping it before using BCP to upload a half-dozen new accounts. It's up to you.

Defaults, Rules, and Triggers

If the table has default values set for particular columns, they're substituted, as required. BCP doesn't necessarily require that the data for each field be uploaded. In the case of Null values being sent, the default value would be substituted. To save time, triggers and rules defined for the target table are *not* executed.

TIP It might be easier just to do an INSERT instead of retesting the rules and rerunning the triggers after the load. You can always set up a stored procedure to run the rules and triggers after the fact. You might want to upload the new data to a parallel table in one step (via BCP) and use another procedure to move the data over to the live table, just to make sure that data integrity and referential integrity constraints aren't violated.

Formatting

You can choose from two different types of automatic conversion. The first is the Character option, which uses Char( ) formatting for all columns. This option creates a format that places a tab between columns and a newline character at the end of rows. Character format is ideal for importing or exporting foreign-database or spreadsheet data, most of which can create a CSV (comma-delimited) file. You can also (when you use the /c Character option) change the interfield delimiters. Use /t followed by the chosen field delimiter, or use /r followed by the chosen column delimiter. Valid BCP field terminators are shown in *Figure 36-1*. What you're trying to do by choosing the right terminator is embed the terminator in the data. For example, if your Name column separates last and first name with a comma ("Farkle, Fred"), using a comma delimiter might not result in a desired output. Here's an example of calling BCP.EXE with this first option:

```
BCP work..Farm_animals out barnyard_tab barn.out /c /t, /r\n
/Smy_server /Usa /Pclyde
```

Figure 36-1
Valid BCP Field Terminators

Terminator	How to Indicate
Tabs	\t
New line (Chr$(10))	\n
Carriage return (Chr$(13))	\r
Backslash	\\
Null terminators (no visible terminator)	\0
Any printable character (up to 10)	Just specify

The second type of automatic conversion available is the Native option, which keeps data in the native (database) data types. This is most useful for porting data from one SQL server (which knows how to create the format) to another SQL server (which knows how to read the format). It also saves some time, since data isn't needlessly converted to or from Char( ). Here is an example of calling BCP.EXE with this second format option:

```
BCP work..Farm_animals in barnyard_tab barn.in /n /Smy_server /Usa
```

Batch Size

You might want to modify the batch size, which sets the number of rows to be processed before performing a Checkpoint operation on the database. This commits all processed rows up to that point and flushes all data from the RAM caches to disk. It also flushes the space allocated in the transaction log. A large BCP operation can fail when the transaction log fills up. Setting the batch size to a smaller value will prevent this. The default value copies all rows in the file in one transaction—one batch. This means that if the BCP program fails partway through, it won't have any effect on the database, and all rows will have to be re-sent. If you use a block count value, BCP will signal for a Checkpoint every n rows. This means that if the BCP fails partway through, only the records that were in the last (uncompleted) batches will have to be reprocessed.

> **TIP** When the BCP fails partway through, you might not have any way of telling how many records made it and how many didn't except by watching the screen. But if this is an automatic, hands-off process, that might not be an option. You could do a query on the database, to see which rows have been added, and truncate the input file. Or you could restart the BCP, skipping down one row for every row that made it to the database (minus one row for every row sent to the error file).

Error File

If you need to capture records that can't be converted for some reason, you'll need to name an error file.

Starting/Ending Row

If you want to copy only a selected set of rows, you'll be able to indicate which row to start on and which to end on.

Interactive Mode

If you don't choose one of the automatic modes, BCP.EXE puts you into "interactive" mode, which asks for field descriptions for each column. It gives you the option of saving this formatting information at the end of the session so that it can be read later in the form of a "format" file.

Alternatives to the BCP API

One of the easiest things to do in Visual Basic is read comma-delimited files. Reading other ASCII-format or binary files is also fairly straightforward. It would probably be a good idea to check out the performance of the entire

process before you walk the BCP plank. When you compare operations, be sure to consider the following points:

- *Development or setup time.* This is a one-time cost, unless you are constantly having to set up different upload and download operations that could benefit from previous development efforts.

- *Run time.* This is certainly a critical component, especially if there are a lot of records to move. If there are only a few hundred or even several thousand records, this might not be a significant factor.

- *Multitasking.* Do you expect your user to be able to work while the copy operation is executing? Will other, more critical applications running on the workstation need CPU cycles?

- *Flexibility.* Do the records being read from the foreign host need to be uploaded to multiple tables? Do current records need to be updated (as opposed to just having data appended to them)?

- *Reformatting.* Do the records need to be prefiltered, audited, or otherwise munged? Do the columns need to be combined or separated? Do the column delimiters change from record to record? Are some records different in format, length, or composition?

- *Postprocessing.* Will you have to rerun triggers, rules, protection schemes, validations, business rule tests, or referential integrity tests after the upload? Does this mean that the data will have to be off line or in a separate table while you do this, or will you merge the questionable data with the verified data and back out the "bad" records later?

Moving Data from Server to Server

If you don't have a giant database to move, you might want to consider using the following method for moving data:

1. Transfer the data to be moved to a separate database. (If the whole database needs moving, don't bother.)

2. Back up the database to a dump device.

3. Make the dump file visible across the net, dump the database to tape or floppy, or move the dump file to removable media.

4. On the target system, create a new database just large enough to hold the data from the dumped database.

5. Restore the database from the dump device.

6. Move table data to the primary database, using stored procedures or just a one-time query. (Accessing multiple databases is easy in SQL Server, as long as they're on the same physical server.)

This isn't a logged operation, but it's fairly simple and relatively safe. It's easy to repeat any of the steps or deal with contingencies as they occur.

Conventional File Translators Using Visual Basic

More often than not, I've relied on Visual Basic to read in the records from foreign files, CSV, DIF, DBM, and other custom formats, including those created with the Scantron mark-sense system. These translators usually took less than a couple of hours to write and less time than that to modify when formats changed. Once I had the records from the files, I created sets of INSERT or UPDATE statements that added records to several tables at once, each in its own transaction.

Transaction Management

The number of transactions seems to be a critical factor in overall performance. If I give the SQL server too much to do at once (say, several hundred INSERT statements in a command batch before I do a SQLExec), SQL Server's thrashing eats up quite a bit of extra time. SQL Server builds a temporary table for all inserted records in an inserted table (an operation replicated for every user doing an INSERT statement). In addition, a table of deleted records is created when a transaction executes a DELETE statement. Both tables are created once an UPDATE statement is executed. They are used to permit triggers to compare the new rows with rows about to be deleted, inserted, or updated. An economy of scale can be realized (because of overhead incurred with each transaction), but it starts to decrease at about 50 INSERT transactions.

The Visual Basic language makes an excellent platform for high-speed record processing, string parsing, and transaction management. Using the conventional API (SQLCmd, SQLExec or SQLCmd, SQLSend, SQLDataReady, SQLOK) can be a very efficient way to send customized TSQL statements to the SQL server. You also won't have to rerun the rules and triggers after you're done, nor will you have to drop the indexes before running. (The indexes might actually help add data to the table, especially if there's no *clustered* index—one that requires the data rows to be in physically sequential order.)

CAUTION
Each call to SQLExec is considered a single transaction, no matter how many statements are in the batch, unless the batch contains multiple BEGIN TRANSACTION–COMMIT TRANSACTION statements. Each transaction either completes as a unit or fails as a unit. If your batch—a single transaction, unless you specifically indicate otherwise—fails, the entire set of commands in the batch fails. And if your UPDATE or DELETE statement encompasses half the rows in the database, you don't want it to fail partway through.

A Bird's-Eye View of the Bulk Copy API

If you decide to use the VBSQL bulk copy functions in your application, you'll have to provide all of the parameters via function calls. For example, you'll indicate the filename, direction (in or out), column and row terminators, error files, and so forth. At logon time, when the connection is established, you'll also have to tell DB-Library and the SQL server that you intend to do bulk copy. This implies that you'll have to dedicate a connection to this operation. The functions you'll be using (and the order in which you'll use them) are shown in *Figure 36-2* on the next page.

Setting up a bulk copy thread is not very difficult—a little tedious, but doable. An application using the bulk copy function doesn't need to be dedicated exclusively to bulk copy operations, but it will need a specially initialized connection. This will permit DB-Library to take over operation of the connection and perform the file operations for you, without your intervention, after it starts.

Figure 36-2
VBSQL Bulk Copy Functions

Function	Description
SQLBCPSetL	Sets flags in the LoginRec for bulk copy operations. Tells SQL Server this connection is going to use bulk copy.
SQLBCPInit	Initializes bulk copy operation. Sets most command-line options.
SQLBCPControl	Changes various default settings for the control parameter. Sets number of errors, rows to skip, rows to copy, and so on.
SQLBCPColumns	Sets the number of columns in the MS-DOS file involved in the copy (in or out).
SQLBCPColfmt	Describes the column format of the MS-DOS file.
SQLBCPExec	Starts the bulk copy operation.

NOTE When BCP copies a file from a specified SQL Server table into another file, it uses the column order specified when the database table was created. It uses the current row order of the table. Thus, if the table has a clustered index, it's physically sorted according to that index and the rows are written to the file in that order. BCP also writes fixed-length table data in a fixed format. If the table data is of variable length, a 4-byte length is used for Text and Image types and a 1-byte length is appended for all other variable-length types (VarChar, VarBinary, and so on). No terminators are inserted into the file.

SQLBCPSetL

This function sets up the logon record for use with bulk copy. This must be called to set a flag in the LoginRec before you call SQLOpen, which means you can't use an existing connection or SQLOpenConnection. SQLBCPSetL takes two parameters:

- *LoginRec*, the result of executing SQLLogin

- *Enable*, a Boolean value—True (1) or False (0)—that indicates the state of the BCP flag in the logon record

SQLBCPInit

This function sets up the DB-Library connection for use with bulk copy. It indicates all of the external files that will be needed, the table to be processed, and the direction (in or out). Its parameters are as follows:

- *SQLConn*, the dedicated (or clean) connection handle.

- *Table Name$*, the name of the SQL server table to be processed.

- *Filename$*, the name of the MS-DOS (or Microsoft Windows NT) file to be processed. (This file will be the source, the receiver, or the data.)

- *Error Filename$*, the name of the MS-DOS file (same rules as for *Filename$*) to which error records are to be written.

- *Operational Direction*, which must be specified as either *DBIN*, to move data into the specified database table, or *DBOUT*, to move data out of the specified database table.

The SQLBCPInit function returns *SUCCEED* (1) or *FAIL* (0).

Your *Filename$* parameter should be in the format of the operating system you are working with—but I'll bet you breakfast that your OS will support only an 8.3 filename (eight characters followed by three characters of extension).

> **NOTE** If the logon name you specified in the SQLOpen function sets your default database correctly or if you ran SQLUse to change the default database, you need not specify the name of the SQL Server table to be processed in SQLBCPInit. Otherwise, you should provide the table name in fully qualified mode: *database.owner.table*. For example, *FarmAnimals.dbo.Cows* will access the *Cows* table in the *FarmAnimals* database.

SQLBCPControl

This function sets up a number of options for the bulk copy operation. It makes sense to use this function only when you are moving data from a file into the specified table (which is also the only time you really have to use this function). You'll have to call this function a number of times to set each of the parameters that need to be changed from their default values. The maximum value for these integers is probably 32767 (although DB-Library will take 65535); you might try using negative integers to get at values greater than 32768. SQLBCPControl's parameters are as follows:

- *SQLConn*, the dedicated (or clean) connection handle.

- *Option*—one of the following parameter flags:

  - *BCPMAXERRS*, the number of errors it will take before BCP gives up. (Default value is 10.)

  - *BCPFIRST*, the first row to copy. (Default value is 1.)

CAUTION

If the BCP engine has a problem with a record, it writes it in the *Error Filename$* parameter, so it can be processed later. If you don't specify a filename, no error data is kept.

- *BCPLAST*, the last row to copy. (Default is all rows.)
- *BCPBATCH*, the size of the batch in rows. (Default is 0; no check-pointing.)
- *Value*, which specifies the value to be applied to the specified *Option*.

The SQLBCPControl function returns *SUCCEED* (1) or *FAIL* (0).

TIP When you specify the value to be applied to the *Option* parameter of SQLBCPControl, you're limited to 65,535 rows at most. If you try to specify starting points or other parameters higher than this number, you'll find yourself up a famous creek where you'll be lucky to find a paddle. You have to specify a negative number if you want to specify anything larger than 32,768—either that or pass a hex value converted to Integer.

SQLBCPColumns

This function tells BCP how many columns are in the specified file. You must call this function whether or not you intend to use all the columns in a file. (The documentation also says that you should call this function only if you intend to use a file whose format is different from the default format, as described by SQLBCPInit.) You won't be able to call SQLBCPColumns until you have called SQLBCPInit. SQLBCPColumns takes two parameters:

- *SQLConn*, the dedicated (or clean) connection handle
- *Columns*, which specifies the number of columns in the file

SQLBCPColumns returns *SUCCEED* (1) or *FAIL* (0).

SQLBCPColfmt

CAUTION
The SQLBCPColfmt function will fail if you don't call SQLBCPColumns first.

Once you have set the number of columns, you'll be expected to call SQLBCPColfmt once for each column. This function provides information about the file format for each column of the file to be created or read. If you don't want to copy a chosen database column, set the Database column number (the last parameter of this function) to 0. For each column, this function passes the following specific information:

- Database column corresponding to this file column
- Data type
- Length of the prefix (if any)
- Maximum data length
- Terminating string
- Length of the terminating string

The parameters for SQLBCPColfmt are as follows:

- *SQLConn*. This is the dedicated (or clean) connection handle.

- *Database Column*. This is the number of the file column to which this column description applies. (Numbering of file columns starts at 1.)

- *File Datatype*. This is the data type of this column in the file. It sets up a conversion (if needed) as data is copied. If you just want to use the database column, set this parameter to 0. Valid data type constants for this parameter from VBSQL.BAS are shown in **Figure 36-3**.

- *Prefix Length*. Each column defined might have a length prefix to indicate the length of the data in the string held in that column. Differing languages and import engines require different-length prefixes. Valid values are 1, 2, and 4 bytes. If you don't want BCP to attach a

Figure 36-3
Valid Data Type Constants from VBSQL.BAS

Constant	Value Hex/Decimal
SQLIMAGE	&H22 / 34
SQLTEXT	&H23 / 35
SQLARRAY[1]	&H24 / 36
SQLVARBINARY	&H25 / 37
SQLINTN	&H26 / 38
SQLVARCHAR	&H27 / 39
SQLBINARY	&H2D / 45
SQLCHAR	&H2F / 47
SQLINT1	&H30 / 48
SQLBIT	&H32 / 50
SQLINT2	&H34 / 52
SQLINT4	&H38 / 56
SQLDATETIM4	&H3A / 58
SQLFLT4	&H3B / 59
SQLMONEY	&H3C / 60
SQLDATETIME	&H3D / 61
SQLFLT8	&H3E / 62
SQLFLTN	&H6D / 109
SQLMONEYN	&H6E / 110
SQLDATETIMN	&H6F / 111
SQLMONEY4	&H7A / 122

1. Not documented

prefix length to the strings (if, for example, you want to terminate your strings with a Null), set this parameter to 0. This field in the data file can also be used to indicate that a Null was passed as data, since BCP will set the length prefix to 0 for null data elements.

- *Maximum Data Length&*. This is a Long. How much data can this field hold? It doesn't count any length prefixes or terminator strings. Setting this parameter to 0 indicates that the system is to consider this data to be null. Setting the maximum data length parameter to –1 tells BCP not to limit the length of data in this column but to expect to use the terminator string to mark the end of the file data. BCP returns an error if no terminator string is specified. BCP expects you to set maximum data length to –1 (no maximum) for fixed-length columns (like Integers)—as long as you expect to include the column in the copy. For variable-length data types like Char(), Text, Binary, and Image, you can set the maximum data length to –1 (no limit), 0 (ignore), or some positive value (copy *n* characters).

- *Terminator Sequence$*. This string specifies what BCP is to add to the end of variable-length data to mark the end of the column's data string in the file. Obviously, this string must be a sequence that won't occur in the data. Suggested terminators are Chr$(0) (Null), Chr$(9) (tab), Chr$(10) (new line), Chr$(44) (comma), and Chr$(13) (carriage return).

- *Terminator Length*. This is the length, in bytes, of the Terminator string. It must be set to –1 if no terminator is desired.

- *Database Column*. This specifies the number (starting with 1) of the column in the database. If it's 0, the column isn't copied. The order of the table columns is the order that's returned by a simple SELECT * query. You must describe each column whether or not you want to copy it.

This function returns *SUCCEED* (1) or *FAIL* (0).

SQLBCPExec

This function executes the bulk copy operation itself. It sets up transactions, checkpoints, and data copying, as required, without further intervention. It doesn't yield to anything during its operation, nor does it return until all specified rows are copied. SQLBCPExec takes two parameters:

- *SQLConn*, the dedicated (or clean) connection handle

- *Rows Copied&*, which receives the number of rows copied by the BCP operation that has been specified

This function returns *SUCCEED* (1) if all the specified rows were copied successfully. If some (or all) of the rows didn't copy, if one of the parameters in a previous function wasn't set correctly, or if SQLBCPInit wasn't called, SQLBCPExec returns *FAIL* (0). In any case, the number of rows successfully copied is returned in the *Rows Copied&* parameter.

PART VI

The ODBC API

Chapter

The Core ODBC API Functions

The ODBC Driver Manager and Driver

Initializing the ODBC Environment

Managing Connections

Error Management

Executing SQL Statements

Visiting a Simple Application

There's danger on the journey ahead. If you're using the ODBC API from Microsoft Visual Basic in a 16-bit environment, your path to a workable application has just been narrowed—by quite a bit. A few fairly significant things have changed since Visual Basic version 3.0 (and 16-bit Visual Basic version 4.0). For example, now that Microsoft Windows 95 has brought Unicode into the picture, the way you handle strings has become far more complicated. If you're going to hitchhike in the dark winding streets and unlighted alleys of the ODBC API, be careful; there are lots of strange characters here, and if you take a ride with the wrong one, you just might bring your whole system crashing down on yourself.

The ODBC API is designed for C developers. DB-Library is also designed for C developers, but the VBSQL interface to DB-Library removes virtually all of the C hazards. It does all the binding, memory allocation for strings, and parameter mungeing you need to make your applications fairly trouble-free. The ODBC API does *not* provide such an interface. (Well, actually, it does. It's called the RDO interface—and we've been there, done that.) If you code directly to the ODBC API, you have to bind each parameter in a parameter query to a data type, bind each column returned in a result set, allocate and initialize the memory for strings, pass the length of strings, convert strings back from Unicode to ASCII, and on and on and on. You get the drift. Let's just say that the ODBC API isn't an exact match as a SQL Server interface.

If you're not used to working with the rigors of a C interface, you need to read this chapter. For one thing, if you're using either of the ODBC approaches and know how the insides of the ODBC API work, you won't be surprised when something goes wrong. You're also more likely to use development techniques that are a better match for the features and data-handling methodologies afforded by the ODBC API. This chapter includes a number of code examples that demonstrate how to access SQL Server. You can also apply them to most remote engine servers, including Oracle and mainframe database servers, if you're so inclined.

This chapter and the next take you through the core ODBC API functions used to connect to SQL Server, submit a TSQL query, retrieve the results, handle any errors along the way, and disconnect from the server. Virtually every ODBC application uses this core set of API calls to perform fundamental operations:

- *SQLAllocEnv,* to establish an environment handle

- *SQLAllocConnect,* to establish a connection handle

- *SQLAllocStmt,* to establish a statement handle

- *SQLConnect or SQLDriverConnect,* to make a connection

- *SQLExecDirect or SQLExecute,* to execute SQL statements

- *SQLGetData,* to retrieve data values

- *SQLFetch or SQLExtendedFetch,* to process results

- *SQLFreeStmt,* to free the statement handle and release the result set allocation and any pending cursors

- *SQLDisconnect,* to close the connection

- *SQLFreeConnect and SQLFreeEnv,* to release the connection and environment handles

ODBC is a different interface from DB-Library, with a different purpose. ODBC's goal is to enable interoperability. DB-Library's mission is to expose all the features and functionality of SQL Server. To say that ODBC entails a performance penalty because it has more layers is too simplistic. For SQL Server, ODBC has exactly *one* more layer than DB-Library, and benchmarks have shown that performance difference between the two is minimal. You can't really stack one up against the other in terms of simplicity or complexity. It's an Apples and PCs comparison.

TIP If you're writing an application targeted at a single DBMS and your application makes extensive use of features unique to that DBMS, use the native interface. If you're writing an application that has to be interoperable, use ODBC. But don't assume that you can't use most of the features of a given DBMS with ODBC just because ODBC isn't the *native* interface. ODBC is extremely flexible and is designed to enable the use of most DBMSs' specific features.

The ODBC Driver Manager and Driver

The ODBC driver is a dynamic-link library (DLL) designed to interface with a specific back-end server like SQL Server. Whenever possible, the driver takes advantage of specific back-end features, such as cursors or parameterized queries. In some cases, the driver itself implements specific functionality to supplement features not supported by the back-end database. There's a separate SQL Server driver for the Sybase versions of SQL Server; the Microsoft SQL Server driver doesn't work with many versions of Sybase SQL Server. The ODBC driver is responsible for the following tasks:

- Implementing the ODBC API functions
- Establishing one or more connections and submitting requests to SQL Server
- Translating and returning results to your application
- Formatting errors into standard error codes
- Declaring and manipulating result set cursors
- Managing transactions

The ODBC Driver Manager provides the interface from your application to the SQL Server ODBC driver. The Driver Manager is responsible for the following tasks:

- Loading the SQL Server driver
- Initializing the interface
- Exposing the ODBC API functions implemented by the selected driver
- Validating parameters and managing serialization of ODBC functions

NOTE If your design can't use the RDO interface or Microsoft Jet's data access objects but you still need the database independence of ODBC, you can code directly to the ODBC Driver Manager through the ODBC API. This programming model uses the same Driver Manager and specific ODBC driver that Jet and the RDO interface use, but you have to manage all aspects of the connection, the query, buffers, cursors, and any errors that are generated.

One of the features of the ODBC API is its ability to morph the ability of the back-end server. If the remote server implements cursors itself, the driver can be written to take advantage of that ability. Without the right driver, however, your application can't take advantage of the server features. The ODBC API provides a whole slew of functions whose sole purpose is to ask the driver, "Can you do this?" Many of these functions don't access SQL Server at all, even though you have to open a connection before using them. They *do* access the SQL Server driver, which is designed to return information on how it works and what it's capable of doing.

The amount of memory that the ODBC API requires varies with the size of the specific ODBC driver. When you're calculating RAM resources, you have to account for the code *and* data segments required. The ODBC driver and Driver Manager can be shared with other applications. For example, if you have a Jet-based ODBC application running, both the ODBC driver and Driver Manager are already loaded. Your application creates instance data segments for these components but can share the existing code segments. Because you can control the cursor keyset size and composition, you can also control the keyset's impact on RAM and disk space when it overflows memory. The ODBC SQL Server driver also supports server-side cursors, which can significantly reduce RAM and disk space requirements on client workstations.

CAUTION
When you take advantage of server-specific features, your application loses some of its portability. For example, if your application uses stored procedures on SQL Server, it can't access other database servers that don't implement the same procedures. It's possible to create applications that can access more than one type of database, but you might have to avoid using some of the more sophisticated features of those databases.

TIP Through judicious implementation of cursors and functions that use local result set buffers, you can control the amount of network traffic your database application generates. You can also create forward-only scrolling and read-only cursors, which have very little overhead, to perform operations over low-speed links like RAS.

Because Visual Basic must handle data values passed to and from the ODBC API Driver Manager DLL in a fairly structured manner, there are some restrictions on how variables are passed and referenced by the DLL. Your code is responsible for passing arguments that provide input to the DLL procedures and pointers to initialized variables that receive the results of the functions. The ODBC function declaration statements define what DLL to use, what entry point to reference, each of the input and output parameters, and the data type of the returned value.

Each argument passed to and from the DLL is specified by data type and by whether the argument should be passed by reference (a pointer to the Visual Basic variable) or by value (a copy of the variable). If you don't specify these correctly, your code can be unceremoniously interrupted by a GPF.

NOTE The ODBC DECLARE statements have been augmented with additional ODBC API function calls to help prevent errors that cause GPFs.

In all cases, the ODBC API functions return an Integer as their result code, even for the 32-bit versions. Your code tests this Integer for one of several error codes, as defined by each call. In some cases, this code indicates success. If the function worked but a message or low-importance error occurred, the return code might indicate "success with information."

Your code provides all numeric input parameters in the form of constants, properly cast variables, or hard-coded values. String values *passed to* a function can be string literals, string constants, or string variables. Whenever a function *returns* a string, you must first declare and initialize a fixed-length string in code. Again, if this isn't done correctly, there's nothing to stop the ODBC API from stepping on your RAM and tripping a GPF. To reiterate, numeric parameter initialization is done automatically, but you *must* initialize string variables in code. Otherwise, vital stack, code, or data memory might be overlaid with unpredictable results. To retrieve a string value directly from a function, you can use the following code:

```
Dim sValue as String * 255     ' Name, allocate space for the string
Dim sValueLen as Long          ' The length of data returned
sValue = String$(255, 0)       ' Initialize the string variable
rc = SQLGetData(hstmt, 1, SQL_C_CHAR, sValue, 100, sValueLen)
```

In some cases, ODBC API functions are declared in such a way that a single argument might have to accept or pass string or 16-bit or 32-bit integers or other binary values. A Visual Basic argument can't assume the role of variables passed both by reference (nonstring values) and by value (string values), so a number of API functions are provided in the ODBC DECLARE files (ODBC32.TXT and ODBC16.TXT) found in the \SAMPLES\REMAUTO\DB_ODBC subdirectory of the main Visual Basic Enterprise Edition directory, as well as on this guide's companion disc. These Visual Basic ODBC API functions are listed in *Figure 37-1*. (If you examine the DECLARE statements closely, you can see that each of these extensions is really calling an aliased function that's listed in the ODBC Software Developer's Kit.)

Figure 37-1
Visual Basic ODBC API Functions (as Extended)

Function	Purpose
SQLColAttributesString	To retrieve information about selected data columns. This function uses SQLColAttributes.
SQLGetConnectOptionString	To retrieve string options for the SQLGetConnectOption function.
SQLGetInfoString	To retrieve string information about the driver and data source. This function uses SQLGetInfo.
SQLGetNumericData[1]	To retrieve data from nonstring columns in result sets. This function uses SQLGetData.
SQLGetStmtOptionString	(Not currently needed, but provided for future compatibility.) This function uses SQLGetStmtOption.

1. Because most column values, such as dates, integers, and floating-point numbers, can be retrieved in string form and quickly converted to native data types, you shouldn't need the SQLGetNumericData function unless you have data types that can't be converted easily.

TIP The 32-bit version of Visual Basic supports Unicode strings by automatically converting them to ANSI when calling DLLs and then back to Unicode when returning them. To support this functionality, you must use Byte arrays to ensure data integrity. When passing data to and from DLLs indirectly, as is done with SQLBindCol, your application must include code to convert strings from the 16-bits-per-character Unicode form to the 8-bits-per-character ANSI form. This additional code is required only with the use of early binding (for instance, with SQLBindCol) and isn't required for the extraction of data with SQLGetData.

To access the ODBC API functions, your application must include the ODBC API header files—ODBC32.TXT (32-bit DECLARE information) and ODBC16.TXT (16-bit DECLARE information—as provided in the \SAMPLES-\REMAUTO\DB_ODBC subdirectory of the main Visual Basic directory or in the ODBC API directory on this guide's companion disc). These files include Visual Basic DECLARE statements for each function and PUBLIC CONST declarations for each ODBC API constant. These DECLARE statements make the individual API functions and constants visible to your Visual Basic application.

NOTE The ODBC 2.10 Software Developer's Kit doesn't include 32-bit versions of the header files or Visual Basic sample applications. To use these API functions with 32-bit Visual Basic, you must substitute the ODBC header files as provided with the Visual Basic Enterprise Edition and on this guide's companion disc.

Initializing the ODBC Environment

Before an application can use any ODBC function, it must initialize the ODBC interface and allocate an environment handle with the SQLAllocEnv function:

```
Dim rc As Integer, henv As Long
rc = SQLAllocEnv(henv)
```

If SQLAllocEnv returns *SQL_SUCCEED*, the ODBC Driver Manager is initialized and memory is allocated to store information about the environment. If this function fails, the ODBC DLLs didn't correctly initialize. You need to execute SQLAllocEnv only once because the returned environment handle supports multiple connections to data sources.

Managing Connections

When your code opens a connection to a remote server or database, the connection remains open until your code closes it. There's no automatic connection timeout and reconnection, as implemented by the Jet database engine. For instance, when you're using the ODBC cursor library, the Driver Manager creates an additional connection to perform updates. This connection is kept open only as required to perform the operation. Generally, using your own connection management scheme to perform browsing and updates is easier and conserves connection resources more effectively. To economize on your application's use of server connections, you should develop a strategy that times out connections that aren't being used and reconnects them when user activity returns.

Allocating a Connection Handle

Before an application can connect to a driver, it must allocate a handle for the connection. The SQLAllocConnect function is used for this purpose, as shown in the following code:

```
Dim hdbc As Long
rc = SQLAllocConnect(ByVal henv, hdbc)
```

If the SQLAllocConnect function returns *SQL_SUCCEED*, memory is allocated for a connection handle. If this function fails, you can use the SQLError function to determine the cause. You must allocate a connection handle for each connection you open. Allocation of the handle has no impact on the SQL server and very little impact on your workstation's resources.

Creating a Data Source Name

When you open a connection to any database or remote database server with the ODBC API, you can reference a data source name or specify the server, driver name, and default database in the connect string. Although you can create DSNs in code with the ConfigDSN ODBC setup function, the easiest way to create or modify a DSN is by using the Control Panel ODBC Administrator program, which is installed if you select the ODBC option during Visual Basic custom installation.

DSN information is stored in the ODBC.INI file in 16-bit operating systems and in the system registry in 32-bit operating systems. If you have both 16-bit and 32-bit applications running on a 32-bit operating system such as Microsoft Windows NT or Windows 95, you must establish both ODBC.INI file and registry entries.

Connecting to a Data Source

Once the environment and connection handles are allocated, your code can open one or more connections to remote database servers by using a different connection handle for each connection. When working with SQL Server, you might need to open more than one connection to support simultaneous updates or multiple query operations. It's better to create several statement handles on a single connection than to create multiple connections with a single statement handle. The process of connecting to SQL Server using the ODBC API is basically the same as using Jet's OpenDatabase or attached table strategies or the RDO OpenConnection function. The connect string you create is identical to the one you create for the RDO interface.

Setting connection parameters

Your code should provide the following arguments to establish a connection:

- *A valid environment handle,* created by SQLAllocEnv for each connection handle

- *A valid connection handle,* created by SQLAllocConnect

- *A registered data source name,* corresponding to a DSN entry in the ODBC.INI file or the system registry; or the server, driver, and default database names

You can also provide the following optional elements:

- *A valid user ID,* which is a logon ID or account name used to access the data source

- *A valid password that corresponds to the user ID*

- *Any parameters that provide information to the driver* (such as information about whether the driver should select a specific default database)

To establish a connection, you can use one of three ODBC API functions for passing these parameters to the ODBC Driver Manager:

- *SQLConnect accepts a registered data source name, user ID, and password as arguments.* To be perfectly clear, you *must* provide SQLConnect with a registered data source name; you can't just specify extra arguments in the connect string. SQLConnect changes the allocated connection handle to the connected state and returns *SQL_SUCCESS*, *SQL_SUCCESS_WITH_INFO,* or *SQL_ERROR.*

- *SQLDriverConnect accepts a string identical to the RDO OpenConnection method's* Connect *argument* and similar to the Connect property of the Visual Basic Data control or the DAO OpenDatabase *Connect* argument. (But it does *not* begin with the *ODBC;* parameter, and it does *not* support the *Timeout* parameter.) To set ODBC connection timeout, use the SQLSetConnectionOption function. If insufficient information is provided in the string, one or more dialog boxes will gather information for missing or invalid parameters. This function returns *SQL_ERROR* if the user cancels or if the driver manager is unable to connect for other reasons.

- *SQLBrowseConnect supports an iterative method* of determining available drivers, data sources, and other parameters. Your application chooses from available data resources.

TIP If you are using Windows NT domain-managed security with SQL Server, you might not need to provide a user ID and password. By passing these arguments as Null values, the ODBC driver attempts to log on with your current Windows NT domain logon name and password.

Once the connection is established, you can use the connection handle with all subsequent functions that need access to the database. You can open as many connections as you need, to as many databases as necessary. You can also set a number of other options on the connection by using the SQLSetConnectOption function.

You can open a connection to a SQL Server database server by using the SQLConnect function. For example, the code provided below connects to a data source named *MyDSN*. (Note that you must pass not only each of the parameters but also the *length* of each parameter, which is fairly standard practice for C-based API interfaces.)

```
Dim rc As Integer, henv As Long, hdbc As Long
Dim Dlen As Integer, DSN As String

' Allocate the environment handle.
rc = SQLAllocEnv(henv)
' Allocate a connection handle.
rc = SQLAllocConnect(ByVal henv, hdbc)

DSN = "MyDSN"
UID = "MyUserID"
PWD = "MyPassword"

' Connect using the arguments provided.
rc = SQLConnect(hdbc, DSN$, Len(DSN$), UID, Len(UID), PWD, Len(PWD))

' Test for a successful connection.
If rc = SQL_SUCCESS Or rc = SQL_SUCCESS_WITH_INFO Then
    Print "Connection open"
Else
    Print "Connection did not open"
End If

DescribeError henv, hdbc, 0
```

You can also open a connection to a SQL Server database server by using the SQLDriverConnect function. The following code connects to a data source named *MyDSN*:

```
Dim rc As Integer, henv As Long, hdbc As Long
Const MaxLen% = SQLMAX_DSN_LENGTH
Dim Connect As String
Dim ConnectOut As String * MaxLen
Dim ConnectOutLen As Integer

ConnectOutLen = 0
ConnectOut = String(MaxLen, 0)      ' Initialize string
Connect$ = "DSN=MyDSN;UID=MyUserID;PWD=MyPassword;"

' Allocate the environment handle.
rc = SQLAllocEnv(henv)
```

```
' Allocate the connection handle.
rc = SQLAllocConnect(ByVal henv, hdbc)

' Connect using the "connect string" technique.
rc = SQLDriverConnect(hdbc, Me.hWnd, Connect$, Len(Connect$), _
                      ConnectOut, 1024, ConnectOutLen, _
                      SQL_DRIVER_COMPLETE)
```

CAUTION
All open connections are left open on the server until you exit Visual Basic, so if you use SQLDriverConnect or SQLConnect repeatedly without using the SQLDisconnect function to release the connection, you can exhaust all available connections on the server.

The ODBC Driver Manager prompts the user if the connect string doesn't contain sufficient information. SQLDriverConnect returns the connect string used to establish the connection. If the user provides different parameters, these are included. If you use SQLDriverConnect, you must provide an initialized fixed-length string to hold the returned connect string. If this string isn't properly initialized, Visual Basic or your code might behave unpredictably.

NOTE If you're debugging your application in Visual Basic and your project ends, any connections that are established but not explicitly closed will remain open. The environment, connection, and statement handles are no longer usable, however. Stopping and restarting your Visual Basic application in Break mode doesn't release connections. Only by exiting Visual Basic can you completely deallocate these handles and any orphaned connections.

Setting connection options

To manage and govern various aspects of your connections, you can use SQLSetConnectOption. With this function, you can perform the following actions:

- Determine whether the access mode is read-only or read-write.

- Optimize transaction management and locking strategies.

- Set the logon timeout value.

- Define how the driver manager uses the ODBC cursor library.

- Turn on ODBC tracing.

- Specify the network packet size.

- Control whether the driver displays dialog boxes.

To set connection options, you can use the following code, which shows how to set both a String value and an Integer value:

```
rc = SQLSetConnectOption(hdbc, SQL_ACCESS_MODE, _
                         SQL_MODE_READ_ONLY)
rc = SQLSetConnectOption(hdbc, SQL_OPT_TRACEFILE, _
                         "C:\SQLTRACE.TXT")
```

Retrieving connection options

To determine how options are currently set, use SQLGetConnectOption to retrieve numeric values and SQLGetConnectOptionString to retrieve string values. The following code fetches two parameters—a Long and a String:

```
Dim iValue As Long, sValue As String * 255

rc = SQLGetConnectOption(hdbc, SQL_ACCESS_MODE, iValue)
Debug.Print rc, iValue

sValue = String$(255, 0)
rc = SQLGetConnectOptionString(hdbc, SQL_OPT_TRACEFILE, sValue)
Debug.Print rc, sValue
```

NOTE The SQLGetConnectOptionString function, added to the list of C-language API calls to support Visual Basic strings, is aliased to the SQLGetConnectOption function, but it casts its return argument by *value* instead of by *reference*. Some drivers support multiple operations on a single connection. To see whether the current driver supports this feature, use the SQLGetInfo function and check *SQL_ACTIVE_STATEMENTS*.

CAUTION

When connection resources are freed on the client machine and the connection to the server is dropped, any connection-specific temporary objects on the server are also dropped.

The ODBC API can't deal with COMPUTE BY result sets or some of the subtleties of the RAISERROR statement. It's also incapable of dealing with asynchronous error and message handling, so you have to poll the interface after each function to see whether an error has occurred. Give me event-driven handlers every time.

Terminating the Connection

To terminate a connection to a driver and to SQL Server, your application must perform the following steps:

- SQLFreeStmt frees the statement handle and terminates all pending cursors.

- SQLDisconnect closes the connection. The application can then use the handle to reconnect to the same data source or to a different data source.

- SQLFreeConnect frees the connection handle and all resources associated with it.

- SQLFreeEnv frees the environment handle and all resources associated with it.

Error Management

When an ODBC API function completes execution, it returns a result code that indicates the degree of success or failure. Not all errors are fatal, so an "unsuccessful" result code might give you a low-severity message or other normal by-product of the requested operation. The result codes that you'll see most often are listed in *Figure 37-2*. Depending on which API function you use, there can be a number of other result codes as well. If the ODBC API function returns a result code other than *SQL_SUCCESS*, your code can examine the set of errors returned, by using the SQLError function. Each call to SQLError removes an error from the error structure.

Figure 37-2
Most Frequently Encountered Result Codes

Code	Meaning
SQL_SUCCESS	Function succeeded.
SQL_SUCCESS_WITH_INFO	Function succeeded; additional status information available.
SQL_ERROR	Function failed.

CAUTION
Overlaying the stack or other vital memory areas by incorrectly specifying or initializing structures or API function arguments usually results in a GPF or some other kind of failure, so be sure to save your work frequently.

TIP If additional status information is available from the function, you can obtain details by using the SQLError function. A single function can generate up to 64 errors, so multiple calls to SQLError might be necessary to extract all the information.

SQL Server returns unique native error codes exposed by the *native* return argument of the SQLError function. For example, in the normal process of establishing a connection to SQL Server, several informational messages are returned, and SQLConnect returns *SQL_SUCCESS_WITH_INFO*. Any SQL Server operation that generates an error with a severity level of 11 or above causes the function to return *SQL_ERROR*. Errors with a severity level of 10 or below are considered nonfatal and cause the function to return *SQL_SUCCESS_WITH_INFO*.

Executing SQL Statements

If your application is designed to work with more than just SQL Server as an ODBC data source, you should use only standard SQL syntax. The specific back-end driver translates these statements to the syntax used by the data source. If an application submits a SQL statement that doesn't use the ODBC syntax, the driver passes it directly to the data source.

To execute SQL statements, you have to carry out the following actions and decisions:

- Allocate a statement handle.

- Decide whether to execute statements more than once.

- Decide whether to use parameter markers or literal values.

- Terminate statement processing.

Using ODBC SQL Syntax

ODBC defines the following extensions to SQL, which are common to most database management systems:

- Date, time, and TimeStamp data
- Scalar functions, such as numeric, string, and data type conversion functions
- LIKE predicate escape characters
- Outer joins
- Procedures

The syntax defined by ODBC for these extensions uses the escape clause provided by the X/Open and SQL Access Group SQL CAE specification (1992) to cover vendor-specific extensions to SQL. Its format is as follows:

```
--(*vendor(vendor-name), product(product-name) extension *)--
```

To make a long story short, all you have to do for most applications is circumvent all this nonsense and use the

```
? = Call myprocedure-name (?, ?, ?, ?)
```

syntax and the

```
{d 'value'}
```

for date literals.

Allocating a Statement Handle

Before an application can submit a SQL query, you must initialize a statement handle by using the SQLAllocStmt function, as shown here:

```
Dim rc As Integer, hstmt As Long
rc = SQLAllocStmt(hdbc, hstmt)
```

You only have to execute this function once because the returned statement handle can be used for any number of SQL statements. With SQL Server, however, you must complete the query on a statement handle before starting another query. Therefore, you can't allocate another statement handle without first opening another connection to the server or waiting until the current statement has finished (just as is the case for the other programming interfaces). If you use server-side cursors, you might be able to create an additional statement handle before the current statement is complete. To discard uncompleted results and free the statement handle for reuse, use the SQLFreeStmt function:

```
rc = SQLFreeStmt(hstmt, SQL_CLOSE)
```

Choosing an Execution Strategy

There are usually two strategies you can implement to execute a SQL statement. You can base your decision on whether you expect to execute the statement more than once. Use the combination of SQLPrepare and SQLExecute in the following circumstances:

- If you need to execute a SQL statement repeatedly

- If you need to execute a SQL statement that requires parameters

- If you need information about the result set prior to execution

Use SQLExecDirect in the following circumstances:

- If you need to execute a statement only once

- If you need to execute a SQL statement that requires parameters

> **NOTE** The combination of SQLPrepare and SQLExecute is similar to the rdoPreparedStatement object, and the SQLExecDirect function is similar to the RDO interface's OpenResultset method.

A prepared statement executes faster than an unprepared statement because the ODBC Driver Manager creates a temporary SQL Server stored procedure that is subsequently passed parameters and executed, which saves recompiling time. In the process of creating a stored procedure for a prepared statement, the ODBC Driver Manager and SQL Server compile the statement, produce an access plan, and return an access-plan identifier to the driver. The SQL server minimizes processing time because it doesn't have to produce an access plan each time it executes the statement. Network traffic is also minimized because the driver sends the access-plan identifier (instead of the entire statement) to the data source.

Statements can be executed just once, with SQLExecDirect, or they can be prepared with SQLPrepare and executed several times with SQLExecute. An application also calls SQLTransact to commit or roll back a transaction, as required.

> **TIP** If your SQL query requires parameters, use the SQLBindParameter function with the SQLPrepare and SQLExecDirect functions. This puppy is *really* fun. I have spent many an afternoon figuring out how to bind a variety of Visual Basic data types to the right data type for the ODBC API.

Setting Parameter Values

A SQL statement can contain parameter markers (basically, just question marks) indicating values that you intend to supply and that the driver retrieves from your application at execution time. For example, your application might use the following statement to insert a row of data into the *Animals* table:

```
INSERT INTO ANIMALS (NAME, AGE, FURTYPE) VALUES (?, ?, ?)
```

Your application should use parameter markers instead of literal values if the following conditions exist:

- It needs to execute the same prepared statement several times with different parameter values. (If the parameters don't change, just use literals.)

- The parameter values aren't known when the statement is prepared.

- The parameter values need to be converted from one data type to another.

To set a parameter value, an application performs two operations. (The order in which they're performed doesn't matter.)

- It uses SQLBindParameter to bind a Visual Basic variable to one of the parameters in the query that you marked with a question mark. The first parameter is 1, the second 2, and so on. At this point, you also specify the data types of the variable and the column associated with the parameter, along with the precision and scale of the parameter. (Precision and scale are used for numeric types and contribute to making this quite a joyful experience.)

- It places the parameter's value in the variable.

These steps can be performed either before or after a statement is prepared, but they *must* be performed before a statement is executed.

Visual Basic variables remain bound to parameter markers until the application calls SQLFreeStmt with *SQL_RESET_PARAMS* or *SQL_DROP*. An application can bind a different variable to a parameter marker at any time by calling SQLBindParameter. An application can also change the value in a variable at any time. When a statement is executed, the driver uses the current values in the most recently defined variables. In other words, when the variable is bound to a parameter argument, the value that is currently in the variable at the time the query is executed is the value used to run the query.

Terminating Statement Processing

To free the resources associated with a statement handle, you can call SQLFreeStmt, which has four options, shown in *Figure 37-3*.

To cancel a statement that is executing asynchronously, an application takes the following steps:

1. It calls SQLCancel. Whether and when the statement actually is canceled depends on the operation in progress.

Figure 37-3
SQLFreeStmt Options

Option	Purpose
SQL_CLOSE	Closes the cursor and discards pending results. The application can use the statement handle later.
SQL_DROP	Closes the cursor, discards pending results, and frees all resources associated with the statement handle.
SQL_UNBIND	Frees all return buffers bound by SQLBindCol for the statement handle.
SQL_RESET_PARAMS	Frees all parameter buffers requested by SQLBindParameter for the statement handle.

2. It calls the function that executed the statement asynchronously. If the statement is still executing, the function returns *SQL_STILL_EXECUTING*. If it has been canceled successfully, the function returns *SQL_ERROR* and *SQLSTATE* S1008 (operation canceled). If it has completed normal execution, the function returns any valid return code, such as *SQL_SUCCESS* or *SQL_ERROR*.

3. It calls SQLError if the function returns *SQL_ERROR*. If the driver has successfully canceled the function, the *SQLSTATE* is S1008 (operation canceled).

Visiting a Simple Application

This section illustrates a simple Visual Basic ODBC API application. The code uses many of the core ODBC functions to access a remote SQL Server database. Generally, the type of database is irrelevant because the same code can be used to access a table on virtually any type of database that is supported with an ODBC driver. If you plan to take this approach, however, you can't reference any of SQL Server's unique features. The code in this section illustrates how the application performs the following actions:

- Creates global variables to hold environment, connection, and statement handles.

- Establishes a connection to an existing data source.

- Submits a SQL SELECT statement.

- Displays results in an unbound Grid control.

- Closes the connection.

- Handles errors.

Note that the code is one continuous example that takes you through the entire process, from allocating handles to closing connections. To try this code yourself, load the first ODBC sample application from this guide's companion disc.

Allocating Handles

Like the VBSQL interface, the ODBC API uses handles to manage the ODBC superstructure. Unlike VBSQL, the ODBC API needs three handles:

- *The environment handle (hEnv).* This handle provides a way to establish global ODBC initialization settings that affect the entire application. In VBSQL, this functionality is handled by SQL Server options that affect all connections; your application needs only one environment handle, and if you allocate another, you get the same value anyway. In the RDO interface, this is implemented with the rdoEngine and rdoEnvironment objects, which expose the environment handle. In the Jet/DAO model, this functionality is provided by the DBEngine and Workspace objects.

- *The connection handle (hDbc).* This handle is returned when a connection is established to SQL Server. The connection handle provides the same functionality as the *SQLConn* returned by the VBSQL SQLOpen or SQLOpenConnection functions or the RDO OpenConnection function, which also exposes the connection handle. Jet relegates this functionality to the Database object. The connection handle lets you set postconnection options and provides a way to create a result set against a specific connection.

- *The statement handle (hStmt).* Each time you execute a SQL query, you must first allocate a statement handle to support preexecution option settings or postexecution management of the result set. An application can have any number of statement handles active at any one time, and they can be reused as they are needed. In VBSQL, there's no handle as such to individual statements, but the SQLResults function activates the next statement. In RDO, the statement handle is exposed directly when you use the OpenResultset function. In Jet, the statement handle isn't exposed, but its functionality is managed by the Resultset object.

The following Visual Basic code creates global variables to hold environment, connection, and statement handles in addition to the return value returned by many of the ODBC API functions:

```
Dim henv As Long, hdbc As Long, hstmt As Long, rc As Integer
```

Establishing a Connection to the SQL Server

The following code establishes a connection to a remote SQL server by using the SQLDriverConnect function with a connect string. We don't use a DSN entry for this connection, since we specify the driver and server names in the connect string. The DescribeError function simply displays any errors that are encountered.

```
Private Sub OpenButton_Click()
Dim Connect As String            ' Holds the connect string
Dim ConnectOut As String * 255   ' Holds the postopen connect string
Dim ConnectOutLen As Integer     ' Holds the length of the connect
                                 ' string that is passed back
ConnectOutLen = 0
ConnectOut = String(255, 0)  ' Initialize the string
' Connect to the Pubs database on MyDSN using a specific
' password and user ID.
Connect$ = "DSN=MyDSN;UID=;PWD=;Database=Pubs;" _
    & "DRIVER={SQL Server};SERVER=BETAV486"
rc = SQLDriverConnect(hdbc, Me.hwnd, Connect$, Len(Connect$), _
ConnectOut, 255, ConnectOutLen, SQL_DRIVER_NOPROMPT)

' Test for a successful open connection.
If rc = SQL_SUCCESS Or rc = SQL_SUCCESS_WITH_INFO Then
    .
    .' If it failed, show error.
    .
Else

    DescribeError henv, hdbc, 0     ' Defined in "Handling Errors"
End If
End Sub
```

Submitting a SQL SELECT Statement

The following code submits a TSQL SELECT statement. First, we allocate a statement handle and, using the SQLExecDirect function, send a SELECT statement to the server. If the query fails, the error is described in a message box.

```
Private Sub SendQueryButton_Click()
Dim SQL As String, RCols As Integer, I As Integer

' Define a SQL query to fetch from the Pubs database.
SQL$ = "Select * from authors"
' Allocate a statement handle.
rc = SQLAllocStmt(hdbc, hstmt)

' Run the query; pass the SQL query and the length of the query.
rc = SQLExecDirect(hstmt, SQL$, Len(SQL$))
' Test for success; if it fails, display the error.
If rc <> SQL_SUCCESS Then _
    DescribeError henv, hdbc, hstmt: Exit Sub
```

Displaying Results

The following code displays the resulting rows in an unbound Grid control:

```
Dim sValue As String * 1024             ' Holds the data row
Dim lValueLen As Long, larg2 As Long, ivaluelen As Integer
Dim sGridText As String
' Note that the number of result columns is retrieved with the
' SQLNumResultCols function; the Grid control size is set to the
' number of returning data columns.
rc = SQLNumResultCols(hstmt, Rcols)     ' Get the number of columns
If RCols > 1 Then
    Grid1.Cols = RCols
    Grid1.Rows = 10
    Grid1.Row = 0
Else
    Exit Sub                            ' No columns returned; just
                                        ' quit
End If


' The column headings are retrieved with the Visual Basic
' function SQLColAttributesString.
For I = 1 To RCols
    rc = SQLColAttributesString(hstmt, I, SQL_COLUMN_LABEL, _
        sValue, 255, ivaluelen, larg2)
    Grid1.Col = I - 1
    Grid1 = Left$(sValue, ivaluelen)
Next I
' Individual rows are fetched with SQLFetch.
' The column data for each row is fetched with SQLGetData.
Do                  ' Loop through all rows of the resultset
    rc = SQLFetch(hstmt)                ' Get a row of data
    ' Test for a successful fetch.
    If rc = SQL_SUCCESS_WITH_INFO Then DescribeError henv, hdbc, _
        hstmt
    If rc = SQL_SUCCESS Or rc = SQL_SUCCESS_WITH_INFO Then
        ' Prepare string for data value.
        sValue = String$(1024, 0)
        ' Make sure there is enough space in the Grid
        ' for this next row.
    If Grid1.Row + 1 >= Grid1.Rows Then Grid1.Rows = Grid1.Rows + 10
        Grid1.Row = Grid1.Row + 1
        ' Get a data value for each column in this row.
        For I = 1 To RCols
            rc = SQLGetData(hstmt, I, SQL_C_CHAR, _
                            sValue, 100, lValueLen)
            If rc <> SQL_SUCCESS Then
                DescribeError henv, hdbc, hstmt
                Exit Do
            End If
            Grid1.Col = I - 1
            sGridText = Left$(sValue, lValueLen)
            ' On the first set of results, the grid's column width
```

```
                    ' is set according to the data returned.
                    If Grid1.Row = 1 Then _
                        Grid1.ColWidth(I - 1) = TextWidth(sGridText) * 1.1
                    Grid1 = sGridText
            Next I
        Else
            Exit Do
        End If
' Continue through all rows in the resultset.
Loop While rc = SQL_SUCCESS
End Sub
```

Closing a Connection

The following code closes the connection, frees the allocations, and ends the application:

```
Private Sub CloseButton_Click()
    rc = SQLFreeStmt(hstmt, SQL_CLOSE)
    rc = SQLDisconnect (hdbc)          ' Disconnect
    rc = SQLFreeConnect (hdbc)         ' Free the connection handle
    rc = SQLFreeEnv (henv)             ' Free the environment handle
    Unload Form1
End Sub
```

Handling Errors

The following code displays all errors returned by the last function. There might be several errors, so SQLError is called until all errors are displayed.

```
Sub DescribeError(ByVal henv, ByVal hdbc As Long, _
                  ByVal hstmt As Long)
' Print an error message for the given connection handle
' and statement handle.
Const SbufferLen = SQL_MAX_ERROR_STRING ' Maximum error string
Dim Cr$
Cr$ = Chr$(13) & Chr$(10)
Dim rgbValue1 As String * 16
Dim rgbValue3 As String * SbufferLen
Dim Outlen As Integer
Dim Native As Long
Dim lrc As Integer
Dim lhenv As Long, lhdbc As Long, lhstmt As Long
rgbValue1 = String$(16, 0)
rgbValue3 = String$(SbufferLen, 0)
' Loop through the errors starting with hstmt, then hdbc,
' and finally henv.
For L = 1 to 3
    Select Case 1
        lhenv = SQL_NULL_HENV
```

(continued)

```
                lhdbc = SQL_NULL_HDBC
                lstmt = hstmt
            Select Case 2
                lhenv = SQL_NULL_HENV
                lhdbc = hdbc
                lstmt = SQL_NULL_HSTMT
            Select Case 3
                lhenv = henv
                lhdbc = SQL_NULL_HDBC
                lstmt = SQL_NULL_HSTMT
            End Select

        ' Get all of the stored error values one at a time.
        Do
            ' Request the next error in the set of stored errors.
            lrc = SQLError(lhenv, lhdbc, lhstmt, rgbValue1, _
                Native, rgbValue3, SbufferLen, Outlen)
            If lrc = SQL_SUCCESS Or lrc = SQL_SUCCESS_WITH_INFO Then
                If Outlen = 0 Then
                    MsgBox "Error--No error information available"
                Else
                    If lrc = SQL_ERROR Then
                        MsgBox Left$(rgbValue3, Outlen)
                Else
                        MsgBox Left$(rgbValue3, Outlen) & Cr & _
                            "Native error:" & Native
                    End If
                End If
            End If
        Loop Until lrc <> SQL_SUCCESS
        Next L
        End Sub
```

38
Chapter

Managing ODBC API Result Sets

Retrieving Results

Using Cursors

Modifying Result Set Data

Transaction Management

Retrieving Information About the Data Source

Accessing Server-Specific Features

To retrieve information from Microsoft SQL Server, you need to understand how to use cursors and how to modify result sets. This chapter explains how to create cursors and simpler result sets with the ODBC API.

Retrieving Results

Once you've submitted a query, you must process the result set, even if it contains no rows. Your query might also generate more than one result set, as is often the case when you execute system stored procedures or SQL batches. Each result set must be processed or discarded before the statement handle can be reused.

TIP   When you're executing system stored procedures that aren't saved in the default database, you must refer to the procedure by using the *database.owner.name* syntax—for example, *Master..sp_who*.

When you use the ODBC API programming model, *every* SQL SELECT statement is associated with a cursor. You can give the cursor a name by using SQLSetCursorName, and you can set the cursor behavior with SQLSetStmtOption. Before you even create the cursor, you can use SQLDescribeCol, SQLColAttributes, and SQLNumResultCol to determine the characteristics of the result set. If your result set generates rows, you can expose the data from the result set columns by using any of the following functions:

- *SQLBindCol assigns a Microsoft Visual Basic variable to one or more selected column(s) of the result set*. Data is placed into the variable with the SQLFetch or SQLExtendedFetch function.

- *SQLGetData fetches character data from a specific column into a Visual Basic string variable*. You set the column characteristics for each string column using function arguments.

- *SQLGetNumericData fetches nonstring data from a specific column into a Visual Basic variable.* You set the column characteristics for each numeric column using function arguments.

NOTE   The SQLGetNumericData function has been added to the list of C-language API calls to support Visual Basic nonstring data types. This function is aliased to the SQLGetData function, but it casts its return argument by reference instead of by value.

Using SQLBindCol

If you really need to make your afternoon extra long, you can use SQLBindCol to associate Visual Basic variables with selected columns of the result set. Although you must repeat binding for each result set, you have to do it only once—before fetching any data rows. You don't have to perform binding in data fetch loops. As you reposition the current-row pointer, the data values in the variable are refreshed with the current row values once a variable is bound to a result set row. I guess you could bind to Visual Basic controls this way as well—sort of a poor man's bound control.

16-bit Visual Basic

In 16-bit Visual Basic applications, you describe the result set on a column-by-column basis. For example, you could use the following code to bind a numeric column in a result set to a numeric Visual Basic variable:

```
rc = SQLBindCol(hstmt, 5, SQL_C_SSHORT, job_id, 4, cbjob_id)
```

This example binds the fifth column of the result set specified by the statement handle to a variable named *job_id*, limits the size to 4, and puts the actual length found in a variable named *cbjob_id*.

When you execute SQLFetch for this statement handle, the ODBC driver fetches the data from the result set and places the data into the variable. Although you can specify a TextBox or Label control to accept the data, your application must save or display these variables in other Visual Basic controls, like ListBox or Grid controls.

32-bit Visual Basic

In using SQLBindCol with 32-bit Visual Basic applications, you must take special care when handling strings. Because of the way Visual Basic converts strings passed from DLLs into Unicode, you can't directly bind result set columns to String or Variant variables. Instead, you must bind each database character column to a Byte array, a flat structure treated as a string of characters and not subject to Unicode machinations. The problem is that once your data is in the Byte array, you have to get it out again before you can use it as a normal String. To use the SQLBindCol and SQLFetch calls to fetch data from the *Employee* table in the SQL Server *Pubs* sample database, you can use the following code, which creates a Byte array and retrieves data from a character column:

```
Private Type Employee
    emp_id(10) As Byte
    cbemp_id As Long
End Type

Dim Emp As Employee
rc = SQLBindCol(hstmt, 1, SQL_C_CHAR, Emp.emp_id(0), 10, _
                Emp.cbemp_id)
```

Notice the user-defined Type declaration. It's not a requirement for handling Byte array data, but it's a useful way to manage data columns.

Converting strings from Unicode to ANSI

Once data is placed in the Byte array, you can access individual bytes one at a time. In most cases, however, you should use the Unicode translation (StrConv) function to convert the Unicode Byte array back into a String:

```
Public Function BytesToStr(ab() As Byte) As String
Dim v As Variant, s as String
    v = ab()
    ' Convert to a string
    #If Win32 Then
        s$ = StrConv(v, vbUnicode)
    #Else
        s$ = v
    #End If
    BytesToStr = s$
End Function
```

NOTE If you want to perform positioned updates with SQLSetPos, you must use SQLBindCol to identify columns in the rows to be updated. Unless all columns are bound, you can't use SQLSetPos to add new rows. To make your life easier, make sure your query includes only the columns you intend to bind.

Using SQLGetData

You can also use SQLGetData to extract character-formatted column data from a result set row. This function doesn't have the same string restrictions as SQLBindCol because retrieval and conversion are performed on a column-by-column basis after the row has been fetched with SQLFetch or SQLExtended-Fetch. In this case, all string manipulations are handled automatically by Visual Basic. Note that you must use preinitialized fixed-length strings to accept the data.

This is a two-step process that uses the Dim and String statements. The following code extracts a character column and an integer column from a result set in a SQLFetch loop:

```
Dim SQLIn as String
Dim A As String * 255, LenRead As Long
Dim MyVal as Integer, LenARead as Long
A = String(255, 0)          ' Initialize the string to hold data
SQLIn = "Select Name, Age from MyTable"
rc = SQLExecDirect(hstmt, SQLIn, Len(SQLIn))
If rc = SQL_SUCCESS Then
    rc = SQLFetch(hstmt)
    Do While rc = SQL_SUCCESS
        rc = SQLGetData(hstmt, 1, SQL_C_CHAR, A$, 254, LenRead)
        rc = SQLGetData(hstmt, 2, SQL_C_USHORT, MyVal, 3, LenARead)
```

It takes slightly longer to execute SQLGetData than it does to prebind with SQLBindCol, but SQLGetData is far easier to use in both 16-bit and 32-bit applications. SQLGetData is *required* when you're using data types like *SQL_LONGVARCHAR* and *SQL_LONGVARBINARY*, which map to the SQL Server Text and Image data types. Because your code has complete control over the variable that receives the data, you can use SQLGetData to place data in a Grid control, a ListBox control, or other data-aware controls.

Ordinarily, you can use SQLGetData to read both character and numeric columns by simply specifying that the numeric columns should be converted to strings as they're retrieved. The preceding code uses this technique to fetch the *MyVal* value. When you *can't* implement this technique, use the SQL-GetNumericData function. It retrieves numeric columns and converts them into numeric Visual Basic variables:

```
Dim SQLIn as String
Dim N as Integer, LenRead As Long
Dim D as Single, LenRead2 as Long
SQLIn = "Select Age, Pay from MyTable"
rc = SQLExecDirect(hstmt, SQLIn, Len(SQLIn))
If rc = SQL_SUCCESS Then
    rc = SQLFetch(hstmt)
    Do While rc = SQL_SUCCESS
        rc = SQLGetNumericData(hstmt, 1, SQL_C_USHORT, N, 3, _
                              LenRead)
        rc = SQLGetNumericData(hstmt, 2, SQL_C_FLOAT, D, 8, _
                              LenARead2)
```

Examining Result Set Attributes

Once the query creates the result set, you can extract descriptor information about the current result set or selected column by using the functions shown in *Figure 38-1* on the next page.

Figure 38-1
Functions for Extracting Information
About Result Sets and Columns

Function	Returns
SQLNumResultCol	Number of columns in the result set
SQLDescribeCol	Column name, type, precision, scale, and nullability
SQLColAttributes	Numeric descriptor column characteristics
SQLColAttributesString	String descriptor column characteristics

Using Cursors

CAUTION
You should use SQLSet-
ConnectOption and SQL-
SetStmtOption only when
they're required, since they
can significantly affect run-
time performance.

The ODBC Driver Manager always creates a cursor when the query returns a row-containing result set. Each time your code calls SQLFetch, the driver positions the current-row pointer at the next row in the cursor and retrieves data for that row. By default, cursors are read-only and forward-scrolling–only. Once you position the current-row pointer past a row, that row is no longer available. Therefore, you must reexecute the query to retrieve it.

You can determine the following information with SQLSetConnect-Option (for ODBC driver features) and SQLSetStmtOption (for statement options):

- Whether the cursor is forward-only, static, keyset, or dynamic

- Whether bookmarks will be used with a cursor

- Whether an operation is asynchronous.

- Whether a result set is read-only or read-write

- The size of the cursor keyset and the number of rows in the cursor rowset

- The maximum number of rows retrieved and the maximum length of the data retrieved

- Whether binding is by row or by column

- The cursor's locking and concurrency attributes

- Whether the driver scans SQL statements for escape clauses (arguments substituted by the driver in a SQL statement on the basis of options or parameters you provide)

- The length of a query timeout

Cursor Types

The ODBC API supports four types of cursors. These cursors are similar to those supported by the other three programming models.

- With *static cursors,* data in the underlying tables appears to be unchanging. The membership, order, and values of the result set used by a static cursor are generally fixed when the cursor is opened. Rows updated, deleted, or inserted by other users aren't detected by the cursor until it's closed and reopened. (This type of cursor is like the Microsoft Jet snapshot-type Recordset object.)

- With *dynamic cursors,* data in the underlying tables appears to be in flux. The membership, order, and values of the result set used by a dynamic cursor are ever changing. Rows updated, deleted, or inserted by all users are detected by the cursor the next time data is fetched. Although ideal for many situations, dynamic cursors are the most expensive and the most difficult to implement. (This type of cursor is like the Jet table-type Recordset object.)

- With *keyset cursors,* membership is static, but the data is dynamic. Membership and ordering of the result set of a keyset-driven cursor are generally fixed when the cursor is opened. As with dynamic cursors, most changes to the values in the underlying result set are visible to the cursor the next time the data is fetched. (This type of cursor is similar to the Jet dynaset-type Recordset object.)

- With *mixed (keyset/dynamic) cursors,* the keyset is smaller than the result set but larger than the rowset. In other respects, a mixed cursor is like a keyset-driven cursor. Within the boundaries of the keyset, a mixed cursor is keyset-driven (the driver uses keys to retrieve the current data values for each row in the rowset). When a mixed cursor scrolls beyond the boundaries of the keyset, it becomes dynamic—the driver simply retrieves the next rowset. The driver then constructs a new keyset which contains the new rowset. This type of cursor is unique to the ODBC and VBSQL API programming models.

To activate one of these cursor types, use the SQLSetStmtOption and SQLSetConnectOption functions. You can make each of these cursor types a forward-only cursor by setting the *SQL_CURSOR_FORWARD_ONLY* option with SQLSetStmtOption. You can also set the size of the keyset, the length of binary data, maximum cursor rows, and all other cursor options in similar fashion.

Positioning the Current Record

Once a suitable result set is created, the current row is positioned before the first row of the result set and is unavailable until you use SQLFetch or SQLExtendedFetch to retrieve the data for the current row. SQLExtendedFetch retrieves rowset data (one or more rows) in the form of an array, starting at a position you specify in code. To position the current record pointer to other rows of the cursor, use one of the following techniques:

Using Bookmarks to Position the Current Row

Like the DAO model, the ODBC API supports the use of book-marks to return the current row to a specific cursor row. If your application needs to use bookmarks, use the SQLSetStmtOption function with the *SQL_USE_BOOKMARKS* option before opening the cursor. To retrieve the bookmark for a fetched row, access column 0 with SQLExtendedFetch or SQLGetData, or use SQLGet-StmtOption with the *SQL_GET_BOOKMARK* option. To reposition the current row to the row specified by the bookmark, use the SQLExtendedFetch function with a fetch type of *SQL_FETCH-_BOOKMARK*.

- To fetch the *next* row in the cursor, use SQLFetch.

- To fetch a *specific* row based on a *bookmark,* use SQLExtendedFetch and the *SQL_FETCH_BOOKMARK* option with the bookmark value.

- To fetch a *specific* row by *number,* use the number of the row to be fetched with SQLExtendedFetch and the *SQL_FETCH_ABSOLUTE* option.

- To fetch a *specific* row starting *at the end of the result set,* use a negative row number relative to the end of the result set with SQL-ExtendedFetch and the *SQL_FETCH_ABSOLUTE* option.

- To fetch an *adjacent* row or the row at *either end* of a cursor, use the *SQL_FETCH_FIRST, _LAST, _NEXT,* or *_PRIOR* options with SQL-ExtendedFetch.

- To fetch a row scrolling *forward* or *backward* relative to the current cursor row, use a displacement value with the *SQL_FETCH_RELATIVE* option of SQLExtendedFetch.

Modifying Result Set Data

You can modify data in the database by using one of three techniques:

- Execute positioned UPDATE and DELETE statements by using a named cursor.

- Use SQLSetPos with a named cursor.

- Process multiple result sets with SQL statements that update or delete rows on the basis of key values extracted from the result set.

The first two techniques reference one or more rows of a cursor. The third technique simply uses a SQL query to make changes.

TIP Updates or deletes that involve cursors are far more expensive than those done directly by the remote database's query processor.

Executing Positioned
UPDATE and DELETE Statements

An application can directly update or delete the current row in the cursor result set. This kind of statement is known as a *positioned* UPDATE or DELETE statement. After executing a SELECT statement to create a result set, an application calls SQLFetch one or more times to position the cursor on the row to be updated or deleted. Alternatively, it fetches the rowset with SQLExtendedFetch and positions the cursor on the desired row by calling SQLSetPos with the *SQL_POSITION* option. To update or delete the row, the application then executes a SQL statement with the following syntax on a different statement handle:

```
UPDATE table-name
    SET column-identifier = {expression | NULL}
        [, column-identifier = {expression | NULL}]…
    WHERE CURRENT OF cursor-name
DELETE FROM table-name WHERE CURRENT OF cursor-name
```

Positioned UPDATE and DELETE statements require cursor names, which you can create with SQLSetCursorName. If your application doesn't create a name for the cursor by the time the driver executes a SELECT statement, the driver generates a cursor name. To retrieve the cursor name for a statement handle, an application calls SQLGetCursorName. To execute a positioned UPDATE or DELETE statement, an application must follow these guidelines:

- The SELECT statement that creates the result set must use a FOR UPDATE clause.

- The cursor name used in the UPDATE or DELETE statement must be the same as the cursor name associated with the SELECT statement.

- The application must use different statement handles for the SELECT statement and the UPDATE or DELETE statement.

- The statement handles for the SELECT statement and the UPDATE or DELETE statement must be on the same connection.

Modifying Data with SQLSetPos

To add, update, and delete rows of data, an application calls SQLSetPos and specifies the operation, the row number, and the method for locking the row. The data source defines where new rows of data are added to the result set and whether they're visible to the cursor. The row number determines both the number and the index of the row to be updated or deleted. If the row number is 0, the operation affects all the rows of the rowset.

SQLSetPos retrieves the data to be updated or added from the rowset buffers. It updates only those columns of a row that have been bound with SQLBindCol and don't have a length of *SQL_IGNORE*, but it can't add a new row of data unless all the columns of the row are bound, can be Null, or have a default value.

Processing Multiple Result Sets

SELECT statements return result sets. UPDATE, INSERT, and DELETE statements return a count of the affected rows. If you batch any of these statements or if you submit them with arrays of parameters or in procedures, they can return multiple result sets or counts of multiple affected rows.

To process a batch of statements, statements with arrays of parameters, or procedures returning multiple result sets or row counts, an application performs the following operations:

1. Uses SQLExecute or SQLExecDirect to execute the statement or a procedure.

2. Uses SQLRowCount to determine the number of rows affected by an UPDATE, INSERT, or DELETE statement. (For statements or procedures that return result sets, the application calls functions to determine the characteristics of the result sets and retrieve data from the result sets.)

3. Uses SQLMoreResults to determine whether another result set or row count is available.

4. Repeats step 2 and step 3 until SQLMoreResults returns the value *SQL_NO_DATA_FOUND*.

Transaction Management

In *auto-commit* mode, every SQL statement is a complete transaction that's automatically committed. In *manual-commit* mode, a transaction consists of one or more statements. When an application submits a SQL statement and no transaction is open, the driver implicitly begins a transaction. The transaction remains open until the application commits or rolls back the transaction with SQLTransact.

SQL Server supports the *SQL_AUTOCOMMIT* connection option; the default transaction mode is auto-commit mode. Use the SQLSetConnectOption function to switch between manual-commit mode and auto-commit mode. If an application switches from manual-commit mode to auto-commit mode, the SQL Server driver commits any open transactions on the connection.

TIP To terminate, commit, or roll back a transaction, you should use the SQLTransact function instead of submitting a COMMIT or ROLL-BACK statement.

CAUTION
Committing or rolling back a transaction, either by calling SQLTransact or by using the *SQL_AUTOCOMMIT* connection option, can cause the data source to close the cursors and delete the access plans for all statement handles on a connection handle.

As with other cursor and transaction models, when a cursor is created but isn't fully populated on the server, the server can establish page locks on some or all of one or more tables in the database. It's best to move to the last record of a result set as quickly as possible to free these shared page locks. By default, the ODBC API model supports low-impact cursor models that can significantly reduce this locking overhead.

Retrieving Information About the Data Source

If you need to examine the database schema itself, the ODBC API provides a number of specific function calls for retrieving information about a data source. These function calls, listed in *Figure 38-2* on the next page, describe the database, its tables, privileges, table columns, and other information about the database schema. Each function returns the information as a result set. You can retrieve these results by calling SQLBindCol and SQLFetch or SQLGetData.

Accessing Server-Specific Features

This section discusses specific SQL Server features and how you can use the ODBC API to take advantage of them. Because the ODBC API is designed to be a universal interface to any database with an ODBC driver, not all server-specific features can be implemented or leveraged as they would be with an API designed for a specific engine. In most cases, however, every attempt has been made to implement mainstream features and to make the ODBC interface as efficient as possible with each server to which it can connect.

Asynchronous Processing

To gain more control over your front-end applications, you can request that the database interface work *asynchronously*—that is, the interface returns control to your application and continues to work before the query or other process is complete. Using this technique, your application can execute other operations instead of just blocking until the ODBC operation completes. By default, ODBC operations are synchronous, which means they must complete before returning control to the calling application. To enable asynchronous operations, use SQLSetStmtOption to set the *SQL_ASYNC_ENABLE_ON* option.

Figure 38-2
Function Calls for Retrieving Data Source Information

Function	Returns
SQLTables	Names of tables stored in a data source
SQLTablePrivileges	Privileges associated with one or more tables
SQLColumns	Names of columns in one or more tables
SQLColumnPrivileges	Privileges associated with each column in a single table
SQLPrimaryKeys	Names of columns that make up the primary key of a single table
SQLForeignKeys	Names of columns in a single table that are foreign keys; names of columns in other tables that refer to the primary key of the specified table
SQLSpecialColumns	Information about the optimal set of columns that uniquely identifies a row in a single table, or the columns in the table that are automatically updated when any value in the row is updated by a transaction
SQLStatistics	Statistics about a single table and the indexes associated with it
SQLProcedures	Names of procedures stored in a data source
SQLProcedureColumns	A list of the input and output parameters, as well as the names of columns in the result set, for one or more procedures

To determine whether the function has completed, check its return code for a value other than *SQL_STILL_EXECUTING*. Once a function has been called asynchronously, only the original function, which is used to check for completion of the operation, can be called on the statement handle or the associated connection handle.

Server-Side Cursors

If your application uses the SQL Server ODBC 2.5 drivers (as supplied with Visual Basic) or other level 2–compliant drivers, the ODBC Driver Manager will use server-side cursors when you set the *SQL_ODBC_CURSORS* option with the

SQLSetConnectOption function. If the database query processor supports SQL cursor syntax, you can also use it to specify cursors and cursor-positioned update or delete operations.

Stored Procedures

Stored procedures and singleton execution SQL statements play an important role in many client/server applications. With the ODBC API, you can execute any type of stored procedure by using either SQLExecute or SQLExecDirect. The ODBC driver automatically passes these statements to the remote database engine's query processor for execution, just as it does with any other SQL statement that uses a server-specific dialect.

To use a stored procedure that returns a result code or output parameters, include an escape clause in the SQL syntax. Here's the escape clause that ODBC uses for calling a procedure:

```
[?=] call procedure-name[([parameter][,[parameter]]...)]
```

Procedure-name specifies the name of a procedure stored in the data source; *parameter* specifies a procedure parameter. A procedure can have zero or more parameters and can return a value.

For output parameters, *parameter* must be a parameter marker. For input and input/output parameters, *parameter* can be a literal or a parameter marker or it can be unspecified. If *parameter* is a literal or isn't specified for an input/output parameter, the driver discards the output value. If *parameter* isn't specified for an input or input/output parameter, the procedure uses the default value of the parameter as the input value. The procedure will also use the default value if *parameter* is a parameter marker and the *pcbValue* argument in SQLBindParameter is *SQL_DEFAULT_PARAM*. If a procedure call includes parameter markers (including the *?=* parameter marker for the return value), the application must bind each marker by calling SQLBindParameter before calling the procedure.

If an application specifies a return value parameter for a procedure that doesn't return a value, the driver sets the *pcbValue* buffer specified in SQLBindParameter for the parameter to *SQL_NULL_DATA*. If a procedure returns a value and the application omits the return value parameter, the driver ignores the value returned.

If a procedure returns a result set, the application retrieves the data from this result set the same way it retrieves data from any other result set. The following statement uses the procedure EMPS_IN_PROJ to create the same result set of names of employees working on a project:

```
{call EMPS_IN_PROJ(?)}
```

To retrieve a list of the procedures stored in a data source, your application can call SQLProcedures. To retrieve a list of the input, input/output, and output parameters, as well as the return value and the columns that make up the result set (if any) returned by a procedure, an application calls SQLProcedureColumns.

CAUTION

Because stored procedures can generate more than one result set, your code must be prepared for the number and composition of the result sets.

RAISERROR and PRINT Statements

When either a SQL Server trigger or a stored procedure executes a RAISERROR Transact-SQL (TSQL) statement, the current ODBC function receives the result code *SQL_ERROR_WITH_INFORMATION*. Your error handler can then use SQLError to retrieve the native error number and message sent by the RAISERROR statement. The query in progress isn't otherwise affected because the ODBC driver doesn't take any action on the basis of an error generated by a RAISERROR statement. TSQL PRINT statements are also treated like RAISERROR statements with a severity of 0.

Appendix

Setting Up the Test Databases

Tips on Using the SQL Upsizing Wizard

Adding the Stored Procedures

Creating a Test "Attach.MDB"

Creating a Test "BIBLIO" DSN

All of the samples I use in this edition are executed against a new test database that's based on the new Microsoft Visual Basic version 5.0 BIBLIO.MDB. I spent many, many hours building this puppy—unfortunately, the correct version didn't make it into Visual Basic version 5.0. What's included is a broken version with some scrambled data.

To use this MDB database as a test database on Microsoft SQL Server, you need to get the data and structure up to SQL Server. I'd like to say "just" use the Microsoft Access upsizing wizard to install it on your SQL server, but it isn't that easy. I tried to re-create the steps needed to do this and got pretty frustrated after a couple of hours. It seems that the upsizing wizard is pretty picky and broke down any number of ways as it balked at the larger tables. If you upload a single table at a time, you might get the job done—just dump the transaction log between operations. I also don't expect that everyone will have a copy of Microsoft Access—and you don't really need it to build successful client/server applications. But you do need to move the data from the BIBLIO.MDB database over to SQL Server. I'm sure you can figure it out.

Tips on Using the SQL Upsizing Wizard

I have included the upsizing wizard on the companion CD-ROM—it's a self-extracting compressed EXE. You need to install it in a separate directory on your system before executing so that the expanded files don't contaminate the local directory. Run Setup from this new directory to install it. Once it's installed, the Tools/Addins/SQL Upsizing Tool add-in is activated. Before you get started, review the items on the following checklist:

- Be sure the SQL Server has a device big enough to hold it. With the pictures and data, I expect 50 MB should do. You'll need to either create new data and log devices or share space on an existing device. Make sure the log is also large enough because many of the operations we'll be doing are really update-intensive—especially when working with the pictures.

- Be sure you have a system administrator DSN pointing to your server. I tried this with a normal user DSN, and it didn't work. The error messages didn't tell me I had permission problems; but once I switched to a system administrator account, I was able to get past the first set of errors.

- Upsize both the structure and data. I asked for Triggers for the RI options.

- Use the upsizing wizard one table at a time. At least do the *Titles* and *Title Authors* tables singly. Be sure to dump the BIBLIO transaction log between steps.

- If all else fails, upload just the structure and create a simple query to upload the data.

Adding the Stored Procedures

I have also included a SQL script to rebuild the test stored procedures I use in the examples and to illustrate how these procedures work. Use the SQL Enterprise Manager or ISQLW to install them on your new *Biblio* database. This script is called MakeSP.SQL, and it's saved on the companion CD-ROM.

Creating a Test "Attach.MDB"

Some of the tests also need to use the Attach.MDB database. This database is simple enough; it has attached tables that point to the *Biblio* SQL Server database and a single query that returns a single result set based on a four-table join. There's a sample on the companion CD-ROM, but you'll have to rebuild the attachments because they point to my server—unless you can figure out how to link to my server, in which case at least give me a call so that I can turn on the server.

Creating a Test "BIBLIO" DSN

Virtually all of the ODBC-based tests use a single BIBLIO DSN. Although I sometimes use the *Biblio* database in these examples, as often as not I simply change the default database to *Pubs* to make the samples more universal. Use the Control Panel 32-bit ODBC applet to create the BIBLIO DSN. You can make it a User DSN or a System DSN, but I don't think you can get away with a file-based DSN for these samples.

B

Appendix

SQL Server Error Codes Decoded

The first of the three tables provided in this appendix lists errors that any front end to Microsoft SQL Server can encounter. In the Microsoft Jet and RDO models, they appear in the Errors collection. In the ODBC API, they're exposed by the SQLError function. In VBSQL, they're trapped by DB-Library and returned in the Error and Message event handlers. (For the exact text of error messages generated by the server, see the *SysMessages* table of the *Master* database, where the messages are enumerated and documented.) The second table lists cursor function errors. No manifest constants or error codes are defined in the VBSQL documentation for the cursor functions. The third table lists the meanings of error severity codes.

Manifest Constant	Value	Severity Level	Error Message	Context/Notes
SQLEMEM	10000	8	*Unable to allocate sufficient memory*	With any function that allocates memory (opens, reads, and so forth)
SQLENULL	10001	7	*NULL DBProcess encountered*	With any function requiring the connection token returned from SQLOpen (connection has died, or integer holding the token returned from SQLOpen was altered)

Manifest Constant	Value	Severity Level	Error Message	Context/Notes
SQLENLOG	10002	11	*Null LoginRec encountered*	With SQLOpen or any of the SQLSetL... functions (SQLLogin not executed before SQLSetLUser, SQLSetLPwd, SQLSetLHost, SQLSetLApp, or SQLOpen)
SQLEPWD	10003	2	*Login incorrect*	With SQLOpen, when logon name isn't a valid user on the SQL server (password used in LoginRec structure or in SQLOpenConnection incorrect for user name provided)
SQLECONN	10004	9	*Search on server failed*	With SQLOpen (Server LAN down, or LAN permissions or resources won't allow connection; too many LAN users on server; too many LAN resources in use on workstation)
SQLEDDNE	10005	1	*DBProcess is inactive or not enabled*	With any function requiring the connection token returned from SQLOpen (bad connection token)
SQLENULLO	10006	11	*Attempt to log in with null LoginRec*	C error code (not listed in VBSQL.BI); see SQLNULLO
SQLNULLO	10006	11	*Attempt to log in with null LoginRec*	With SQLOpen; see SQLENLOG
SQLESMSG	10007	5	*General SQL Server error has occurred*	Usually after opening, during row processing; fairly common (check messages from the SQL server)
SQLEBTOK	10008	9	*Bad token from SQL Server: data stream out of sync*	Rarely encountered (suspect network error or alteration of the Tabular Data Stream data)
SQLENSPE	10009	7	*General nonspecific DB-Library error*	Rarely encountered (not described in Visual Basic programmer's reference)
SQLEREAD	10010	9	*Read from SQL Server failed*	Usually after opening, during row processing (suspect LAN protocol error)
SQLECNOR	10011	7	*Column number out of range*	When SQLData column reference doesn't match SQL query

(continued)

Manifest Constant	Value	Severity Level	Error Message	Context/Notes
SQLETSIT	10012	1	*Attempt to call SQLTsPut with an invalid TimeStamp*	With SQLTsPut (error in VBSQL documentation)
SQLEPARM	10013	11	*Invalid parameter in DB-Library function reference*	With any function call
SQLEAUTN	10014	7	*Attempt to update the TimeStamp of a table that has no TimeStamp column*	With SQLExec, SQLSend (invalid query)
SQLECOFL	10015	4	*Data conversion resulted in overflow*	Unlikely; no conversion in DB-Library for Visual Basic applications (data conversion errors done via TSQL CONVERT verb reported via SQL Server error messages; possibly applicable to Visual Basic)
SQLERDCN	10016	4	*Requested data conversion does not exist*	Unlikely; no conversion in DBLIB for Visual Basic applications (data conversion errors done via TSQL CONVERT verb reported via SQL Server error messages; possibly applicable to Visual Basic)
SQLEICN	10017	7	*Invalid ComputeID or computer column number*	With SQLAData or any of the Compute columns (*ComputeID* passed back from DB-Library by SQLNextRow)
SQLECLOS	10018	9	*Error in closing network connection*	Rarely encountered
SQLENTXT	10019	7	*Attempt to get Text identifier or Text TimeStamp from a non-Text column*	With SQLTxPtr, SQLTxTimeStamp, SQLTxTsNewVal, SQLTsNewVal
SQLEDNTI	10020	7	*Attempt to use SQLTxTsPut to put a new Text TimeStamp into a column whose data type is neither Text nor Image*	With SQLTxTsPut
SQLETMTD	10021	7	*Attempt to send too much Text data by using SQLMoreText*	With SQLMoreText

Manifest Constant	Value	Severity Level	Error Message	Context/Notes
SQLEASEC	10022	7	*Attempt to send an empty command buffer to SQL Server*	With SQLExec, SQLSend (execute SQLCmd before executing SQLExec; SQLSendCmd has no query)
SQLENTLL	10023	1	*Name too long for LoginRec*	With SQLSetL... functions
SQLETIME	10024	6	*SQL Server connection timed out*	With any query after SQLExec or SQLSend
SQLEWRIT	10025	9	*Write to SQL Server failed*	When there are network problems or libraries are out of sync (error number might be unused)
SQLEMODE	10026	9	*Network connection not in correct mode; invalid SQL Server connection*	Rarely encountered
SQLEOOB	10027	9	*Error in sending out-of-band data to SQL Server*	Rarely encountered
SQLEITIM	10028	7	*Illegal timeout value specified*	With SQLSetTime, SQLSetLoginTime
SQLEDBPS	10029	8	*Maximum number of SQL Server connections already allocated*	With SQLOpen (memory constraints limit number of possible connections on workstation; use SQLMaxProcs to allocate more)
SQLEIOPT	10030	?	*Attempt to use invalid (Visual) Basic option*	Rarely encountered (unknown severity level)
SQLEASNL	10031	7	*Attempt to set fields in a login record with LoginRec% set to 0*	With SQLSetL... functions (call SQLLogin before setting any LoginRec fields)
SQLEASUL	10032	7	*Attempt to set unknown LoginRecfield*	With SQLSetL... functions; rarely encountered
SQLENPRM	10033	7	*Option cannot have a null string as a parameter*	
SQLEDBOP	10034	7	*Invalid or out-of-range parameter for the option*	
SQLENSIP	10035	7	*Negative starting index passed to SQLStrCpy*	With SQLStrCpy

(continued)

Manifest Constant	Value	Severity Level	Error Message	Context/Notes
SQLECNULL	10036	7	*You have used 0 as an identifier for a Text TimeStamp*	
SQLESEOF	10037	9	*Unexpected EOF from the SQL server*	At SQLOpen time (named-pipe connection to the SQL server closed unexpectedly; SQL server might have gone down, or net might have closed your pipe connection; suspect no more connections available; later, suspect network failure)
SQLERPND	10038	7	*Attempt to initiate a new SQL Server query before processing the previous result set*	With SQLExec, SQLSendCmd, SQLSend (results pending)
SQLECSYN	10039	4	*Attempt to convert data stopped by syntax error in source field*	Unlikely; no conversion in DB-Library for Visual Basic applications
SQLENONE	10040	9	*Network interface layer not in place*	SQLInit (usually, required DLLs not in place)
SQLEAB SQLEBNCR SQLEAAMT	10041– 10046[1]	7		
SQLENXID	10047	3	*Server did not grant a distributed transaction ID*	Not applicable to Visual Basic (used only in two-phase commit)
SQLEIFNB	10048[2]	7	*Illegal field number passed to BCP_control*	Possibly with SQLBCPControl (not listed as valid VBSQL error)
SQLEKBCO	10049	1	*1000 rows successfully copied to host file*	With bulk copy operations
SQLEBBCI	10050	1	*Batch successfully copied to SQL Server*	With bulk copy operations
SQLEKBCI	10051	1	*1000 rows successfully copied to SQL Server*	With bulk copy operations
SQLEBCWE	10052	3	*I/O error while writing a BCP data file*	With bulk copy operations
SQLEBCNN	10053	1	*Attempt to bulk copy a Null value into a SQL Server column that does not accept Null values*	With bulk copy operations

Manifest Constant	Value	Severity Level	Error Message	Context/Notes
SQLEBCOR	10054	11	*Attempt to bulk copy an oversized row to SQL Server*	With bulk copy operations
SQLEBCPI	10055	7	*SQLBCPInit not called before BCP operation*	With bulk copy operations (error in VBSQL documentation)
SQLEBCPN	10056[3]	7		
SQLEBCPB	10057	7		
SQLEVDPT	10058	2		With bulk copy operations (for bulk copy, all variable-length data must have a specified length prefix or terminator)
SQLEBIVI	10059	7	*Use SQLBCPColumns and SQLBCPColfmt only after SQLBCPInit*	With SQLBCPColumns, SQLBCPColfmt (error in VBSQL documentation)
SQLEBCBC	10060	7	*Call SQLBCPColumns before SQLBCPColfmt*	With SQLBCPColfmt
SQLEBCFO	10061	1	*Host files must contain at least one column*	With bulk copy operations
SQLEBCVH	10062	7	*Call SQLBCPExec only after SQLBCPInit has been passed a valid host file*	With SQLBCPExec
SQLEBCUO	10063	8	*Unable to open host data file*	With bulk copy operations
SQLEBUOE	10064	8	*Unable to open error file*	With bulk copy operations
SQLEBWEF	10065	3	*I/O error writing BCP error file*	With bulk copy operations
SQLEBTMT	10066	7	*Attempt to send too much data with BCP_moretext*	With bulk copy operations (error in VBSQL documentation)
SQLEBEOF	10067	3	*Unexpected end of file encountered in BCP data file*	With bulk copy operations (data file might not be structured as described; suspect comma-delimited files not properly converted)
SQLEBCSI	10068	11	*Host file columns may be skipped only when copying to the SQL server*	Not listed as VBSQL error
SQLEPNUL	10069	11	*Null program pointer encountered*	Not listed as VBSQL error

(continued)

Manifest Constant	Value	Severity Level	Error Message	Context/Notes
SQLEBSKERR	10070	11	*Cannot seek in data file*	Not listed as VBSQL error
SQLEBDIO	10071	7	*Bad bulk copy direction*	With bulk copy operations
SQLEBCNT	10072	1	*Attempt to use bulk copy with nonexistent server table*	With bulk copy operations
SQLEMDBP	10073	?		Not listed in VBSQL or C documentation
SQLINIT[4]	10074	?		Not listed in VBSQL or C documentation; unknown severity level

1. Not applicable to VBSQL; pertain to errors in binding possible only with C interface.
2. Error codes 10048–10100 not defined in SQL.BI; functions not supported in VBSQL interface.
3. Not applicable to VBSQL.
4. Same spelling as SQLInit$() function.

Manifest Constant	Value	Severity Level	Error Message	Context/Notes
SQLCRSINV	10075	7	*Invalid cursor statement*	With cursor operations
SQLCRSCMD	10076	7	*Attempt to call cursor function when there are commands waiting to be executed*	With cursor operations
SQLCRSNOIND	10077	1	*One of the tables involved in the cursor statement does not have an index*	With cursor operations
SQLCRSDIS	10078	7	*Cursor statement contains one of the disallowed phrases COMPUTER, UNION, FOR BROWSE, or SELECT INTO*	With cursor operations
SQLCRSAGR	10079	7	*Aggregate functions are not allowed in a cursor statement*	With cursor operations
SQLCRSORD	10080	7	*Only fully keyset-driven cursors can have ORDER BY, GROUP BY, or HAVING phrases*	With cursor operations
SQLCRSMEM	10081	7	*Keyset or window scroll size exceeds the memory limitations of this machine*	With cursor operations

Manifest Constant	Value	Severity Level	Error Message	Context/Notes
SQLCRSBSKEY	10082	7	Keyset cannot be scrolled backward in mixed cursors with a previous fetch type	
SQLCRSNORES	10083	1	Cursor statement generated no results	
SQLCRSVIEW	10084	7	A view cannot be joined with another table or a view in a cursor statement	
SQLCRSBUFR	10085	7	Row buffering should not be turned on when using cursor APIs	
SQLCRSFROWN	10086	1	Row number fetched is outside valid range	
SQLCRSBROL	10087	7	Backward scrolling cannot be used in a forward-scrolling cursor	
SQLCRSFRAND	10088	7	Fetch types RANDOM and RELATIVE can be used only within the keyset of keyset-driven cursors	
SQLCRSFLAST	10089	7	Fetch type LAST requires fully keyset-driven cursors	
SQLCRSRO	10090	7	Data locking or modifications cannot be made in a read-only cursor	
SQLCRSTAB	10091	7	Table name must be determined in operations involving data locking or modifications	
SQLCRSUPDTAB	10092	7	Update or insert operations using bind variables require single-table cursors	
SQLCRSUPDNB	10093	7	Update or insert operations cannot use bind variables when binding type is NOBIND	

(continued)

Manifest Constant	Value	Severity Level	Error Message	Context/Notes
SQLCRSVIIND	10094	7	*The view used in the cursor statement does not include all the unique index columns of the underlying tables*	
SQLCRSNOUPD	10095	1	*Update or delete operation did not affect any rows*	
SQLCRSOS2	10096[1]	7	*Cursors are not supported for this server*	Cursors aren't supported on Sybase SQL Servers?
SQLEBCSA	10097	?		Unknown; no description of this error shown in C or or VBSQL documentation
SQLEBCRO	10098	?		Unknown; no description of this error shown in C or VBSQL documentation
SQLEBCNE	10099	?		Unknown; no description of this error shown in C or VBSQL documentation
SQLEBCSK	10100	?		Unknown; no description of this error shown in C or VBSQL documentation

1. These error codes are listed in VBSQL.BAS but aren't otherwise documented.

Severity Level Constant	Severity Level Number	Description
EXINFO	1	Informational, nonerror
EXUSER	2	User error
EXNONFATAL	3	Nonfatal error
EXCONVERSION	4	Error in VBSQL data conversion
EXSERVER	5	Server returned an error flag
EXTIME	6	Timeout period exceeded while user waits for response from server; *SQLConn* still alive
EXPROGRAM	7	Coding error in user program
EXRESOURCE	8	Resources running low; *SQLConn* possibly dead
EXCOMM	9	Failure in communication with server; *SQLConn* dead
EXFATAL	10	Fatal error; *SQLConn* dead
EXCONSISTENCY	11	Internal software error; need to notify Microsoft Technical Support

INDEX

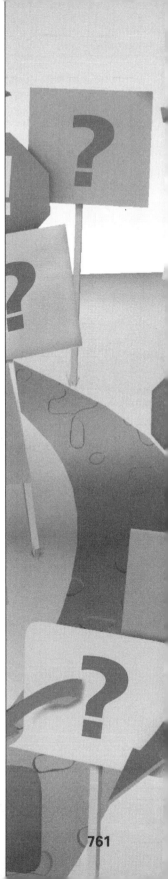

CHARINDEX function, 476
Char SQL data type, *211, 212*
chunk data, 497–501
client, role in client/server architecture, 71–72
Client Batch cursor library
  defined, 122, 180
  and ODBCDirect, 339–40, 456
  and optimistic batch updating, 339–40, 456, 457
client cursors, defined, 629
client/server architecture
  client's role, 71–72
  cursors in, 115–20, *121*
  and DAO/Jet, 98
  database size, 90
  vs. distributed-engine configuration, 69, 83, 89–93
  hypothetical example, 75–83
  implementing front end, 95–99
  input/output ratio, 90–91
  interface in, 74–75
  and ODBC API, 97–98
  overview, 70
  performance issues, 80–83
  and RDO model, 98, 351
  server's role, 70, 72–74
  six ways to access data, 8–10
  typical configurations, *78,* 78–79
  typical costs per user, 80
  and VBSQL, 95–97
CloseButton_Click event procedure
  in Jet DAO sample application, 33
  in Jet Data control sample application, 27
  in ODBC API sample application, 59
  in ODBCDirect sample application, 42–43
  in RDO interface sample application, 40
  in VBSQL sample application, 51
Close method, 39, 206, *208,* 209, 365, 367, 448, 479
Clustered property, *216*
coding
  CloseButton_Click event procedure, 27, 33, 40, 42–43, 51, 59
  error handlers, 51–52, 55
  FillTextBoxes procedure, 50, 57–58

coding, *continued*
  Form_Load event procedure, 30–31, 38, 45, 49, 56
  message handlers, 51–52
  SearchButton_Click event procedure, 26–27, 31–32, 38–39, 42, 46, 50, 56–57
  ShowRecord procedure, 32
  support procedures in ODBC API sample application, 55–56
collections
  and DAO model, 194–95
  defined, 194–95
columns. *See also* fields; TimeStamp data type
  assigning data to Visual Basic controls, 510
  term used by RDO model, 356, 452–54
ColumnSize property, 453, 500
COM. *See* Component Object Model (COM) architecture
CommitTrans method, 205, *209,* 367, *527*
compacting databases, 242, 316
Component Object Model (COM) architecture, 200–201
COMPUTE clause, 661, 665–67
concatenation (&), 163
concurrency
  and Jet, 272–73
  and RDO model, *432–33,* 434, 435
connecting to SQL Server
  active vs. idle connections, 145–46
  basic VBSQL code, 573–74
  checklist for, *138*
  ConnectionTimeout setting, *226,* 228–29, 237, 238
  error messages, 147–54
  exhausting connections, 571–72
  managing connections, 144–47
  overview, 138–54
  pooling connections, 145
  timeout values, 147
  using Jet, *138,* 234–41, 244–45
  using ODBC API, *138,* 717–22, 728–29
  using ODBCDirect, *138,* 328–32
  using RDO model, *138,* 379–87
  using VBSQL, *138,* 541–42

Int SQL data type, *211, 212, 213*
IPX/SPX networks, VBSQL libraries for, *557*
ISAM databases, Jet access, 185, 186
IsolateODBCTrans property, 203
ISQL application, 109

J

Jet. *See also* DAO model
   accessing SQL Server data, 205–7
   access to remote databases, 185–90
   and asynchronous queries, *169,* 189, 228
   and attached tables, 205–7, 241–42
   backing up databases, 317–18
   and centralized vs. distributed engines, 94
   connecting to SQL Server, *138,* 234–45
   cursor and buffer support, *121,* 186–88, 254–59
   and custom controls, 19
   Data Access Objects, *194,* 200–217
   Database object, 203–9
   DBEngine object, *194,* 201–2
   error handling, 276–77
   error messages, 295–98
   evaluating constructs locally, 309–11
   generating SQL to send to server, 313
   libraries, 190–91
   limiting scope of operations, 190
   linking databases to SQL Server tables, 205–7, 243
   message handling, 293–97
   and Microsoft Access, 189
   and MSysConf table, 231–32
   object models, 191, *192*
   and ODBC, 98, 226–32
   and overlapping queries, 168
   overview, 11–12
   populating DAO model, 196
   query processor, 186–90, 308–13
   and Recordset objects, 186, 188
   registering Data Access Objects, 20, 23, 29–30, 44
   relocating current-row pointer, 265–69

Jet, *continued*
   sample application using Data Access Objects, 28–33
   sample application using Data control, 22–28
   and server security, 272
   speed of, 12
   and SQL pass-through, 12, 280–81
   and SQL Server, 12, 69–70, 184–85, 308–13
   syntax, 249–50, 281
   transaction model, 274–75
   type libraries, 11
   updating SQL Server data, 270–76, 318
   using cursors to access SQL Server data, 248–54
   using to access data, 248–77
   versions of, 8, 11–12, 190–91, *200*
   and Windows registry, 220–25
   and Workspace object, *194,* 202–3
JetTryAuth ODBC setting, *227,* 230

K

keyset, defined, 635
keyset cursors
   ODBC, 739
   overview, 119, *121,* 635
   RDO, 427, *431*
   VBSQL, 631–32
KeysetSize property, *525*

L

LANs. *See* local area networks (LANs)
LastModified method, 266
LastModified property, 447–48
LCASE function, *310*
LEFT function, *310*
LEN function, *310*
libraries. *See also* DBLIB
   Jet DAO versions, 190–91
   list of alternatives, *557*
   troubleshooting, 148–50
   for VBSQL, 556–57
licenses, 152–53, 358–59

programming models. *See also* DAO
model; ODBC API; ODBCDirect;
RDC/RDO model; VBSQL
comparing sample applications, 60, *61*
design decisions, 122–27
overview, 8–10, 95–99, *121*
Prompt property, 38, 524, *525*
properties, defined, 193

Q

queries
active statements, 236
ad hoc, 168, 660–70
asynchronous, 169–70, 228, 438–41,
676–82, 743–44
and buffered rows, 609–11
building, 159–71, 577–82
comparing techniques, 290–91
completing, 590–91
converting to stored procedures,
580–82
and cursors, 115–17
dates in, 668–69
executing in ODBCDirect, 332–36
fixed vs. on-the-fly, 579
with multiple result sets, 168–69,
493–97, 742
ODBC query syntax, 313, 481, 482,
490–92, 723, 724
overlapping, 167–68
overview, 156–57
parameter, 166–67, 480–90
processing options, 671–76
quote management, 164–66, 581–82
select vs. action, 156–57
sending, 582–88
single-row result sets, 175–76
timeouts, 171, *227*, 228, 229, 545–47,
589–90
tips for optimizing performance,
157–59
troubleshooting, 171–72, 542
types of, 156–57
undocumented options, 672–73
and UserConnection Designer,
390–407
using drop-down lists, 579–80
when to use cursors, 176–77

Query. *See* Microsoft Query
QueryCompleted event, *528*
QueryComplete event, *440*, 449
QueryDef data access object
and attached tables, 243
Connect property, 283, 288, 292
and Data control, 305
defined, *194*
LogMessages property, 295, 296
in ODBCDirect, 332, 333–36, 344–45,
346
ODBCTimeout property, 229
RDO model equivalent, *357*
vs. rdoQuery object, 335–36, 344–45
ReturnsRecords property, 283
and SQL pass-through, 282–84, 288
SQL property, 282, 292
temporary, 282, 292
and Transact-SQL, 281, 282–84
QueryTimeout event, *440*, 449
QueryTimeout ODBC setting, *227*, 228,
229
QueryTimeout property
Database object, *208*
RemoteData control, 478, *525*, 526
quotation marks
in Transact-SQL statements, 164–66,
581
Visual Basic, 581–82

R

RAID, 179
RAISERROR statement
and Jet, 276, 295
and ODBC, 746
and TSQL, 548–49
and VBSQL, 588
RAM, 561–62
RAS (remote-access service), 77–78,
105–6
RDC/RDO model. *See also* RemoteData
control; UserConnection Designer
adding data, 514–15
asynchronous operations, *169*,
383–84, 438–41
building cursors, 422–54
connecting to SQL Server, *138*,
379–87

William R. Vaughn

(Bill to his friends) was born in Washington, D.C. and was raised as an Army brat. He traveled with his family all over the world to Germany, Thailand and all over the U.S. He attended Augustana College, in Sioux Falls, South Dakota; the University of Kansas at Lawrence; Mary Hardin-Baylor College, in Killeen, Texas; and the University of Texas at Dallas. As a result of all this diverse schooling, Bill earned his pilot's wings from the Army, an associate's degree in systems analysis, a bachelor's degree in computer science, and a master's degree in interdisciplinary studies.

In the early 1970s, Bill started working in Austin, Texas, as a mainframe programmer for the Texas Department of Public Safety, where he developed a statewide database management system that is still in use today. Bill might still be there today if Electronic Data Systems hadn't moved him to Dallas. He eventually worked as a microsystems consultant to Ross Perot and developed an accounting system on the IBM 5110 (IBM's *first* attempt at the PC).

Bill spent about a decade in the Dallas area, working for Mostek, Challenge Systems (you never heard of it), Digital Research, and CPT Corporation. He wore many hats in those companies, learning about hardware systems as well as writing, designing, marketing, supporting, and implementing a number of Z80 and PC-based systems, but he kept his focus on microcomputers.

About 10 years ago, Microsoft moved Bill up to Redmond, Washington, to work in the Windows development liaison group. Bill went on to spend more than 5 years at Microsoft University, developing and teaching courses on DB-Library, Transact-SQL, OS/2, and Visual Basic. After some time off to write the first edition of the *Hitchhiker's Guide,* he joined the Microsoft Visual Basic team. He spent 5 years there as a senior technical writer in the User Education unit, with responsibility for much of the Visual Basic data access documentation, especially where client/server systems and front ends are concerned. In addition to writing the Visual Basic 3.0 data access guide, he wrote the back half of the Visual Basic 4.0–specific *Building Client/Server Applications with Visual Basic* and about a bazillion help topics for Visual Basic 3.0 through 5.0. In September of 1996, Bill was promoted to Visual Basic Enterprise Product Manager. In this role, he gets to listen to customers and tell them (and the press) what Visual Basic is capable of doing.

Bill's younger daughter, Christina (a.k.a. Fred), is attending Whitman College, where she is working on a Liberal Arts and Journalism degree. When she is not being serenaded by one or more of the fraternities, she stays in shape by playing soccer. Bill's older daughter, Victoria (a.k.a. George), is graduating this year from the University of Washington with a degree in Chemical Engineering. She has made the Dean's List and will make a dynamite engineer. Well, at least a very good one. She has just been accepted to the Civil Engineering Graduate school at UW—perhaps *they* can make her more civil. Victoria is getting married this summer to a gentleman who plans a career in the Air Force. When she marries Mr. Michael Ballard her new initials will be V.B. (of course).

The manuscript for this book was prepared and submitted to Microsoft Press in electronic form. Text files were prepared using Microsoft Word 7.0 for Windows 95. Pages were composed by Microsoft Press using Adobe PageMaker 6.0 for Windows 95, with text in Stone Serif and display type in Stone Serif Semi Bold. Composed pages were delivered to the printer as electronic prepress files.

Cover Graphic Designer
Gregory Erickson

Cover Illustrator
George Abe

Interior Graphic Designer
Kim Eggleston

Illustrator
Joel Panchot

Principal Compositor
Sandra Haynes

Principal Proofreader/Copy Editor
Richard Carey

Indexer
Julie Kawabata

Create ActiveX™ controls and Internet-*enabled* applications— *fast!*

U.S.A. **$44.99**
U.K. £41.99 [V.A.T. included]
Canada $60.99
ISBN 1-57231-436-2

MICROSOFT® VISUAL BASIC® 5.0 DEVELOPER'S WORKSHOP, Fourth Edition, is a one-of-a-kind book-and-software package that gives you the recipes to build powerful, full-featured graphical applications for Windows® 95 and Windows NT® This book demonstrates everything from creating a screen saver to building ActiveX controls that can be used in a Web page. You'll learn by example how to:

- Build 32-bit applications for Windows 95 and Windows NT
- Develop reusable objects to enhance your productivity
- Extend the language by calling Windows API functions
- Take advantage of ActiveX technologies
- Access data on an Internet server
- Install applications over the Internet

Create full-featured Windows 95 and Windows NT–based applications faster than ever before with MICROSOFT VISUAL BASIC 5.0 DEVELOPER'S WORKSHOP!

Get active!

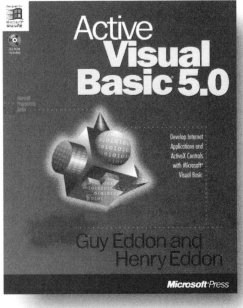

ACTIVE VISUAL BASIC® 5.0 introduces the features and capabilities of Visual Basic that allow for the creation of Internet-enabled applications and interactive Web content. After a technical overview of the Internet and the Internet-related capabilities of Visual Basic, the book covers the Internet Control Pack, ActiveX™ control creation, and creating Doc Objects. Advanced topics in the final section include overviews of developing Internet servers and accessing the Windows® Internet API. If you're entering this exciting growth area for Visual Basic development, you'll want this book.

U.S.A. **$39.99**
U.K.   £37.49 [V.A.T. included]
Canada $54.99
ISBN 1-57231-512-1

Microsoft·Press

IMPORTANT—READ CAREFULLY BEFORE OPENING SOFTWARE PACKET(S). By opening the sealed packet(s) containing the software, you indicate your acceptance of the following Microsoft License Agreement.

MICROSOFT LICENSE AGREEMENT

(Book Companion CD)

This is a legal agreement between you (either an individual or an entity) and Microsoft Corporation. By opening the sealed software packet(s) you are agreeing to be bound by the terms of this agreement. If you do not agree to the terms of this agreement, promptly return the unopened software packet(s) and any accompanying written materials to the place you obtained them for a full refund.

MICROSOFT SOFTWARE LICENSE

1. GRANT OF LICENSE. Microsoft grants to you the right to use one copy of the Microsoft software program included with this book (the "SOFTWARE") on a single terminal connected to a single computer. The SOFTWARE is in "use" on a computer when it is loaded into the temporary memory (i.e., RAM) or installed into the permanent memory (e.g., hard disk, CD-ROM, or other storage device) of that computer. You may not network the SOFTWARE or otherwise use it on more than one computer or computer terminal at the same time.

2. COPYRIGHT. The SOFTWARE is owned by Microsoft or its suppliers and is protected by United States copyright laws and international treaty provisions. Therefore, you must treat the SOFTWARE like any other copyrighted material (e.g., a book or musical recording) except that you may either (a) make one copy of the SOFTWARE solely for backup or archival purposes, or (b) transfer the SOFTWARE to a single hard disk provided you keep the original solely for backup or archival purposes. You may not copy the written materials accompanying the SOFTWARE.

3. OTHER RESTRICTIONS. You may not rent or lease the SOFTWARE, but you may transfer the SOFTWARE and accompanying written materials on a permanent basis provided you retain no copies and the recipient agrees to the terms of this Agreement. You may not reverse engineer, decompile, or disassemble the SOFTWARE. If the SOFTWARE is an update or has been updated, any transfer must include the most recent update and all prior versions.

4. DUAL MEDIA SOFTWARE. If the SOFTWARE package contains more than one kind of disk (3.5", 5.25", and CD-ROM), then you may use only the disks appropriate for your single-user computer. You may not use the other disks on another computer or loan, rent, lease, or transfer them to another user except as part of the permanent transfer (as provided above) of all SOFTWARE and written materials.

5. SAMPLE CODE. If the SOFTWARE includes Sample Code, then Microsoft grants you a royalty-free right to reproduce and distribute the sample code of the SOFTWARE provided that you: (a) distribute the sample code only in conjunction with and as a part of your software product; (b) do not use Microsoft's or its authors' names, logos, or trademarks to market your software product; (c) include the copyright notice that appears on the SOFTWARE on your product label and as a part of the sign-on message for your software product; and (d) agree to indemnify, hold harmless, and defend Microsoft and its authors from and against any claims or lawsuits, including attorneys' fees, that arise or result from the use or distribution of your software product.

DISCLAIMER OF WARRANTY

The SOFTWARE (including instructions for its use) is provided "AS IS" WITHOUT WARRANTY OF ANY KIND. MICROSOFT FURTHER DISCLAIMS ALL IMPLIED WARRANTIES INCLUDING WITHOUT LIMITATION ANY IMPLIED WARRANTIES OF MERCHANTABILITY OR OF FITNESS FOR A PARTICULAR PURPOSE. THE ENTIRE RISK ARISING OUT OF THE USE OR PERFORMANCE OF THE SOFTWARE AND DOCUMENTATION REMAINS WITH YOU.

IN NO EVENT SHALL MICROSOFT, ITS AUTHORS, OR ANYONE ELSE INVOLVED IN THE CREATION, PRODUCTION, OR DELIVERY OF THE SOFTWARE BE LIABLE FOR ANY DAMAGES WHATSOEVER (INCLUDING, WITHOUT LIMITATION, DAMAGES FOR LOSS OF BUSINESS PROFITS, BUSINESS INTERRUPTION, LOSS OF BUSINESS INFORMATION, OR OTHER PECUNIARY LOSS) ARISING OUT OF THE USE OF OR INABILITY TO USE THE SOFTWARE OR DOCUMENTATION, EVEN IF MICROSOFT HAS BEEN ADVISED OF THE POSSIBILITY OF SUCH DAMAGES. BECAUSE SOME STATES/COUNTRIES DO NOT ALLOW THE EXCLUSION OR LIMITATION OF LIABILITY FOR CONSEQUENTIAL OR INCIDENTAL DAMAGES, THE ABOVE LIMITATION MAY NOT APPLY TO YOU.

U.S. GOVERNMENT RESTRICTED RIGHTS

The SOFTWARE and documentation are provided with RESTRICTED RIGHTS. Use, duplication, or disclosure by the Government is subject to restrictions as set forth in subparagraph (c)(1)(ii) of The Rights in Technical Data and Computer Software clause at DFARS 252.227-7013 or subparagraphs (c)(1) and (2) of the Commercial Computer Software — Restricted Rights 48 CFR 52.227-19, as applicable. Manufacturer is Microsoft Corporation, One Microsoft Way, Redmond, WA 98052-6399.

If you acquired this product in the United States, this Agreement is governed by the laws of the State of Washington.

Should you have any questions concerning this Agreement, or if you desire to contact Microsoft Press for any reason, please write: Microsoft Press, One Microsoft Way, Redmond, WA 98052-6399.